The

Natural

Genesis:

OR SECOND PART OF *A BOOK OF THE BEGINNINGS*, CONTAINING AN ATTEMPT TO RECOVER AND RE-CONSTITUTE THE LOST ORIGINS OF THE MYTHS AND MYSTERIES, TYPES AND SYMBOLS, RELIGION AND LANGUAGE, WITH EGYPT FOR THE MOUTH-PIECE AND AFRICA AS THE BIRTHPLACE.

Gerald Massey

Volume 1

ISBN 1-56459-119-0

Kessinger Publishing Company
Montana, U.S.A.

" In the customs and institutions of schools, academies, colleges, and similar bodies destined for the abode of learned men and the cultivation of learning, everything is found adverse to the progress of science. For the lectures and exercises there are so ordered, that to think or specu- late on anything out of the common way can hardly occur to any man. And if one or two have the boldness to use any liberty of judgment, they must undertake the task all by themselves : they can have no advantage from the company of others. And if they can endure this also, they will find their industry and largeness of mind no slight hindrance to their fortune. For the studies of men in these places are confined and as it were imprisoned in the writings of certain authors, from whom if any man dissent he is straightway arraigned as a turbulent person and an innovator."—BACON.

They needs must find it hard to take Truth for authority who have so long mistaken Authority for truth.

> The Shadows of the past, substantialized,
> Environ us ; we are built about from birth
> With life-long shutting-out of light from heaven.

" The few who had the courage to call the child by its right name, the few that knew some- thing of it, who foolishly opened their hearts and revealed their vision to the many, were always burnt or crucified."—GOETHE.

> 'Tis a truth, howe'er unheeded,
> Work least wanted is most needed.

There is, however, an ineradicable tendency in human nature, howsoever few may cultivate it at one time in the same direction, never to rest short of the attainable ; and however mini- mized its value may appear in the process of attainment, we cannot rest until we know the truth.

Certain insects have developed the instinct to lay up food for their offspring which they never live to see.

In Africa the natives still dig round about the modern gum-trees to find the buried treasure that oozed from other trees which stood on the same spot in the forests of the far-off past.

" ὦ ἀμαθεῖς ἄνθρωποι, διδάξετε ἡμᾶς, τί ἐστιν ὁ θεὸς ἐν τοῖς ἀποκεκλεισ- μένος?"

" Bind it about thy neck, write it upon the tablet of thy heart, ' Everything of Christianity is of Egyptian origin.' "—Rev. ROBERT TAYLOR, Oakham Gaol, 1829.

" It is easy to show that this fabular relation borders on the verity of physical science."— PLUTARCH.

" As for wisdom, what she is and how she came up, I will tell you, and will not hide mysteries from you ; but will seek her out from the beginning of her nativity, and bring the knowledge of her into light, and will not pass over the truth."—Wisdom of Solomon, chap. vi. v. 22.

" Why does not some one teach me the constellations, and make me at home in the starry heavens, which are always overhead, and which I do not half know to this day ?"—CARLYLE.

" The time is near when these mysteries shall be revealed."—SOHAR.

" Now Joseph, the son of Rabbi Joshua, being sick, passed into the state of trance. His father inquired of him, ' What seest thou ?' He replied, ' The world turned upside down. The lofty are laid low, and the lowly are lifted up on high.' When his father heard this, he said unto him, ' Verily, thou hast seen the age of Selection.' "—Pesachim, f. 50, 1.

DEDICATORY.

At times I had to tread
    Where not a star was found
To lead or light me, overhead ;
    Nor footprint on the ground.

I toiled among the sands
    And stumbled with my feet ;
Or crawled and climbed with knees and hands,
    Some future path to beat.

I had to feel the flow
    Of waters whelming me :
No foothold to be touched below,
    No shore around to see.

Yet, in my darkest night,
    And farthest drift from land,
There dawned within the guiding-light ;
    I felt the unseen hand.

Year after year went by,
    And watchers wondered when
The diver, to their welcoming cry
    Of joy, would rise again.

And still rolled on Time's wave
    That whitened as it passed :
The ground is getting toward the grave
    That I have reached at last.

Child after Child would say—
    " *Ah, when his work is done,*
Father will come with us and play—"
    'Tis done.   And playtime's gone.

A willing slave for years,
    I strove to set men free ;
Mine were the labours, hopes, and fears,
    Be theirs the victory.

GERALD MASSEY.

EGYPTIAN PLANISPHERE OF ZODIACAL AND NORTHERN SIGNS.

(*According to Kircher.*)

EXPLANATORY.

"THE NATURAL GENESIS" contains the second half of "A BOOK OF THE BEGINNINGS," and completes the author's contribution to the new order of thought that has been inaugurated in our own era by the writings of Darwin and Wallace, Spencer and Huxley, Morgan and McLennan, Tylor and Lubbock. It was written by an Evolutionist for Evolutionists, and is intended to trace the Natural Origines and teach the doctrine of development. The total work is based upon the new matter supplied by the ancient monuments, ranging from the revelations of the bone-caves and the records of the Stone Age to the latest discoveries of hieroglyphic inscriptions, the cuneiform tablets, and the still extant language of gesture-signs. The work is not only one of original research, it is emphatically aboriginal, and the battle for evolution has here been continued amongst the difficult defiles and mountain fastnesses of the enemy.

After reading the first two volumes, Mr. Alfred Russel Wallace expressed the fear lest there might not be a score of people in England who were prepared by their previous education to understand the book. Few of its reviewers could be included amongst that number ; and some of them were as remote from the writer and his meaning as the apes from man, gibbering across the chasm of the missing link. But the author's mode of treatment, which was deficient in the art of bridge-building, and the exigencies of publishing according to a plan that (so to speak) caused the Exodus to precede the Genesis, may have been unfortunate.

Much of the matter is pre-eval, so that the method could not be historical ; nor could it be chronological, because of the links missing in series and sequence. The method is typological ; and these two volumes of "*Typology*" are necessary to the proper understanding of the previous ones, which were written with the matter of these in

mind.   In the preceding part of the work the author took very
extended views of Egypt's enormous past and the age of her pre-
monumental mythology.   Some of the conclusions set forth therein
were characterized by Dr. Samuel Birch as interesting and ingenious.
But at that time these suggestions and conclusions were announced
in direct opposition to the accepted authorities.   Since then, however,
the inscriptions discovered at Sakkarah have come to corroborate the
present writer.   They contain allusions to Sirius the Dog-star, which
show that at least two Sothiac cycles of 1,460 years each had been
observed and registered previous to their time—even if they are not
copies of indefinitely older documents—which carries the chronology
back to some 9,000 or 10,000 years from the present day.   Various
myths, hitherto supposed to have been the growth of later centuries
or of Asiatic origin, including the most important of all, that of Sut-
Horus, were then extant and of immemorial antiquity.   In this case
it is but just to say that "A BOOK OF THE BEGINNINGS" happened
to be the farthest advanced upon the right road.

The German Egyptologist, Herr Pietschmann, who reviewed the
"BOOK OF THE BEGINNINGS," was startled at the many "*unheard-of
suggestions*" which it contained, and thought the work was "*inspired
by an unrestrained thirst for discovery*," but he adduced no evidence
whatever to rebut the conclusions, and gave no hint of the author's
being wrong in his derivation of facts from the monuments upon
which those conclusions in a great measure depend.   The writer has
taken the precaution all through of getting his *fundamental facts* in
Egyptology verified by one of the foremost of living authorities,
Dr. Samuel Birch, to whom he returns his heartiest acknowledg-
ments.   He also sincerely thanks Captain R. F. Burton and
Mr. George St. Clair, F.G.S., for their helpful hints and for the
time and labour they have kindly given during the progress
of this work.   As a matter of course, the author will have
blundered in manifold details.   Discoveries are not to be made
without mistakes, especially by those who do not cultivate the
language of non-committal.   But up to the present time I have not
been shown nor do I perceive any reason for doubting the truth of
my generalization that Africa and not Asia was the birthplace of
articulate man, and therefore the primordial home of all things
human ; and that the race which first ranged out over the world,
including the islands of the north and the lands of the southern
seas, was directly Kamite ; the Blacks of Britain (who left the

flattened tibia, the negroid pelvis, the Australoid molars, and gorilla-like skulls in our bone-caves) and the Blacks of Australia being two extreme wings extended from the same African centre. Professor Huxley recognizes in the native Egyptian the most refined form of the same anthropological type that survives at a far lower stage in the Australian black. My further contention is that both issued from Inner Africa as the human birthplace, and that Egypt itself is old enough to be the mouthpiece of the first articulate language, the oldest intelligible witness to the natural genesis of ideas, and the sole adequate interpreter of the primary types of thought.

Professor Huxley has asserted that the Iberian (or African) blood remains in Britain even though "*all traces of language may have been obliterated.*" But all traces of a language can never be obliterated. We hear of a Pictish language disappearing along with a lost race and only leaving a word or two on the surface. That is impossible. The Cornish race and Cornish words live on after a particular dialect has ceased to be spoken. The structure of language changes, dialects dislimn and transform, but words do not pass away; the oldest are preserved in our dialects. Neither Kymraig, Gaelic, nor Irish Keltic is spoken in Dorsetshire, yet "*Rimbury*" remains with its place of urn-burial to prove that it was so named as the "*Roimh*," a burying-ground, the meaning of which is repeated in the Bury.

The present writer has been charged with being "sublimely unconscious that words have a history;" but he knew that certain words were also prehistoric, that they are older than languages, and that words, like myths, customs, laws, or beliefs, do not always begin where we may first meet with them. The prehistoric is everywhere the dominating difficulty with which we have to deal. It is said that you can do anything with words, but the illustrations chiefly relied on by the present writer were precisely those words and names which the current etymology could do nothing with, neither account for nor affiliate them. These proved to be Egyptian, and that pointed to an extension of their history, or of ours. Moreover, it was found that the Kamite typology offered a principle of naming which determines the primary nature and significance of words. This the writer applied to the type-names of places, waters, hills, and caves in Britain. The result is to show that the most ancient names and words are Kamite, not Aryan nor Semite.

That is they are words still extant in Africa, which can be brought
out of that land together with the black race, but cannot be got
into it backwards from Europe or Asia, America or Australia. For
example, it was suggested that the name of *Deruthy*, the place of
the bone-cave, at the junction of the two rivers Gave, was identical
with the Egyptian *Teru*, for the river-branch. But the writer did
not then know that the name was applied in Egypt at *Teruta*,

⸗] ᛚ ⊗ , the land (*ta*) of the river-branch, which is the

name of an Egyptian town situated on the Nile *at the junction* of
the Bahr-el-Yussuf.[1]   Here the type is the Tree, whence the branch,
and this is the *Teru* in Egyptian and numerous other African
languages.   Again, in the earliest known mention of the Cimbri,
Philemon the poet says they called the Northern Sea, from their
own country as far as Cape Rubeas, the *Morimarusa* or Dead Sea.[2]
This has been compared with *Mor-marwth* in Welsh for the Sea
of Death.   But in Egyptian *Mori* is the sea, *Meru* means the
dead, and *Sa* denotes the hinder part, the back, behind, *i.e.* the
Kamite North.   Thus read, *Mori-maru-sa* would signify the Dead
Sea North.   Such type-words—and I have adduced hundreds—are
equal to archaic coins for comparative purposes, and these pre-
historic words, which are not derived from language in Asia, bear
the stamp and superscription of Egypt.   Hence my claim that the
recognized non-Aryan (or pre-Aryan) residuum constituted the
African origines.

It has now been amply shown in these volumes that certain root-
words run through all language, and thus point back to a unity of
origin which has to be sought for in the most primitive conditions.

The main thesis of my work includes the Kamite origin of the
pre-Aryan matter extant in language and mythology found in
the British Isles,—the origin of the Hebrew and Christian theology
in the mythology of Egypt,—the unity of origin for all mythology,
as demonstrated by a world-wide comparison of the great primary
types, and the Kamite origin of that unity,—the common origin of
the mythical Genitrix and her brood of seven elementary forces,
found in Egypt, Akkad, India, Britain, and New Zealand, who
became kronotypes in their secondary, and spirits or gods in their
final psychotheistic phase,—the Egyptian genesis of the chief celestial signs, zodiacal and extra-zodiacal,—the origin of all mythology

[1] Champollion, *L'Égypte sous les Pharaons*, tom. i. pp. 297, 298.
[2] Pliny, *Hist. Nat.* iv. 16.

in the Kamite typology,—the origin of typology in gesture-signs,—
and the origin of language in African onomatopœia.

At least sufficient evidence has been produced to prove that all
previous discussions, speculations, and conclusions concerning the
genesis of language, mythology, fetishism, theosophy, and religion
are inadequate if only because the Kamite element has been hitherto
omitted, and to show that the non-evolutionist could not possibly
bottom any of the beginnings. One object aimed at in these and
the previous volumes is to demonstrate that the true subject-matter
of "Holy Writ" belongs to astronomical mythology; the history
first written in the book above, that was sacred because celestial;
and that this has been converted into human history in both the
Old Testament and the New. The "Fall in Heaven" was an
Egyptian mythos previous to its being turned into a Hebrew history
of man in the garden of earth. The Exodus or "Coming out of
Egypt," first celebrated by the festival of Passover or the transit
at the vernal equinox, occurred in the heavens before it was made
historical in the migration of the Jews. The 600,000 men who
came up out of Egypt as Hebrew warriors in the Book of Exodus
are 600,000 inhabitants of Israel in the heavens according to the
Jewish *Kabalah*, and the same scenes, events, and personages that
appear as mundane in the Pentateuch are celestial in the *Book
of Enoch*.

It was my aim to be foundational and accomplish a work that
should be done for the first and last time: to ascertain how the
oneness in primitive thought bifurcated in duality and was differentiated in expression by visible and audible signs,—how natural
gestures got stereotyed as ideographs and hieroglyphics,—why the
letter A should win the foremost place in the alphabet,—why mankind should come to worship a supposed divine being alleged to
divide all things into three, as a mode of representing its own
triune nature. All through the object was to reach a root-repre-
sentation of the subject-matter. Evolution teaches us that nothing
short of the primary natural sources can be of final value, and that
these have to be sought in the Totemic and pre-paternal stage of
Sociology, the pro-religious phase of Mythology and the ante-
alphabetic domain of Signs in language.

One clue to the writer's mode of elucidation may be found in
his treatment of mythology as the mirror of prehistoric sociology,
and his beginning with the mould of the motherhood which

preceded a knowledge of the individualized fatherhood. Also, such phrases as " *Serpent-worship*," " *Tree-worship*," " *Water-worship*," and " *Phallic-worship*" have but little meaning from the present standpoint. Nowhere did the Cultus originate in religion, but in a system of typology, a primitive mode of expression, a means of representation. The natural need of making signs by gesture-language led to the gradual adoption of certain things that were used as typical figures, a medium for the exchange of meanings, the earliest current coinage ever stamped and issued from the mint of mind. Such types were adopted for use, and became sacred in the course of time, the fetishtic or religious being their final phase. The present writer has sought for the natural genesis of the primitive mode of expression which created the types that were continued in the typology that is held to be fetishtic in Africa but religious in Europe. The oldest types, like the Serpent, Tree, or Water, were feminine at first, not because the female was then worshipped, but because the motherhood was known before paternity could be identified. The serpent sloughed periodically, so did the female. The tree was the producer of the fruit, as was the female. Water was the female fount of source. The ancestral spirit that preceded the individual ancestor, which was represented as creating or continuing by transformation of itself, might come to be typified by the serpent that sloughed and renewed, because a type once founded could be variously applied, but the serpent was a feminine ideograph from the beginning, and *only the natural genesis of the type will enable us to interpret the later typology.* Much of my matter has been fetched from far, and may be proportionately long in obtaining recognition. Being so remote from ordinary acquaintanceship, it could not be made familiar at first sight by any amount of literary skill. The appeal has to be continually made to a lapsed and almost lost sense of the natural genesis of ideas, customs, and superstitions. Nothing short of the remotest beginnings could sufficiently instruct us concerning the origin of religious rites, dogmas, and doctrines, that still dominate the minds of men without being understood, and years of intense brooding had to be spent in *living back* to enter the conditions and apprehend the primary phases of the nascent mind of man, so as to trace the first laying hold of things by the earliest human thought of which the cave-dwellers of the human mind have left us any record ; and the writer believes that no such sustained, or at least prolonged and elaborate, endeavour has hitherto been made to interpret the mind of primitive and archaic man by means of the types—found to be extant from the first—which are herein followed from their natural genesis in phenomena to their final phase of application. To trace the natural genesis of mythology and typology is to write a history or present a panorama of man's mental evolution ; and every type pourtrayed or traced in these pages proves the lowly status of the beginnings, and tends to establish the doctrine of mental evolution in accordance with the physical.

My work is written long and large, and the evidence is faithfully presented in every part for each conclusion drawn, so that the reader may test its truth. Indeed a certain absence of personal showmanship or explanation by the way in marshalling the long array of data may be set down to a dominant desire that the serried facts should speak for themselves and tell their own tale as far as was possible. A judgment of facts is now asked for, not belief in a theory ; the judgment of those who have time and patience to study and the capacity to comprehend. Belief has no more to do with the reading of this book than theoretical speculation had to do with the writing of it. From the peculiar nature of the work it is almost inevitable that its critics will have to learn the rudiments of the subject from the volumes offered for review; and great patience may be needed to reach the root of the matter, or to perceive the author's drift through all the mass of details. Each section is complete in itself, but the serious student will find the whole of them correlative and cumulative. They are called sections to denote that they have not the continuity of narrative ; but they are parts of a whole.

The claim now to be advanced on behalf of the work is that it sets forth a physical basis for the human beginnings in thought, language, and typology; shows the mode in which the primitive and archaic man attained expression in terms of external phenomena ; demonstrates the natural genesis of signs and symbols, recovers the lost foothold of mythology in the phenomena of space and time, and traces the typology of the past into the mytholatry of the present; that it represents the ancient wisdom, the secrets of the mysteries, numerical, physiological, and astronomical, according to the mode in which the Gnosis was expressed ; that mystical subjects previously dabbled in are for the first time sounded to the depth ; that the foundations of the phallic cult are laid bare without the

grin of the satyr in Greece or the libidinous leer of the subject in
its Italian phase, by a process as purely scientific as the origin
was simply natural. The writer has not only shown that the current
theology *is*, but also *how* it has been, falsely founded on a misinterpretation of mythology by unconsciously inheriting the leavings
of primitive or archaic man and ignorantly mistaking these for
divine revelations. The work culminates in tracing the transformation of astronomical mythology into the system of Equinoctial
Christolatry called Christianity, and demonstrating the non-historic
nature of the canonical gospels by means of the original mythos
in which the Messianic mystery, the Virgin motherhood, the incarnation and birth, the miraculous life and character, the crucifixion
and resurrection, of the Saviour Son who was the Word of all Ages,
were altogether allegorical.

During a dozen years the writer has put his whole life into his
labour, fully facing the fact that the most important parts of his
work would be the least readable, and that the more thorough the
research, the more fundamental the interpretation, the more remote
would be its recognition and the fewer its readers. But the work is
warranted to wait, and the author does not doubt that its comparatively few friends at first will be continually increased from many
generations of genuine men and women.

SUMMARY OF CONTENTS.

SECTION V.

SECTION VI.

SECTION VII.

SECTION VIII.

THE NATURAL GENESIS.

SECTION I.

NATURAL GENESIS OF THE KAMITE TYPOLOGY.

IN an epistle to the Egyptian Anebo, assigned to Porphyry, the learned Greek writer asks, "*What is the meaning of those mystic Narrations which say that a certain divinity is unfolded into Light from mire ; that he is seated above a lotus, that he sails in a ship, and that he changes his form every hour according to the signs of the zodiac ? If these things are asserted symbolically, being symbols of the powers of this divinity, I request an interpretation of these symbols.*"

According to Proclus, in his Commentary on the Enneads of Plotinus, Jamblichus wrote his work on the Mysteries as a reply to the pertinent questioning of Porphyry.[1] But Jamblichus, like so many who have followed him, began with things where he first met with them, on the surface, in their latest phase. He represented the Egyptians as worshippers of the one God, uncreated, unique, omnipotent, and universal. He starts with this as *their* starting-point, and affirms that all the other gods of the Pantheon are nothing more than the various attributes and powers of the Supreme personified. In short, he makes Monotheism the foundation instead of the summit of the Egyptian religion. This view has been maintained by several Egyptologists.

Champollion-Figeac says, "*A few words will suffice to give a true and complete idea of the Egyptian religion. It was purely monotheistic, and manifested itself externally by a symbolical Polytheism.*[2] According to De Rougé,[3] one idea pervades the total cult—*that of a single primordial God.* M. Maspero is likewise of opinion that all the forms

---

[1] Jamblichus, *De Mysteriis Ægyptorium, cum notis Gale*, fol. 1670.
[2] Champollion-Figeac, *Égypte Ancienne*, p. 245.
[3] E. de Rougé, *Conference sur la Religion des anciens Égyptiens*, p. 13

and names of the innumerable gods were for the worshipper only so many terms and forms of the one God. M. Chabas declares that all the gods and goddesses are but different aspects or attributes of the one sole God who existed before everything.[1]

M. Pierret asserts that *the ignorant were held in abject fetishism by the despotism of the priests, but the initiated recognized one sole and hidden God.*[2]

Mariette, in reply to Jamblichus, has denied this interpretation point blank, and *in toto.* He says, "*Neither in these temples nor in those which were previously known to us does the 'one God' of Jamblichus appear. We find everywhere deities who are immortal and uncreated; but nowhere do we find the one and invisible God without name and without form, who presides from on high over the Egyptian Pantheon. No indication to that effect is given by the Temple of Denderah, the most hidden inscriptions of which have now been thoroughly examined.*"[3]

Dr. Samuel Birch, our great English Egyptologist, in conversation with the present writer, agreed with Mariette. Renouf asks "*Was there really, as is frequently asserted, an esoteric doctrine known to the scribes and priests alone, as distinct from popular belief?*" His answer is, "*No evidence has yet been produced in favour of this hypothesis.*"[4]

Nor was there a one God known to Jamblichus. He quotes two by name, as *Ichton* and Ἡμήφ.[5] Bunsen says no notice of the latter name appears elsewhere. But it is evidently intended for *Iu-em-hept*, the Greek Imothes, whose mother's name was *Jusâas*, she who was great with the Coming One; and his father is Atum. The one God in this case was the solar trinity of Heliopolis, the Hebrew *On.*

There never was a subject which demanded the evolutionary mode of manipulation more than this of the origin of Egyptian mythology and the expansion of religious ideas in the Valley of the Nile. Nothing but the application of the evolutionary method can rescue us from the traditions we have inherited as survivals of the primitive system of mythical interpretation. It takes the latter half of all one's lifetime to unlearn the falsehood that was instilled into us during the earlier half. Generation after generation we learn, unlearn, and re-learn the same lying legendary lore. Henceforth our studies must begin from the evolutionist standpoint in order that they may not have to be gone over again.

In vain the non-evolutionist, who is likewise a metaphysician, would deal with the problem of the religious origines. None but the evolutionist can go back far enough. None but the evolutionist

---

[1] Chabas, *Calendrier des Jours Fastes et Néfastes*, p. 107.
[2] *Le Panthéon Égyptien*, Introd. p. 7.
[3] *Monuments of Upper Egypt*, Eng. Trans. pp. 24, 25.
[4] Hibbert Lectures, p. 217.   [5] Cap. viii. 2.

can commence early enough. None but the evolutionist is entirely freed from the falsehood of the "Fall" and the hallowed beginning at the wrong end of things, called the "Creation." Only the evolutionist can present the facts in their natural sequence and the true order of their development. The non-evolutionist can begin at any time, and anywhere, except at the right place. But neither in Egypt nor out of it did mythology *commence* with the causative interpretation of phenomena assumed by the non-evolutionist. Reverence for an unseen power apprehended as mind and conscious cause was preceded by a recognition of powers and potencies in nature exterior and superior to men, which were estimated by the force of their physical manifestations; and the fear and dread of these were operative long ages before the existence of that reverence which can be called religious—that which Shakespeare designates the "*Angel of the World.*" *Primos in orbe deos fecit timor.*

An unfathomable fall awaits the non-evolutionist misinterpreters of mythology in their descent from the view of a primeval and divine revelation made to man in the beginning, to the actual facts of the origines of religion. A "*primitive intuition of God,*" and a God who "*had in the beginning revealed Himself as the same to the ancestors of the whole human race,*" [1] can have no existence for the evolutionist.

The "*primitive revelation,*" so-called, had but little in it answering to the notion of the supernatural. It was solely just what the early men could make out in the domain of the simplest matters-of-fact. Theirs is *the profundity of simplicity, not of subtlety.* Their depth, like that of the Egyptian soil, is the result of constant accumulation of silt between us and the solid rock. Moreover, an Egyptologist may know the monuments from first to last, and yet be unable to give any satisfactory account of the *rise and development of the Egyptian religion,* because its roots are hidden in an unknown past. All that would be of supreme interest and primordial value to the evolutionist is out of view and untested by the comparative process. Egypt comes into sight upon a summit of attainment. The non-evolutionist is still infected with the notion of a primeval monotheism and a lapse into polytheism and idolatry, whereas mythology arose out of typology, and religion was developed from the mythology, not the mythology from religion; but to begin with a conception of the one hidden God is to make religion precede mythology. A religion had been established in the time of the earliest monuments, but the mythology no more begins at that point than the Nile springs in Egypt. M. Pierret, for instance, is right as to the ideographic types being figures for use rather than fetishes for worship, but utterly wrong as to their origin in a manifold expression of monotheistic thought.

[1] Max Müller, *Chips*, vol. i. pp. 366—368.

It is easy, of course, to take the later texts and then read the monuments backwards. It is easy to assume that all the divine types are modes of manifestation for the one God ; but the idea of the one God belongs to religion ; this was preceded by mythology, and these types were extant before either. We require to know what they signified in their pre-monumental phase, and what was their origin. We cannot tell who or which the gods are until we have ascertained what they represented or typified—in short, what was their natural genesis.

Egyptologists who talk of the one primordial God as the father of souls, never seem to recognize the fact that the individualized fatherhood was comparatively late as a human institution, and that the father could not be recognized in heaven before he had been discovered on earth. There is no fatherhood in the first pleroma of the gods, who are a family of seven, born of the genitrix of gods and men. Those of the seven that can be traced, such as Sut, Kebekh, Kak, Kafi (Shu), and Horus, had no father. Hence, *when we do get back to a one God on any local line of Egyptian mythology, it is the mother alone, and not the father, we find to be the first.* No matter which cult we question, the genitrix of the gods precedes the primordial God, whether as Taurt, the Mother of the Revolutions, who presides in the birthplace at the centre ; or Neith, who came "*from herself,*" and who boasted significantly at Sais that her *peplum* had never been lifted by the male generator; or Mut, Ank, or Hathor. The mother is everywhere first and foremost, as she was in nature where the bringer-forth was observed and typified long before the human mind could enter into the realm of creative cause, or the fatherhood had been established. *Hence the female was continued with the male in the image of the one God,* and there is no one God that is not a biune being, a twin form of the "double primitive essence," like Ptah ; in fact, a "*Male-Mother,*" which is the meaning of "Ka-Mutf," a title of Khem ; because the mother-mould of the producer was primordial.

When at last attained, the "one God" of Egypt is as much a result of evolution and survival of the fittest type, as in the case of any other species, ranging through the four series of elemental, stellar, lunar, and solar deities. The unity is final, not initial, and when the one has been aggregated from the many, which is the sole followable process of attaining unity, the last result is a dual deity who brings forth from and with the womb. Manifested "*existences are in his hand ; unmanifested existences are in his womb* (kat)." [1] This is the language of various other texts that might be cited.

If there be a one and only god, according to the language of certain inscriptions, a father of beginnings endowed with all the attributes of the sole god, it is Amen-Ra, the *Hidden* Sun. But his creation is comparatively late—the solar *régime* being last of all—he

---

[1] *Ritual,* ch. xxxii.

was later than Ptah, Atum, Horus, Seb, Shu, Osiris, and Sut, and his birth was as a *Time-Keeper*. In the inscription from the Temple of El-Karjeh it is said that he was "self-produced," and that in "making his body," and "giving birth to it," "*he has not come out of a womb—he has come out of cycles*."[1]

Like Taht, the moon-god, and Seb, the star-god, he too was a birth of time. This is the "only one," as the sun-god, of whom the Osirian says, "*Let me cross and manage to see the Only One, the sun going round, as the giver of peace*."[2]

The language of monotheism reaches its climax in the hymns and addresses to Amen-Ra, the one god, one in all his works and ways. Yet he was a god with a beginning, and his piety to his parents is on record. He paid an annual visit to the Valley of the Dead, and poured out a libation to his father and mother on the altar of propitiation. The one god is simply the culminating point of all the immeasurable past of polytheism.

The world of sense was not a world of symbol to the primitive or primeval man. He did not begin as a Platonist. He was not the realizer of abstractions, a personifier of ideas, a perceiver of the *Infinite*. In our gropings after the beginnings we shall find the roots of religious doctrines and dogmas with the common earth, or *dirt* even, still clinging to them, and showing the ground in which they grew.

Metaphysical explanations have been the curse of mythology from the time of the Platonists up to the present. All interpretation is finally futile that is not founded on the primary physical phenomena. Fortunately, this basis of the earliest thought is more or less extant in the types that have been left us to interpret as best we may ; and on this concrete foundation we have to build. Nor is there any origin of religion worth discussing apart from these foundations of mythology which are verifiable in the phenomena of nature.

Instead of a monotheistic instinct, or a primeval revelation of the one god, mythology exhibits a series of types as the representatives of certain natural forces from which the earliest gods were evolved, and finally compounded into a one deity, who assumed their attributes as his manifestations, and thus became the supreme being and god over all. It will be demonstrated that Egyptian mythology began with the typifying of seven elements or seven elemental forces, such as fire and water, earth and air, born of the Typhonian genitrix, as the Abyss. These were the eight in Am-Smen, the place of preparation, who were *born of space or chaos before the formation of the world, or the establishment of order and time. Their types were continued in the secondary phase—that of time—as intelligencers to men.*

The primordial, or supreme deity in Egypt, then, was not a god one, or one god of the beginning, but the one who had been com-

---

[1] *Records of the Past*, vol. viii. p. 137.   [2] Ch. cxlviii.

pounded and elevated to the supremacy as solar type of the godhead and representative of a pleroma.   Neither Ra, Atum, Amen, nor Ptah was one of the eight original gods.   The processes will be shown by which the latest deities were compounded or developed from characters previously extant, who were gods of the earliest time, as these were of the latest.

Ra, as a total god, comprises the seven spirits, or souls that preceded his creation, as the seven spirits of the Bear.[1] So the one god of the Avesta, Ahura-Mazda, is made up of the seven spirits, or Amshaspands, who preceded his supremacy. One title of the sun-god Ra is "Teb-Temt," and *temt* means totalled, from *tem*, the total, as in the English *team*. His total, as Teb-temt, consists of seventy-five characters.   These seventy-five manifestations of Ra—which correspond to the seventy-five zones of suffering in the Hades, whence came the cries of those who were in greatest need of knowing a name to call upon—are repeated in number in the Ormazd-Yasht of the Avesta, where the divinity gives to Zarathushtra his seventy-five names. The Parsees say the number should be seventy-two, correlating them probably with the seventy-two Decans, but the seventy-five correlate with the original Egyptian unknown to them.[2]

The primordial god, as Ptah, was not divided into four couples as M. Pierret argues, but the four couples, or the eight great gods previously extant, were represented by Ptah ; they were resolved into his attributes, or manifestations, when Ptah as a solar god had been created.   Everywhere, inevitably, the non-evolutionist reverses the process of development.

Canon Rawlinson has lately re-affirmed the statement that there was an esoteric and exoteric system of teaching, by which the Egyptian priests, with whom the "*primary doctrine of the esoteric religion undoubtedly was the real essential unity of the divine nature,*" *taught the people at large* "*a polytheism of a multitudinous, and in many respects, of a gross character.*"[3] This is the portrait of the Egyptian priest commonly presented by modern monotheists, who surreptitiously interpolate the ancient texts.

Here, however, the seventeenth chapter of the Ritual, which is designated the gospel or faith of the Egyptians, and is the kernel of their religious creed, contains a complete refutation and reversal.

It happens that in this chapter we have the text mixed up with the glosses, which were intended to be kept oral ; the two corresponding to the written and oral law of the Hebrews. Thus, for once the exoteric and esoteric teaching appear together. A text or saying is announced followed by the "*Petar ref su,*" = "let him (the esoterist) explain it;" and in many instances he does explain the text. The result is that *the announcement contains all the monotheistic matter, the*

[1] *Ritual*, ch. xvii.   [2] *Litany of Ra*, cf. Bleeck, vol. iii. p. 23.
                                     [3] *History of Egypt.*

supposed esoteric doctrine, whereas the glosses which secreted the hidden oral wisdom relate to the materialistic beginnings, and tend to identify the abstract god once more with the origines in phenomena, the spiritual god being explained physically—mark, not in the exoteric but in the esoteric teaching.

The theosophy is continually rendered in terms of physical phenomena. The deceased speaks in the person of various gods. He says, for example, "*I am Tum, the only being in the firmament.*" Now Tum is the "one god," the father of souls. But the abstract idea is in the text, and the commentary, gloss, or esoteric teaching keeps the mind anchored fast to the natural genesis in physical phenomena. The god of the exoteric teaching is all through the actual *sun* of the esoteric.

The "*sun in his rising,*" the "*sun in his disk,*" the "*great god*" in the pool is the "*sun himself.*" The "father" is "the sun." The one who "*orders his name to rule the gods*" as Horus, the "son of Osiris," is explained to be "*the sun himself.*"

These explanations, which usually remained unwritten, show that the cause of concealment in later times was the simple physical nature of the beginnings out of which the more abstract ideas had been gradually evolved.

There is undoubtedly a dislike in the later stage of ideas to having them expressed in those terms of phenomena which serve to recall the physical origines, and a great desire to keep their primitive nature clothed and out of sight, requiring all the unshrinking honesty of modern science —"whose soul is explanation"—to counteract such diffidence. Yet it was necessary for the learned to retain a knowledge of the beginnings. This it was that led to the *hidden* wisdom, the Gnosis, the Kabalah, the inner mysteries. *The knowledge was concealed because of its primitiveness, and not on account of its profundity.*

According to the statement of the Bishop of Cæsarea, the learned Egyptian Chaeremon acknowledged no *intellectual* principles in the earliest mythology of Egypt. This shows that he knew the matter to the root, and the nature of the eight Elementaries whose origin was entirely physical.

It is certain, then, that Egyptian polytheism was not monotheism intentionally disguised with various masks for one face, and equally sure that the image of the one god and supreme being was evolved from many preceding gods, and that the process of this evolution can be followed and fixed.

Cicero asks, "*Do you not see how from the productions of nature and the useful inventions of men have arisen fictitious and imaginary deities, which have been the foundation of false opinions, pernicious errors, and miserable superstitions?*"[1]

And he affirms rightly that the sacred and august Eleusina, into

[1] Book ii. 28.

whose mysteries the most distant nations were initiated, and the solemnities in Samothrace and in Lemnos, secretly resorted to by night, if they were properly explained and reduced to reasonable principles, would rather explicate the *nature of things* than discover the knowledge of the gods.[1]

A few hints may be found in Plutarch's ever-precious fragment " *Of Isis and Osiris* "; also in the "Hieroglyphics" of Hor-Apollo, which have been considerably undervalued by certain Egyptologists. But the mysteries remained unpublished. The Greeks could not master the system of Egyptian mythology, and the hieroglyphics were to them the dead letter of a dead language.

What Herodotus knew of the mysteries he kept religiously concealed. What Plato had learned made him jealous of the allegories to which he did not possess the clue ; but he would have banished the poems of Homer from his republic, because the young would be unable to distinguish between what was allegorical and what was actual; exactly on the same ground that many sound thinkers to-day would banish the Bible from our schools for children.

Outside of their own mysteries the Greeks stood altogether outside of the subject. They, as their writers allege, had inherited their mythology, and the names of the divinities, without knowing their origin or meaning. They supplied their own free versions to stories of which they never possessed the key. Whenever they met with anything they did not understand, they turned it the more effectively to their own account. All that came to hand was matter for metaphysics, poetry, statue, and picture. They sought to delight and charm the world with these old elements of instruction, and with happy audacity supplied the place of the lost nature of mystic meaning with the abounding grace and beauty of their art. Nothing, however, could be more fatal than to try to read the thoughts of the remoter past through their eyes, or to accept the embellishments of these beautifiers for interpretations of the ancient typology ; and the reproduction of the primitive myths from the Aryan stage of language in Greece is on a par with the modern manufacture of ancient Masters carried on in Rome.

In his Commentary on Plato's Politics, Proclus, speaking of the symbolism of the ancients, and their sacerdotal system, says truly that from this mythology Plato himself derived or established many of his peculiar dogmas.[2]

The utterly misleading way in which Egyptian physics were converted by Plato and his followers into Greek metaphysics, makes Platonism only another name for imposture. Time, says Plato finely, is the moving image of eternity. But the foundation of the image is planetary, or stellar motion, and on this basis of visible things he sought to establish all that was invisible, and build up the human

---

[1] *On the Nature of the Gods*, book i. c. 42.   [2] Taylor, p. 372.

soul backwards, according to the celestial geometry of the Egyptians.[1] Philo complains that the Greeks had brought a mist upon learning which made it impossible to discover the truth. The same charge may be substantialised on other grounds against his own countrymen. In India the myths have been vapourised. Their poets are at play with the shadows of ancient things, and the mere fringe of phenomena. It is not that the mythical characters in the Vedas have not yet been evolved into a definite form. It is not the indefiniteness of beginning that we find there, but of dissolution. The definite representation was earlier, and in the Vedas the shapes are in process of dislimning and being evaporated into doctrinal abstractions; the concrete facts of early earth are passing off into the fading phantoms of cloudland.

The decadence of mythology is to be found in the Greek poetising, Hebrew euhemerising, and Vedic vagueness. What the myths have to tell us depends on their having preserved the earliest shape; they have reached their decay when made to speak falsely through the interfusion of later thought. They preceded our civilisation, are not a birth of it, nor a descent from it; and their value is in proportion to the marks of their origin which have not yet been worn off them.

It is with mythology as with language. In vain we look for the lost likeness of language simply in the structure of a thousand languages. The genius of language has been at work for countless years to diversify and divaricate in structure. We must seek the primitive unity in the original matter of human thought, and in the earliest modes of expression; and the further we go back the nearer we shall find ourselves approaching to the origin in unity, for the bole of the tree is extant as well as the branches above and the roots below.

It is solely in the symbolic stage of expression that we can expect to recover the lost unity. This is preserved in the gesture-signs, ideographic types, the origin of numbers and the myths, the imagery scattered over the world that still remains unread by us; and in the religious rites and ceremonies, popular customs, and other practical forms of typology which have been wandering dispersedly about the earth. Any single shape of registered tradition is no absolute guarantee for fidelity to the lost original. It is, as it were, only an individual memory. We have to appeal to the memory of the whole human race, by gathering up the scattered fragments and various versions of the general tradition. Many incoherent witnesses may testify to one truth when we are in possession of the clue. Their disconnected evidence is all the more express when they are too unconscious to connive.

We shall find the human race has kept its own buried records of the pre-historic pre-literary ages almost as faithfully as the earth its

[1] See especially the "Timæus" with Proclus' *Commentary*.

geological register. So far from the process having corrupted or dissipated the ideas entrusted to its keeping (as Gibbon alleges), these have been preserved because they were branded and bitten into the memory more permanently than they could have been stamped in metal or engraved in stone.

The most perfect, that is the most primitive, forms of the myths and symbols out of Africa are those which for thousands of years have been kept by living memory alone. Having to trust to the memory in the absence of written records the Oral method of communication was held all the more sacred, as we find it in the ancient priesthoods, whose ritual and gnosis depended on the *living memory* for their truth, purity, and sanctity. It was the mode of communication from "mouth to ear," continued in all the mysteries, including Masonry,—that Monotheism in Polytheism !

In Sanskrit, the tradition which has been borne in mind from the beginning, delivered by mouth and learned by ear, to live in memory alone, is "*Smriti.*" *S'ruti*, a form of the same word, signifies hearing. *Sem*, in Egyptian, also denotes hearing ; *rut* means repeated ; and on this hearing of the oral wisdom has been based a theory of the Vedas having been communicated by *audible revelation !* But the revelation was simply made from mouth to ear.

So ancient was this mode of making sure of the treasures of knowledge, so deeply were these engrafted in the mind, so painfully scored in the flesh by the marks and symbols of tattoo, as if one should bury his jewels in his own body for a safe ; so permanently was the record inscribed that it still lives and underlies all literature or artificial registers in the world. It reaches down to the origines of human thought, however far from those we may be who dwell on the surface to-day, where we keep our own written records of the past. This matter, preserved by the universal memory, belongs to the symbolic stage of expression, and can only be understood by reverting to the symbol. The symbol is the true Tower of Babel and point of dispersion in language. *The symbolic extends beyond the written or the spoken language of any people now extant.*

With the Chinese, for example, *their symbols can be read in various parts of the empire by words and sounds so entirely different that the speakers who interpret the typology cannot understand each other when they talk.*

The symbols underlie two other languages, and at that depth the scattered readers meet once more.

So is it with the typology of tattoo. The African Oworos and the Basas do not speak one language, but they have the same tattoomark, and that is the link of a connection earlier than their language as spoken at the present time.[1]

The Khoi-Khoi, or Hottentots, form one branch of a wide-spread

[1] Koelle, *Introd.* p. 6.

race which has been divided into ever so many tribes. These differ totally in language, but they preserve a primæval relationship in the use of certain peculiar sounds, of which the clicks constitute the essential part.[1]

Among the Tembus, Pondos, Zulus, Ashantis, Fantis, and various other African tribes there are many *people of the same family title. These are unable to trace any relationship with each other, but wherever they are they find themselves in possession of ceremonial customs which are quite peculiar to those who bear that name.* Thus the particular customs observed at the birth of a child are exactly the same in different parts of the country among those who have the *same family title*, although they have never heard of each other's existence, whilst their neighbours of the *same clan*, but of *different family names*, have altogether dissimilar customs.[2] Here the name and the typical custom lead down to that unity of origin which is lost sight of on the surface. This equally applies to such typical customs and names on a far larger scale than that of the Kaffir tribes. Also it shows how the name, the mark, and the custom have persisted together from time immemorial.

So is it on the American continent. Not the remotest affinity can be detected by grammarians between the languages of the Pawnees and the neighbouring Mandans,[3] but when it comes to a type like that of the four quarters and the cross, together with the customs and super-stitions associated with the type, then the earlier connection becomes apparent and the possession is found to be in common.

James describes the Kiawa-Kaskaia Indians as nations united "under the influence of the Bear-tooth," yet they were totally ignorant of each other's spoken language, and when two individuals of different nations wished to converse *they did so freely by the language of gesture-signs.*[4] That was the earlier and simpler medium of communication reverted to when the spoken language was dispersed. The primal unity was shown by the Totemic "Bear-tooth" and by gesture-signs. Here, then, we get down to a record of the past that lies beyond spoken language, the living memory of man, or of the tribe, the local race, or the human race itself. This record is the language of symbolism, a skeleton of all other forms of human speech, whose bones are like the fossil remains that exist as proofs of an original unity between the lands that are now severed, just as the bones of the Mammoth in Britain and France show that the two lands, though divided now, were originally one.

As Emerson has it, "*a good symbol is a missionary to convince thousands.*" When Europe was first converted to Christianity, it was by making use of the same symbols that were hallowed in the Pagan

[1] Hahn, *Tsuni Goam*, p. 2.   [2] Theal, *Kaffir Folk-lore*, p. 198.
[3] Brinton, p. 71.
[4] James, *Expedition to the Rocky Mountains*, vol. iii. p. 52. Burton, *City of the Saints; Gesture Signs.* Tylor, *Primitive Culture and Early History.*

Cult ; the rooted Types being indefinitely more potent than any later sense engrafted on them.

Whether for good or ill the symbol has proved all-powerful. The hold of symbolism is in its way as strong in civilised society as in the savage world. CRESTOLATRY is as nearly a form of devotion as Christolatry, Totemism, or Fetishism, except that a Briton who had the fish, stag, or vine in his coat-of-arms, would not now-a-days think of totally abstaining from fish, venison, or wine in consequence ; as would the Bechuana of Southern Africa or the Kol of Nagpore ; although the time was, in these islands, when he would have done so, as may be seen by the non-eating of the pig, hare, and eel in the past.

The king, as sacred ruler, acquired the vesture of his divinity and the halo of awful light because he was made to personate or reflect the deity on earth, and thus became vicariously divine. Kingship, *in this phase*, was not founded on the human character, however supremely able, however exalted in the forms of chieftainship, but on the typical and representative character. Hence the "divinity that doth hedge a king," which did not emanate from him but was conferred upon him ; he wore it from without, as a lay figure invested with the drapery of deity.

The *Ank* (Eg.) or the *Inca* (Peru.) represented the living and ever-living one, who was therefore not a human being, and on this ground was based the fiction of the king being the undying one. So the king never dies. This was not directly derived from the natural genesis, but is in accordance with the typology formulated in Egypt and extant wherever the title of Inca, Ying, or King is found.

Hence the king becomes the life and the master of life to his people, as in Siam, in a very literal later fashion, where the typical character is superstitiously interpreted. The king in Egypt was the living image of the Solar God. He was the divine child, the Repa, god-begotten, who grew up into the god in person on earth. And just as the king was glorified as the sun, *so were the earlier rulers glorified under more primitive types of power*. In Madagascar the monarch, like the Pharaoh of Egypt, was the potent bull. The king of Ashanti is glorified as the snake and the lion; the Zulu king as the tiger, lion or mountain. In Guatemala the king was the tiger of the wood, the laughing jaguar, the mighty boa, the op-pressing eagle. The Norse king *Gorm* was the great worm (or Crom) the dragon-king. The chief in a Kaffir folk-tale is a snake with five heads. By the earliest titles the bearers were assimilated to the most terrible types of power and the most primitive forms of force, and, therefore, to the elementary gods, which preceded the sun, moon, and star gods of the cycles of time.

When the symbol has lost its significance, the man or woman still remains to receive the homage of ignorance and the sacrifices that once were offered intelligently to the visible and living image of the god, as it was in Egypt, or to the demon in Africa beyond. So potent is the influence of symbols over the mind that the world's welfare cannot afford to have their indefinable appeal perverted by cunning or ignorance.

Symbols still dominate the minds of men and usurp the place of realities. A symbol may cause humanity proudly to rise in stature or grovel pronely in the dust. Who has not felt the flutter of the flag in one's pulses and been stirred with rapture to horripilation at sight of some war-worn, shot-riddled remnant, stained with the blood of its bearers, which had braved and beckoned forward the battle on some desperate day, that made all safe once more for the dear land of our love? Whether used for good or evil the symbol, that outward and visible shape of the idea, is supreme. Most helpful of servants, most tyrannous of masters. Expression still attains the summit in a symbol. It belongs to the universal language, the masonry of nature, the mode of the immortals.

In the case of the flag the link betwixt the fact and its sign is not lost, but precisely where it is lost and we have no clue to the natural verity signified, the origin is there claimed to be supernatural, and credited with the power of conferring a divine sanction on all sorts of devilry. The same influence will prevent the Hindu, if starving, from tasting a bit of cow, or killing the monkey that is devastating villages.

The ancient symbolism was a mode of expression which has bequeathed a mould of thought that imprisons the minds of myriads as effectually as the toad shut up by the rock into which it was born.

The human mind has long suffered an eclipse and been darkened and dwarfed in the shadow of ideas, the real meaning of which has been lost to the moderns. Myths and allegories whose significance was once unfolded to initiates in the mysteries have been adopted in ignorance and re-issued as real truths directly and divinely vouchsafed to mankind for the first and only time! The earlier religions had their myths interpreted. We have ours mis-interpreted. And a great deal of what has been imposed on us as God's own true and sole revelation to man is a mass of inverted myth, under the shadow of which we have been cowering as timorously as birds in the stubble when an artificial kite in the shape of a hawk is hovering overhead. The parables of the primæval thinkers have been elevated to the sphere, so to say, as the "hawk" or "serpent," the "bull" or the "crab" that gave names to certain groups of stars, and we are in precisely the same relationship to those parables and allegories as we should be to astronomical facts if we thought the serpent and bull, the crab and hawk were real animal and bird instead of constellations with symbolical names. The simple realities of the earliest time were

expressed by signs and symbols and these have been taken and
applied to later thoughts and converted by Theologists into problems
and metaphysical mysteries which they have no basis for and can only
wrangle over *en l'air*, unable to touch solid earth with one foot when
they want to expel opponents with the other.

The Greek and still more *modern misinterpretations of ancient
typology have made it the most terrible tyranny in the mental domain.*

Much of our folk-lore and most of our popular beliefs are fossilized
symbolism. The fables and allegories that fed the minds of the
initiated, when interpreted, became the facts of the ignorant
when the oral teaching of the mysteries was superseded by letters
and direct reading, because the hidden wisdom had never been
published. Misinterpreted mythology has so profoundly infected
religion, poetry, art, and criticism, that it has created a cult of the
unreal. Unreality is glorified, called the ideal, and considered to be
poetry, a mocking image of beauty, that blinds its followers, until
they cannot recognise the natural reality.

In the great conflict of the age between the doctrine of evolution
and the dogmas of mythology, between the Marvellous and the
Impossible, our art and poetry are continually found on the side of
the mytholators. The myths still furnish lay-figures for the painter
and poet, and lives are spent in the vain endeavour to make them
live by those and for those who have never known what they signified
at first. Youth yet falls in love with them, and has the desire to
reproduce; Humanity is re-cast in the present according to a lion-
browed, ape-toed Greek type of the past (described later on), and
the humanly heroic is superseded by the counterfeit divine. The
prostitute of primitive intercourse, the great harlot of mythology, is
continued as a supreme personage in poetry, whether as Helen of
Troy or Gwenivere of Britain, or Iseult of Brittany, the Welsh
Essyllt, one of the " *three unchaste maidens*" of British mythology.
It is on the assumption that these lay-figures of poetry, art, or
religion, were human once that an interest is taken in them now.
But the assumption is false, and falsehood, however attractive, is
always fraudulent.

These divinities of the bygone time may serve to beguile the
children of to-day as dolls for dandling, but they are outgrown by
all who have attained the stature and status of real men and women.
Shakspeare, we are told, has no heroes. Happily to a large extent
he drew from nature instead of the models of mythology.

The Jews are caught and confined in a complete net-work of
symbolism, so closely woven round them that they are cramped and
catalepsed into rigidity from long keeping of the same postures, and
the interstices are almost too narrow for breath to pass through.
So is it with the Muhammedan and Parsee ritual of rigid rule and
ceremonial routine; a religion of form in which the trivial is stereo-

typed for all time because of its mystical, that is emblematical, character.

The world of thought is thronged with false births and malformations which were entirely bred of perverted typology. The theological doctrines of evil, the depravity of matter, the fallen nature of the flesh have no other basis and had no other beginning.

Religion itself is sick and daily dying in the process of unliving and sloughing off that which has been imposed upon it by a misinterpretation of symbolism.

It is not the ancient legends that lie; the creators of these did not deal falsely with us. The falsehood is solely the result of ignorantly mistaking mythology for "revelation" and historic truth.

They did not teach geology in the ancient mysteries. The Christian world assumed that they did, and therefore it was found in opposition to scientific geology.

They did not teach the historic fall of man in the myths. Theologists have assumed that they did, and consequently were found to be utterly opposed to the *ascent of man* unveiled by the doctrine of evolution. The earliest limits of the human mind have been re-imposed upon it as the latest, in the name of religion, until it looks at last as if all that faith accepted is arrayed against and at enmity with everything that science affirms to be true.

As the later people of many lands no longer recognise the Celt stones for things of human workmanship, but consider them to have fallen ready-made from Heaven, so has it been with the simplest ideas of the primitive or Archaic men which have been unrecognised because out-grown. These were picked up and preserved as divine. They are believed to have come direct from Heaven and are treasured as such in that repository which is in reality the European Museum of the Kamite mythology.

Nor were the symbolists insane as they appear to Max Müller.

There is nothing of insanity, nothing irrational in the origines of mythology, when the subject is considered in the light of evolution. The irrationality arises from and remains with the non-evolutionist view. It may be affirmed here, for it will be proved hereafter, that the ancient Wisdom is not made up of guesses at truth, but is composed of Truths which were carefully ascertained and verified; that the chief character of the myths in their primitive phases is a most perfect congruity and that they have the simplicity of nature itself.

The only work of value left to be written on mythology or typology is one that will account for the facts upon which the myths and religions are founded by relating them once more to the phenomena in which they originated, so that we may know how and where we stand in regard to a beginning. That is now attempted. This work aims at getting to the root and discovering the genesis of those ideas that have caused more profound perplexity to the human mind in modern times, without benefit to the individual or the race, than all the problems solved by science, with its glorious gains and rich results for universal humanity.

The idea of De Brosses that "*these fetishes are anything which people like to select for adoration, a tree, a mountain, the ocean, a piece of wood, the tail of a lion, a pebble, a shell, fish, plant, flower, cow goat, elephant, or anything else*," is entirely erroneous, as regards the origines. We might as well expect to select our words by the promiscuous heaping together of *any* of the letters at random. What he calls fetishes are types which were almost as much the result of natural selection as are any other things in nature, so little conscious choice had man in the matter, so slow was the process of adoption, so great the economy of means on the part of nature. But once evolved they were preserved as faithfully as any other types. De Brosses had no glimpse of the origin of symbolism which he called Fetishism.

Men did not "set to" to select and adopt their symbols, they made use of things to express their thoughts, and those things became symbols in what grew to be a system of Homonymism which was created by the human consciousness so gradually under the guidance of natural law, that individual authorship was unknown.

Mr. Spencer has rightly denied that "*conscious* symbolization" is at the *foundation* of certain ceremonial customs and rites of what he terms "ceremonial government." He has argued that there is just as little basis for the belief that primitive men deliberately adopted symbols as that they deliberately made rules of social contract. Symbolism was *not* a conscious creation of the human mind ; man had no choice in the matter. He did not begin by *thinging* his thoughts in intentional enigmas of expression.

Necessity, the mother of invention, was the creator of types and symbols. The type is but a first pattern which becomes the model figure because it was first. *Tepi* (Eg.) the type, signifies the first. The earliest signs that were made and adopted for current usage were continued as the primary types which had to serve for several later applications.

We have to remember that *doing* was earlier than *saying*, and the dumb drama was acted first. When all allowance has been made for the influence of heredity, the deaf-mute who imitates faces and peculiar features and gestures to represent the likeness of certain persons is an extant specimen of the primitive and pre-verbal mimic. Naturally picture-making by gesture signs preceded the art of picture-writing or drawing of figures on the ground, on bones, stones and the bark of trees. Also the earliest figure-drawing was by imitation of objects as they appear, and not as they are conceived by *thought*. Things were pourtrayed before thoughts by those who were thingers rather than thinkers. The men who first employed signs had not attained the art which supplies an ideal representation of natural facts ; they directly represented their meaning in visible forms. The signs enter a second phase as the representatives of ideas when they become ideographic and metaphorical.

The figure of an eye directly represents sight and seeing, but the eye as reflector of the image becomes a symbol. The eye of Horus is his mother as mirror and reproducer of the babe-image. The Uta eye signifies health, welfare, safety, and salvation, because when placed with the mummy in the tomb it denoted reproduction for another life. The Macusi Indians of Guiana say that when the body decays in death the "Man in the eyes will not die," the image reflected by the eye being emblematic of the shadow or soul. The Nootkas of Nootka Sound were found, by Lord, to be in possession of a precious *medicine ;* a solid piece of copper hammered flat, and of an oval or eye-shape, the chief device on which was an EYE represented in many sizes. This *medicine* was most carefully preserved and shown only on extraordinary occasions.[1] This was identical with the symbolic eye of health, welfare, and salvation in Egypt.

The Hottentots to this day will take the root of a shrub called kharab, cut it up and pound it on stones. When one is hungry he takes a pinch of the dust and goes to the house of his neighbour where instead of asking for food, he throws the powder on the fire and expects food to be given to him.[2] The charm is known as the food-provider. Here the action is elaborately symbolical. In the earliest stage of sign-language it would have sufficed to point to the mouth and the food. Again the tip of the crocodile's tail is the hieroglyphic sign for *black*, not because it was black, for it is but slate-coloured when darkest, and is often of a reddish brown. The *type* therefore in this case does not depend directly on the complexion. According to Hor-Apollo the tail of the crocodile signifies dark-ness because the animal inflicts death on any other animal which it may have caught by first striking it with its tail (?) and rendering it incapable of motion.[3] That is one idea. The crocodile likewise denoted sunset. Its two eyes typified the sunrise, its tail the sunset or darkness. All day long the animal lay on land and when the night came down it disappeared in the waters. The tip of its tail was the *end of it*, and the black signified was night ; the colouring matter, so to say, was mental and this sign became its ideograph. The crocodile, his mark! that had been made on their minds by actual contact, and the wrestling for supremacy during ages of watching of this intelligent one of the deep, or the deep one, not unmixed with a sense of relief at the nightly-vanishing tip of its tail.

[1] It was seen by Lord, *Naturalist*, vol. ii. p. 257.
[2] Hahn, *Tsuni-Goam*, p. 83.   [3] Book i. 70.

A distinct statement of the symbolic nature of the sacred fish may be quoted from the Ritual.[1] One of the forty-two sins was the catching of "*the fish which typify.*" These then were sacred because symbolical.

The meaning of many curious customs and rites cannot be directly ascertained, for the memory is lost, and the ritual of the cult was unwritten. Nor can it be directly derived from nature, which has outgrown that infantile age of humanity, however lucky the guesses we may make. True, the evolutionist is able to affirm that such customs as we now call symbolical are not accounted for until we can trace them to their natural genesis. Here is the imperative need of the typological phase of these things to interpret that which was once the natural; the directly representative, which is still reflected for us by the older races of the world in the primitive customs, religious rites, superstitious beliefs, folk-lore, and fetishes; also in the mirror of mythology. Betwixt us and the natural genesis of ancient customs, rites, ceremonies and religious beliefs, lie the culture represented by Egypt, America, Babylonia, and China, and the decadence and obliviousness of the dying races; and at least we need to know what Egypt has yet to say on these earliest simplicities which have become the later mysteries; she who is the contemporary of time, or rather its creator; the chronologer, the revealer, the interpreter of antiquity; the sole living memory of the dark, oblivious land (the very consciousness of Kam), the speaker for the dumb, unfathomable past, who gave, in graven granite, permanence to the primitive signs of thought, and types of expression; whose stamp or mint-mark may be found generally on this current coinage of the whole world. Without some such clue as Egypt offers, any direct or literal rendering of that which has become symbolic, is likely to be erroneous. The decaying races can but seldom tell what is the intention underlying the type. They have their symbols without the means or desire to interpret them for us. They have their thoughts, for which they do not find expression; their feelings, that may not be transfigured into thought; but for us they are dumb in the awful shadow of the past that hangs over them, and they cannot explain the meaning of its mystery; they have no interpreter between themselves and us for the language of symbols, and until these are understood we shall never understand them. We English mix with 250,000,000 of natives in India, and can rule over them, but cannot comprehend them. Yet those natives who read the present work will penetrate its significance far more profoundly than the writer's own countrymen, whose knowledge is too late a creation, and whose minds live too extensively on the surface of the present for them to get *en rapport* with their remoter ideas, and establish any real *camaraderie* of relationship with the peoples of the far-off past.

[1] Ch. cxxv.

Egypt can help us to enter the primordial domain of human thought. Egypt or Kam is the parent of all primitive typology, and she alone can adequately explain it, as she was the great conscious recorder of that which had been unconsciously created for the commonest use in the inner African birthplace.

What is here termed Typology had its origin in gesture-language, where a few signs supplemented by a few sounds served all purposes for expressing sensations, feelings, and ideas. Gesture-language was (so to say) developed and made permanent in typology. The origin of both may be traced to the fact that men visualised thought in pictures, which they pourtrayed to the eye, and reflected things in their mental mirror long before they could speak in words, just as the deaf-mutes tell us they thought before mastering the alphabet of gesture-signs. The origines of mythology, symbolism, and numbers have all to be sought in the stage of gesture-language, which was the first mode of figuring an image. For instance, a pin made crooked to throw into the "Wishing-well" is a prayer made permanent. It is a survival of gesture-language; a kind of drawing made by the dumb for the invisible powers to see. The sign can be interpreted by the hieroglyphic *Uten, a twisted bit of metal*, signifying an offering, a libation, the appeal of sacrifice, therefore a type of prayer. Such sign-language is yet extant, and is illustrated at a distance by the Chinaman who failing to convey his meaning by words will draw the ideographic character on the palm of his hand, or with his fan in the air, saying, "*I mean that!*"

Stanley tells us how the Waganda frequently have recourse to drawing figures on the ground to illustrate imperfect oral description, and that they show surprising cleverness in the truthfulness of their rough-and-ready delineations. The skill of the Bushmen, Kaffirs and some Negroes in the drawing and modelling of figures is a result of the primordial gesture-language transferred from the air to solid earth.

Leibnitz has said that the writing of the Chinese might seem to have been invented by a deaf person, its formation was so near to that of gesture-signs addressed to the eye. The oldest Chinese characters, two hundred in number, are called *Siang-Hing*, that is images or ideographic representations. A considerable number of Chinese ideographs are identical with the Egyptian.

The most ancient Egyptian hieroglyphics are those which convey their meaning by direct representation or imitation. In a later phase these were still continued as ideographic determinatives, so that notwithstanding the development of the hieroglyphics the links are complete from the gesture-signs down to the alphabet.

Man invoking, praying, adoring, rejoicing, dancing, striking, building, sculpturing, tilling the ground, fighting, reposing, ruling, carrying, walking, old man and young child, are represented directly

C 2

in the act of making the appropriate gesture-signs or visible speech which all men can read at sight. Things belonging to sight are indicated by an eye. An arm outstretched is the sign of offering, and making a present. The ear is an emblem of listening, hearing, judging ; the nose, of breathing, smelling, and the delight of life or existence. A pair of legs going denotes the transitive verb ; and the legs *in transitu* were first.

A comparison of certain Egyptian signs with those of the North American Indians tends to the conclusion that they had a common origin.[1] The Egyptians engraved such hieroglyphics in granite and the Indians still figure them in the air. But the typology is at times identical and the two continue to meet in one and the same meaning.

With the Indians one sign serves to convey several meanings according to a prototypal idea. The index finger lifted above the face signifies over, heaven, great Spirit, and day, or to-day. So in the hieroglyphics *Her*, the sign of Heaven, denotes above, over, superior, a spirit, and the same word means day. Thus, one form of the sign is the face (Her), above, and the Indian sign is made above the face.

In making the signs for day, morning, noon, to-morrow, or yester-day, the subject must face the south with his back to the north, and right hand to the west. This attitude shows the Sabean and pre-solar standpoint in which *the south was the face and front and the north the hinder part*, whereas in the solar reckoning the east was the front and the west was the back.

In Egyptian imagery the south is the front, the north the hinder part. The male emblem as the *bahu* denotes the front, and is the figure of "*before.*" The female is the image of behind and the hinder part, probably in relation to primitive usage, when woman was as the animal. This typology is illustrated by the Bongos, who bury the male facing the north, or frontwise, and the female facing the south or hinderwise, according to the Kamite reckoning.

It is probable that the Indian sign of *before* is an equivalent for the Egyptian ideograph. "*The left hand representing an imaginary line, the action of the right makes it the front, or before ;*" the forefinger is pointed outward, and the hand thrust forward forcibly and rapidly. These gestures tend to identify the original meaning with the Egyptian masculine sign. When the Indians, according to Dunbar's list of gesture-signs, denote *the man* by closing the hand and with the extended fore-finger drawing a line down over the stomach from the upper to the lower part of the body, they are indicating the male as *the front one,* just as the *Bahu* hieroglyphic of the male signifies

[1] *Introduction to the Study of Sign-Language among the North American Indians*, by Garrick Mallery : Washington, 1880. *A Collection of Gesture-Signs and Signals of the North American Indians*, by Garrick Mallery : 1880. *Sign-Language*, by Garrick Mallery : 1881.

"*before.*"   *Behind* is pourtrayed by making the gesture for before, and then swinging the hand *backwards from the thigh*, with a motion quickened as the hand goes back.[1]   Behind (Khepsh the North, or Khept the Rump) is represented in the hieroglyphics by the *hinder thigh*.

The typology of the left as the lower hand, the feminine half, corresponding to the hinder part and the nethermost of two, runs through all the Indian signs.   The lower, hinder part, and the left hand are feminine in the quarters north and west.   The Indian sign for the female (squaw) is made by passing the flat extended hands with fingers joined down the sides of the head as far as the shoulders to denote long hair.   Then the *left* hand is held transversely before the body, pointing to the right.   The right hand, index downwards, is then passed beneath the *left* hand along the abdomen, and the sign is made which signifies "*of woman born.*"[2]

"*Below,*" as with the Egyptians, is identical with the *left* hand ; the indicatory movements being made with the left, or lower, hand, palm downwards, and the eyes kept looking down.   Also to rub the back of the left hand with the fingers of the right, is a sign of black, (Dakota, 4) the lower, night side, the English *Car-hand*, for the left hand, and *Car-land* for low-land.

This identifies the left hand, the Car-hand, with the *Kar*, or *Karh* (Eg.) of the lower, the night side, the dark.   In gathering the selago herb, Pliny says, the Druids plucked it with the right hand wrapped in a tunic, the *left* being uncovered, as though they were stealing it.[3]   This is the pictograph of stealing according to the Indian sign-gestures.   In these, the left hand and night, or the dark side, being identical as the *under* hand.

The action of stealing is pourtrayed by holding the left forearm a little in front of, and across the body for cover and concealment, then the seizure is suddenly made with the right hand, which feels furtively, grasps, and withdraws ; the act being performed under the security of darkness or night, typified by the left hand.   Stealing is yet described as " underhand work."

The *left* hand plays the same part in the mimograph of *fruitless*. It is brought forward ; the *left* index punches the right palm, and is then swept backwards and downwards by the left side.   This sign of negation and deficiency is employed by the Hottentots, who describe a stingy chief as being *Gei-âre*, or greatly left-handed ; *âre*, with the click, being identical with the English *Car* for the left hand ; the Egyptian *Kar* for underneath.

Some antique statues have been lately found by M. de Sarzil in the mounds of Tello, belonging to an art and civilisation which preceded those of Babylonia and Assyria.   They have all one attitude, the arms being crossed on the breast with *the left hand clasping the right.*

[1] Mallery, *Collection*, p. 35 (Ojibwa 4).   [2] Mallery, p. 57.
[3] *Book of Beginnings*, vol. i. p. 88.

This is a gesture-sign to be read at sight. The left hand being the lower and inferior, this is the attitude of humility, or an act of worship. Whether the object be human or divine must be determined by the surroundings, but the gesture-sign belongs to gesture-language, and tells its story according to one system wherever found.

The significance of giving the " right hand of fellowship," and in making a covenant, or of being seated on the *right* hand still depends on the origin in gesture-language, the right being the superior hand. The symbolism of the left hand is also applied by the Indians to the representation of death, in which it is held flat over the face with the back outwards, when the right hand similarly held is passed *below* the other, gently touching it (Wied).[1] This sign likewise denotes the passage under ; death itself being described as " *going under.*" In the representation of " dying," the *left* hand is held as in the sign for dead and the right is passed under it with a slow, gentle, interrupted movement.

The signs for death point to drowning as the typical end and mode of " *going under.*" One illustration is by reversal of the hand, which reads " *upset,*" " *keeled over.*" Water is the most primary and permanent of types, one of the Two Truths of Egypt ; the natural opposite or antithesis of breath. The Egyptian ideograph of *negation, no, not, without, deprived of*, is a wave of water ; and the Indian representations of death include a downward movement of the hand outstretched with the palm upward. The hand is lowered gradually with a wave-like motion. In another sign the palm of the hand is placed at a short distance from the side of the head, and then withdrawn gently in an oblique downward direction, at the same time the upper part of the body bends, leans, and the sinking motion is thus imitated twice over. The word " Ke-*neeboo*" is pronounced slowly. Colonel Mallery points out that in Ojibwa the word *Nibo* means he dies, he sleeps, the original significance being he leans, from *Anibeia*, it is leaning ;[2] but the leaning, keeling over, and sinking, all indicate death by water, and in the chief Indian languages, *Nibo*, for " he dies " is the type-name for water, as

Neebi, Ojibwa.	*Nepee*, Knistinaux.	*Nippe*, Massachusetts.
Nebee, Potowatami.	*Nepee*, Skoffi.	*Nip*, Narragansetts.
Nipish, Ottawa.	*Nepee*, Sheshatapoosh.	*Nape*, Miami.
Nipi, Old Algonkin.	*Nabi*, Abenaki.	

Death by drowning was a form of sinking and going under that was obvious to the earliest perception, and this negation of life by means of water is figured in the hieroglyphic sign of *negation*.

It has been said that there is no negative in nature[3] but the men

---

[1] Mallery, p. 86.   [2] *Collection*, p. 83.
[3] *Negation.*—" *Now we come upon a feature which is inconsiderable in its bulk. . . . but yet one which covers with its influence half the realm of language. This is the apparatus of Negation. . . . Where in the outer world is there such a thing as a Negative ? Where is the natural phenomenon that would suggest to the human*

who made water the sign for *no, en,* or *nun* had observed that it was the negation of breath, and the hieroglyphics show the type of negation in running water. Also the word *skhet* (Eg.) which means to slay, signifies to *capsize. Khem* (Eg.) is a form of no, not, and the word likewise means dead.

With this waving and sinking of the hand to indicate death we may connect, and possibly interpret, the Indian signs of *no,* the emphatic negative. One of these is made by moving the hand in front of the face ; another by oscillating the index finger before the face from right to left. This latter sign, made by the Pah-Utes, is said by Canon de Jorio to be in use also among the Neapolitans, and in many parts of Southern Europe. Oscillation shows negation whether made with the head or the hand. This sign is extant among the Japanese.

The shake of the head is another mode of negation corresponding to the wave and the waving motion. Also the natives near Torres Straits have a gesture of negation in which they hold up the right hand and shake it by turning it half round and back again two or three times,[1] which corresponds to our shake of the head as a sign of "*no.*" The essential feature is the *waving* or *wave* which imitates the wave of water that constitutes the hieroglyphic *no,* emphatic negation, none (Nun).

A Chinese character signifying *law* is composed of "water" and "to go," why is unknown ; but, as water denotes the negative, the two signs read "no go," or "thou shalt not," which was the earliest formula of law.

Darwin, on *The Expression of the Emotions,*[2] remarks that "the waving of the hand *from right to left,* which is used as a negative by some savages, may have been invented in imitation of shaking the head ; but whether the opposite movement of waving the hand in a *straight* line from the face *which is used in affirmation* has arisen through antithesis or in some quite distinct manner, is doubtful." The left hand in the Kamite typology is the negative, feminine, nether, underhand ; the emphatic negative being expressed by both hands held low down, whilst the *straight* is the *right* and thus the *right* hand waved in a *straight* line has the value of yes.

Straight is synonymous with true or right and true, that is with *Må,* which also means "*come,*" "*you may,*" and is therefore an affirmative. So the Dakota signs of yes and truth are identical. Possibly this sign of *Må* or *Måi,* for "come," "you may," can be read at root by "*Maaui*" (Eg.) which signifies "*in the power of.*" More fully "*You may come, I am in your power, truly, or empty-handed ; see the palm of my hand.*"

mind the idea of Negation ? There is no negative in Nature."—Earle, *Philology of the English Tongue,* pp. 421—425.
[1] Jukes, *Letters, &c.,* p. 248.   [2] Ch. i.

In the Egyptian ideograph of the verb to pray and beseech the palms of the two hands are presented *outward*, showing that the hands are empty.

In a similar manner the sound of " *Cooey*," which the Australian settlers have adopted from the natives, affords its intimation. In the Yarra dialect the word *Kooo-ey* signifies " *Alone*," or " I am alone ;" and this intelligence is first uttered by the messenger from one tribe to another whilst he is yet a mile from their place of encampment.

In the Apache, Comanche, Kaiowa and Wichita sign, the palm of the right hand is afterwards thrown against the horizontal palm of the left hand, showing in another way that *both hands are empty*, although only one was lifted in invitation.

This reading may be illustrated by the Yoruban saying, " *The Palm of the hand does not lie*," or it never deceives one. The same fundamental meaning survives in the phrase of clear or " clean-handed."

The Egyptian Ideograph of peaceful and gentle actions is the arm with the hand fallen thus ⌒◻ . Whereas the determinative of forcible actions is the clenched hand uplifted.

The Indian intimation of No, Not, Negation, is conveyed by the hand being waved in refusing to accept the idea or statement presented. This action is in keeping with the hieroglyphic sign for No, Not, Negation, with the two hands waved apart and extended palm-downwards ⌐⌐. In the Dakota sign (67) the hand is held flat and pointing upwards before the right side of the chest, then thrown outward and pressed down. Also there is a strong coincidence between the negative particle " *Ma*," given by Landa, and the Egyptian emphatic negative.

According to Fornander, the same gesture sign for " No " prevails throughout Polynesia. He says, " *Ask a person if he had such or such a thing, and, two to one, instead of saying ' No,' he will turn his hand or hands palm-downwards, in sign of a negative answer.*" [1]

This figure of negation, of forbidding and prohibiting represented by the hieroglyphic ⌐⌐, is yet made by our railway signalmen for staying the train and preventing it from starting. It is still the " *No*" of gesture speech.

The explanation as given by Captain Burton of the Indian signs for Truth and Lie, is sufficient to affiliate the gestures to the " Two Truths " of Egypt, which are manifold in their application as two aspects or phases of the one idea, such as yes or no, before and behind, good and bad, right and wrong, the dual justice or twofold truth. Captain Burton says the forefinger *extended straight* from the mouth is the sign for telling truth, as " one word," whereas two fingers denote the " *double-tongue*," or a lie. Truth is that which comes straight from the heart or mouth. Speaking the truth is straight speech.[2] Among

[1] Vol. i. p. 243.   [2] Mallery, *Ojibwa*, i.

the Khoi-Khoi, law means that which is straight, right, true, in a straight line, in exact agreement with *Maat*, for the law as inflexible rule. Also the gentleman's or great man's word is the true word (Amab).[1]

Although comparatively superseded by the cubit measure, yet the finger is at times found to be an Egyptian determinative of *Mā*, the True, Truth, or Goddess of Truth. *Mā* signifies to *stretch out* (*protendere*), to hold out straight before one, just as the Indians extend the finger. This stretching out straight is the sign of right rule, the finger being an early form of the rule measure, or the straight, right, and true. All the meanings meet in the Zend *erezu* for rule, straight, right, true, and the name of the finger.

The extended finger was the rule-sign of Truth, of *Mā*, which has two phases, positive and negative, or true and untrue, the untrue being indicated by the second finger as the dual *Mā*. If we read Mâti as Makti, that IS double-tongue. Here it may be remarked that one sign of *Mā* is the hand outstretched in offering the sign of *stretched-out*, but *not* of hand, and that the Mexicans pourtrayed a hand—*Ma* (itl)—to signify the sound of *Ma*, and *not the word hand*.

The Egyptian Ankh, to pair, couple, clasp together, duplicate, naturally includes marriage, and, as we still say, the marriage-tie. The Ankh-knot is made in gesture-speech by forming the loop with the tips of the thumb and forefinger. When Goat's-Nose (in Pantagruel)[2] makes this sign by softly coupling the nails of the two members together, Pantagruel says the sign denotes marriage. This is the modern Neapolitan sign for "love," and was a sign of marriage and of Venus in Italy from remotest times.

This sign of coupling, unity and marriage is made by Vishnu with his right hand, in the act of embracing Lakshmi with his left.[3] When the Ankh tie was formed, that served the purpose, but the gesture made with the thumb and forefinger was first.

The knot or tie (Ankh) is a hieroglyphic sign of life and living. Ankh also means to clasp, and the Indian sign of life and alive is made with a particular mode of making the clasp with the thumb and middle (root) finger of the right hand.[4]

In the sign for death (Comanche) the Gesture-maker might be undoing the Ankh-sign of life as the instructions are : "*Bring the left hand to the left breast, hand half clinched, then bring the right hand to the left with the thumb and forefinger in such a position as if you were going to take a bit of string from the forefinger of the left hand, and pull the right hand as if you were stretching out a string.*"[5] This reads "*Soul going to happy hunting grounds;*" and as before said looks

[1] Hahn, *Tsuni-Goam*, p. 18.   [2] Rabelais, book iii. chap. xx.
[3] Moore's *Hindu Pantheon*, plate ii. fig. 1.   [4] Dakota, 4.
[5] Mallery, *Collection*, pp. 20—84.

like the loosening of the Ankh-knot of life. Moreover, the untying in the sign of death is the right natural antithesis to the tie or clasp (Ankh) as the symbol of life.

The death-sign described by Host is made by placing the "*Left forefinger and thumb against the heart, act as if taking a hair from the thumb and forefinger of the left hand with the thumb and forefinger of the right and slowly casting it from you, only letting the left hand remain at the heart and let the index finger of the right hand point outward toward the horizon.*"[1] Here also we have the sign of the knot or cord which formed the Ankh-symbol of life, and the pantomime of loosing it ; that loosing of the silver חבל (Eg. *Kabu* the Cord) described by the Hebrew writer, which also probably applies to the noose-symbol of life.

The mode of describing the meaning *destroyed, all gone, no more*, is by an action of the palms. These are rubbed together, signifying *rubbed out*. The hands are held horizontally and the palms are rubbed together two or three times circularly ; the right hand is then carried off from the left in a short horizontal curve. They are *rubbed* out. This is an express signification of "*ter*" (Eg.) for killing, running through, transfixing, obliterating, literally to *wipe* and *rub out*.

One mimograph of the personal pronoun I, myself, is made by striking the breast repeatedly with the clenched hand, and it is noticeable that *Ank* (Eg.) the personal pronoun, the I, I the king, also means to clench or clasp the hand. Others touch the top of the nose with the index finger, or lay it along the ridge with the top resting between the eyes. So in Egypt.

"*He pronounced an oath by the sovereign Lord* (the Pharaoh) *striking his nose and his ears with both hands upon a rod.*"[2]

In some languages the man, the I, and the nose have one name.

The personal pronoun I is—

Nira in Illinois.	*Nal*, Ostiac.	*Nyr*, Ziranian.
Nir in the old Algonkin.	*Nol*, Vogul.	*Onari*, Guaque (Carib.)
Nil, Micmac.	*Nyr*, Votiak.	*Naran*, Ticunas.
Nel, Etchemin.	*Nyr*, Permian.	*Nyore*, Mose (African).
Nelah, Shawni.		

In Egyptian *Nra* is the man, *Nra* the neb of the vulture. In Tsheremis *Ner* is the nose. In Latin *Nare* is a nose ; also the nostrils of a hawk. Here the three types of man, the personal pronoun, and the nose meet under one word, and are in keeping with the Indian sign of " I."

The Arapahoes make a gesture sign, which denotes their name, by taking the nose between the thumb and forefinger.[3] And as in other Indian gesture signs the nose is the ideograph of the personal pronoun I, and as the nose is an equivalent for Ankh (Eg.) I, I am,

---

[1] Mallery, *Introduction*, p. 21.
[2] *Spoliation of Tombs*, p. 5—7 ; *Recoras*, vol. xii. p. 109.
[3] Mallery, *Collection*, p. 154.

the king, these according to the typology are claiming a supremacy among men. If interpreted by the Nar or Nose of the vulture they would be the sure hunters, the far-sighted, the victorious.

The Todas of the Neilgherry Hills have a mode of salutation, supposed to be one of respect, in which they raise the open right hand to the brow and rest the thumb on the nose. The hieroglyphic nose when human signifies pleasure and delight; glad to smell you as it were.

The nose as the Ank or personal pronoun I is equivalent to the Eskimo *Innuk*, a type-name for man. In one of the dialects (Kuskutshewak) *nikh* is the name for the nose, which is *Kinaga* in Kadiak. *Innuwok* in Eskimo is life and to live. In the Maya we have *Inic, Winic, Winak;* in Javanese *Wong*. The Iroquois *Onnhe*, to live, is a modified form of the same archetypal word, and probably the *Wong* or spirit of Inner Africa is the *Unku* (Eg.) a spirit; the spirit was primarily the breath, hence the connection with the nose as an organ of breathing, and a type of the I, the *Ank*, who in Egypt had become the king, the living one.

The nasal sound *Nug* of the Cherokee language is the Inner African *Nge*, the most common form of the personal pronoun "I," in Africa, or the rest of the world. This represents the nose, and the personal pronoun "I," the Ankh itself *in the domain of sounds*.

The mouth, eye, nose, and ear are all forms of the Ankh-type of life and living; the being, the one who IS, the *I am*, the I see, or I hear, I breathe, I smell out, I perceive, with the particular organ for Ideographic determinator. Hence the mouth, eye, nose, and ear became natural hieroglyphics of the I in person, sufficient to distinguish four different ideas or persons, and to furnish four totemic signs. The Chinese have five officials of the human body, the mouth, nose, ear, eye, and eye-brow. The strong eye-brow is a preserver of long life; and in the Egyptian hieroglyphics the *Anhu*, eyebrow, is a modified *Ankhu* or emblem of life; the natural being primary.

The teeth are touched by the Indians to indicate the meaning of *White*, and in Egyptian the tooth is "*Hu*" which is also the name for white as *Hut*. Black is signified by touching the hair, and in Egyptian black and hair are synonymous; they have one name as *Kam*. Another sign for black is made by pointing to the sun and executing the sign for no; no sun or sun-setting being equal to black. So the Chinese ideograph of the setting sun which is similar to the Akkadian and like it has the value of *Mi* sunset, night, black, is one with the Egyptian *Am* or *Mmi* for the west, the place of sunset. The mode of indicating a period, applied to the end of a lifetime, as in the address of *Kin Che-êss*[1] is by the gesture-sign of "*Cut off*." Ever, always, or eternal is "Never cut off." This ideograph belongs to the oldest representation of time in Heaven. In the

[1] Mallery.

planisphere of Denderah [1] the goddess of the seven stars and mother of time is pourtrayed holding a knife, the Kat (Eg.), English cutter, in her hand. That is the sign of time cut off, separated, distinguished. One revolution of the Bear was one year cut off; the annual quota cut off, *quotannis*. A long time is expressed by placing the thumbs and forefingers as if a thread were held between the thumb and forefinger of each hand; the hands first touching each other, are then slowly drawn apart as if stretching a piece of gum elastic. Colonel Mallery compares this act with the Greek τείνω, to stretch.[2] In Egyptian *Ten*, denotes time, measure, to stretch and to reckon. *Ten* is to extend, lengthen out; *tens* is a stretcher. Ten is to complete fill up, determine, and the variant *Tem* (our time) has the same meaning. A *tent* is a length of time, a fortnight; *temt* is a total.

The Egyptian gesture-sign for *Ter* to interrogate, ask, inquire, question, English tell me, is made with both hands scooped upwards exactly as the one hand is employed in making the common Indian sign for "tell me."[3] This gesture is used by the natives of Australia and is common with all orators as a mode of inquiry. Another link may be established between *Teru* for time, and *Teru* to draw. The sign-gesture for drawing was first, but *teru* (Eg.) to draw had become pictorial, applied to colour and painting. *Teru* to draw, is also a measure of land, or of time, the *gesture* is a measure of time, indicated by the *drawing out*.

Hor-Apollo observes, "When we would denote the loins or constitution of a man we depict the backbone, for some hold that the seed proceeds from thence."[4]

Mr. Long says:—"*If an Indian wishes to tell you that an individual present is his offspring, he points to the person, and then with the finger still extended, passes it forward from his loins in a line curving downward, then slightly upward.*"[5] Captain Burton tells us, "*A son or daughter is expressed by making with the hand a movement denoting issue from the loins.*" Offspring, read literally, is "*out of the loins.*"

The signs for male and female, boy and girl, are made by direct imitation, the fore-finger taking the place of the Egyptian Ideograph. To depict the female the two outstretched thumbs and forefingers are joined, and placed in position to form the ovoid figure represented by the hieroglyphic Ru ◯. The sign for the female is also made with an almond-shaped opening between the thumb and forefinger, with the tip of the one resting on the tip of the other.

One sign for woman is also European. The *left* fore and second fingers are extended and separated with the other fingers closed. The thumb is then placed against the palm in such a manner that

---

[1] Plate in *B. B.* vol. ii.   [2] Mallery, *Address*, 1881, p. 26.
[3] Mallery, *Sign-Language*, Fig. 71.   [4] Book ii. p. 9.
[5] Mallery, p. 54.

the top is visible in the crotch thus figured. This represents a likeness to the form *et staturigo veneris* in the *pudendum muliebre*.[1]

It is common among the English peasantry, and constitutes a most deadly sign of insult with the Latin races, who give the Fico, or Fig, in a similar manner. The insult lies in the gesture indicating the female, and reads, " *You are effeminate,*" " *Behold your sign.*" So our English boys who shoot (at marbles) with the thumb tucked in are chaffingly said to play " cunny-thumbed."

A form of this feminine mimograph is given by Colonel Mallery under the heading of " *Challenge,* Florentine Sign." " A fist clinched with the thumb thrust out under the forefinger." The thumb thrust out is a sign of mockery and contempt with various African races. One of the Oji proverbs says, " *If you go to the sabbat* (or 'customs') *making the sign with the thumb* (*i.e.* thrusting out the thumb) *you will be answered with blows.*" One mimograph for woman is made by imitating the action of combing the long hair.[2] This sign has the same value as the comb found on the tomb of the Lars, in the Akkadian pictographs, or on the Scottish stones along with the mirror, both being feminine, both symbols of reproduction by the pubescent female. The comb is a female sign in the hieroglyphics, and is equivalent to the sign of combing. Another of the ideographs for "woman" is to point to or express the *mammæ* (Chesney). This is the same as the sign of the two breasts in hieroglyphics, the determinative of menâ, the wet-nurse, and menâ, to suckle. Menâ (menkat) had become a goddess in Egypt, and her vases had taken the place of the *Mammæ*, but the living type is still retained in the Indian sign. The primary natural signs remain for use where vases, breast-shaped or womb-shaped, are no longer manufactured. The vase of Menâ was both mammæ-shaped and womb-shaped, and in the gesture-sign for the female, as rendered by Matthews, " *the arms were flexed and the hands held fist-like at either side in the position of the female mammary glans, then swept semi-circularly downwards.*" The sign reads, one with prominent *mammæ*, who can bring forth young, and who thus represented the blessings of the Hebrew Shadai. The vase of Mena was also imitated by making the cup-shape over each breast.[3]

The Egyptians indicated pregnancy in the female by a swelling abdomen, and the hieroglyphy is the same, although only drawn in gesture-sign for the moment, when the Indians express the same fact pantomimically by passing the two hands slightly arched from the pubis in a curve upward and in toward the pit of the stomach, and thus depict the rotund shape of the abdomen.[4]

For birth, delivery, to produce the child, the Egyptians represent the woman in the act of emaning the child, whose head and arms

[1] Mallery, *Collection*, p. 289.   [2] Mallery, p. 288.
     Mallery, pp. 287, 288.   [4] Mallery, *Collection*, p. 204.

are visible. The Indians enact the process of parturition, and imitate the pubic arch and the curve of carus with the two hands, which is followed by the head of the child during birth. This sign is used generically.[1] With additions it means mother, father, grand-parent. The Egyptian sign reads *pâ-pâ*, for the human species; *pâ*, the race, men; *pâpâ*, to produce and be delivered. To denote the babe, or nursling, the back of the right hand is laid crosswise in the palm of the *left*, on the *left* side of the breast, and the movement up and down is then made as though holding and dandling an infant (Dakota 1). So in the hieroglyphics, *renn*, to dandle, and *renn*, the nursling, are identical; and the babe is shown in the arms of the nurse, who is dandling it up and down, and who is named the dandler, as Rennut.

The child, or suckling, is pourtrayed by the thumb and fingers being brought to the mouth, or by the finger placed in the mouth. This is the Egyptian hieroglyphic for the child. The primary idea was probably in reference to the suckling child. Still the infant and *infans* are inseparably connected, and the Greeks were not so wrong as some Egyptologists have supposed in making the child Har-pi-kart, the god of silence, or the silent god. The child and silence have the same name in Egyptian.[2] Khart, the child, also means silence. It is always perilous to limit an ideograph to one meaning. The chief sign for astonishment, surprise, and wonder is made by placing the right hand before the mouth, which is supposed to be open. This gesture is generic in the hieroglyphics, where it is used for expressing various emotions; it likewise signifies to speak, whisper, meditate, and to kiss, as in Job's description of idolatry or adulation conveyed by kissing the hand. It also has the meaning of thinking and meditating, and would therefore apply to being lost in astonishment, or speechless. It serves as the determinative of "dumb," "mouthless." Hiding the mouth, with many Asiatic races, is equivalent to being mouthless, *i.e.*, dumb. The negroes on the West Coast of Africa clap their hands to their mouths when surprised, saying, at the same time, "*My mouth cleaves to me*,"[3] that is, I am speechless, dumb with amazement. In spite of all assumptions to the contrary, this gesture is a sign of the child as the speechless one, the dumb Horus, or silent khart, who was the opposite of the True Voice. The sign has really to be read by childhood being the type of speechlessness. The gesture says, "I am voiceless, a child again, a ninny who has nothing to say." The Australians, the North American Indians, and the Africans all make this gesture-sign of wonder. Darwin remarks that it has been observed among so many races of men it must have some natural origin.[4] We may add, that there must also have been *consensus*. The mimograph

[1] Mallery, *Collection*, p. 42.
[2] See *Dictionary*, Birch, p. 421.
[3] Winwood Reade.
[4] *Emotions*, ch. xii.

for silence and the child, are both expressed by the one word *Khart* (Eg.).

Mrs. Barber says the Kaffirs and Fingoes express astonishment by a serious look and by placing the right hand upon the mouth, uttering the word "*Mawo*,"[1] which is the Xosa exclamation for wonderful! prodigious! The word also signifies "alas." The fuller form of the expression in grief is "*Mame-Mawo*," or "Alas! my mother!" In this the mother is added to the type of the child. So in Egyptian the *Mam*, *Mum* or *Mu* is the mother, and *Mahui* denotes wonder, to be full of astonishment, like the vulgar English "*O moy!*" The word "adore" really means "with hand to mouth."

For the sign of companion, as the husband, or to accompany, the forefinger of each hand is extended pointing straight to the front and joined, all other fingers of both hands being closed, the hands held horizontal, with the backs upwards, signifying "inseparable, united, equal."[2] A similar sign is made by the native Australians when they offer the woman to a visitor as a rite of hospitality, the fingers of both hands being closely interlocked. In the hieroglyphics *Teka*, to join, adhere, mix, and multiply with the sign of the cross X is equivalent to the two or the ten digits, or to the two hands being interlaced to signify conjunction. To denote a basket, or wicker-work, the separated fingers of both hands are interlaced in front of the body.[3] So *Tekar* (Eg.), the digit, is the type of *teka*, to join, cross, cleave, twist, intertwine, as do the fingers, or the withies in making baskets.

The sign of counting, and of enumeration in general, is made by stretching out the ten digits. Also many, much, quantity, multiplicity, are expressed by stretching out the fingers and clutching at the air several times. This action, says Kohl, is often confounded with that for counting. The native Australians likewise denote many, multitude, large numbers, by holding up the hand, spreading out the fingers, and shutting and opening them rapidly.

Now the first and most universal reckoning was digital, and the name of the digits and the number ten of many languages is *Tek*, or Tekh (Eg.). Tekh is a title of the reckoner, who was both *Tekhi*, the goddess, and *Taht*. *Tekar* is the Egyptian digit, a finger. The sign of TEK is the cross X, the Roman figure of ten, or *Decem*, and this is the hieroglyphic symbol of multiplication.

One sign of ALL is made by moving both hands horizontally, palm downwards, in a large circle, two feet in front of the face.[4] The Egyptian ALL, as NEB and TEMT, is a total and a circle of two halves.

Among the signs for Day, one is described by Titchkemátski, the Shienne Indian, as ending with the palms of the hands being

[1] Quoted by Darwin.   [2] Mallery, p. 71.
[3] *Dakota*, i.   [4] *Dakota*, iv.

outspread upward, to indicate the opening out of day. Wied also
describes this gesture as consisting in both hands being placed apart,
some distance from the breast, with the palms upward. This sign
for Day, or this Morning, is an Egyptian gesture. It is made with
lifted hands, and the palms outspread upwards, signifying "all open,"
"everything is open," the reverse of the sign for Night, or "everything is closed." This is the hieroglyphic for *Tuau*, or *Seb*, which
has the meaning of the *opening* day, morning, morrow, and also to
worship. So certainly is the sense of "opening out" conveyed by
the words *Seb* and *Tuau*, for the dawn of day, that they also denote
the *gateway* of the light; the gate or gate-opener being a star.
One sign of the night is made by the two hands crossed horizontally.[1] The cross is a well-known Indian sign of night and darkness.
This is connected with the crossing of the sun by night, who is
represented as the black god.

It was the custom in Egypt to reckon the year by the Inundation.
The month of Mesore is named from the new birth of the waters.
In like manner one of the Indian signs for rain or snow is the ideographic sign for a year.[2] The year as a rain marks the same mode
of computation as that of the Unyamwesi and the Hottentots, who
reckon time by the rainy seasons, as the Egyptians did by the
inundations.

The hand and language have one name in Egyptian, as "Tut."
Also the tongue and hand are the two Egyptian hieroglyphics of
speech. The sign-language of the Indians is known as Hand-Conversation. Burton says the open hand is extended from the mouth.
·Various other gestures of hand and mouth likewise denote speech.

The Egyptian sign of *Kà*, to beckon, call, and say, with the
uplifted hands, agrees with the *Oto* sign for an interview—"*Approach,
I will open myself to you, I will speak to you.*" One Egyptian
determinative for *Tet*, speech, address, to tell, shows both hands
held up and waving level with the mouth.[3] Both hands are used
for "conversation" in the Arikara and Hidatsa gesture-signs. An
Egyptian tradition, recorded in Plutarch, tells us that until the god
Taht taught men speech they used mere cries like other animals; and
it is true that Taht, the Lunar Logos, is later than the god Shu, or
Kafi, and the Typhonian genitrīx *Kefa*. The Kaf ape was a type
of "hand-conversation" and gesture-language. The ape is the hand
of the gods, has the name of the hand, is the hand personified, and
its name, Kaf, is the earlier form of Kà, for calling and saying; thus
the hand is an earlier sign of speech in Egyptian mythology than
the mouth or tongue as Taht, the Lunar Logos.

In the scenes of the Hades appear four monkeys, each holding an
enormous hand.[4] Moreover, the descent of the hand-type can be

[1] Dunbar.   [2] Burton.
[3] Bunsen, vol. v. p. 520.   [4] *Book of the Hades*, 11th division.

traced in language from the *Kaf*, monkey, to the human hand of
Taht. One name of the oldest genitrix, the Kaf-nosed hippopotamus,
is Tept. *Tept* is the tongue, and she was depicted with her tongue
lolling out as a symbol of utterance. *Tept* modifies into *Tet*, for the
tongue, the human hand, and the later equivalent for *Kaf*, the hand,
to take, to utter language. Typology and mythology agree in this
beginning with the *Kaf*, which is solely African, and neither Asiatic,
European, nor American. *Tep* in Egyptian means to taste, breathe,
inhale. It is also the name for the tongue and palate. This is a
common type-name for the tongue or mouth, the organ of taste, as—

Tupe, Coropo.	*Topono*, Yarura.	*Tavas*, Cornish.
Tope, Purus.	*Debe*, Alege.	*Teppa*, Comanche.
Tib, Soiony.	*Tafod*, Welsh.	*Tupa*, Wihinasht.

Tofo, in Polynesian, and *Tovolea*, Fijian, mean taste ; *Tubbu*, Fiji, is
to be sweet to the taste, and *Dovu* is the sugar-cane. *Teb* (Eg.) is
the fig, the fruit that is sweet to the taste. In Santa Barbara salt is
Tipi; and in San Luis Obispo it is *Tepu.* A variant of the word
Tef (Eg.), *Tyffen*, Cornish, is to spit ; also *Tuf*, in Persian.

The Indian sign for *Taste* is to touch the tip of the tongue.[1]
In the Shienne gesture-sign for " *Sweet*," the tip of the fore-finger
is pressed on the tip of the tongue.[2] The same sign is used for
" *Sour*." The Dakota sign for *Sour* includes spitting. Now the
tongue (Tep) was touched in tasting, and gave its answer in saliva
before there was a word *Tep* to express the sensation, or to name the
organ or the act.

Colonel Mallery says :—

" *A lesson was learned by the writer as to the abbreviation of signs
and the possibility of discovering the original meaning of those most
obscure from the attempts of a Shienne to convey the idea of* ' OLD
MAN.' *He held his right hand forward bent at elbow, with fingers
and thumb closed sidewise. This not conveying any sense, he found a
long stick, bent his back, and supported his frame in a tottering
step by the stick held as was before only imagined. There, at once, was
decrepit Age dependent on a Staff.*"[3]

The bent old man leaning on a long staff is likewise the Egyptian
sign of age, elders, the *old man*.

In this description we see a mode of reducing the earliest direct
ideograph to a secondary representation, or kind of hieroglyphic
short-hand corresponding to the reduction of the Egyptian ideographic signs in the demotic phase on the way to their becoming
letter signs. The mimic finding the symbolic and secondary phase
ineffectual had recourse to direct representation, as we do when
we revert to the primary gesture-language.[4] In like manner the
deaf mutes will contract and reduce the natural, or spontaneous
gesture, into an artificial sign that loses all obvious likeness to the

---

[1] Burton.   [2] Mallery, p. 259.   [3] *Ib.* 244.   [4] *Ib.* introd. p. 55.

natural one, but is understood by them, and serves the purpose of expression.[1]

Gesture-language was, and still is, continued in religious rites and ceremonies. In holding up the holy water the Parsee ritual prescribes that at certain words it is to be lifted *level with the heart* of the officiating priest, and at others it is to be held *level with the arm* of the priest, so that the warriors fighting for their country may be *fuller of breath*, and the husbandmen *stronger of arm* in tillage and cultivation of the world.[2]

The principle is the same if the action is not so primitive as that of the Hottentots, who, when out on the war-path, will take the heart of a crow and calcine it to dust. This is then rammed into a gun and fired off with powder. As the heart is blown into air it is held that the enemy will lose heart and fly off like timid crows.[3] Both had their origin in the acting drama and the signs that preceded spoken language. Our popular beliefs still talk to us or make their dumb show of meaning in gesture-speech. The noose of the hangman or the suicide is not only held to be healing on account of its having taken life ; it loses its efficacy if allowed to *fall to the ground*, and the touch of the dead hand must be applied whilst the body is still *hanging*. Why ? Because the symbol of *suspending* or of being *suspended* was taken to *suspend* the disease.

These primates of human expression have now to be traced on another line of thought. In the early dawn of the human consciousness man would observe that the animals, birds, reptiles, and insects excelled him in various kinds of contrivance, modes of getting a living, and power over the elements. The fish could breathe in the water which was fatal to him. The frog could engender and suspend on the flood a floating foothold of life, a base of being that began in the water and ended on the land. The hippopotamus could dive and disappear for an hour together. In attack or retreat many of the animals were superior to himself. The dog made a better hunter and watchman ; the cat could see and pounce on her prey in the dark ; the bee, bird, and beaver beat him in building ; the spider in spanning empty space, with the woven means of crossing it. The serpent managed the art of locomotion without visible members, and renewed its garment periodically by changing its skin. The monkey, with his four hands, excelled man, who had lost two of his in the process of metamorphosis and descent from the four-fold foot-hold in the tree to the two-fold standing on the earth. Animate or inanimate things were adopted of necessity for use as a means of representing his primitive thought, and these things in the later phase became sacred objects, and thus Africa and the world were filled with fetish images which are only another kind of hieroglyphics not yet interpreted ; a

[1] Dr. W. R. Scott, *The Deaf and Dumb*, p. 12, 2nd ed.
[2] *Shayast La-Shayast*, ch. xiii. 9.   [3] Hahn, *Tsuni Goam*, p. 90.

rendering of which was brought on, almost intact, by the Egyptians. Tradition, customs, and language in many lands, still preserve the ancient types, where their meaning is no longer understood. But the notion that the primitive man fell straightway to worshipping these types is wholly erroneous. Greek writers, like Porphyry, mystified themselves with thinking that the Egyptian respect paid to animals arose from their belief in the transmigration of souls. This was their guess at the hieroglyphics they could not translate, and the symbolism they did not comprehend. Our remotest ancestors were not so simple as to regard the brutes as gods, or the birds as angels, or the reptiles as devils. Such a reading postulates gods, angels, and devils, which were not then extant. They observed the keen instincts, the ingenious works and ways of the creatures as something remarkable and imitable, so far as was possible, without suspecting the presence of divinities or demons in animal disguise.

The Bushmen venerate or pay homage to a kind of caterpillar, to which, or in presence of which, they pray for success in hunting after game.[1] The caterpillar is the stealthy crawler. In Egyptian, *Hefa*, to crawl, is the name of the caterpillar and viper, or snake. It would supply a type of that crawling stealthily along the ground which was a necessity with the early man in pursuit of his prey. And the so-called praying to the image would be equivalent to saying, *may we slide along as silently and successfully as the caterpillar*, only as they expressed themselves by means of things, this was their sole way of saying it.

The Mantis, a perfect type of the most deadly deception, is also highly honoured by the Bushmen and Hottentots. The noiseless movement of the caterpillar, or snake, and the deceiving appearance of the Mantis, were enviable and admirable to the primitive huntsman. They are living ideographs, which were afterwards pourtrayed in Egypt as hieroglyphic determinatives of ideas.[2]

The enormous fecundity of the frog was the cause of the tadpole being adopted as the ideograph of a million, and also designated the lord of life. The time was when people in England, who wished for offspring, would swallow frogs to ensure children. The frog was eaten not for any virtue which it could communicate, but because it was an ideograph of fecundity. So the Malays of Singapore eat the flesh of the tiger, and pay highly for it, not that they like it, but they say that the man who eats tiger "acquires the sagacity, as well as the courage, of that animal."[3]

Captain Burton remarked that in the heraldry of the Abeokutans, which is tattooed into their own flesh, the lizard was an especial favourite. This on the monuments is an ideograph of multiplying,

[1] Spencer, *Descriptive Sociology, African Races*, table 18.
[2] Champollion, *Dictionnaire*, 168.
[3] Keppel, *Expedition to Borneo*, v. i. p. 231.

to be numerous, and, like the frog, was a type of fertility and reproduction, whether applied to this life or the next, or both. So in the
Hervey Islands the custom of tattoo was said to be derived from
their most fecund fish, whose name (Tini) signifies innumerable, and
whose striped pattern they copied.

When the nature of symbolism is understood, such phrases as
"*zoolatry*" and "worship of animals" will be superseded. Animals
were the living hieroglyphics, among the first figures of speech, and
means of thinging thoughts; pictures painted by nature to illustrate
the primary language. A bull-man, a cow-mother, a serpent-woman,
are modes of expression; ideographs adopted for use, having no
necessary relation to animal or reptile worship.

Cicero makes the apposite remark, that the Egyptians held no
beasts to be sacred, except *on account of some benefit which they had
received from them*. The barbarians, he says, paid divine honours to
the beasts because of the advantages they derived from them, whereas
the Roman gods not only conferred no benefit, but were idle and did
nothing whatever to get their living [1]—as we say.

The ichneumon will destroy the cobra-di-capello, and consequently
was greatly honoured as a serpent-killer. Pigs, as is well known, are
determined enemies of snakes. So soon as a pig sees a snake he
rushes at it, and the snake immediately makes off at sight of a pig.
Pigs have been employed in America to clear out districts that were
infested with rattlesnakes. Even the hedgehog in England will attack
and devour the viper. The sow was a type of Rerit, the goddess of
the Great Bear. The numerous mammæ were one cause of the personification, but the picture of the mother devouring snakes—man's
fatal and most subtle enemies—in defence of her young, would arrest
early attention. In recognising his friends and defenders the early
man would not overlook the hedgehog and pig. Accordingly we
find the hedgehog was sacred to Pasht or Buto, the Great Mother.
In the Pahlavi Vendidad [2] the hedgehog is termed "*the slayer of the
thousands of the evil spirit*," and in the "*Shayast La-Shayast*" it is
said the high priest taught "*that it is when the hedgehog voids urine
into an ant's nest that a thousand ants will die*." The ant being
considered a noxious creature because it carried off grain.[3]

The Ibis received great honour from its destroying all deadly and
venomous reptiles, so that any person who killed one was punished
with instant death. The Thessalians protected the stork for the
same reasons.[4] Darwin mentions the "secretary hawk" as having
had his whole frame modified for the purpose of killing snakes with
impunity.[5] This bird is named the *gxangxosi* in Xosa Kaffir. It
lives on snakes and other reptiles, and is protected by law from being
killed.[6]

---

[1] *Of the Nature of the Gods*, b. i. c. 36.　　　[2] xiii. 5.　　　[3] Ch. x. 31.
[4] Diod. i. 83 ; Pliny, x. 23.　　　[5] *Emotions*, ch. iv.　　　[6] Davis.

Major Serpo Pinto in the account of his crossing Africa, tells us of an intelligent creature.   He says no sooner does the traveller penetrate into one of the extensive forests of South-Central Africa, than the *indicator*[1] makes its appearance, hopping from bough to bough, in close proximity to the adventurer, and endeavouring by its monotonous note to attract his attention.   This end having been attained, it rises heavily upon the wing, and perches a little distance off, watching to see if it is followed.   If no attention be paid, it again returns, hopping and chirping as before, evidently inviting the stranger to follow in its wake, and when the wayfarer yields, it guides him through the intricacies of the forest, almost unerringly, to a bees' nest.   Whether the action arises from the bird's desire to communicate the secret or to make a cat's-paw of the new-comer, it is very arresting if true, and worthy of the land which we look upon as the nursery of the human mind.

These birds were honoured for work done.   Besides which the Ibis, that represented Taht, who amongst other things was the god of medicine, taught men the use of the enema, or clyster, by administering it to herself, as Plutarch relates, she being observed to be after this manner washed and purged by herself.   So that those of the priests who were the strictest observers of their sacred rites, when they used water for lustration, would fetch it from some place, where the Ibis had been drinking, for she will neither taste any infectious, nor come near any unwholesome water.[2]   Hor-Apollo says when the Egyptians symbolise a man that conceals his own defects they depict an ape making water, for when he does so he conceals his urine.[3]   The cat, another curiosity of cleanliness, would also present a worthy example as a concealer of its own defects.   That such animals were among the teachers of the primitive and prehistoric men, is witnessed by the way in which their portraits have been preserved in the picture-gallery of the hieroglyphics.

The Chinese are still in the habit of using the eye of the cat for a time-piece.   No matter whether the day is cloudy or dull, they will run to the nearest cat, pull open her eyes, if closed, and at once determine the time by the contraction of the iris and size of the pupil.[4]

Hor-Apollo writes : " The Egyptians say that *The male cat changes the shape of the pupils of his eyes according to the course of the sun.* In the morning, at the rising of the god, they are dilated, in the middle of the day they become round, and about sunset appear less brilliant ; whence the statue of the god in the city of the sun is in the form of a cat."[5]   In the Ritual (ch. xvii.), one of the transformations of

---

[1] The Kaffirs tell the same story of the *Ngende*, or Honey-bird.   Davis.
[2] Of Isis and Osiris.   [3] Hor-Apollo, b. ii. 67.
[4] *Knowledge*, Feb. 17, 1882.   [5] B. i. 10.

the solar god is into a cat. As such he "makes the likeness of Seb," or Time, which shows the timepiece as the cat.

When the dog turns round before lying down to rest, he is said, in the Isle of Wight, to be "making his *doke*." He has no need to do so now, as his wild ancestors had when they made their nightly bed in the long grass and liked to have it well beaten down, with a clear and ample space around for the purpose of watching; but he still continues the habit on bare boards, with no enemy to apprehend. The *Doke* is a furrow, a hollow, a division, a small brook. It answers to the Egyptian *Tek*, a boundary frontier, dyke, cutting. It supplied the name of the district or nome as *Tek*, variant Tesh, when the Nomads who came down into Egypt had made their *Dokes* and *Dykes*. Doke and dog are synonymous for a boundary, fence, defence; that which incloses and *guards*, as the dog-irons fence the fire. In the celestial divisions the first Nome, or *Doke*, was given to the Dog, who had taught the primitive man a lesson in making his *Doke* ; and the dog as Canis Major or Canis Minor continues to make his doke, and to be the doke, tekh, or dog in heaven for ever.[1]

The Egyptians had no "tide-predicting machines," but, according to Plutarch, the beetle khepr and the crocodile were the natural prognosticators of the height of the *coming* inundation. He affirms that in whatsoever place in the country the female crocodile lays her eggs, that may with certainty be regarded as the *utmost limit to which the rise of the river Nile will reach for the year.* For, "*not being able to lay their eggs in the water, and being afraid to lay them far from it, they have so exact a knowledge of futurity, that, although they enjoy the benefit of the approaching stream at their laying and hatching, they still preserve their eggs dry and untouched by the water. They lay sixty eggs in all, and are just that number of days in hatching them, and the longest-lived of them live as many years ; that being the first measure (No. 60) made use of by those who are employed in the celestial reckonings.*"[2] The crocodile was also honoured as a purifier of the holy water of the Nile.

Yarrell, in his book on British birds, tells the story of a swan on the river at Bishop's Stortford which was sitting on four or five eggs. One day, previous to a very heavy downpour of rain, she was observed to be most diligently adding to her nest, which she raised some two and a half feet higher. That night the rain fell and the flood rose, but her nest had lifted the eggs just beyond the *coming* water's reach, and they were safe. Man had no such prescience of impending danger. He made no preparation, but the swan did.[3]

[1] The DOG. *Tekh*, or *Takh* is a name of Taht, one of whose types is the dog. The name is applied to the tongue of the Balance which was represented by the Cynocephalus as well as by the Vase The dog is the tongue or voice of the gods. But *Tekai* (Eg.) means the *Adherer*, a most appropriate name for the dog or doggie !   [2] Of Isis and Osiris.
[3] Yarrell, *British Birds*, vol. iii. p. 207, 2nd ed.

. The beetle, in Egypt, during the Inundation, would have been washed out of life altogether but for its Arkite cunning in making ready for the waters by rolling up its little globe, with the seed inside, and burying it in the dry earth until the Inundation subsided. How they must have watched the clever creature at work; no font of letter-type employed in radiating human thought could shed a clearer light of illustration on the idea of resurrection from the earth than this living likeness of the process of transformation into the winged world. How the primitive man observed the works and ways and on-goings of the intelligence thus manifested around him; how he copied where he could, and gradually found a line of his own in the scheme of development; how he honoured these his early teachers and instructors, and made their forms the pictures of the primal thoughts which they had evoked from his mind, is at length recorded in the system of hieroglyphic symbols and mythology; and the illustrative proofs are extant to this day.

One of the workers that caught the attention of primitive men was the spider, as the spinner. In Inner Africa the ten-legged spider, called *Ananse* in Ashanti, serves as the type for the Creator of man. This can be interpreted. The spider, as the first weaver, made the suspended woof. Heaven is the blue woof, the weaver of which was therefore the spider, according to the typology. They always represent Ananse as talking through his nose. The nose is an organ of breath. The god Khnef is called the breath of those who are in the firmament. Ananse, as spinner of the blue woof above, was a deity of breath, or the nose as a type of life.

The spider is an object of great reverence with the Maori, who are most careful not to break any webs or gossamers. The Bishop of Wellington said their priests taught that the souls of the faithful went to heaven on gossamer threads.[1] The insect's name will show how this was to mistake the typology. The spider, in Maori, is the *Pungawerewere*; from *Punga*, to anchor, and *werewere*, to be suspended. Thus it was the type of an *Anchorage above*. Poetry has no finer image.

This type of the spinner is British as well as African, and by the type we can explain the custom of shutting up the large house-spider alive in a pill-box or in a nutshell, to be worn round the neck as a cure for ague. The type of spinning and reproducing from itself is laid hold of as the representative of disease, for when shut up it *cannot go on spinning, nor sustain itself,* and as it dies the disease is supposed to be suspended and to die out. The type is one whether it represents the good or the evil power.

Hor-Apollo has been unduly depreciated by Bunsen, Wilkinson, and Sharpe for his hints respecting the symbolical and allegorical values of the hieroglyphics. They are symbols in relation to an

[1] Trans. of Ethnol. Society, 1870. p. 367.

occult knowledge of their application to dogma and doctrine not yet possessed by readers of the hieroglyphics, who know that a certain ideograph is the determinative of a special meaning, without knowing *why* it is so.

Hor-Apollo now and again gives us a valid reason for the adoption of the type. He tells us that the lion is one of the signs of the Inundation *because* half of the new water is supplied whilst the sun is in the sign of Leo. Hence it is that those who anciently presided over sacred works have made the spouts of the fountains in the form of lions.[1] The lion's head was commonly used as a waterspout in Egyptian temples, and has been continued in Europe. In three months the waters ceased to flow, and the exhalation began with the sun in the sign of *Serk*, or the scorpion. This is suggestive of the Egyptian origin of the Zodiac. The scorpion is borne on the head of the goddess Serk, who is associated with the four quarters.

" *When the Egyptians symbolise one enemy engaging with another equal to himself, they depict a scorpion and a crocodile, for these kill one another.*"[2] Whether this be a fact in nature or not, the Egyptians placed the crocodile in the sign or as a paranatellon of Scorpio, at the place of the equinox, when the year began with Scorpio, the place of poise and equal power. The scorpion likewise represented breath and dryness; the crocodile, water; two other forms of the twinship of upper and lower in heaven, and the Two Truths of life.

To denote connubial intercourse, says Hor-Apollo, the Egyptians depict two crows, because these birds cohabit with one another in the same manner as does a man by nature. Another reason is because the bird lays two eggs; one of these produces a male, the other a female; these two make a monogamous marriage and repudiate polygamy altogether for the rest of their lives. So faithful are they to each other, that they hold no intercourse with any other crow, and when one of them dies the other does not wed again, but ends its widowed life in solitude. Hence, when men meet with a single crow, they look upon it as an evil omen, because they have met with a widowed creature. On account of the remarkable custom and concord of these birds, he says, the Greeks in their marriages exclaim *ekkori, kori, korone*, although " *unacquainted with the import of the words.*"[3] We have the same symbolry in Britain with regard to the magpie; " *one's a funeral, two's a wedding,*" says our folk-lore; and if you see a single bird you ought to turn round three times to avert ill-luck. Possibly it was the faithful crows that converted the ancient Egyptians, or Kamites, from polygamy to single marriage, and first instituted the prohibition of marriage with the wife's sister; they seem to have held the doctrine which is still maintained by many modern clerical *Rooks*.

A night-raven signifies death *because* it pounces suddenly on the

---

[1] Book i. 21.   [2] Hor-Apollo, ii. 35.   B. i. 8, 9.

young of the crows by night, as death overtakes men.[1] Death, or
darkness, the Hebrew *Ereb*, or *Ghareb*, means either *Erebus* (darkness) or the raven, Arabic *Ghuráb*, and, according to Damascius, the
Sidonians made the bird an emblem of Erebus. This type of death
in the dark had thus a very natural origin before it was invested
with supernatural power to become the prophetic bird of death with
many other races of men.

Livingstone describes the Ibis flying by night and crying "*Aah-
Aah*," a duplicate equivalent in Egyptian to "*Aah-ti*," a name of the
moon-god, who was represented by the ibis, and who was the
lunar tongue, mouth, or speech of the gods. Thus the ibis, as testified
to by the modern ear, and mode of pronunciation, named itself as the
Aah, or *Aah-Aah*, *i.e. Aah-ti*, in Egyptian. Aah is the moon, and
Aah-ti, or *Aah-aah*, is the ibis-headed divinity.

A Cretan story tells how a poor woman once sat down, and for
very weariness sighed "*Ah*," whereupon a *Moor* instantly appeared
whose name was "*Ah*."[2] The *Moor* is the dark side of his dual
character. He, too, transforms into a radiant youth, as the old dark
moon renews itself, and the Kaf-ape transforms into the ibis-headed
Taht, or Aah-ti. *Aah*, whether male or female (for there is a feminine
Aah-ti), or both, has two aspects, like the moon, with a continual
metamorphosis.

The stork, or crane is the European representative of the lunar ibis,
and the transformation of Taht; and the bird is extant in the folk-lore
of Friesland, where the changing of storks into men, and men into
storks is still an article of popular belief.[3]

In parts of Germany it is forbidden to hurt the stork, for, it is urged,
"*he is elsewhere a man*." It is recorded, likewise, by Gervase of
Tilbury, that the stork is also a man. So Taht, the ibis-headed god
was also pourtrayed in the human form as a man. A Flemish legend
relates that a citizen of Bruges once met a man near Mount Sinai,
who told him they were near neighbours in Bruges, for the nest of one
(as the stork) was next door to the home of the other : and the stork-
man showed the other a ring which he had stolen from the Fleming
once upon a time ; he gave this back on condition that the stork's nest
should be protected.[4] Bruges and Mount Sinai answer to the two
opposite sides of the moon's circle, where the moon-god, as in Egypt,
was a stork in one region and a man in the other.

The moon is considered to be masculine in Egyptian mythology,
but Aahti was also a goddess. Sefekh was the consort of Taht, and
Hathor was a lunar divinity. In the Ritual we read, "*I am the
Woman, the orb* (hour) *of darkness ; I have brought my orb to darkness,
it is changed to light. I have prepared Taht at the gate of the moon.
Its feathers are on my body*." Here the woman is the bringer-forth,

---

[1] Hor-Apollo, ii. 25.   [2] Hahn, No. 73.   [3] Kelly, p. 94.
[4] Kelly, p. 94 ; Liebrecht, G. T. 157.

apparently under the feathered or ibis image, and Taht the young moon is her messenger.

So the stork in Germany, Denmark and Holland is the typical bringer of the babies, and messenger of the Genitrix Frau Holda. The stork keeps its character too as the fisher of the waters. The ibis was depicted as the fisher with the fish in its mouth, and thus furnished the type of the fisher-up of the moon out of the waters. In the ballad of Sir Patrick Spens the new moon is described in popular phrase with the old moon in its arms, and the crescent of light which clasps the orb of darkness was represented by the curving beak of the ibis as bringer.

The German genitrix is pourtrayed sitting in her stately subterraneous home beneath the waters, the nursery of unborn children, and the refuge of those who are lost or strayed. Hence her connection with the fountains so popular in Germany, the *Kinderbrunnen*, where the stork finds the little ones and leads them home. The lady of the fountains has her Queckbrunnen or fonts of life in Dresden out of which the " clapper-stork fetches the Dresden children." [1] The Fisher of the hieroglyphics is yet extant in the stork, whose figure surmounts the chapel holding one babe in its beak and two more in its claws.

Birds and beasts are the divine personages of the Australians. The native cat represents the moon. Its name is Bede or Bude. In Egypt the cat-headed lunar goddess is Buto or Peht.

The Mangaians say that the gods first spake to man through the small land birds. [2] The little bird that tells is with us a living relic of the same mode of revealing. Now when the Aztecs lived in Astulan there was a certain Huiziton who heard the voice of a bird crying *tihui, tihui*, rendered " let us go," " let us go." The little bird in this case was called the humming bird, but another typical leader, Quetzalcoatl, was represented by the sparrow. The sparrow in Egyptian is the Thuu ; and the word Tehu signifies speech and to Tell ; Tehu or Tekhu being one of the bird-headed tellers ; speech personified. All such sayings are readable in the hieroglyphics.

Regarding the bird ashozusht, which is the bird Zobara-Vahman (cf. the Persian Zûlah, a sparrow or lark), and also the bird *Sôk* (cf. Persian Sak, a magpie), they say that it *has given an Avesta with its tongue*. [3] *Mak* (Eg.) signifies the tongue ; and to *mag* in English is to chatter.

" *Regarding Karshipt they say that it knew how to speak words, and brought the religion to the inclosure which Yima made and circulated it. There they utter the Avesta in the language of birds.* [4] Karshipt is the *bird-shaped Karshipta* of the Gujerat Version of the Vendidad. [5] The birds here, as elsewhere, were the time-tellers set in heaven,

---

[1] Mannhart, pp. 280—83. [2] Gill. [3] *Bundahish*, ch. xix. 19.
[4] *Ib.* ch. xix. 16. [5] ii. 139.

because they returned and told of time and season on the earth. Karshipt is the *Roc*, the Persian Simurgh.[1] This bird is said to be the first created, but not for this world.[2] Its resting place is in the tree of life and of all seeds; and every time it rises, its wings shake down the seed of future life:[3] which the hieroglyphics will explain. The Egyptian *Rukh* is a form of the phœnix, and a type of immortality. More than one bird served as a phœnix. The bennu is pourtrayed in the Asru tree over the tomb of Osiris.[4] The *Rukh* represents the pure spirits; it may be termed the phœnix of 3,000 years, in relation to the life in Hades.

It should be noticed that the mythical Roc of the Arabian tales (and the Sim-*urg*, or Kam-*rosh* of the Persian scriptures) has been lately discovered in reality. Captain Burton says: "*The French missionaries brought to Zanzibar from Udoe, on the Upper Wami, the tips of the flippers measuring two and a half feet long. They declare that the bird is said to have had its habitation about the equatorial African Lakes; and Herr Hildebrand, a well-known naturalist and traveller, accepts the discovery.*"[5]

Thus the real Roc or Rukh of Inner Africa, although extinct, has been preserved as an ideographic type in the pictographic museum of Kam, and was set in heaven as the phœnix. The "*Rukh* of Madagascar" lays an egg said to contain the equivalent of 148 hens' eggs.[6] With us the type of the long-lived blackbird is extant as the rook.

Hor-Apollo says, "*When the Egyptians would symbolise an aged minstrel they pourtray a swan, for when it is old it sings the sweetest melody.*"[7] The usual form of the tradition is that the song of the swan when dying is the perfect sweetness of music: this has to be interpreted. The Swan constellation of the Greeks was the Bennu, or Phœnix of the Egyptians, in which the dog-star Sirius was so conspicuous a luminary. From being a celestial type of Repetition in time the phœnix or swan became the symbol of continuity or immortality, and the more imminent the end of the cycle that it represented, the more near was the new era which it prophesied; hence the death-song was the sweetest on account of the future life proclaimed by the bird of resurrection. The reason given by Hor-Apollo[8] for the hawk being adopted as the type of soul is because it did not drink of water, but drank blood, by which, likewise, the fœtal soul is fed, nurtured, and sustained. This agrees with the name of the hawk-headed *Kabh-senuf*, whose refreshment is blood.

The *Gemsbok*, now found chiefly in the Karoos of South Africa, is

---

[1] *Bundahish*, ch. xiv. 11, 23, 24.   [2] *Ib.* xxiv. 11.
[3] *Ib.* ch. xiv. 11, 23; ch. xxiv. 11; *Minokhird*, 62, 37—39.
[4] Wilkinson, fig. 194.   [5] Camoens, *Commentary*, vol. ii. p. 405.
[6] *Comptes Rendus*, xxxii. p. 101, 1851.   [7] *Hor-Apollo*, B. ii. 39.
[8] B. i. 7.

the *Oryx* of the hieroglyphics. This was a Typhonian type, and as such was turned into an image of impurity. Hor-Apollo says the Oryx shows such antipathy to the moon that when she rises the beast howls with anger and indignation. This it does so punctually as to form a kind of gnomon.[1] It would be honoured at first as a time-teller in the pre-lunar or Typhonian stage, and then superseded as a bad character, one of the unclean animals.

Darwin says, "*It is a remarkable fact that an ape, one of the Gibbons, produces an exact octave of musical sounds, ascending and descending the scale by half-tones.*" And Professor Owen has observed that this monkey, "*alone of brute mammals, may be said to sing.*"[2] This, then, was the first teacher of the scale in Africa.

Possibly the typology may tell us something more of the cause and origin of the ape's singing. Hor-Apollo says of the Cynocephalus, the personified speaker, singer, and later writer, that the Egyptians symbolised the moon by it on account of a kind of sympathy which the ape had with it at the time of its conjunction with the god. "*For at the exact instant of the conjunction of the moon with the sun, when the moon becomes unillumined, then the male Cynocephalus neither sees, nor eats, but is bowed down to the earth with grief, as if lamenting the ravishment of the moon. The female also, in addition to its being unable to see, and being afflicted in the same manner as the male, ex genitalibus sanguinem emittit; hence even to this day Cynocephali are brought up in the temples, in order that from them may be ascertained the exact instant of the conjunction of the sun and moon. And when they would denote the renovation of the moon, they again pourtray a Cynocephalus in the posture of standing upright and raising its hands to heaven with a diadem on its head.*[4] *And for the renovation they depict this posture, into which the Cynocephalus throws itself, as if congratulating the goddess, if we may so express it, in that they have both recovered light.*"[5] This presents us with a picture of the ape in the act of crying or singing, and supplies a motive for the music, such as it is, in the loss of the lunar light. Want or desire must have been the earliest incentive to the development of the human voice. Virility becomes audible in the voice of animals and birds in their respective breeding times, whether this be in spring or in autumn, as with the rutting deer. The call of the male to its mate, and the mother to her young, is incessant in their seasons. The joy of various animals becomes vocal at meeting and greeting each other. But the sharpest sounds, the tones of highest pitch, are evoked at parting, and by the sense of loss. The bleat of the parent in pain for her lost young ones; the cry of the bird that hovers wailing round the robbed nest; the roar of the lion rising higher and higher

---

[1] *Hor-Apollo*, B. i. 49.   [2] *Descent of Man*, vol. ii. p. 332.
[3] B. i. 14.   [4] The crowned Kafi. Cf. the crowned Kepheus.
[5] B. i. 15. Captain Burton tells me the idea survives in modern Africa.

in the presence of death, as he realises the loss of his companion, or cubs, tend to show how the sense of loss, when added to desire and want, will increase the upward range of voice. In Hor-Apollo's description, the

> Monkey crying in the night,
> A monkey crying for the light,
> And with no language but a cry,

illustrates this sense of loss, and the consequent increase of the higher tones, when the loss is that of the lunar light. The sense would be still more quick, and the voice more emotional, when the companion of life was lost.

Thus we may infer that sitting in the darkness of night and of the deeper darkness of death the Gibbon evolved and by degrees formulated his voice, his scale of sounds, until at length the notes by which he had expressed his perception of darkness and loss of companionship became a solace and a source of pleasure through constant repetition, and he was like a poet who transmutes his sorrow into the music of his song. The ape was certainly the predecessor of man, and the singing of the Gibbon was therefore an earlier phase of utterance than human speech; and as the ape has been continued for the typical singer and divine bard it looks as if a form of musical sounds may have been practised by the primitive man in imitation of the ape, who was not only the first singer, as the bewailer of the lost light and saluter of the re-illumined orb, but the earliest teacher of a musical scale and composer of songs without words.

The hieroglyphics of Egypt may not contain all the signs made by the ape-men in their earliest phase of mimesis, but the essential types have been continued. The Hand KAF bears the name of the Kaf monkey, which is the typical *Hand* on the monuments—the hand of the Gods. From this we may gather that the Kaf idea was derived from the Kaf animal, that could climb and made such dexterous use of its forepaws; and that the hand-type of speech was identified with the language of gesture-signs, beginning with the Kaf, who presented the picture of hand-conversation and demonstrated the idea of *Kaf* to seize with the hand, which is registered by Kaf becoming the name of the hand, and by the monkey and hand being two types expressed under one word. The Kaf is likewise the clicker, and was continued in Egypt as the Image of Language, the Word of Speech, and type of the Lunar Logos. The Clickers were the earliest articulators of sound, which could be understood before the formation or evolution of verbal speech. They are identified by name with the Kaf as the Kaffirs.

In the hieroglyphics the Ibis which cries "*Aah-Aah*" and supplies the type of "*Aah-ti*" became finally a phonetic **A**. The eagle and a bird of the goose kind, also the fish, became signs of the letter **A**. The sparrow-hawk, Nycticorax, and Ram are forms of the letter **B**.

The Cerastes snake supplied the phonetic **F**, and its horns are still extant in the shape of that letter. The lion furnished one of the signs for **H**, the frog and beetle two others. The jackal and perch are found as forms of the **T**. The ape and the crocodile's tail supply two shapes of the **K**. The owl and the vulture figure as signs for **M**. The fish and another kind of vulture appear as **N**. A water-bird and the lioness are variants of the letter **P**. The **R** is a lion; later this was the phonetic sign for **L**. The goose and jackal supply a form of the **S**. The **T**'s include the snake, a bird, and the beetle. The chicken, swallow, and hare are among the different **U**'s. The fish is a supplementary **K** (Kha or Gha) as well as the calf (Kha or Aâ). These are ideographs reduced to phonetics.

With them we may compare the Kamilaroi "sayings" (Gurre) or ideographic letters.[1]

B. *Bundar*, Kangaroo.	K. *Karagi*, duck	P. *Pilar*, lance.
D. *Dinoun*, emu.	M. *Mullion*, eagle.	T. *Tulu*, tree.
G. *Giwir*, male.	N. *Nurai*, snake.	W. *Waru*, bird.
I. *Inar*, female.	Ɔ. *Ɔarumbon*, stork with fish.	Y. *Yaraman*, man going.
J. *Jimba*, sheep.		

Now, we can understand how these types and symbols got misinterpreted in popular beliefs and superstitions.

The connecting link of the beast fables of Europe and Inner Africa is not only extant in the Egyptian ideographs, the fables themselves as found in Æsop are Egyptian. In one of these the mouse is about to be devoured by the lion, whereupon he reminds him that when he was caught in the net of the hunters, he the mouse released him.[2]

Enceinte women in Hertfordshire still hear with alarm of a lioness having brought forth young; the present writer had proof of this a few years since, when an accouchement was announced at the Zoological Gardens that caused great consternation in the country. It was held to be an unlucky omen for all who were child-bearing. This is the result of misinterpreting a nearly-effaced type. The Egyptians, says Hor-Apollo, when they would symbolise a *woman that has brought forth once, depict a lioness, for she never conceives twice.*[3] The lioness having brought forth, bequeaths the blank future to the woman not yet delivered.

The Little Earth-Men of the German folk-lore are said to have the feet of geese, the print of which they leave on the ashes that are strewn for them. This may be explained by the type of Seb, who is the representative of the earth, and whose image is the goose!

The ancient Peruvians used to beat their dogs during an eclipse to make them howl. In Greenland the women also pinched the ears of

---

[1] Ridley.
[2] Lauth, *Moses der Ebräer*, p. 14; *Munich Sitz. Ber.* 1868, vol. ii. p. 42; J. Zundel, *Revue Archéologique*, 1861.   [3] B. ii. ch. lxxxii.

their dogs during an eclipse; and if the animals howled lustily, it was a sign that the end of the world had not yet come. It was the dog's duty to howl at such a time. For this reason, the dog in Europe took the place of the Dog-headed Ape of the Mysteries in Egypt, the howler during the moon's eclipse, and was bound to fulfil the character, willy-nilly.

Many games are typical, and constitute a kind of picture-reading, as well as picture-writing of the past. The cockchafer still suffers in another symbolical ceremony belonging to the cruel rites performed by boys. The chafer, in Egypt the scarab, called khepr, was a type of time and turning round. It *was* the turner round. And it is a pastime with boys to thrust a pin through the middle of the cock-chafer, and enjoy his spinning round and round, as the circle-maker.

All who have ever suffered mentally from the misinterpretation of ancient myths in the name of Theology, and felt its brand of degradation in the very soul, ought to sympathize with the treatment of the ass, for it is a fellow-victim who has likewise undergone unmerited punishment, and had its fall, and still awaits its redemption. The ass was once in glory, sacred to Sut, and a type of the Hebrew Deity. But Sut was transformed into Satan, and the ass who carried the Messiah in the Mysteries, having borne him for the last time, was degraded and assailed with stripes, kicks, and curses. The ass that carried the mythical Messiah was treated as the beast that bore the real one, or carried the Cross at the time of the Crucifixion—as proved by the mark between its shoulders—and "beating the ass" became a Christian sport, a humorous pastime in which the pagan past was figuratively kicked out in the real kicking of the ass. The animal being cast down from his primitive estate was associated with all that was ignominious. The adulterer and the cuckold were mounted on the ass with their faces turned to its tail, when the animal received the rain of bountiful blows, and suffered the worst part of the punishment.

The hare is considered unclean in various countries; the animal whose form was assumed by the witch, solely on account of its having served as a type. It is the sign of UN (Eg) to open. Un is also an hour, a period. The opening period is that of pubescence, whether of the male or female. When the Egyptians would denote an opening, says Hor-Apollo,[1] they delineate a hare because this animal always has its eyes open.

In relation to feminine pubescence, it signifies "it is lawful" or "unprohibited," therefore *open*. But the hare, as the emblem of the period, had a double phase, and delivered a double message to men. It is likewise related to the egg of the opening that was laid at Puberty.

[1] B. i. 26.

According to Pliny, the hare is of a double sex.   It was simply the type of periodicity which had a double phase, whether lunar or human and these two are signified by the hare and egg, the hare being considered a feminine, and the egg (of puberty) a masculine symbol.

"*The Easter Hare,*" says Holtzman, "*is inexplicable to me ; probably the hare is the animal of Astara ; on the picture of Abnoba a hare is present.*"[1]   Easter was the opening of another year, hence the emblem of the hare of March or Easter.

It is on this account that the hare is associated with the egg of Easter, which is broken as an emblem of the opening period.   In Saxony they say the Easter hare brings the Easter egg, and in Swabia children are sent in search of the hare's egg.   In some parts the Easter eggs are made into cakes in the form of a hare ; in others the babies are said to come out of the hare's form.   The uncleanness of the hare was solely symbolic.

Rats and mice in Germany were held to represent the human soul. One story relates that at Saalfeld, in Thuringia, a girl fell asleep whilst her companions were shelling nuts.   They observed a little red mouse creep from her mouth and run out of window.   They shook the sleeper but could not wake her, so they removed her to another place. Presently they saw the mouse creep back and run about in search of the girl, but, not finding her, it vanished, and at the same moment the girl died.[2]

The goddess Holda was said to lead an army of mice, and she was the receiver of children's souls.   Now, in Egypt, the shrew-mouse (*mygale, mus araneus*) was consecrated to the Genitrix Buto, and the mummies, together with those of the solar hawk, were buried in the City of Buto.[3]   The animal was held to be blind, and the hawk was the personification of sight.   These furnished two types of the soul or being, only to be understood in accordance with the "Two Truths," one of which will account for the red mouse.

Plutarch[4] says the mouse was reverenced for its blindness because darkness was before light.   The hawk was the bird of light.   Buto was the nurse who concealed Horus, and the mouse was a type of Horus in Skhem, the hidden shrine and shut-place, also known as a region of *annihilation.*[5] The mouse typified the mystery of shutting up the red source of life, the flesh-maker, which was looked upon as the first factor in biology.   And it was by its being shut up and transformed in the region of annihilation that the future life was created.   The mouse thus represented the soul of flesh, so to say, the mother-soul, the eyeless and unseeing soul, before the fatherhood was acknowledged ; the first, the blind Horus, who had to be blended

[1] *Deutsche Mythologie*, p. 141.
[2] Baring-Gould, *Curious Myths*, vol. ii. p. 159.
[3] *Herodotus*, ii. 67.
[4] *Plutarch Symp*. iv. Quæ. 5.
[5] *Mon. Brit. Museum.*

with the second, as the two halves of the complete soul. According to this primitive mode of thought and expression we can account for the shrew-mouse in England being made the victim of sacrifice.

It is well known that amongst other charms for healing and saving the shrew-mouse was selected to be offered up on or in the tree; the shrew-ash or elm being the most popular for the purpose. A deep hole was bored in the bole, and a shrew-mouse was thrust in alive, the hole being plugged up behind the victim.[1] This represented the Horus in Skhem, the saviour-victim who was sacrificed in the physiological, solar, and lastly Christological drama of redemption, according to the doctrine of blood-sacrifice. " To denote *disappearance*," says Hor-Apollo, "the Egyptians pourtrayed the mouse." And the disease or ailment prescribed for was supposed to disappear with the imprisoned and decaying mouse.

It came to be believed of this type of a disappearance, that if the heart were cut out of a mouse when alive and worn round about the arms of a woman, it would prove fatal to conception.[2] The Hebrew abomination denounced as "*eating the mouse*," may have had a kindred significance. On the other hand, *during an eclipse of the moon*, the Mexican women who were *enceinte* and terribly alarmed lest the unborn child should be *turned into a mouse*, were accustomed to hold a bit of *iztli* (obsidian) in their mouths or in their girdles to guard against such a fatality.[3] The moon in eclipse represented the period opposed to gestation. The stone was a symbol of founding and establishing, and the mouse an emblem of a disappearance.

The shrew-mouse in Britain is a sufferer from the later sense read into words. *Shrew* in Anglo-Saxon means to curse (cf. Eg. *sriu*, curse), and denotes something wicked; hence the poor shrew-mouse is accounted wicked and accursed. But this is not a primary meaning or form of the word, which is *skrew* in Somerset, and *scro* elsewhere. The animal was named as the digger; so the German *Schormaus* and the Dutch *Schermuys* are the mole as the digging mouse, named from *schoren* or *scharren*, to dig. The shrew is the earlier *scro*-mouse, and the digging is retained in the Gaelic *sgar* and Breton *skarra*, to tear open, to dig. In Egyptian, *sru* is to dig, with a prior form in *skru*, to cut and plough, the plough or digger being the *ska*, whence *skru* and *screw*. The shrew-mouse would not have typified a disappearance but for its being the digger. The digging to bring forth its young was the cause of its adoption as a sign of the Shut-place in Skhem, the mythological shrine of re-birth for the Solar God in the underworld, where the sun disappeared to be re-born on the horizon of the resurrection.

---

[1] Brand, *Physical Charms.*
[2] Richard Lovell, *Panzoologicomineralogia*, 1661.
[3] Sahagun, *Hist. Gen.* tom. ii. lib. viii. p. 250.

E

There is a Bohemian legend in which the Devil creates the mouse to eat up "God's corn," whereupon God creates the cat to destroy the mouse.[1] This belongs to Egyptian Mythology, where we find the cat that killed the rat that ate the malt in the house that Jack built. It appears as the "*abominable rat of the sun*," which was looked after by the cat-headed Great Mother, Pash (whence the Arabic *Bisseh* or tabby); the cat being a type of the moon as the luminous eye of the dark.

To a great extent modern superstition is symbolism in its state of dotage, when it cannot remember what the types originally meant. The Abipones are said to see the souls of their ancestors in certain birds, the widgeon or other water-fowl that fly by night, and make their cry; and in the hieroglyphics, not only is the bird a symbol of the soul but one of these, the Pâ, a sign of the soul of breath, is the widgeon or a wild goose in the act of hissing as the bird of breath issuing from the waters. So that the hissing duck or goose was the symbol of a soul in Egypt, and, as Pâ (or Pepe) means to fly, of a flying soul. The hieroglyphics are still unwittingly preserved by the Abipones.

The Eskimos say that all living beings have the faculty of soul, but especially the bird.

The Hurons of North America are reported to believe that the souls of their deceased friends turned into turtle-doves. The turtle-dove, in Hebrew תור, bears the name of the Genitrix *Tef*, English Dove. The dove as well as the hawk was associated with Hathor, who was the habitation of the hawk (Horus, her child) or more literally the birdcage of the soul.

The priestesses of Western Sarawak make the figures of birds which are said to be inhabited by spirits. But the bird as a type of the spirit or soul must be read all round.

The Egyptians did not think the soul turned into a bak-hawk when they depicted or embodied the Ba (soul) in bird shape. It is a mode of expression which may be variously interpreted according to the mental stage. The hawk of fire, or spirit, is the one of the seven elementaries which became the solar Horus; and in Britain we have seven spirit-birds that fly by night, known as the "seven whistlers."

The learned and conscientious Montesinos relates that when the worship, or veneration, for a certain stone had ceased, a parrot flew from that fetish and entered another stone, which was held as an object of adoration instead. In this story the parrot takes the place of the hawk, the bird of soul, or the dove, the bird of breath. The soul (or spirit) is thus represented as typically passing out of the one type into the other. The bird imaged the object of worship, and the fetish-stone its dwelling place.

[1] Ralston, *Russian Folk Tales*, p. 330.

According to a Muhammedan tradition, the souls of the martyrs are said to rest in the crops of green birds, which eat of the fruits and drink of the waters of Paradise.[1] This is the Egyptian imagery in which souls are represented as human-headed birds being fed with the fruit and nourished by the water of the Tree of Life ! Also green is the colour of renewal, and of Ptah the revivifier.

The soul of the hieroglyphics, depicted as winged, with the human head, is the original of the winged race of men in the Phædrus of Plato and the winged angels of Iconography. All such types belong to the hieroglyphical and symbolical mode of representation, not to the human race pre-Adamite or otherwise.

When told that the natives of West Africa look upon monkeys who are seen near a burial-ground as being animated by the spirits of the dead, we turn to the hieroglyphics for interpretation. There we find the ape (Ben) is a type of the Resurrection, elevated in the Ritual[2] to the status of a Divinity. The *Ben*-ape is a form of the phœnix, whose name it bears, and the dead turning into monkeys is the same typologically as the ape being an image of the transforming dead.

The ape, as the imager or imitator, offered a natural model for the transformer. Shu, the star-god, transformed under this type ; and the moon made its great change in the character of Aan, the ape. Lastly, the same type was applied to the soul in death as a mode of representation. In Egypt the animal was known to be ideographic. But in Inner Africa the real animal became a fetish-image confused with the spirits of the dead, the original link of connection being more or less missing in the mind of the modern natives, and absent altogether from that of the missionaries.

It is often reported that such and such a people, like the Kaffirs of South Africa, believe that the spirits of their dead ancestors appear to them in the shape of serpents.[3] Zulus are said to recognise the spirits of their ancestors in certain green snakes that are harmless. This means that in such a case the serpent, not the bear, ape, or dog, is the particular token. The green colour also identifies the type of immortality. Green is the hue of the resurrection from the earth ; the colour of the stone-axe and amulet of Jade ; the colour of Ptah, Num, and Shu, as the sign of rising again.

Also, as the serpent was a type of the eternal by periodic renewal, an emblem therefore of immortality, the belief that their ancestors survived in spirit was expressed by the serpent symbol, and this is independent of any perversion of the matter, whether by the native mind or the missionary. The true significance can be recovered in Egypt with whom survived the consciousness of Kam.

The goddess Renen, the Gestator, is said to receive in death the

---

[1] Sale, *Prelim. Discourse*, sect. iv.   [2] Ch. xxxi.
[3] Casalis, *Basutos*, p. 246.

breaths (souls) of those belonging to her.[1] The serpent was one of her symbols, consequently these souls, or breaths, would enter the serpent-woman to be born again ; and as the serpent was a type of renewal before *Renen* was personified in Egypt, we hear the Inner Africans talking in the same figures of speech that were made visible by Egyptian art.

When the Greenlander who has been at point of death in an exhausting illness, recovers his health and pristine vigour, they speak of his having lost his former soul and had it replaced by that of a young child, *or a reindeer*. But this also is only a figurative mode of speech ; the language is that of the hieroglyphics ; the imagery that of the bone-caves.

The bone of the calf, or of the child, was an emblem of renewal, buried as such with the dead. The horns of the reindeer were indicative of *renewal coming of itself*, and, like the bone of the child, simply supplied a type of rejuvenescence.

The underlying typology is in many instances obscured, but seldom quite extinct. Nor do the older races mistake the symbol for the thing signified, so much as is represented. The totemic nature of the type is made significant every time the supposed worshippers slay their god in the shape of a bear, crocodile, or other fetish with apologies and appeasing rites offered to the animal they have killed. They recognise in some dim way that it was only a type of the hidden meaning, not a real deity ; a representation, and not an incarnation. The reporters are mainly responsible for the doctrine of incarnation. It was because the image was representative that it acted vicariously, and was beaten at times by the irate worshipper, not as the god in person, but as some sort of likeness. The doctrine of vicarious sacrifice and atonement dates from this origin in the most primitive stage of thought—in thus laying hold of something that imaged and represented the absent, invisible, intangible — which culminated at last in Christology and in the waxen image of witchcraft as it had done earlier in the mummy-figure of the Egyptians.

The Basutos are said to think that if a man should walk along a river's bank and cast his shadow in the water, a crocodile may seize it and draw him in ; his shadow, or *Seriti*, being one with his soul.[2] This, too, is connected with the Egyptian typology. The crocodile was one of the animals into which the soul passed or was transformed in order that it might cross the waters in death. The crocodile was a form taken by the Goddess of the Great Bear, who was a crocodile in her hinder-part, one of her four types.

The eighty-eighth chapter of the Ritual is named the *Chapter of Making the Transformation into a Crocodile ;* and the vignette is a crocodile-headed snake—two forms of the Genitrix in one. The speaker (deceased) says : "*I am the crocodile whose soul comes from*

---

[1] *Ritual*, ch. clx.   [2] Casalis, *Basutos*, p. 245.

*men.   I am the crocodile whose soul comes from men; I am the crocodile
leading away by stealth.   I am the great fish of Horus, the great one
in Kam-Ur.   I am the person dancing in Skhem."*   The crocodile (as
Ta-urt or Typhon) was the earliest form of the Fish-mother, the
Derketo, Atergatis, Hathor or Venus, who brought forth from the
waters.   The speaker personates the crocodile who leads away the
souls of men by stealth.   The Skhem is the shrine of re-birth, and
this therefore is represented by the crocodile.   He is in the crocodile
(or *is* the crocodile), and so crosses the waters as did the sun-god,
whether as Horus or Herakles, inside the fish during the three days
at the winter solstice.   Thus the tradition of the crocodiles seizing
the souls of men in the shape of their shadows, can be traced to the
typology.

"In North-west America," says Dr. Tylor, "we find some Indians
believing the spirits of their dead to enter into bears, and travellers
have heard of a tribe begging the life of a wrinkle-faced old grizzly
she-bear as the recipient of the soul of some particular grandame,
whom they fancied the creature to resemble.   So among the
Esquimaux, a traveller noticed a widow who was living for conscience'
sake upon birds, and would not touch walrus-meat which the
Angekok had forbidden her for a long time, because her late husband
had entered into a walrus."[1]

A Chiriquane woman of Buenos Ayres was heard by a missionary
to say of a fox: "*May not that be the spirit of my dead daughter?*"[2]
These were thinging their thought according to the ancient typology
which is yet interpretable by means of the Kamite Mythology.
In this the Great Bear Constellation (the hippopotamus, seal, walrus,
or other water-type) was the Great Genitrix who became the reproducer of souls in a later phase of thought, because she had been the
mother of the revolutions or time-cycles in heaven, and of the
Elementary Gods.

From being the mother of the beginnings in space and time, she
was made to impersonate the womb of a new life.   She formed the
principal Car (Urt) in Heaven which the thought of man mounted to
ride round and ascend up out of the darkness of the depths when the
constellation was the "*dipper*" below the horizon.   It is the *bearer*
still, as the Wain of Charles.   It was the car of Osiris in Egypt, and
the Coffin which the Osiris deceased entered to be re-born in the
eternal round.

Thus the souls of the Egyptian dead entered the bear or hippopotamus as with the American Indians, among whom the aged
she-grizzly represented the most ancient Genitrix, the recipient of
souls, who bore them and brought them to re-birth.   The same type
is continued in the Arabic daughters of the bier (Ursa Major)
and the Chinese coffin of the seven stars, in which a board is placed

[1] *Prim. Culture*, vol. ii. p. 6.   [2] Brinton, p. 254.

for the dead to rest on. This board contains seven holes which are regarded as representing the seven stars, and it is therefore called the "*seven-stars-board*." It is fluted as well as perforated, and a quantity of lime and oil is deposited between the board and the bottom of the coffin.[1]

The fox or jackal was a type of Anup, the conductor of souls, who led them up to the horizon of the resurrection, as the divine embalmer, chief of the mountain in which the dead were laid. The jackal in two characters tows the bark of the sun and the souls, and these two are called "Openers of the Way." One opens the road of darkness to the north, the other the road of light to the south.

The spirit of the dead girl being identified with the fox in Buenos Ayres is the exact parallel to the souls of men becoming jackals in the belief of the African Marawi.[2] With them, however, there is another connecting link. It is the soul of the bad man that becomes the jackal; the soul of the good man becomes a snake. The jackal, or seb, was a type of the earth; the lower world of two, whereas the snake was a symbol of renewal and immortality.

The practice of killing and burying a dog with a deceased person is not uncommon, and the custom can be read by the hieroglyphics. Cranz relates that the Esquimaux laid the head of a dog in a child's grave as the type of the intelligent animal that was sure to find the way. Bishops used to be buried in this country with a dog lying at their feet. One of the chief funeral ceremonies of the Aztecs was to slaughter the Techichi, a native dog which was burnt or buried with the corpse, a thread being fastened round its neck, and its office was to guide the deceased across the Waters of Chiuhnahuapan on the way to the land of the dead.[3]

The custom of bringing a dog to the bedside of a dying person, as an escort and guide to the soul, was common with the Hindus and Persians.[4] A corpse which had not been seen by a dog was held capable of polluting a thousand men. But when the corpse had been shown to an observant dog, that removed the power of pollution. The dog was supposed to be its guardian against the fiend of corruption, by the Parsees. In Egypt, the dog as Anubis was the embalmer and preserver of the dead. Hence the protection afforded to the corpse by the presence of the dog.

In a recent work on Japan, the dog of the dead is described as being the messenger of spirit-mediums, whose stock-in-trade consists of a small box (supposed to contain some mystery known only to the craft) of somewhat less than a foot square. It is said that, in the south, a dog is buried alive, the head only being left above ground, and food is then put almost within its reach, exposing it thus to the

---

[1] J. H. Gray, *China*, p. 283.   [2] Waitz, vol. ii. p. 419.
[3] Tylor, *Prim. Culture*, vol. i. p. 426.
[4] *Shayast La-Shayast*, ch. ii. 65; ch. x. 33.

cruel fate of Tantalus. When in the greatest agony and near death, the head is chopped off and put in a box.[1] This cruel treatment is intended to make the animal return in spirit, and thus the dog (which was the wolf-dog, or the golden dog—the Egyptian Mercury) fulfils the character of the Psychopompus.

So the hound of Hermes, in Greece, came to guide the passing soul to the river Styx. And still, when the soul of the dying is about to go forth, the dog is supposed to utter its howl with prescient instinct.

This intelligent friend and faithful companion was sacrificed to become the guide of the poor cave-dwellers when benighted in death.

The Barrow at Barra was *a central room with seven other chambers* that contained the skeletons of men and dogs.

The bones of a dog were found buried with the human skeleton in a cave of the Pyrenees, showing that this faithful friend of man, at that remote time, was looked upon as a kind of Psychopompus, an intelligent shower of the way through the dark. Here it may be thought that a creature so intelligent as the dog might be independently adopted in various lands. But the dog was a creation of man, who made the animal domesticated. The dog is a civilized descendant of the wolf and jackal, and both these types are earlier than the dog, in the Egyptian mythology as in nature.

Colonel Hamilton Smith in opposing the theory of the dog's descent from the wolf and jackal, suggested by Darwin, has rashly asserted that a thorough *philological* inquiry would most assuredly show that in no language and at no period, did man positively confound the wolf, the jackal, or the fox, with a real dog. This of course could only apply to the name. And it happens that the name of the wolf in Greek, *Lykos*, is confounded, or is identical with the Akkadian name for the dog, *Likku*, which again answers to *Arigu*, the dog in the Ai-Bushman tongue. The names of the wolf and dog are found to be equivalent in the pre-historic languages.

Tsip is the dog in Inbask (Yukahiri), and in Egyptian *Tseb*, Arabic *Dîb*, is the wolf. In the Hottentot language the jackal is named *Girib*, and in the abraded form *Årib* is the name of the dog. In Egyptian one name of the dog is *Anush* or *Unush*, and this is likewise a name of the wolf, which not only confounds the dog with the wolf, but tends to show the derivation of the dog from the wolf, as is acknowledged by the continuity of the name of the wild animal for that of the domesticated dog.

The star Sothis is the well-known star of the dog. The dog was identified as its type *when there came to be a dog*, but its still earlier forms were the jackal (or golden dog), the wolf, and the fox-dog of Abyssinia, called the Fenekh. All three preceded the domesticated dog, and all three meet in the dog of the Dog-star. Before this

[1] *Fu-So Mimi Bukuro*, by C. Pfoundes.

domesticated dog could have been adopted as a type Anubis as jackal, wolf, or fenekh, was the still earlier guide of the sun and souls through the under world. Anubis is designated the " preparer of the way of the other world." " I have made way," says the deceased, " *by what Anup has done for me.*" [1]

The Osirian in the *Ritual,*[2] in the 10th gate of his passage to Elysium, brings with him the head of a dog as a kind of talismanic toll. He pleads with the gate-keeper: "*I have anointed myself with red wax. I have provided myself with a dog's head.*" The keeper replies: "*Thou mayst go: thou art purified.*"

The Kamite types are to be found the world over, in one stage or another. They can be traced to Upper Nilotic Africa as their birthplace; and wheresoever they are extant, Egypt alone is their interpreter.

The Khoi-Khoi declare that if the jackal discovers an ostrich nest he will scream for the white vulture. This bird then follows him, and when they come to the nest, which is covered by the ostrich hen, the vulture claws up a stone and ascends the air vertically over the nest to drop the stone down plumb on the breeding hen. The ostrich, startled and frightened by the blow, scuttles off, and then Reynard breaks the eggs, and both he and the vulture feast on them in the most friendly manner.[3]

These sly rogues furnished two divine types. The vulture is Egyptian (*Neophron perenopterus*), and a representative of the great Mother Neith, whose guide and companion, her Mercury, is the jackal! The vulture is also a prophetic bird with the Khoi-Khoi as it was in Egypt. The jackal, Anup, who was such a subtle thief in Inner Africa, was the typical thief, and god of thieving, and he became the Greek Hermes and Roman Mercury.

The *fainche* is a fox in Irish-Keltic and the *fenekh* is the fox-dog of Abyssinia, which was a type of the dog-star, the announcer of the Inundation.

In Europe the fox is still the announcer, the prophesier, as was Anup, the jackal or fox (fenekh) in Egypt. When the fox is heard barking in the woods at night in England, he is said to prophesy a sharp winter.

Egypt, who brought on certain types of things in the simplest condition from Inner Africa to develop and send them forth into the whole world at different stages in her own development, can still give the sole intelligible account of their origin and significance.

Thus in Inner Africa the chief type-name of the lion and leopard is *gfa*. In Egyptian *kafa* denotes force, puissance, potency, the abstract forms of power. But it also means to hunt and seize by force. The *kafau* are the destroyers and desolators. *Kafi* (Shu)

---

[1] Ch cxlviii.　　　　　[2] Ch. cxlvi.
[3] Ha'ın, *Tsuni-Goam,* p. 84.

a divine type of power, who forces the sun along, wears on his head the hind quarter of the lioness as the emblem of his force.

The lion and leopard were the live types first-named, and Egyptian shows the later application of the same word to a more abstract or recondite meaning.

Gray describes the treatment of a Mandenga who had killed a lion, and who was considered guilty of a great crime because he was only· a subject, whereas the lion was a lord or sovereign.[1]   This status of the animal was continued in the ideographs where the lion (*Ha*) signifies the lord, the ruler, the first and foremost, the glory (*Peh*), a type of the double force.

The tail of a lion suspended from the roof of a Xosa-Kaffir chief's hut as the sign of his power, has the same meaning when worn by a Rameses as Pharaoh of Egypt.   Other animals (as already mentioned) which were first named in Inner Africa can be traced by those names in Egypt where they have become divine types in mythology, that is gods and goddesses. *Nome* is the serpent in Bidsogo and the deity *Num* is serpent-crowned in Egypt. *Nam* is a goat in Kiamba, and the goat in Egypt is another type of the god *Num*.

The *Numu*, in Vei, is an enormous kind of toad. *Num* (Eg) is called the king of frogs, and *Hek* is his frog-headed consort in Egypt.

The monkey is named *Kefu* in Krebu ; *Kebe* in Kra ; *Éfie* in Anfue. In Egypt this is the *Kaf* ape, a figure of Shu (*Kafi*) and Hapi, a type of one of the seven elemental gods.

In the Makua language *Paka* is simply the cat. In Egypt *Pekha* is the cat-headed goddess. She is also known as Buto (*Peht*), and the cat is named *Boode* in Embomma, and *Boude* in Malamba.

Azi is the cow in the Kaffir dialects ; *Esu* in Isiele. This is the type of Isis the cow-headed Genitrix called *As* or *Hes* as the Egyptian goddess. *Gbami* is the cow in the Pika, and *Khebma* is the water-cow the most ancient type of the Genitrix in Egypt.   The type-name for the woman in Inner Africa is—

Manka in Ekamtulufu.	*Menge* in Bayon.	*Mangbe* in Momenya.
Manka in Udom.	*Mengue* in Pati.	*Mengue* in Param.
Manka, in Mbofon.	*Mengue* in Kum.	*Mana-Nube* in Kisawahili.

The position of the woman was that of concubine and slave, like the Kaffir *Ncinza*, rather than of wife, and in this double character she is named—

Manka in Ekamtulufu.	*Mengu* in Param.	*Mangbe* in Bagba.
Manka in Udom.	*Mengue* in Bayon.	*Mengbe* in Momenya.
Amanka in Mbofon.	*Mengue* in Kum.	

In Egypt Manka or Menka (Menâ) reappears as the wet nurse, the suckler, another type of the Genitrix who was divinized as the great mother in mythology.   Here, and elsewhere, Inner Africa shows

---

[1] Gray's *Travels in Western Africa*, p. 143.

the natural genesis, the primitive forms, the earliest status of things which became symbolical and were held to be divine in Egypt, and these underlying facts show a more profound relationship between Inner Africa and Egypt than those of syntax and grammar in language. They belong to the same ancient order of evidence as the totemic signs, gesture-language, and the oldest primitive customs that are likewise found to be the most universal in their range.

SECTION II.

NATURAL GENESIS AND TYPOLOGY OF PRIMITIVE CUSTOMS.

(The symbolical and superstitious phases of customs once primitive can only be explained by means of ir natural genesis.)

THE thesis here maintained is that inner Africa was the birth-place of the animal typology, which is at the base of the hieroglyphics, of heraldry, totemism, and of the so-called beast-epic of the Red Indian, Australian, and Aryan folk-lore.

It is the original home of various natural prototypes, which became the earliest symbolic types, and Egypt remains interpreter of the land of the origins.

The animals, reptiles, birds, and insects, which talk in the tales of the Bushmen and in the beast-stories of Europe, Australia, America, and India were adopted amongst the earliest means of expression for the primitive man, because they had been his tutors. We know what they said to him, for they continue to say the same things as types. He adopted them of necessity, made use of them for himself, stereotyped them for us, and we have but to learn this language of animals to know that the same system of typology which has spread all over the world and been eternized in the stars of heaven, must have had one origin and emanated from one centre, now claimed to have been African.

Totemism and heraldry are two extant modes of making signs by means of typical zoology. According to *Boece* the ancient Britons used the figures of beasts after the manner of the Egyptians, "*from whom they took their first beginning*," more particularly in the "*inscriptions above their sepulchres.*" These are still to be found on the stones, the coins or talismans, and in the hieroglyphics of heraldry.

Herodian mentions the "*shapes of the heavenly bodies and of all kinds of beasts and birds*" as the tattoo-marks of the Picts.

The zoological nature of British naming is shown even by the following coats of arms in Canting Heraldry :—

Keats, 3 cats.	Heron, 3 herons.	Cunliffe, 3 conies.
Head, 3 unicorns' heads.	Ramsden, 3 rams' heads.	Lamb, 3 lambs.
Coote, 3 cootes.	Colt, 3 colts.	

The warriors who fought at Cattraeth included bears, wolves, and ravens.[1]

The *Bibroci* were the biber (Cornish befer, Gaelic beabhor) or beaver tribe. The *Brockdens* are the badgers (unless named from the den of the brock), the Gledstanes are kites or hawks.

The *mertae* of Sutherlandshire were the cow-men, whose mother was possibly represented by the British goddess *Rosmerta*.

The *luga* were the calves. The men of Essex and the Isle of Wight are still known as the " calves "; the " calves " were also located near Belfast. Some of these totemic types became the blazons of counties.

People were once known in these islands as the taverns are now, by their signs ; each being the symbol of the group, clan, or tribe. The formative suffix in numberless names shows them to be derived from the " tun " and " den," the " ham " and " combe," the " leigh," " ford," " worthe," " ing," " stock " or " stow," which were place-names before they became personal.[2]

The first name was given at puberty to him of the totemic mark. Next to him of the common land, the tribal settlement. There is a form of the 'ham' extant at Gloucester with peculiar common rights and liberties. Even when land was made *several*, and became individual property, the man, like John-o'-Groats, was called after the land, and the right to bear a crest is based *primarily* on a claim of descent from a particular tem, ham, ing, tun, or other group which was known by its totem. Heralds still profess to trace back the branches to the stem of the family tree, if they do not penetrate to the root that once grew in the place so named.

Totemism was as purely a form of symbolism as English heraldry and coats of arms, and both emanate from that inner African system of typology which was continued by the Egyptians, North American Indians, Chinese, Australians, British, and other ancient races.

Sir John Lubbock has called totemism a "*deification of classes*"; but it originated in the need of names and the adoption of types for the purpose of distinguishing the groups from each other. The

---

[1] Aneurin's *Gododin*.

[2] It may be very deceiving where the earliest place-names have become the later race-names. Take that of the *Menapii* for example. They are found by name in Menevia (St. David's, Wales), at Dublin, and at the mouth of the Rhine. Were these Menapii then of one race? That depends on whether the name be a race-name or a place-name. My contention would be for the place-name. *Men* in Egyptian means to arrive, warp to shore, and anchor. The *Mena* is a landing-place, a port, or harbour; Persian *Miná*. This is continued in the Cornish *Min* for the coast, brink, border, boundary. Thus Menapia is the place of landing, and would be so named in the language of the first comers. Ap (Eg.), is the first, and Apia as country denotes the first land attained. This would apply to the first landing-place on any coast, Welsh, Irish, or Belgic. "Menapii" as a folk-name, the Menapii of Cæsar, is more probably derived from the Kamite *Menefia*, for soldiers, as the German is the war-man. If the Menapii as later settlers were named from the place, their name can be no clue to their race.

deification, if any, consisted in venerating or divinizing the totemic type, the family crest first adopted of necessity for use.

Totemism, however, is not what the same writer thought, a system of naming *individuals first and then whole groups after some animal.*

Mr. Freeman also is wrong in asserting that the clan grew out of the patriarchate.[1] Who was the British patriarch in this sense when, as Cæsar tells us, ten or a dozen totemic brothers held their wives in common ?

When the brothers, uncles, and nephews held their wives in common as with the Tottiyars of India, there were none among them that could be distinguished as fathers except they were the old men, the elders, the collective patriarchate, as among the Galactophagi, with whom the only fathers known by name were the "old men"; the young men being the "sons."

Descent was first traced from the mother, then from the sister; *the "two women"* from whom the Kamilaroi tribes claim to descend ; then from the uncle, and finally the father.

Bowditch says of the Ashantis, "Their extraordinary rule of succession excludes all children but those of a sister, and is founded on the argument that if the wives of the brothers are faithless, the blood of the family is entirely lost in the offspring, but should the daughters deceive their husbands it is still preserved."[2]

In Central Africa, according to Caillié,[3] the sovereignty always remains in the same family, but the son does not succeed the father ; the son of the king's sister is the chosen heir.

With the Kenaiyers of North-West America a man's nearest heirs in the tribe are his sister's children. With the Nairs, as amongst all polyandrists, no child knows its own father, and each man counts his sister's children to be his heirs.

Among the Malays, if the speaker be a female she salutes her sister's children as sons and daughters, but her brother's children as nephews and nieces. The sister of the brother was reckoned of more account than the wife. The marriage of brother and sister, which was continued by the Pharaohs of Egypt, no doubt originated and was preserved as a type of this blood-tie; the custom was sacred to them alone. This marriage of the brother and sister was continued by the Singhalese, who likewise limited the custom to the royal family. So was it in ancient Persia.

Indefinite progenitorship gave more importance to the brother's sister's son, the nephew, because in him the blood-tie was traceable. Of the Fijians it has been said, "*however high a chief may be if he has a nephew he has a master.*" The nephew was allowed the extraordinary privilege of appropriating whatever he chose belonging to

[1] *Comparative Politics*, p. 3.
[2] Bowditch, *Ashantee*, p. 185. "So all over Africa."—Captain Burton.
[3] *Travels*, vol. i. p. 153.

the uncle, or those who were under his uncle's power. The nephew of his uncle was an Emperor by nature. These two, uncle and nephew, were recognised personages before the father and son (as the son of the father).[1] So when Vasouki, the Serpent King, desired an heir, instead of marrying himself, he had his sister married, and the nephew succeeded to the supremacy.

This social status is reflected in the Egyptian mythology. Nephthys (*Neft*) was the sister of Osiris; *the child, as Anubis, being mothered by the sister;* and *Nift* in old Icelandic is the sister still. *Neft* is expressly designated "*the sister*"; "the benevolent *saving* sister," the "mistress of the house." It is she, not the wife, who *carries the seed-basket* on her head; she who *preserves the seed in its purity;* her basket (neb) *being the purifier of the seed.*

The genitrix as *Neft* is the bearer of the brother's son, the *nephew*; and in Lap the sister's son is named the *napat*. At this stage the seed (nap Eg.) was reckoned as the child of the sister, not of the wife, or concubine, on purpose to trace the line of descent.[2] In this way mythology becomes a mirror that reflects the primitive sociology.

There are customs extant which show the father assuming his right to claim his son by direct descent.

The Limboos of India, a tribe near Darjeeling, had a custom for the boy to become the father's property on his paying the mother a price for him, when the child was named and entered into his father's tribe. The girls remained with the mother, and belonged to her tribe.[3]

Aristotle[4] says the Libyans have their women in common, and distribute the children *according as they favour the men in likeness.* This, says Captain Burton, is the general rule in Africa.

The Fijians have a feast called *Tunudra,* in celebration of the birth of a child, but which, says Williams,[5] appears to have more relation to the mother than the child. This fact is implied by the name; *tuna* is the mother, and *dra* blood, in Fijian. The *Tunudra* is in celebration of the mother-blood, or mother-right.

When the child is the *first-born* there are games and sports; one of these consists in the men *painting on each other's bodies the woman's tattoo.*

Tattooing is a custom typical of becoming men and women as parents. And at this festival of the eldest child and mother-right, the men in sport marked each other's bodies with the women's tattoo;

---

[1] *Fiji and the Fijians,* vol. i. p. 34.
[2] *Nap, or nephew.* Nap (Eg.) is the seed. In the inner African languages the *boy* is the *napat* in Kanyop; *nabat,* Sarar, and *nafan* in Bola. Both the brother and sister are named *nofi* in Anfue; *novi,* Mahi; *anaefi,* Hwida, and *nâwie* in Dahome. In English, the *knave* is a lad.
[3] Lubbock, *Origin of Civilization,* p. 123.
[4] Pol. 2, 39.
[5] Williams, *Fiji and the Fijians,* vol. i. p. 175.

the mother symbol being transferred to the male, in the process of making game of each other.

The Fijians had superseded the mother-right, with descent on the father's side, but it looks as if we here recovered a primeval picture of the communal system in which it was impossible to father the child, and that this was being done jokingly in a game of guesswork, and by aid of the maternal type or *tat*, or tattoo. It is the way of many very primitive customs to end in harlequinade like the British pantomime, when they have found no ecclesiastical place of refuge.

So far from the patriarchal family being first, it is the last but one; the monogamic being last of all. It was preceded by the gregarious horde, undistinguished by name or totem or law of sexual intercourse. Next by the organization on the basis of sex, with later rules for the checking of incest; then by the family in which marriage was by single pairs, pairing at pleasure, or cohabiting until the child was born; then followed the patriarchal or polygamic family, with property in cattle and wives; and finally the monogamic family founded on the individualised fatherhood, and the polyandry of less civilized societies.

The totemic types originated when the undistinguished herd was first discreted into groups, and the groups were discriminated by some particular sign, clan, or tribal name.

The types adopted to distinguish the groups were the earliest ideographs that served for signs when these were without other names, and the *tem*, or body, of persons was only known from the gregarious mass by means of the natural figures which were at first branded into the flesh at the period of puberty.

Men and women still clothe themselves in the wool, fur, and feather of beast and bird. Earlier races wore the skins with the hair on. The still earlier clothed themselves as it were in the figures of birds and beasts. They dressed like them in their symbolical dances, and imitated their cries, by which they would be identified still further with their totemic sign; and this typology is continued in the personal names derived from the same mould of thought. Nor had the deification of animals any place in the origines of symbolism. The animals *are* the symbols. They were so in the absence of later hieroglyphics, and were continued as and for symbols into the domain of personal names.

If, as Schoolcraft alleges, the totem of the Redskins had become to them a symbol of the name of a progenitor it was not that the Indians thought a beaver or serpent, a turtle or a hawk, a stone or a tree, was their progenitor;[1] nor that they fancied the souls of their ancestors had entered into the particular totemic types. That is only a suggestion made by the modern ignorance of symbols. *Totemism began long before the male progenitor was known.* The tribe

[1] *Indian Tribes*, vol. ii. p. 49.

was the progenitor, with descent only on the mother's side; and the animal was the type of the whole group.

The coyote, or prairie dog, was honoured as the bringer into the world of the ancestors of the root-diggers of California. The wolf is respected by the Lenni Lenape Indians as the animal which released mankind from their subterranean abode. Coyote and wolf represent the golden dog, Anup, in Egypt, one of the first types of time, as the dog-star; who, in the planetary character of Mercury, passed through the underworld and rose again as a guide, deliverer, and saviour.

The totem is not the name of the dead ancestor, but of the clan, or communal type, which is *any animal* rather than a human ancestor, or male patriarch. The distinction of an individual name was the latest of all. Lichtenstein describes the Bushmen as having no personal names, although they did not appear to feel the want of such a means of distinguishing one individual from another. *Their society had been arrested in the totemic stage of nomenclature.*[1] In Dahome the personal name can hardly be said to exist at all. It changes with every rank of the holder.[2] These distinctions of rank and class-titles are another form of naming the division first, as is shown also by their being hereditary.

The Japanese have a different personal pronoun for various *classes* of persons, each class being compelled to use their own, and not another. "*There are eight personal pronouns of the second person peculiar to servants, pupils, and children.*"[3] These told *which* "thou" was intended, as *one of a class*, and therefore show a continuation of the totemic mode of naming and distinguishing by the group only. Eight classes of the personal pronoun answer to the eight totems of the Kamilaroi or eight of the Iroquois Indians; the principle of discreting from the undistinguished mass and naming by subdivisions is the same, although applied to a later stage of society. The Japanese people themselves were really divided into eight primary classes, corresponding to the universal eight original gods, or proto-types, in the various mythologies of the world.

By whatever names the Redskins might be known in their lifetime, it was the totemic, not the personal, name that was recorded on the tomb, or the *Adjedatig*, at the place of burial.[4] So is it with us. In death the individual still reverts to the totemic style, as is manifested by displaying the coat of arms on the scutcheon, in front of the house. The Scottish wife, whose married name is changed for her maiden name in death, still makes the typical return to her own tribe, or totem.

In the Ojibwa dialect the word *totem* signifies the symbol or device of a *Gens;* thence the figure of a wolf was the totem of the

---

[1] Lichtenstein, vol. i. p. 119; vol. ii. p. 49.   [2] Burton, p. 97.
[3] Steinmetz, *Japan and her People*, p. 299.
[4] Schoolcraft, vol. i. p. 49.

wolf *Gens ;*[1] the figure of a serpent was the totemic sign of the Tuscaroras.

The original of the word totem is supposed to be the Algonkin *Do-daim*, the type or mark of the *Daim*, as a town. The *Daim*, as the especial name of the town, is still extant in Central Africa, where the people are divided into the dwellers in " *Tembes*." In dispersing the mob at Ugogo, and sending them to their homes, the chief shouted, " *To your Tembes, Wagogo, to your Tembes.*"[2]

The town is also the

Edume, in Adampe.	*Demgal*, in Goboru.
Diambo, in Kisama.	*Dsamei*, in Buduma.

The Zulu *Tumu-tumu* is a large assemblage of huts, a big *Tumu*. The Vei people have a religious rite, performed at the time of puberty, which is called the *Beri*. A new name is then conferred on the youth, and a totemic or national mark is made on the back, by a *masked man who acts the part of a being from the unseen world ;* this mark is termed the Beri-*tamba*, or mark of the pubescent male, who is thus adopted into the *Tem*. *Tembe* in Vei also means to stand in a row, or fall into rank, like the English *Team*. *Tem* and *Tun* permute, and in Inner Africa the *Tembe* is also called the

Tan in Koama.	*Tanasu* in Gbandi.	*Tunk* in Dselana.
Tan in Bagbalan.	*Tenga* in Mose.	*Sa-ten* in Guresa.
Idon in Anan.		

In Egypt the totemism of the tribal system had been continued in the towns and cities which bore the names of the zoological types, such as the hippopotamus, crocodile, lion, ape, dog, wolf, hawk, fish, and others. The *"Temai"* had become the town, village, district, fort, or city; and this agrees with the Gothic *Dom* as the whole of anything. The Tem (Eg.) also means the total ; Maori *Tamene*, to be assembled together. The *Tem*, as a whole, under the king, became a kingdom. The primordial *Tem*, as a birth-place, is preserved by name in the West Australian *Dumbu*, for the mother's womb.

The *Daman* in Pahlavi is the dwelling ; the Latin *Domus*, the abode or domicile. The *Toms* in Scotland are relics of the same primary type of the dwelling in life, and the *Tomb* in death.

The Attic township was a *Dem*. The second member of the Greek organic territorial series comprised the ten *Demes*, as parts of the larger district. The Magars of India had an organization of twelve *Thums*.[3]

The Brehon joint family, the Hebrew twelve tribes, the joint Hindu family, the Zadruga house-community, of the Southern Sclavs, the Keltic *fine*, the *rekh*, ing, and many other of the primitive units that held a domain and property in common, and the land itself as

---

[1] Morgan, p. 165.　　[2] Stanley, *How I Found Livingstone*, p. 198.
　　　[3] Latham, *Descriptive Ethnology*, vol. i. p. 475.

"*perpetual man*," were all forms of the *Tum*, which permutes with *Tun*, and did not descend from the common ancestor, the patriarch of the *Tent*, because they existed when the male ancestry was *too common* to be individually identified.

· Nor was it the ancestor as male that was eponymous, but the totem, the type of the *Tem*, *hence the true ancestor so frequently claimed in the totemic animal*, and the confusion of the symbol with the thing signified. When the Sumatrans speak of tigers as *Nenek*, or Ancestors, it is because the tiger was a totemic animal. When the Dyaks of Borneo caught the alligator or crocodile they saluted it as their grandfather.[1]

The Yakuts of Siberia address the bear as their "*beloved uncle*." This title reflects the pre-paternal phase, as the uncle was acknowledged before the father was known, because he was the brother of the mother.

The animal is but a symbol, the *Sept*, or tribe, is the fact signified. This view is corroborated by the Australian "*Kobang*," which is not primary when applied to the type, but to the thing signified, that is to the family, or *Ank*,—for the *Ank*, Egyptian Ankh, Chinese Heang, applied to the people of a district, is very general as a type-name. Mungo Park gives a clan-name of the Mandengas of North Africa, which they bear in addition to the personal name as that of the *Kont-ong*. The Japanese *Kob-ong*, answering to the Australian *Kobang*, is a superstitious life-tie between two persons. This was once the tie of the Ankh or Tum. And such ties were supposed to exist between the brethren of the Ankh and their namesake of the Totem, which might be the leopard, (*Inko* in Kisama; *Yingue*, Songo, *Onnchu* Irish, or *Hanchi*, the lynx·in Cornish), or any other ideographic type.[2]

The British were known to Tacitus as the *Ing·gau*, the men of the *Ing*, the dwellers in a certain district, who preceded the people of Engla-land. The *Ing* is an inclosure. The *Hank* is a body of people confederated. *Enec* in Irish means the protection of the Clan or Ing. The *Aonac* (Gaelic) is an assembly; those who dwell together.

Ank in Sanskrit is to mark, stamp, or brand. *Ang* in West Australian signifies belonging to. The Maori *Ngt* is a mark applied to the division of land also called a *Tio*, equivalent to the Algonkin *Do*, or mark of the *Daim*. *Ngatahi* signifies "together." The Narrinyeri of South Australia have a totem for each tribe or family, called the "*Ngaitye*." This Ngaitye has also passed into individualized heraldry, and is regarded as the man's tutelary genius.[3]

[1] St. John, *Far East*, vol. ii. p. 253.
[2] Captain Burton tells me the brotherhood (*ntwa*) of the totems is uniformly recognized, on the Gold Coast by means of zoological symbols that denote consanguineous descent.
[3] Morgan, *Anct. Society*, p. 375.

The totemic type, whether as leopard, alligator, serpent, bull, dog, or others, stood for the general ancestor of the Tem and Ankh long before the individual fatherhood was known. Hence the style of "grandfather," or old one, conferred on the crocodile, and "uncle" on the bear.

"*They say, moreover, that all the animals of each species have an elder brother, who is as it were the principal and origin of all the individuals, and this elder brother is marvellously great and powerful. The elder brother of the beavers, they told me, is perhaps as large as our cabin.*"[1] Here the *big elder brother* was the human archetype.

Totemic signs served for various purposes of social intercourse. The Magar tribes of India are divided into totemic sections, and the law is that no two members of the same section may intermarry. These sections are the "*Thums.*"

With the *Tsim*sheen Indians of British Columbia who are *temmed*, divided into totems, and have their "Crests" of the whale, tortoise, frog, eagle, wolf, and other types, the relationship of the "Crest" is nearer and dearer than that of blood or any other tie which we may consider near; and it dominates that of the tribe. Members of the tribe may intermarry, but not the bearers of the same crest.

Those of the same totem are not allowed to marry under any circumstances; that is, a whale must not marry a whale, nor a frog unite with a frog.[2] So is it with the *Tin*neh Indians, and if a man should defy the law and marry a woman of the same totem he is laughed at and ridiculed as *the man who has married his sister*, even though she may not have the slightest connection by blood, and has come from a totally different tribe. So is it still with the Somali of East Africa.[3]

The Munnieporees and other tribes round Munniepore are each and all divided into *four* families, the *Koomrul, Looang, Ankom*, and *Ningthaja*. A member of any of these families may marry a member of any other, but the intermarriage of the members of the same family is strictly prohibited.[4]

The totemic name still implied an original totemic relationship. And this continued dominant after men were known by the individual surname. The Ostiaks held it to be a crime to marry a woman of the same surname;[5] that likewise implied, as it had carried on, the totemic name still known with us by the heraldic type. In China marriage between those of the same surname is unlawful, and this rule includes all descendants of the male branch for ever.[6]

The first formation of society recognizable is the division into two totems.

[1] *Le Jeune in Rel. des Jes. dans la Nouvelle France*, 1634, p. 13.
[2] Hardisty, "Notes on the Tinneh," *Smithsonian Report*, 1866, p. 315; *Metlah katlah*, p. 6, published by the Church Missionary Society.
[3] Burton. [4] *Account of the Valley of Munniepore*, pp. 49 and 69.
[5] Pallas, vol. iv. p. 69. [6] Davis, *The Chinese*, vol. i. p. 282.

The Aborigines on the river Darling, New South Wales, are still divided into the two castes or totems of the earliest separation, which are rigidly preserved, and the children still follow the rank of the mother.[1] This is the oldest social formation on earth, the very bifurcation of the promiscuous herd.

Among the North American Indians the Chocta gentes were united in two phratries, and the first phratry was called the *divided people.* The second was the "beloved people."[2] These two brotherhoods were subdivided into eight totemic tribes, for breeding purposes. Here we meet by name with those who were distinguished as the "divided *ones.*" Nor is this an uncommon type of name. The "beloved," apparently, indicates the sexual purpose of the earliest division.

A tradition of the Senecas affirms that the bear and the deer were the original two totems, of which the eight (gentes), bear, wolf, beaver, turtle, and deer, snipe, heron, and hawk, composing the two brotherhoods of the Seneca-Iroquois, were subdivisions.

The Kamilaroi were organised in two primary totems, which are subdivided into eight groups from the most archaic form of society hitherto known. These two, male and female, are—

Male.	Female.		Male.	Female.
1. *Ippai.*	1. *Ippata.*		3. *Murri.*	3. *Mata.*
2. *Kumbo.*	2. *Buta.*		4. *Kubbi.*	4. *Kapota*

All the *Ippais* of whatever gens are brothers to each other and are theoretically descended from one common female ancestor. The *Kumbos, Murris,* and *Kubbis* are the same respectively, for the same reason.

Male.	Female.		Male.	Female.
1. *Ippai* can marry *Kapota* 4.			3. *Murri* can marry *Buta* 2.
2. *Kumbo* „ *Mata* 3.			4. *Kubbi* „ *Ippata* 1.

If any *Kubbi* meets an *Ippata* he can treat her as his *goleer* or spouse. And so of the others according to the name.

Male.	Female.			Male	Female.
Ippai marries *Kapota.*	Their children are	*Murri.*	*Mata.*
Kumbo „ *Mata.*	„	„	*Kubbi.*	*Kapota.*
Murri „ *Buta.*	„	„	*Ippai.*	*Ippata.*
Kubbi „ *Ippata*	„	„	*Kumbo.*	*Buta.*

"Ippai" begets "Murri" and "Murri" in turn begets "Ippai;" in like manner "Kapota" begets "Mata," and "Mata" in turn begets "Kapota," so that the grand-children of "Ippai" and "Kapota" are themselves "Ippais" and "Kapotas," as well as collateral brothers and sisters, and as such are *born* husbands and wives.[3]

The Two Totems are those of the Iguana and the Emu, both feminine symbols. "Iguana-Mata" must marry "Kumbo;" her

---

[1] Bonney, F., British Association Meeting, 1882.
[2] Morgan, *Ancient Society.*   [3] Morgan, p. 425, note.

children are "Kubbi" and "Kapota," and necessarily *Iguana* in Gens, because descent is in the female line.

In like manner, "Emu-Buta" must marry "Murri;" her children are "Ippai" and "Ippata," and of the *Emu* gens. "Emu-Ippata" must marry "Kubbi;" her children are "Kumbo" and "Buta," and also of the *Emu* gens.

By following out these descents it will be seen that in the female line *Kapota is the Mother of Mata*, and *Mata*, in turn, *the Mother of Kapota*. *Ippata* is the mother of *Buta*, and *Buta* the mother of *Ippata*; and thus return is for ever made to *the dual feminine ancestry!* The Tem is maintained by keeping in its membership the children of all its female members, and each Tem is made up theoretically of the descendants of the "*two women*" of the most primitive sociology; the two sisters of mythology who were two forms of the Mother, whose children were first divided and distinguished from those that lived in the state of primal promiscuity. This is shown by the two feminine types of the two Totems, the Emu (bird) and Iguana (reptile). The bird is the type of the woman above, the mother heaven; the reptile of the woman below, the bringer-forth from the abyss, as the crocodile (Typhon) or dragon (Tiamat) of the waters. This elaborate-looking device is but the result of the uttermost simplicity, working within the narrowest limits.[1]

The first division and the cause of it can be ascertained. The Kamilaroi eight tribes of the original Two Totems declare that they all descend from "two women." Now, the mother was the first individual recognised, and mythology says the next was the sister. The two sisters of our sociology were the two female ancestors of the Australians.

The earliest tie perceived was uterine; the next was that of the blood relationship; and the two sisters of one blood were the primary cause of dividing the offspring into the two first Totemic castes. Hence the descent from the two women, whose signs of the Iguana and Emu distinguished the earliest separate groups. The two women were the mother and her sister, and the two castes were cousins, who at first might intermarry.

The Totemic Heroes of the Caribs, in the West Indian Islands, were seen by them in the figures of the constellations! The clan, gens, or Tem being represented by the star-group, we see the later link of connection between the individual soul and the star. The star and soul are identical as *Seb* (Eg.); this identity is common with various races, and as the star and soul have the same name, this may account for the notion with which the Fijians are credited, that shooting-stars are souls of the departed. Each starry family was composed of individual stars.

[1] The two primary divisions and the later eight are also extant on the Gold Coast.

The Hottentots, in blessing or cursing, will say, *May good or evil fortune fall on you from the star of my grandfather!*[1] This was a totemic type, however, before it signified a translated soul.

The Twelve Signs of the Zodiac are totemic with the Chinese. These are—

Shu	Rat	Aries.	*Ma*	Horse	Libra.
Niu	Ox	Taurus.	*Yang*	Sheep	Scorpio.
Hu	Tiger	Gemini.	*Heu*	Monkey	Sagittarius.
Tu	Hare	Cancer.	*Ki*	Cock	Capricorn.
Lung	Dragon	Leo.	*Kuen*	Dog	Aquarius.
She	Serpent	Virgo.	*Chu*	Boar	Pisces.

The twelve signs are likewise represented by or in connection with the Chinese horary of twelve hours.

Each of the animals is still recognised as a totem, and they are all believed to exert a great influence on the lives of persons, according to the hour and its special sign under which they were born.

Star-totems were in use among the ancient Peruvians. Acosta describes the people as venerating the celestial archetypes of certain animals and birds found on earth. It appeared to him that the people were drawing towards the dogmas of the Platonic ideas.[2] Speaking of these star-deities he says, the shepherds looked up to a certain constellation called the Sheep, and the star called the Tiger protected them from tigers. His theory is that they believed there was an archetype in heaven of every likeness found on the earth in the animal shape. This was the Platonisation of the starry hieroglyphics, the archetypes of which were found on earth, and the types that had been configurated in the heavens for totemic signs ; these being reflected back again in the minds of men ; and this *platonisation* of mythology is the ground-rootage of Plato's system of celestial archetypes carried out in the region of more abstract thought. It is but a step from the celestial to the spirit world. The origines, however, are visible and physical, although the earlier type is employed to convey a later significance. We have to take the prior step from the natural animal to the celestial, and also to read the thoughts and things of earth at times by means of the imagery *Stelled* in the heavens.

The chief totemic signs of the North American Indians are to be found in the heavens, ranging from the Great Bear to the Stone of the *Oneidas* (the Stone or Tser Rock in Egyptian), but the Indians did not figure them there as constellations. These are the eternal witnesses above to the Kamite origin of mythological typology.

It has already been suggested that the first mapping out of localities was celestial before the chart was geographically applied, and that all common naming on earth came from one common naming of the heavens, commencing with the Great Bear and Dog. The mapping out of Egyptian localities, according to the

---

[1] *Tsuni-Goam*, p. 85.　　　　[2] Tylor, *Prim. Culture*, vol. ii. p. 222.

celestial Nomes and scenery, is described in the inscription of Khnum-hept, who is said to have "*established the landmark of the south, and sculptured the northern—like the heaven. He stretched the Great River on its back. He made the district in its two parts, setting up their landmarks like the heaven.*"[1]

It is said that: "*Thebes is a Heaven upon earth. It is the august staircase of the beginning of time.*"[2] Thebes is Teb or Apt, the birth-place, and the mother of birth, first personified in the abyss; next in the heaven of the Great Bear, and lastly as Apta in the Solar Zodiac.

The twelve signs of the zodiac were the twelve Totems of the Hebrew Tems. The system was full-blown under another type in the Kabalistic Tree of the world, with its seventy-two branches corresponding to the seventy-two duo-decans of the zodiac.

The tree of seventy-two branches, as the figure of the seventy-two duo-decans, is of Egyptian origin.

They use the ape (Aan), says Hor-Apollo,[3] "to symbolize the world, because they hold that there are seventy-two primitive countries of the world." This world was in the heavens, where the station of the ape was at the equinox, the point of completion. The stars were totemic with the ancient Arab tribes. Jupiter was the star of the Jôdam and Lakhm tribes; Mercury of the Asad tribe; Sirius of the Kais tribe; Canopus of the Tay tribe. Others recognised constellations as totemic types. From these we come at last to the ruling planet and the individual's guiding star. These things did not begin with any vague general worship of the heavenly host. The God of Sabaoth is the deity of the *Seven* Stars, not of Argelander's map of millions, or the diamondiferous dark. Those stars were observed and honoured by which time could be reckoned, and position in space determined. The constellations were figured for use, the types were made totemic, and became fetishtic; but, the non-evolutionist who looks on fetishism as a primæval religion degraded to idolatry, might just as well look on the black race as a very discoloured or dirty kind of white. He has to be forced back-ward step by step with face set all the while the clean contrary way. Fetishism began with typology, and both mythology and religion were the outcome, not the origin.

A very comprehensive designation for the divinities of all kinds, says Gill,[4] is the Mangaian "*te anau tuarangi,*" the heavenly family. This "*celestial race includes rats, lizards, beetles, sharks, and several kinds of birds. The supposition was that the heavenly family had taken up their abode in these birds and fishes.*" All such supposition is gratuitous and European. The Mangaian mind was still in the symbolic stage, and these animals were all types. The animals

---

[1] *Records of the Past*, xii. 68.   [2] Inscription of Queen Hatasu, *Rec.* xii. 133.
[3] i. 14.   [4] *Myths and Songs*, pp. 34-35.

are still named in heaven, and the stars are hieroglyphically grouped for us as for them. The writer explains that he takes these things "*apart from mythology and symbolism.*" But they cannot be taken apart; they had no other origin, and have no other meaning. What they once signified in Africa was their meaning in Polynesia, however dim in the native memory.

The Mound-Builders of America, particularly in Wisconsin, shaped the outlines of their inclosures in the forms of animals, birds, and serpents, which appeared on the surface of the country as huge hieroglyphics raised in enormous relief. One serpent figure has been traced a thousand feet in length; this was in Adams County, Ohio. These in all likelihood were delineated as the Totems of the buried dead; each *Daim* having its own mound, where the chief or the principal male and female were interred, with the common people around.

The Acagemans of California worship the God TOUCH, or *Tacu,* who appears at times in a variety of animal forms. He is said to send to every child that enters its seventh year some animal to be its protector or guardian. In order that the child might ascertain what animal shape the protecting spirit wore, the diviners took narcotic drinks, or the child fasted and watched in the Vanquech, a sacred inclosure, beside the image of the god, looking at the figure of some animal drawn on the ground by one of the Mages, until mesmerised. Then the animal seen in vision was adopted as his type or fetish figure. This was branded on his arm, and it was intended to give him a surer *touch* on the bowstring.[1]

Totemic types were not adopted without reason. The earliest two of the Kamilaroi, the Iguana and Emu, show the two powers of the Water and Air; the first two elements, like the dragon and bird, the serpent and bird, or the feathered serpent elsewhere. These *manifested powers superior to the human in relation to the two elements.*

Gesture-language and names show that, as the man was first distinguished by his pubescent attributes, so there were totemic types derived from ankh, the ear; ankh, the eye; ankh, the nose; ankh, the mouth, the hair, the beard, the tooth; and that these were represented by the animals, birds, &c., as the *ear of the jackal,*

---

[1] At the Congress of "Americanists" held at Madrid in September, 1881, a Mexican *savant* professed to have discovered the clay bust of a god *Cay* or *Tsaa* (unless these denote two different deities) amongst other antiquities which he had exhumed at Uxmal in Central America. Near the image of the Mexican deity was an altar upon which there is a *hand* of iron. Was this a form of the god *Touch?* *Touch* is an Egyptian divinity named Ka or Sa. With the prefix this is Teka (Eg.) to touch, attach, join together. This Egyptian *Ka* (still later *Sa*) is the deity of emblematic types; the *Ka* image being the spiritual likeness in the future life; the double of one's self in 'this. These types include the mummy image, the Karast, the tie-type of reproduction, and many other forms of the amulet and protective charm, the *Ka, Sa, Tesa,* or *Feitiço. Ka, Sa* or *Touch,* was the god of fetish images in Egypt, as was the god Touch in America.

or dog; the *eye of the hawk*; the *nose of the vulture*; the *claw or nail of the lion*; the *horn of the rhinoceros*, and *tooth of the bear*; *because they offered types of superior powers*. Such types are preserved in mythology. The hawk of Horus represents Sight; the sow and hippopotamus, the mouth of the Genitrix Rerit; the ear of the jackal, Sut-Anup; the nose of the kaf-ape, the God of Breath; the tooth of Hu, the Adult.

The Kamite typology can also be traced into the domain of primitive practices which are symbolical, to be read by the hieroglyphics. Some of these strange customs and consequent superstitions originated in zoological typology, and the acting of a primitive drama according to the animal or totemic characters. Specimens of them were extant to a late period in British plays and pastimes, and survive at present in the " pantomime."

In the Kanuri language of Bornu (Africa), the name of the hyena is *Bultu*, and from this is formed the verb *bultungin*, which signifies " *I transform myself into a hyena*." There is a town named *Kabultiloa*, the inhabitants of which are said to possess this faculty of transformation.[1] These doubtless originated in the hyena *Totem*, and the donning of the hyena skin in their religious masquerade. The hyena is one of the transformers or phœnixes (the Benn) in the Ritual.[2]

Hor-Apollo[3] says when the Egyptians would symbolise one that is unsettled, and that does not remain in the same state, but is sometimes strong, and at other times weak, they depict an hyena, for this creature is at times male, and at times female. This belief is still held by the Arabs. It *originates in the shedding and transforming phase being considered feminine*.

It was the practice at certain ceremonies, as we know from various sources, for the totemic people to masquerade in character, and appear as the typical beasts of the Totem, transformed into the earliest images of the gods or prototypes. Among the North American Indians, the Buffalos wore horns, and danced as buffalos.[4]

The natives of Vancouver's Island had a religious ceremony in which the performers stripped themselves naked and plunged into the water, no matter how cold the night, and crawled out again, dragging their bodies along the sand like seals; then they went into the house and crawled around the fire, and at last they transformed and sprang up to join in the " *seal-dance*."[5] They represented the seals, as the Mangaians did the crabs in character when they danced the crab-dance.[6]

This transformation, and the meaning of their names, may be considered to constitute two factors of the belief in the magical powers possessed by the Munda of India for changing their shape into wild beasts at will. In these customs the symbolism is acted, and becomes

---

[1] Koelle, *Afr. Lit. and Kanuri Vocab.* p. 275. [2] Ch. xxiv. [3] B. ii. 69.
[4] Catlin, vol. ii. p. 128. [5] Sproat, p. 66. [6] Gill, p. 256.

a drama of typology, scattered fragments of which are now found in the form of inexplicable superstitions and beliefs.

In writing of the Guatematlecs, old Gage delivered himself on this matter thus:—"Many are deluded by the devil to believe that their life dependeth upon the life of such and such a beast (which they take unto them as their familiar spirit), and think that when that beast dieth they must die; when he is chased their hearts pant; when he is faint they are faint; nay, it happeneth that by the devil's delusion they appear in the shape of that beast."

Plutarch refers to the idea "*that the gods, being afraid of Typhon, did, as it were, hide themselves in the bodies of ibises, dogs, and hawks,*" and repudiates it as "*a foolery beyond belief.*" This, however, is a matter of interpretation.

We know that such representations were part of the drama of the Mysteries. Many descriptions might be quoted to show that in their religious ceremonies the actors performed their masquerade in the guise of animals.

Diodorus has it that the gods were at one time hard pressed by the giants, and compelled to conceal themselves for a while under the form of animals, *which in consequence became sacred.* In this version the giants displace Typhon, the gigantic Apophis, or dragon of the dark, as the representatives of dissolution and chaos.

The gods taking the shape of animals to oppose the Typhonian powers means the typification of the time-keepers and celestial intelligencers, as the hippopotamus, dog, ape, ibis, hawk, crocodile, lion, ram, and others by the aid of which the time-cycles were made out and order was established (or the world was formed); but for which, chaos, Typhonian discord, dissolution, and destruction would have prevailed for ever. The lunar goddess assumed the form of the cat as a watcher by night. Horus escapes through the nets of Typhon as a fish, or soars heavenwards as a hawk. The sun-god is seen taking the shapes of animals that represent time (Seb), and thus comes between men and chaos, or timelessness. Ra passed through the signs, and this in the language of symbol was designated his transformation into the shape of the signs.

It is not more than three or four centuries since, in England, the Zodiac was called the "bestiary." The sun then passed through the bestiary, as he did in Egypt. In the Pool of Persea he made his transformation into the cat; in the height of his power he transformed into the lion; at one equinox into the hawk, and at the other into the phœnix, the emblem of rising again from the Hades. In the *Ritual* the deceased who transforms into the various animals, fishes, or birds, emphatically states that he himself is the respective intermediate type which he adopts in the process of being assimilated to the highest. He flies as a hawk, crawls as a serpent, *cackles as a goose.*[1]

[1] Ch. 17.

He says, "*I establish myself for ever in my transformations that I choose,*" [1] just as we say the sun passes through the signs ; only their metaphors identified and did not compare the person with the type.

Herodotus was told that the Neurian wizards amongst the Scythians, settled about the Black Sea, became, each of them, a wolf for a few days *once a year.* [2] The Texan tribe of the Tonkaways did the same when, clothed in wolf-skins, they celebrated the resurrection of the wolf from the Hades. The head of a wolf was worn in the mysteries of *Isis,* because the wolf (Anup) was her warder and guardian during her search after Osiris in the underworld. The wolf, jackal, or dog, was the guide of the sun and of the souls of the dead. The station of the wolf in the Egyptian planisphere is at the place of the vernal equinox, a point of commencement where we find the double holy house of Anup. [3] The candidate as the *Loveteau* of French Masonry still enters as a young wolf: also the "wolf" that was the *guide* of the Great Mother and of the sun is still made use of as the "*guide*" (called the wolf) in tuning the piano !

The transformation into the wolf or other animal, was no doubt connected at times with abnormal trance-conditions which are now better, but by no means sufficiently understood. In the Shetland Isles, the transformers are known as the *Finns.* These are sometimes human beings, and at other times seals. By means of a "*skin*" the men and women are able to turn themselves into seals, like the natives of Vancouver's Island, and if the sealskin be stolen from one of the seals when it has transformed into the human figure, it is compelled to retain that shape. It was exactly the case with the swan-maidens, who, when deprived of their skin of feathers, could not re-transform until they had re-clothed themselves in the stolen skin.

In the far north it was the seal that supplied the typical skin which was furnished by the lion, leopard, bear, wolf, cat, hyena, or cow in other regions. The seal must have been a totemic sign of those who boasted of their descent from the *Finn* women. It is noticeable that *Ven* is a Cornish name for woman. Also the *Phynnodderee* is a Manx spirit, said to have been an outlawed fairy, whose name signifies the "*hairy one;*" and in the mysteries of puberty the initiate *was transformed into the hairy one,* and became a Finn, or Phynnodderee, so to speak, at that period of his life, as a member of the Totemic tribe.

That the *Finn* represents the *Benn* (Eg.), or transformer, may be seen by the stories of transformation. When one is caught in a net, or on the line of the fishers, it begins to change and swell and swell until its bulk threatens to sink the boat ; or it will cut a chip off the vessel and turn that into a boat.

The hieroglyphics show various types of transformation under this name, such as *Benn,* the snake ; *Benn,* the palm, or phœnix-tree ;

---

[1] Ch. 72. [2] B. iv. 105. [3] Pl. i. vol. ii. *Book of Beginnings.*

Benn, the ape; *Benn*, the phœnix-bird; *Benn*, the hyena. We also have several kindred types in the *Bunnan* (Irish), a crane, heron, or bittern; the *Finenn* (Gael), a buzzard; the *Faing* (Irish), a raven; the *Feannog*, a royston crow; the Shetland *Vanega*, a mythical cat; and in the *Fainche* (Irish), for the fox, we have the phœnix, or Fenekh, the fox-dog type of Sut.

The Danes are said to know the man, who is a Were-wolf or transformer, by his eyebrows meeting, and thus resembling a butterfly; a type of the soul. The beetle, however, is the better type, and we describe such a person as *beetle-browed*. The flying beetle is a chafer, Egyptian Khepr, and both meet in the Welsh *Cyfaeliawg* for beetle-browed. The beetle being a special emblem of the transformer (as the god Khepr), is thus extant as the *same type* in the beetle-brows, and *Cyfl* is identical by name with *Khepr*.

The Mexicans assigned twenty symbols, some of them animals, to the different parts of the human body as types of the ruling powers. In the Ritual (Eg.), in which the body of the deceased is reconstructed, he is put together again and there is not a limb of him without a god.[1] Being attached to the person of the god or assimilated to him is literally being joined to him limb by limb or piecemeal. And these types represented the parts assumed bit by bit by the deceased, in order that he might effect his total transformation. Nineteen divinities constitute the types or ruling powers in place of the twenty Mexican. "*The hair is in the shape of that of Nu,*" Nu being the flowing, as water; and, in Mexican, water is the symbol of the hair. So in the Indian hieroglyphic signs rain was depicted by a dot or semicircle filled with water and placed on the head. The typology is all one.

In Egypt the various types had attained the status of divinities. Nu or Nu-pe, the celestial water bears the jar or vase on her head as the lady of heaven; and in the Peruvian mythology the lady of heaven pours out the water of heaven from the cross-shaped vase.

The deceased was transformed into these types of gods, birds, animals, as a mode of preservation during the passage of the Hades, where dwelt the destroyer and *obliterator of forms*. His chances or means of getting through the thicket of opposing enemies were represented by these types. He clothed himself with them as super-human powers. He could make his way through the earth as a tortoise; through the mire as an eel; through the water as a crocodile; see in the dark as a cat; soar through the air and the fire of the sun as a hawk. *The early men had no other means of expressing their thought!*

This typology explains its deposits as in the belief of the Pimos and Maricopas that in a future state the several parts of the body will be changed into separate animals; the head into an owl; the

[1] Ch. xlii.

feet into a wolf, just as it is in the Mexican and Egyptian apportionment of the parts to the presiding types, or prototypes.[1] The Moquis *identify the types they will be turned into with the original animals from which they came*. Others recognize in the animals the representative figures of their gods, because the gods were these prototypes of power.

The New Zealanders apportion out the body in the same manner to the evil deities or powers which inflict pains, ailments and diseases on mortals.[2] This shows the earlier stage of the idea, when the actual physical pains were the powers represented as a sort of ghosts or demons. It was simply a mode of expression.

The system of thought and manner of representation are one wherever found, and had their first origin in expressing ideas by means of external things; the animals, fishes, and birds being the ideographs in living forms; and the art of representing personifying, and imitating these, remained amongst the earliest races, even as it existed before the art of drawing figures had been discovered; and this form and mode of pourtrayal was continued by the Christians. It survived in the mysteries and has descended to us in the Christmas pantomime—the supreme feature of which is still the scene and act of *transformation from the animal shapes into the human or divine*.

In the primitive masquerade the performers clothed themselves as animals, so in various other practices they acted like them, and thus preserved the earliest natural customs in the later symbolical phase, which was continued after the link in the chain of descent had been lost.

The Maori custom of *Hongi*, and the Malay *Chium*, is a mode of saluting by rubbing or touching noses and smelling, breathing, and sniffing each other; a practice known also to the Fijians, Eskimos, Laps, Africans, Chinese, and other races. In Zulu Kaffir *Nuka-nuka* is to discover by the sense of smell. In Maori the word *Hongi* means to smell, sniff, salute, by touching noses. We have now the means of reading this ideographic custom. The nose is an organ of the breath, which is the *Ankh* (Eg.) or life. *Ankh* as a word is equivalent to "*Live*," an expression which is used by some races when one sneezes, as a formula for sneezing.

The inner African "*Nge*" is a type-word of the whole world of language. *Ma-hungoa* in Basa; Me *Nueg* in Anan means "I breathe." *Nga* in Maori signifies to breathe; *Wakanga* to make or take breath. *Ang* in the Yarra (Aust.) dialect denotes breathing. In Egyptian "Ankh" means life, living, and certain organs of life.

Ankh-uta-snab was the salutation to the Ra; it was their "*Long*

---

[1] Bartlett's *Personal Narrative*, vol. ii. p. 222.
[2] Shortland's *Traditions*, pp. 97—125.

live the King." It means "*Health and long life to you!*" More briefly, Ankh is "life," of which breathing or sniffing was the sign, the *Hongi.*

The word *Nge,* which is breath or life in Maori ; *Ponga-ponga* being the nostrils, is used by the Zulus to express a wish or desire, whilst *Nuki* in Barba (African), and *Nkowu* in Pati, signify " I love thee," *anka* in Xosa Kaffir denotes kissing. Breathing, smelling, and coupling were the earlier modes of demonstrating affection and desire.

The evocation expressed by wishing " life " is enacted in the touch of noses. This is a most primitive gesture-sign that would serve several purposes before speech had been formulated. It goes back to an animal mode of saluting by smelling. The primitive man was led by the nose. The first appeal made by external nature is to the sense of smell. It has been demonstrated that if the olfactory nerves of a puppy are destroyed it will not learn to suck, and that the action of sucking is excited through the sense of smell.[1]

" *Think'st thou to breath me upon trust?* " asks the woman in Heywood's play.[2] To breath or breathe was also synonymous with to smell under one word, connected with more than one organ, and here it signifies *futuere.*

The Maoris, Australians, Papuans, Esquimaux, and others would seem to have gone out from the African birth-place before kissing was discovered and adopted as a natural language of affection, for some African races, the Somali, for example, do not kiss.

Doubtless, the custom of smelling and inhaling was the far older mode of manifesting desire. This kind of salutation had been continued from the animal condition into a recognized form of ceremonial. Such customs would survive as automatic actions when and where the symbolic meaning was forgotten ; that is the final form of their continuity. But they were natural at first, and became typical by consensus in the secondary phase as current coin of intercourse.

In this secondary or symbolical stage to touch noses and breathe was tantamount to expressing a wish for long life or a declaration of love. Whilst by taking a prolonged sniff they were complimenting each other as if they had said, "*You are my life ; you are the breath of life to me.*" To breathe, sniff, or smell any one in salutation signifies symbolically "*I breathe new life from you,*" or " *Your presence renews my life* " ; " *You are as the breath of life to me.*"

There is a comment on the in-breathing of life from one another by this mode of salutation in the 91st chapter of the Ritual, which is entitled, " *The Chapter of not Allowing a Person's Soul to be Sniffed out of Him in Hades.*"

The Chittagong Hill people have a form of invitation—" *Smell me* "

---

[1] Darwin, *Expression of the Emotions,* ch. i. The present writer, however, would rather not have known the fact than that the dog should have been vivisected to prove it.   [2] *Royal King,* 1637.

—answering to our " *Give me a kiss*," and they place the mouth and nose upon the cheek to *inhale* the breath strongly.[1] This is breathing rather than merely smelling, so that "*Breathe me*" is really the true rendering.

Timkowski describes a Mongol father who from time to time kept smelling the head of his youngest son, a mark of paternal tenderness, he says, among the Mongols, instead of embracing. This reminds us of Isaac smelling his son in salutation and saying, "*It is the smell of a field which the Lord hath blessed.*"

The custom was still kept up by the conservatives of Egypt for us to find it in the Book of Genesis. It cannot be directly shown from the monuments that taking a good hearty sniff of each other was an Egyptian mode of salutation. When they come into sight they had probably attained the custom or art of kissing, though the smelling of the lotus as a means of indicating and giving delight is universal. Also the name of the nostrils, *sherau*, is derived from *sher*, meaning to *breathe with joy*.

In the hieroglyphics, *sen* is breath and to breathe. It is associated with smell by means of the nose determinative. The nose, *senti*, is the double breather. *Sent* is the English *scent ; sen* is the French *sentir*, to scent. "*Sen-sen*" has the signification of to *fraternize*, in brotherly (and sisterly) union, and it is an equivalent for "breathe-breathe," and for the transmigration of spirits as breaths. Also *sen*, to breathe, denotes the act of profoundest respect, compliment, and homage, which, in the ceremony of *Senta*, is paid by breathing the earth ; bowing down and breathing the ground by inferior persons having taken the place of sniffing the person among equals ; prostration on the earth adding profoundness to the homage of inferiors.

Mr. Spencer finds the origin of ceremonial obeisance in the intrinsically coercive character of militant rule, and he deduces politeness from the prostration of slavery and inferior station. Here, however, the genesis of the act of smelling from animal desire (the smell of blood, &c.), the primal phase, and, next, out of compliment to the person, is nearer to nature. It belongs to the language of lust, later affection, in the lowliest range of expression, at the meeting-point of man and the less specialised animals.

The custom was then applied to sniffing the ground as an obeisance of later law and ceremonial, after *men had made their own masters* and *elevated their human* (or inhuman) *lion, panther, snake, thunderbolt, Moon-God or Sun-God to wield supreme power over them*, as chief of the tribe or people. For example, when Jacob bowed himself to the ground seven times in presence of his brother, the number has a recognised significance to be sought for in the astronomical symbolism.

The Chinese at the present time make *eight* obeisances, increasing in humbleness, the eighth being the highest in number and the lowliest

[1] Lewin.

in posture, due only to the emperor and to Heaven. *This number answers to the Egyptian eight adorations to the eight great gods.* The Chinese eight, being represented by Heaven and the emperor, probably personate the genitrix of the seven stars and the son, whose name was Sevekh or Seven ; also the seven primary and elementary powers, which were born of her. In Bootan the form of obeisance rigidly observed demands that all who are permitted to approach the Raja, must make *nine* prostrations in his presence.

The number nine sacred to the Raja (Egyptian Râ), belongs to the nine solar months of gestation, and the sun in the nine dry signs of the twelve. *These numbers are figures quoted at their known value in the system of symbols,* and they are not to be read apart from the rootage of ceremonial customs in mythology, where they have even a chronological sequence, as well as diversity of religious significance, and contain *dates* in their data.

In Fijian the salute by smelling and taking a good strong sniff is named *regu.* It is also applied to kissing, &c. In Maori, *reka-reka* is tickling and otherwise pleasantly provoking by means of contact. *Roke* in English is to scratch, also *futuere.* *Lick* is a form of the same root-meaning. *Rak* in Akkadian is to beget. These are all modes of knowing, and in Egyptian *rekh* is to know and denotes relationship. This knowledge, this relationship, was once limited to smelling, licking, and other animal modes of knowing.

Smelling and breathing were primitive means of *knowing,* and the language of the animal was continued, and is traceable in human language, as well as in human customs.

Our words *new* and news; Breton, *nevaz ;* Latin, *novus ;* Greek, *νέος ;* Gothic, *ninjo ;* old Norse, *nyr ;* Gaelic, *nuadh ;* Sanskrit, *nava ;* Arabic, *Nafs ;* are all related to *nef* (Eg.), for the breath, and to perception by means of smell. To *nose* is to smell. The Danish and A. S. *nys,* to get news of a thing, is to get wind or scent of it. The Dutch *neuselen,* means to sniff after. The nose obtained the earliest news. In Egyptian, *khnum* is to smell, with the nose for determinative. The same word means to choose and select with the nose. It is also the name for the nurse, tutor and educator ; the nose being a primary teacher. Khnum is to *ken* by the nose, and the word modifies into num, to guide, direct, accompany, go together, in such an act as " numming " with noses, and other forms of kenning or knowing each other.

The act of smelling passed into the domain of sacrifice, and survived in the mysteries where the branch and other emblems were smelled. The Divinity of Israel threatens not to continue to be led by the nose in this way any longer. " *I will not smell the savour of your sweet odours,*" [1] " *I will not smell in your solemn assemblies,*" i.e. on the day of feasting. This divinity, like the Kamite (Gold Coast) Ananse,

---

[1] Levit. xxvi. 31.

the spider-god, *talks through his nose.* It is the primitive god of the primitive man.[1]

Charlevoix mentions a tribe of Indians on the Gulf of Mexico, who continued the custom of *blowing* or *breathing* into each other's ears,[2] as a mode of salutation. This is but a variation of the same ceremony, having the same significance.

The ear, and ears, are named *ankh* in Egyptian, and in Inner Africa.

Anko ...... is the ear in Faslaha.			*Ngoli* is the ear in Mende.	
Tino-cingtu	,,	Bushman.	*Nguli*	,,	Gbandi.
Engiok	,,	Ukuaĥ.	*Nogu*	,,	Kra.
Ngou........	,,	Landoro.		

It is a world-wide name for the ear, as for the nose and mouth.

The ear is *Nakhu* in Karen.		The ear is *Inaka* in Shoꞓhoni.	
,,	*Nachit* in Garo.	,,	*Inako* in Wihinasht.
,,	*Nekho* in Limbu.		*Nakoha* in Mandan is ears.
,,	*Inkon* in Maram.	,,	*Naughta* in Osage.
,,	*Nak'h* in Punjabi, &c.	,,	*Nicioca* in Moxos.
,,	*Ungn* in Armenian.	,,	*Nikobko* in Mongoyos.
,,	*Yang* in Honduras.	,,	*Ngureong* in Lake Mac-
,,	*Nacaz* in Mexican.	,,	quarie, Australia.

The custom, like the *hongi*, denotes breathing and actually communicating life in place of wishing it. Analogous to this was the practice of the Egyptians, who placed a form of the ankh-sign in the ears of their dead. In the Ritual, the 13th chapter is "*said over the drop of an earring of the ankham flower placed on the left ear of the spirit.*" That was the flower of life worn as an eardrop by the mummy. It was also an ancient custom in England to wear a rose in the ear.

When the ear, or ankh (Eg.) was eaten by the female *Ariki* as a sacrifice, the Maori identified the offering with the heavenly *Henga* and cried,

> "*Lift up his offering,*
> *To Henga a te Rangi;*
> *His offering:*
> *Eat, O invisible one, listen to me,*
> *Let that food bring you down from the sky.*"[3]

The food was a human *ear,* the type of hearing; and the sacrifice was a mode of prayer, with the ear for an ideographic determinative.[4]

In like manner, *motoi*, in Maori, means to beg, to pray. And this

[1] This mode of stating a Scriptural fact may be considered offensive by those who never consider the offensiveness of the fact itself. I repudiate the Voltairian mode of treatment; but it was not unwarranted.

[2] Vol. iii. p. 16.

[3] Taylor, *New Zealand*, p. 182.

[4] When the Egyptians would symbolize a man who hears with more than customary acuteness they pourtray a she-goat, for she respires (or hears) both through her nostrils and ears (Hor-Apollo, B. ii. 68). Of course the sense of perception was one, the organs varied.

is also the name of an ear-ornament made of *green* stone, which, placed in the ear, like the ankham flower, becomes a visible prayer, a gesture-sign addressed to the unseen power as the hearer.

In the following illustration of the ankh-sign, the nose and ears have a remarkable meeting-point. If a cow during the night is heard to groan in her sleep, it is a custom with the Hottentots to catch her next morning, and a piece of skin just above her nose is cut so that it hangs down in the shape of an ear-ring or *eardrops*. If this be neglected the owner will die.[1] Therefore the eardrop shape is a symbol of life or the ankh (Eg).

The name and tribe-sign of the Arikara Indians denote them to be the wearers of " big earrings." [2] The name of the Oregones or Orejones is derived from *or-ejo*, the ear, as the large-eared people, and the large-ear supplied a type-name to various American and European tribes from the lobe of the ear being perforated and artificially enlarged in accordance with a most ancient and world-wide custom ; the size of the hole being a sign of the hero who had bravely borne the pain and suffering.

The Incas had this type-name of the ear ; and they only permitted the Aymaras to cultivate the large ear-lobe a long while after the conquest. The jackal, the fenekh and the ass were typhonian representatives of the hearer.

In John's Gospel we read—" *And when he had said this he breathed on them, and saith unto them, receive ye the Holy Spirit*" (ch. xx. 22). This was a survival of the breathing in the ear and the rubbing noses of an earlier time, and only in the primitive stage can the typology be fathomed. In this aspect the invitation " Come smell me," or *Breathe me*, signified, give me life, inspire me. It was the language of the female animal converted into verbal speech. The general object of these salutations is to wish or to give life and health, and in the custom of the people of Carmana, mentioned by Athenæus, they used to offer life itself—the blood being the life—by " breathing" a vein and holding forth the red drops to drink. This was the exact equivalent of the Egyptian practice of offering the ankh, the emblem of life ; the blood being an earlier reality. Ankh (Eg.) life, liquid of life, is the name of blood in the Garo *anchi*.

Hunga means medicine in the Omaha (Indian) language and in the African tongues.

To be *well*, or healthy, is—

Nga in Kanuri.	*Inga* in N'godsin.	*Nkindei* in Nalu.
Nga in Munio.	*Nga* in Bagrimi.	*Aingete* in N'kele.
Nga in N'guru.	*Ngo-dodo* in Tiwi.	

Lastly, the healer and lifegiver in many Kamite languages bears the type-name of life, living, to live, breathe, and of the organs of

[1] Hahn, *Tsuni-Goam*, p. 87.   [2] Mallery, *Collection*, p. 295.

breathing, the name being chiefly found in the duplicated form. The doctor is designated—

Ngange in Isuwu.	*Nganga* in Kanyika.	*Nganga* in Kisama.
Nganga „ Kum.	*Nganga* „ Mutsaya.	*Ngana* „ N'Kele.
Nganga „ Kabenda.	*Nganga* „ Bumbete.	*Ngan* „ Konguan.
Nganga „ Mimboma.	*Nganga* „ Nyombe.	*Nanga* „ Kiriman.
Nganga „ Musentanda.	*Nganga* „ Basunde.	*Ngan* „ Eafen.

Another ceremonial custom known to be wide-spread is that of invoking a blessing when one sneezes. This is intimately related to the salutation by breathing and sniffing, and is founded on the same principle. Sneezing is a sign of life because connected with the breath. The first sign of life in the man made by Prometheus was a sneeze, which connects the sneeze with the breath of life. The sneeze is a vigorous expulsion of the breath.

Sneezing with the Zulus is a token that a sick person will be restored to health. The sneeze is typical of the good spirit being with him. If he cannot sneeze they judge the disease to be very bad indeed. The sneeze is a sign of health. "*He hath sneezed thrice, turn him out of the hospital,*"[1] is an English proverb.

Sneezing is not only a vigorous form of breathing, but it is involuntary; hence inspired, or of an extraordinary origin. A hearty sneeze when ill and faint would imply a sudden accession of the breathing power, which was inwardly inspiring and outwardly expelling; the good spirit enters and the bad spirit departs, cast out by the sudden impulsion. The expulsion and repudiation implied in sneezing is yet glanced at in the saying that such a thing is "*not to be sneezed at.*"

A sneeze, say the Zulus, gives a man power to remember that the spirit is with him. The *Tongo* (i tongo) is a spirit like the *Wong* and others founded on the Ankh type of life.

Sneezing, according to Hor-Apollo, was held to be the antithesis of the spleen. He says the Egyptians depict a dog to denote smelling and sneezing, because the thoroughly splenetic are unable to smell, or sneeze, or laugh; that is, be open, blithe, and frank-hearted. The dog, he avers, of all animals, has a very small spleen, and what spleen he has is the cause of his madness or rabies.[2] This is supported by a statement in the "Litany of Ra,"[3] "*his spleen is the God Fenti,*" i.e. the God of the Nostrils. This may serve to connect the sneeze with something to be got rid of, and breath as the means.

The foundation for such customs, beliefs, and sayings which are connected with sneezing was laid in the time when the spirit *was* the breath and the breath *was* the life. Hence the object of provoking the sneeze and invoking the good spirit.

It is common for people to take a pinch of snuff to cause a sneeze for the expulsion of headache, and in this connection the British

[1] Brand on Sneezing.   [2] Book i. 39.   [3] Ch. iv. 8.

custom of placing on the dead a plate full of snuff is most remarkable. If a pinch of snuff were efficacious in expelling the bad spirit, stuffiness, or pain by means of a sneeze, then the plateful of snuff laid on the breathing-place—the bosom of the dead—was typically intended in relation to the breathing of the future life, and wishing well or well-wishing. This also was a mode of saying, "*Life to you*," with the type on a large scale. The sneezing away of obstruction and blowing the nose to expel the disease would lead to the primitive practice of "*blowing away disease*," which is still extant among the early races. To blow into the left hand is an Indian sign for medicine and healing.[1]

The breath being the soul, a sneeze was a breathing sign of soul or the good spirit, the expeller of the bad and evil one, the opponent or adversary. The Negroes of Old Calabar shake off evil influences with a sneeze. The sneeze, then, was a sign of life, soul, or spirit. Jacob prayed that the soul of man might not depart with a sneeze, *i.e.* die with the breath. When the Hindu sneezes the bystanders cry "*Live!*"[2] The Jews say, טובם חים or "good *life*."[3] The Samoans exclaim "*Life to you!*"[4] A blessing is still the rule in southern Europe.

When the Zulu sneezes he exclaims, "*I am now blessed!*" the spirit, the *good* spirit, was with him, and that constituted the very nick of time for wishing and invoking. "*Tutuka!*" is an exclamation used by the Xosa Kaffirs. *Tutu* is the ancestral spirit, *Ka* denotes an attempt. *Tutuka* may be rendered "the ancestral spirit tries to speak," as it was supposed to do in a sneeze. A tree also named *tuti*, or *tati* is the sneeze-wood of the colonists.

It was a common belief that no idiot could sneeze, and that there was no surety like a sneeze for the new-born child's having a soul. British "howdies," or nurses, held the child to be under the fairy spell until it showed signs of spirit by sneezing. "*God sain the bairn*," said an old nurse when the little one sneezed at last; "*its no a warlock.*" The ancestral soul had descended. This mingling and confounding of "*spirits*"—that of the Breath and the Manes—is shown in the Maori rite of infant baptism. On the eighth day after birth the ceremony was performed at the side of a stream. A native priest sprinkled the child with a twig, or branch, when the little one was not immersed. The priest kept calling over the names of its ancestors until at last the child sneezed. *That* was its name thus chosen by the child itself, or the ancestral spirit manifesting through it.[5]

With the Parsees the rule is that when a person sneezes "*one is to speak a Yatha-ahu-vairyo, and one Ashem-vohu; and also when one hears the sneezing of any person to speak in like manner is so considered*

---

[1] Wied. [2] Ward, *Hindus*, vol. i. p. 142. [3] Buxtorf.
[4] Turner, *Polynesia*, p. 348. [5] Taylor, *New Zealand*, p. 184.

as an action of good." It is asked : What causes sneezing ? And the reply is "*hungry living.*" The remedy for its existence is the *Ahunaver*, and praise of righteousness ; the *Honover* of the Avesta ; *i.e.*, the Egyptian *Un-Nefer*, or the *Revealer of Good.*[1]

The invocation made on sneezing is a part of the same ritual relating to the breath, as the Parsee rule for uttering one Ashemvohu with every coming and going of the breath on lying down to sleep.[2]

Sneezing is certainly a spontaneous act enough, but without some idea connected with the act and attached fast to it no such universal ceremonial custom as invocation at the time of sneezing could have become world-wide. The sneeze would not have been a type of the same idea without some pre-agreement and consensus.

"*Do you not see that all the world is one ?*" said Hernando de Soto when he perceived the Floridans had the same custom of salutation on sneezing as the Spaniards.[3]

Mr. Haliburton brings forward the universal habit of saying "*God bless you,*" or making an invocation when one sneezes, as his strongest case for concluding that such primitive customs have been inherited from one common source, and that they owe their origin to an era anterior to the dispersion of the human race. The typology is certainly one, and Egypt, the explicator, vouches for the Kamite origin.

Our word *sneeze* is identical with the Egyptian *snesh*, to open, discover, open of itself, which is connected with *sen*, the breath, as the opener, and *senn*, to make the foundation and passage by opening. *Snes* also signifies salutation, to invoke, wish, evoke, adore —Sanskrit, *sans*, to wish, desire, invoke—all that accompanies the ceremony of sternutation is expressed by the word *snes*, our English sneeze.

The doctrine, so to speak, of the sneeze was eminently Inner African. The name of the sneeze is

Siani in Krebo.	*Suana* in Balu.	*Dsune* in Bagba.
Sani in Gbe.	*Tison* in Soso.	*Dsuna* in Momenya.
Usiane in Isoama.	*Dsisin* in Bulom.	*Dsieni* in Bayon.

"The Indian nations," says Morgan, "after treating, always exchanged belts, which were not only the ratification, but the memorandum of a compact. When agreements were covenanted by the Iroquois, belts of wampum were exchanged as determinatives of their intentions to keep troth."[4] "*This belt preserves my words,*" was a common remark of their chiefs in council, the belt being symbolic of the bond and covenant. The speaker then delivered a

---

[1] *Shayast La-Shayast*, ch. xii. 32.   [2] *Ibid.* ch. iv. 14.
[3] Theodore Irving, *Conquest of Florida*, vol. ii. p. 161.
[4] Morgan, *Ancient Society*, p. 138.

belt to the other side in token of faith and honour in the execution of the treaty or promise. "*Here's my belt*," was the equivalent of "*Here's my hand on it*," or "*I give you my word of honour.*"

The belt of wampum was a sign of the same significance as the Egyptian tat, a belt-buckle, an emblem of eternitizing in the region of Tattu. The buckle is based on the tongue, but *the act of tatting with the human tongue* preceded the tongue of the buckle, and was its antetype, with the same meaning of establishing the covenant of affection, mutual agreement, or ownership, giving and taking; the first form of which had been effected by *licking with the tongue.*

Covenants *were* made by tonguing in this way, before speech was formulated. Hence, when it was evolved, we find language called by the name of the member, the tongue, the tat.

The tongue as a tat is identical with language, and the use of the member as a sign of expression was earlier than words. Licking with the tongue is a part of the language of animals, and must have been of the primitive man. By licking each other the animals establish a covenant with their tongue, and this custom can be followed into the human phase, both of act and language.

When anything is presented to the Esquimaux, they have the habit of licking it at once as a sign of ownership. In New Zealand, according to Dieffenbach, the natives had the same practice, only *their licking was done by the givers of the present.*

Licking it was *tonguing* it, anointing it, and consecrating the gift whether received or given; and the act, as explained by aid of Egyptian, is one of the customs belonging to the time of gesture-language. The one word "*tat*" includes the gift, given, taken, and assumed.

In the symbolical stage *licking* was a mode of anointing. In provincial English a "*good licking*" alternates with "*anointing*," as a nick-name for a thrashing or beating. Also spittle was a form of unction made use of for anointing in baptism, and in exorcism. In Egyptian, *tat*, the name of the tongue and mouth, also signifies *unction* and a ceremony; and "*tatting*," by *spitting*, follows the custom of licking as a mode of establishing and covenanting. Bruisers have the habit of spitting in their hand before the fight begins in token of a covenant of good-fellowship.

"In the north of England," says Brand, "the boys have a custom amongst themselves of *spitting their faith* (or, as they call it, 'their saul,' *i.e.* soul) as a form of oath-taking."

The Newcastle colliers, in their combinations, are said to pledge themselves to keep faith by spitting on a stone, and there is a popular saying, applied to persons who hang together, "*They spit upon the same stone.*"[1]

This mode of covenanting may have a bearing on the figures of the hand found in the Australian caves. These symbols are supposed

[1] Brand on Spitting.

to have been imprinted on the walls by placing the human hand on the clean stone and *spitting some colouring matter all around it*, and so leaving the impress of a hand.[1] The hand and spitting were two signs of tatting or establishing a covenant to which the hand would remain a witness. The word *tat*, for hand and typing, abrades into *tâ*, and *tā* in Maori is a name of the tattoo ; to imprint and paint ! *Tete* is to stand fixed in the ground ; *titi* to stick or stamp in and make fast. *Tutu*, a messenger ; also to summon and gather in a solemn assembly.

Captain Cooke says the natives of the Tongan Islands "*have a singular custom of putting everything you give them to their heads, by way of thanks as we conjectured.*"[2]

Here the head was the "tat," and *tat* (Eg.) French *tête*, *is* the head.

The Ashantis had a war-custom of sending a head with the Messenger-Sword (this head was found to show considerable likeness to ancient Egyptian work, especially in the beard [3]), said to intimate "*I mean to cut off your head.*" Head, messenger, and sword [4] are each named the *tat* in Egyptian.

The young Sioux Indian is obliged to take a head or scalp to win "the feather" before a girl will marry him. So the young Somali of Africa, or the Dyak of Borneo must take a head in order that he may take a wife. "*It need not,*" says Mr. J. G. Wood, "*be the head of an enemy ;*" it is a token, not merely a trophy, showing the typical nature of the head. This is an ancient symbolic institution, conflicting with later law, as both tribes award punishment for murder.

As late as the seventeenth century, a Russian petition began with the words "*So and so strikes his forehead*," and petitioners were termed the "*forehead strikers.*"[5] The custom was Kamite, and Egyptian will explain it. The forehead, temples, ears and nose were struck by the petitioner. The meaning (which may vary) is then interpreted by a gesture sign. To *strike* the flag is to lower it ; and "I strike my head," means I bow to you; I acknowledge you *as my head !* But the gesture was voluntary before it was made compulsory, and only when the custom becomes coercive do we reach the degradation of smelling the earth, or striking the ground with the forehead.

The personal member or feature had to stand in place of a personal pronoun in gesture language ! In Egyptian, he who speaks to himself is he who speaks to his *head*.[6]

---

[1] "The hand-print on the wall is commonly used by the Jews to avert the evil eye ; care is taken to put it in a conspicuous place outside the house before a marriage, birth, or other festival. In the ruins of El Barid, near Petra, Professor Palmer and I found a cistern whose cornice was decorated with hand-prints alternately black and red. At the present day both Moslems, Christians, and Jews hang hands, rudely cut out of a thin plate, of silver or gold, round the necks of their children to preserve them from the evil eye."—C. F. Tyrwhitt Drake, in *Qtly. Statement of Pal. Explor. Fund*, January, 1873, p. 16, *notes*.
[2] *Voyage towards the South Pole*, vol. i. p. 221.
[3] *Archæological Journal*, vol. xxxi. p. 29.
[4] Bowditch *On Superstitions Common to Egyptians and Ashantis.* Paris.
[5] Spencer, *Ceremonial Institutions*, v. p. 141.   [6] *Litany of Ra*, 7 and 57.

Lifting the hands to the forehead or temples is also a sign of obeisance. The oriental salute of an inferior includes the putting of his fingers to his forehead. The Sumatrans touch the forehead or temples. This gesture may be read by the Egyptian name of the temples of the forehead, *Teb*, a word that means to pray, implore, seal, answer, *be responsible for.*

The Fijian *Teb* or *Tobe* is a kind of pig-tail, and when tributaries approached their master, they were commanded by a messenger to cut off their Tobes, and all of them docked their tails.[1] This was a sign of subjection, or token of ownership. The Egyptian " *Tebnt* " is likewise a sign of hair cut off, a lock of hair.

The Khonds have the custom of holding their two ears in their hands as the symbol of submission, or as it is here represented, the token of a covenant, a mode of swearing by the *Ankh*, which denotes the two ears, the oath and covenant, in Egyptian. Such a custom would lead to cutting off the ears of the outlaw.

" *No one*," says Mr. Spencer, " *can suppose that hand-shaking was ever deliberately fixed upon as a salute.*"[2] Such customs grew by degrees, and the type was passed on from one thing to the other as the special ideograph of the gesture-sign. The Egyptian "tatting" had become handshaking. " *Two men joining their hands denote concord*," says Hor-Apollo.[3] The sign is found as the determinative of amity, covenant, alliance.[4]

Dogs and apes will spontaneously offer the paw. Here at least we can shake hands with our predecessors. In offering the paw, or hand, they were *tatting*, making the present, and establishing an understanding of friendship by this mode of invitation; a stage in advance of smelling and licking. The custom of making presents is based as lowly as this in the desire to make friends—a desire evinced by the animals the more they enter into a mixed condition, and are drawn out of their primal isolation. Mixing together is for them a mode of civilisation.

The hieroglyphic " Tat," as hand, denotes the offering presented, to give and take possession. The next phase is the clasp-sign of a covenant (Ank, Eg.); in this the give-and-take are enacted. Then the clasp and shake of the hand become a symbolical custom in the covenant of good-fellowship. Deep down in the English nature there yet lingers the ancient sense of its almost superseded sacredness. It is a form of *tat*-ing with the hand as in the other cases with the tongue or head. " *By the Haft*," is a common English oath, and " loose in the haft," means " not quite honest." In this the *handle* follows the hand as the type of a covenant.

The Egyptian Ank, to clasp and squeeze, is found in the Maori

[1] Erskine, Capt. J. E., *Cruise among the Pacific Islands*, p. 454.
[2] *Contemporary Review*, May, 1878, p. 7—89.   [3] Book ii. 11.
[4] Birch, *Egyptian Texts*, p. 93.

Anga, for the cockle-shell, and the *Angarite*, a bivalve molusk. *Rite* denotes the likeness of the *Anga*, or clasping shell. *Anga-anga* signifies agreement, and *Rite* means agreed to, performed. Thus *Ank* (Eg.), to pair, to clasp, make a covenant, as in clasping hands, is equivalent to the perfect two-oneness of the bivalve, which is here one of the Ank-types by name. The shell of the bivalve, which closed to clasp and protect the life in the waters, would thus acquire its significance as a type of twinning together, a token therefore of agreement, of unity, in the belt of Wampum ; of covenant, as the currency used for bartering ; and possibly of *re-uniting*, when shells (coffins—are still called shells) were heaped above the bones of the dead. *Oyster* and *mussel*-shells were sacredly preserved by the Wenya among their treasures,[1] together with the beads, which denote reproduction or resurrection.

The clasp of hands in shaking them was a final token of the Ank-covenant.

We have to think our way back to the time and condition when the human body supplied the chief symbols of expression, and there were no manufactured forms, no loop or knot, or Crux Ansata ; no Tat-pillar, or belt, or buckle ; no sword, or book, or Mamit to swear by ; almost nothing but the human organs, limbs, and gestures. These supplied the hieroglyphics in the language of gesture-signs ; and the customs in which the typology was continued are the hieroglyphics where there are no others. In this. language, to " *cross the palm for good luck*," is an ideograph of equivalent value to that of the Tat (hand) and Tat Cross.

In the present researches the clue has been continually found in the most primitive phase of the thought, after long seeking for it vainly in the later stages. The idea of founding and establishing by *opening* was developed by the Egyptians into a doctrine of creation. Ptah was a form of the *opener;* that is one meaning of his name. He carries the Tat image of founding and establishing. The " opener " is a title of the rising sun. The title of Un-Nefer is that of the good *opener. Sut opened the Genitrix whom Horus sealed.* This may be read either in the physiological or the astronomical phase. If we take it in the latter, Sut, as star-god, opened the year with the rising of Sothis, and on his rising was the Great Bear cycle founded. Now when this opening was first observed, the earth being considered as a flat surface endlessly extended, the star Sothis had to break its way up through the earth, according to appearances ; and so the *opener* became the founder of a circle of time. The born child did the same ; and in the passage quoted Sut represents the child ; Horus is the pubescent male, the generator. The tooth which cut its way through the gums was a perfect type of that which opened. The testicle was another. The pubes another.

[1] Stanley, *Dark Continent,* vol. ii. p. 254.

We are now in a position to read the typology of certain primitive customs and ceremonial usages of the Stone and Bone Age, which have survived to the present time amongst the elder races of the world; such as semi-castration, or the knocking out of teeth at the period of puberty, or filing them to make the *opening* visible between. "*Gat-toothed I was, and that became me well,*" says the jolly wife of Bath, with *her* interpretation of the cut or opening. Cut or indented teeth are still considered an ornament to the female in England, and that is a modified form of the African charm which the "hussies"—denounced by Livingstone—produced by filing their teeth.

In the hieroglyphics, *Un*, to open, be open and periodic, has the open-eyed hare for determinative. This open condition thus denoted means "it is lawful;" "I am open to you," or, "unprohibited." The filed teeth of the females and the tooth forced out of the male, thus represent the open condition of lawful intercourse.

The Vei people perform a rite called the *Sande*. When the female becomes pubescent she undergoes a sort of circumcision, or rather a rite of being *founded* as the woman *by opening*, from which time she can be bought or hired (*Sande*) as she too is SENNT, or established, by being "opened." In the rites of puberty, the cutting and opening are at times performed by those who impersonate the gods or supernatural powers. This suggests the genesis of other customs like that of the Babylonians mentioned by Herodotus,[1] who says that every native woman was compelled to sit in the Temple of Venus (Belit) once in her life and have intercourse with some stranger. Many wore a crown of cord round their head, the top-knot of puberty.

It was a custom in India for virgins to present themselves in the temples to be opened and made free to marry.[2]

This rite of opening was Totemic first and became religious afterwards. In this way certain corporate and temple rights were founded. The offerings made by or to the females were the property of the priesthood. Theirs was primarily the "*droit du seigneur*" (the right and rite of *pucelage* and *cuissage*) to open the young virgins—a right that was claimed by the elders among the Australian blacks.

The priest represented Priapus, the generative power. His rights were farmed out in Babylon as in India, and the temple was thereby enriched.

"*Thou shalt not bring the hire of a prostitute into the House of the Lord*" is the command which proves the practice amongst the Hebrews (Deut. xxiii. 18).

This traffic in the rights of the priesthood introduced a mode of commutation and a principle of compensation, whether the price was claimed by the temple or the tribe. The right of the reverend

---

[1] Herodotus, b. i. 199.
[2] Dulaure, *Histoire Abrégée des Cultes*, vol. i. p. 431 ; vol. ii. p. 108.

seigneur was waived on payment of a price; and this mode of commutation probably indicates the origin of compensation for the bride who was captured in marriage.

The time came when there was a revolt of youth against the rights of the elders, and a price was set upon virginity, to be paid by the lover.

When the Kaffir female has attained the marriageable age, which was primarily that of puberty, she is at liberty to woo her intended husband by sending him an "um-*lomo*." The *lomo* is symbolically her mouth. But the word signifies *any opening*, or the opening of anything. This means that she is *open* to him, or has undergone the opening rite.[1]

Here, as everywhere else, the natural genesis only of the primitive custom can interpret it in the later symbolical or superstitious phase. The tooth established a foundation by opening the ground; therefore a tooth was knocked out at the time of puberty as the type or token of another foundation by opening the ground.

When the testicle descended, pubescence was founded by its opening of the ground. Hence, in the semi-castration of the Bushmen (in times past) as a rite of young-man-making, the opening was made by extraction of one testicle. In the fanatical and religious phase, when the male devotee was assimilated to the *Eternal Child*, the foundation was established and the consecration completed by total castration.

What has been termed fashions in deformity did not originate in the senselessness of the modern victims of the prison-house of pride. These customs were ideographic, and had their meanings and uses.

The Zulu "*Hlanhla*," for the opening between the teeth, also means good luck, prosperity, and plenty of progeny. "Tapu" (Maori), according to Shortland, signifies to be "thoroughly-marked," and this agrees with Tebu (Eg.) to be sealed, to become responsible.

Gesture-signs were not the only human hieroglyphics; the body itself was the first book of pictographs. A picture is still called a cut, and the earliest pictures were cut in the live black flesh for uses belonging to the system of primitive signs. This was continued and modified in the customs of tattoo as the human skin grew somewhat lighter.

The incisions which are cut in the flesh from the shoulder to the hip of the pubescent males among the Australian aborigines are called *Manka*. These are of such a secret significance that they must never be spoken of when women and children are present.

Manka relates to puberty and to clothing. The *Manaeka* in Maori is a garment. *Menkha* (Eg.) denotes clothing. The first clothing was the *toga virilis* assumed at puberty, consisting mainly of hair and

[1] Dugmore, *Kaffir Laws and Customs*, p. 47.

slashes in the flesh.   We find the impubescent are the naked, and the pubescent are the clothed.   Tattoo was a form of clothing the human body with the marks of manhood, pictures (cuts) of puberty, and of heroic triumph over pain, that illustrated the bearing of the brave.

The Maori fashion of wearing the hair tied up in a knot at the forehead is called *Ngou-ngou*, and the top-knot put on at puberty is named the *Ngoi*.   The earliest *Ankh*-tie in Egypt was the knot-sign of femine pubescence and of putting on clothes.

In Inner Africa the *Gree-Gree* as a bracelet or necklace is a form of the ankh called—

Wanka in N'goala.	*Wuanga* in Lubalo.	*Nganga* in Songo.
Wuanka in Kisama.	*Owanga* in Pangela.	

In the Kaffir languages the ground-root of this NG or *Nek* may be studied in the most primitive relationships.   The *skin* beaten by women to make the music which circumcised lads keep time to in the dance of the pubescent, is a NGQONGO, and the word which denotes the sexual gestures and contortions made in the dance that is performed when a girl attains puberty is *Ngqungqa*.   This is identical with the Maori *Ngangahu*, a dance, and to distort the features, or make game of, and *provoke*, as was done by the women in the mysteries when the boy was made a free man.

The *Coco* is a ring worn on the heads of the Zulu men to distinguish them from the impubescent boys, and the custom includes the rings worn in the ear, nose, or lip of the women.

With the Bongas, as soon as a woman is married, her lower lip is bored, and the orifice plugged to extend the circle.   The plugs are gradually increased in size until the hole in the lip is five or six times its original proportions.

The plugs employed are cylindrical in form, and often not less than an inch thick; they are exactly like the pegs of bone and wood and straw worn by the Musgoo women.   Other pegs and rings are worn in the lips, nose, and ears, but the plug in the lower lip is alone the *sine quâ non* for the married women.[1]   It is here the same token then as the marriage ring in Europe.   But the custom dates from a time before metal rings were made, and the *circle had to be incised* and formed in human flesh; when a bone, a stone, or other emblem filled the place of the later ring worn in the orifice.   Not that the ring originated with marriage in the modern sense, but it was a token at first that the maiden was marriageable, or ready to bear young.   In Egyptian, for example, the completed course, the circuit, is written with the Shen-ring of reproduction.   In the Balu and Bayon dialects, *Sin* is the name of the nose-ring; in Mfut the ear-ring is

---

[1] Schweinfurth, *Heart of Africa*, vol. i. p. 297.

Tsen, Sannu in Bambara, and the *Dzeni* is a Gree-Gree ring in Limba.

The bones and stones inserted in the holes bored through the nose, lip, and ear, were images of the *founding by opening*, in relation to puberty ; the opening period of the woman ; the founding and establishing of the man.

Here it may be noted that *Renka* (Eg.) the Pubes, the period of pubescence, and the *Renk*, English, for the man, are related by name to the *ring* (Chinese Ling), which was a type of some period completed ; the circle being a visible figure of the cycle.

The ring, the synonym of Renka is represented in the Inner African languages by

Lunga, the Ear-ring, Kabenda.	*Belingu*, the Ear-ring, Kasands.
Nlunga „ „ Mimboma.	*Lingben* „ „ Nso.
Nlunga „ „ Basunde.	*Alongo*, a Gree-Gree, Orungu.

The arm-ring is a

Lenke in Lubalo.	*Longa* in Orungu.	*Nlunga* in Nyombe.
Longa in Baseke.	*Nlungo* in Mimboma.	

It is the same word as LINK and *ring*, and the name coincides with those of the other types of puberty, the hair, bone, and stone which we shall find retaining the same name in the most diverse of languages.

The Hindu *Langi* is a peculiar boddice, and *Langiam* means fit to be joined (or *linked*), as in marriage.

In the Parsee " *Shayast La-Shayast* " instructions are given for the woman, the *moment menstruation begins* (*not* for the first time) to *take off first her necklace, then her ear-rings, then her head-fillet* (Kambar), and apparently she is prohibited from wearing *leather* covering or shoes.[1] These are the very ornaments put on by the most primitive races *in token of the female having attained pubescence.*

The Kustik girdle of the Parsees is assumed at the time of puberty, when they have turned fourteen years of age. Until then there is no sin in the male or female running about uncovered, as in Egypt and Inner Africa.[2]

The hieroglyphic *Khekh* (Eg.) is a collar with nine beads, the sign of gestation. *Khekhru* is a generic name for " ornaments." These are founded on the necklace and collar, the ornaments of the pubescent maiden and the *enceinte* genitrix.

In the portrait of a Lobah woman, figured by Schweinfurth in the " *Heart of Africa* " the plugs that fill the holes with which the ear is perforated are *nine in number ;* the same as the number of beads (bubu) worn in the sacred collar of Isis. This many-plugged female likewise wears a round disk in the upper, and a pointed cone in the lower lip.[3]

[1] Ch. iii. 2, 3.   [2] *Shayast La-Shayast*, ch. iv. and x.
[3] Also copied by Flower, *Fashion in Deformity*, fig. v. p. 24.

A stick and a straw were two of the types employed as plugs for the apertures. These can be paralleled in Britain as the two signs of establishing a covenant. When land was given by the proprietor to his tenant for one or more years, it was a custom to give the tenant a stick of wood in one hand and some straw in the other, which was then returned to the master, and this act was the deed and bond of the lease.[1]

In Egypt the collar called *Menâ* or *Menka* was the ring of the wet nurse. It had nine or ten beads, according to the reckoning, and relates to the nine months or ten moons of gestation. In the N'goala dialect *Menu* is the name for the nose-ring; *emenga* in Bola, Ka-*menga* in Sarar. The *Menkua* is an armlet in Afudu. *Ark* (Eg.) denotes a period, a covenant, to surround, tie up, be perfected, and it is a form of the Ankh-knot of life. In Ebe the ear-ring is an ark-ring called *Arukâ*, and in Nupe the armlet is an *Uroka*.

The Thlinkeet female children have a slit made in the under lip, parallel with the mouth, about half-an-inch below it. The recognised size is produced by putting in larger and larger objects, and at puberty a block of wood is inserted. This is usually of an *oval* or elliptical shape, the same as the *Ru*, ⬭ the symbolical mouth in the hieroglyphics, and is therefore the female emblem, the Loma or opening.

The suggestive shape of the same oval figure has been observed in the whitish cicatrices raised by cuts in the black flesh of the African females. The ovoid circle, with the stone, bone, or metal inserted, is finally the emblem of the female and the male. Moreover, the block employed by the Thlinkeet matrons to fill the oval was of an ovoid or egg-like shape, corresponding to the egg of the male. It is at the time of young-man making or pubescence that the Batoka tribes knock a front tooth out of their children's mouths.[2]

The earliest piercing of the lip is performed by the Eskimo, on approaching manhood, which identifies it with the rites of the Maori and Batokas as sexual. This is corroborated by the religious festival or sacred feast with which the ceremony is accompanied.

Haygarth tells us of a young Australian native, who had become servant to a settler, that he said one day, "*with a look of importance, he must go away for a few days, as he had grown up to man's estate, and it was high time he should go and have his teeth knocked out.*[3]

The Peruvian traditions affirmed that it was a practice "*very serviceable to the gods,*" for fathers to take out their children's teeth.

In Java the opening is made by hollowing out the canine teeth,

[1] Martin, 125. "The keen-darting Gwrnerth slew the largest bear that ever was seen *with an arrow of straw*."—*Welsh Arch.* vol. ii. p. 68. *Vide Herod*, B. iv. 33, for an offering of straw. "If she converses no more," sings the Welsh bard, "*break the straw with my fair one.*"

[2] See vol. ii. p. 647.

[3] Haygarth, *Bush Life in Australia*, vol. i. p. 103.

sometimes so deeply as to penetrate the pulp cavity. In Borneo the teeth are drilled, and the hole is filled with a plug of brass, having a round or star-shaped knob. Sometimes the teeth were so filed as to leave a lozenge-shaped white piece of enamel untouched.[1] This agrees with the ovoid figure cut in the lip or on the inner arm. Blackening the teeth and lips, a custom very widely spread, had the same origin, as a sign of feminine pubescence. To have *red* lips *after the age of puberty* was a great reproach to the Maori women, and the colour was *covered*, put out of sight by tattooing the lips; if they were not tattooed elsewhere, this sign of adultship was never *omitted*, and many were tattooed only on the mouth.[2] Blacking the teeth would be a modified kind of tattoo, and of putting on a covering.

The Rejang women of Sumatra are in the habit of making their teeth jet black, but some of them, particularly those of the Lampong country, *file them right down to the gums*,[3] so that they are made invisible that way.

The Egyptians had got beyond this blacking of the teeth and lips but the typology was continued by the women blacking their eyes ; painting the ovoid circle round them, and elongating the natural shape. The eye is a mirror, an emblem of reproduction, and this was *underlined* at the time of puberty. This did Jezebel when she *stimmied* her eyes, like the Egyptian women. Black, however, was not the only symbolic colour. At one monumental period the female eyes were painted underneath with a band of green, the colour of reproduction. We still use the term of "green-sickness" in a like sense. Customs that are at last degraded into a fashionable form of meaningless mimicry were consciously begun for use, and continued into the stage of superstition.

The Unyamwezi girl, says Stanley,[4] "*waits with impatience the day when she can be married, and have a cloth to fold around her body ;*" till then she wears no garment. So the Egyptian maiden went naked up to the time of puberty. The earliest revelation taught the need of a monthly covering. Hence the figurative "fig-leaf" and the loin-belt. To attain this dignity was the earliest of woman's rights. In the Vei language the virgin (which means the pubescent female) is named after the loin-cloth. This is a *Bere*, and the wearer becomes a *Beremo*. There is a significant Accra saying, "*He has no cloth (or mama) and calls for a woman*"—meaning he is too poor to provide the least bit of a garment to cover her shame.

The *beginnings* of morality were of a nature too lowly to be noticed by writers on ethics. Yet the origin of the sense of shame may be traced to the period of feminine puberty, and the first natural need of concealment by means of the fig-leaf, liku, or ankh-tie. A feeling of proud pleasure must have preceded any sense of shame at this proof of

---

[1] Flower, *Fashion in Deformity*, p. 31.   [2] Dieffenbach, ii. 35.
[3] Marsden, *Sumatra*, p. 52.   [4] *How I found Livingstone*, pp. 5 and 6.

womanhood, but the tribal consciousness demanded the covert, and the sense of something to hide would evolve the feeling of shame in presence of the male. Then it was held to be a shame, a mark of the monkey, to violate the tapu, and it grew to be wrong in the man to look on the woman during her period. By this token Nature revealed the time of reproduction, and therefore for reproducing. The first covenant was founded on this ground of fact, and to break it became morally wrong.

When the Hottentot boys come of age at puberty, they are taught to speak the truth, *respect the female sex, and not to commit rape,*[1] or, it may be added, violate *tapu.*

In the Australian ceremonies called *Mur-rum Tur-uk-ur-uk,* a covenant is made with sticks or twigs, which are thrown by the young men at the pubescent girl, as a token that they will not assault her, but will accord her their protection until she is given away lawfully to her betrothed; whilst, on her side, she may meanwhile entertain any one of them as her lover.[2]

The top-knot of puberty was and still is worn by the women in some parts of France. Montaigne describes the females of his neighbourhood as shaping the male image in their kerchiefs, and wearing it as a fore-top, and when they come to be widows they turn it round and hide it beneath their caps.[3] This knot was identical with the Ankh-tie of Egypt, and the *Ngoi* of the Maori, which denoted the period of putting on clothing, and the covering of the hair by the *femme couverte.* As a symbolic custom, it is identical with the African flesh-cutting and tooth-filing, the Maori tattoo of the lips, and the Japanese blacking of the teeth.

This right of cover, however, is denied in various of the Inner African Courts, where womankind is still reduced to the pre-pubescent status, or childish condition elsewhere. "*Women may only enter the presence of the Sultan of Melli in a stark naked condition. Even his own daughters must conform to the custom.*" At the Court of Uganda, according to Speke, the valets were stark-naked, full-grown women.

It should be noted however that at a later stage the "naked Goddess" in Egypt and India is also the unchaste, a type of the prostitute, as the opposite to the *femme couverte.*

In Egypt the women were clothed, but Diodorus has described them as exposing themselves naked in presence of the God Apis. Also, in the Inscription of Pianchi Mer-Amen,[4] we read that the king had "*peace-offerings*" brought to him; then followed "the queens and princesses to adore the king after the wont of women"—or literally with the things (*choses*) of women. "But his majesty did not turn his countenance upon them."

The woman in Proverbs makes her invitation to the young man

[1] Hahn, *Tsuni-Goam,* p. 18.   [2] Smyth, B. i. p. 61—2.
[3] On some verses of Virgil.   [4] Inscription, line 63.

with the statement that she has peace-offerings to proffer. One mode of proffering peace-offerings was by exposure of the person in the dance; a primitive form of which survives in the French "*can-can.*" The Fijians dance the *can-can* called *gini-gini*, a religious ceremonial dance with which women welcome back the returning heroes with wanton gestures and motions, or those peace-offerings that were the reward of the warrior, the bull of battle, proffered with the simplicity of gesture-language.

It was a feminine form of *kotouing* to the male, or the bull. The North Americans likewise danced a *can-can*. Penn said the worship of the Leṅape Indians consisted of sacrifice and *cantico*, the latter being a round dance performed with shouts and antic gestures. "*Gentikehn*" in the Algonkin Delaware means to dance a sacred dance.

The Maori also danced the *can-can*. *Kani-kan* is to dance and to move backwards and forwards. *Kanu-kana*, in Kaffir, is to lust after one another. The Hindus call the Wag-tail (*Montacilla alba*) Matta-*Khanjana*; but more particularly—that is, typically—at the pairing season. The Wag-tail in love as the "Matta-*Khanjana*" dances the *can-can* of love. *Khanjana* denotes going, moving; the secret pleasures of the Yatis; the cohabitation of saints. *Khan-khana* (Sansk.) is the tinkle-tinkle of a bell.

The Egyptian *kan-kannu* is to dance and leap; *kan* is to dance, and *kannu* is victory. It has survived because it was a sacred dance, and it was sacred because it was sexual.

The Egyptians continued the leaping dance, or *kan-kannu*, from Inner Africa, and gave to it a symbolical significance. Plutarch tells how they represented generation by means of motion, though less grossly doubtless than in the Africa beyond. He says of the Sistrum of Isis, an emblem of the female in two phases, those of Isis and Nephthys, "*they tell us that the Sistrums frighten away and avert Typhon, insinuating that as corruption* (i.e. *the menses*) *locks up and fixes nature's course, so generation resolves and excites it by means of motion.*" [1] And so the Sistrums were shaken, and the waving to and fro of their limbs and bodies was a sign of Typhon's dismissal, and the time of peace-offerings.

In the sacred dance the idea illustrated was that with the departure of Typhon all need of secrecy and seclusion was gone, hence the motive of the festival, and freedom of the dance.

The universal name of the dance and dancing in Inner Africa will tell us where the *can-can* came from. This is:—

Kina, Mbamba.	*Kina*, Songo.	*Gani*, Kanem.
Kini, Ntere.	*Kena*, Kisama.	*Kina*, Lubalo.
Kini, Mutsaya.	*N'kan*, Limba.	*Kina*, Nyamban.
Kine, Babuma.	*Gani*, Tumbuktu.	*Yani*, Salum.
Kena, Bumbete.	*Kan*, Padsade.	*Yini*, Krebo.
Gina, Kasands.		

[1] Of Is. and Os.

Partial exposure of the person is still an African mode of showing homage, because it is a return to the status of childhood, intended to be a contrast to the person who is clothed with dignity, which first began with the investiture of pubescence, the *toga virilis*. Moreover, the wives of the Zulu King, Dingairn, said that when he was present they were only allowed to appear on all fours, and always moved about on their hands and knees. In Loango this was the prescribed attitude for wives in general in presence of their husbands. Captain Burton says the *Dakro*, a woman who bears messages from the King of Dahome to the men, goes on all fours before him, and "*as a rule she goes on all fours to these men, but only kneels to smaller men.*" So the oriental women are not compelled to veil the face before slaves or men of inferior position, they being more on an equality as mere women.

The earliest Genitrix went on all fours, as she is pourtrayed in mythology, and personified as the hinder part; a type continued from the time when woman was the female animal.

In Africa it is found to be almost as at first in the action of the woman, who goes on all fours to the male. That which was once natural is continued wholly or partially as a typical mode of doing honour. The wives of a great man among the Soosoos, bend their bodies to him with one hand resting on each knee. This attitude is also assumed when he passes by.[1]

Among certain African tribes the women greet the men—and even half-grown youths—by bending their backs until the tips of their fingers rest on the toes of their feet; or, by turning their bodies *sideways*, clapping their hands, exclaiming *wake, wake, waky, waky, huh, huh.*[2]

In some parts of India[3] and in certain of the Pacific Islands it is considered a token of respect and an act of homage to present the back-side to a superior. The most precious offering to the Deity of Israel even when the male idea dominated, continued to be the rump (Aliah)[4] the hinder thigh which from the beginning had been an emblem of the female, a sacrificial type of that which was once offered in the custom of the feminine Kotou, the hieroglyphic "*Ur-heka*" the great magic power, or potent charm of primitive man.

The most striking feature in the females of the Bushman race is their protuberant hinder part; this is peculiar enough to cause perplexity to the Anthropologist. Descriptions have been given that recall the saying of Proclus in Timæus, "immense nature is suspended from the back of the vivific goddess." But the doctrine of sexual selection and the customs of Kotou may suggest an explanation of

[1] Winterbottom, *Account of the Native Africans in the Neighbourhood of Sierra Leone*, vol. i. p. 122.
[2] Stanley, *How I Found Livingstone*, p. 551.
[3] Dubois, *Description of the People of India*, p. 210.
Lev. iii. 9; vii. 3; viii. 25; ix. 19.

this feminine formation of an earlier time that made peculiar appeal to a primitive taste. In the Maori language *Kotua* means respect, regard, to pay homage, *with the back turned towards one*. This denotes a primordial mode of *Kotou*. *Khetu* in Egyptian signifies reversal. One meaning is conveyed by the Hebrew קדש. In Zulu Kaffir Uku-*Kota*mela is to stoop or bow down towards a person. The genesis of such a custom is not far to seek. It belongs to the stage at which the female performed the Kotou animal-fashion, and the African belle was of the Bushwoman type of beauty.

Invertions of the custom of Kotou still abound, and are performed with much ceremony in every royal European court. In these the obeisance is still made by the persons *going backwards*. Such is the persistence of customs, natural or unnatural, that have once become symbolical; and so the bishop wears his *Liku* or shent apron of puberty, and the courtly flunkey bows backwards in happy ignorance of the excessively simple origines of such specimens of survival.

In some regions of Inner Africa it is a practice for the females to pluck out the hair of their eyebrows; special pincers for that purpose forming a part of the outfit of their toilette. This is a kind of *Kotouing* to the male; a poor-thing sort of mode in being unmasculine, or more feminine and servile; a negational distinction of the sex.

Acosta describes the Peruvians as pulling out their eyebrows and eyelashes, and offering the hairs to the gods, and it was a practice when in the temples to perform the pantomime of plucking out the eyebrows and of blowing the hairs towards the Idol.

What the African female performs in kotouing to the male was also practised in sacrifice to the gods, whether by the Peruvians, or by Lucian at Hierapolis, or by Paul in Cenchrea.

The women of New Zealand, Samoa, New Caledonia, and Tasmania, the brown race and the black, have their hair cut short or cropped close, whilst the men all wear theirs long.

The Chinese continue the custom, said to be a Tartar one, of fixing the espousals by sending a matron from the bridegroom with a pin to fasten up the hair of the betrothed female. Hair is an emblem of pubescence which applied to both sexes. In Egyptian AN for the hair, is the name for beauty of appearance, to become beautiful, and sexually inviting. But the hair type is found to be the especial glory of the male, the bearded one.

In the Tasmanian rite of young-man-making, a girdle of human hair sometimes of the *pubes* forcibly extracted was presented to the initiated to be worn as the token of their manhood.

The Australians of Botany Bay plaited strings of human hair and wore them as girdles round their waists. The Australian Dieyeri manufacture a form of the " *Ankh*-tie " called a Yinka, to be worn by the male at puberty. This is a string of twisted human hair which is worn round the waist, and is ordinarily 300 yards in length. The *Yinka*[1] is greatly prized but is exceedingly rare on account of the difficulty in procuring human hair.

This emblem of the male was suppressed or diminished in the female, hence her covering, cutting, or plucking out of the hair. Nor was this all. The feminine pubes were turned into ornaments for masculine wear, in the mysteries and out of them. It was a custom with the ancient Irish for the women to present their lovers with rings and bracelets made of their own hair.[2] The hair became a symbol so essentially masculine and potent, that the dead of both sexes were represented by an image of the *bearded* male, as the Egyptian *Shebti*. St. Austin also refers to those who think that woman will rise again in the male image rather than her own ; although he does not assign the true reason for making the type of resurrection masculine.

From so simple an origin arose the practice insisted on by St. Paul, of the female wearing her head covered in presence of the angel, and in the worship of the male deity. At Hierapolis, the devotee offered her hair, or pubes, as a commuted form of feminine sacrifice.

In the Egyptian paintings, baldness is a mode of representing non-virility in the pigmy Ptah, the crook-legged abortion ; a phase of the god as Ptah-Sekari, the infantile and infertile. The bald head agrees with the *penis manu compressa* of his portraits, and both betoken the impubescent one, the *Ren* in opposition to the *Renka*.

The Osirified in the Ritual rejoicing in his having retained ALL the tokens of his manhood in death says, amongst other things, " *My eyebrow is not plucked out.*"[3] " *No injury is done to my body.*" There is another reference in the words, " *I knew that eye ; the hair of the Man was on it !*"[4]

Hair is one of those human types that lead us back to gesture-language in many lands.

The Pai-Ute Indians make the sign for *the Chief by grasping the fore-lock of their hair and lifting it up at full length. A lesser length of hair* denotes a lower rank.[5] The more hair the greater the man. So, under the order of chivalry it was a token of respect for the gentleman to pull at his moustache when in presence of a lady ; and pulling the forelock is still a provincial mode of making an obeisance to a superior ; as it is also with English sailors.

In Mediæval Europe the inferior classes of the people were prohibited by statute, or edict, from wearing " Fur." Rank was then denoted by the skin of the animal, as in Africa to-day. Indeed the word " rank " is one with the Egyptian *Rnk* for the *pubes*, which

---

[1] " YINKA." The Zulu Kaffir " *Yinga* " is a necklace of coloured beads. The " *Ingu* " in Aku, is made of beads ; the *Hanga*, Basunde, is a chain-fetter.
[2] Gough's *Camden*, vol. iii. p. 658.   [3] Ch. clv.
[4] Ch. cxv.   [5] Mallery, *Introd.* p. 19.

constituted the first rank of the male, and founded his supremacy over the female.

The Welsh Rhenc or Breton Rhenk is primarily the status attained at puberty which afterwards became the rank in the Male line of descent.

The name of the man was originally conferred, like the white stone in the Mysteries, at the time of puberty. Thus the name, the stone, and *pubes* or hair, were homotypes. According to Hans Stade the Tupi warrior took away the name of the man whom he slew and bore it himself; and when the young Creek Indian brought in his first scalp he won his war-name, and became a Brave.

The Osage Indians are reported as killing an enemy on purpose to suspend his scalp over the grave of their own buried warrior, with the view of sending the murdered man's spirit to him as his slave in the other world; and this interpretation is supported by the fact that when the Chichimec scalped his enemy alive, the vanquished man became the conqueror's slave by the loss of his scalp and hair, the tokens of his manhood. Childhood, widowhood, bereavement, ignominy, and slavery, were all indicated by the hairless condition.

With some races the woman shaved her head on losing her husband. The same word *Mundai* in Toda, is the name of the widow and the bald. In the Hieroglyphics the determinative of the Kharu or widow, is the detached scalplike tress of hair. Also plucking out the hair was a gesture-sign of grief and mourning.

Loss of hair was degrading, and humiliating, whether voluntary or enforced; and shaving is the symbolic act of rendering non-virile, monkish, unsexual, whether applied to the pubes, beard, or crown, as it was in Egypt, and still is in the Cult of the Virgin Mother and her impubescent Bambino in Rome.

This is recognized by Isaiah who threatens Israel with a razor that will shave it at both ends, *and " it shall consume the beard."* [1]

As hair was the emblem of virility and reproduction, baldness was the natural antithesis; and the loss of the hair was enforced as a later form of penalty, because it had been held so sacred as a voluntary offering. The hair being a symbol of reproducing potency, this will account for the lock of a person's hair being considered the representative of the person's self, when his life is sought to be taken, or blasted by magic, i.e. *enacting of the malignant desire in gesture-language* according to primitive usage.

It is believed that the hair and nails ought never to be cut on Sunday, the day of Khem-Horus, or on Friday, the day of the Genitrix.

The Lion Paru in the Ritual is called the "*Lord of numerous transformations of skins,*" i.e. repeatings of the hair; and time was, in England, when people would make a point of having their hair cut

---

[1] Ch. vii. 20.

whilst the *Moon*, the female reproducer, was in the sign of the Lion or the Ram ;[1] two chief types of male potency.

When we know the symbolic value of nail from the origin we can understand the reason why biting the nail by way of scorn should be considered an insult.[2] The act was equal to plucking the beard or cutting the hair ; it was aimed at the person's manhood, on the ground of nail being a representative of virility in gesture-language and the primitive typology.

The nails as an equivalent for the hair, a type of "*renewal coming of itself*," will account for a custom like this :—"*The ancient Frenchmen had a ceremony that when they would marry, the bridegroom should pare his nails and send them to his new wife ; which done they lived together afterwards as man and wife.*"[3] The act had the same significance as when the pubes or locks of hair were offered to the divine Genitrix, or the foreskins were piled in the circle of the twelve stones at Gilgal. Each was dedicated to re-production.

Captain Cook describes the Maori as wearing the nails and teeth of their dead relations.[4] These were equivalent to the phallus worn by the widows, as a type of re-production.

It was an Egyptian custom to gild the nails, teeth, and membrum virile of the embalmed mummy. These were glorified in the gloom of the grave because, as types of production, they served in a second phase as emblems of foundation, and visible basis of renewal and resurrection.

It was a theory that the hair, beard, and nails of the Japanese Mikado were never cut. They had to be trimmed furtively while he was sleeping. This corresponds to the assumption that the king never dies. He was not reproducible. He only transformed. He was the living one, like the Ankh (Eg.) ; an image of the ever-living, a type of the immortal.

The male emblem of virility, like the scalp, was a trophy to be cut off in battle. On the monuments there are heaps of these collected as evidence of conquest. In one instance the "spoils of the Rebu" consist of donkey-loads of phalluses (Karunatu) and severed hands. 12,535 members and hands were cut off from the dead after the battle of Khesef-Tamahu, and deposited as proofs of victory—an enacted report—before the Pharaoh Rameses.

By aid of the hieroglyphic values conferred on the image in life, we can read the significance of the emblem in death. By its excision the enemy was typically annihilated ; the last tribute paid thus was the forfeiture of his personality in a spiritual sense ; for without the member the deceased, according to Egyptian thought, could not be *reconstructed*. He would not rise again ; resurrection,

---

[1] Brand, *The Moon.*   [2] Brand, *Hand and Finger-nails.*
[3] Vaughan's *Golden Grove*, 1608.
[4] Cook, *Hawksworth Voy.* vol. iii. 457.

as in the case of Osiris, depended on repossessing the member. The type of individuality here was the emblem of existence hereafter.

We have only to become acquainted with the doctrines of the mummy in the Ritual, and see the fearful anxiety of the deceased to get all his members intact and solid, to avoid dissolution; see how he rejoices in the firmness of his phallus, the hardness of his heart, the soundness and indissolubility of his vertebræ, to apprehend what terrible meaning there was in the custom of dismembering the body, swallowing the eyes, eating the heart, or pulverising the bones to drink them in water as an ocular demonstration of dissolution. The New Zealanders are said to think that a man who is eaten is thus destroyed soul and body.[1]

In the Atharva-Veda it is affirmed that when the dead passed through the sacrificial fire to heaven, Agni (fire) does not consume their generative organ; whereas in the earlier thought of Kam it would have been held to do so, or to efface the type, which came to the same thing, symbolically, on the most physical plane of thought.

Because the custom was typical, it permitted of modification and commutation in the interchange of types. Thus the "*bloody foreskin*" of the slain came to be adopted in place of the total emblem, as with the Abyssinians, described by Bruce, and the hundred Philistine foreskins demanded by Saul of David, and doubled as the dowry of Michal.[2] The foreskin, or prepuce-cover had precisely the same symbolical value as the *sign of manhood*, hence its excision at the age of puberty, for that was the earlier period, and the Jewish custom does not retain the primary significance, except in its being a commutated offering to the paternal deity.

Scalping had a similar origin. The hair being a token of manhood and potency, the scalp bore these values as a typical trophy. Cutting off the head was but a less refined mode of taking the scalp without the trouble. In other forms of mutilation the hair was the primary object as a type of the male potency now utterly vanquished in the dead, or transferred, still living, to the living.

It was not only the act of killing that was consecrated by the mutilation of the dead. Among the Shoshones, taking an enemy's scalp was an honour quite independent of the act of vanquishing him. To kill your adversary was of no importance unless the scalp was secured; and if a warrior slew any number of foes in battle and others obtained the scalps, they who took them had all the honour; this went with the trophy, that is the type.

There was a recent massacre of the Kultas by the Khonds, in which one of the latter picked up the head of an old man, who had just been decapitated, and was carrying it off in triumph, when the leader called out to him, "*Why carry about a head without hair?*

---

[1] Taylor, *New Zealand*, p. 101.   [2] 1 Sam. xviii. 25.

There will be no scalping of him!" and he threw away the useless trophy.[1]

It was a practice with the Maori for the victor in battle to scoop out the left eye of his dead enemy and swallow it. This was done, says Dieffenbach, because the soul was supposed to have its seat in the left eye.[2]

The left eye of a chief was believed to become a star after his death; and Shungie, a New Zealand chief, declared that he had swallowed the left eye of an enemy whom he had killed for the purpose of increasing the glory of his own when it shone in the firmament above.

According to the typology of Egypt, the left symbolic eye is the eye of light by night—the eye of the moon in the dark. It is said to Ra in the inscription of El Karjeh—*"Thy left eye is in the disk of night. Thou shinest in the morning out of the earth, thy right eye is the essence."*[3] The right eye was the sun.

In the story told by Plutarch, Hermes (Taht) is said to cut out Typhon's muscles, and turn them into lute-strings. Typhon tears out the eye of Taht and swallows it. That is the *left symbolic lunar eye.* Then the sun restores the eye when the moon is renewed.

According to the Kamite typology the Maori warrior swallowed that which would have been his enemy's light by night—his moon in the darkness of death, and thus extinguished him utterly.

There can be little doubt that a religious cannibalism had its origin or derived its significance from the victors eating portions of the vanquished, and finishing them that way. The Kongo Namaquas, like many other Africans, eat human flesh in time of war,[4] and then only.

Many unintelligible forms of thought may be interpreted by an original type when once we obtain the clue to the origin—and very little short of the origin in these customs is really worth knowing—which enables us to follow them in their later phases of survival.

The idea of reproduction and continuity, symbolled by the Hieroglyphic skin, is the primary cause of the belief as expressed in popular lore, that the cow's hide has the quality of stretching and extending endlessly. Hence the garment of cow's hide worn by Vishnu in the *Mahâbhârata.*

According to the Vulgate, the Maker stretched out the heaven *like a skin.*[5]

It is by means of a SKIN which they possess that men and women are enabled to change themselves into seals, in the folklore of Shetland. And through the same type of transference, the Seals are looked upon as human beings who have been transfigured.

---

[1] *Globe* newspaper, August 24, 1882.   [2] Vol. ii. p. 129.   [3] Line 21.
[4] Koelle, *Polyglotta Africana*, Introd. p. 15.   [5] Ps. civ. 2.

All turns on the skin, whichever way the transformation may take place. When the *Finn* woman is once in the power of the Shetlander, it is because he has possession of her skin, without which she can never transform back again or escape from her captor.

In the "Orphic Fragments" we read, "*No one has seen Protogonos with his eyes, except the Sacred Night alone ; all others wondered when they beheld in the ether the unexpected light, such as the* SKIN *of the immortal Phanes shot forth.*"[1] The skin is here the same type of transformation as that of the *Fenn*. The type is one whether it be the wolf-dog or jackal of Anup, the lion of Shu or any other form of the Phœnix-skin, including the Seal of the Shetlanders, and of the Ahts of North America.

The natural origin of all the transformations, by assuming the skin, hair, or feathers of the animals or birds, may be traced to the ritual and ceremonial of puberty. When the boy became pubescent, he transformed into the hairy one. The first clothing was hair, and this was followed by fur and feather, and the skin with hair on, worn in later times. He made his transformation in the likeness of the totemic animal, and became a bear, a wolf, a bull, a dog, a seal, a crow, hawk, or other tribal type of the ancestral descent. This mode of transformation was then continued in the religious mysteries, and applied to other changes. For example, we *speak* of a "change of heart," but the Egyptian "change of heart" was represented by taking the old heart out of the mummy's breast to embalm or preserve it apart, and replacing it by the beetle, a type of change and transformation.

That which we can *talk, say,* and *write* was first *enacted,* and the most primitive customs were the sole *records* of such acting by men who *performed* those things that could not otherwise have been memorized. These customs had their origin in gesture-language ; they constitute the drama of dumb humanity, and volumes might be filled in showing the (to us) unnatural-looking results of an origin that was quite natural.

Seeing the primitive importance of the skin as a type of prowess and a symbol of reproduction adopted on account of its shooting the hair and renewing itself, it is more than probable that the custom of throwing the old shoe after the newly-wedded pair is connected with the skin-type of repetition (Nem). We have to think back beyond leather to the time when the sandal was made of skin, and worn with the hair on. The shoe of Vair fur or hair which fitted Cinderella was of the same symbolic value. The Prince was in search of the reproducer. The shoe is thrown for good luck, which in this case means progeny. For the typology is actually identified by the Esquimaux, who seize an old shoe of the English with great avidity, cut it up into strips, and turn them into talismans to make barren

[1] Ed. Cory, p. 296.

women fertile, or teeming.[1] This may be adduced as the connecting-link, still extant, with the custom of throwing the old shoe for good luck in marriage, and the non-wearing of skin or leather during menstruation by the Parsee women.

Such an application of the skin of the animal in the shape of the shoe will also explicate the custom of putting shoes on the dead or burying a pair with them, as was done in England and other northern countries. In Scandinavia the burial shoe is called helskô or Hell-shoe. The shoe would have the same significance as the skin in which the Inner Africans still inter their dead, and the Bes or Nem skin that was held to give warmth, protection, and the hope of a joyful resurrection or reproduction to the mummy in Egypt. At the famous Duke of Wellington's funeral a pair of boots were carried to St. Paul's Cathedral in the stirrups of the dead warrior's horse; as is the rule at the burial of a field-marshal.

The shoe-skin being a sign of supremacy, as shown, for instance, by the declaration of the Hebrew Deity—"*Over Edom will I cast my shoe*,"[2] this will account for its being taken off as an acknowledgment of inferiority. The earliest skins worn were trophies of the victor and types of his virility, proofs of his potency.

The *pubes* supplied a supreme type of male power. The vesture, the shoe, and hat, were made of skin, fur, or feather, which are interchangeable as symbols. These being worn proudly, were doffed in humility. The Cossacks of the Don elected their Hetman by casting their skins or hairy caps at him, which were reckoned as votes.

The hat is put on by the Speaker of the House of Commons as the chief sign of his authority. The hat, or beaver, was also a form of the skin. The bear-skin Busby continues the Bus-skin of Egypt, which was a sign of protecting power and of transference; it is a genuine relic of the primæval skin wherewith the conqueror clothed himself, and sought to frighten his foe. The tall silk hat is an imitation of the hairy one, and in this the man still tries to look martial, and the boy pubescent. In the shape of the hat the skin is still a type of transformation from boy to man.

The relationship of the skin to the hair and renewed life is demonstrated by the ancient custom of presenting a pair of gloves to the culprits who had been condemned to die, but who received the king's pardon, whereby the glove became the type of life renewed. This custom was followed by a pair of gloves being given to the judge before whom no prisoner had been capitally convicted at what is termed a "Maiden Assize." The same theory of origin will also explain why gloves should have been given at weddings. In the time of Queen Elizabeth the bridegroom wore gloves in his hat as the symbol of good husbandry, and this identifies the type

---

[1] Egede, *Greenland*, p. 198.　　　　　　[2] Ps. lx. 8.

The glove hung up in churches and in the pews of those who had died young is a sign of the same significance as the skin buried with the dead as the symbol of a future life.

Some amorous pleasantry is connected with the belief that if a woman surprises a man when he is sleeping, and kisses without waking him, she is entitled to receive a new pair of gloves. It was especially applicable on Valentine's Day, when lovers were chosen by lot or captured. The covertness of the act has the look of the lady's having earned the right to be covered, or to become the *femme couverte*, as if it were a form of feminine capture.

The skin was made use of in the ceremony of bride-capture; the bride in some instances being carried off in the symbolical skin. In the Sutras it was provided that at one important part of the marriage ceremony, the bridegroom and a strong man should compel the bride to sit down on the skin of a red ox. The skin was the same emblem of reproduction as if thrown after the wedding pair or buried with the dead. Nor is the type limited to reproduction. *Bus*, the skin, also signifies transference, to pass, change from one to another. Thus the skin or shoe is a double Ideograph when applied to the bride.

Much has been written of late years on the subject of capture in marriage. The present writer, however, is not concerned with tribal endogamy and exogamy. The act of capture goes back of necessity to the state of utterest promiscuity. The capture of the female by the male is so ancient that it may be compared with the capture of the hen by the cock. Next lawless capture was regulated and applied to periods of time and to persons within and without the Totemic tribe.

Under the sign of *Fekh* in the hieroglyphics, we have the meaning of to capture, inclose, clasp, untie, undress, denude, burst open and in short ravish the female as was done *even in accordance with the regulated customs of capture*.

The hieroglyphic tie, noose, or knot, is the determinative of *Fekh*, and all the ideas connected with capturing, tying, making a bond and covenant. It is the determinative of *Ark* and *Ankh* to surround, envelop, clasp, pair, couple, and duplicate. The *knot then is the sign of capture and covenant*, which include all the various modes of marriage. The knot is still the symbol of marriage, described as tying the knot. The ring, the wreath, the scarf, are other circular and corroborative symbols. But the knot did not originate with the ceremony of marriage, whether of capture or covenant. It is the hieroglyphic sign of life and reproduction. As such it was carried by the Great, the *enceinte* Mother, as her emblem. It is the ideograph of periodicity, and was primally the determinative of *Ark*, the end of a period, to end, be perfected; and applies to the period of feminine pubescence. It is the determinative of *Ankh*, to put on clothes, to dress; the nature of which is shown by linen hung up to dry. The first *Ankh*-tie was put on at puberty, by the leaf-wearers, some of whom still clothe themselves with a leaf-girdle to-day, as do the *Juangs* of India—described by Colonel Dalton—whose name is possibly based on their early type of the *Ankh*-tie, whence the Juang. This tie is still made of leaves in the Kaffir *Cacawe*.

Fekh (Eg.), the tie, girdle, band, or knot, is identical with the Zulu *Foko*, a woman's top-knot, the sign of pubescence, and the status of womanhood. The origin of the tie then can be traced to the simplest necessity of nature. It was next adopted as the sign of reproduction, because it had become the token of feminine pubescence, and the period of possible pregnancy; therefore a symbol itself. The type was continued in the Egyptian and Inner African custom of tying up or *snooding* the hair after that period. Here again the tie, or knot, signified that the wearer was capturable—ready for marriage, and it constituted a primitive means of distinguishing between the right and wrong, according to the rude inter-tribal code of ravishing.

The laws of regulated capture are illustrated by the Narrinyeri tribes of Australia, with whom members of the different clans are present at each other's ceremonies of young-man-making to see that they only enter those youths who are of the proper age, so that they may not claim more females from another tribe than properly belong to them, or than they *have the right to take*.[1]

The *Arku* (Eg.), tie, is represented by the Fijian *Liku* (a variant of the word Arku), or loin-cloth which is assumed at the time of puberty. The Liku is likewise known to the Australian Aborigines. The young females of Victoria put on a girdle or very short skirt made of opossum fur, called a *Leek-Leek*.[2]

When the daughter of a Fijian chief was betrothed in infancy, the mother carried a *Liku* as a present to the intended husband, in token, and as a pledge that her daughter should be his wife. The Liku is the feminine loin-cloth, zone, girdle and apron all in one. The message conveyed to him by this sign would tell him that when the girl put on the Liku at puberty she would become his wife. In return, he presented to the mother some whales' teeth as his pledge, and sign of the covenant.[3] The tooth emblem of Adultship—Hu (Eg.), tooth, ivory, and the Adult Solar God,—was one with the Nails of the Frenchmen, or the lock of hair sent in later times, to be worn by the woman. The tooth, and loin-cloth, were typical of pubescence in the two sexes, hence their relationship to marriage.

The Fijian Liku and Victorian *Leek-Leek*, is Inner African, as the

Lok, Waist-cloth, Wolof.	*Loga*, Shirt, Kore.	*Halak*, Shirt, Soa.
Liga, Shirt, Kano.	*Lugod* ,, Dsarawa.	*Halak* ,, Wadai.
Liga ,, Kadzina.	*Ariga* ,, Mbarike.	*Melagiye* ,, Beran.
Dolokie ,, Timbo.		

[1] Smyth, vol. i. p. 65.　　[2] Smyth, vol. i. p. 272.　　[3] Williams, *Fiji*, vol. i. p. 168.

Also the Ark and Ankh Nooses are names for cord or rope :—

Orugba, a Cord, in Igu.	*Olugba*, a Cord, in Egbira-Hima.	*Aruka*, Ear-ring, Ebe.	
Orugba ,, ,, Opanda.	*Oruka*, Ear-ring, Ife.	*Uroka*, { Armlet or Bracelet. } Nupe.	

The Ankh tie is likewise Inner African, as

Ngeha,	{ Rope or Cord, }	Landoro.	*N'ket*,	{ Rope or Cord, }	Bamom.	*Nek*,	{ Rope or Cord, }	Konguan.	
Ngeya	,,	Mende.	*Nke*	,,	Momenya.	*Nganga*,	Gree-gree,	Songo.	
Nke	,,	Bayon.	*Nke*	,,	Papiah.	*Wuanka*	,,	Kisama.	
Nke	,,	Pati.	*Nkui*	,,	Param.	*Wuanga*	,,	Lubalo.	
Nke	,,	Kum.	*Ongoi*	,,	Pangela.	*Owanga*	,,	Pangelo.	
Nke	,,	Bagba.	*Ungos*	,,	Runda.	*Wanka*	,,	N'gola.	
Nket	,,	Balu.	*Nkoi*	,,	Matatan.				

The typical knot on the head, called by the Maori, *Ngoi*, made the same communication as the knot in the handkerchief, used for "kiss-in-the-ring," which signified to capture and kiss, because the time had come. And so the type was carried on in the bridal knot, and representative *ring*, when coupling had attained the status of monogamous marriage.

Such types founded in the necessities of nature—the sole revealer in the matter—were continued as signs or symbols, and still survive in hieroglyphical customs where they are no longer read.

Max Müller has remarked, that :—

"*The Sanskrit name for love is Smara; it is derived from Smar, to recollect; and the same root has supplied the German Schmerz, pain, and the English, smart.*" [1]

In Egyptian, *Mer* is to love, to kiss, attach, bind; the *Merti* (our married) are persons who are attached and bound together. *Mer* is determined by the noose, or tie of binding; hence Hor-Apollo says truly *a noose denotes love*.[2] S is the causative prefix to verbs, whence *Smar* (and *Smart*) to bind, twist, slaughter, which serves to connect the word with pain and smart. *Smara* (Eg.) to bind, also means to *collect*, and is applied to the *collecting* of taxes,[3] and the Sanskrit *Smara*, to re-collect, is the metaphysical phase of *Smaru* (Eg.) to collect, which again agrees with *mer*, to be attached, or bound together.

This meaning of love began in collecting and capturing or binding the females, as the primitive mode of *abstracting*, whether legally or illegally, not in sentimental recollection, or an abstract kind of word. Forcible and legalized capture preceded the bondage of affection and the name of the one was continued for the other.

Such is the part played by words in obscuring the meaning they had in the past with the sense they bear at present; *i.e.* in the Aryan stage.

In one shape or other the knot, tie, Ankh, Ark, or Mer-circle, is universally worn, figured, and pourtrayed in the coupling or marriage

---

[1] *Lectures*, vol. i. p. 383, ed. 1862. [2] B. ii. 26.
[3] Goodwin, R. A. 1861, 125.

ceremony. Enacting the knot came first. Hence the noose-sign of capture under the term *Fekh*. In the marriage of the Aztecs a priest tied a point of the bride's gown or *huepilli* to the *tilmatli* or mantle of the bridegroom; this was their marriage ceremony, and mode of tying the knot. At other times the circle was traversed. The bridegroom carried the bride on his back and made the circuit of her house.

The Veddahs of Ceylon, who, according to Tennant, have no marriage rites, are said by another writer to use a symbol of duration for the union of the man and woman who pair together. The woman twists a cord, and on the wedding day she presents this to her mate who puts it round his waist to wear till death.[1]

The supposition still prevails amongst the working classes in some English counties that a husband may lawfully sell his wife to another man provided he puts her up to auction, and delivers her over to the buyer *with a noose about her neck*. The fact is continually cropping up in the newspapers. In this ceremony the noose-sign of capture and covenant continues to do duty in the act of transfer and the making of a new bargain; and the *hank* is still the hieroglyphic *Ankh*.

The religious ritual of the moderns also is crowded like a kitchen-midden with the refuse relics of customs that were once natural and are now clung to as if they were supernatural in their efficacy, because their origin is unknown. Such customs are like those rudimentary organs of animals that nature suppressed and superseded, which only tell of uses long since passed away.

Some of these lost all their significance when they were transferred from one period of life to another, as the rites and ceremonies of pubesence were transposed to the time of infant baptism. At the period of puberty *the youth was inducted into the tribe; the tribal mark and totemic name were conferred on him in a baptism of blood*. His Totem-tattoo was scored into the flesh of his back. The brand of the deserter shows this custom on the reverse of the coin. A front tooth was knocked out and the prepuce cover either excised or the mark was made by the longitudinal slit of the Australian Aborigines and the Fijians. By the one cut he was dedicated to the clan as its kinsman; by the other he was consecrated as a future generator. Hence the name of the rites of "young-man-making." The mutilation took various forms at different times amongst many peoples.

The Burmese for example bore their ears and the custom takes the rank of a baptism. It was primally the making and sacred sealing of a bond and covenant in the blood of a responsible individual who could understand the nature of it. But when the custom of circumcision was transferred to the time of childhood, as it had been by the Jews, to be performed on the infant of eight days old, then the natural (*i.e.,* according to the savage condition) in transforming

[1] Quoted in *Primitive Manners and Customs*, p. 236, Farrer.

into the symbolic custom, loses its sense; and it becomes cruel in its dotage.

The custom of shaving the head of an infant, or cutting its hair at the time of conferring the father's name, can only be explained by the first intention. The Peruvians also cut the babe's hair ceremonially with a stone knife when the name was conferred at the age of two years. It is a common Moslem custom in Africa for the child to have its hair cut when the name of the father is given to it.

Park in his travels into Inner Africa says it is a custom among the Mandengas for the child to be named when it is seven or eight days old, and the ceremony commences by the priest shaving the infant's head. In Europe too cutting the hair of the child or young man was a mode of adopting and fathering. Clovis offered his beard for Alaric to cut in token that he adopted him for his son, and Charles Martel sent his son, Pepin, to Luithprand, the Lombard king, that he might cut his first locks and thus adopt him as his son.[1]

The custom was continued as symbolical, but the transfer of the rite from the time of puberty leaves the natural genesis so far behind that it is lost sight of. *At the period of young-man-making the shaving and hair-plucking represented a typical return to infancy, and the pubescent male was thus reborn and adopted into the community as its child.* But when the ceremony is enacted in infancy it is meaningless and becomes inexplicable.

There is abundant evidence to prove that the earliest tattooing was done by cuts in the flesh, and that these were totemic signs. Burton testifies that in Abeokuta every tribe, sub-tribe, and family had its blazon printed on the body ranging from great gashes down to a diminutive pattern-prick.

The totemic preceded the individual ancestor as father; and affiliation to the Totem was first. At a later stage such symbols became ancestral, but they originated as tribal marks and were primarily adopted for use in the earliest societary phase. They were signs of the bond of fellowship before they were turned into the badges of bondage to an individual tyrant.

The same loss of sense occurs in transferring the rite of baptism from the age of puberty to that of infancy. The Kaffir and Hottentot girls undergo the baptism of water at this time. Casalis describes one form, yet to be quoted; Dr. Hahn another. It is a Hottentot custom for pubescent girls to be exposed stark naked to the first thunder-storm that follows their period, and, as an eye-witness, he describes them running to and fro in this manner when the thunder roared incessantly, and the sky appeared to be one continued flash of lightning, and the rain drenched them in a deluge.[2]

[1] Spencer, *Ceremonial Institutions*, p. 63.
[2] *Tsuni-Goam*, p. 87.

Baptism at puberty was also a rite of consecration by means of blood, because blood was the announcer of the female period of pubescence. So lowly of status was the " primæval revelation." Nature herself wrote the first rubric ; and her red was blood. This was next applied to the male at puberty by the bond made in his blood. Adult baptism, whether with water or blood, was a consecration of the generative powers to righteous use and a cleanly life. But a baptism of the unconscious babe as a rite of *re-generation* by ministers who are profoundly ignorant of its origin and significance, becomes an imposture, all the greater for its sanctity. The continuity of the custom is shown by the child's taking the father's name instead of the tribal one of old. The re-generation doctrine, however, is nought but a delusive shadow of the past, the Manes of a meaning long since dead. Indeed, the whole masquerade of Roman Ritualism in these appurtenances of the past is now as sorry a sight to the Archaic student as the straw crowns and faded finery of the kings and queens whose domain is limited to the asylum for lunatics.

Not that the evolutionist can justly complain of these specimens of survival. " As it was in the beginning," is the gospel found to be continued by them ; and no written record in the present can compare with the unwritten records of the past which are preserved in symbolical customs.

When we know that the human race first dated from the dark, the lower side, and reckoned the place of darkness in the north by the left hand, that will explain numerous customs connected with the left hand.

The Talmudists assert that man was created from the left hand. Sut was born from the left side. In the Roman worship of the Great Mother, a left hand was borne in the sacred procession with the palm expanded,[1] because the left hand was a feminine type. The Vamacharis, or left-hand worshippers of Siva are Yonias, those who recognise the female as primary. In English churches and chapels the men used to sit on the south side, or right hand ; the women to the north on the left hand, which is precisely the same symbolical custom as that observed in the burial of the Bongo dead. A custom like this yet affects the Ritualistic controversy. The followers of the female still lean to the left side and the place of the Genitrix in the north. In the year 1628, Prebendary Smart, in preaching against certain innovations made in the Ritualistic practices of the Reformed Church says the Communion-Table must " stand as it had wont to do. Neither must the table be placed along from north to south, as the altar is set, but from east to west *as the custom is of all Reformed Churches*, otherwise the minister cannot stand at the north side, there being neither side towards the north. The Lord's table eleven years ago was

[1] Apuleius.

turned into an altar, and so placed that the minister cannot stand to do his office on the north side, as the law expressly chargeth him to do, because there is no side of the table standing northward."

As in the Hebrew arrangements, the north side represents the birth-place of all beginnings, the mouthpiece of emanation. Prebendary Smart was an English Vamachari, and the Eucharistic table standing "in the sides of the north" represented the Virgin Mother just as surely as if she had been the Vāmorū-tarā of the Tantras. When the "Sohar" declares that *the left side will have the upper hand and the unclean will be the strong, till the Holy God shall build the temple and establish the world; then will His Word meet with due honour, and the unclean side shall pass away from the earth*, it is the same conflict of the male with the female, that is yet current in modern Ritualism.

It is the English rule of the road in driving for each to take the left side, because that is the inferior hand, and thus each offers the place of honour to the other. The Toda Palal (priest), who has always used the right hand for the purpose of washing, when exalted to the divine office, always uses his left hand to wash his face and teeth on first rising in the morning.[1]

The left hand being first, the earliest progression was made from left to right. This was illustrated in the ceremonial of the "*Sabbath*" when the witches always went "Widdershins," *i.e.* from left to right in their circular dances, and thus represented the "backward way" of the moon which passes through the stellar heaven from west to east, contrariwise to the apparent diurnal motion. In the later Solar Cult this was reversed; the worshippers went "deasil," from right to left. The right hand had become foremost of the two.

As with the left hand, which is the inferior put first, so is it with the lower that preceded the upper, and—to take one illustrative custom—the lower is so sacredly the first with the natives near Lake Maro, that if a child cuts its upper teeth before the lower, it is killed as unlucky.[2] Captain Burton tells me the custom is common in Africa. A practice like this is unconsciously typical, and all such customs have unwittingly registered facts for the evolutionist.

Also as certain animals like the ass, the cock in the springtide pastimes, and others have suffered for the parts they once played in symbolism, so has it been with woman, as the widow, the step-mother, and others, who have been victimized on account of their typical characters in mythology, which reflected the pre-monogamous status of woman.

"*Don't have the mother-in-law to live in your house*," is a prevalent piece of advice at the time of marriage. Dislike to the mother-in-

[1] Marshall, *A Phrenologist among the Todas*, p. 141.
[2] Livingstone's *Last Journals*, i. 276.

law is cultivated by such sayings, independently of the person. The mother-in-law is thus a generalized character.

The Zulu Kaffirs have a custom which is termed being "*ashamed of the mother-in-law*," and the Kaffir and his mother-in-law are taught to avoid each other, not to look each other in the face when they meet, and not to repeat each other's names. Should they chance to pass each other, he will hide his blushes behind his shield, and she will seek the protection of a bush.[1]

This is current in Zululand, in Ashanti, and other parts of Africa. With the Beni Amer, the wife, as well as her husband, hides herself at the approach of the mother-in-law.[2] The custom belongs to the laws of Tabu. According to Richardson, when any of the Cree Indians live with the wife's parents after marriage, the etiquette of the family demands that the husband's mother-in-law must not speak to him nor even look at him.

Philander Prescott, writing of the Dacotahs, says he had heard of instances in which a violation of this law had been punished by stripping the offender piecemeal, and leaving him stark naked by casting every rag of clothing away.[3] This, too, would be a typical custom.

With the Arawaks of Guiana, it was unlawful for the son-in-law to look on the face of his mother-in-law. They were partitioned off from each other in the same house, and sat back to back in the same boat.[4]

Among the Australian Aborigines, the son-in-law must shun his mother-in-law, and she may not look on him. If they chance to meet he will hide behind his shield, and she will squat down in the bush-grass. If she is near her tribe when he goes by, they endeavour to screen her, but they do not mention his name. It is believed that if they were to look on each other, both would become old prematurely and die. This strict etiquette commences from the moment the female child is promised to the man, and belongs to the same class of ideas as that of the. *Liku* being presented by the future mother-in-law to the intended husband.[5] In the lowest castes of Hindus, however, the man sleeps with his mother-in-law until the promised bride comes of age.

There is an Indian story of the man who *looked on* his mother-in-law, or, in other phrase, made love to her, whereupon she threw a handful of ashes at him. These scarred his face for ever. The man was the lunar god. Hence when it is new moon he turns the burnt and blackened side of his face to us, and the blots are still to be seen. The custom had become typical, but there is a natural genesis beyond.

Certain rules of courtesy and etiquette look ridiculous to us, chiefly

[1] Wood, *Nat. History of Man*, "Africa," p. 87.   [2] Munzinger, p. 325.
[3] Schoolcraft, vol. ii. 196.   [4] Tylor, *Early History*, p. 285.
[5] Smyth, vol. i. pp. 95-96.

because they were so simple in their origin, but so sacred in their end and aim. So much is apparently made of so little. But we have to go back a long way to attain the true standpoint. When we learn that among the African Khoi-Khoi (or first men), the son-in-law was compelled to spend his earliest years, like Jacob, in the service of his father-in-law, and to be the *old man's* constant companion, we see at a glance why he was bound not to look on, or to have intercourse with his mother-in-law. One kind of intercourse was then interpreted by another, as a mode of memorizing the law.

Again, the highest oath that a man can take, and still takes, is to swear by his eldest sister; and if he should perjure himself in taking her name, she is allowed to carry off the finest cows or sheep from his flock.

Also, a man may not address his own sister personally. He must speak to another person who addresses her in his name: or, if no one else is present, he has to be overheard by her as he expresses a wish that somebody would tell his sister what he wants.[1] This looks as ludicrous as the sight of a dog scratching the air whilst some one is scratching him. Still the dog goes upon the ground of the real scratch, and the etiquette of the Hottentot is but the shadow of a primal reality.

We see in this custom a relic of the earliest code of morals as ancient as the time when incest was prohibited. The eldest sister can still inflict punishment on the grown-up brother who violates that traditional etiquette which now typifies the power of protecting her own person. It is noticeable that the Tamil "*Aunei*," for the mother, is honorifically the elder sister!

With the Veddas of Ceylon the brother might marry his younger sister, but was prohibited from taking the elder to wife. On the Isthmus of Darien the people have a tradition that the man in the moon was guilty of incest with his elder sister.

The Esquimaux likewise charge the man in the moon with an unnatural love for his sister who daubed his face over with mud to frighten him away. Thus the *sister* and the *mother-in-law* meet in the same myth.

The Chaldean Magi and the Thessalian Charmers are credited with the power of bringing down the moon to the earth. The Greenlanders told Egede, the missionary, that the moon frequently came down on a visit to their wives, who, on the occasion, were accustomed to anoint themselves with spittle. But what moon? That on which the feminine fertility depended; and when it did not descend, or rise, it was a part of the sorcerer's work to charm it and "*bring down the moon.*"

The Arabic saying that "*When a woman has a husband, she can*

[1] Hahn, *Tsuni-Goam*, pp. 18-21.

I 2

turn the moon round her little finger," goes to the root of the matter, and identifies the moon.

One of the most curious of all symbolical customs is known as the Basque Couvade, called by the French *faire la couvade*, or the act of hatching. In this we have another ceremony which survives when the clue to its origin and significance has been lost. Another of those enactments that belong to the system of a common typology, the key to which has been mislaid, as was that of the Egyptian hieroglyphics previously to the nineteenth century. The custom belongs to some of the most diverse races of the world. It has been found amongst the Iberians, Basques, Corsicans, Navarrese, West and other Africans, Caribs of Arawak, the Tamanacs, Abipones, Dyaks of Borneo, Tupis of Brazil, the people of West Yunnan in China, the Greenlanders, Indians of California, and other primitive or pre-Aryan races of men.

In performing the couvade the father takes the place of the mother ; goes to bed with the new-born child and "lies in" instead of the female.

The following account is given by Du Tertre of the Carib couvade in the West Indies :—

"When a child is born, the mother goes presently to her work, but the father begins to complain, and takes to his hammock, and there he is visited as though he were sick, and undergoes a course of dieting which would cure of the gout the most replete of Frenchmen. How they can fast so much and not die of it is amazing to me, for they sometimes pass the five first days without eating or drinking anything ; then up to the tenth they drink oüycou, which has about as much nourishment in it as beer. These ten days passed, they begin to eat cassava only, drinking oüycou, and abstain from everything else for the space of a whole month. During this time, however, they only eat the inside of the cassava, so that what is left is like the rim of a hat when the block has been taken out, and all these cassava rims they keep for the feast at the end of forty days, hanging them up in the house with a cord. When the forty days are up they invite their relations and best friends, who, being arrived, before they set to eating, hack the skin of the poor wretch with agouti teeth, and draw blood from all parts of his body, in such sort that from being sick by pure imagination they often make a real patient of him. This is, however, so to speak, only the fish, for now comes the sauce they prepare for him ; they take sixty or eighty large grains of pimento, or Indian pepper, the strongest they can get, and after well mashing it in water, they wash with this peppery infusion the wounds and scars of the poor fellow, who, I believe, suffers no less than if he were burnt alive ; however, he must not utter a single word if he will not pass for a coward and a wretch. This ceremony finished, they bring him back to his bed, where he remains some days more, and the rest go and make good cheer in the house at his expense. Nor is this all ; for through the space of six whole months he eats neither bird nor fish, firmly believing that this would injure the child's stomach, and that it would participate in the natural faults of the animals on which its father had fed ; for example, if the father ate turtle, the child would be deaf and have no brains like this animal ; if he ate manati, the child would have little round eyes like this creature, and so on with the rest."—Du Tertre, *Hist. Gén. des Antilles habitées par les Français*, Paris, 1667, vol. ii. p. 371, and fol. According to Rochefort's account the very severe fasting was *only for the first* child.—Tylor, *Early History of Mankind*, 3rd ed. p. 292.

Dr. Tylor's suggestion is that *" couvade"* shows the *" opinion that the connection between the father and child is not only, as we think, a mere relation of parentage, affection, and duty, but that their very bodies are joined by a physical bond ; so that what is done to the one acts directly on the other.*" If so, surely some of the parent's sufferings attending the ceremony were calculated to kill any number of children ; and this fact is fatal to the reason assigned for the one part of the performance which was intended to insure the safety and well-being of the child.

Bachofen suggested that the custom of *couvade* originated as a ceremony that was typical of a transfer in the line of descent from the motherhood to the individualised fatherhood, as if the male parent were performing an act symbolical of his superseding the female parentage. But *with the Macusis of Guiana, amongst others, the father and mother both lie in, and there is no transfer from the mother to the father.* So with the Arawacs. The act did *not* transfer the child to the father ;[1] they continued to trace the line of descent from the mother.

The custom shows that the parent identifies himself with the infant child. He takes no more nourishment than would keep a mere child alive, and this is limited at times to the most infantile food. If the child dies, it is because of some sin of omission or commission with which the father is chargeable. He has "*neglected to shave off his long eyebrows,*"[2] or he has handled metal, or injured his nails. For the Macusis of Guiana might not *scratch themselves with their own nails* (a type of pubescence), and a rib of the palm-leaf was hung up for use instead. An Abipone resisted the luxury of a pinch of snuff for fear it should make him sneeze and the sneeze bring some danger upon the child.[3]

When the child is born the father exhibits the offspring as his. He receives the congratulations of friends instead of the mother. The father not only takes the mother's place in bed with the child ; *He makes a typical transformation into the character of a child.* He becomes as a little child in his habits and diet before the child is born.

Among the Coroados as soon as the woman was known to be pregnant the strict regimen began and the man lived chiefly on fish and fruits ; his infantile diet. The men of the Caribi and Acawoid nations abstained from certain kinds of meat lest the expected child might be injured in some mysterious manner by the father's eating of them.[4]

Thus the father represents or *impersonates the child before birth* and religiously abstains from everything that could hurt an infant. He did also take the place of the mother, but the still more arresting phenomenon is found in his *becoming as the child.*

[1] Spix and Martius, *Travels in Brazil*, vol. ii. 247.
[2] Dobrizhoffer on the Abipones.   [3] Dobrizhoffer.
[4] Brett, *Indian Tribes of Guiana*, p. 355.

There is no modern meaning in the act itself; nothing rational; and no natural genesis will directly account for it. · It is done in violation of the natural law of nursing, whether animal or human, and must have been utterly humiliating to man unless dominated by some idea which protected him from ridicule and derision.

What then did the *couvade* mean symbolically, and what was the natural phenomenon in which the custom originated? The Kamite typology alone can tell us; and the present writer is prepared to stake the authenticity of his rendering of the primitive system of dramatic representation, with Egypt as the mouthpiece of Kam, on the truth of her interpretation of *couvade*.

The act of couvade is a ceremony typical of the transformation of the father into the child, which can be read by the doctrine of Khepr, the Scarab-god, who was the *creator by transformation*. Khepr signifies to create, but it also means to transform; and the name of couvade agrees with the Egyptian khep, to change and transform in giving birth to, or in hatching.

It is said in the Litany of Ra, " *Homage to thee, Ra, the beetle* (Khepr) *that folds his wings, that rests in the Empyrean, that is born as his own son.*"

One of the titles of Osiris, who changed into Horus of the Meskhen, the place of re-birth, is the "*old man who becomes young*"; and the word for this transformation is "*khepat.*" In the inscriptions, Khepr is designated "*the Scarabaeus which enters life as its own son.*"

Ptah, who was a form of Khepr-Ra, is addressed thus :—"*O God, architect of the world, thou art without a father, begotten by thine own becoming, thou art without a mother, being born through repetition of thyself.*"[1] In another text we read :—"*O divine Substance, created from itself. O God, who hath made the substance which is in him. O God, who hast made his own father and impregnated his own mother.*"[2]

"*To denote an Only Begotten,*" says Hor-Apollo, "*the Egyptians delineate a Scarabaeus, because the Scarabaeus is a creature self-produced, being unconceived by a female. The Scarabaeus also symbolises generation and a father, because it is engendered by the father solely.*"[3] And in the Egyptian mythology Khepr, the beetle whose name means the transformer, makes his transformation into his own son. In the Ritual[4] the re-born spirit makes the transformation of Khepr in its manifestation to light or re-birth in the likeness of the young sun-god. *Khepr, the beetle, buried himself, with his seed, in the earth, there he transformed, and the father issued forth as the son.* In the *couvade* the beetle's proceeding is imitated in all simplicity.

Doubtless the act of Couvade did imply an attempt to individualise the ancestral spirit believed in before it could be personally

[1] Text cited by Renouf, *Hibbert Lectures*, p. 222.
[2] From a papyrus rendered by M. Chabas.
[3] B i. 10.   [4] Ch. lxiv.

recognised, and was a mode of fathering the child, and demonstrating the line of continuity and renewal by the transformation of the parent into his own child. So far Bachofen's suggestion was right. It belonged to a very primitive interpretation of phenomena. The act of couvade was a representation of the creative process, not by the father incarnating himself in his seed, but as transforming into his own seed or other self, like the beetle, said to procreate without the female. It was the transformation of that which was recognised as the *ancestral spirit* before the individual fatherhood was known! Also, the father's sufferings, which far exceeded those of a mother, were probably intended to do so in proof that he was worthy of being reckoned as the parent of the child. How faithfully the drama was represented and the typology preserved intact may be seen in the Carib Couvade, in which, *for six months*, the father ate neither fish nor fowl, the two images of the two truths of air and water.

" *They say also that the beetle lives six months under ground and six above.*" [1] That is as a solar symbol representative of the sun in the six lower and six upper signs. Hor-Apollo also describes Khepr as a lunar type, and observes : " *The beetle deposits its ball in the earth for the space of twenty-eight days ; for in that number of days the moon passes through the twelve signs of the zodiac.*" This would correspond to the lying-in or abstinence from certain food for *one month*.

On the nine-and-twentieth day—the day of the creation and re-creation of the world—occurs the baptism of the beetle. Khepr casts his ball into the water, where it opens, and the young beetles issue forth ; the old Scarab being renewed in its young by this act of immersion or regeneration. [2]

Khepr was said to form his own body continually [3] from self-originated substance, and the father acts as if he were the gestator and bringer-forth of the child before the time of lying-in ; as if he too were the former of his own future body. Taht, the lunar god, is called the "self-created," "never-born."

Every time the sun was represented as lying-in, and transforming, he performed the *couvade* annually as the " *Great Cat which is in Annu,*" the solar birthplace, where the father was reproduced by the cat as his own son.

The father had to *cut off his long eyebrows.* This cutting of the hair was also typical. The non-virile Ptah was depicted bald-headed, as the pigmy or child who represented the fire of the sun in its dwarfage. So the god Tum, in his resurrection, makes the transformation into his *anbu*, his *eyelashes* (or eyebrows). [4] The long eyebrows answer perfectly to the horns of the Scarabaeus, on which such stress is laid in the Ritual.

The forty days are identical with the forty days of suffering found

---

[1] Clement Alexander, *Strom.* 5.   [2] B. i. 10.
[3] Rit. ch. xvii.   [4] Lepsius, *Todenbuch*, lxxviii. 12.

in many myths, including the forty days of Lent, the forty days of (comparative) fasting in the solar drama. Forty days was the period of seclusion after childbirth appointed for the woman by the Parsee and Levitical Law.[1] So in the transformation of Apis, when the old bull died, its successor remained during forty days shut up in an island of the Nile. This, too, was a form of the *couvade;* the bull, or beetle, or the sun which they both typified, did not die, but was changed, the old into the young one. The father was a follower of the suffering sun-god, and the *scoring* of his back answers to the cutting in pieces of Ptah, or the dismemberment of Osiris. *Sekari* is the title of the suffering Ptah, and *sekar* means to cut; cut in pieces; *sacrifice;* or, as we have the word in English, to *score* and scarify.

Couvade can be explained, then, by the doctrines of the solar drama. But the beetle type of transformation was lunar first, and the lunar transformation and renewal were the earliest observed and imitated.

The natural genesis of the doctrine is visible in the lunar phase, where the parental moon (as male) is seen to reproduce itself as the young one. In the solar phase it had become symbolical.

Couvade goes back to the time of the mother and child before the individual fatherhood was ascertained, and the Hottentots have the myth of the virgin mother and her self-begetting babe in the most primitive form. The deity of the Hottentots, Heitsi-eibib, is Lunar. He was the transformer and renewer, like a tree; the tree being his especial type instead of the beetle or cat.

Heitsi-eibib is the young moon-god who is born without the fatherhood. In one account of his birth it is said there was grass growing, and a cow came and ate of the grass, and she grew pregnant, and brought forth a young bull. In another version the young girls went out to fetch fire-wood, and one girl took a *hobe-ga* (a juicy kind of sweetish grass), chewed it, and swallowed the juice; and she became pregnant from this juice, and was delivered of a son, who was very clever, and she called that boy Heitsi-eibib, and all the other young women came and helped her to nurse the boy.

Once on a time, when the mother and her friends were travelling, he was very naughty and fretful, so that his mother had to stop whilst her friends went on. Again he was naughty and dirty, and detained his mother until at length her friends were out of sight. Then all of a sudden he became a big man, and forced his mother to the ground and committed incest. (In Khoi-Khoi the word is Xai-si, *cum matre coïit.*) Then he transformed into a baby once more, and when she came to *her* mother, she put him down on the ground and took no notice of him. At last her mother said, "*Don't you hear your*

---

[1] *Shayast La-Shayast,* ch. iii. 15 ; *Levit.* ch. xv. 19.

child crying ?"   The daughter replied, "*I hear; but let big men help themselves as big men do.*"[1]

This is the myth according to naked nature, and to naked nature we must go to read it.   Nor does it contain any irrational element when once it is fathomed in phenomena.   The irrational or insane element is introduced only when the mythical is assumed to be historical and human.

In this myth Heitsi-eibib personifies the male moon.   As a child his mother carries him on her back in the Hottentot fashion. The moon reproduces itself visibly, but the first part of the re-begettal is out of view.   It occurs when the friends of the mother are all gone out of sight.   He is said to throw her down to commit the rape on her.

In the Ritual the lunar goddess or mother of the moon describes this re-begettal on herself.   She say, "*I have prepared Taht at the gate of the moon,*" i.e., the young moon-god who, in the Khoi-khoi myth, is Heitsi-eibib.   Previously she has said, "*I kiss, I embrace him, I come to him, I have fallen down with him in the Eastern Valley.*"   "*I have united Sut* (the Child) *in the upper houses, through the old man with him.*"   "*I have brought my orb to darkness, it is changed to light.*"[2]

As the genitrix preceded the fatherhood in mythology, the first mother is the Virgin Mother, and the god or child begotten of her is self-begotten.

The Moon in Egypt, as Taht, was male, and the male Moon, transforming into the child, affords a natural genesis for couvade. From the origin in lunar phenomena, the type of the male child renewing himself was evolved as in "Heitsi-eibib."   It was applied to Sut, Shu, Ptah, but especially to Horus, who is pourtrayed with the god Bes standing behind him.   This representation shows us the "old man who becomes young," and the custom of couvade offers the best interpretation of the meaning of that group in which the grinning jolly Bes acts the part of the male gestator or reproducer of the child by transformation.   The word Bes signifies to change from one to the other.

Bes was a great favourite with Egyptian women as an ornament to the toilet-table, and a symbolic figure at the head of their beds.   My conclusion is, that his wide-legged pose, his protruding tongue, and *parturient* expression (cf. *Bis*, Sans. to split ; *Bishkala*, parturient), are intended to pourtray the bringing forth of the child ; as the old one who becomes young.

The particular transformation signified by the Bes-Horus group is that of the Elder Horus into the youthful Virile one, at puberty, and therefore only typical.

In Egypt the doctrine appears midway between the primitive nature of the Hottentot myth, and its culmination in the christology

---

[1] Hahn, *Tsuni-Goam*, p. 69.   [2] Ch. lxxx.

of Rome. A theosophical doctrine like that of the Virgin Mother and the Child-Christ, as commonly accepted, can find no explanation in science, and has no foundation in human nature. It must be referred back to the mythical origines to be understood for the first time, by the aid of known phenomena. In its latest inexplicable phase it becomes a part of the grossest superstition the world has ever seen.

It is in accordance with the natural and mythological origin here suggested, that in Germany similar superstitions cluster around the godfather, who partially plays the part of the father in the couvade. "*It is believed that the habits and proceedings of the godfather and godmother affect the child's life and character. Particularly the godfather at the christening must not think of disease or madness lest this come upon the child; he must not look round on the way to the church lest the child should grow up an idle stare-about; nor must he carry a knife about him for fear of making the child a suicide; the godmother must put on a clean shift to go to the baptism or the baby will grow up untidy.*"[1]

Not until we have penetrated to this depth in an artesian attempt to bore to the bottom, do we get at the origin of religious doctrines into which far other meanings have been interfused. Here we find the indefinitely earlier form of the *only-begotten Son,* and the real origin and primæval illustration of attaining eternal life by *conversion*—the later name for transformation—"*into a little child.*" In the *couvade* that conversion was religiously enacted, with a pathetic childlikeness, by the male performing the two characters of the child and the pubescent male, as well as that of the mother, and thus representing a trinity in unity, which became the later theological mystery.

The wonder is not that the father and husband was made to suffer so much in the "*couvade,*" but that he was not altogether effaced. The old moon or sun never emerged again from its lying-in, except in the regenerated shape of its own child; and some approximation even to this phase of utter effacement and extinction appears to have been attempted, and may be at the root of other primitive customs.

The *Bechuanas* in public orations call themselves sons of the late king.[2]

The passing away of the father would be actually realized by the arrangement of the Andaman Islanders, in which the father and mother remained together until the child was weaned, when they separated as a matter of course, and each sought a new partner.[3]

In the celestial allegory the son preceded the father as bull of the mother, and the boy became the husband of his own mother.

---

[1] Tylor, *Early History*, p. 304, 3rd ed.   [2] Spencer, A. R. table 21.
[3] Belcher, *Trans. Ethn. Society*, vol. v. p. 45.

And amongst the Reddies of Southern India, there was a singular custom that may have realized this mythical relationship of the child-husband to the mother. With them a young woman is married to a boy of five or six years of age. But the marriage is consummated by her living with some adult male, it may be with the boy-husband's own father, who begets the children which are fathered on the boy. When the boy himself grows up, he in turn takes up with some other boy's wife, and procreates children for another boy-husband.[1]

The priority and supremacy of the son which is reflected in the mirror of Egyptian mythology was acknowledged in Tahiti, where the monarch abdicated so soon as a son was born to him. The son became as it were the husband of the mother. Under the same system the land-owners lost the fee-simple of their land and were turned into trustees for their own sons, who became the actual possessors.[2]

In Sumatra the father is called Pa-*Rindu* (from *Bapa*, the father of), the father of the child, which, as the nursling, is in Egyptian the *Renn*. Also it is the first child, the Renn, that he is named after : he himself was the second or grown-up form of the child, the *Renpu* of the mythos. So Khem-Horus is the secondary form of the child Horus.

It followed from the social condition that the father should be called *after* the child, which was first named after the mother. In Australia, when a man's eldest child was named, the father and mother both were called *after* the child, and took their place in the rear of it. The child being named Kadli, *Penna* the father (*Penna*, man), becomes *Kadlitpenna*, the man of the child ; the mother (from *Ngangki*, the female, as woman) becomes *Kadlingangki*, the woman of the child.

This pre-eminence of the son is shown by the Egyptian titles of "*Atef-nuter*," the father of the Divine One, and "Mut-Suten," mother of the king, the Suten being named from *Sut*, the child. The son was the great male divinity and type before the fatherhood was established. Here the boy precedes the father as the husband of the mother ; he grows up to become the later father, as did Sut and Shu in the Stellar, and Sevekh or Khem-Horus in the Solar mythos. In such wise the Inner African origines which passed out over the world as natural customs, were enshrined for ever in the Kamite typology.

It has been shown how the most ancient customs practised in common by different races may be a guide to the pre-historic past where language fails to lead us farther. Symbolic customs and usages are among the oldest data extant, and the more primitive

[1] Shortt, *Trans. Ethn. Society*, N. S. vol. vii. p. 194.
[2] Ellis, *Polynesian Researches*, vol. ii. pp. 346—7.

of these preserve the most fundamental human relationship and speak of a unity of origin in a kind of universal tongue.

The primordial customs, usages, ceremonies, and other modes of thought and expression still survive in Inner Africa, where they have been continued because never outgrown by culture and development.

Fish were considered an abomination by the ancient Egyptians, who did not use them as an article of diet. So is it with the Somali and other Africans. The Kaffirs to this day eat no kind of fish, and call them all snakes without distinction.[1]

The Stone Age of the Hottentots, or "Khoi-Khoi," is proved to have existed by the fact that their priests preserve and still use the sacred stone knife made of a sharp shard of quartz. This is employed in the rite of young-man-making, and in the sacrifice of animals offered to the manes or the gods.[2] The Bongos of Abyssinia yet employ flint chips as their fleams for bleeding, just as the Egyptians preserved the stone knife for embalming. It is a strict injunction in the rubric of the Ritual that the 100th chapter should be *painted* with the point *of a graver of green felspar* (with yellow colour). The incisor of hard, green stone, the *Uat*, being sacredly used in the later painting, as it had been and because it had been in scraping and cutting the stone and bone. *Wampum of cockle-shell was found in the bone-cave at Aurignac (in the year* 1842), *along with the bones of the mammoth and other giant mammals of the Quaternary epoch.* And wampum, the common wear, in what Burton terms the pre-historic adornment, is still extant in South Africa, consisting of shells ground down into small thin disks for threading.

It was a practice in the old Stone Age of Europe, as revealed by the bone-caves, to bury the dead in a sitting posture, and in obvious imitation of the fœtus folded in the mother's womb. This was a custom of the Tasmanians, who placed the corpse in the hollow tree (for a coffin) in a sitting posture, with the knees drawn up to the chin. The custom has been universal. The type is extant in the Peruvian mummy, and Nature herself suggests the primary model.

The Hottentots, Bongos, Kaffirs, Bechuanas, and Baris, amongst others, still bury their dead according to this likeness of the embryo in the uterus. Explorers of Inner Africa have not yet got to work with the mattock and spade; when they do, a custom like this ought to yield up some valuable relics of the pre-historic past.[3]

---

[1] Theal, *Kaffir Folk-lore*, p. 16. [2] Hahn, *Tsuni-Goam*, p. 22.

[3] It was recently reported from South Africa that in making the "*Umgeni*" cutting (through red loam, gravel, and limestone rock), at fourteen feet from the surface, from which a dense forest had been previously cleared, the navvies came upon the remains of a fire, charred sticks, &c., in the red loam. Close by the engineer found what he describes as a well-made and beautifully-finished flint adze head, the cutting-face sloping from one corner to the other, with a bevelled edge like a chisel, and the other end finished off with a round flat knob. Again, at forty feet from the surface, in the hard gravel, he found a *good many* flint instruments, the two most remarkable ones being a round stone, about the size of a large orange, very much

It is certain that this was the intention in burial, because the tomb and womb are identical under various names.

Some of the large mounds left in Mississippi were called "*navels*" by the Chickasaws, although the Indians are said not to have had any idea whether these were natural mounds or artificial structures. They thought Mississippi was at *the centre of the earth*, and the mounds were as the navel in the middle of the human body.[1] Navel, belly, and uterus, are synonymous in the pre-historic languages. An Egyptian name of the navel, as *Khepa*, is also the name of the womb, the concealed place, the secret intimate abode, the sanctuary. The tomb being founded on the womb will account for these mounds as burial-places being identified as navels. The navel is a type of the birthplace, and a sign of breath, which in Egyptian is Nef; the gestator and breather of life being personified in Neft (Nephthys in the Greek).

Nyefe	is	the belly,	in Bulanda.	*Nufuo*	is	the female breast, Ashante.		
Nefo	,,	,,	,, Alege.	*Nafo*	,,	navel in the Avesta.		
Navvo	,,	navel	,, Ankaras.	*Nape*	,,	,, in Lap.		
Navvo	,,	,,	,, Wun.	*Napa*	,,	,, ,, Finnic.		
Navva	,,	belly	,, Wun.	*Nabba*	,,	,, ,, Esthonian.		
Neben	,,	female breast,	Mbofon.	*Nabhi*	,,	,, ,, Sanskrit.		
Nipele	,,	,,	,, Meto.	*Napoi*	,,	belly ,, Andaman.		
Nibele	,,	,,	,, Matatan.	*Nubo*	,,	,, ,, Musu.		

The Osirian, speaking as a re-born spirit, says, the "Gods rejoice when they see him coming forth from the womb, *born of his mother*."[2] That was from the mount of the horizon, called the "Tser Hill." Anup, the Psychopompus, is called chief of the mountain in which the dead were laid.

An Egyptian formula for the living and the dead is literally those who are on earth and *on the mountain*. The mountain being a solid figure of the celestial dome and breathing-place above, as well as a type of the mount that is still known as the *mons veneris*.

We shall find that the Great Mother was represented by the natural mount, the earliest burial-place. Next, the mounds were reared as artificial mounts, places of re-birth, wombs, or navels, or both in one, as is the Hindu image, called the Nabhi-yoni, or female umbilicus. The mound then, identified with navel, is further identified as an enormous swelling Nabhi-yoni. And such, it may be suggested, was the Nebbi-yunus, one of the two great mounds opposite Mosul, called Jonah's Tomb, figured as a mound instead of the vast Hindu

flattened at each pole, with a three-quarter-inch hole drilled through it, and by the side of it a stone handle seven or eight inches long, one end just fitting through the hole, and the other end rounded off; when put together it had the appearance of a small stone-mason's mallet. At a short distance from this was a stone quoit, almost exactly like the iron ones at present in use, except that, from where the indentation for the thumb is, the circle was cut straight across, for about a quarter of the circumference, by a round handle. . . . (*Knowledge*, June 23, 1882). (A page of the remotest past is missing in Africa generally in consequence of the lack of flints).

[1] Schoolcraft, i. 311.   [2] Ch. lxxix.

umbilicus of stone. "*Omphale gês,*" the navel of the earth, was a Greek designation of Delphi. The *Nafedhrô apâm,* or umbilicus of the waters, is the sacred mount of the Avesta; the Alborz of the Bundahish, the breathing-place that rose up out of the Abyssal Sea. The original birthplace of mankind was thus externalized on a vast scale.

We have the navel mound in Britain by name, as the *Knap* Hill, the mount, or a rising ground. There is a Knap Hill about three miles from Silbury Hill.

This mother-mould of the beginning, the base of all building, has been continued up to the present time. The *nave* still shows the church to be a navel-mound, the swelling image of the procreant mother. "Beloved of the Adytum, come to *Kha,*" exclaims Nephthys, to Osiris, the "fructifying bull." Kha is represented by the vagina[1] emblem, the entrance or porch; the womb was the adytum, argha, nave, or lady chapel; the holy of holies in Egyptian temples. This may account for the custom of the marriage ceremony being commenced in the porch, and concluded within the body of the church.

The Navel was not the sole feminine type of the Hill. The Pap and Mammæ were also applied. This will account for the "Mam" —as in "Mam-Tor"—a breast-shaped hill. Nipple and Navel are two forms of the same name; and the types are interchangeable. In Africa the womb or belly is the *Memba* in Nyamban, and *Mimba* in Marawi. So the "Tut" hill is identical with the *Teat* and the Hieroglyphic △ mammæ or teat-sign of the female, which is still extant as the letter D. The Hill, as burial-mound, was the uterus of Mother-Earth within; her navel or mammæ without; and the interchange of types will also account for the teat or τιτις being the Yoni in Greek.

The Vase is another identifiable type. This was found in the Mound or Mount of Hissarlik as a vase with breasts. The pot, or Vase, typified the mother's womb. *Menka* (Eg.) is the vase and the Genitrix, hence the vase with female breasts. The type was continued in the Roman catacombs, when it had passed into the vessel of glass. The vase was personified in Europe as the woman-figure offering her womb, or emblem, in the shape of a vase, in a pitiably pathetic manner.[2] The vase was an important and prominent symbol in the Aztec and Maya mythologies. The Yumanas, also the Tupis, were accustomed to bury their dead doubled up in an earthen pot.

The mound-builders were far advanced in the art of pottery. Some of their work has been found perfect as that of the ancient Peruvians. An urn holding forty-six quarts was dug up near Harrison Mound, in South Carolina, which had been buried with a quantity of beads,[3] just

---

[1] "Lamentations of Isis and Nephthys."—*Records,* vol. ii. p. 123.
[2] Plates in *The Worship of the Generative Powers.*
[3] Baldwin, *Ancient America,* p. 24.

as the beads were entombed with Egyptian mummies; the beads of Isis, a symbol of gestation and reproduction. In the Bongo burial the vase or pitcher is placed on the summit of the cairn of stones erected over the grave.

The genesis and development of the coffin or shell is an interesting study. The mother's womb was the natural type for the Palæolithic cave, or the navel-mound. This was continued in the vase with female breasts. The tree was the earliest coffin of wood. The Scottish Cos, a hollow tree, agrees with the Kas (Eg.), for the coffin, which was followed by the Kist (chest) or family Ark for the bones. The link between the domestic bone-ark and the hearse was extant in certain Scottish villages not long since as a general burial-chest.

It was stated in the Paris *Moniteur*, during the month of January, 1865, that in the province of Venice, Italy, excavations of a bone-cave were made, and bones of animals, chiefly post-tertiary, were found together with flint implements, a needle of bone, having both eye and point, and a plate of an argillaceous compound, on which was scratched a rude figure of the male organ of generation ; and that these things were dug from *beneath ten feet of stalagmite*. That emblem was a type of resurrection, formed on the most natural grounds. According to the Gnosis, this rude figure had the same significance, denoting a place of burial for those who expected to rise again, and its image in the tomb can be read by the Egyptian " *Litany of Ra* " (34). " *Homage to thee, Ra! supreme power, the ray of light in the sarcophagus! Its form is that of the progenitor.*"

The self-erecting member was the type of resurrection, as the image of Khem-Horus, the re-arising sun, and of Khepr-Ra, the re-erector of the dead. The widows of the aborigines of Australia are in the habit of wearing the dead husband's phallus round their necks, and the significance of the custom is the same as in Egypt and the bone-caves. The emblem was sacred as the type of reproduction. The same type was worn as an ear-drop by the ladies of Latium, and is yet worn in southern Italy.

"*Images of pollution have been found at Hissarlik,*" exclaims the author of *Juventus Mundi,* and the voice of the primitive consciousness says the phallus typified the earliest ray of light that penetrated the darkness of the grave ; indeed this primitive type is found in a fourfold form in the Christian iconography of the Roman catacombs.[1]

The branch of palm has now taken its place in the imagery of heaven and the typology of the eternal. In the Book of Revelation those who stand before the throne are pourtrayed with palms in their hands. Horus is represented in the monuments as defending himself against his evil enemy, Sut, or Satan, with a palm-branch in his hand. The branch of palm was, and still is, an emblem of renewal. But

[1] *Vide* Drawing in Section vii.

the branch of birch that was buried with the dead in the barrows had the same meaning. A barrow at Kepwick was found to be lined with the bark and branches of the birch. That is the *Bedwen* of the British, which was also the maypole and the phallus. The Bedwen was typical of resurrection equally with the palm.

As already shown, the beetle type of Khepr, the transformer, was also buried with the dead in Britain as it was in Egypt. Beads were likewise buried with the British dead as they are with the Africans, and with Egyptian mummies. As these were imperishable it should be noticed that a kind of bead which is made in Africa has been found buried in Britain. Beads denote reproduction, and were worn by the genitrix Isis when *enceinte*, as the beads and *berries* are worn by pregnant women in Africa to-day. Beads in the tomb typified re-birth, whether in Africa, America, Australia, or Britain. The *Glainiau Nadredd* of the Welsh were the serpent beads which symbolized renewal; the Glains, as the bard Meilyr tells us, represented a resurrection.

In the Ritual, Ptah is the re-clother of the soul of the deceased *in flesh*, or, as it is said in the 64th chapter, "*I have made the dress which Ptah has woven out of his clay.*" The god himself tells Rameses II. that he has re-fashioned his flesh in *vermilion*.[1] That is, the red clay which represented the flesh.

"*Having had my flesh embalmed,*" says the Osirified deceased, "*my body does not decay;*" and the bones were coated with the red earth long before the body could have been embalmed. Ptah's dress of clay was imitated in the rudest mode of embalming the bones of the dead in the red earth used by the Maori, the Australian aborigines, the North American Indians, and the mound-builders in Britain, at Caithness.

Now, all the conditions for the natural genesis of this custom meet in Africa, and in that land alone did it *culminate* in a supreme art of embalmment. The red earth was used there to preserve the dead, because it was first necessary to protect the live flesh from the fury of the sun. The red Indian, the black Australian, and the palæolithic Briton had no such need of protection from the solar fire.

From beginning to end the custom is traceable in Africa to-day. The Kaffirs still cover their living bodies with an ointment of fat and red clay, which makes them shine like statues of polished bronze.[2] The practice of the living was applied to the dead, and is still continued by the Bushmen, who anoint the head of the corpse with grease and red powder, and embalm their dead as rudely as did the Inner Africans (or the men of the mounds) ages before the Kamites of the Nile Valley had developed the natural custom into an art of absolute perfection.

The practice survives in the Maori Hahunga, (named from *Hahu*,

---

[1] Inscription of Abu Simbel, line 9.   [2] Theal, *Kaffir Folk-Lore*, p. 12.

to disinter the bones of the dead, and remove them to their last resting-place), in which the bones of the deceased chief are taken up and scraped clean. They are then re-fleshed, as it were, with a coating of red earth, wrapped in a red-stained mat, and placed in a box or a bowl smeared with the sacred colour, and deposited in a painted tomb.[1]

The Australian black warriors are anointed with grease and embalmed or ornamented with red-ochre. The corpse is then doubled up, and tightly wrapped in the opossum-rug, like the Bongo, Bari, or Bechuana of Africa.

After the body has lain in the ground for some months it is disinterred, the bones are scraped and cleaned, and packed in a roll of pliable bark. This is painted and ornamented *with strings of beads*. It is then called "*Ngobera*," and is kept in camp with the living. It had undergone a transformation which, in Egyptian, is denoted by *Khepra*.

And just as the Egyptians had their mummy image carried round at the banquet as a type of *Khepra*, a reminder of immortality, so the *Ngobera* is still brought forth by the Australians into the midst of the domestic circle at the gathering of relatives and friends.[2] The custom and mode are indefinitely older than embalment in Egypt, and these have persisted both in Inner Africa and Australia, all through the ages during which the long procession of Egyptian civilisation was slowly filing past. The typology is the same, and the *Ngobera* is identical, even by name, with the Egyptian *Khepra* (Ptah), the transformer, the divinity who re-fleshes the dead with his red clay.

The strings of beads correspond to the network of beads with which Egyptian mummies were wrapped as the symbol of the Net that recovered Horus or Osiris from the waters of the Nile; the beads that were worn by Isis, during gestation, in the Collar containing nine in number.

The bones of the dead were buried in the ancient British middens after they had been rudely embalmed and preserved in red earth and sea-shells. An old name of the English midden is a *Miskin*; the *Muschna*, a heap or pile in the Grisons. Now the *Meskhen* is the Egyptian place of burial and re-birth, and the typology of the burial customs shows that the dead were buried for their re-birth.

Further, in the eschatological phase, the *Meskhen* became the place of re-birth for the soul. It was the Egyptian Purgatory, and the Irish have the Miskhen as the Purgatory.

In the comical *Pilgrims' Pilgrimage into Ireland*, it is said, "An *Ignis fatuus* the silly people deem to be a soul broken out of Purgatory;" and in a *Wonderful History* (1704) we are told that in superstitious times the Popish Clergy persuaded the ignorant people

[1] Taylor, *New Zealand*, p. 95.   [2] Smyth.

that the "Will-o'-the-Wisps" were *souls come out of Purgatory all in flame,* to move the people to pray for their entire deliverance.[1]

In Ireland the "Will-o'-the-Wisp" is known as "*Miscanne Many,*" as may be seen by an allusion in the story of Morty Sullivan and the Spirit-Horse in Croker's *Fairy Legends of the South of Ireland.* "*Man*-in-the-Oak" is an English name for the *Ignis fatuus,* and *Miscanne* repeats the Egyptian *Meskhen,* which *is the name of the Purgatory,* as the place of burial and re-birth for the Stars, the Sun, and the Souls, in the region of the under-world.

The Inner African mode of burying the dead wrapped up in the skin of an animal is identical with that of a remote age in the British Isles. General Sir J. Alexander has described the most ancient woman in Scotland who had been buried deep in a bog, and was well-preserved in a deer skin. The Bongos and Bechuanas still wrap their dead in a cow's skin.[2]

The ritual and hieroglyphics of the Egyptians contain the typology of the skin. The *Nem* (skin) means repetition, to renew, a second time or form.

The deceased whose body has been laid aside, says to the God, "*Thou makest to me a skin,*" and "*I make to Thee a skin, my soul.*"[3] This part of the ritual is especially Inner African. It comes from the land of Kens or Nubia.

The skin was of course a preservative in itself. But the deer-skin goes with the deer's horn as a type of renewal, and so the natural image of preservation becomes symbolical.

It has often been a subject of wonder why the men of the Neolithic age should have buried the axes and other amulets of green stone, the polished jade, with their dead. The custom was Kamite; and if the Egyptians had no jade for the purpose, they had other green stones called Uat. We read again, in the Ritual, "*I have said the opposite of evil. I have done what they* (the wicked) *could not when I was* (or when I represented) *the amulet of green jasper protecting the throat of the Sun.*"[4]

This is in the chapter of propitiating the *Ka,* or double of a person, in the spirit world.

In the "Hall of Two Truths," the Egyptian judgment hall, the reason for this custom was explained. It is said in the 125th chapter of the Ritual, "*Explain to him* (the deceased) *why thou hast made for him the amulet* (handle) *of green stone after thou buriest him.*" And it must be admitted that they are the right authorities to consult in such mystical matters, who *can* explain them.

The axe of the Stone Age was Egypt's especial emblem of power

[1] Brand, *Will-with-a-Wisp.* It likewise looks as if the Egyptian *Mammesi* another name for the place of burial and re-birth of the Mam (Mummy), had survived by name in the Gaelic *Mamsie,* a tumulus.
[2] See *Book of Beginnings,* vol. ii. p. 664.
[3] *Rit.* ch. clxvi.   [4] *Ibid.* ch. cv.

and divinity, the type of founding by opening the ground, making a passage, and therefore appropriate to the buried dead, as another image of resurrection. Axes of green stone were also buried in the ancient mounds of Japan, and an emerald was made the base or heart of the Aztec mummy.[1]

The custom has its representative likeness in the most mystical parts of the Book of the Dead. In the chapter said over a tablet of Felspar, the speaker personates the green stone called *Uat*, our Jade, and says, "*I am the Felspar tablet. It hates all injury. It is well; I am well. It is not injured; I am not injured. It is not scraped; I am not scraped.*"[2]

It was a type of duration impenetrable to the tooth of time and corrosion of decay, that also retained its polish.

And again, in the same paragraph, it is said of the mummy awaiting its re-erection: "*Shu has walked to him under the name of Felspar,*" or Uat. Shu is the god of breath and soul; and here it should be remembered, the parturient "*Bes*" is a form of Shu. Also, as the god in green, the colour of reproduction from the under-world, Shu is the heaven-bringer. But the god and the soul are not only represented by the green stone; according to the idiomatic mode of expression they impersonate it; IT was them. The green stone therefore was not only the symbol of divinity in general, but of the god of breath, soul, and reproduction (like the green things) *from the under-world*. This chapter was placed at the throat (breathing place) of the mummy; and the green stone was one of the amulets worn by the dead.[3]

Long before the axe of jade could have been cut and polished for a type, the flake of flint, the stone, or deer's horn, and the typical branch served the same purpose.

These talismanic tokens buried with the dead were emblematic of preservation, continuity, and renewal; stone, bone, and horn being types of permanence. As Hor-Apollo says, the symbol of the stag's horn signifies *duration*.[4] The symbol of bone denoted permanence and safety.[5]

If the rite were only prompted by mere desire for the continuity of the dead, the living who buried these types of power and stability were already founding for another life by putting, as it were, a bottom into the grave; a physical foothold. For this purpose a shard of pottery was as good a type of duration as the stone of power. And so many of the ancient British barrows are found to have been strewn with shards of pottery along with flint stones; a shard of pottery being equivalent to a flake of felspar. This mode of interment with "shards, flints, and pebbles" is recognised by Shakspeare

---

[1] *Book of Beginnings*, vol. i. pp. 93—4.
[2] *Rit.* ch. clxi. Birch. [3] *Rit.* ch clxi.
[4] B. ii. 21. [5] B. ii. 10.

as non-Christian, and therefore a pagan form of burial, reserved for suicides.[1]

Such primitive customs are like the actions of the dumb, or gesture-signs addressed to the eye, that preceded speech for the ear.

The axe of Anup the Opener was continued in the stone *purgatory Hammers* of the Irish, with which the dead were supposed to knock at the portals to get free passage through.

The Hair brought by Anup (the Dog) for his work of embalment is alluded to in the *Ritual*.[2] He was the hairy god of the Dog-star, and of the planet Mercury, who came for the dying, and conducted the dead through the darkness of the nether-world; and here the hair, which is another type of reproduction, is used by him in the work of embalment—the preparation for the resurrection. That is, so to say, the hair of the dog of Death is employed in the restoration to life and health. This offers good ground for the origin of the belief in the efficacy of a hair of the dog that bites you.

In the Edda (Havamal, 138), it is said "*Dog's hair heals Dog's bite.*" This was a faith so firmly founded in Britain that a few years since a woman of Oldham prosecuted the owner of a dog which had bitten her. She said she would not have done so if the owner of the animal had given her some of its hair to protect her against any evil consequences from the bite.[3] Hair as the sign of *reproduction* will explain the custom of cutting it from the tail of a weanling calf and stuffing it into the ear of the cow from which the young one had been taken: an action emblematic of future production (of milk, or young) which may be paralleled in the human domain by the practice of inserting the bones of young children into the skulls of the adult dead, as they are found in the caves of France. The same primitive phase of thought is exemplified by the Hottentot hunter, who if he has wounded game without causing immediate death, will, as the lamed animal limps off, take up a handful of sand from its footprints, to throw into the air and bring it down by this obliteration of its track.

It is an English superstition that hair when cut off or combed out should be buried, never burned, because of a tradition that the owner will come and search for it at the time of the resurrection! The hair being a type of pubescence and reproduction is the same here as the hair of Anup, or the tuft worn on the chin of the mummy by *both male and female* alike, as an emblem of the rising again, or re-erection in the next life. Tradition and custom preserve the typology intact.

The Bongos, as remarked in the previous volume, continue to bury their dead in a symbolic fashion, which they themselves do not understand. The male and female are interred with their faces turned in opposite directions; the male facing the north, the female the south. And in the Egyptian typology the south is the front of

[1] *Hamlet*, A. v. S. 1.   [2] Ch. xc.
[3] *Notes and Queries*, vol. v. p. 581.

heaven, the male being before, and the north is behind, the female being considered the hind part. Hor-Apollo tells us that when the Egyptians would denote an amulet, they pourtray two human heads, one of a male looking inwards the other of a female looking outwards. This is a type of protection, for they say that no demon will molest any person thus guárded. Without inscriptions they protect themselves with the two heads.[1] Here the typology is identical with that of the Bongo burial, and explains it. So the Dayaks will make the rude figures of a naked man and woman and set them face to face with each other on the way leading to their farms as a mode of protection against evil influences.[2]

The Hottentots, the Bongos, and other African tribes still raise the same memorial mounds of stones over their dead, or above the grave of their god (or chief), who rises again, as did the earliest cairn-makers of the remotest past. The nearest likeness to the British long-horned cairns, is extant in the long cairns of the Hottentots, one of which was seen by Alexander in a cleft between two eminences. This was a heap of stones eight yards long by one and a-half high. And these "*Heitsi-Eibega*" are found scattered wherever the Hottentot race has lived in East and South Africa.

Lastly, it is possible that some of the Cup-markings on the British stones may be read by the Egyptian typology. Many of them are oval or egg-shaped. The egg was a most primitive type of birth and re-birth. "*Oh! Sun in his Egg!*" is an exclamation in the Ritual.- The sun, or the dead *returned as it were to the egg-stage in the under world for the re-hatching or couvade.*

Now the Egg ☾ is an Egyptian ideograph of *enveloping* and *embalming the dead;* and these egg-shaped signs are incised on the cap-stones and coverings of the dead.

It is also noticeable that many of the cups are *dotted at the centre,* and in the hieroglyphics the eye is the ideograph of watching, to be watched over, to sleep, to dream. A plain circle also served as an equivalent for the eye; and twin circles were the same as a pair of eyes. These cups or eyes are known to have received offerings, especially of *fat!* And if the dotted circles represented eyes, then we are able to read the custom of filling the cup with fat or oil by the Egyptian doctrine of "*filling the eye.*" Filling the eye of Horus is synonymous with bringing an offering of holy oil. In fact Dr. Birch reads, "*I have filled for thee the eye of Horus,*" where M. Naville has it, "*I have anointed thee with the offering of holy oil.*"[4]

The eye, as reflector of the image, was turned into a type of re-producing. The year was re-born from the eye, whether at the vernal equinox, as in the zodiac of Denderah, or at the summer solstice.

[1] *Hor-Apollo,* B. i. 24.   [2] St. John, *Far East,* vol. i. p. 198.   [3] Ch. xvii.
[4] Birch; *Ritual,* "Address of Horus to Osiris," line 39 ; Naville, *Records,* vol. x. p. 164.

Hence it is said of the deceased, "*His eye* (his spirit) *is at peace in its place or over his person at the hour of the night; full the fourth hour of the earth, complete on the 30th of Epiphi* (June 15th). *The person of the eye then shines as he did at first.*" Here the eye and spirit are identical; so that to feed the eye with fat was to feed the spirit; a primitive mode of glorifying and causing to shine, which, like anointing the body with fat, was pre-eminently African.

The Osirified deceased boasts that he obtains assistance by his eye, *i.e.* the eye filled with oil or fat;[1] and this becomes a Lamp to dazzle and daze the powers of darkness.

In the North of England the pupil of the eye is called the candle; and in the hieroglyphics the "AR" is both the eye and the candle. This serves as a link between the lamp of light and filling the symbolic eye with oil or fat.

The offering of fat or oil to the eye would be made with intent to make the spirit of the person shine in glory. Supplying the eye with fat was an earlier mode of feeding the lamp of light which was placed in the graves of later times after lamps were made. In like manner the pot or cruse of oil is carried by the Ram as the light of the dead in the iconography of the catacombs. Also, some of the Roman lamps have the shape of an eye.

Thus the *Ritual* or "Book of the Dead," which was so sacredly buried with the Egyptian mummy, becomes a live tongue in the mouth of Death itself, the interpreter of the typology of the tomb and of customs the most primitive, most obscure, most universal.

[1] Birch, ch. cxlviii.

SECTION III.

NATURAL GENESIS AND TYPOLOGY OF THE TWO TRUTHS.

"I have penetrated the region of the Two Truths."—*Egyptian Ritual*, ch. i.
"I follow the Two Truths."—*Egyptian Ritual*, ch. lxxii.

THE words myth, mythos, and Mythology are derived from the Greek μύθος, *Muthos*, which is usually taken to mean a saying, a word, and is sometimes equivalent to *Logos*. In consequence, Mythology has been declared to have originated in *mere sayings*, the clue to which was lost before Mythology proper could have existed. For it has been affirmed by Max Müller and maintained by his followers that the radical meaning and primitive power of certain words (and sayings) must be obscured or lost for them to become mythological; and that *the essential character of a true myth consists in its being no longer intelligible by a reference to the spoken language.*[1]

Such teaching of "comparative Mythology" is the result of its being limited to the Aryan area; and if the myth be no longer intelligible in the later languages we must look for it in the earlier.

The Greek *Muthoi*, for sayings, represents the Egyptian *Mutu*, for ejaculations or brief utterances. *Mutuni* (Eg.) means *Lo it is*, or *It is verily so*. In a similar sense, "So *Mote* it be" is used by our free-masons, which brings on a saying and an ancient mode of saying under one word. *Mut* (Eg.) signifies the *pronouncing of conservative formulas*. And these formulas and wise sayings were part of the *Muthoi* in Egypt. The muthoi or myths did not begin in Greece or originate in any other Aryan language; nor with the sayings which are the fading metaphors of Mythology, and the utterances of its second childhood. Nor is the Myth a mere word in Greek. *Mutheo-mai* is not simply to say, but to feign and fable, represent and invent.

Μυθικὸς signifies that which pertains to fable and Myth in an early sense; Μυθολογεω, is to recite fables. In Attic prose the Myth was commonly a legend of early Greek times, before the dawn of history. The Mythoi were no mere sayings in a modern sense;

[1] *Comparative Mythology. Chips*, vol. ii. pp. 73—77.

they were mystical. In them the mysteries were uttered by word of mouth to the ear alone; like the *Smriti* of India. The myths are sayings because they were only to be said, not written; hence *Muthos* denotes anything delivered by word of mouth. They are myths because uttered by word of mouth alone, but they were so uttered because they contained the hidden oral wisdom and *dark sayings of old*. The Mythoi are the Logia, and the Logia, or sayings, are assignable to a Sayer or Logos, who was personified as the utterer in the Mythology which preceded Theology. The Sayings, or Logia, in Egypt, were assigned to Taht, the Moon God, who was the measurer of time; the reckoner and registrar of truth in the hall of the Two-fold Truth, or double justice. In consequence of his being primarily a representative of the dual lunation, Taht was the Sayer, Utterer of the divine words, and a Logos, tongue, or Word in person.

The Sayings or Logia were likewise attributed to the youthful Solar God Iu-em-Hept (the Egyptian Jesus of the Book of Ecclesiasticus),[1] and the "second *Atum*," who was another of the Sayers of whom we read, "*I have heard the words of Iu-em-Hept and Hartataf. It is said in their Sayings*," etc.

The ass (Aai) and the cat (Peht) are the Sayers of great words in the house of Pet, or Heaven.[2]

The Christian Gospels were founded on and originated in the Logia or sayings as Papias emphatically declares. The Christ of John is the Word, Logos or Sayer in person. His teaching, according to John and Matthew, was conveyed by the Sayings, Logia or Mythoi.[3]

Now, it is immaterial whether the Greek *Muthoi* or Mythoi be connected at root, not merely etymologically, with the Egyptian *Mâti* who represents the "Two Truths," but Mu and Ma are interchangeable, and these Sayings were held to be the words of truth and wisdom personified. When Paul speaks of a *true* saying he means one of the sayings of Truth, of Aletheia.

So far from Egyptian Mythology being founded on words that have lost their senses, it is the science of Truth in a twofold phase or character, called *Mâti*. Mâti, as Divinity, is the goddess who presides in the hall of the twin Truth. Mâti is also a title of Taht in relation to the two Truths. The two Truths (or twinship of Mâti) appear in the Sanskrit *Mithuna*, a twin couple, the zodiacal Gemini, the state of being dual, Greek *Meta;* and one form of the Mâti as Ma and Shu was that of the zodiacal Gemini in Egypt. *Mati* in Sanskrit signifies measure and exact knowledge. In Egyptian *Maât* as a noun means an inflexible rule of right; that which is strictly accurate in measure, and perfect as the poise of scales, the straightness of the plumb line, or the stretcht-out finger.

Mythology proper—by which is meant its relation to time as

[1] *Book of Beginnings*, vol. ii. pp. 106—109, 290—302.   [2] *Rit.* ch. cxxv.
[3] Matthew xv. 12; xix. 11. John vi. 60; vii. 36; viii. 51; xv. 20; xviii. 9.

distinguished from space, which will be hereafter described—began with the measuring and establishing of periods. Mâ, earlier Mak, in Egyptian denotes measure, to measure, the measurer who in the dual character is Mâti. Mata in Sanskrit is the *Mother*, also the moon as the measurer of time ; time being measured and reckoned both by the Mother and the Moon. The Mother measured time in the two phases of feminine pubescence and gestation. These are signified by the double serpent. *Matoti*, in Lithuanic, is to measure ; *Muthi*, in Toda, is the new moon. *Mata* signifies ten fishes in Fiji, that is a total equal to two hands or the two feet, which are also *Mâti* in Egyptian ; and *Mêt* is No. 10 in Coptic.

Taht and Maât then are two personified forms of the Measurer and the Utterer of truth. This has two aspects like the Mother, or the Moon, in her dual Lunation ; and these *Sayers* in Egypt, preceded the *Sayings* in Greece. Moreover, Myth and Logos are interchangeable in Greek ; and one sense of the word Logos is a *true* narration ; as it is said, in the Georgias, the fable differs from λόγος, because the latter is true. Thus the Logos or myth is identical with the *Ma-Kheru* or "True Word" of the Egyptian Theosophy, the word that was made Truth when impersonated in the god Har-Ma-Kheru.

It is now intended to show that Mythology is at root the science of the two Truths or *Mâti*, which are at the foundations of Egyptian thought and expression. For instance, the *Moth* is a perfect type of Mâti, on account of its transformation from the Grub. *Mato* in Fin is the Grub or Worm ; *Mato*, Lap, the Caterpillar or Grub ; *Mathu*, Gothic, a Worm. In English the Moth is the winged Worm, sometimes called a Soul, in the second of two phases.

Mâti may denote Water and Breath, Decay and Renewal, a pair of Feet, the two Waters, the two Solstices, the double Lunation, the Twin Lion-Gods, Light and Shade, Menstruation and Gestation, Wet and Heat, the Circle and Cross (in the knot or Ankh), the Collar and Counterpoise, the house of the Two Truths, or any other *type of twinship in which the beginning at First bifurcated.*

For, *it may be affirmed*, generally, *that all veritable Beginning in typology, mythology, numbers and language, can be traced to the Opening of a Oneness which divides and becomes dual in its manifestation.*

So far as the evidence reaches back, all *beginning* is synonymous with *opening*. In Egyptian, to found is to open. In Maori and Mangaian, to begin, or *tupu*, is to open as the bud and flower. So the place of opening is the *Teph* (Eg.), the *Tuba* in Kaffir ; and the earliest ascertainable human thought was related to *opening*. Night opened the starry heaven. The black cloud opened with its quivering Assegai of the lightning. Darkness opened into day. The mother opened to give birth. The child opened into the woman or man at puberty. The male opened the female. The eye opened for seeing ;

the ear for hearing. The nostrils opened with the breath of life. The mouth opened to utter forth; hence the mouth and mother are one by name. In the act of opening things became dual, and this was the bifurcation signified by the Kamite "Two Truths" of all beginning.

Max Müller asserts that "*as soon as Sûryas, or ἥλιος, appears as a masculine form, we are in the very thick of Mythology*";[1] that is, as soon as sex is distinguishable in words. Nay; *but we are caught in the thicket before language was sex-denoting at all;* and it is at *that* stage we have to read some of the hardest riddles of the Sphinx of Mythology.

The Hottentot, amongst other languages, reaches back to that stage. "*Thou son of a red 'she-bull'*" (*i.e.* of a heroine), is a Hottentot address to a hero.[2] This agrees with "*The Bull called Sothis at her time.*"[3] Language had but one name then for the beast of both sexes. So *Nin,* in the Assyrian, denotes both the Lord and the Lady, because *Nin,* or *Ninu,* was the name of the child, the English Ninny, and the child was named before the two sexes were discriminated by different terminals. *Nin,* for the child, was not a sex-denoting word, and the child so named might be of either; and, so far as the type goes, of *Both.*

The Egyptian type of Divinity is the Nunter, or Nuter, our neuter. The *Nnu* is the Ninny, the impubescent boy, or young one, the Khart of either sex, as is the child or the colt. This type-name is found in English, Greek, Italian, Javanese, Fijian, North American Indian, and other languages, and it is Inner African for the *young one,* as

Nina in Mende.	*Nina* in Gbandi.	*A Nene* in Soso.
Neni in Kirıman.	*Nunina* in Toma.	*A Nene* in Kisekise.

Also for the younger brother, as

Nan in Koama.	*Nyan* in Yula.	*Ninda* in Biafada.
Nana in Bagbalan.	*Nyena* in Dselana.	*Ninda* in Landoma.
Neneye in Pangela.	*Nyene* in Kiamba.	*Nande* in Nyanban.
Nuane in Isiele.		

It is likewise applied to the younger sister.

As the child, *Homo* was born twin (within the limits of language), and was separated and distinguished at puberty. We shall find the two sexes are said to have been divided by the lizard or serpent, or severed by the stone of the opener; and it will be shown *how* the one statement is related to the female, the other to the male.

The Totemic mysteries reveal the fact that individual personality was constituted at the period of puberty, and determined as twain by the manifestations of sex, the "Two Truths" of reproduction. Until that time the child-name was not distinguished by gender. In Egyptian it was also the *Nakhen,* or young one, as the *Impubescent.*

---

[1] *Selected Essays,* vol. i. p. 604.   [2] Hahn, *Tsuni-Goam,* p. 72.   [3] *Rit.* ch. cx.

Nakh denotes pubescent or virile power, which the terminal *en* negatives. Nicholas, the good genius of children, who was always a child himself, is the Nakhen, or Nakh-las.[1] The *A-nak*, in Malay, Salayer, and Javanese, is the child in the same sense.

Nakhen (Eg.) reappears in the Sanskrit *Nagna*, and *Nagnaka* for the girl who is yet impubescent, and on that account allowed to go naked. In Zulu, *Nguna* means to be quite naked, or to expose the person, and in English *Nakne* is to make naked. The naked were the impubescent, those who did not need to be clothed. Hence the two classes in the Hall of " Two Truths," the Good and the Evil, are called the " *Clothed and the Unclothed*," in accordance with this simple origin of the typology.

Again, the Hottentot language shows a primitive mode of distinguishing the one sex from the other. In one of the chaunts the Mother of the Lion calls him "*the yellow child of the Lion-tail*," *i.e.* of herself as female Lion.[2] She is the *Liontail*, the hinder part, just as it is in the hieroglyphics where the forepart of the animal is masculine, the Lord or Leader, that which goes first, the " Ha !" whereas the hind part denotes the female sex. There was then but *one being*, whether as human or beast, and the front was the male, the back female. This is the secret of the Sphinx. The orthodox sphinx of Egypt is masculine ⟋ in front and feminine behind. So is the image of Sut-Typhon, ⟋ a type of horn and tail, male in front and female behind. The Pharaohs, who wore the tail of the Lioness or Cow behind them, were male in front and female behind. Like the Gods they included the dual totality of Being in one person, born of the Mother, but *of both sexes as the Child*.[3]

It was a common tradition with the Jews and other races that man, Homo, was formed of both sexes at first, and afterwards divided. It is so stated in "Genesis." The Rabbi, Jeremiah Ben-Eleazer, also supported this view with the authority of the text,[4] " *Thou hast fashioned me Behind and Before*."[5] Other Rabbis affirm that Homo was male in front and female behind ; just as we find it was in language and is imaged in the Typology, which alone can explain it.

Within such limits of expression *Homo*, or Khem, was born twin ; the male and female were distinguished by their sex as two forms of one being ; and these limits of early thought and expression were the cause of the dual and epicene types, and of the later superstitious beliefs. Sex was first denoted by gesture, and next by images, which were retained in the mythological figures like those of the Sphinx, the

---

[1] *Book of Beginnings*, vol. ii. p. 165.   [2] *Tsuni-Goam*, p 73.
[3] The present writer has suggested, and he maintains, that the *Pharaoh* was not founded on the Rā (who was the earlier Rek or Rex) but on the double Har, who preceded him as the Har-Iu ; whence *P-har-iu*, the dual Horus, the effeminate (or feminine) and the virile one united.
[4] *Berachoth*, f. 61 ; Bartolocci, *Bibl. Rabbin*, iv. p. 66.
[5] Ps. cxxxix. 5. *Talmud, Tract.*

Centaur, Sut-Typhon, Pan, the God, or Pharaoh, with the feminine tail.

Not only typology but language itself was also evolved from this primary phase that contained and divided into the Twinship of the Two Truths.

As already affirmed, there was a stage at which language was not sex-denoting and different words or signs were used by the two sexes (as such) to distinguish them. At first the genders were dramatised, so to say, and the speech was according to the character or sex of the speaker. Doing, demonstrating, in relation to sex (from which peculiar customs have descended) preceded saying in sex-denoting speech. Language began without distinction of gender. The Kinyamwezi and other African languages have no genders. There is a formal absence of gender in the Australian dialects. The Algonkin language has no direct distinction of gender. In the Fula language of Central Africa there is no distinction between the masculine and feminine genders, but it divides beings into two classes. In one is everything belonging to humanity; in the other everything belonging to the brute creation and to inanimate objects; these have been termed the human and the brute genders. There are two genders in Iroquois known as the noble and ignoble, the first being applied to divinities and the male of human beings, the second to all other things. The Dravidians also have a "*high caste or major gender*," which is that of the divinities as well as great men. The Mexicans evolved a dual kind of language on this principle, one form of which is used solely by the superior castes, the other by the inferior in social position.[1] In the Aryan languages the father and mother occur without the signs of gender, which shows the *neuter* was first; and the distinction between animate and inanimate which forms the genders in the North American Indian dialects is visibly earlier than the distinction by sex. The sign of gender in the Bonus Pater and Bona Mater is obtained by means of the adjective. The person, so to say, remains neuter. So papa, (Eg.) to produce, may be applied to either the father or the mother. The Mother is the Papa in the Australian dialects.

The Kaffir custom of Hlonipa shows us language in the act of becoming twain. It is negatively sex-denoting. The especial language of the female becomes so by her avoidance of male names and masculine terms. It is similar to the woman distinguishing her sex by denuding herself of her eyebrows and pubes, to be un-masculine, or become more feminine. Hlonipa was not assumed at first as a sort of fig-leaf apron of the feminine consciousness, although it may look so now. Certain words, expressions, or sounds were only used by each sex because they were sex-denoting, and the primitive mode of denoting the sex was by each keeping to its own words. In

[1] Gallatin, *Notes on the Semi-Civilised Nations of Mexico*, vol. i. p. 28.

this way the genders were dramatised, and the human being was made twain, as were the two castes in other languages.

In the American Indian dialects women use different words from the men to denote various *degrees of relationship, the custom being confined to such words and to the interjections.*[1] For example, among the Araucanian tribes the brother calls his brothers *Peni*, and his sisters *Lamnen*. But the sister calls both sexes *Lamnen.*[2] In the woman's mouth the distinction based on sex is effaced.

Peni, as in other languages, denotes the male organically, and this name the female avoids, not primarily from shame or modesty, but because it was representative of the male at first, and was afterwards prohibited to the female. The Kaffir women are forbidden to pronounce the names of any of their husband's male relatives in the ascending line, or to use any words in which the chief syllables of these names occur.

The Fijians have an interjectional *Neu*, which is prohibited to the men, and is used only by the women. This is a universal form of the negative ; and in the hieroglyphics *Nnu* is No, Negation, and the woman menstruating. The woman was being limited to her own negational sign expressed in sound ; just as she was the hinder part, as Liontail to the *Ha*, or front; or as the North to the South for the front. Although the first, she became negative to the male. In Egyptian the feminine article is also found to serve for the neuter one, which preceded sex.

The Apaches "*Nyau*" is an exclamation strictly limited to the females, whereas "*Ah*" is the exclamation confined to the males. In the African Hausa language the two genders of sex are distinguished by the terminal *Ia* used for the male, and *Nia*, the force of which has not been determined, for the female. So in a Murray dialect (Australia) the word *Purragia* signifies "You lie" *when addressed to a man ;* and "*Purragaga*" is "You lie," *when addressed to a woman.*[3] The reason for this is unknown.

Ia and *Nia* are common forms for Yes and No. In Egyptian, *Ia* is Yes, positively, certainly. *Na* is No, negative ; these contain the Two Truths, however applied. Hence they served as signs of the male and female nature ; the male claims to be the superior one, according to the Two Truths, a division answering to that of the "noes" and "yeas" of the two castes of people in Australia. Even when the genders of language had to be expressed by gesture-signs and interjectional sounds or clicks, the Two Truths or diverse aspects of the one were represented by signs and clicks ; for with the Zulus, to this day, the woman expresses contempt by a sound like that of the c click, whereas a man does it with the x click, and this is according to the secret signs or sounds of "*Nci-fila*," and a very primitive Gnosis.

[1] *Archæologia Americana*, v. ii. p. 163.   [2] *Ibid.* p. 264.
[3] Smyth, *Aborigines of Victoria.*

Such a manner of distinguishing the sexes was developed in the Ibu "*Nna*," for the father, and "*Nne*" for the mother ; and in the Kooch *Nana* for the paternal grandfather, and *Nani* for the paternal grandmother, by means of a vowel-intonation in a name instead of a personal click, or sexual gesture-sign.   In the Sonorian dialects of America the gender is indicated by the addition of words denoting the *Man-word* and *Woman-word*, which took the place of earlier signs, on the way towards a sex-denoting terminal for single words.[1]

In the hieroglyphics the natural ideographic *Signs of Sex* can be traced into sex-denoting suffixes.   The feminine terminal and article "*The*" is the sign ◠ of the female sex ; it is one of the two Mammæ separated from the body.   This phonetic T is an ideographic *Tt*, the English Teat and Titty, for the female breast.   The masculine article *The* is Pâ, ideographic Paf (The) ; and Paf signifies the Breath.   This sign then denotes the Breath-giver, who was at first the quickening female and afterwards the *causative* male, *Pepe* having the same meaning as "engender," the papa as Engenderer.   These signs are related to the "Two Truths," and to the breath and liquid of life, and they became the two masculine and feminine articles and sex-denoting suffixes.   Thus Gesture-Signs of Sex were first ; next the Words of Sex ; lastly the Woman-Sign, the teat or mammæ, becomes a terminal t, to denote the feminine gender of words.

In the Nagari alphabet there are two peculiar signs for symbolic sounds which may also be related to the Two Truths of the Water and the Breath.   The one . represents *N*, and is the symbol of nasal sounds. The other : is the symbol of H, and the sibilant called Visarga. N denotes the negative element (water) in many languages, including Sanskrit, Egyptian, Chinese, Japanese, Akkadian.   Visarga is a distinctly audible aspirate.   This and the H therefore represent Breath. The Rabbins have a saying that all came out of the letter H.

The Two Truths appear in the Chinese division of the roots of their language, the full and the empty words, designated *Chi-tsen* and *Lin-tsen*.   Grammar, they say, is an art which teaches us how to distinguish between the full and the empty words.   Full and empty have great nearness to the original nature of the Two Truths, the Yes and No, Positive and Negative, Breath and Water, Light and Darkness, of the primitive typology.

The Melbourne blacks used to distinguish their language as *Nuther galla*.   Galla is language, and *Nuther* means *No*.   Judging from the Egyptian Nuter and the English *Neither*, it may be inferred that this is negative in the sense of the *Neuter* that becomes either. The language of "No" is equivalent to the "*No*" or Negative people of Australia.   The Egyptian Nu-ter contains the elements of *Nnu*, Negative ; and *ter*, for the type, image, or status.   The pre-pubescent

Buschmann, *Abhandlung d. Berlin. Akademie*, 1869, i. 103.

period of the child was neuter in.this sense of neutral, which became dual at puberty, and the language formed before *Homo* could be sexually distinguished by the name, would be *Nuther* or *Neuter* speech.

In the Kamkatdal and Koriak dialects of the Aino language, man, as Homo, is called *Nuteira* and *Nuteiran.* The name included both sexes, but distinguished neither. It was because the Nuter preceded sex that it became a type of divinity beyond sex and the Neuter remains the sexless gender. The Neuter of deity is either he or she'; in the negative sense neither, but potentially both. At this primitive stage the type of a biune deity was founded in the likeness of the child, which is of either sex, as the dual being. It has been said that in no language does the plural precede the singular. But the one, as group, was earlier than the personal I, and the bifurcation and individualization from the group or from the typical one, the Mother, who preceded the dual child, is one of the *Cruxes* of all beginning. Those who date from the Mother, the Negative one, are the No-people.

They who begin as her children are both Yes and No, male and female, no longer Neuter. With them there is a dual that precedes the singular. It belongs to the pre-pubescent period of the child. The Egyptian " Heir Apparent," the *Repa*, has a name that signifies either, the Repa being the royal or divine *Child* of either sex, of two characters, or typically of both. The twofold oneness of the primordial Neuter is still attained or preserved in the various duals of dignity, the " We," " Our," and " Us," of Royalty, which is an equivalent for the Cow-tailed Râ, and is represented in literature by the infallible " We " of the Reviewer and Editor. In Samoa this is continued to the extent of asking the single chief,[1] " Have *you Two* come?" " Are *you Two* going ? " Thus " Your Twinship " is a perfect plural of dignity. This plural is pourtrayed by the hieroglyphic sign of Nakh (or Ankh, the pair), ☖ the type of pubescent power in the male, who has doubled, and become "You Two."

The personal pronoun, I, is a dual in several ancient languages, as in the Hottentot. The Egyptian *Ank* (I) is plural in Ankh, a pair. *U*, the I or Me, is also a plural for they or them. *Penti* in Egyptian is emphatically *the* one, *because* the word is plural and indicates a dual nature, like that of the pubescent male, the doubled Horus, or the female in her second phase of the Two Truths.

Here, as elsewhere, the dual does precede the singular in language and was necessitated by an earlier stage of expression, the I being twin in sex. The human being was broken in two (as it were) to be divided into male and female. This led to the primitive legends of the split men, the half men, the one-legged race, who fancied the Zulu maiden must be a pair of people. " You Two," or the Twinship, restores this original unity. The parent when

[1] Turner, *Nineteen Years in Polynesia*, p. 340.

enacting the Couvade might also have been addressed as "You Two!"

The Baroling regard their god as a person with only one leg, and they hop round in his image on one leg in their sacred dances. The Single Leg, says Rowley, is emblematic of Unity. This one-legged divinity was continued in the mummy-type of Ptah, which type includes the male and female, and shows the process of individualizing.[1]

In death the Egyptians returned to the type beyond sex. The mummies were bound up in the undivided image of the single-legged Ptah, or Osiris, whose legs were at first undivided. The Shebti or *double* of the deceased shows no distinction of sex for the male or female, but served for both. The unity of the lower part corresponds to the pre-pubescent period of the child in which the sexes were as yet undistinguished, or, as they called it, undivided.

In the sacrifices to the Mexican god Tlaloc, children were selected who had *two whorls* in their hair, or were what we call "double-crowned."[2] These were held to be the most agreeable offering to the gods, because as we read the symbol, the double-crown, like that of the divinities and kings of Egypt represented the Two Truths of the biune one. This the present writer considers to have been the reason why Twin children were especially chosen to be offered up in sacrifice and not from any absurd notions connected with the infidelity of the mother and a double fatherhood. Such customs and ideas date from a time when there could be no such thing as female fidelity. Hoho was the Dahoman god of Twins. These being sacred to him would be sacrificed to him. The Twin Being in Mythology is the complete one, the dual child, and the Twins according to the same idea would furnish the perfect offering. The same typology is continued in the custom of "Wishing" over the double kernel found in a fruit-stone called a "phillipine."

When words become sex-denoting in themselves we are *out of the thicket of Mythology or Typology ;* and the "Two Truths" of Egypt relate to this primary phase, short of which there is no beginning.

The "Two Truths" may be said to commence with the natural antithesis of the positive and negative. As Day and Night embrace the whole world in two halves, so do "Yes" and "No" cover the two hemispheres of the world of language ; and these may be indicated even by the nod and shake of the head in Gesture-language.

The "Two Truths" originated in there being but one name or type for the dual manifestation of an object, person, or thing. Shen (Eg.), for instance, is a circle, an orbit, a whole. It was the circle of the year. But Shen is also Twin, and Two ; the circle of the year, being first divided into the Two Times ; and the *Shen*, Tunic, was first put on at puberty when the *second of the two phases* was attained. The *Shen* as the brother and sister were Shu and Tefnut (also the Shenti)

---

[1] Rowley, *Religion of the Africans*, p. 24.   [2] Bancroft, iii. 332.

the Lion-Gods of the two gates North and South in the earliest halving of the circle.

This form of the bi-une one was finally fixed in heaven as the Twins of the Zodiac. Thus the Shen (as one) includes both sexes, two halves, two times, and the Shen-ring is a symbol of reproduction or duplicating. The knee-joint and elbow are both *Shena* (Eg.), or *Shenat*, the equivalent of *joint*, as the hinge of juncture and point of unity. Shen and Sen are interchangeable. Sen is Two or Twin. Also Sen (Eg.) means Blood and Breath, the dual foundation of being, the Two Truths in a biological sense; the Twin as two principles of life under one and the same name. Sen means to be made, to become, to be founded, by means of the Mother-Source, and secondly, by the quickening breath or spirit, first observed through the Mother, and lastly assigned to the Father.

The Serpent, on account of its sloughing became a pre-eminent type of the Twin Truths, or two manifestations of the one, especially in the two phases of the female. In India the Serpent still images the two primary Truths represented by the elements of Wind and Wet; it is invoked in the one character for fine weather; in the other for rain. In the time of Hioun-Thsang, that traveller records how the people of Cashmere would go to the spring accompanied by the priest, and " *snapping their fingers would invoke the Dragon and at once obtain their wishes.*" [1]

The rootage of Language and of Mythology has to be sought here where the oneness bifurcates in duality according to the Egyptian doctrine. The Ojibwa signs or hieroglyphics contain a unique symbol of the Two Truths, consisting of a serpentine *double* line which represents the *River of Words* in a twofold flow. This serves as a visible figure of unity bifurcating into duality.

It is an Accra saying that men have Two Ears but these do not hear Two Stories; and when the one tongue spoke falsely that became the double-tongue. In like manner the Human Being was named as *one*, before the two sexes were distinguished by genders. There were two forms of the primary one. The genus had to be identified before sex and species could be distinguished by name. So that the root of the present matter is not reached on any line of research until we have attained the starting-point in a twofold oneness.

The name of the Goddess Aahti is the name of the womb, the moon, and a pair of bellows, legs or shanks. *Aah* denotes the house, moon, or the thing which is duplicated by the *ti*. Thus the womb Aahti is the dual house, the place of the Two Truths of the Water and Breath, or of duplication in reproduction. The Lunar Aahti is the manifestor of the Two Truths in the waxing and waning of the moon. The Ibis Aahti was Black and White, thence representative of the dark and light of the lunar orb.

[1] *Voyage*, Vol. ii. p. 152.

The two eyes of the crocodile denoted sunrise, the tip of its tail was an ideograph of sunset.

The earliest division of the human being is founded on sex, whatsoever the terminology; and the ideographic signs are the members. The He is the head and She the tail of the first dual coinage, as well as in the latest currency. The He is before, in front, and She is the hinder half. He is the outer and the right hand, She the inner and the left hand; He being the type of *out*, and She of *in* and *within*. He is the upper and active; She the lower and passive when the one becomes Twain.

All the earliest imagery in the Planisphere is arranged according to these Two Truths, or the dual one. There are two Bears, the Greater and Lesser; two Dogs, the Major and Minor; two Lions, as the Lion-Gods; the double Anubis or dual form of Sut; two Fishes; two Mothers, the Virgin and Gestator; one in the sign of Virgo, the other who brings forth the Solar Child in the sign of Pisces. The Twins (who in Egypt were the two Lion-Gods); the Ass and its foal; the Polar Dragon, North, and Hydra, South; with the Scales figured at the equinoctial level, the division as the connecting link of two heavens and the express emblem of the Two Truths.

One of the symbols of *Ma* is the Ostrich Feather, which is the sign both of Light and Shade, Ma and Shu. There can be nothing older than Day and Dark, and as the Ostrich Feather was an inner African sign of the Two Truths, and as Hor-Apollo says the symbol was adopted because of the *equal length* of the ostrich feathers, it has been suggested that the type was first made use of in a land of *equal* day and dark, or equatorial Africa.[1]

This would be a form of equal poise and of the *balance* before the equinoxes were made out in higher latitudes.

With the Chinese the Two primal principles called *Yang* and *Yin*, the Male and Female, or Father Heaven and Mother Earth, were originally known as *Light* and *Shadow*.[2] These are the Two Truths of Ma and Shu, or Mâti, in Egypt.

The Hebrew deity is represented according to the Two Truths, studying in the Scriptures by day and the Mishna by night.[3] Also it is said that when Moses was with the Lord during forty days and forty nights he was taught the written law; then he understood it was day, and when he was taught the oral law he knew it was night. These also are the Two Truths of Light and Shade, *i.e.* of *Ma-Shu* (Eg).

The White and Black ermine worn by English judges continues the typology of the Two Truths or the dual justice, and corresponds to the feather of Light and Shade which was worn by the Goddess Mâti

---

[1] *Book of Beginnings*, vol. ii. p. 484.
[2] Chalmers, *Origin of the Chinese*, p. 14.
[3] *Midrash*, f. xcvii. c. 3; Buxtorf, *Synag. Jud.* c. iii. p. 54, Basil, 1661.

in the Judgment Hall.   The ermine, says the Bundahish, was the first
of the fur animals that was produced.[1]

The Two Truths of Light and Shadow appear in the Bundahish
represented by Two antagonistic spirits, personified as Ahura-Mazda
(the spirit of Light), and Aharman (the Angro-Manyus, or Black Man
of the Avesta).   " *The region of Light is the place of Ahura-Mazda,
which they call endless Light, and his omniscience is in vision* (sight) *or
revelation.*"   Aharman " *in Darkness, with backward understanding
and desire for destruction, was in the abyss, and it is he who will not be*
(he only exists negatively), *and the place of that destruction, and also of
that Darkness, is what they call the endlessly dark.*" [2]   In the earliest
phase these two were simply the Light and the Darkness.

In many lands the waxing and waning moon conveyed two messages to men as its form of the Two Truths.   According to a Lithuanian
precept, boys should be weaned whilst the moon is waxing, and girls
during the wane.   The Orkney Islanders prefer to marry when the
moon is waxing.   The present writer has personally met with a
prejudice entertained by English villagers against killing the pig in
the wane of the moon, because the meat will waste so in cooking !
The Two Truths conveyed by the moon's message to men, are set
forth in the Hottentot legend.

The Moon once sent an insect to men with this message :—" *As I
die and dying live, so ye shall also die and dying live.*"   On its way the
insect was overtaken by the hare, who, being a fast runner, proposed
to convey the message to men.   The insect consented.   When the
hare arrived she said, " *As I die and dying perish, in the same way ye
shall also die and end.*"   The hare then returned to the Moon and
told her what she had said to men.   This made the Moon so angry
that she struck the hare on the mouth and slit it.[3]   So the hare-lipped
mouth became a type of the double (cf. the double tongue) or lying
lip.   " *We are still angry with the hare,*" said an old Namaqua, " *and
dislike to eat its flesh because of the message it brought.*" [4]

Shu, the feather of Light and Shade, also reads Ma ; and Shu-Ma or
Shu, and his sister (Tefnut) represent the Two Truths of Breath and
Moisture.   These in one form may be the Breath of heaven, and its
Dew, as *Tef* is to drip and drop.   They likewise denote the breath of
soul and the blood of source, the mystical water of life.   Also, Shu-
Ma is a name for the " Pool of the Two Truths."

When Thales, the Milesian, said water was the mother of life, he
did but formulate the first perception of the primitive man in a thirsty
land.   Water and Breath were the two elements of life earliest
identified ; and water, *having to be sought for* and supplied as drink,
whereas the air came of itself, would make the earliest appeal and first

---

[1] Ch. xxiv. 12.   [2] *Bundahish*, ch. 1, 2, 3.   West.
[3] Bleek, No. 31.   [4] *Ibid.* p. 7.

demand for recognition. Hence, in Mythology, *Water is the primal Element.* All begins with or issues from the Water, the first of our Two Truths. The " Revelation " concerning creation in the forty-first chapter of the Korân, says the Lord set His mind to the creation of Heaven, and it was darkness or smoke. Al Zamakshari affirms that this smoke or vapour of darkness ascended from the waters under the throne of God and rose above the waters and formed the heavens. In the Hindu creation it is said that " *From the foam of the water was produced the wind,*" [1] that is the Breath or Anima, the Egyptian *Pef* (or *Beb*), the exhalation.

According to the Vishnu Purana,[2] the creation proceeds from the quality of Darkness called Sesha. Sesha shows that Breathing out of the Waters which is represented under the waters by Vishnu and Ananta. And in Egyptian, *Ses* is to breathe ; *Susu*, in the Inner African languages is smoke, and to breathe. The god Shu, who represents the element of breath and air, is the born child of Nun, the firmamental water. The doctrine had a natural genesis, and was derived from observation. Breath, or vapour, *is* a secondary condition of water in the form of mist. Heat is a means of converting water into breath or vapour. The Breath of Heaven is born of the firmament, which was called the celestial water ; water in its second, upper, aerial or ætherial condition.

The name of the Genitrix *Uati* signifies both Wet and Heat, and the water was converted into breathing life by the Mother when in heat, or gestating, *i.e.* life-making. The soul of man, say the Australian blacks, was breathed into him through his navel. The two primal principles of Wet and Heat are the bases of beginning in the Vedic Hymn,[3] as everywhere else, however mystified by later rendering, and obscured by still later translation. The one like Uati consists of the water and heat ; and although the latter may be expressed as fervour and desire, fervour, desire, and heat are yet synonymous. We read in the Ritual, [4] " *Oh the Being dormant within his body, making his burning in flame glowing within the sea, raising the sea by his vapour. Come give the fire, transport the vapour to the Being.*" The vapour was the breath, the later spirit or soul.

In drowning it was observed that the vapour was transported *from* the being, when the breath of life ascended in bubbles of air. Beb (Eg.) is to exhale ; and they saw the Beb or Pef (gust or wind) was exhaled in bubbles or in foam, and so the earliest wind, breath, the second element of life, came visibly from the water. Hence the element had two aspects, the Water of Life was also the Water of Death ; for water as the drowning element would impress the primitive man as profoundly as did the deadly sting of the Serpent. The Two Truths of life as the first and second are well illustrated in an inscrip-

---

[1] In the *M. Bh. S'antip.* 6812 ff. Muir, *San. Texts*, vol. v. p. 357.
[2] B. ii. ch. 3.　　　　[3] *Rig-Veda*, 129.　　　　[4] Ch. clxiv.

tion on an Egyptian vase. The Goddess Nut stands in her sycamore tree from which she pours the Water of Life. The deceased awaiting his resuscitation cries, " *Give me the water and the breath of life*." The Goddess replies, " *I bring thee the vase containing the abundant water for rejoicing the heart by its effusion, that thou mayest breathe the breath of life resulting from it*." The Water precedes and is the creative cause of the Breath of Life, and such is the relationship and sequence of the Two Truths. Water is the first form of matter in all the oldest Mythologies or so-called Cosmogonies. It is the mother of substance, and mother and matter are one. Water is called by Plato " *the liquid of the whole vivification;* " and again he alludes to it mystically as a " certain fountain." That fountain was the mother-source, in the mystical rendering of the water of life.

. Water was the First *cause* in Egypt. So was it in India, or, as it was put by later theology, the first *creation* ; and one of the most curious ceremonies in the festival of the Water-Goddess Ganges is to make her image and cast it into the river. " *The Pundits*," says Sir William Jones,[1] " *of whom I inquired concerning its origin and import, answered that it was prescribed by the Veda, they knew not why*."

Ganga, the Water, like

Khenka in Chinese,	*Ngi* in N'guru,	*Nke* in Bamom,
Ngongi in Maori,	*Ngi* in Kanem,	*Nki* in N'goala,
Engi in Munio,	*Aningo* in Orungu,	
Nki in Kanuri,	*Nke* in Balu,	

is a form of *Ankh* (Eg.) the liquid or water of life. The goddess *Ank* represented the mystical water, with her crown of hemp, as the *clother* in flesh, and the casting of the image into the waters was typical of the human formation from the waters.

One of the Hawaiian expressions used to designate the death of a man was " *He has gone to the moist earth and the muddy water* (soil) *from which he was made*." [2]

Images modelled in honour of the Genitrix were a symbolical offering of the human form which was clothed and shaped by her in the womb. It was a commuted kind of human sacrifice, once fulfilled by offering a virgin to the waters, as the Bride of Nile, which we hear of in Egypt and can read by the images made to be resolved by the Nile or the Ganges, as a mode of return by proxy to that source from whence we came. The Romans at one time used to make fetish images or dolls to cast into the river Tiber as proxies for the earlier sacrificial victims.

The confusion of vapour that rises from the water with spirits or apparitions ascending from the lakes is common in Africa. For instance, in the Vei language *Dsina* is a Ghost, Spectre, or Wraith. *Dsi* is water, and *Na* means to come. Thus the *Dsina* comes from the water. The Vei ghosts manifest from the water as one of their

---

[1] *Gods of Greece, Italy, and India.*   [2] Fornander.

Two Abodes. The other is considered to be on the summit of Cape Mount, their aerial abode,[1] the high land of Breath.

The Maori have a race of beings called the *Ponaturi* (from *Pona*, the joint, and *turi*, the knee,) who are literally the people of the division, the join of the upper and lower worlds, typified by the knee-joint. Their country was underneath the waters, but every night they ascended to sleep on dry land in a large house called *Manawa-tane*, or breath for the suffocated. They were obliged to come up to breathe, and the place was at the division or crossing, the level of the Two Times, where land or breathing-place was attained. But they had to leave before sunrise under penalty of death; for, like the Norse Trolls, if the sun saw them they perished. Exactly the same expedient is adopted in the Maori legend of "Tawhaki," and the Norse story of "Lord Peter," to kill the Ponaturi and the Troll. The myth belongs to the division by two of a world of water and breath, and the Beings of the water-half ascend by night to breathe the air of the upper half, but as they are mere vapour-spirits the sun consumes them with its glance.

The Two Truths of the Inner African beginnings were further emphasised and enforced by the peculiar conditions found in Egypt. Every year when the new inundation had poured forth its water of life, the welcome wind of the north arose with its breath of life and spread the tide of the stream out over the thirsty soil. The beatitude of Paradise pourtrayed in the Ritual is to drink of the Nile and breathe the bliss of the vivifying wind of the north which had brought coolness to the burning land.

"*She's hit between wind and water*" is a provincial English expression for one who is more likely to be a mother than become a wife. According to that typology the dead in Egypt were buried between wind and water, or in the womb of a new life. The Great Pyramid was a symbolical sepulchre containing a Well supposed to have some communication with the Nile. Where there was no water, this was still represented by the well. The wind or breath was allowed for in the small air-hole of the *serdab* left open to the north quarter from whence came the revivifying breath of life.

These Two Truths of Life are illustrated by the wind and water; the two primary and supreme elements of Life, the givers of breath and bringers to life, in the American myths. The Quiché four ancestors, are four forms of the spirit of breath as males, who were created by Hurakan, the air in motion; and their four wives the mothers of the human race were four forms of water, Falling Water, Beautiful Water, Water of Serpents, and Water of Birds.[2]

At this mental stage the primal biology was formulated. In relation to the Two Truths of water and breath Empedocles may be quoted

[1] Koelle, *Vei Grammar, &c.* p. 161.
[2] Brasseur de Bourbourg, *Le Livre Sacré des Quichés, &c.* pp. 203—205. Note.

who said :—"The earliest breath was drawn by the first animal when *the moisture in infants was separated and by that means an entrance was given to the external air* into the gasping vessels from which the moisture retired." [1]

In the beginning all came out of the *Nu* (Nun) the waters of the firmament ; and existence is *Nuti* or *Enti* (Eg.) as entity. *Enti* means *out of ; froth ;* existence in a negative phase ; Water being the negative of Two Truths when the Breath is included. *Nuti* as *froth* shows the breath of life issuing from the Waters as it might in frog-spittle or the breath-bubbles of the submerged Water-cow, or Aphrodite personified as kindling into breathing life and beauty as she rises from the foam. *Nuti*, for froth, is the same word as *Neith*, and Aphrodite was the froth or breathing life of the waters. Neith is Hathor, the Egyptian Venus, Aphrodite from the froth or Nuti (*i.e.* Neith) in whom the breathing power was *entified* and named as that which came "out of" and was afterwards personified or represented as the mother of life, who had two characters derived from the liquid of life and the breath of being. The primordial image of power and type of time was set in heaven as the Hippopotamus (Ursa Major) the great breather in and out of the water.

One form of *Mâti* signifies to float on the surface of the water ; to be going in the cabin, which denotes the second phase, that of the breathing life. Water also imaged the visible type of existence ; air or breath the invisible ; hence the priority of water.

The "secret of Horus in An" is how his mother made him or caught him in the water. Neith, or the Net, as it were, fished the child from the water. The Fish being a type of the Breather in the water.

In several languages birth, beginning, *Natalis*, is identical with swimming. This is seen in Latin as well as in the Egyptian *Enti*, out of (the water), and Mâti, to float, in the cabin or Argha-Yoni. In Tamil *Nid* or *Nitt* is to swim and also to be born. Being born of the water is equivalent to being borne upon it. Man was not a born swimmer and never could live under water, hence this type of birth and existence was found in swimming on the water and in coming *out of it.*

In the most ancient typology (the Typhonian) life was emaned from the waters by the genitrix imaged as the Water-cow. There were no human fishers then. When the goddess Neith was created men had learned how to catch fish. The perch on the head of Neith, or Hathor, is a symbol of birth from the waters. Neith also carries the Shuttle or Knitter of the Network. Her name is synonymous with Net. So Ank, the goddess who wears the bundle of hemp or flax on her head, shows that men were weavers when she was created. Neith was the Knitter or Netter and typifies the mother as the

[1] Plutarch, *Morals, Sentiments of Philosophers,* ch. xxiii.

catcher of fish who netted Horus from the water, or in other words
gave him birth under the type of the fish. She is pourtrayed as
suckling her fish in the shape of a crocodile.

Being, existing, then is figured as an escape (Net) out of the waters,
a drawing out (Net, to draw) and thence a Netting as the means of
being born, saved, fished from the drowning element. The Maori
language has various forms of " *Net* " with this primary meaning;
Noti, is to draw together with a cord ; *Nati*, to make fast, hold firm ;
Ngita, to make fast, secure, carry, bring forth; *Noto*, is to shut.
Notan, an oyster that keeps shut and safe under water. That which
could breathe and keep its life under water was the object of deep
attention to the earliest observers.

The West-Australians used the term " *Netingar* " to signify their
ancestors or beginnings. They also reckoned to come from the waters.

A Maori meaning attached to the word " *Ewe* " or *Uho*, the Placenta, retains the idea of the primæval land, earth and foothold ; the
Mud of the mythical waters. *Ewe*, the placenta, the after-birth, is
likewise the "land *of one's birth.*" *Whenua*, another name for the
placenta, also means one's own land, country, native place. The
Whenu is a warp, a form of the Net. *Ea*, to appear above water,
means to be performed, to be produced, or evolved.

This mode of attaining land and breathing-place gave especial
significance to the placenta and the umbilical cord. *Tangaenga*
(Mao.) the cord, and *Tangahangha*, the fish, are both derived from
nga, to breathe, the breather, to take breath. Likewise *Nef* (Eg.)
for breath and the navel, as breathing-place, are identical. *Nef* (Eg.)
is the sailor, and the aboriginal natives of Australia consider that
children with large navels will be famous swimmers.[1] The navel is
the Bilyi (belly) and a good swimmer is called Bilyi-Gadak, that is
having a good navel. One name of the navel in English is the
Nathe.

When the umbilical cord drops off the child, the New Zealanders
put it in the mussel-shell with which it was severed, and place the
shell with its freight on the water. If the shell should swim it is a
lucky omen ; but if it capsizes that portends an early death.[2] Others
cast the cord into the waters as an offering.

The Placenta (Lat.) is a cake, and the cake sign is the Egyptian
ideograph of land. The goddess Hathor (Venus) in the tree of life
pours the water with one hand from the vase, and in the other she
holds the cake emblem of land [3]—the two types of the Two Truths of
the beginning. Hathor was that Queen of Heaven to whom the
Israelite women offered their cakes, which are called *Placentas* in the
Vulgate.

In Kanuri one's native place is *na dabu kambe*, or literally, where

[1] Moor, *Aust. Vocab.*   [2] Hooper, *Journal of Ethnological Society*, 1869.
[3] Wilk, *Mat. Hierog.* pl. 24.

one's umbilical cord was buried. The Placenta thus identifies the place of birth, in relation to one's native land. Amongst the Wanyamwizi, when a child is born the father cuts the cord and travels with it to the frontier of his district, and there buries it. If the frontier be a stream (the natural boundary) he buries it on the bank. Then taking the root of a tree (in exchange), he carries it home and buries it at the threshold of his door.[1]

It was this beginning that gave such importance to the navel as a kind of mesmeric disk which the Ecstatics and Seers of India gaze at until they enter the state of trance. They concentrate their thought or vision on the navel because it was one of the first oracles; it taught them how the child breathed in the womb, and we shall find the early men were very loyal and worshipful to every educational fact of this kind that offered any response to their wonder, and they gave it apotheosis. "*Hear, O sons of the Gods, one who speaks through his navel* (Nabha), *for he hails you in your dwellings*," cries the Brahman Seer.[2] Whatsoever his idea of the Gods and their dwelling, the imagery belongs to the simplest beginning of human thought and expression. Through the navel was the first manifestation of *Nef*, or breath. That way the life was held to be inspired into the child by the mother, or the later God. And that way they sought the breathing power.

The navel was one of the earliest doorways between two worlds, and as such maintained its symbolical value. Through the navel men were told of the breathing source, and they made the navel a type of foretelling. Naba, in Hebrew, is to prophesy, to utter forth. This is a secondary sense, apparently unknown in Egyptian. It was the oracle of one of the Two Truths, that relating to Breath, and then made the type of another meaning. Both Pliny and Solinus say that when Apis was led in the solemn procession if children could get to smell its breath they were thought to be thereby gifted with the power of predicting future events.

The navel of the waters is personified in the Avesta. It is said to take possession of and to guard the imperishable majesty, *i.e.* the soul of breath, which is preserved amid the waters by means of this Mount. In the Sirozah,[3] the navel appears as the navel of the kings, or more anciently, the "*navel of women*," the feminine producer being first. This navel of the waters was the typical mount and mound, the navel-mound, as breathing-place. The Hindu Nabhi-Yoni was a dual type of the Two Truths of the breath and the waters of life; the navel being an image of breath in the waters of the womb.

When the male Vishnu takes the place of the female, the sacred navel loses significance, because the male has been made the source

---

[1] Stanley, *How I found Livingstone*, p. 544.
[2] *Nabhanedishtha Hymn*, v. 4.
[3] *Zamyad-Yasht*, viii. 51.

of breath, or soul, whereas the female was first.   There is no malè Vishnu, however, without the female nature.

Nef (Eg.) not only means the sailor, it is likewise a type-name for the knitter, spinner, and weaver in the Sanskrit *Nabhi* and *Nabha;* Greek, *Nabh;* Maori, *Nape,* to weave (also a fishing-line), Egyptian *Nebt,* a basket of woven wicker-work; *Napet,* in English, woven linen.   Hence she who inspired the breath of life into the child was the weaver or spinner of the web of life personified in Mythology.   She was both Argha and sail (the Egyptian hieroglyphic of breath), and the sail and mast were afterwards given to the god as Argha-Nautha.   In the Athenian festival in honour of Athena, called the ΠΑΝΑΘΗΝΑΙΑ, the ark or boat was carried in a procession, and on it was hung, in the manner of a sail, the sacred garment of the Goddess, the peplum that no man had lifted.   This sail, the Egyptian sign of breath, derives its name from *Pef* (Eg.), breath.   The Two Truths of breath and water were being celebrated, as shown by the boat and sail, and the water-pots following the sign of breath.[1]   The sail was a lady's smock or body-garment, mystically a veil, the veil of Isis or *Neith.*[2]   And this sign of breath, the *Net* of *Neith,* is to be realized at last in one form, as the *caul.*   The caul in which some children are enveloped at birth is the network of Neith.

In this they were netted and fished from the waters.   The caul in English is synonymous with the smock.   It is an old saying, " *Oh, you are a lucky man; you were wrapped up in a part of your mother's smock,*" when born in the caul.   The caul was the work, and the type of *Neith* the knitter, and *Athena* the weaver.   One English name of the spider's web is a caul.   Also the caul was a head-dress in which the hair of the pubescent maiden or married woman was *Snooded,* as was the mythical Gestator.

Egyptian mummies awaiting their re-birth in the tomb were invested in a network of bugles or beads, that represented the net of Neith, in which the child Horus was fished from the Nile.   Buckley states that the Australian mothers likewise made nets of hair and twisted bark, in which they placed the bones of their dead children, and wore them tied round their necks by day, and laid them under their heads by night.   The net-type is the same in both cases.   It represents the caul of birth and afterwards of re-birth.

The caul of fat that forms the network of the kidneys was to be especially offered to the Hebrew deity.

---

[1] Potter. *Antiq.* vol. i. p. 421.

[2] The most occult signification of the saying of Isis, at Sais, that no man had lifted her veil or peplum may now be interpreted.   The first clothing or veil was assumed on natural grounds at puberty.   Isis or Hes is the liquid of life personified, the flow which ceases with generation.   But Isis always wore her veil as divinity.   She came from herself, and the Generator had not put aside her mystic veil.   In the same sense, the Nun (cf. nun (Eg.), for negation) takes the veil that remains unlifted by the male in marriage.   The profoundest mysteries are the simplest.

"*Thou shalt take the caul that is about the midriff and the two kidneys, and the fat that is upon them, and burn them upon the altar as a 'sweet savour.'*"[1]

The same caul of fat is still sought for and highly prized by the Australian blacks; but it must be human. They make an incision in the flank of the live victim, and extract a portion of the kidney-caul to anoint themselves with, leaving the sufferer to die slowly.[2]

It is in this connection that the caul, or network, and sign of saving from the waters, acquired such significance for sailors. Mid-wives used to sell the caul to them as a preservative against drowning; also to Advocates, for the purpose of making them eloquent. The first connects it with the saving from the flood; the second, with the *Nabi*, because it was a sign of the revealer and maker known. Navel, naval, and nautical, are derived from this origin, and the sailor still holds on to the hieroglyphic signs.

On launching a canoe a Fijian chief has been known to slay several men for "rollers" to facilitate the launching; the "rollers" being afterwards cooked and eaten. Time was when a chief would kill a man, or men, on laying down the keel of a canoe, and try to sacrifice a life for every fresh plank added. Why was this? It was because the life was the breath in one aspect, the blood in the other. *Nef* (Eg.) breath, is the sailor, the wind, the breeze. The dead men were eaten as "*food for the carpenters;*" but the souls let out were the breath that was *to fill the sails*, and make the voyage prosperous. If a chief did not lower the mast of his vessel within a day or two after arriving at the place, some poor creature was sacrificed, and taken to him AS the "*lowering of the mast,*"[3] or letting out the breath of his sail. When a canoe arrived at a place for the first time after the death of a chief, the mast was not only lowered, the sail was also flung away into the water to be scrambled for. The typology is the same when the English or other ships still make the death-salute with lowered masts or flags at half-mast high. The sail was an Egyptian symbol of breath and soul, and the lowered flag now takes the place of the earlier sign.

The Two Truths of the water and the breath are especially oper-ant in certain primitive and traceable customs, some of which are universal.

When the Brandenburg peasant empties a pail of water on his doorstep after the coffin has crossed it-on the day of the burial, to "hinder the ghost from coming back," the custom is based on the antithesis of Water and Breath, and on the spirit or soul being founded on the breath. So is the belief that the ghost cannot cross a running stream without some kind of bridge, if only formed of a single thread.

[1] Ex. xxix. 13: Lev. iii. 4, 10, 15.   [2] Smyth.
[3] Williams, *Fiji*, vol. i. p. 206.

Dapper, in his description of the Hottentots,[1] says, some of them wear round the neck certain roots, which they find in the rivers far inland. When on a journey they set light to these in a fire, and then *blow the smoke* and ashes about, believing that the fumes or smell will keep off wild animals ; or they chew the root and *spit out the juice* around the spot where they encamp for the night to ensure protection. When the Hottentot goes out hunting, his wife will kindle a fire, and she must do nothing else but tend it and keep it alive, for if it should go out, her husband will not be successful ; or, if she elects the other element, she must pour water on the ground. When she is tired, her servant, or some one, must pour the water ceaselessly, or the hunter will not be lucky.[2] We shall not find a simpler application of the Two Elementary Truths.

On the last night of the year the Strathdown Highlanders form themselves into bands and fetch home great loads of juniper bushes, which are ranged round the fire to dry until morning. A discreet or wise man is then sent to the Dead-and-Living-ford to draw a pitcher of water in profound silence, without letting the vessel touch the earth. On his return they all retire to rest. Early on New Year's morning the *usque-cashrichd*, or water of the Dead-and-Living-ford, is drunk as a charm that is potent till the next New Year's Day. One of them then takes a large brush, with which he performs an act of lustration by sprinkling the occupants of all the beds. When this is ended, the doors and windows are completely closed, and every crack and cranny carefully stopped. The juniper collected in the various rooms is brought in and set fire to, and a rite of fumigation is performed by aid of the suffocating vapour. The more intense the *Smuchdan*, the more propitious is the solemnity. Horses, cattle, and other live-stock, are then smoked to preserve them from evil or inimical influence during the coming year. The effusion of the spirit following this baptism of water is also represented by the drinking of whisky. As soon as the gude wife has sufficiently recovered her breath to reach the bottle *dhu*, she does her best to regenerate the wheezing, coughing, nearly choked sufferers.[3]

These Two Truths of the Water and Breath are illustrated in like manner by Herodotus, who describes the way in which the Scythians made use of Indian hemp in their rite of purification after the burial of their dead. He says. "The Scythians having buried their dead, purify themselves by washing their own bodies. Then they set up the tent of fumigation." "*When the Scythians have taken some seed of the hemp they creep under the clothes, and then put the seed on the red-hot stones; this smokes, and produces such a steam that no Greek vapour-bath could surpass it.*" The Scythians, transported with the vapour, shout aloud with delight.[4] He likewise relates how the

[1] P. 621.   [2] Hahn, *Tsuni-Goam*, p. 77.
[3] Stewart, *Superstitions of the Highlanders.* Dyer, p. 17.   [4] Book iv. 73, 74.

Massagetæ had discovered trees that produced a peculiar kind of fruit, which the inhabitants threw on the fire, and sat round it in a circle to inhale the odour till they became intoxicated; then they rose up and betook themselves to singing and dancing.[1]

In Russia custom requires that on the third day after child-birth the mother shall take a vapour bath. The results are often evil, but the practice is typical, therefore sacred, and thus continued. The Two Truths of the Water and the Breath are combined in the vapour bath. Vapour is the breath of water. The vapour or sweating bath is a prominent and hitherto inexplicable feature in the mysteries of the American Indians, Aztecs, and other races. Vapour produced from water by heat was a primitive illustration of the breath of life. It was the marvel, the mystery called *Kepu* (Eg.), the mystery of heat, of fermentation, of breathing spirit into the embryo. *Kept* (Eg.) also means to fumigate. This was performed with vapour or other fumes produced by fire.

At a festival of the Delaware Indians said to have been held in honour of the God of Fire, a small hut-oven was set up inside the house of sacrifice, made of twelve poles tied together atop, and covered over with blankets. It was heated with *twelve* stones made red-hot, and *twelve* men crept within. An old man then threw *twelve* handfuls of tobacco on the stones, and the fumes narcotised the sitters, who were carried out swooning.[2]

The smokers and fumigators with tobacco were inhaling spirit, and in-breathing an inspiring life, a delirium of delight. Intoxication by tobacco was held by the North American Indians to be a supernatural ecstasy in which they saw spirits, as did the Brazilian sorcerers by the same means. Breath, breathing, vapour, were synonyms of the Spirit, and the North American Indian yet adores the Great Spirit, the master of breath, by breathing the smoke of his tobacco-pipe toward the sun.

When the Canadian Indians killed a bear, one of the hunters placed the stem of his pipe between the bear's teeth and, breathing into the bowl, forced the tobacco-smoke backwards into its mouth, adjuring the soul of the animal not to be offended![3]

The smoke was a temporary revivification, a typical giving back of the breath, or a mode of spiritual communication by means of the breath here represented by the smoke. The smoke of sacrifice and of incense represents the breath or spirit. The Chinese burned beasts and rich silks and jewels for their vapour to ascend as an offering to the celestial spirits.[4] The Jews were commanded to burn a perpetual incense before the Lord.[5] The household deity of the Siamese was supposed to delight in the fragrant steam of hot rice and Arrack.

[1] Book i. p. 203.   [2] Loskiel, *Ind. of North Am.* pt. i. p. 42.
[3] De Plancy, *Dict. Inf.*   [4] Author, pt. ii. p. 65.   [5] Ex. xxx. 37; Lev. x. 1.

In offering flowers to Coatlicue the Aztec Goddess of flowers, it was forbidden to smell them before they were presented to the Goddess. Scent was considered the spirit of the offering, the breath of the flowers, by the primitive races. The Limboos in offering their sacrifices dedicate the "*life-breath to the gods, the flesh to themselves.*"[1] The Kaffirs eat the animals which they offer to the Manes; the hunger of the spirits being satisfied with smoke. The Seminoles of Florida held the babe of a woman who died in childbirth over her mouth in order that it might receive her spirit with her parting breath: the breath was the spirit! So with the Romans, the nearest of kin had the right to inhale the breath or soul of the dying.

At the Jewish feast of Tents or Tabernacles a golden pitcher that held three logs of water was filled from the fountain of Siloah. When they came with it to the water-gate the trumpet was blown, the priests ascended the stair of the altar and turned to the left, where two silver basins stood. Each was perforated at bottom with a small hole *like a nostril*. The one toward the west was for the water; the one to the east for the wine.[2] The wine to the eastward was the Water of Life, and represented the effusion of the Holy Spirit, the second of the Two Truths. The double basin with the nostril-like aperture repeats the hieroglyphic vase with the two spouts, the name of which has been read Khent and Fent, and probably includes both in relation to the Two Truths, for it signifies the nose (which is fent), and it is at the same time a water-vase, or a vase of the Two Waters.

At the moment of pouring out one of the waters, in this case the Water of Life, considered by some Talmudists to be the *effusion of the Holy Spirit*, a strange transformation scene occurred. The priests suddenly cast off their belts and breeches; tore them into shreds and then made use of the strips as candle-wicks to which they set light.[3]

This was the analogue of the rising up to play in the Exodus, and conjoining promiscuously as in the Witches' Sabbath, the first mode of celebrating an influx of the Spirit.

The Jewish breeches were not a masculine garb. The *Makanase*[4] was a form of the primordial garment of womankind, still put on first by the priests, the same as the Egyptian *Ank*, the dress and strap, which often appears as linen hung up to dry. The tearing up of this was typical of the negative period past, and the setting light to the strips as candles was the equivalent of procreation. To light a candle *Sta* (Eg.) is synonymous with begetting a child.

The unleavened bread of the Egyptians and the Jews was symbolical of the first feminine period. Fermentation (*Kepa*) was the primary form of spirit, and of the second of the Two Truths represented by the

[1] *Trans. Eth. Soc.* new series, vol. vii. p. 153.
[2] *Mishna, Treatise Succah,* iv. 9.   [3] *Ibid.* v.
[4] Josephus, *Ant.* bk. 3, ch. vii. p. 1; also *Wars,* bk. 5, ch. v. p. 7.

leavened bread. *Sekha-hut* (Eg.) is leavened or inspirited bread. Dough, when leavened began to show holes and rents; it commenced *breathing*. In the Mishna instructions are given to the women who make unleavened bread, that they are to plunge their hands into cold water to prevent its breathing, or to hinder the dough from rising.[1]

It was likewise a law that during Passover no man was allowed to chew wheat for laying on a wound, because it set up a process of fermentation on the way to becoming leavened.[2]

Bread, when fermented, and breath are synonymous, and in English the breathing-place is called the Bread-basket. So the Goddess *Neft* whose name signifies the Breathed, or the Breather, carries the bread and seed basket on her head; and she who is the Lady of Breath or Seed is the later Llafdig, or Lady of the Loaf.

The Jews also apply the Two Truths to fruit, and make a distinction between Biccurim, the fruits of the soil in their natural state, and the fruits in their prepared condition of wine, oil, and flour called *Therumoth*.

Before milk is considered *fit for the use of men*, with the Kaffirs, it needs to undergo the process of fermentation. New milk is only fit for the young, the adults hold it puerile for them to drink it. Fermented milk represents virility and spirit.[3]

Of the Passover feast the Rabbins say: "*On all other nights we dip what we eat once; on this night we dip twice.*" Other ceremonial observances show the unification of the Two Truths.

The "Passover of the Resurection" is spoken of by the two brothers in the Gospel of Nicodemus.[4] They state that they were "*baptized along with other dead who had arisen,*" and that afterwards they celebrated the *Passover of the Resurrection*.

The child Horus was fabled to be drowned, and the Osirified in this character enters the water. Bacchus, lord of the humid nature, in being raised again ascends from the waters and in the character of the twice-born was called the *Fanman* or winnower.[5] The initiated in the greater mysteries were purified with water and breathed on, fanned, or winnowed by the purifying spirit.

"*Tis the Lenæan feast* (Bacchic). *But we ourselves now, at least, are winnowed* (pure).[6]

The Two symbols held in the hands of the Egyptian Gods, the *Hek* or Aut Crook and the *Khi*, are signs of these Two Truths. The Hook which denotes laying hold is the determinative of matter as "*Aut.*" The *Khi* is a fan, the sign of breath or spirit.

[1] *Tract. Pesachim*, ch. iii.   [2] *Mishna*, Treatise 4, ch. ii. p. 7.   [3] Dugmore, p. 125.
[4] Ch. xi. pt. 2.   [5] Plutarch, *Isis and Osiris*.   [6] Aristophanes, *Acharn.* 471.
[7] The Crook is an Inner African symbol. Hurd says of certain tribes, "*they place fetishes before their doors, and these titular deities are made in the form of grapples or hooks which we use to shake our fruit-trees.*"—Hurd, p. 374. From this natural genesis the type becomes the Crosier of the Pope of Rome, and of the Lama in Tibet, the Symbol of the Gods in the temples of Japan. But the Inner African fetish image is primary.

The " Two Truths " are represented by the Water and the Spirit or ghost in the dual baptism practised in many lands, and in all the known Mysteries. The Two Baptisms of the Gnostics were recognised by them as the animal and the spiritual.[1]

In the New Testament records we find the Two Baptisms contending for supremacy. John is represented as the Baptizer with Water and Paul with the Holy Ghost.[2] They are likewise illustrated by the Two Baptisms of John and Jesus. John says, "*I baptize with Water*," but Jesus is "*He which baptizeth with the Holy Ghost.*" The double baptism is pourtrayed in Jordan by John baptizing Jesus with water, and the Spirit descending from heaven like a dove, one of the symbolic birds of soul, and by the fire which Justin asserts was kindled in the river Jordan. The Two Truths are recognizable even in the formula of the Christians, applied to heretics who were "to be baptized or burnt."

The " Two Truths" of Biology survive in their primitive perfection as the " Blood and Fire" blazoned on the banners of organized ignorance by the "Salvation Army." The blood of the female and the vivifying fire of the male are the two factors in the human creation. These bringers to birth in the natural genesis,—the " double primitive force" of the Creator Ptah,—were continued as types of re-birth in the symbolical representation of the Mysteries, where the soul was supposed to be regenerated in baptism, reborn and saved, as by Fire and Blood, or the Water and Breath, that were made use of in the purifying rite. When divorced from their origin and un-explained by the Gnosis, such doctrines and dogmas culminate in publicly profaning all that was once held sacred under the Seal of Secresy because they were so natural in their genesis.

Among the Jakun Tribes of the Malay Peninsula the Two Truths of the water and breath are recognised in their dual baptism. When a child is born it is carried to the nearest stream and washed. There a fire is kindled, *fragrant* wood is burned, and the child is passed to and fro through the fumigatory incense-smoke, or breath of fire.[3] When the child is born the Khoi-khoi kindle a fire with the Dorob, a fire-drill ; no flint, steel, or matches being allowed. This fire has to be maintained until the navel heals and the umbilical cord drops off. Nothing must be cooked on that fire. If these injunctions be not duly observed the child will surely die.[4]

The old Pahlavi Rivayat, or Miscellany of Traditional Memoranda called the *Shayast La-Shayast*, gives instructions for the fire to be stirred and made to blaze high the moment the navel-cord of the new-born infant is severed, and for three days and three nights no one is to pass between the child and the fire.[5] The Placenta is still offered up as a burnt sacrifice by all good nurses ; fire being the superior

[1] Irenæus, bk. 1, ch. xxi. p. 2.   [2] Acts xix.   [3] *Journal Ind. Archip.* vol. ii. p. 264.
[4] Hahn, *Tsuni-Goam*, p. 77.   [5] Ch. x. 15.   Author.

element of life; the fire that vivifies; the solar or masculine fire. It is also an English custom for the parturient woman to *breathe* in her *left hand* to bring away the after-birth.

In ancient Mexico the first act of lustration took place at birth. The child was washed by the nurse in the name of the Water Goddess to remove the outward impurity. Next she *blew her breath* on water held in *her right* hand, and prayed the invisible deity (the Holy Spirit) to descend upon the water for baptism of the inner nature and deliverance from sin, foulness, and misfortune. Four days later there was another ceremony (the *Nem*, or second festival of Egypt), at which the babe was named, and it is said the child was passed four times through the fire.[1] These customs were continued in the Mysteries.

Modern writers may begin their account of the religious origines with the "Perception of the Infinite"; but such thinkers, whose

> "*Nimble souls*
> *Can spin an unsubstantial universe*
> *Suiting their mood, and call it possible,*
> *Sooner than see one grain with eye exact*
> *And give strict record of it,*"[2]

are not calculated to interpret the thought of primitive men who began with a perception of the Definite. They saw the breathing image of life issue from the water in various forms. They found that water was an element opposed to breath. They observed the fish the frog and the hippopotamus could keep under water and live; the water did not extinguish their breath as it did that of the human being. Hence when they tried to express the perception of a power beyond themselves, it took one shape as the power of breathing in the water. Such is one of the great facts registered in the Kamite Typology. This perception led to the pourtrayal of powers in the image of the frog, the eel, the perch, the hippopotamus, the crocodile, and other types of that which could cross the waters and live beneath them.

In one figure of life issuing from the waters the Lotus is the type of the bearing and breathing power. It is noticeable that the Greek word στέγω, which is used for bearing, means to hold water, and in gestation the bearer as vessel is water-tight in the mystical sense. Hence the pregnant Water-Horse was adopted as a type of the bearing Mother; the Lotus on the Water is the early type of the natural Argo. The Womb, or Argha-Yoni, was the primary form of the boat that goes of itself without sail or wind in the mythical tales. But the Water and Lotus are both female emblems at first. The Lotus represented Her who came from herself or from the Water of Life, *i.e.* the blood source. The Papyrus-Sceptre, the *Uat*, is the express sign of the feminine nature of *Uati* who impersonated both

---

[1] Tylor, *Primitive Culture*, vol. ii. p. 394.   [2] *Spanish Gipsy.*

Truths of Wet and Heat, Water and Breath, or Body and Soul. It was the blue and red Lotus in Egypt, where red denoted flesh and blood, blue signified the soul.[1]

To image Source as Water, they identified Water first as Source. This was the one existence with Two Manifestations, or two aspects; the water of life in one sense might become the water of death in the other, according as it was drink of life or drench of death.

In the mystical phase it was the water of life when it nourished the embryo, and the water of death to the seed that was mixed with it through the non-observance of time and season.

A mythical form of the Twin Waters of Source was supplied by the Red and White or Spotted Cow, as the menstrual fluid and milk; the water of the womb and breast; the red source being reckoned first as it is in nature. Maka, Menka, or Menkhat, the genitrix, carries in her hands two Vases, the symbol in a dual aspect of the two Waters of the Motherhood.

In the Bundahish there is a physiological account of the Two Waters of Source considered as female and male. In this the seed of the male becomes the uppermost of the two, and is a form of the spirit that broods over the water in creation or incubation. *It says in Revelation—*

"*The seed of the females which issues beforehand takes a place within the womb, and the seed of the males will remain above it and will fill the space of the womb; whatever refrains therefrom becomes blood again, enters into the veins of the females, and at the time any one (child) is born it becomes milk and nourishes him, as all milk arises from the seed of the males, and the blood is that of the females.*"[2]

According to the Parsee Ritual the rule is that "*That which comes from the menstruous woman to any one or to anything is all to be washed with bull's urine (gomez) and water.*"[3] These also are two opposite forms of the Waters as male and female.

The Two Waters are divided, and one of them is underlined with red by John as the water *and* the blood.[4]

The double baptism of the Mysteries was also by water and by blood. The blood represented the *Hesmen*, the menstrual purification, and the water the masculine source, as may be learned from the Ritual and the process of regenerating; hence the water of *purifying* and the water of *vivifying*, the Pool of Natron and the Pool of Salt.[5]

Considered as Liquid or Uat the Two Waters are One, but they were divided to distinguish them. They were One when the Water and the Breath constituted the Two Truths. When distinguished as the male and female of source there are Three, including the Breath,

---

[1] See plate in Bonwick's *Egyptian Belief and Modern Thought.*
[2] *Bundahish*, ch. xvi. p. 5. West.   [3] *Shayast La-Shayast*, ch. x. 38.
[4] 1 John v. 7, 3.   [5] Ch. xvii.

and John identifies the later three as the Water, Blood, and Spirit. "The Christ came," he says, "by Water and Blood." The *Alexandrine* version distinctly says He came by Water *and* the Spirit. Another version gives the Water, Blood, and Spirit.

This uninterpreted Gospel mystery is only explicable by aid of the Two Truths, and by distinguishing their variations. John has taken the Two Truths of the Water (male), the Blood (female), to evolve the Spirit as the third witness of his Trinity; "*and these three agree in one.*" There were but Two Truths, but these were blended to produce the Son who was a Third to the preceding two as the one in whom they united and were reproduced ; the Spirit of Life being here evolved from the Two Waters, male and female.

The negroes of St Croix, West Indies, on becoming Christianized objected to be baptized by the water from the earth ; they insisted on using rain-water which came down from heaven.[1] Such a superstition belongs to an earlier form of faith than the Christian, which, especially in the Protestant phase, is smilingly ignorant of any distinction between the two. The Catholics sanctify the water of earth by adding salt, and this turns the water of *Hesmen* (blood) into the Pool of Salt according to the Egyptian Ritual.[2]

When the Two Waters are distinguished as male and female, existence, healing, and purity are made dependent upon their not being mixed. Various legends inculcate the never mixing of the white source with the red. The Talmudists say the waters of Jordan are unfit for healing the unclean because they are *mixed* waters. This is a relic of naming from the Two Waters considered as male and female continued from the time when distinction of season was first taught.

In the Book of Enoch, when the world is destroyed it is described in the same typical language. Destruction depends upon the *Waters mixing*, the water above being considered as masculine source. "*The water which is above shall be the agent (male), and the water which is under the earth shall be the recipient, and all shall be destroyed.*"[3]

Unlike the Jordan described by the Rabbins, the Welsh Bala, or going forth from the source at the head of the twin river Dee was famed for not mixing its dual waters which ran into one lake but were reputed to pass through it in separate currents that never blended together. The same was said of various other waters. Homer describes the river Titaresius flowing from the Styx as pure and unmixed with the waters of death ; and gliding like oil over the surface of the waters by which the gods made their covenants.

The Twin Waters are also localised in Dumfriesshire, where the river Esk takes the double form of the white and black Esk. The

[1] *Contemporary Review*, 1875, p. 773.   [2] Ch. xvii.
[3] *Book of Enoch*, ch. liii. 7—10.

M 2

place where the one water bifurcates was once sacred to most ancient rites; a fair was formerly held there annually, at which it was
the custom for unmarried persons of both sexes to choose a companion
with whom they were to live for the year following. This was called
hand-fasting. If they liked each other they were then united for life,
and if not they separated and made a fresh choice.[1]

The Kabala Denudata says there are *two dews, the dew of Macro-
prosopus* (the primal cause) *and the dew of the Seir.*

In the inscription of Darius at El-Kharjeh the two waters appear
as the young and the old *Han* or *Mu ;* Youth and Age being the two
aspects there assigned to the same element for typical purposes.

The Twin Waters are found at the centre of all in the Assyrian
place of beginning, in the realm of Hea and Nin-ki-Gal, the Great
Lady of the earth, or the Great Mother Earth. Here, according to the
Assyrian mythos, rose the stream Miebalati, or waters of life, and here
also the "*waters of death which cleanse not the hands,*" in consequence,
probably, of being like the Egyptian *tesh* and *pant,* the red source.
The Basutos have a mysterious region in the world of spirits called
Mosima, the Abyss. The Baperis on the *northern* shore of the Fal
river affirm that the entrance to this region is in their country.
Here the universal Two Waters are located; one is a kind of Styx,
the river of death; the other, in a cistern, is the water of life and
nectar of the gods.[2]

The natives of Millbank identify the water with Two rivers guarded
by two huge portals and flowing from a dark lake. The good enter
the stream to the right hand, this is the water of life from which they
are eternally supplied. The wicked enter the water on the left hand
and suffer from starvation and perishing cold.[3] In this, the Two
Waters appear just as in the Ritual, and the myth presents the eschatological aspect of the Egyptian judgment. Even the island answers
to the Isle of the Blessed in the celestial Nile.

The Water that divides in space is a type of bifurcation in the
beginning. The heaven or firmament, (the Nun,) was first apprehended, or named as the water above. This was divided in creation
as we find it in the Hebrew Genesis where the water is separated
into upper and lower, and was represented by the two manifestations
of day and dark, the water of life and water of death. Various
legends may be read by an application of this type. The Chinese
have a saying that Chaos opened and unfolded at midnight, and
therefore they date their day from that hour; the one time of the
"Two Truths" of Light and Shade.

The separation was next marked on the two horizons of dawn
and darkness. The one water that is divided in the Ritual became twain in forming Two Lakes;[4] the Northern being the lake

[1] Sir John Sinclair's *Statistical Account of Scotland.*, vol. xii. p. 615. 1794.
[2] Casalis, *The Basutos,* p. 248.   [3] Bancroft, vol. iii. p. 519.   [4] Ch. cix.

of primordial matter; the Southern, the lake of sacred principles or seminal (later spiritual) essences. Thus the South, as the region of light, and the North as the domain of darkness, were the bright and the dark waters of the Two heavens. This was in the vaguest stage of distinguishing before the Two Solstices could be determined by Two constellations or stars. We find the water of life is sometimes said to be concealed between two lofty mountains which shut closely together. But for two or three minutes in each day they open, and the seeker of the healing and vivifying water must be ready on the instant to dash through the opening, dip his two flasks and as instantly rush back.

There is a Slovak version of the myth, which makes the cleft in one mountain open at *mid-day*, the other at *mid-night*. The mid-day cleft discloses the water of life, the mid-night one reveals the water of death.[1] In this version the division is that of mid-day and mid-dark, and the heaven is the water of light and shade, as it is in Egyptian when the pool of the two waters is called Shu-Ma, or Ma-Shu, *i.e.* light and shade. Similar stories are told of the Moslem Mount Kaf.

This imagery of the cloven mountain is applied by Zechariah on the grand scale to the great year when the Lord shall go forth and stand upon the Mount of Olives, " *And the Mount of Olives shall cleave in the midst thereof toward the East and toward the West, and half of the Mountain shall remove toward the North and half toward the South.*"[2] This is the Mount of the Equinoxes, yet to be described. When the vast cleft shall open into a deep valley the " *living waters shall go out from Jerusalem : half of them toward the Southern sea* (in front or before) *and half of them toward the Hinder sea* (*i.e.* the north, which implies the other being south).[3] These are the Two waters of the earliest division.

" *Generator of Years* " is another name of the Two Pools—the Pool of Natron and the Pool of Salt—in which the Sun was re-born by day and the Moon was renewed by night. This shows the waters in relation to the keepers of time and period. The first definite indicators of the Year were the seven stars of the Great Bear, and the " Well of the Seven Stars " the Hebrew Beer-Shebâ, was an early form of the primordial water of the nocturnal heaven, from the depths of which the constellation arose in latitudes where it dipped below the horizon. Then it became the Pool of the Sun and Moon on the two opposite sides of the Circle, when the waters were divided. The Muhammedan traditions speak of the two waters as the Pool of the Sun and the Pool of the Moon.[4]

In Polynesia the god *Tane* was the mythical divider of the heaven from earth, or the waters into upper and lower; and the divided or

[1] Wenzig, p. 148.   [2] Zech. xiv. 4.   [3] Verse 8.
[4] Sprenger, *Leben Muhammed.*, p. 111.

dividing waters are still represented by the constellation Eridanus, the Iarutana (Eg.), or River of the Division. In a Maori myth the Waters of Tane are the Waters of Life and renewal for the Moon. At their only festival, that of the New Moon, the women assembled and bewailed those who had died during the last moon, crying, "*Alas, thou, O Moon, hast returned to life, but our departed ones come not back. Thou hast bathed in the living Waters of Tane, and had thy life renewed, but there has been no fountain of living water to restore life to our departed ones.*" [1]

Following the division of light and shade the two Solstices were established, north and south, by means of two stars, such as the double Law-giver Kepheus (Kafi or Ma-Shu) north, and *Cor Leonis* in the zodiac. Kepheus was known in India as Capuja [2] and in New Zealand *Kupe* (a name of Maui the Maori Shu) is *celebrated as the Divider of the north from the south islands and as the Former of Cook's Straits.*

This first division of the heaven, the water, or the circle, is possibly symbolised in the custom of the Algonquin Indians who, when on the war-path, drink out of small bowls which are marked across the middle. In going out one side of the circle is placed to the mouth and in coming back the other. In such customs the original meaning continued to be enacted when otherwise forgotten.

The Chinese have the Two Waters of the Egyptian *Ann* as Two Rivers in the Valley of Han or Han-mun. It is said to have been in this valley that Hwang-te the first mythical Emperor of China obtained the Map-writings in red lines and in the Seal character. The dragon-writing was derived from the River Ho ; the tortoise-writing from the River Lo, the two waters which are still represented by the double stream of Aquarius. [3]

At the time and place of receiving the writings there were three days and nights during which all was wrapt in vapour. When the mist removed the Emperor saw a great fish and sacrificed to it. Three days and nights was the length of time during which the hero was immured in the fish's belly. It was when the fish floated off to sea that Hwang-te obtained the map-writings in the Valley of Han (Egyptian Ann) the Birth-place, where the one water of heaven was divided in two for the earliest mapping-out. The Fish was in all likelihood the *Pisces Australis* which contains the great Star Fomalhaut (the mouth of the fish), one of the determinatives of the four quarters. This was an early sign of the solstitial division ; and the Fish, Crocodile, or Water-cow, was the primordial type of the genitrix who brought forth the writings from the waters.

As before said one name of the Egyptian pool is *Shu-Ma*, or Ma-

[1] *Te Ika a Maui*, 54.　　　　　[2] Wilford, *Asiatic Researches*.
[3] *Annals of the Bamboo Books.* Notes. Legge's *Chinese Classics*, vol. iii. p. 1 ; *Prol.* p. 109.

Shu, in relation to the Two Truths represented by *Ma* and *Shu*, and the Chinese have a curious ceremony designated the *Mae-Shuwy*. On the death of a parent the eldest son living puts *two* small copper coins into an earthen vessel which he takes in his hands and goes, accompanied with other mourners, to the city-moat, or to the *well* at the village gate, where he deposits the money and takes some water, with which the face of the dead is washed. Whoever brings this water is entitled to a *double* share of the property. When there are no children or grandchildren the next of kin purchases the water, and this ceremony determines the heir to the *double possession*.[1] In this typical ceremony the water at the gate, the two copper coins, the twofold property all tend to identify the *Mae-Shuwy* rite with the Two Truths of the pool called *Ma-Shu* in Egyptian mythology.

The Great Hall of the Two Truths in the Ritual stands at the place of the double pool or lake. This is in *Ann*, which is an Egyptian name of the Valley and of *Fish*.

The Pool of the Two Waters was also formed at the place of the great Serpent Temple, Nagkon-Wat, in Cambodia. On either side of the immense causeway, 725 feet long, is an artificial lake fed by springs, each lake covering about five acres of ground.[2] Popular tradition assigns the foundations of the temple to the prince of *Roma*, whose name is mentioned by the native historians. Now the Fish was a sign of the birth-place from the beginning. It was there the prince, the Repa and heir-apparent, was born, that being the sign of re-birth out of the waters, which was fixed at last as the sign of Pisces in the solar zodiac.

It was there that Semiramis or Derkêto, the fish-tailed genitrix, brought forth her son ; and in the temple of *Roma* there is a representation of the child as Vishnu issuing from the mouth of the emaning fish, holding in his hand the Word, which has been rescued from the waters. *Rama* is another Egyptian name for the fish, and for the throat out of which issues the Word. It has been previously suggested that *Semi* (Eg.), the image, and *Rami* (Eg.), the fish, supplied the name of the fish-tailed Semiramis. It is the celestial locality that will account for Roma in Cambodia and Rome in Italy. Rumo was an ancient name of the River Tiber, and from this the city was undoubtedly named as the birth-place of the twins, Romulus and Remus. Ram (Eg.), the fish and the throat, is still represented by the mitre, shaped like the fish's mouth, worn by the Pope of Rome ; and Roma, called the mother of the twins, is one with Semiramis of Nineveh.

The Pool of the Two Waters, denominated the Twin Pools, was represented in Jerusalem as the Two Pools called Bezatha by Eusebius in his Onomasticon. He says, "there is a pool

[1] Kidd, *China*, pp. 175, 176.
[2] Vincent, *Land of the White Elephant*, p. 209.

at Jerusalem, which is the *Piscina Probatica*, that had formerly five porches, and now is pointed out as the twin pools there, of which one is filled by the rains of the year, but the other exhibits its water tinged in an extraordinary manner with red, retaining a trace, they say, of the victims that were formerly cleansed in it." The red one answers to the Pool of Pant and Hesmen; the other to the Water of Life. Jerusalem, the Mount of Peace, the Nabhi-Yoni of the earth, was one of those sacred cities that were mapped out according to the Kamite model in the heavens. As such they include the Well of the Abyss (Egyptian "*tsta*," the depth) and the Water from the source.

Thus the miracle of the healing[1] belongs of necessity to the Astronomical Allegory. The "moving of the waters" is periodic, as in all other forms of the mythos. It depends on the coming of the Angel—the very impersonation of periodicity—and on his washing in the water first. "*An angel of the Lord washed at a certain season.*"[2] So in the Ritual the deceased is restored to life by the water in which Osiris, the good opener (Un-Nefer), has washed.

The Pool of Two Truths was in Ann (Heliopolis) and Ann is the name of the Fish. In Jerusalem it is the Fish-pool, and when the Zodiac of the twelve signs was formed the solar birth-place was figured in the sign of Pisces, as the outlet from the northern quarter, and the Waters of the Abyss, the depth, or *Tesui-ta* (Eg.) from which come the Hebrew Bethesda or *Bezatha*, and the Assyrian Bit-*zida*—for the same imagery is found in the Assyrian mythology and mundane mapping out from the one original pattern. In the Greek text[3] the pool is said to be *by the sheep*, not by the sheep-market, and the Fishes of course are next to the sign of the Sheep or Ram in the zodiac.

The twin-pool was located in Ann, the white water being Southward and the red Northward. Here the Church of Anne answers to the Temple of *Ann* in Egypt. Near the Church was a reservoir of water which is mentioned by Brocardus, corresponding to the pool or well that supplied the two waters. The Assyrians likewise have their Bit-Anna "A shrine of *Anna* was built on the Mound near Bit-ziba;"[4] just as the ancient British had their well and water of "*St. Anne.*"

The well *Zem-Zem* at Mecca, into which the moon is fabled to have fallen, is an extant form of the Pool of the Two Truths. The waters also preserve their dual character as of old. They are the Water of Life to the true believer. Every pilgrim who visits the shrine seeks its well, and both drinks of the water and pours it over his body. It is still the water of purification or regeneration in accordance with the meaning of *Sem-Sem* in Egyptian. *Sem-Sem* (Eg.) denotes the regenesis. The Ritual says: "*Inexplicable is the Sem-Sem, it is the greatest of all secrets.*"[5]

The Pool in the Ritual is the Well of *Sem-Sem*. It was the place

[1] John v. 2—4.   [2] Alexandrine version.   [3] Griesbach, John v. 2.
[4] *Book of Beginnings*, vol. ii. p. 512.   [5] Ch. xv.

not only where the Moon fell but where both Moon and Sun were renewed. In accordance with which doctrine the deceased seeks the well to receive baptismal regeneration and be purified and renovated. He says : " *I wash in the Pool of Peace. I draw waters from the Divine Pool under the Two Sycamores of Heaven and Earth. All Justification is redoubled on my behalf.*" [1] "*The Osiris is pure by that Well of the South and the North.*" [2]

The water of *Zem-Zem* is sent forth to Muhammedan devotees abroad as the water of life and spiritual healing. And it is very literally the water of death ; for a late analysis made by Dr. E. Frankland showed it to be sheer sewage " seven times more concentrated than London sewage," and containing 579 grains of solid matter per gallon.[3]

The division of the water is likewise pourtrayed on the monuments by the figure of Hapi-Mu. Hapi, being of both sexes, denotes the one in whom the two were united (Hapi), hence the epicene personification. From the mouth of Hapi issues the one water which enters two other figures that emane it from their mouths in two separate streams.[4] Thus the one water is visibly divided into the two waters of Mythology just as the one Nile became two in the Blue Nile above and the Red Nile below, in the land of Egypt. Hapi-Mu is painted red and blue. One source of the Two Waters of Hapi-Mu called the " Abime of Karti," was localized at the Ivory Island, Elephantine.[5] This personification of the Waterer was finally fixed as the Waterman pouring out the Two Streams in the zodiac. But long before the zodiac was formed the Two Waters were said to issue from the mount, a figure of the height, sometimes called the Rock of the Horizon. The "two-topped mount divine" was a form of this rock that divides in two in various myths. The double rock which marked the Solstices first, and afterwards the Equinoxes. The well or pool of Ma-Shu (Eg.) bubbles up from this mythical mount or rock of the horizon in a legend of the people called *Shu*-Paropamisans, south of the Hindu-Kush. At the top of a rock near the fort of Khornushi there rises a spring of brilliant water, hot in winter and cool in summer, in a basin always brimming. "*Nu-Shu*" is said to be the sound made by the murmur of the water. Shu having been the *opener* of the rock from which the water sprang at first. In this legend Shu appears as the grandson of Noah. Nu (Eg.) is water and a variant of Mu or Ma; thus Nu-Shu is equivalent to Ma-Shu, the name of the pool in Egyptian. Shu was the divider of the rock whence came the water as the god of the two Solstices or divisions in

---

[1] Ch. xcvii.   [2] ch. cxxv.
[3] Report in *Times* newspaper, Sep. 9, 1881.
[4] Pourtrayed on the tomb of Rameses III.
[5] Inscription of Seti I. at Rhedesieh.

heaven. This, like the Hebrew legend of Moses or Mashu smiting the rock, is another version of the same original mythos.[1]

In Maori the Two Truths of Mati find expression the most perfect. *Matua* signifies the first; the parent and parents. *Matauai* denotes the fountain-head. *Matatu* is to begin to flow. *Matahae* means the stream diverging from the main channel where the water becomes the Two Waters. *Mata-mata* is the source of all, the bifurcating or dual point of beginning; an exact equivalent for the dual Mati (Eg.). *Motu* means dividing, to be severed; and *Matahi* is the name of the two first months of the year.

One ancient Egyptian name of the birth-place in the beginning where the water divided into two—as in the double stream of the Waterman—was *Mat*, the middle; later *Ann*, and this is extant by name in the Mangaian and Maori mythology. Rangimotia, or the centre of the heavens, is the point of commencement marked by a hill,[2] as it was in Mat, the boundary, division, middle of the heaven. It was on Rangi-Motia that Ru, the sky-supporter, planted the trees upon which the heaven was raised up from the earth. The division of Mangaia was based on that of the hill Rangimotia, the centre of the heavens; and in accordance with this mapping out of the land it was the custom in ancient times, whenever a large fish was stranded, to divide the fish in two, straight along the back-bone, and then apportion it in shares, the head going to the two eastern chiefs, the tail to the two western, and the middle to the two central chiefs of Mangaia.[3] Again, the divided fish typifies the one fish of the primordial division which is represented for us by the twin fishes of the zodiac. Also the Annamese consider it bad luck for a fish to leap out of the water into the boat. When this happens the fish must be cut in two and thrown into the water again, one half on each side of the boat.[4] Such customs are correlative, however widely scattered. The whole round of the world is a reflector of the celestial imagery.

In the kingdom of Udyana, or " the garden," a form of Eden, near Cashmere, there is a sacred mountain called " *Mount Lan-po-lo*," by Hiuen-Tshang. At one time it was identified with Mêru. It is the source of the waters as is Alborz, in the Bundahish, and the Gan-Eden in Genesis. The Buddhist pilgrims describe the tree of life, or periodicity, Kalpatura, as growing on the summit, where there is a lake from which a large river issues, and in the water lurks a dragon. In many mythologies the " Two Waters " are localised along with the tree and the great serpent (or dragon). The Three are inseparable in the Ritual, where the Pool of the Two Truths is also the pool of the two trees as well as the two waters, and the Apophis serpent that lies in the Pool of Pant.

---

[1] Latham, *Comparative Philology*, p. 241, note.
[2] Gill, *Myths and Songs*, p. 58.   [3] *Ibid.* p. 128.
[4] Consul Tremlett, *Trade Report on Saigon and Cochin China*, 1881.

In a Russian story a flying snake brings two heroes to a lake into which a green bough is cast, and the green bough forthwith breaks into flame and is consumed. Into another lake they flung a decaying log, and this immediately burst into blossom.[1] The legend preserves its two branches of the two trees and the two waters of life and death as found in the Pool of Ma-Shu. These narratives belong to the same original myth as the burning bush of Moses and the budding rod of Aaron, the flying serpents, the bitter waters, with the log or tree cast in to make them sweet. As such they have been preserved in the northern folklore instead of being converted into Hebrew history out of the Kamite mythology. In the Russian stories these Two Waters also appear as the water of strength and of weakness. They are often among the precious treasures guarded by the Serpent in a cave, cellar, or other hole of the under-world. One of the Skazkas tells of a wondrous garden in which there are two springs of healing and life-giving water, and around this garden coils a mighty serpent like that of Midgard hidden in the waters, which encircles the world until the last day. The Egyptian pool of the Two Truths is represented in the Bundahish by the Abyssal waters. These are identifiable by the tree and the lurking monster. Here it is the Hom tree, the tree of healing and immortality. The Apophis dragon of the Egyptian pool is here the lizard with a log-like body, which is at eternal enmity with the good mind, and for ever tries to injure and destroy the Tree of Life. The waters, in a modern Greek story, are guarded by a Lamia, a serpent-woman, and these flow from a rock. In another, the cleft of the mountain opens at midday, and the springs are disclosed. Each of these cries " *Draw from me*," but the bee flies to the one that gives life.[2]

The Healing Water that is periodic in the Gospel according to John is one with the water that only heals periodically in this form of the Mythos.

The Mount, or Rock, and the Tree, are co-types with the water at the point of all commencement, and these can be traced in many localities. For example—

The same Pool of the Two Truths, along with the Tree of the Ritual, is found in the story told by Varro of the origin of Athens. It is related that a double wonder appeared springing out of the earth—the olive tree and water. The oracle declared that the olive was the sign of Athena, the water of Poseidon; and the people were to choose from which of the two—tree or water—they would name their city, the name of Athens being adopted.

The Two Waters are also described in the "Bundahish" as belonging to the "beginnings of creation." They are said to flow from the north, where the Aredvivsur fount of the waters is the source of all.

[1] Ralston, pp. 233—234, also 250.   [2] Hahn, vol. ii. pp. 234—280.

Ardvi-sura, in the Aban Yasht, is a title of the Goddess Anahita, who is the female Angel of the Waters; and the name of Anahid is applied to the planet Venus in the Bundahish. Anahita is the Persian form of the Egyptian Anit (Neith) and the Assyrian and Syrian Anne. The waters come "*part from Alburz and part from the Alburz of Ahura-Mazda; one towards the west, that is the Arag, and one towards the east, that is the Veh River.*" Of these it is said: "*Through those finger-breadth tricklings dost thou pour and draw forth such waters, O AhuraMazda!*" The fertilization of the world arises from these two waters.[1]

Here, as elsewhere, the mythical waters have been confused with actual rivers with which they were identified, but the celestial Egypt and the Nile of the Waterman are indicated as the originals of the common Mythos. The Arag is described as passing through the "land of *Spêtos*, which they also call *Mesr*, and they call it there the river *Niv*." Mesr is Egypt, the Mes-ru, or outlet of birth, and *Spêtos* therefore represents the word Egypt.[2] The S in Pazend being equivalent to the Avesta G or Pahlavi ik or ig, *Spêtos* is a form of Egypt like Coptus or Egyptos. *Niv* is also identical with *Num* (Eg.) or with *Nil*, if the Pazend form of the word be transcribed through Pahlavi.

The Tree, the Water, and the Serpent, which are clustered together in various myths at the point of commencement, may be identified at last as Inner African, for these are the three supreme types of divinity with several races. The Water, the Serpent, and the Tree, sometimes classed as a triad, are the objects of worship in Hwida. Three deities only are adored by the Negroes of Guinea—the Water, Tree, and Serpent.[3] This myth of the Heaven that divided into the Two Waters of Day and Dark, of South and North, of Life and Death, is universal, and belongs to a total system of typology that is one and indivisible.

It takes years to fathom the simplicity of the primitive thought and expression; the knowingness of the "ignorant present" is totally antipodal to such matters as are herein interpreted. The Two Truths were also typified by *motion* and non-motion, or *arrest* in relation to the female. This is shadowed forth by Plutarch in a somewhat abstract and remote manner, but thoroughly illustrative of the way in which the simplicities of the early time have been transmogrified into the "Mysteries" of the later, especially by the Greeks :—

"The generative and salutary part of nature hath its motion towards him (Osiris), and in order to procure being; but the destroying and corruptive part hath its motion from him, and in order to procure not-being. For which reason they call the former part *Isis*, from *going* and being *born-along* with *knowledge*, she being a kind of a living and prudent motion. For her name is not of a

---

[1] *Bundahish*, ch. vii. 15; ch. xx. 2; West.
[2] *Bundahish*, ch. xx. 8; West, footnote.
[3] Butron, *Dahome*. Bosman's *Voyage*, p. 195.

barbarous original; but as all the gods have one name (*Theos*) in common, and that is derived from the two first letters of *Theon* (*runner*) and of *Theatos* (*visible*), so also this very goddess is both from *motion* and *science* at once called Isis by us and *Isis* also by the Egyptians. So, likewise, *Plato* tells us that the ancients opened the nature of the word *Usia* (or *substance*) by calling it *Isia* (that is, *knowledge* and *motion*); as also that *Neosis* (*intellection*) and *Phronesis* (*discretion*) had their names given them for being a *Phora* (or *agitation*) and a kind of *motion* or *Nûs* (or *mind*), which was then, as it were *Hiemenos* and *Pheromenos* (that is, moved and agitated), and the like he affirmeth of *Synienay* (which signifies to *understand*), that it was as much as to say *to be in commotion*. Nay, he saith moreover, that they attribute the very names of the *Agathon* (or *good*) and of *Arete* (or *virtue*) to the *Theontes* (or *runners*) and the *Euroüntes* (or *well-movers*). As likewise on the other hand again, they used terms opposite to motion by way of reproach; for they called what clogged, tied up, locked up, and confined nature from *Jesthai* and *Janai* (that is, from *agitation* and *motion*), *Kakia* (*baseness* or *ill-motion*), *Aporial* (*difficulty* or *difficult motion*), *Deilia* (*fearfulness* or *fearful motion*), and *Anina* (*sorrow* or *want of motion*). As corruption locks up and fixes Nature's course, so generation resolves and excites it by means of motion."[1]

The simple foundation for this doctrinal abstruseness is that the early men perceived and taught that there was a time to go, and a time not to go, or a time of motion and a time of arrest. Some of the strangest matter in all folk-lore is related to this subject. The Hottentots speak out more plainly. Bleek tells us how in their folk-tales it is affirmed that by the glance from the eye of a maiden (this, he says, is *probably at a time when she would be usually kept in strict retirement*) men became fixed in whatever position they then occupied, with whatever they were holding in their hands. They were also transformed into "trees that talked."[2] That is, as other legends show, during the ordinary menstrual period, which was looked upon as the opposite of motion, an end of time, a solution of continuity, a phase of arrest.

At a later stage of thought it is said: "*The fiend or demoness Geh is so violent that where no other fiend can smite with a look, she smites with a look.*"[3]

This arrest was transferred and reflected in the persons of those who looked on the maiden at the *tabu* time. Many legends of a transformation of living things into stone originated in this way, and the petrifying is often assigned to water. The water of life, represented as the water of death or negation in the occult sense, is afterwards externalised.

The Polynesians and North American Indians call water that flows living water, and when it ceases to flow it is dead water. Also, during the negative period, or the solution of continuity in time, it was the dead water, or water of death, according to the symbol. The water of life flowed, was in living motion, and motion was equivalent to generation, whereas corruption, as Plutarch has it, "*locks up and fixes Nature's course,*" and this corruption was that of the dead water, the Typhonian torpidity which required to be aroused by means of motion in generation.

[1] Plutarch, *Morals*, vol. iv. p. 119; London, 1704.   [2] Bleek, p. 14.
[3] *Shayast La-Shayast*, ch. iii. 29.

Remembering the *Liku* token of a marriage covenant and other customs connected with the reckoning of intercourse between the sexes from the time of feminine puberty, it is more than probable that the myth of the *Sleeping Beauty* and her water of life is founded on the condition of the pre-pubescent and un-open female. This, too, was a condition of not going, non-motion, arrest, passivity, the first lock-up to primitive man, which was also applied to menstruation as the opposite of motion in another sense, both meeting in the one meaning of non-going during the time of *Tabu*.

One of the Two Waters is described as a magic fluid flowing from the hands and feet of a fair maiden, who is a form of the "Sleeping Beauty." In a variant of the same Russian story, the precious water is contained in a flask concealed beneath the pillow of the Sleeping Beauty, who lies on her couch in the Enchanted Castle amidst the realm that is locked in magic slumber, until the Prince comes to wake all up and to carry off the prize, here represented as the feminine Water of Renewal, which is sought for the purpose of turning age into youth, or, in other phrase, for reproduction.[1]

The Russian Folk Tales almost invariably recognise Two Waters as being made use of for the miraculous restoration or transformation One is called the Water of Death. This is employed in healing the wounds of a corpse. The Living Water is held to restore the body to life.[2]

The Norse tales speak of two waters; one—the Water of Death —induces a magic sleep, from which the Water of Life alone can recover.

These waters in the Folk-lore make the blind to see and the lame to walk, as they do in the Russian story of the Blind Man and the Cripple, both of whom are cured by one of the Two Waters; the witch being destroyed in the other;[3] this correlates with the belief that evil spirits, when exorcised, flee to and find their place of disappearing in the Red Sea; the Sea or Pool of Dissolution in the Ritual.

Both Truths of the Water and Breath were at first represented by the Great Mother of Mythology in accordance with the earliest appearances. The mother gave the Water of Being as flesh-maker to the child, and breathed the quickening breath of life into the embryo through its navel. Breath was the second element of life—the spirit that fluttered over the mystical waters. The Two Truths were also assigned to the genitrix, in two characters, those of the two sisters, Isis and Neft, one of whom represented the Red Source, the other the Breath, or Nef. Next the male was made the breather, and the female represented the water. He was the Inspirer of soul, and she the Former of flesh. The Phallus, as Nefer, becomes the male breather. A Yoruban saying

---

[1] Ralston, *Russian Folk Tales*, p. 235.   [2] *Ibid.* p. 231.
[3] *Ibid.* p. 240.

affirms that "*Marrow* (*cf.* the Hebrew שׁמֶן) *is the Father of Blood.*" Observation had then extended to the region of causation, and the male principle had been made primary. The Bât (Eg.) is the Father as the Inspirer of the Breath or soul, called the *Bâ*, earlier Paf. And the male as *Bat* or Pater, the Inspirer of Breath, is strangely illustrated in an Indian sculpture from the Cave-Temple of Elephanta, now in the British Museum. The critic of the present work should take a lesson in symbolism from this sculpture. To the eye that is unfamiliar with, and the mind that is uninstructed in such teachings of the past, it is ghastly in its grossness; a fragment from Sodom, a damning proof against the carnal heathen mind. Yet denunciation is altogether beside the mark. Such things, of course, are not reproducible now, but they have never been explained. Once the meaning of these representations was piously expounded in the Caves of the Mysteries, where the primitive pictures were drawn on the walls of the Chambers of Imagery. The group here referred to very simply sets forth the male as the supplier to the female of the Breath and the Water of Life, as in the dual emanation proceeding from Khem in the drawings at Denderah. The male is the breather of life in a twofold character, and the act of natural congress could not have represented the meaning as does this biological allegory.[1]

When this repellent subject was carved it was to demonstrate the idea that a *male* source was the nourishing potency of nature, and the breather or inspirer of the female; and both the Water and the Breath of Life are here assigned to the male, as the active agent of a Biune nature, in which the female, as the passive recipient, is being fertilised. The Hindus reduced the feminine to mere nonentity, and here ascribe both the breath and the liquid vivification to the male: the *female being now pourtrayed as the receiving instead of the emaning double-mouth.* This transfer of the breathing-source from the female to the male can be traced in Egypt.

In the Ritual the speaker in the new life says he has been "*snatched from the Waters of his Mother,*" and "*emaned from the nostril of his father Osiris.*" At this stage the father had become the breather of life. But the mother was primordial.

When the two Divine Sisters invoke Osiris to come to them to *Kha,* as the beloved of the Adytum, the *Lord of the sixth day's festival,* the fructifying Bull, Isis says: "*thou comest to us from thy retreat to spread the water of thy soul; to distribute the Bread of thy being, that the Gods may live, and men also.*"[2] Bread and Breath are homotypes, and thus the Male Divinity is here the Lord of the Two Truths, and supplier of the Water and the Breath, as in the Indian drawing.

The Two Truths of Water and Breath were likewise represented by the God Num or Khnef. He is the Lord of the inundation; the

[1] In the British Museum. Copied by Paine Knight.
[2] *Records,* vol. ii. p. 122.

King of Frogs; the Sailor, the Spirit breathing on the waters in creation. He is characterised as the *Great God making* (like a Potter) *the Son of his race with the good Breath in his Mouth.*[1]

In the Hebrew version of the Mythos the water of life flows from the Rock Tser until the time of Miriam's passing away. She represented the feminine source. The change to the masculine occurs when the water gushes for the first time from the Rock Sela, by command of Moses.[2] This was the Water of Meribah, and in Egyptian *Meri* is water, and *Bah* signifies the male. In Chinese *Fu-Mu* for the parents is now understood to mean the father and mother. Both, however, were feminine names at first, and *Fu* (Chin.) is still a name of the wife; *Fu* (Eg.) signifies dilatation, swelling, bearing, the mother as gestator. *Mu* is water and the mother. Fu, fuf, or puf, denotes the breath of life, whether represented by the male or female, and the two parents are identical by name with the two elements of breath and water.

When the masculine deity had taken the place of the mother, and the sun had been adopted for the creative type, the same imagery of the Two Waters and the Twin Source was applied to the Solar God. We read in the "Magical Texts": "*When the sun becomes weak he lets fall the sweat of his members and this changes to a liquid ; he bleeds much.*"[3] Then he was called the sun in linen; he was bound up as a woman; or he was Osiris-tesh-tesh in his bloody sweat, in *Smen.*

In another of the sun's weepings or sheddings he is figuratively said to "*let water fall from his eyes ; it is changed into working bees ; they work in the flowers of each kind, and honey and wax are produced instead of water.*" Shu and Tefnut (an equivalent of Shu and Ma) are said to weep much. "*Shu and Tefnut give it* (the liquid) *to the living members.*"[4] But the sun is the deity who in the later Mythos sheds one water that turns to blood, and a liquid source of life which is typified by wax or sperm. The English Ritualists still cling to their long sperm candles as the sign of the Light of the World, the Solar Messiah; the red source being symbolised by the bloody wafer of the Papists. The tallest wax candle in Rome is the same, symbolically, as the most elongated Linga of Siva in India, and both meet where they can be explained in the typology of Kam. The Hebrew deity is also represented as shedding two creative tears, a more abstract form of the primæval Two Waters.[5]

In a Hindu picture[6] of Mahadeva and Parvati, the waters of Soma are seen issuing from the head of the male deity, and from the mouth of the Cow, the feminine personification. Siva is the mouth of the Male Source, and Parvati, the great Mother, the Mouth (Mut) of the feminine source.

[1] Birch, *Gallery*, p. 9.
[2] Num. xx. 8.
[3] *Records*, vol. vi. pp. 115-116.
[4] *Ibid.*
[5] Bartolocci, tom i. 596.
[6] Moor's *Hindu Pantheon*, pl. 17.

The golden rod standing amid the waters is a hieroglyphic of the biune one.   The reed as Vetasa in Sanskrit, is synonymous with the male emblem.   He who knows the golden reed standing in the midst of the waters is the mysterious Prajapati, as generator. This golden reed is described standing in streams of butter [1] (Ghrita). Opposite as it may seem to any direct resemblance, butter is the representative of female source, not of the male.

And rightly too.   It came from the female, the cow, the nourisher, and in the sacrificial rites Soma was typical of the male origin; Butter of the female.   Thus the golden reed and the butter are the biune source imaged in Prajapati.   Ghritaki, the Butterer or female Anointer is an epithet of the Goddess Saraswati.   "*May the waters, the mothers, cleanse us ; they who purify with butter, purify us with butter*," [2] is one of the invocations, and Saraswati was this Purifier personified.

The golden reed of Prajapati is the Priapus.   The linga and reed also cross by name in the Kaffir *Hlanga* for the reed and for the name of the Zulu Prajapati or progenitor, the great, great Father of all.

Porphyry tells us that Zaratusht consecrated a cave in a mountain on the borders of Persia, where he represents the powers of nature by painted symbols, as the souls *descending into birth.*   "For," he remarks, "*the ancients thought that these souls are incumbent on the water which is inspired by divinity, as Numenius says, who adds, that on this account a prophet asserts that the Spirit of God moved on the waters.*" [3]   In this later phase the souls *descend* instead of ascending in froth, foam, vapour, or breath.

The Two Truths of Egyptian biology, the blood and breath named *Sen* or *Sun* (the u being earlier than the e) are apparently extant as English in relation to the *sound* of fishes.   The cod-sound is scientifically known as the "swim-bladder," and popularly as the aorta or great blood-vessel.   These two are organs of breath and blood, both of which are named *Sen* in Egyptian, where alone after all superficial philological discussion, we can reach the root of the matter.

Sen (Eg.) means to make a foundation by opening, as is done by the breath and the blood.   It also signifies to pass.   From this comes the *sennt* or *sunnt* as in the Sound, a strait, a sea passage, and the *snout*, a passage for the breath (sun).   *Sunnt* is that which is founded, the very self-hood, from *sun* which in biology is the blood or the breath.   *Sunnu* in Assyrian and *Sen* in Chinese denote foundation. If we take the fish-sound to be the air-vessel or swim-bladder, then *sun*, to breathe, is the root of *sound*.   *Sne*, in English, is to swim.   If the aorta, then *sun*, the blood will account for it as a blood-vessel. And if the name of the "sound" belongs to both, as it well may, we have the Two Truths of Egyptian biology under one word.   Sun (Eg.) being breath and to breathe, *Sound* is likewise that which is breathen ;

---

[1] Muir, *Sans. Texts*, vol. v. p. 384.   [2] *Ibid.* p. 338.
[3] Taylor's *Porphyry*, pp. 174-7.

and the *snout*, like the sound, is an organ of breath or air. The Two Truths may be followed in manifold directions.

The author of *Juventus Mundi* has elaborately demonstrated that Homer's colour-phrases all resolve at last into epithets of brightness and darkness,[1] and that in his use of words for light and dark he is unerring, whereas his other epithets are confused and indefinite and his colours all run.

From this undoubted fact he infers that the author of the *Iliad* and *Odyssey* was especially sensitive to light and dark, but that the perception of colour was almost absent. He remarks that " *a child of three years in our nurseries knows, that is to say, sees, more of colour than the man who founded for the race the sublime office of the poet.*" [2]

It may be the archaic or primitive man set out with a limited perception of colours. But Homer could in nowise have represented the primitive man. The world was very old when Greece was young. In the beginning all was luminous and non-luminous. This stage is expressed by the Two Truths of Light and Shade as the two aspects of one truth which determined the earliest classification of colours.

The double Sut, as Sut Nub, is typified as black and golden by the bird of darkness and the gold hawk. The moon is black and white, and these were imaged by the black and white ibis. White and black were equated by the blue and red of the solar colours, those of the blue heaven and red sun which are also found in the tongue of Hu and in the two colours of spirit (blue) and flesh (red).

These pairs conform to the primary dual of light and shade, upper crown and lower. Black and red permute in Homer or in Egypt as the lower of two colours. The Two Truths dominate in Homer's system of colour, which is symbolical. Scientifically, all colours resolve into light and its negation dark. Light and dark were the two primaries, and in the sacred writings all other colours were affiliated to the parental pair. So Homer founded upon light and darkness as the two opposite poles, because in the beginning there were but Two Truths of what came to be called colour—those of light and shade. This has nought to do with colour-blindness or defective perception of colours. It is a relic of the past, religiously preserved. The colour-blindness, like much of our modern blindness, was not natural but sacerdotal. And when the limits are thus imposed they are held to be divine; the boundary is the most sacred part of the domain occupied; the fetters are more highly prized than any freedom.

Plato bears witness that for ten thousand years the religious art of Egypt was forcibly held in bonds like these and doomed to repeat itself without innovation or change. The twilight of the Two Truths was perpetuated ; the past for ever reproduced, as the most hallowed thing that could be done by Art. This was the sacred sign of the

---

[1] *Juventus Mundi*, p. 539.   [2] *Nineteenth Century*, October, 1877.

religious writings, the note of the initiated, and, as it turns out, incontrovertible evidence for the Kamite origines, and the doctrine of mental evolution.

In like manner an important ethnological fact was registered by the Greek artists, through their following the Egyptian canon. In the Apes the second toe is considerably longer than the first, and the long great toe is an attribute especially human. But the Greeks represented the first toe as being shorter than the second, and this has been conventionalised in modern art.[1] They copied from the Egyptians who had derived and retained the type from the negro on the way from the ape, and so it was perpetuated as the token of a well-proportioned foot. But the Greeks were no more Ape-toed than Homer was colour-blind.

The same limitation to the law of the "Two Truths" found in Homer can be traced in the colours of the Wampum belts used by the American Indians of the North Atlantic coast. In these the Light shades of colour were all in one class of signs denoting peace and pleasantness in different degrees, whereas the Dark hues were all in the second, signifying gradations of warfare, and other dangers.

One frequently meets with proofs that the ancient symbolism survived more or less in the secret societies. For example, Jacob Böhme, who was one of the illuminati, observes,[2] "*We must be silent concerning the Times of the ancients, whose number shall stand open in the Rose of the Lily.*" And he further remarks, "*Those who are ours will know what I mean.*"

Here is an allusion to the two times of the Two Truths, whose perfect flower-symbol was the Lily-lotus of Egypt. The Lily-lotus, the *Sushenin*, or Sushen, was the flower of the Two Truths and two colours, the breather in and out of the waters. Isis was said to have conceived by smelling this flower. So Gabriel, the Announcer, offers the lily to Mary at the time of *her* conception. The Greek Muses were said to speak with the *lilied* voice of the gods.[3] The Lily-lotus, or rose of the lily, is the only flower really identifiable in the Hebrew Bible.[4]

There were two mirrors made use of in the Mysteries. It is said in the Talmud, "*All the prophets looked into the non-luminous mirror, while our teacher Moses looked into the luminous mirror.*"[5] The non-luminous mirror was the dark water that first reflected a face or likeness, when the creative spirit looked into it. This was symbolled by the Black Mirror of the Magi and Mysteries. The monthly prognosticators in the occult sense looked in the black mirror, and

---

[1] Flower, *Fashion in Deformity*, page 67.
[2] *Works*, ch. xxx. sec. 54; Lond.: 1654. [3] *Iliad*, iii. 152, *Theog.* 41.
[4] In Spanish a Lily is still called *Azuçena*, that is the Egyptian *Sushen* (from *Sushnin*), the Lily and Lotus in one. *Sush* is to open, to unclose; and *Nn* or *Nu* is the Water. Also Sushen was continued in Arabic, and as the English female name of Susan. [5] *Jebamoth*, 49 *b*.

prophesied. Paul alludes to this black mirror when he says we see as in a glass darkly. That is, we only see in the non-luminous mirror of the Mysteries. *Ma*, to see, is also to mirror with the eye for the mirror. The water of life and of death was a form of the Twin-Mirror of Ma. Also a mirror of steel and one of water were employed, as in the temple of Neptune, described by Pausanias. The steel, Ba (Eg.), identifies the one with Ba, the soul ; the water represented the female source. The Initiates in the Greater Mysteries were designated magicians of the steel mirror. The Ba or steel was also a type of the Blue Heaven.[1] The Two Mirrors also represented the Two Trees—of Life and the knowledge of Good and Evil.

The Mysteries of Masonry are founded on the "Two Truths" of the goddess Mâ, who survives in them, even by her name. "*How few newly-made Masons but go away* (from their initiation) *imagining that it* (the word communicated with mouth to ear, and at low breath) *has some connection with the 'marrow in the bone.' What do they know of that mystical personage known to some adepts as the 'venerable Mah'?*" This question is asked and left unanswered in "Isis Unveiled,"[2] by an Initiate in various mysteries.

The essential idea of Masonry is that of a Company or Brotherhood of builders working under the Master Architects, just as the Company of the Seven *Khnemmu* work under the direction of Ptah and *Mâ;* Ptah being the artisan who built with Truth ; that is, with Mâ. The Seven Khnemmu are their operatives. Egypt will re-identify Masonry as *a mystic craft*, with foundations in facts that go beyond the religious Mysteries of the Hebrews, Romans, or Greeks. Here, for example, is Masonry. An Egyptian scribe addresses the gods as the "*Nutriu, who test by their Level* (the Mason's level) *the words of men; the lords of law (i.e.* Maât). *Hail to you, ye gods, ye associate gods.*"[3]

A mason in Egyptian is a *Makh* (Makht), and *Mâ* has an earlier form in Makh, for rule and measure. Also the goddess of rule and measure had a prior personification in *Makha* (or Menka), who came

---

[1] *Mirror.* The Mother of the Gods was their Mirror. Tef is the genitrix and the Pupil of the Eye, and the Eye was a Mirror. The Japanese make much of this type. A correspondent sends me the following:—The Japanese have an ancient myth to this effect—In the beginning the earth was comparatively dark, because the sun-goddess was concealed in a cave, and would not appear. The gods decided to entice her out by means of her own image shown to her in a mirror; for this purpose they made a mirror with steel got from heaven, and hung it on a tree opposite the cave, whose petulant tenant was to be aroused by the dancing and singing of a certain lovely goddess, while all the gods made music. This goddess danced, like David, "with all her might," and her excitement and her action rising together, loosened her dress, thus revealing more and more of her loveliness, till at last, to the intense delight of the gods, her garment slipped from her altogether! The laughter of the gods shook the heavens (ἐσβεστος γελως !), and the sun-goddess rushing out of her cave, saw her beautiful image in the mirror, and rushing up to it, was caught, and obliged ever after to perform her office of light-giving.

[2] Vol. ii. p. 388.   [3] Text cited by Renouf, *Hibbert Lectures*, p. 208.

into these islands as *Macha*, the wife of Nevy, whether accompanied by any Masonic mysteries or not. Sen (Eg.) denotes a brother or brotherhood; Sen-sen means to fraternise. Thus derived, the Mâ-sen or Makh-sen would be the Brother-Mason of the craft, and the fraternity would be that of Mâ, not only as masons, but as that of Truth. The Masonic Brotherhood is founded on "Truth," as one of its primordial tenets; and Mâ is Truth. The Initiate is instructed to be true and trusty, and is consecrated to the *Truth*, which alone is immutable and eternal. This Truth was first founded and expressed by the stone-squarers and polishers in the typology and language of building. Hence the symbols, the square, compasses, and other Masonic emblems.

One sign worn by Mâ is the ostrich feather, which denotes both light and shade, or black and white. The Masons likewise wear a suit of black, with white aprons, gloves, stockings, and sometimes white shoes, which are the exact equivalent of the feather of light and shade worn by the goddess Mâ. In their processions the Masons always walk Two and Two; and Mâ is dual; *Sen* means two. The eye is one of the Masonic signs. In Egyptian Mâ is the eye, and the word also signifies seeing. The hand is proffered in greeting to make the peculiar sign of the Brotherhood, and the hand extended to offer and give is an ideograph of *Mâ*. The hands crossed in making the circle of the mystic chain form another hieroglyphic of *Mâ* or *Mah*, the crossed loop, tie, wreath, or crown. Masons read the twenty-four inch rule as a sign of the twenty-four hours, or day and night. The twenty-four inch rule represents *two feet;* and two feet in Egyptian read *Mâti*, a pair of footsoles, as well as the Two Truths of Mâ; the Two Truths that were the basis on which all stood.

The pair of shoes occasionally found with the pair of half-opened compasses on the tombs of masons in Rome,[1] are the same symbolically as the pair of feet on the ancient stones of Britain and Ireland and in Polynesia or other parts of the world, and these may be interpreted by the pair of feet or the "footstep and the sole" of the Two Lion-gods of Egypt who kept the gates or divisions of the Two Solstices, north and south. The half-closed compasses which accompany them denote the midway of the equinoctial level.

The council-chamber of the "knight of the east" degree is illuminated by seventy-two lights, erroneously supposed to be in memory of the seventy-two years' captivity of the Jews, but which relate to the seventy-two duo-decans of the zodiac of twelve signs; these were also typified by the tree with seventy-two branches and by the Parsee Kustik or Sacred Girdle formed of seventy-two threads which represents the girdle studded with stars that was first prepared in heaven according to the good Mazdayasnian Law.[2]

[1] Dallaway, *Discourse on Architecture*, p. 401.　　　　[2] *Yasna*, ix. 81.

English Free-Masons in Australia have felt convinced that the aborigines were in possession of some of their own secret signs. Dr. de Plongeon is certain that he detected traces of the mystic craft among the ruins of Uxmal. There is nothing incredible in this. Some of these signs have persisted from the earliest times because they belong to those gestures which are the oldest form of language.

Under the Totemic system certain signs were given to each fraternity whereby their brotherhood was known, and this mode at least is extant in the signs of Free-Masonry. Red is the colour of Ma, and Sen (Eg.) is blood. Blood is sworn by in Masonry, and thus supplies the true colour. Seng in English is both blood and true. This type of Mâ, the true, used to be the chosen colour of the English felon about to be executed, who held a red handkerchief in his hand when on the scaffold to show that he had betrayed no secrets, but died "bloody true." [1]

When the candidates were initiated into the Eleusinian Gnosis the holy Mysteries were read to them out of a stone book called *Petroma*, the book being of stone and formed of two stones fitly cemented together. [2] But the Petroma meant more than the Stone Book. *Petru* (Eg.) is to show, explain, interpret. Hence the "Peter" or interpreter of the mysteries who became the typical interpreter or "Peter" of the Roman Church. The *Petroma* was the book of *Mâ* written on stone, and the two leaves or tablets corresponded to the Twofold Truths of Mâ, the Truth in its dual aspect. The double tablet of stone is yet represented in English churches with the Ten Commandments inscribed on it, and every Sunday the Petar, interpreter, goes to the *Petroma* and reads the Ten Commandments just as the *Peter* of the mysteries read out of the Stone-Book to the Initiates. The same mysteries are now performed by daylight.

The Two Truths are likewise illustrated by the numbers nine and ten. The number ten is lunar; it is the number of Menat, the Wet-Nurse. *Ment* denotes number ten and liquid measure. The number nine of Mâ and Ptah is that of dry measure, and the reckoning by nine solar months. Nine solar and ten lunar months are the Two Truths relating to feminine periodicity; the Two Truths of *Mâti*.

In an inscription on the San-tablet these two numbers meet. There was an order of priestesses called the Didyma or Twins, who were allowed ten gallons of oil of sesame with nine bushels of barley a month, in addition to a provision of three loaves daily. The Didyma were keepers of the Two Truths.

The Great Pyramid was built according to these two reckonings, its slope being that which builders call nine by ten. Another illustra-

---

[1] Rawlinson, *Report to General Board of Health from the Parish of Havant, Hampshire.*
[2] Potter, vol. i. p. 391.

tion may be found in the English game of skittles with either nine pins or ten pins.

The one Truth of all Beginning is probably extant under the name of *Nuter*. In the ancient languages of India this is the name for blood, as *Netru*, Budugur; *Netturu*, Canarese; *Netteru*, Telugu; *Netra*, Kohatar, and others, and this source was typified by Neith (Isis) who was designated *Nuter.t*, the feminine *Nature*, out of whom all issued in the beginning; the *One Blood* of the Motherhood which became dual through the typical "Two Sisters," when the fountain-head was divided into the first two Totemic lines of descent.

By degrees the first of the Two Truths in the primitive biology was degraded from its primacy of place. When the soul was assigned to the male, the water as feminine source was made the passive factor; the negative element that only served to give life by vanishing away. It became the *Unreal* one of the Two, and on this was founded the doctrine of *Maya* or illusion in India, and in Egypt, of Annihilation in the Pool of Pant, or the Red Sea of the Ritual. Further illustrations of this natural genesis of primitive ideas might be adduced.

There are Two Times, says the Sûrya Siddhânta.[1] Time the destroyer of worlds, and another Time which has for its nature to bring to pass. This latter, according as it is gross or minute, is called by two names, *real* (murta) and *unreal* (amurta). That which begins with respirations (prana) is called real, that which begins with atoms (truti) or matter, is called unreal. The real and unreal applied to time is akin to the Parsee doctrine applied to Vohu-Manyu, the Good Mind that dominates the hemisphere of Reality, or of all things good, perfect and true; and Akem-Mainyu, the Extinguisher in the hemisphere cf Non-reality.

The "Two Spirits" of the Parsee writings also illustrate the Two Truths, or the Truth in its twinship. Ahura-Mazda is the teller of Truth, and the evil spirit the teller of lies, hence the double tongue, as it is represented by the Indian gesture-sign with the two fingers diverging from the corners of the mouth. Two minds or intellects and "two lives" are also spoken of in the Gathas. These two intellects are called the First and the Last, which came to be applied to the here and hereafter. The Two Lives correspond to the Two Truths as Matter and Spirit, or Body and Soul.

The origin of Good and Evil in the nature of man considered as a being of flesh and spirit, and as the embodiment of two opposite principles with a spontaneous tendency toward good, supposed to originate in the spirit, and an antagonistic impulse towards evil assumed to be engendered by the blood (or flesh) which are destructive of individual responsibility, not to say of personal identity, has no other foundation except in the perversion and misapplication of the dualism of the primitive Two Truths.

[1] Book i. v. 10.

There was no new point of departure in phenomena, nothing added to nature or human knowledge in these later views of the Metaphysicians and Theosophists. It was but the transformation of Mythology into Metaphysics, Philosophy, and Theology, in which the supposed revelation of a newer truth was largely founded on a falsification of the old.

From these "Two Truths" of all Beginning the total system of Typology and Mythology was telescopically drawn out joint by joint, and as we shut up the glass again in the return process and attain the early stand-point and focus of vision we perceive with more or less exactness what the early thinkers saw.

SECTION IV.

NATURAL GENESIS AND TYPOLOGY OF NUMBERS.

The limits are here identical with the origines; and to demonstrate the one is to define the other.

WE have seen that the first *Beginning* is figured as Opening; and this bifurcation of the one in the commencement may be compared with the opening of the oyster. The present Section will determine whether the writer has securely inserted the knife into an hitherto unopened bivalve of the "Two Truths" type, because NUMBERS furnish a crucial test of this beginning with the Two Hands as demonstrators of the Two Truths.

NUMBERS constitute a true connecting link between the earliest gesture-signs and spoken language. Hand-reckoning with digital numerals is one of the primitive customs found to be universal; our English Hundred—the Arabic *hand*—is founded on the Hand-type of counting up to ten.

The Omagua gets his number five from the hand, *Pua*, and his ten by duplication from *Upapua*. *Tallek*, a hand, serves also for the Number 5 in Labrador. The Lower Murray natives of Australia express 5 by one hand, and 10 by two hands. *Tut* (Eg.) is a hand, also the Number 5. *Kep* is the fist, and the Variant Seb is Number 5.

The Hottentot *Kore* for Number 5 means the *Palma cava*, the *Inner* or female *hand*. In the Kamite Typology the outer or second of the two is considered the male type, an equivalent for Number 2 or Number 10.

The Latin V sign for Number 5 is obviously a hand, conventionalized to represent the divided thumb and fingers. The Phonetic V or F was a syllabic *Fa*, *i.e.* a hieroglyphic hand; originally a *Kafa* or *Kaph*.

Tatlemat in the Eskimo (Tshuktshi Nos.) is Number 5, and the word is connected with the arm in Greenland, whilst in Egyptian *Tat* is the hand (a Number 5), and lem denotes the arm.

An Irish A, the first, the one, as a letter, is named *Acab*, corresponding to the hand, the Kep (Eg.), Gap Akkadian ; Kaph, Hebrew. The British letter " Cailep " is the 10th and it signifies the double or second hand. *Khep* (Eg.) to make the figure also denotes the figure as the fist, of five digits. So in French, *Chiffre*, for the figure, is the name of the digit.

Number 20 in the African Pika, is *Kobolo*, literally two heads or two *upper halves*. This agrees with the Number 10 of the Towka Indians of South America, which means half a man ; the Number 20 being equivalent to a whole man. In Egyptian *Ten* is one half. The Vei numeral for Number 20 is called *Mo bande*, and in Kono *Mo odon bande ;* these denote a person completed.[1]

The Tamanacs reckon Number 5 as a whole hand, and 10 as both hands; 15 a whole foot, and 20 a whole Indian. The Aztec 10 is Matlactli from *Ma*, hand, and *tlactli*, one half; 10 is the upper or hand-half of a man. The Greenlanders, Eskimos, and others, count by the hands and feet, with a whole man for 20. The Rajmahli tribes still reckon by twenties in this way, although they have the Hindi numerals as well. In the memoria technica of the Hindu Sages the *Nail* is a sign of Number 20. The Nail is a type of Virility and of manhood as previously shown. The Number 20 is equivalent to a whole or completed man, the man of twenty years, as well as the 20 Nails.

Thus when the Buddha is represented with a Nail in the palm of his hand (as in a statue now at Birmingham), instead of denoting the crucified, it distinguishes the completed male from the Child-Buddha; the Nail as *Clavus* serving instead of *Unguis*. So the clavus was used in the ancient Roman reckoning of years in place of the Unguis.

Man and the Number 20 have the same name at times in the same group of African languages. Thus Man is *Momba* in Bala, Pati and Momenya, whilst *Momba* is Number 20 in N'goten and Melon. But 20 implies an advanced stage of reckoning. The 2, 5 and 10 were the earlier limits. Various African tribes only count up to five, or one hand. In the Mbamba they reckon up to *Betan*, 5 ; in N'Ki, to *Mitan*, 5 ; in Tiwi, to *Witan*, 5 ; in N'Kele, to *Tane*, 5 ; and then they begin again.[2] The *tan* is their division, end, a place of division, and cutting off, of *tenning*, so to say.

In Algonkin Ten is the five more than the first five, equal to the second of the two hands. In the Makua numerals *Pili* is 2 and 7, *Taru* is 3 and 8, *Cheshe* is 4 and 9 ; that is, 2, 3 and 4 on *either* hand, according to the gesture-sign. So in the Aht language there is but one name for Numbers 1 and 6, and one for Numbers 2 and 7. Also, Guii is 1, Guisa, 6 ; Gam, 2; Gamana, 7 ; Nona, 3, Nonadi, 8, in the Ai-Bushman. This mode frequently survives and the hand type is

[1] Koelle, *Vei Language*, p. 27 ; *Polyglotta Africana*, p. 14.
[2] Koelle.

implied where the principle of naming has been lost sight of altogether.

The oldest Australian languages show that originally they had no *names* for numbers beyond two. The Tasmanians counted one, two, plenty. The New Hollanders reckoned one, two, many. But they had the means of reckoning up to ten in their digits, which would serve to signal *how* many, although they had no names for the numbers. Here we have a test of the unity of origin. For, as the two hands, or rather two arms, were reckoned first, and the ten digits afterwards; as one hand is a figure of 5, and two hands form the 10, it follows on the development theory that the names of No. 1 as arm or hand, will often agree with those of No. 5; and the names of two, as hands, with those of No. 10.

This is what we do find. The hand and No. 5, the two hands and No. 10 are constant equivalents *under the same name.*

"*Keba,*" in Kra, and other dialects, is an Inner African type-name for the hands, or other two limbs. This is continued as the *Kab, Kaf, Kep,* or *Khep,* for the hand in Egyptian, *Kaph,* Hebrew; *Gap,* Akkadian; *Cab,* Mexican; *Chopa,* Movima; *Tcapai,* Pujuni; *Gaupen,* a handful, in Scotch. *Keb* (Eg.) signifies double, to duplicate, and the hand, arm, or leg, is a dual member. The hand, then, is a figure of five or ten according to the gesture-sign. We see by the hieroglyphics that *Kep,* a fist (of five) preceded the modified *Seb* for the Number Five. And this type-name will be often found as the title of Ten.

In the Yukahiri Tungus language the Numbers Two and Ten are both named *Dzhur,* the two hands being equivalent to the ten fingers. In Egyptian *Shera* is the boy or girl, the child of either sex; the two sexes being likewise equivalent to the two hands. So in the Norway Gipsy *Dy* is Number Two, and *Ty* Number Ten.

Lekh (or rekh) in Egyptian is to count; *Lokket* in Finnish is to reckon, *Lokke* being Number 10, or the reckoning; and in Russian *Ruka* (Luka) is the hand. *Kaks* (modified Kâs) Number 2 (or twin) in Akkadian; *Kaksi,* Olonets; *Kaksi* Karelian; *Kaks,* Fin; *Kasi,* Vod; *Kaks,* Esthonian; *Kaûs,* Kamkatkan; are explained by the name of the hand, which is *Kâsi,* Karelian; *Kâsi,* Olonets; *Kâssi,* Esthonian; *Kêsi,* Fin. The Egyptian Khekh, or *Khaûsu,* for the beam of the balance, is another form of the one that is twin in its two arms. Also *Khkha* (Eg.), is the name of Number and to number.

The names of Numbers throughout all language show an incessant interchange in this way under one and the same type-word. *Kefto* is the Number 2 in Mordvin; and *Khepti* is the two hands, *Kabti* the two arms in the hieroglyphics. The Mexican *Quipu,* knot (Egyptian *Khabu*), is a tie of 10, yet it agrees by name with *Kep* (Eg.) for the fist of five. So the Hebrew Jad is one hand, but it suffices for the numeral sign of 10. With the exception of Number 1, all the numerals of the Absné (Circassian) language are based on this hand-type of name,

Seka is No. 1.	*Khuba* is No. 5.	*Akhba* is No. 8.
Ukhba ,, ,, 2.	*Ziba* ,, ,, 6.	*Ishba* ,, ,, 9.
Khpa ,, ,, 3.	*Bishba* ,, ,, 7.	*Zheba* ,, ,, 10.
Pshiba ,, ,, 4.		

The foot is *Shepeh*, in the same language.

The Assyrian numbers are digital. *One* is the hand. Two signifies duplication. Three means after, or following. Five is a fist. Six denotes the other hand. Ten means together, the total expressed by two hands, or ten fingers in detail.

The Akkadian *Ua* for the sole, chief one, and the Fijian *Vua* for the one only, agree by name with the Egyptian *Uâ* for the one, the one alone; the only one. This *Uâ* (Eg.) has the hand for determinative, and is probably a worn-down form of *Ufa*, from Kufa, the hand or fist. *Uâ* is written with the barbed hook; a later type of laying hold. *Kefa, Shâ, Api, Fa, Uâ, â* are all Egyptian forms of the first one, Number 1, or one hand. The Egyptian *Ua* or *Uat* (Coptic *Ouat*, Toda *Vodd*, for the one) is Number 5 in the Ostiak *Uet*, that is the one as a hand.

Pairing the two hands would be a primary mode of signifying or reckoning two. Clasping the hand, the earliest manner of *fiving*, by making the fist, and the two hands clasped together and cut off at the wrists form the hieroglyphic sign of Number 10, ∩.

The root of the words *Numero* and *Number* may be found in *Num* (Eg.) to join, or put together, add, repeat, again, twice, second. *Nema* in Sanskrit, for the other, one-half of a whole, thence the other or second half, is identical with the Egyptian Num or Nem, which is as early as adding another one to the first to reckon two. *Num* for twice and second has a variant in *Nub*, the all, as a twin-total; the male and female, or the two hands.

In the Manyak language Number 2 is *Nabi*, and in the North American Indian languages it is

Nopa in Yankton.	*Nompiwi* in Winebago.	*Nomba* in Omaha.
Noopah in Minetari.	*Nompah* in Dacotah.	*Noomcat* in Crow.
Naperra in Catawba.	*Nombaugh* in Osage.	*Nompah* in Mandan.

Here the digital origin is likewise shown by the name for the hand itself, which is

Napai, Yankton.	*Nomba*, Omaha.	*Nimel*, Shabun.
Nahbeehah, Winebago.	*Numba*, Osage.	

But there is more than one way of duplicating, and *the earliest is by division of the one, not by addition to it.* The Gallas obtain their two as two halves of the one, by breaking a cake of salt; a broken piece, from *Tchaba*, to break, having the meaning of one-half. This is the Egyptian *Kab*, double; Xosa *Gabu*, to part in two, double; *Gabha*, Sanskrit, to be cloven in two; *Kapala*, one half; *Koporo*, Maori, truncated; *Kabili*, doubly, Zulu; *Kuppoa*, the elbow, Murray (Aust.); Akkadian *Gab*, for the female breast, to be abreast, or duplicated. The body is one, but when divided the hand or foot becomes *tchaba*, *Kaf, Khep, Kab*, or *Gap* (Akk), by name as the divided or duplicated one. The principle may be illustrated by the *Gab* for the mouth; the *Geb* for the bird's beak, and by the *Gape*. The *Gab* becomes dual in the gape. *Gcaba*, Xosa Kaffir, is to crack open, as in the *Chap*. "*I Cebo*" is true and good counsel when the word is used in the singular number, but in the plural it means false or bad advice.

Pidu is an Akkadian name of Number 1 or the first one. *Bat* is the Basque name for Number 1. *Foda* is Number 1 in Bulanda. These denote the opening one that divides and duplicates. Put or Pet in Chinese signifies the very beginning, by opening, putting forth. *Puthu* (Eg.) is to open the mouth, or other member that divides in two. *Pita* (Ass.) is to open; פ (Heb.), the opening; Arab, *Fath*.

Pepu and *Pû* (Eg.) are to divide. This the Wings do for flight. Hence *Ppat* means to fly. Ppat, to figure forth, is by dividing. So the Wing or foot divides to become a figure of two.

The New Caledonians count ten with a prefix to the names.

Oua-nait	is No. 1.	*Oua*-naim	is No. 5.	*Oua*-naim-guein is No. 8.	
Oua-dou	,, No. 2.	*Oua*-naim-guik	,, No. 6.	*Oua*-naim-bait	,, No. 9.
Oua-tugien	,, No. 3.	*Oua*-naim-dou	,, No. 7.	*Oua*-doun-hic	,, No. 10.[1]
Oua-tbait	,, No. 4.				

This *oua* is otherwise rendered *Paih* and *Wae*, and in Tahitian *Pae* denotes the division or portion divided off as a hand, or one half. *Wae* in Maori signifies the limb and to divide, part, separate. Applied to the hand it would denote the dividing of the one hand into two, and the two hands into ten digits in accordance with the natural process. The Hebrew *Sephr*, to number, also denotes a splitting and dividing into parts.

The principle of derivation through division may be illustrated by the Hebrew Achad for the *only one*. This is a common name for the Numeral one. In Africa, for example,

Gade is one in Bode.	*Kado* is one in Afudu.	*Keddy* is one in Begharmi.
Gadsi ,, N'godsin.	*Kuden* ,, Legba.	*Kadenda* ,, Darrunga.
Gudio ,, Doai-	*Kudum* ,, Kaure.	*Hido* ,, Batta.
Kede ,, Bagrmi.	*Kudom* ,, Kiamba.	*Ahad* ,, Hurur.
Ket ,, Anan.	*Kidem* ,, Soso.	*Adde* ,, Tigre.

These can be followed by

Ahad, Arabic.	*Kat* in Lepcha.	*Khuta* in Pumpokolsk.
Achad, Hebrew.	*Kat* in Magar.	*Chuodscha* in Kamacintzi.
Ahad, Assyrian.	*Kate* in Gyarung.	*Ikhet* in Watlala.
Hhad, Syriac.	*Khatu* in Tengsa.	*Akt* in Lap.
Kotum, Omar.	*Katang* in Nowgong.	*Yet* in Tharu.
Keteh, Insam.	*Ektai* in Kirata.	*It* in Milchan.
Hets, Yengen.	*Akhet* in Khari.	*It* in Sumchu.
Kitol, San Antonio.	*Kadu* in Pwo.	

---

[1] Latham, *Comparative Philology*, p. 381.

This is also a type-name for the Woman, as

Kat in Karıgas.   *Kota* in Kwaliokwa.   *Kīthia* in Chetemacha, &c.

Likewise for the hand and the uterus, as in

Geta,	hand,	Cape York.	*Qatu* or }	womb, Figi.	*Ucht*,	womb, Gaelic.
Geta,	,,	Massied.	*Kete*, }		*Kutte, Cut* }	womb, English.
Geta,	,,	Kowrarega.	*Quida*,	,, Old Norse.	or *Cat*, }	
Ket,	,,	Lap.	*Quithi*,	,, Alemannic.	*Chedar*,	,, Hebrew.
Kat,	,,	Assyrian.	*Cwythu*,	,, Welsh.		

The Hebrew name of the one, as *Chad* or *Achad* is related to Chadi חדי the Middle, *that which divides in two*, as the Breast; also the *place where the two halves divide.*

Achad is applied to unity as well as to the unit, hence it means together.

The Hebrew rites of Achad, the Only One, denounced by Isaiah (Ch. lxvi. 17) in a confused but conscious passage, applied to that primordial unity only to be found in the female nature, which was personified in the mother, as *Kat*-Mut and *Hat*-hor; the British *Ked; Katesh*, an Egyptian form of the naked goddess Kên or Chivn; and *Kotavi*, the naked type of Durga in India. The female alone divides to become Two and she therefore was the only One who is still worshipped by the Yonias as the one alone from the Beginning.

Under the type-word *Ankh* we also get back to a oneness, or a one in phenomena which is represented by the *Ankh*-tie, the *Hank* or *Ing* as a community, and the *Ng* as first person who duplicates.

Inek is number 1 in the African Shiho, *Inneke* in Danakil. This one is the Man in the Eskimo *Inuk* or *Innuk*. In Egyptian Ank is the one as the King, the first person, the I or A one. *Enika*, Aku, is oneness applied to personality.

Ankh also denotes duplication, and Ank the Mother is the one who duplicates. Several other types of oneness and the one that duplicates are extant, in the *Ankle, Knuckle*, and the *Neck*, the *Hinko* in Nyamwezi: the *Ancha*, Arabic; *Hanche*, French; *Haunch*, English, for the hip; the *Inoku* for the Navel, Nyamwezi, as the place of duplication where the two were joined together, and severed. *Naka*, Maori, means connection; *Niko* is the tie. The *Anga*, Maori, is a bivalve fish. *Hangi*, Nyamwezi, is repetition, and duplication.

Here then we have a type-word which signifies the one (like the hand, foot, or ear), as the initial point of reckoning.

Under such a type-name we may expect to find the numbers 1 and 2; 5 and 10 because of the two sexes, the two hands, and the digital origin of reckoning.

In keeping with these initial limits the Maori *Anake* is *the* one, only, unique, without exception.

The Xosa *Onke*, for one (one loaf of bread) every one, is also a plural, and signifies the All which, as the typology shows, may be comprised in the dual one or oneness of the Beginning, that divided and became twain.

In the Kaffir languages *Nye*, earlier *Nge*, signifies oneness, unity. *Hanac* is the one in Quichua. Nge or Nye is the African guttural-nasal, NO, the Sound of Negation which was first, whether represented by the Water, the Motherhood, or the left hand.

The English *Ing* or *Hank* is one as a body of people; the Hottentot *Hongu* is one as a group of Seven; and the Number 1 is

Onji in Tulu.	*Nɔksh* in Piskaws.	*Jungkihkh* in Winebago.
Nge in Kakhyea.	*Hongo* in Chetemacha.	*Quenchique* in Bayano.
Nkho in Atna.	*Wanche* in Yankton.	*Ingsing* in Karaga.

Ankua	is No.	5 in	Faslaha.	*Ango*	is No.	5 in Dofla.
Ankua	„	„	Agaumidr.	*Panj*	„	„ Gadi.
Nga	„	„	Sak.	*Panch*	„	„ Deer.
Nga	„	„	Tablung Naga.	*Panch*	„	„ Kooch.
Anju	„	„	Yerukali.	*Penjeh*	„	„ Persian.
Anju	„	„	Tamul.	*Panka*	„	„ Sanskrit.
Anja	„	„	Malayalim.	*Penki*	„	„ Lithuanic.
Anje	„	„	Kohatar.	*Bunch* (of five)		English.

Ankh or *Nak* is also a common type-name for Number 2.

Ankh, two ears, Egyptian.	*Ainak*, Kushutshewak.	*Neguth*, Shienne.
Hanak, No. 2, in Banyun.	*Aniko*, Miri.	*Nakte*, Tuscarora.
Ahinka, Tumbuktu.	*Nkhong*, Singpho.	*Nhaik*, Rukheng.
Onogha, Nubian.	*Nyik-ching*, Changlo.	*Niokhtsh*, Kolyma.
Nakha, Dog-rib Indian.	*Onkong*, Kakhyen.	*Niyoktsh*, Koriak.
Nakhei, Kutshin.	*Naghur*, Chepewyan.	

Nak permutes with *Nas*, and in this form of Number 2 we have

Nyis, Tibetan.	*Nes*, Darnley Island.	*Nes*, Etchemin.
Nish, Milchan.	*Naes*, Erroob.	*Niss*, Abenaki.
Nish, Sumchu.	*Neish*, Potowatami.	*Neis*, Arapaho.
Nis, Magar.	*Neezhwand*, Ojibwa.	*Nass*, Adaihe.
Nishi, Sunwar.	*Nishuh*, Knistinaux.	

The Ankh (Eg.), as Ear, is both one and two. So is it with the Hand or Panka (Sanskrit). In the Portland dialect (Australia) the ear is named *Wing*, which reminds us that the wing also duplicates and becomes a pair, like the ear or the hand. *Pankti* (Sanskrit) number 5, a set or cluster of five, is also the number 10, because the Pair, as Arms, sub-divides into 5 and 10 as fingers.

Ango is five in Dofla, and *Inge*, in Abor (the same group of languages), is Number 10.

Onger in Amberbaki.	*Wonka* in Tshuvash.	*Ongefoula* in Cocos Island.
Inge in Abor and Miri.	*Iangpono* in Tagala.	*Nokolou* in Fonofono.
Ongus in Yeniseian.		

The type-names, then, for number 1 include various forms of THE one that became two, or had a dual manifestation and are not limited to the hand. These may be the one·Being that bifurcates as *Omoroka;* the one Mother that divides into Mother and Sister or Mother and Child; the one species of the two sexes; the male front and the female hind parts.   One person with two halves, upper and lower, or hands, right and left.

The notion of oneness and firstness preceded that of one in reckoning, and this had several types.   The Mother was first; Darkness was first; Water was first; the Left Hand was first.   The Hebrew ה, or He, which the Rabbins tell us "*all came out of*," has the numeral value of 5, the equivalent of one Hand, hence it interchanges with the Jad (hand).   The Left, inner or female hand, is the first that was used in reckoning the number five.

The Australian *Ngangan*, for the Mother, signifies the Thumb.   So in Maori *Matua* the first, the Parent, denotes the thumb, the *Koro-Matua*, as the first or fifth, the one or the sum of the five.   The first one and five were those of the *left* hand, the Mother-hand, or *inferior first*.   Whereas "*Tupa*," the other Thumb, in Xosa Kaffir, is also the name for number 6.   This was a male type.   Reckoning from the left hand as the first and foremost is yet extant amongst the Kaffirs in whose social system the wife of the left hand is the great lady; the wife of the right hand is the secondary and lesser one.   Also the son of the left hand is the elder, superior—who is the principal heir, and the chief of the first clan; the son of the right hand being the inferior one—the head only of a secondary clan.[1]   This progression from left to right illustrates the bifurcation of beginning in the societary phase, just as the Circle of heaven was divided to become two, as Night on the left hand, and Day on the right.

The Egyptian *Un* or *one* is the round of an hour.   The Circle is represented by the Cipher, as the first figure or one.   The Circle, the Nought, the Cipher, is still the primordial figure, as the sign of zero.   It has gone down low, or rather remains first; it is the repeater and dominant determinative of figures, and still gives significance to all the rest.

The Welsh *Cyfr*, English *Cipher*, French *Chiffre*, Arabic *Sifron*, Italian *Zephiro*, Swahili *Sifuru*, Hebrew ספר, may all be derived from the Egyptian *Khefr* or *Khepr*.   Khepr means to figure, to make the figure, form, or type which in the Cipher is a Circle: In Africa the Beetle, *Khepra*, was an early form of the Cypherer or *Chiffrer* (French), because he was observed to roll up his ball in the shape of a cipher, or of the world.   His name is derived from *Khep*, to form and figure forth.

The figures made use of in Africa, which are called the "*Gobar*" figures, bear the name of Khepr,—a name probably derived from the Scarab (Khepr) as the figurer.   "Gobar," says Max Müller,[2] "*means dust, and those figures were so called because, as the Arabs say, they 'were first introduced by an Indian who used a table covered with fine dust for the purpose of ciphering.*'"   *Ghubár* is dust in Arabic; *Gobar*,

---

[1] Theal, *Kaffir Folk Tales*, p. 6.
[2] *Chips*, vol. ii. p. 292

cow-dung in Hindustani; but, if we read *Khepr* for the Indian who used dust for his figures we shall recover the original Cipherer of the legend in the Beetle (khepr) that rolled up its ball of dung and dust and *covered* its seed in making the first figure or Cipher.

The Beetle was a lunar emblem before it was assigned to the solar god, and the figure made by the renewing moon was that of the horned crescent orbing into a circle. The figure of the new moon is *Kupra* in Etruscan, and *Kibulia* in the African Guresa language. These correspond by name to *Khepra*, the figurer of the Circle in Egypt, and to the "*Gobar*" figures of the Africans. But the earliest maker of the Circle in Heaven that is related to time and number was the genitrix *Kep*, the goddess of the Seven Stars, who carries in her hand the Noose sign ∝ of *Ark*, a period, an ending, a turn round, *i.e.* a time. She was the Mother of the first revolution, registered as a figure, circle and cycle of time, in a latitude where the Great Bear was the Dipper below the horizon at the Crossing in the north. Her symbolic figure combines a Circle and a Cross, the image of the Circle above the horizon and the Crossing below. In making her circle and in crossing she formed the Cipher and the Cross-sign of Ten; and *Kep* is the first ONE in Egyptian mythology—the genitrix whose hands are said to be the Two Bears. *Kep* or *Kef* was the Mother of Beginnings, and in Bambarra *Kufolo* is the beginning.

So *Uâ* (Eg.) in the feminine gender is *Uat*, the genitrix, and *the one* in Coptic; *Uata*, the Woman, as Mother, in Hausa; and *Uat* is another form of this Goddess of the North.

The Mother then is our chief type of number One or the first in figures and numbers, as she is in nature and in the mirror of Mythology.

Hor-Apollo tells us the Vulture, Mu, represented *Two Drachmas*, "*because among the Egyptians the Unit of money was the two drachmas, and the Unit is the origin of every number; therefore, when they would denote two drachmas they, with good reason, depict a Vulture, inasmuch as, like Unity, it seems to be Mother and Generation in one.*"[1] This was as a type of the Two Truths, or the dual one.

The Alexandrine interpreters of the Old Testament always reckon the Hebrew money by the *Didrachma*. For the Drachma they use the half of a Didrachma, τὸ ἥμισυ τοῦ διδράχμου. The Vulture, *Mu*, was the sign of the gestator, the royal mother, the woman of the "Two Truths," who wore the double crown; the one that first duplicated. This, too, shows a beginning with bi-unity of type in which the dual may be said to precede the singular.

In the Inner African languages the Mother is identical with the number 1 as the *Mama* (variants Nga-Nga, Nana, and Kaka). Number 1 is:—

Mom and *Momu* in Tiwi.	*Mumo* in Mutsaya.	*Momos* in Babuma.
Momo in Bumbete.	*Mmo* and *Mo* in Bayon.	*Mbo* in Ndob.

---

[1] Book i. 11.

Mbo in Tumu.	*Moi* in Bute.	*Mô* in N'goala.
Mbo in Aro.	*Mô* in Mbe.	*Mô* in Bamo.n.
Mfu in Isiele.	*Mô* in Pati.	*Mô* in Balu.
Umot in Penin.	*Mô* in Papiah.	*Mô* in Bagba.
Èmot in Konguan.	*Mô* in Momenya.	
Îmo and *Mo* in Param.	*Mô* in Kum.	

In the Tungus dialects :—

Mu, ômu or *momu* } is No. 1.	*Moe* in Ka is No. 1. *Moe* in Khong is No. 1.	*Mue* in Mon is No. 1.

This reduced form of the primary *Momu* takes on the terminal t and becomes *Mot*, number 1, Cochin ; *Mot*, number 1, Tonquin ; just as *Mmu* and *Mu* become *Mut* in the African languages. The full form is *Momo* or *Momu ;* Mô, as in Bayon, is the reduced word. *Momo, Mom* or *Mam*, for *the one* enables us to identify this name of the one with the Mother. *Mmu, Mu,* or *M*, denotes the Mother, in Egyptian ; and *Mu*, the Vulture-type of the genitrix. *Mam, Umam, Umma,* and *Ma*, are the Mother in the Kiranti dialects. This type-name for the Mother is wide-spread.

Mam is the Mother in Welsh.	*Mamma* is the Mother in Murrumbidgee.
Mma is the Mother in Akaonga.	*Ama* is the Mother in Erroob (Australia).
Momo, moo, or *mu* is the Mother in Chinese.	*Memi* is the Mother in Barre (America).
Mu is the Mother in Amoy.	

In the African languages the Mother is :—

Mama in Makua.	*Mama* in Kanyika.	*Maman* in Nyamban.
Mama in Songo.	*Mama* in Ntere.	*Mama* in Landoma.
Mama in Mose.	*Mama* in Mutsaya.	*Mame* in Koro.
Mma in Guresa.	*Mama* in Babuma.	*Mama* in Undaza.
Mma, Mema and *Mua* } in N'goala.	*Mama* in Kasands.	*Mma* in Benin.
	Mama in Nyombe.	*Omma* in Wadai.
Mno or *Mmae* in Momenya.	*Mama* in Basunde.	*Mame* in Kaffir.
Mmae in Papiah.	*Mametu* in Kisa.na.	*Mam* (woman) Dsarawa.
Mama or *Mamame* } in Mimboma.	*Mma* in Kiriman.	*Momare* in Baseke.
	Amama in Meto.	

These, with their variants and reduced forms, show a general type-name for the Mother in Africa.

It is still more to the purpose that the Grandmother, the old, first Mother should bear the same name almost universally as the Mama, or the Mâ.

Mam	Grandmother	Wolof.	*Mama*	Grandmother	Toronka.
Mame	,,	N'kele.	*Mama*	,,	Dsalunka.
Mama	,,	Kano.	*Mma*	,,	Bambara.
Mama	,,	Landoma.	*Mama*	,,	Kono.
Mama	,,	Bulanda.	*Mama*	,,	Vei.
Mama	,,	Gadsaga.	*Mame*	,,	Solima.
Memeo	,,	Param.	*Mama*	,,	Kisekise.
Mama	,,	Biafada.	*Mama*	,,	Tene.
Mama	,,	Padsade.	*Mama*	,,	Gbandi.
Mama	,,	Baga of Kalum.	*Mama*	,,	Mende.
Mama	,,	Kisi.	*Mama*	,,	Adampe.
Mama	,,	Mandenga.	*Mama*	,,	Anfue.
Mama	,,	Kabunga.	*Mama*	,,	Hwida.

The Mother, then, was the first person, as the *Mama*. *Mama* (Eg.) to bear, to carry, denotes the *enceinte* Mother. In the single form of

the word this becomes *Mâ*, *Mu*, or *Mo*, for the Mother, and for the
number 1. In Egyptian the reduced Mâ or Mû takes on the feminine
terminal t to become the *Mât* or *Mût*, the Mater and Mother;
whence came those words. The Mother being the first person
recognized as Primus, we may expect to find hers is the first personal
name, or the pronoun of the first person. This appears in the
African languages as

Mom,	I, in Yagba.	*Mem*,	I, in Nki.	*Mem*,	I, in Mutsaya.
Mam,	,, Legba.	*Momi*,	,, Idsesa.	*Memfo*,	,, Param.
Memi,	,, Mbamba.	*Mumi*,	,, Dsebu.	*Mam*,	,, Bushman.
Mampe,	,, Padsade.				

The Mô, Mâ, and Mi being likewise universal for the I, or, as we
have it in English, the *Me*. This is *Mam* in the Avesta; *Memet*,
Latin; *Mu*, Akkadian; *Mû*, Proto-Median; *Mâ*, Finnic; *Ma*, Ostiac;
Me, Etruscan; *Me*, Ziranian; *Mi*, Welsh and Irish. The primordial
personality was not that of Self—not the I or Me, but that of the
Mammy, the Mother, the MY ONE, mine. The African *Mame*, in the
Kaffir languages, is the abstract form of the Motherhood; and
" *Mame* " is *my Mother*. Captain Burton says the African Negro is
still a child who, in his fear or distress, will call on his " *Mama* "
above, like any other infant. The Hindu does the same, to quote
no others. " *Mame* " is a Kaffir exclamation, a call to stop, and
an invitation to a feast. *Momi*, in Maori, is to suck; *Mama*, to
ooze through a tiny aperture, as does the milk from the *Mammæ*,
—the *Maameyhu*, or mother's breast, in the Carib languages. *Mamma*,
Fin, is the Mother's breast; *Mamme*, Dutch, is the Mother, Nurse,
and Breast; *Mamman* is to give suck. The African " *Mama*," interchanges with *Nana*, for the Mother, the first one, and this also is a
type-name in language for number 1, as,

Nein, in West-Shan.	*Unieen*, in Appa.	*Nengui*, in Fonofono.
Nung, in Siamese.	*Unnane*, in Manx.	*Nyoonbi*, Lachlan (Aust.).
Nung, in Khamti.	*Onan*, in Cornish.	*Nin-gotchau*, in Ottawa.
Onnon, Koriak.	*Unan*, Breton.	*Nancas*, in Adaihe.
Ennene, in Reindeer Tshuktshi.	*Onna*, in Malayalim.	*Unin-itegni*, in Mbaya.

The Inner African N is commonly sounded Ng, and *Nana* represents *Nga-Nga*. Thus the mother is named

Nga in Soso,	*Noki* in Hwida,	*Ngoro* in Mbamba,
Nga in Kisekise,	*Engo* in Kiama,	*Nga* in Dsarawa,
Nga in Tene,	*Ngue* and *Ngie* in Orungu,	*Ngo* in Tiwi,
Nge in Mende,	*Ngua* in Musentandu,	*Ngob* in Mbe—

which furnishes another form of the first personal pronoun.

Nge is I in Mende.		*Nga* is I in N'gola.	*Ng* is I in Dahome.
Nge and *Nya* } ,, ,, Gbandi.		*Nge* ,, ,, Songo.	*Ngi* ,, ,, Bola.
		Ngini ,, ,, Fulup.	*Nko* ,, ,, Marawi.
Ngo ,, ,, Landoro.		*Nga* ,, ,, Kise-Kise.	*Ngi* ,, ,, Mimboma.
Ngo ,, ,, Kasands.		*Nga* ,, ,, Gbese.	*Ngi* ,, ,, Musentandu.
		Ng ,, ,, Mahi.	

This supplied a universal form of the first personal pronoun, ranging through

Ngs in Æthiopic.	*Naika* in Kamilaroi (*Ngai*	*Naika* in Chinook.
Ank in Egyytian.	is My).	*Hang* in Thara.
Anaku in Assyrian.	*Ngo* in Chinese.	*Nga* in Burman.
Anokhi in Hebrew.	*Ink* in Palouse.	*N̦ai* in Tarawan.
Nga-Nga in W. Australian.	*Inga* in Limbu.	*Ayung* in Cherokee.
Ngai in Port Lincoln.	*Ung* in Khaling.	*Nak* in Gundi—
Ngatoa in Wiradurei.		

and numbers more. This root of The One gave the name to the *Ank* (Eg.) for king; Greek *Anax*; Peruvian *Inca*; Maori *Heinga*; Irish *Aonach* (prince); Arabic *Aunk*; Malayan *Inchi* (master); the Basque *Jainco* (Jingo) for the divin:ty. These were applied to the male who came to the front as the chief one, the ruling I of later times. The earliest male Ankh, however, was not the *father*, but the *uncle*, the Kaffir Nakwabo or sister's brother, on account of the blood-tie; he who became Nakh or Ank (Eg.) at puberty. With the Hottentots, the *Uncle* is the Naub or-Ancestor. The Mother of Life, *Ank*, the goddess of life in Egypt, and the Ankh or Hank of people, were still earlier. The female was the first known reproducer of the particular child, and therefore was recognised and named as the primal parent, the one, the earliest Ankh or Ancestor.

The primary mode of duplicating in language was by repeating the word, syllable, or sound. And Ankh (Eg.) to duplicate, to double, a pair, is the name of the mother in the duplicative stage, as

Nâ-nga and *Nga*, Tene.	*Nyongo* or *Nyongongo*, Diwala.	*N̦gangi*, in Xo:a, is the
Nyang:, Mende.	*Nguâku*, Musentandu.	first in time.
Ninge, Landoro.	*Nyangei*, Nalu.	

This dual form is perfectly preserved in the Australian and Maori languages, where *Ngangan* is the mother in the West Australian. *Ngoingoi*, Maori, is the typical old woman, answering to *Ank* (Eg.) the mother of life. *Nêing-Menna*, Tasmanian, is the mother. *Nga-ango* in Yarra (Aust.) is the breath. In the Pine Plains (Aust.) dialect, *Ngango* signifies the very beginning.

These show the Ankh of the beginning under the duplicated form of the name, the mother being the first duplicator. This primordial type-name is that of the woman, as

Nike in Eafen.	*Ankona* in Bushman.	*Naijah*, Woman, Uta.	
Nkas in Marawi.	*Nyoka*, thy Mother, Kaffir.	*Nogahah*	,, Winebago.
Negne in Bute.	*Enga*, Mother, Ho.	*Yeh,ng*	,, Seneca.
Onogua in Akurakura.	*Unnaach*, Woman, Chemmesyan.	*Nickib*	,, Attakapa.
Ungue in N'goala.	*Ehnek*, Woman, Santa Barbara.	*Neŷau*	,, Baniwa.
Nkelo in Nyombe.			

Nga wears down to the Eka, Ich, and I. It did so in Africa, as

Iga, Bini.	*Ai*, Tumbuktu.	*I*, Bidsogo.
Gi, Bola.	*A*, Ka:m.	*I*, Landoma.
Gi, Sarar.	*I*, Egbele.	*I*, Kisi.
Gi, Toma.	*I*, Bini.	*I*, Timne.

Again, water, drink, or suck, is another form of the first one, as the element of life derived from the Mama and Mammæ. It is the primary truth of the Two in Mythology. And water is

Mema in Lubalo.	*Mmeli* in Isoama.	*Mambia* in Biafada.
Mmi in Isiele.	*Momel* in Fulup.	*Mambea* in Padsade.
Mmeli in Aro.	*Momel* in Filham.	

With many variants and worn-down forms in *ômi*, *ûmi*, *âmee*, and *mâ*. Blood, the mystical water of life, is *Mme* in Abadsa; *Mmei* in Aro, African. *Mum* in Japanese signifies that which is primordial, the first, and in the Assyrian creation the *Mumu* or *Mami* are the waters of creation. *Mamari* in Polynesian is the spawn of the waters. This Inner African type-name for Water and the Mother-source still survives, as

Mem, Upper Sacramento.	*Momi*, Tsamak.	*Mimil*, Reindeer Tshuktshi.
Mehm, Copeh.	*Mumdi* (River) Sekumne.	*Mimlipil*, Karaga.
Mem, Mag Readings.	*Mimal*, Koriak.	*Mampuka*, Willamet.
Momi, Pujuni.	*Mimal*, The Kolyma.	*Mimpo*, or *Ampo*, Lutuami.

The Mother and Water are one in Mythology, and both have the same name in the earliest stage of language—that of the mere duplication of sounds to constitute words.

It is now suggested that *Ma-ma* signifies the mother (bearer) in Egyptian—

Momo in Chinese.	*Mama* in Fin.	*Mamma* in Australian—
Mam in Welsh.	*Memi* in Barre (American).	

because of the origin in Inner Africa as the birthplace of language.

The Number 2 in the African languages is—

Beba in Melon.	*Mba* in Puka.	*Mba* and *Pipa* in Param.
Biba in Baseke.	*Mba* in Pati.	*Mfa* in Okam.
Beba in Udom.	*Mbê* in Kum.	*Mva* in Yasgua.
Beba in Diwala.	*Mbê* in Bagba.	*Vëi* in Fan.
Beba in N'kele.	*Mbê* in Bamom.	*Epfa* in Egbele.
Befe in N'Ki.	*Mbê* in Momenya.	*Eva* in Bini.
Befai and *Mbefai* in Afudu.	*Mbâ* and *Pa* in Papiah.	*Eva* in Ihewe.
Bepai in Konguan.	*Mbâ* in N'halmoe.	*Eba* in Ekamtulufu—
Mbê in Tumu.		

and others.

The Param language shows that *Pipa* is a modified form of *Mpipa* or *Mbipa*; as *Befai* is the abraded form of *Mbefai* in Afudu. The *Mb* of the primitive pronunciation having been worn down to the simple B in "Befai." As abraded forms of the original *Momo* for number 1 and *Mbefa* number 2 we have

Mô, No. 1; *Mba*, No. 2; Pati.	*Mô*, No. 1; *Mbê*, No. 2; Bamom.
Mô, No. 1; *Mbê*, No. 2; Bagba.	*Mô*, No. 1; *Mba* and *Pipa*, No. 2; Param.

The father in Africa is a type of *Papa* or *Mbefa*, number 2.

Pupa,	Father,	Songo.	*Mfa,*	Father,	Vei.	*Baba,*	Father,	Yagba.
Papa	,,	Limba.	*Mba*	,,	Kanem.	*Baba*	,,	Eki.
Papa	,,	Landoma.	*Mba*	,,	Basa.	*Baba*	,,	Dsumu.
Papai	,,	Filham.	*Baba*	,,	Bidsogo.	*Buba*	,,	Oworo.
Papa	,,	Bola.	*Baba*	,,	Wun.	*Baba*	,,	Dsebu.
Paba	,,	Sarar.	*Baba*	,,.	Gadsaga.	*Baba*	,,	Ife.
Papa	,,	Pepel.	*Baba*	,,	. Nalu.	*Baba*	,,	Ondo.
Bapa	,,	Baga.	*Baba*	,,	Bulanda.	*Baba*	,,	Karekare.
Fafa	,,	Kabunga.	*Baba*	,,	Barba.	*Baba*	,,	N'godsin.
Fafa	,,	Tene.	*Baba*	,,	Tunbuktu.	*Baba*	,,	Doai.
Foba	,,	Mose.	*Babi*	,,	Bagrmi.	*Baba*	,,	Kamuku.
Mfafe	,,	Kisekise.	*Baba*	,,	Kadzina.	*Baba*	,,	Kiriman.
Mfa	,,	Toronka.	*Baba*	,,	Timbo.	*Baba*	,,	Biafada.
Mfa	,,	Dsalunka.	*Baba*	,,	Salum.	*Baba*	,,	Wartashin.
Mfa	,,	Kankanka.	*Baba*	,,	Ota.	*Baba*	,,	Goburu.
Mfa	,,	Bambara.	*Boba*	,,	Egba.	*Baba*	,,	Kano.
Mba, *Ba,* *Miba* }	,,	Gurma.	*Baba*	,,	Idsesa.	*Abba*	,,	Wadai.
			Baba	,,	Yoruba.	*Aba*	,,	Arabic.

Here the father coincides by name with the number 2, and as the foot is also a figure of two, this will account for its being named *Pupu*, *Ipupo*, etc. in the Carib languages, as well as for

Bofo, No. 10 in Eafen,   *Papo*, No. 10 in Padsade,   *Baba- lnecrahuk* } No. 10 in Timboras,

being equivalent to the two as feet.

These Inner African type-words for the mother and father are found in various other groups of languages. The African *Mb* is also preserved in the Barre dialect of America.

Memi,	Mother;	*Mbaba,*	Father,	Barre.	*Ama,*	Mother;	*Babai,*	Father,	Pakhya.
Mama	,,	*Papa*	,,	} English & others.	*Ama*	,,	*Pha*	,,	Tibetan.
Amma	,,	*Apa*	,,	Murmi.	*Ama*	,,	*Aba*	,,	Serpa.
Ama	,,	*Aba*	,,	Dhimal.	*Momo* or *Mu* }	,,	*Fu*	,,	Chinese.
Amma	,,	*Appa*	,,	Singhalese.	*Ama*	,,	*Bab*	,,	Eroob, Aust.
Ami	,,	*Ahpa*	,,	Burmese.	*Hammoh*	,,	*Baab*	,,	} Lewis' Murray Island.
Ama	,,	*Aba*	,,	Garo.					
Amo	,,	*Abo*	,,	Lepcha.	*Ama*	,,	*Aba*	,,	Hebrew.

The worn-down forms are also African, as—

Ma,	Mother;	*Ba,*	Father,	Mose.	*Ma,*	Mother;	*Ba,*	Father,	Dewoi,&c.
Mai	,,	*Pai*	,,	Lubalo.	*Omma*	,,	*Abba*	,,	Wadai.

M (Mam) and B (Bab) as signs of the first and second, the Mother and Male, are numerically equal to One and Two, or the singular and plural numbers in language; and in the Kaffir dialects the *Um* prefix stands for the singular number, and *Aba* is the first plural. Thus *Um*-fazi is a (one) woman; *Aba*-fazi, women. *Um-Ntu* is a person; *Aba-Ntu*, these persons (from which we may derive the *Bantu* name).

It was not the individualised father, however, who was first named; the *Babe*, *Bube*, or *Bébé*—

Pupombo, the Boy, Kisi.	*Popen,* Boy, Toda.	*Bubboh,* Little Boy, Fernando Po—
Bafet, Boy, Baga.	*Bube,* Boy, German.	

was the earliest male.

The *Pup* is the young one. The *Pubes* constituted the one who was *pubens*, whence the *Papa* as begetter. In Egyptian, *Pa-pa* means to produce, and this is first applied to the female being delivered of a child, she who was the primordial Producer. *Pepe* (Eg.) signifies to engender. The name for mankind, the race and the male, is derived from this root, based on *Pub*erty. *Papa*, or *Pepe* (Eg.), contains the elements of "the He;" the him or it of a masculine gender. The reduced *Pâ* also becomes the masculine article. The "Papa," or Inner African father, whether as the *Second* of Two, or as the *re*-producer and male duplicator, is indicated in the duplicative stage of sounds. This is continued in *Pepe*, to engender. It is visibly reduced to *Pâ* for the masculine pronoun, and then instead of the *pa* being repeated, as in "Papa" for the father, a dual terminal T was added, and we have *Pât* or Bat (Eg.) as the name for the Pater, Vater, or Father, and *Pati* (Sanskrit) for the Husband. Instead of *Pepe*, to engender, *Bat* is to inspire the soul (or *Paba*), give breath to by means of the male. With the addition of T, ti, or a sign of 2, for a terminal, we have the plural in a more workable form, and *Pât* serves for mankind in general, whereas *Papa* was limited to the producer. In the same way *Sen-Sen* is the Coptic word for *Sound*, based on *Sen-Sen* to breathe, or breathe-breathe. But in the secondary stage of formation *Sen-Sen* is represented by *Sen-t* (Eg.), the English *Sound*. The T or D being used *instead of repeating the same sound.* So "Papa" served as a sign of Number 2, reckoned by the repetition of a sound; but, with the figure of two added in the T, RECKONING was superseded, and the sign for reading took the place of the sound repeated for the ear.

Egyptian shows the visible passage from this Inner African stage of mere duplication of the same sound to denote the second, the reproduced, or the reproducer, to the later mode of indicating the duplication by means of a dual terminal, in which process the *Papa* or *Baba* as re-producer became the *Bâ.t* or *Pât*, and the *Father* of later language; as the *Mama* became the *Mât* or *Mut*, the Mother. *Papa* then was reduced to *Pâ*, and the terminal T (or ti) was added to form the word *Pât* (Bat), as the name for the second, or *dual one*. In Egyptian, for example, *Peh-peh* is synonymous with *Pehti*, and these likewise show the two modes of duplication. Peh-peh, or Pehti, is the Lioness in two halves. *This dual one was the Child, at first, on account of the Two Sexes.* Also it was the male child at two periods. In various African languages the boy is known by two different names—the one before, and the other after, puberty.

Another type of the dual one is the *foot* or Put (Eg.), and the *pud* or hand, the one that divides and becomes twain. *Fut* (Eg.) is to be divided and separated, and the foot is a type. Thus *Pat* (Eg.) is two handfuls.

Bit, Chinese, is to separate and be doubled.
Bheda, Sanskrit, dividing.
Path, Tamul, division.

Futa is No. 2 in Japanese.
Piti ,, ,, Tahitian.
Pitco ,, ,, Riccari.
Peetkoo ,, ,, Pawni.

Bitya, second, Avesta.
Pe is No. 2 in Batta.
Bi is No. 2 in Akkadian.
B ,, ,, Avesta.

In this final form the letter B suffices to *figure the duality of Pat*, the earlier Pa-pa, to the eye; and in the hieroglyphics a double P deposits or represents the sound and sign of B.

The foot is a type of Number 2. It was named in the Inner African languages as—

Pĕta, foot, Musu.	*Ebĕta*, foot, Esitako.	*Afota*, foot, Anfue.
Pĕta, „ Gugu.	*Bŭta*, „ Puka.	*Fata*, „ Isuwu.
Bĭta, „ Kupa.	*Afota*, „ Adampe.	*Fodu*, „ Bulanda.

And this type-word is universal for the foot.

Put, foot, Egyptian.	*Bitis*, foot, Pampango.	*Pilna*, foot, Victoria.
Put, „ Soiony.	*But*, „ Karagas.	*Aftia*, „ Rotuma.
Put, „ Pianoghotto.	*Pud*, „ Votiak.	*Pud*, „ Sanskrit.
Pat, „ Batta.	*Patula*, „ Singhalese.	*Pudha*, „ Pahlavi.
Pats, feet, Lutuami.	*Ptari*, „ Tamanak.	*Pedis*, „ Latin.
Puta, foot, Rossawn.	*Pethl*, „ Ulea.	*Fotus*, „ Gothic.
Pado, „ Javanese.	*Petchem* „ Tobi.	*Fŏot*, „ English.
Pada, „ Malay.	*Pitiran*, feet, Cartaret Bay.	

But the primordial type of the one that divided to become two is the female or uterine abode, which is the

Bed, in English.	*Patu*, in Malay.	*Fud*, in Bavarian.
Butah, in Basque.	*Baat*, in N. W. American.	*Pudendum*, in Latin.
Beth, in Hebrew.		

We have now got *Pat, put, fut*, for the typical Two, in place of *Papa;* and *Pat* (Eg.), for two handfuls, when applied to the digits, is equivalent to Number 10. Thus *Putolu*, two hands or two feet, is Number 10 in the Micmac Indian. And this will explain why Number 10 has the same name, especially in the old non-Aryan languages of India.

Bud is 10 in Khotovzi.	*Padi* is 10 in Telugu.	*Putte* is 10 in Kohatar.
Pade „ Gadaba.	*Patta* „ Malayalim.	*Avataru* „ Thug.
Pothu „ Yerukali.	*Pattu* „ Tulu.	*Paduri* „ Thochu.
Pudth „ Gundi.	*Pattu* „ Irular.	*Petiran*, two feet, Australian.
Patta „ Tamul.		

So in the African languages the name for Number 10 is a form of the Number 2, as—

Papo, 10, Padsade.	*Opoa*, 10, Basa.	*Ubo*, 10, Eregba.
Bofo, „ Eafen.	*Opa*, „ Kamuku.	*Evuo*, „ N'goala.

The one is followed by two, either through dividing or adding. The mother became two by dividing or bifurcating at the link of the umbilical cord. This accounts for other type-names of the Number Two. One of these is *Pek, Pak*, or *Bak*. The Goddess *Pekh* divided into the two halves of the Lion which was masculine in front and female behind.

The Brahmans say, " *The supreme Spirit in the act of creation became, by Yoga, Two-fold.*[1]

Pik, in Chinese, is to cleave; *Pakohu*, Maori, is the cleft or division; *Pakato*, Zulu, the uterus; *Pake*, Maori, denotes the sound made in

[1] Wilson, *Brahma Vaivartta Purana.*

dividing or rending in two; and in Toda, the umbilical cord is the *Pokku*, that which is severed at birth, when the one becomes twain.

Abeka, in Kaffir, is to divide by spontaneous or internal action; *Pagu* in Tamul, is to divide; *Phaka*, Vayu, means by halves; *Posh*, English Gipsy, is one half, a halfpenny.

When the human being is divided into front and hind part, the pekh (Eg.), or rump, is the *Back*, the hinder of two halves. Thus *Piga*, Gundi, is the hind part; *Pak*, Chinese, the back. The *Page* is one side of the leaf, which divides in two. The *Peg* is divided, or serves to divide. The word *Epoch*, for a solemn date, denotes the division applied to time. And in the African Isubu language, the *Epoke* is the native name for the division. So primitive is the application, that the people divide their day into three *Epokes*, and have no other reckoning of time.[1]

According to Cæsar, Gaul, of the Keltæ, was divided into forty-three *pagi*, clans, or communities. In this instance the *pagi* is tribal, and the divisional name is applied to the people on the land.

The *Pekha* or *Fekh* (Eg.), for a reward, signified the *division* as a *Share*, and this was the primary form of *Fee* and *Pay*, both in nature and by name.

In Java and Tibet the number Two is expressed by *paksha*, a wing or other member that is twofold. A *pick*-axe is a double weapon. A *Pikel* is a two-pronged fork. Pie-bald is *pick*-bald, or two-coloured as is the Magpie, and in Devon this duality is called Pie-*picked*.

The Pigeon, or Dove, like the Pye, is a parti-coloured bird.

The Bat is a twin-type, and the Scotch call this winged mammal a "*Bakie*" Bird; the Maori name for it is *Peka-Peka*; both "*Bat*" and "*Bakie*" denote the twofold nature, and both are derived (with two different terminals) from an original Baba, Papa, or Pepe, to divide, be double, become twofold.

Number 5 is the dividing number on the left hand, and number 6 on the right. In the African languages number 6 is named both

Pagi and *Padsi*, in Sarar,   *Pagi* and *Padsi*, in Kanyop,   *Mpagi* and *Mpadyi*, in Biafada,

just as Bakie and Bat are two names of the winged mammal in Scotch.

"The *Bat*," says Hor-Apollo, "was an Egyptian image of the mother suckling her child."[2] It represented that biunity of being which was first seen in the mother who had "bagged"; and next was typified in the Bach or Bacchus, the Child of both sexes.

Bak and *Pak*, to be dual or divide, will explain the name of the foot; as—

Pog, foot, Avar.   *Pog*, foot, Tshari.   *Bisi*, foot, Ceram.
Pog, „ Antshukh.

---

[1] Koelle.   [2] Book ii. 52.

Also the Moon, which is dual in its lunation, is

Biga, in Nertshinsk.   *Bega*, in Yakutsk.   *Bekh*, in Lamut.

The Frog is the divider, named *Bheki* in Sanskrit.[1]

To *Bag* in English is to become pregnant, to duplicate in being with child. *Bok*, in Vayu, is to be born.

The human being divided as the mother and child. Next, the little one is the *Bach*, Welsh, the little boy ; *Beg*, Keltic ; *Beag*, Gaelic ; and from *Bach* or *Bog* comes the name of the *Boy*. This is the Xosa *Baxa*, for the young child of either sex ; also the fork in the branch of a tree.

The child is the *Bag*arai in Tasmanian ; the *Pick*aninny in North Tasmanian ; a *Pick*le in provincial English.

The Boy, or Bach, as the little one, is the Second of two, and of a dual nature. This is the Bacchus or eternal Boy ; *the Child which may be of either sex, and so was divinized as the type of both.*

In England twins of both sexes are called a *Pigeon*-Pair. *Bak*, then, denotes the dual, the Second, in various languages, and thus becomes a type-name for Number 2, as—

Biga, in Basque.   *Poquah*, in Darien.   *Pec'h* (a piece), in Breton.
Bagu, in Savara.   *Vocua*, in Cunacuna.

As Bacchus represented the Bach, or little one that was of either sex, and the boy in two phases, so did Bar (Sut), the Hebrew Bâal the son of Typhon. The Hebrew form of the name as *Bagal* (בנל), and the New Forest *Bugle* for the Bûll, show the root Bag or Pekh, to divide and become twain, as did the Child in Boy and Girl. In sex the Bar or Bâal was twin, hence the biune being ; so that there is a meeting-point between *Bar* and *Pair*. The child being what is still termed a *pigeon*-pair (*i.e.* Boy and Girl) or Twin, because of either sex. *Bala*, in Sanskrit, denotes the child of either sex up to the age of puberty. This was Bala-Rama.

Abela, Kaffir, is to divide ; *Bil*, Sanskrit, means to split, cleave, divide in two. The *Bill*, as weapon, is the divider, equally with *Bar*, the fœtus, in Persian. *Bhurij* (Sans.) denotes the two hands, two halves of heaven and earth, a pair, as Shears, or Scissors. *Baru* (Ass.) is one half ; *Paru* (Eg.) one half of the double house. In Tasmanian the feet are named *Perre*,—*Berre* in some Australian dialects. And, by duplication, *Purre-purra* is Number 4 in Catawba.

Bara, in Vei, is the umbilicus, the place of dividing ; *Begel*, whence

---

[1] *Pekh*. A type-word like this may be followed in language under numerous co-types. It is an Inner African name for the knife, as the divider, which is

Poko, in N'gola.   *Poko*, in Kisama.   *Faga*, in Kra.
Poko, in Lubalo.   *Lipoko*, in Kasands.   *Pagbe*, in Gbe.

In the Tinneh (American) group of languages this supplies the name of the knife ; as

Pesh, Apache.   *Paas*, Dogrib.   *Paysche*, Pinalero.
Pes, Coppermine.   *Pesh*, Navajo.   *Pesh*, Mescalero.
Bess, Chipewan.

Bêl (Cornish), is the Navel; *Bal* (Akk.), the Axe or Hatchet; *Palû*, Assyrian, an instrument for dividing.

The first instrument used for dividing was the Stone; and this in the African languages is the

Pulag, in Kanyop.	*Pulak*, in Bola.	*Fulagu*, in Bulanda.
Pulak, in Pepel.	*Pulak*, in Sarar.	

Pelek is the Axe in Greek.

Peleg, in Hebrew, signifies the first division of Mankind into the Gens, Tribe, or Totemic family, and this type of Number 2, which is the second stage, promiscuity being the first, is world-wide under the same name. We are told it was in the days of Peleg that the earth was divided.[1] It certainly was under that name the mass or horde was discreted to distinguish the one from the other, or to discriminate them at all. The Hebrew *Peleg* is the Akkadian *Pulugu*, and the Assyrian *Bulugu*, for the division or dividing. This primary division was Inner African, for *Piliku* (or Piriku) is an ancient name of the tribal divisions of the Kaffirs. The name had crossed the world; it reappears as the "*Bulluk*," an Australian (Ja-jow-er-ong) name for the tribe; and the *Palleg*, or body, in Lap. It was also brought into the British Isles as the *Bolg*, the Irish Fir-Bolg. The *Belgæ* and *Bulgars* likewise continued this name, which has survived from the earliest division of the race into communities, companies, partnerships, such as the Swedish *Bolag*, Icelandic *Felag*, Turkish *Buluk*, Sclavonic *Pulk*, Gaelic *Burach*, and English *Borow*, in which the division was by Ten, the base of our Cantreds, Hundreds, and the Counties that became the final divisions of the land.

The Flag-stone is the divided one, and the flag (banner) is the sign of the division. One name of the Korân·is *al Forkan*, from *faraka*, to divide. The Avesta *Fargard* is a division. So the Hebrews employ the word *Perak* or *Pirka* for a section or division of Scripture. These are identical with our word *fork*, for the divided body. The Month Nisan is called *purakku* in Assyrian, the dividing Month; and the Veil of the Jewish Temple was the Dividing Veil named *Parakah* (פרכה) because it divided in twain like the Circle of the Year.

The Foot being dual, is named

Pilge in Mordvin.	*Bhori* in Kooch.	*Berre* in Australian.
Bale in Murmi.	*Fiyolu* in Maldive.	*Poro* in Mayoruna.
Bhale in Gurung.	*Balankeke* in New Ireland.	*It-pari* in Tocantins.
Pali in Newar.	*Perre* in Tasmanian.	*Da-para* in Cherente.
Pal in Korean.		

The Arm being dual, is named

Bulo in Mandenga.	*Belare* in Tene.	*Brech* in Cornish.
Bulo in Dsalunka.	*Belarai* in Kisekise.	*Braich* in Welsh.
Bulo in Kankanka.	*Balarai* in Soso.	*Porene* in Pinegorine.
Bulo in Bambara.	*Bera* in Udsɔ.	*Ibarana* in Ombay.
Buro in Vei.	*Brech* in Breton.	

---

[1] 1 Chron. i 19.

The Breech is divided, the Brogue (shoe) is double ; as speech, it is a mixture; Breeks are the divided garment, following the naming from the limb. *Brach* is speckled ; *Braggled* is brindled. A *Brocket* is a two-year-old stag. *Bragged* (English) is to be pregnant or in foal. The *Brat* is a child of either sex. The *ballok* is twin.

This root supplied a type-name for Number 2. In the African languages Two is—

Bar, Mobba.	*Belu*, Karekare.	*Fila*, Toronka.
Birr, Darrunga.	*Bali*, Dselana.	*Fila*, Dsalunka.
Biri or *Bili*, Swahili.	*Biele*, Ntere.	*Fila*, Kankanka.
Bella, Dalla.	*Peli*, Meto.	*Fela*, Kono.
Beli, Kiriman.	*Peli*, Matalan.	*Fele*, Gbandi.
Bate, N'kele.	*Vere* and *Pfere*, Gbese.	*Fele*, Landoro.
Bele, Nalu.	*Pere*, Gio.	*Fele*, Mende.
Biele, Mbamba.	*Pere*, Mano.	*Fele*, Toma.
Bol, Mutsaya.	*Fila*, Mandenga.	*Fillo*, Gadsaga.
Buol, Babuma.	*Fila*, Kabunga.	*Fali*, Ham.
Bolo, Pika.		

These are Inner African, and this is the type-name for Number 2 in the Australian dialects, as—

Bulla, Morton Bay.	*Bular*, Karaula.	*Buloara*, Wiradurei.
Baloara, Lake Macquarie.	*Pulla*, Wollondilly River.	*Bularr*, Kamilaroi.
Bula, Wellington.	*Bullait*, Witouro.	*Burla*, Queensland.
Bulia, Lachlan.		

Number Two is also—

Bar in Khong.	*Pir* in Kambodia.	*Barria* in Sonthal.
Bur in Ka.		

And as 2 and 10 are equivalents in the two hands, the Number 10 accordingly is—

Bela bu in Gbe.	*Fulu* in Batta.	*Puluh* in Malay.
Fer in Dselana.	*Pulu* in Atshin.	*Peru* in Akkadian.
Fura in Kasm.	*Fulu* in Malagasi.	*Borow* (a tenth) in English.
Fura in Yula.		

Bar, the child, in Egyptian, Hebrew and Assyrian, is an Inner African name for the boy who became the *Vir*.

Bira, a Boy, in Mose.	*Bara*, a Boy, in Yula.	*Bela-kuro*, a Boy, in Mandenga.
Bear ,, ,, Dselana.	*Pera* ,, ,, Legba.	
Bila ,, ,, Guresa.	*Efilera* ,, Kaure.	*Belin* is the Young One.

In Persian *Pur* is the boy, or son ; *Bor* in Suffolk ; *Ballach*, in Irish is the boy. *Per* (Eg.) denotes the male manifestor. From this root-name of the Boy came that of the brother as one of two ; the sister being the other. In the African and other languages the brother is—

Eburo, Aku.	*Aburo*, Dsebu.	*Brathair*, Irish.
Aburo, Idsesa.	*Aburo*, Ife.	*Phratar*, Greek.
Aburo, Yoruba.	*Brai*, Zaza.	*Bhratar*, Sanskrit.
Aboru, Eki.	*Brat*, Slavonic.	*Frater*, Latin.
Aburo, Dsumu.		

Paltr or Paôtr is the Breton name for the Boy.

The type-name for Number 2 in Egyptian is *Shen*, and *Shen* denotes the brother and sister ; two in sex. *Shen* is also the double or mummy-type of the second life ; *Shen*, the seal-ring (and circle) of Reproduction ; *Shena*, the knee-joint and elbow.

Znauh, the Two Arms, Coptic.	*Dsin*,	No. 2,	Kandin.	*Song*, Laos.		
Shana, feet, Luchu.	*Sani*	,,	,, Wadai.	*Song*, Siamese.		
Sinee, No. 2, Hebrew.	*Seneni*	,,	,, Beran.	*Sang*, Ahom.		
Sina ,, ,, Assyrian.	*Eshin*	,,	,, { San Louis Obispo.	*Song*, Khamti.		
Sen ,, ,, Berber.				*Tsong*, Shan.		
Essin ,, ,, Tonareg.	*San-dah*	,,	,, Mandara.			

As the two are also two hands, this name will account for the Number 10 in some other groups of language. Thus—

Dzhun, is No. 10, Mantshu.	*Dzhan*, is No. 10, Yakutsk.	*Dzhan*, is No 10, Mangasela.
Dzhan ,, ,, Mid-Amoor.	*Dzhan*, ,, ,, Tshapodzhir.	*Dzhuon* ,, ,, Mille.
Dzhan ,, ,, Nertshinsk.		

In the last-quoted language (Mille, Tarawan group) *Dzhuon* is the base of all their reckoning ; their 1 as well as 10 ; 6 is *Dildzheno* ; 7 is *Adzheno* ; 9 is *Me-Dzhuon* on this foundation, corresponding to the Shen-ring which is dual by name, and is the sign of duplicating.

The nursling and effeminate child of either sex is the *Renn* in Egyptian. In Inner Africa *Len Yahare* is the daughter, in Gadsaga ; *Lonufi* in Anfue. *Rinmer* is the child in the Australian languages. In English we have the *Runt* for the little one, the dwarf, and for the castrated ox. The *Loon*, Cornish *Lin*, a fool or simpleton, is a form of the *Renn* or *Lenn*. The impubescent child of early times furnished a type-name for the grown-up simpleton of later language.

The *Renn* as child is equivalent to Number 2. In the African Agaw dialects the Number 2 is *Lin*-ga. In others—

Paren, is Two, in Baga.	*Silin*, is Two, in N'godsin.	*Rendu*, is Two, in Malayalim.
Firin ,, ,, Solima.	*Silin* ,, ,, Doai.	*Irandu* ,, ,, Tamul.
Firin ,, ,, Kisekise.	*Erndu* ,, ,, Irular.	*Rendu* ,, ,, Yerukali.
Firin ,, ,, Tene.	*Rendu* ,, ,, Telugu.	*Rendu* ,. ,, Gadaba.
Selin ,, ,, Boue.		

Another Egyptian name of the nursling child is *Rer* or *Ru-ru*. This also is a dual applied to companions, steps, and to the horizon as the place of the two lions. It applies to the child or children. *Ru-ru* is two by repetition. This furnishes another name for the Number 2. In the Moor dialect, New Guinea, Number 2 is *Roeroe* still and answers to *Ruru*, for the child, the children, or the double horizon.

We likewise have the *rere* as a dual in the " *rere*-mouse," the winged mammal ; the rere-supper, a second course, the *rere*-tail, and the *Rear* for the hinder part or following after. R and L are interchangeable, and in the Fonofono dialect of New Caledonia *Lelou* is Number 2, and *Lolai* in Mangarei. The duplicate was first because the number two depended on repetition, but this was modified when it passed out of the phase of reckoning. Thus we find—

Rererua, Twins, Maori.	*Rua*, No. 2, Figi.	*Lelou*, No. 2, Fonofono.
Roe-roe, No. 2, Moor.	*Rua* ,, Polynesia.	*Lua* ,, Polynesian.
Oroo ,, Pelew Isles.	*Rua* ,, Maori.	*Loa* ,, Cocos Island.
Wa-roo ,, New Caledonia.	*Rue* ,, Malagasi.	*Lua* ,, { Kanaka, Sandwich Islands.
Erua ,, Manototo.	*Rua* ,, Timur.	
Arua ,, Bauro.	*Rua* ,, Saparua.	*Lo* ,, Uea.
Roe ,, Salawatti.	*Rua* ,, Mille.	*Loua* ,, Mami.
Ero ,, Annatom.	*Lolai* ,, Mangarei.	*Luete* ,, Lifu.

Another Egyptian name for the child of either sex is the *Sherau*, the youth, the son, or daughter. This too is a twin-title for the child in two characters; and the kindred name for Number 2 is—

Shiri, Mingrelian.	*Dzhur*, Tshapodzhir.	*Dzhur*, Yakutsk.
Serou, Papuan.	*Dzyur*, Yenesei.	*Dzhur*, Tungus.
Dzur, Lazic.	*Dzhur*, Lamut.	*Dzur*, Amur.
Tshiri, Coroato.		

Sher (Eg.) for the Adult, the Male in his second phase, also agrees with and accounts for the names of Number 10 as—

Ashiri in Kaffa.	*Assur* in Hurur.	*Asar* in Hebrew.
Ashur in Tigré.	*Assir* in Yangaro.	*Sher* in Egyptian.
Assur in Arkiko.	*Ashar* in Arabic.	

All Beginning in language and typology is bound up with the *one becoming twain*, in accordance with the doctrine of the " Two Truths." The Mother was the one that duplicated in the child, which was the twin or *two-one* because of either sex.

Number 3 is the pubescent Male. The Mother was first recognised as the *Producer*, because she was the Bringer-forth, therefore she was the Primus, the typical number 1 under several names. From her the Children traced the earliest descent, and the Child was the second as the one reproduced, therefore the Child is number 2. The begetter was last, and *where three were distinctly recognised he was third person in the series.* This was the order of Nature which passed into the primitive Sociology and Mythology; for, as it was on earth so is it in Heaven. Hence it follows that in the oldest Cult, there is no Father in Heaven, but only the Child of the Mother who becomes pubescent to reproduce Himself in the celestial *Couvade*, because the system was founded before the Begetter could have been recognised as the individual Father of the Child. This was the Cult of the Mother and Child, in which the Child included both sexes, because it could be Boy or Girl, and the Boy at puberty becomes the Consort of the Mother to reproduce the Babe. So excessively simple in Nature was the origin of this great Theological Mystery.

When the Otomacs signify the number 3 they unite the thumb, the fore-finger, and the third or root-finger, *the other two digits being held down.* This same sign of the *trinity in unity* is made by the Hindu Compound Being Arddha-Nārī, with the hand that holds the *Trisula.*[1] Arddha-Nārī is a biune being as male and female; and yet of a triadic nature, because the Mother, the Child, and the Virile one were represented as the totality of being that was triune in nature and biune in sex. The contention between this *Triadic-Dyad*, and the later, more orthodox Egyptian Trinity of Father, Mother, and Son, is also found in language with regard to the names of the Boy and Man.

[1] Moor's *Hindu Pantheon*, pl. 24.

Tutu (or Tet) in Egyptian is the Child, the Son of the Mother. This is an Inner African type-name for the young one, as

Teto, Ota.	*O Tutu*, Oworo.	*Tito*, Dsekiri.
Tutu, Dsumu.	*Tuto*, Eki.	*O Tito*, Ondo.
Tutu, Dsebu.	*Tutu*, Ife.	*Teto*, Idsesa.

The name is applied to the young, renewed Moon, which was reproduced by the old Moon (*Cf.* Ishtar, as Goddess 15), considered to be the Mother of the Child; the full Moon representing the Genitrix who was the one alone. The young Moon is

Tutu, Egba.	*Tutu*, Dsebu.	*Tutu*, Ife.
Toto, Yoruba.	*Teto*, Yagba.	*Tito*, Dsekiri.
Tutu, Oworo.	*Titu*, Ota.	

In Egypt, this name of the new Moon was continued in Tet, Taht, or Tahuti, the God who carries the young Moon on his head. Tet, Tat, or Tahuti, is a dual form answering to two or the second of two, the young one of two. *Ti* written ♄ *shows the duplication* of the T, and the Inner African *Tutu* is just the sound of double T. So that the name of the young one, the child, the repeater, the second of two, is expressed by repetition and duplication of the T-sound, and Tet (Tutu) is afterwards depicted by one T, with the *sign of duplicating as a terminal.* Because it was the sign of the one *reproduced* as the Child, *Tut* or *Tat* could be, and was, extended to become the name of the *Reproducer* as the individualised Father in later times. In Egyptian, *Tat* is the generative organ; it also means to engender, to establish, and denotes the Begetter; the Welsh *Tat*, English *Dad*, Scottish *Dod*, Omaha *Dadai*, and Kaffir *Doda.*

In forty different dialects of Inner Africa, the radical *Tat* furnishes the same name for the Father as for the number 3, and the Begetter is the Third by name, as he was in the reckoning of the Mother (number 1), the Child (number 2), and the Adult Male (number 3).

Tata	is father,	Babuma,	and *Tet*,	No 3.
Tata	,,	Bumbete,	and *Mitatu*,	No. 3.
Tata	,,	Kasands,	and *Tatu*,	No. 3.
Tata	,,	Nyombe,	and *Tatu*,	No. 3.
Tata	,,	Basunde,	and *Tatu*,	No. 3.
Tata	,,	Pangela,	and *Ta'u*,	No. 3.
Atate	,,	Marawi,	and *Tatu*,	No. 3.

In like manner the Boy-name as *Bach* becomes a later type-name for the man, or Virile Male. The Boy was, literally, father to the Man, and just as the father took his name from the child, according to one custom, so he continued the Boy-name for the man or Head as

Boie in Nertshinsk.	*Boya* in Tunguska.	*Bash* in Teleut.
Beye in Mantshu.	*Boyo* in Mangasela.	*Bash* in Baraba.
Boye, Yakutsk.	*Baz* in Kirghiz.	*Bash* in Tshulim.
Bye in Lamut.	*Bash* in Uzbek.	*Pash* in Tobolsk.
Boya in Yenesei.		

Naturally enough the Boy and Man meet under the one name of *Bar*, on account of the Male principle *and the Boy's Second Character.* *Boro*, in Sena is the Membrum Virile; *Phallus* in Greek; *Beron* in

Tasmanian. *Bala* in Sanskrit, and *Bura* in Fiji, are the masculine Source. *Bara*, in the Mandenga dialects, signifies pubescence, the pubes or beard. This is a type-name for the male as *Vir*, which is

Viri in Kusi-Kumuk.	*Fir* in Irish.	*Veres* in Zirianian.
Vir in Latin.	*Feru* in Magyar.	

The Hair or Pubes is

Bal, Ghagar.	*Vols*, Malagasi.	*Barba* (beard), Latin.
Bolo, Tagala.	*Parpee*, Comanch.	*Broda*, Sclavonic.
Bol-bol, Bissayain.	*Folt*, Irish.	*Barzda*, Lithuanic.
Bul-bul, Pampango.	*Folt*, Scotch.	*Beard*, English.
Bulu, Malay.	*Folt*, Manx.	*Varvara* (hairy), Sanskrit.
Bulu, Dyak.		

In Inner Africa the Male also attained the Status of Man (Vir) under the name of *Bar* (the Boy) as

Baro in Yura.	*Abalo* in Legba.	*Fela* in Gura.
Balga in Babuma.	*Abalo* in Kaure.	*Vale* in Kambali.
Bala in Bagbalan.	*Ebalo* in Kiamba.	*Baro* in Yula.
Mbal in Koama.	*Balera* in Bumbete.	

Thus *Ômakuru* or *Ômakuri* is the Khem-Horus, the Virile type of divinity, with the Damaras, their Father in Heaven; and this God bears the type-name of the Boy, who is

Omakuri in Fulup.	*Omo-Kuri*, in Egba.	*Oma-Kure* in Yoruba.
Oma-Kurei in Ondo.	*Oma-Kuri*, in Dsuma.	

Here the name is the exact equivalent of *Khem-Har*, the Adult and Virile Horus, the Man-Child of the Mythos. Bar-Typhon was the great Stellar type of the double Child of the Mother, and the Khem-Horus was the later Solar type.

The male child, then, had two characters. In the Second of these it was Khemt, and became the Khem-Horus or Virile One (the Sun as Generator). Khem signifies the male potency of the *Homme fait*. And in Egyptian *Khemt is the name of number* 3. The God Khem shows the primordial type of the Begetter. *Camo*, in Zulu, denotes the male parts. *Chem*, Chinese, signifies the Manifestor, fulcrum and stand-point. This is imaged by the Creator *Khem*. Khem is the master, the prevailer in the sexual sense ; and in Irish, *Coimhdhe* means the being master. *Kum*-Kani (Xosa Kaffir) denotes kingship, rule, authority. The *Kumara* (Sans.) is the prince, the heir-apparent, as is the Egyptian *Khem*-Ar (or Har). Various titles like the *Emir* or *Amir* were derived from the KHEM-AR (Eg.), or pubescent Child, who became the Begetter, as Consort of the Mother. *Kaumatua* in Maori is the adult ; *Kiamat* in Bolang-Hitam is the father's title. In Hebrew the male ass is a *Chamor*. In several African languages the male elephant is *Kama*. Khem, the *Homo*, being the complete man, accounts for *Gamru* to be complete in Assyrian. *Camani*, in Quichua, is to create, enjoy sexually ; and *Camac* is the Creator. *Comoun* (Eng.) denotes intercourse. *Kama* (Eg.) is to create, form, produce. *Khem* (Eg.) for desire, to go, supplied the later name of love as in *Kama* (Sanskrit); *Kim* (Comanche), to love; *Kamakh* (Shoshone), to love; *Cam* (Eng. Gipsy), to love, desire. *Khem*, the virile Male, is the earlier form of the *Homme* or *Homo*. Thus, *Man* is—

Kame and *Hame* in Soso.	*Hemi* in Maring.	*N'gome* in Mare.
Gme in Boko.	*Kamolan* in Andaman.	*Chamhani*, Vir. Ib.
Khoim in Khoi-Khoi.	*Kuayuma* in Tawgi.	*Comai* in Oregones.
Gemsenen in Bode.	*Kum* in Mid-Ostiak.	*Cuuimahe* in Apiaca.
Gemseg in N'godsin.	*Kume* in Pumpokclsk.	*Comoley* in Peba.
Koombai in Nyamnam.	*Kum* in Obi.	*Kmari* in Georgian.
Kamere in Darrunga.	*Kuim* in Ostiak.	*Umo* in Itonama.
Heme in Kisekise.	*Kem* in Vogul.	*Kami* in Burmese.
Omoi in Egbele.	*Kjmshan* in Koriak of	*Guma* in Gothic.
Nsami in Esitako.	the Tigil.	*Gem* in English.
Khem in Egyptian.	*Kamzhan* in Kamkatkan	*Hemo* in Latin.
Kami in Kami.	of the Tigil.	*Amha* in Irish.
Kumi in Kumi.	*Kaimeer* in Erroob.	*Amme* in Sibsagar Miri.
Chamai in Koreng.		

To be Khemt (Eg.) is to be pubescent, attain the Second character of the Male Child and become the Creator. Here it may be remarked that in Tahitian *Huru* is number 10, and the word originally signified *Hairs*. So in Egyptian Har is number 10, and the name of Horus the pubescent or hairy one, the Khem-*Horus* who was Second of the Two. Huru and hairy agree with the second of two characters just as ten includes the second of two hands. In like manner the name of the Two Truths and the Twins is *Ma-shu* in Egyptian, and in Chemuhuevi *Mashu* is the number 10.

It has been confidently asserted by the Aryanists that Man was self-distinguished by naming himself from his Mind; that *Man* signifies to think, the Sanskrit *manu* originally meaning the Thinker and then Man. Whereas the typology, the ideographs, and the oldest language prove him to have been designated the *Homo, Homme*, or *Khem* and the *Man*, Egyptian *Men*, from his attributes of pubescence. *Men* (Eg.) means to erect, to fecundate, to found. *Men* is the Bull, the typical male. In gesture language the sign for Man is made in front of the crotch, not of the forehead.

The North-American Indian signs for Man include one made with the typical forefinger extended and denoting him who stands like *Men, Mentu,* or *Khem*.[1] The Indian Wife makes the sign of Husband by imitating the male emblem with the right fist denoting " *Man* I have." [2]

The Man dated from puberty *as third in the Triad*, and the types of his virility, including Hair, Beard, Stone, Tooth, and Voice, will be found under the pubescent names. *Khem* is one name for the Man, and the hair or pubes is :—

Tchame, beard, in Tigré.			*Gamboei*, hair, in Biafada.		
Hamoi	,,	Bishari.	*Chham*	,,	Thaksya.
Sameyga	,,	Nubian.	*Cham*	,,	Changlo.
Gamur	,,	Mobba.	*Syam*	,,	Bramhu.
Kommo	,,	Woratta.	*Chham*	,,	Magar.

[1] Mallery, p. 52.   [2] Dakota, iv.

Achom, hair, in Lepcha.			*Kumi Kumi*, beard under the chin, Maori.	
Kumi	,,	Sak.	*Kambissek*, beard, New Ireland.	
Sham	,,	Kami.	*Koom*, hair or beard, Myfoor, New Guinea.	
Sam	,,	Songpu.	*Gemi*, beard in Hausa.	
Sam	,,	Kapwi.	*Hamber*, hair in Tumbuktu.	
Sam	,,	Khamti.	*Kampu*	,, Songo.
Umde, beard, in Middle and Upper Obi.			*Kaman*, beard in Garo.	
Gumi	,,	Tagala.	*Amu*	,, Zapara.
Tshim, hair, in Tobi.			*Gume* is tooth in Kajunah.	
Kum-Kum, beard, in Rotuma.			*Kambe*	,, Serawulli.
Kumi-Kumi	,,	Marguesas.	*Camablee*	,, Maya.
Umi-umi	,,	Kanaka.		

The Horus-Child was represented as silent or dumb (*Kart*, Eg.) whose *Virile or True Voice* came with puberty, when he was Khemt as number 3. So the name of Hu, the God whose symbol is a Tongue, signifies the Adult.

In the Australian, African, and Mexican languages, *Kame* denotes voice, speech, utterance, and mouth. In Van Diemen's Land *Kamy* signifies tongue, mouth, and tooth, each a synonym of puberty, like hair and beard. Khem-Horus was the adult Horus who could open his mouth and had got his virile voice, hair, or beard. *Gemi* is the mouth in Wolof; *Kambi* in the Agau dialect; *Agema* in Motorian, and *Kamatl* in Huasteca.

Although there were three in series and development there were but two in sex, as there are only two hands. Hence the name of *Khem*, the pubescent male, is also identical with the second hand and number 10 in the African languages.

Kum is No. 10 in Mutsaya.			*Kumi* is No. 10 in Nyombe.			*Guma* is No. 10 in Bode.				
Kum	,,	Babuana.	*Kumi*	,,	Basunde.	*Goma*	,,	Doai.		
Kumi	,,	Kabenda.	*Kumi*	,,	Muntu.	*Gum*	,,	Bayon.		
Kumi	,,	Mimboma.	*Kumi*	,,	Kiriman.	*Gum*	,,	Kum.		
Kumi	,,	Musentandu.	*Kumi*	,,	Marawi.	*Gum*	,,	Bagba.		
Kumi	,,	Mbamba.	*Komi*	,,	Nyamban.	*Gum*	,,	Bamom.		
Kumi	,,	Ntere.	*Goma*	,,	Hausa.	*Gum*	,,	Momenya.		
Kumi	,,	Bumbete.	*Goma*	,,	Kadzina.					

Ten is likewise

Cumme in Vod.	*Kymmen* in Karelian.		*Hamish* in Palaik.	
Kamen in Mordvin.	*Kummene* in Olonets.		*Samfor* in Papuan.	
Kuemme in Estonian.	*Amar* in { Basque (cf. *Am*, Eg.		*Samfor* in Mefur.	
Kymmemen in Fin.	the Fist).		*Sampulu* in Bima.	

Such interchange was necessitated by the unity of the types and early limits of language.

The Renn, or nursling Child, became the *Renka*, the Man, at puberty, *Renka* (Eg.) being the pubes. Hence the Man is the

Ranuka in Tanema.			*Oreng*, the Man, Sumenap.	
Renk, the Pubescent Knight, English.			*Oreng*	,, Madura.
Runā	,,	,, Quichua.	*Langai*	,, Patos.
Reanci	,,	,, Sabipoconi.	*Langai*	,, Parigi.
Orang	,,	,, { In the Batta, Malay, and other groups.	*Lonco* (Man and Pubes), Auraucanan.	
			Loonkquee, Oneida.	
			Langa, Virile Male, Sanskrit.	

These names of the Man are one with the Sanskrit *Linga*, and the *Linch*-pin of the stag; the Zulu *Hlanga*, or *Lungu*, a reed; the typical Reed from which the human race originated, the Male Member. Other primitive emblems of virility can be traced under the same type-name.

In the Australian and other languages

Lung, is Stone, in Yarra.			*Long*, is Stone, in Kakhyen.			*Along*, is Bone, in Abor.		
Walang	,,	,, Wiradurei.	*Lunggau*	,,	,, N.Tankhul.	*Along*	,,	,, Miri.
Longa	,,	,, Tasmanian.	*Ngalung*	,,	,, Luhuppa.	*Irang*, is Teeth, in Bathurst.		
Orungay	,,	,, Tuscarora.	*Thullung*	,,	,, Khoibu.	*Irang*	,,	,, Wellington
Nlung	,,	,, Singpho.	*Khlung*	,,	,, Maring.	*Irang*	,,	,, Wiradurei.
Talong	,,	,, Jili.	*Lung*	,,	., Thoung-lhu.	*Leeangy*, is Tooth, in Boraiper.		
Ta-lun	,,	,, Sak.	*Arung*, is Horn, in Sak.			*Leeang*	,,	,, Yarra.
Ka-lun	,,	,, Kami.						

Among the Australian names for the Beard and Hair types of Virility are

Yearnka, Menero Downs.	*Ooran*, Regent's Lake.	*Yaren*, Sidney.
Yerreng, Morton Island.	*Uran*, Wellington.	*Wurung*, Lake Macquarie.

In Inner Africa

Nlenge, is Hair, in Basunde.	*Elungi* or *Eluni*, is Hair, in Oworo.

The Nail of the finger or toe is

Lenyal in Mutsaya.	*Rentoli* in Bumbete.	*Orunyara* in Pangela.
Lenyala in Babuma.	*Lunzoana* in Lubalo.	*Serene* in Gadsaga.

But the Second of the Two in Sex was Third in the Series of Mother, Child, and Vir. Hence Khem or Khemt signifies number 3.

Khemt, Egyptian.	*Angom*, Abor.	*Sam*, Siamese.
Shemt, Coptic.	*Kasam*, Gyarung.	*Sam*, Ahom.
Kumot, Tsheremis.	*Som*, Murmi.	*Sam*, Khamti.
Chami, Cochetimi.	*Swom*, Bramhu.	*Tsam*, Shan.
Kuim, Zirianian.	*Sumzho*, Chepang.	*Zam*, Canton.
Kacham, Mijhu.	*Sumya*, Kirata.	*Ssum*, Tanguhti.
Kimsa, Aymora.	*Syumsh*, Limbu.	*Semi*, Suanic.
Kimisa, Cayuvava.	*Sam*, Lepcha.	*Sami*, Georgian.
Yameenee, Yankton.	*Sum*, Takpa.	*Sumi*, Mingrelian.
Yahmani, Dacotah.	*Sum*, Lhopa.	*Sam*, Canaan.
Homeka, Kulanapo.	*Sum*, Milchan.	*Asam*, Nowgong.
Hamuk, Cuchan.	*Sum*, Theburskud.	*Asam*, Tengsa.
Hamuk, Dieguno.	*Som*, Thaksya.	*Asam*, Khari.
Hamoka, Cocomaricopa.	*Sam*, Changlo.	*Azam*, Joboca.
Hamoko, Mohave.	*Sum*, Tibetan.	*Azum*, Mitham.
Hum, Sumcha.	*Sam*, Laos.	*Masum*, Singpho.
Dshumi, Lazic.		

Basnage says the World was formed by analogy to the Hebrew alphabet, which is numeral.[1] The first three letters of this, Aleph, Beth, and Gimel, are types of our numbers, 1, 2, and 3. Aleph is called the Steer in Phœnician, the Calf in the hieroglyphics, an image of the Primordial One, who was Cow-headed, as Hathor; Calf-headed, as Ahti (Typhon) ; and the Water-Cow, as Kheb. The Beth is Both, Twin, Two. Gimel is the Camel, a type of potency answering by name to the *Third*, who is *Khemt* (3) in Egyptian.

This origin of the Three is not only shown by names, it is visibly demonstrated in the *shape* of our figures 1, 2 and 3 ; the NUMBER 3 being *third in series and dual in form*. The same law governs our

[1] *History of the Jews*, p. 190.

three first Notes of punctuation—the comma (,), semi-colon (;), and colon (:) ; in which the colon is likewise *third in series and an ideographic two in shape*. The duadic-triad is also figured in the Hebrew letter Shin ש. This sign is a Tooth. The Tooth, *Hu* (Eg.) is a type of Adultship, and the name signifies the Adult. The Shin is a *Double* Tooth ; its fangs made it a *figure of the trinity* in unity, and its numeral value is 3 in the series of hundreds. *Khemt* (Eg.) is also the Trident, another figure of the triune being. The author of the *Book of God* gives the sign of ̆30 for the mystical *Ao* as the Hindu *Aum ;* and No. 30 is the numeral value of "*Khemt*" expressed in Tens ; the symbol of the triune one.[1]

Tree and *Three* are also synonymous. First, the Tree was the Mother, as Producer ; the Child was the Branch. But number 3 implies the notion of *Cause*, or the *Root* of the Tree. This was masculine. The Ren, as Renpu (Eg.), is the male root or plant of renewal. In Inner Africa the Root is

Ran in Nso.	*Aron* in Anan.	*Lun-ganzi* in Kabenda.
Ren in Wolof.	*Lun-Kandzi* in Nyombe.	*Lingi* in Tumbuktu.
Erona in Okam.		

The Root likewise agrees in name with the *Sheru* (Eg.) for the Adult or pubescent Youth, and with the *Tser* Rock or Stone, as

Sila, the Root, Mandenga.	*Suru*, the Root, Vei.	*Zori*, the Root, Pika.
Suluo ,, Kabunga.	*Suro* ,, Kra.	*Nzoran* ,, Dsarawa.
Sulu ,, Kono.	*Suro* ,, Krebo.	*Osire* ,, Akurakura.

The number 3 and the Tree are identical in the Hottentot *Nona*, Three, and *Nonas*, the Root, the radix of the tree.[2] The third digit, counted either way, is the root-finger. Here it may be noticed that the *Morindo Citrifolia* Tree, which has the most "wonderfully tenacious" root, is called by the Mangaians the *Nono* tree.[3]

The genealogy of the first family Tree was the Mother (number 1 as Stem), Child (number 2, as Branch), Adult (No. 3, as Root). This may explain why the Egyptians wrote their first plural with the sign of 3 instead of 2; and why the Greeks used the oath, or typical expression, "By Three am I overthrown." *Three* is likewise identical with *Throw*, and a Throw is Three in number with the Letts, who, in counting crabs, throw three at a time; the word METTENS meaning Three, or à throw. Three is the first and Nine is the full Egyptian plural, the highest number on the right. The masculine Hand, as Ten, resolves once more into the Twin-total, the Two-One, the Alpha and Omega of the Beginning. The word *Three* (as well as Tree), in its various forms, is a universal type-name, derived from this origin. The Third was the Adult male, and *Ter* (Eg.) is to engender, *Turreti*,

[1] Introduction, p. 327.
[2] Hahn, *Tsuni-Goam*, p. 14.
[3] Gill.

in Lithuanic. Ter (Eg.), as agent, is the Phallus; the Vayu *Tholu*; English Tolly (and Dil), the Fijian *Droi*, and Maori *Tara*.

The well-known Phallic *Ters* of Antwerp was an impersonation of *Ter*. In Egypt Khepr-*Ter* was the Erector or re-erector of the dead. The Negro God *Til* (Tir) who created the first human pair out of the knee-caps of the Hermaphrodite Mother was likewise a form of the God Three as the Virile Male, who followed the Mother and Child and became a begetting God. The Yurecares also have the God *Tiri*, who is said to have divided the human being into male and female. The first mortals, they affirm, were one at root, and appeared in the bole of a tree. This the God *Tiri* split in two, and the man and woman emerged. Tiri is a form of the God Three, who represents the distinction of the sexes at puberty, when the child becomes the *Khemt* Horus, the Horus as *Third*, the *Homme fäit*, the Lord, the root of the Tree.

In Inner Africa, No. 3 is

Tere in Koama.	*Taru* in Kiriman.	*Tar* in Nso.
Tore in Bagbalan.	*Taru* in Meto.	*Tare* in Tiwi.
Tere in Okuloma.	*Taro* in Matatan.	*Itar* in Mbarike.
Taru in Udso.	*Teraro* in Nyamban.	*Tal* in Gura.
Ter in Papiah.		

Outside of Africa we have

Toru in Maori.	*Tullu* in Savu.	*Three* in English.
Tolu in Fiji.	*Telu* in Ende.	*Tria* in Greek.
Toru in Polynesia.	*Telu* in Sasak.	*Try* in Sclavonic.
Tolou in Mami.	*Telu* in Malagasi.	*Trys* in Lithuanic.
Toro in Pome.	*Telu* in Batta dialects.	*Tres* in Latin.
Bo-toro in Seroci.	*Dre* in West Pushtu.	*Trui* in Kashkari.
Toroe in Dasen.	*Tre* in Gadi.	*Triu* in Arniya.
Toro in Wandamin.	*Trah* in Kashmir.	*Tri* in Sanskrit.
Tolu in Mayorga.	*Tra* in Tirhai.	*Tre* in Siah Posh.
Tolou in Cocos Island.	*Tholth* in Syriac.	*Turrun* in Khurbat.
Toru in Marquesas.	*Thaleth* in Arabic.	*Trin* in Tater.
Tilu in Mille.	*Tri* in Breton.	*Trin* in Gipsy of Norway.
Tulo in Bissayan.	*Tri* in Welsh.	*Toluke* in Kenay.
Tallo in Iloco.	*Try* in Cornish.	*Teli-ko* in Tatalui.
Talu in Cayagan.	*Tri* in Irish.	*Tula-ka* in San Raphael.
Tolo in Timur.	*Tri* in Scotch.	*Tulu-bahi* in San Miguel.
Tellu in Rotti.	*Tree* in Manx.	*Tarani* in Garura.
Etellu in Manatoto.	*Tra* in Tirhai.	*Terewaid* in Jaoi.

This type-word for No. 3 is identical with the name of the *Two Times*, or *Teru* (Eg.) and the *Second phase* of the male child, who became the " Bull of the Mother" at puberty as *Ter* the engenderer. Also the African name of the Bull is

Tura in Biafada.	*Tura* in Bambara.	*Tur* in Adirar.
Tura in Mandenga.	*Tura* in Landoma.	*Tor* and *Adarif* in Beran.
Tura in Kabunga.	*Turana* in Soso.	*Tur* in Arabic.
Tura in Dsalunka.	*Dalo* in Bornu.	*Taurus* in Latin.
Tura in Kankanka.		

Tur and Sur or Sar are interchangeable for No. 3 in the African languages, and

Sara is No. 3 in Kisekise.	*Saran* is No. 3 in Tene.	*Salasa* is No. 3 in Beran.
Saran „ Soso.	*Silasa* „ Wadai.	*Selaste* „ Tigré.

These correspond to *Salas* for No. 3 in Assyrian.

This agrees with the *Sheru* (Eg.) for the Bull or adult male, and with the name for hair and other types of virility in various languages. It is by the nature of the types alone that anything final can be determined about the names. The Hairy one and the Hero are synonymous because the first hero was the pubescent male.

The Egyptian *Sher*, the hairy, is applied to barley and to the adult male. In English *Share* is hair, the pubes of the male; Hebrew שׂיר. This is the natural root of the *Sire*, English; the *Sar*, Akkadian *Sarru*, Assyrian; *Sar*, Persian; *Tzar*, Russian; *Sur*, Hindi; and *Sar*, Gaelic for the Hero; the *Kaiser* and *Cæsar*, who are all founded on the pubescent male, the bearded and hairy one. The root reappears in the latin *Cæsaries* for the hair. The Cæsar represented the *Sheru* (Eg.), and there was a popular Roman belief that Julius Cæsar was long-haired when born!

The name identifies the male ruler with hair, and number 3, and the Triad of Mother, Child, and pubescent Male was completed in the Sar, Sheru, Sir, Sire, or Cæsar.

We are now able to affirm that, beyond the Two hands as the means of signalling numbers, the archetypes of *One*, *Two*, and *Three*, running through many groups of languages, are the Mother, *One*, the Child (twin) *Two*, the virile Male, *Three*; these three being the typical trinity in unity, under various names.

The divinity Pan or Phanes, for example, is a form of this triune total or collective All. Pan is the hairy, horned one of a mystical compound nature. Hair and horn are his types of pubescence, which show the second phase of the male child. *Ân* (Eg.) for hair, to be hairy and wanton, is a reduced form of *Fan*, *Pan* or *Benn*, the Phœnix. Phanes was the Phœnix that transformed at the time of puberty. The Benn or Aan was the hairy Ape. The Phœnix (Nycticorax) wore the double plume; a kind of feather of the Two Truths. Hair and feather are interchangeable types, and the double feather of the Phœnix is still worn by the Kaffirs who don the feather of the Blue Crane.

This is the sign of the hero, but it is related to puberty; hence the winning and wearing of "the feather" by the virile Indian, who takes a scalp to become a Brave. Hence also the Mexican myth of the feather which caused conception in the Virgin Mother.

Our own popular "Punch" is likewise a Pan, or Phœnix, a personification of puberty in the character of the All, the Supreme Being, who acts as if he were everybody; and the drama of "Punch and Judy" is the celebration of his coming to power. *Puns* in Sanskrit denotes the same typical male, the masculine attributes, the virile member; *Bangi* in Zulu, the virile male.

Pan's *animal* type is the Goat. In English the *Buncus* is a Donkey, and the *Bingo* a Dog. In Welsh the *Baingu* is a Bull; this was the Bull of Hu, the pubescent Son and Consort of Kedy (who possibly survives as Judy) the Great Mother. As Khem, the virile male became the Bull of the Mother, as Punch he is the bully.

In his explanation of the cardinal numbers Bopp says "he does not think that any language has produced especial original words for the particular designations of such compound and peculiar ideas as three, four, five, etc." He admits that the appellations of numbers resist all comparison with the verbal roots, and he tries to explain them by the prenominal roots. Being limited to the Aryan group he is compelled to derive the Gothic *Fidvor* for number 4 from the Sanskrit *Chatwar* for number 4.[1] But if *Fid* were *derivable* from *Chat* there would be an end to all foothold in language. It is possible of course for these to become *equivalents* in later language because both may be derived from an earlier word that will account for them, Ch (or K) and F being the twin phonetic deposits of an original ideographic Kf.

The Gothic Fid, in Fidvor, is one form of the type-name for number 4 to be found in the most ancient and diverse languages. It is Inner African, to begin with, as—

Fudu, Hausa.	*Fudu*, Bode.	*Ufade*, Mandara.
Fudu, Kano.	*Fudu*, N'godsin.	*Fadyg*, Bishari.
Fodu, Kadzina.	*Fudu*, Doai.	*Fat*, Batta.
Fedu, Karekare.		

It was continued as—

Feto, in Coptic.	*Pidwar*, *Fethera* and	*Feother*, in English (*Betty-*
Futu and *Aftu*, in Egyptian.	*Phedair*, in Welsh.	*Bodkin*, the 4th finger).
Erbaht, in Tigré.	*Patsar*, in Cornish.	*Effat*, in Malagasy.
Aybatta, in Gafat.	*Fidvor*, in Gothic.	*Pi-ffat*, in Guebé (Papuan).
Arbat, in Arabic.		

(*Pi* is a prefix, as in Pi-leure for five).

Po-bits, Yengen.	*Puet*, Atshin.
Boat, Amberbaki (New Guinea).	*Opat*, Toba Batta.
Fat, Salawatti (New Guinea).	*Mpat*, Sasak.
E-vatz, or *Ta-vatz*, Mallicollo (New Hebrides).	*Opat*, Bima.
Tbait, New Caledonia.	*Apat*, Bissayan.
Eppat, Iloco.	*Apat*, Tagala.

This type-name for number 4 is one of the primaries of the present work, one of the radicals of language, one of the words of the world. The types that lead to the one proto-type of the number 4 are preserved in the hieroglyphics. Fetu and Aft (Eg.) are variants for the number 4, the four quarters or the four-legged thing. Aft is the hinder part or quarter of the four-legged animal. The four-legged crocodile was one type of Aft or Apt (as goddess). We have the same figure of 4 by name in English as the *Eft*.

The hippopotamus is another type of Aft (Apt), and this four-legged animal has four toes on each foot. The word foot, pat, or pode is identical with Fut for number 4, and this points to the origin of the

[1] Bopp, *Comparative Grammar*, vol. i. p. 427. Eng. Tr.

type-name in that of the four-footed animal the Aft or Fut of Egypt. Thus, by name and nature, the type of number 4 is *Quadrupedal*.

And the reason why the type-name of number 2 and the two feet is also a name for number 4 is because in the latter case the type was four-footed. *Every primitive word has to be determined and differentiated by the type intended.* Aft or fut may be the chair, the couch with four legs, the abode with four corners, or the heaven of four quarters. When the type is human the heaven above is represented by a woman arching over and resting on the earth with her hands and feet. In this case the quadrupedal type is pourtrayed by the two hands and two feet. It may be the four-footed fyl-fot Cross of Thor is named from the four as *Fut*. But the great type of number 4 was the ancient Typhon, the Mother of beginnings.

Aft is an abraded form of Kheft (Variant Khept) for the hind quarter which was the north in the heaven of the two halves, and west in the heaven of the four quarters.

The Khept is the *hind quarter of the Quadruped*, and Fet (or Aft) is number 4 and the four quarters. By return to the earlier Khaft or Khept we reach an original for *Chât* as well as *Fid*. Khaft modifies into both Khat and Aft (or Fet), and thus furnishes two different words with one meaning to later language. The Khât (Khept) as the hinder thigh is the seat nearest to nature. So the Kati in Sanskrit is the seat or buttocks. In English we have the *Fud* for the tail. Both are contained in the word *Khaft*, equally with *Chat* and *Fid*. One form of the seat is the chair, and the Irish *Ceathar* and Manx *Kiare* for number 4 agree with the Chair, Kadair and quadrangular Caer, the seat-type of the four, and therefore with *Khept* the hinder thigh of the beast, and with Aft the seat, hinder part, also to squat or go down, as the animal on all fours. The prototypal idea of number 4 then is quadrupedal, and the *Quadra, Quadruped, Chatwar,* and *Ceathar* preserve the fact in their names.

The Assyrian Arbata, Irbitti or Irbit, for number 4 is usually derived from *Rab,* to be great. But the *Rep* (Eg.) is the typical quadruped.

Rabe, Wolof, Cattle.	*Laboi*, Greek, Bear.	*Rebi*, No. 4, Manyak.
Rabu, Coptic, Lion.	*Læp*, Victoria, Sheep.	

Also, רבע applied to the couch,[1] and to the lying down of four-footed things, agrees with the Egyptian *Rep*.

There is no such chance or coincidence as the Aryanists have unwittingly assumed, and would make us believe, when we find that—

Fima is No. 5 in Marquesan.	*Pemp* is No 5 in Breton.	*Pemajala* is No. 5 in Eslen.
Fimf ,, Gothic	*Pymp* ,, Cornish.	*Pumazho* ,, Chepang.
πέμπε ,, Æolic Greek.	*Pump* ,, Welsh.	

And that in the Yesso dialect, one of the Aino group, *Fambe* is the

---

[1] Ps. cxxxix. 3.

name for Number 10. These are explained by the hand itself. In old English one name for the hands is *fambles*. This agrees with the Egyptian *âm* or fam for the fist, and the Botocudo *impo* for the hand. The hand is called a bunch of five. To *five* or to *fim*, πεμπάζειν, is to make the fist; the Egyptian *âm* (or fam); and *Five*, *fimf*, *fim*, or *fam* are variants of one original word. In English *Pimp* is applied to coupling together; hence the *pimp* as a go-between and as a faggot of sticks. So in Xosa Kaffir *Famba* means to heap, pile, cluster together, as in making the fist. The radical is Inner African.

Poma is the hand in Mende. *Asi Pome* in Adampe. In Xosa Kaffir the *Pambo* is the handle or handles of a pot or other vessel. *Fumbata* is to close the hand in the form of a fist; to grasp in the closed hand and hold fast what it contains.

The Egyptian *âemf* (or *famf*) is a handful of food, and as *âm* is the fist as well as to eat, this is the equivalent of the Gothic, Greek, Breton, Cornish, Welsh and other names for "five" as the handful of digits, or one fist. Here the Numbers 5 and 10, the fist, fambles, the clustering and handle, are all related by name to the hand, and there is as surely a unity of origin for the word and types as there is for the numbers in the digits.

Under the name of Tat (Eg.) the hand is the type of offering and giving. So, here, the hand as a type of giving is related by name to the Inner African words for giving.

Pem in Yula.	*Fima* in Soso.	*Femao* in Tumu.
Fema in Tene.	*Fiumo* in Momenya.	*Wema* in Baseke.
Fima in Kise-Kise.		

In Egyptian, one name of the finger is *Teb*; the fingers are *Tebu*, and Tebu is the name of the number 10 in the series of Thousands. Also four Tebu make one Palm, and seven palms (twenty-eight fingers) make the Royal Cubit, or Sutem-Mah.

In Inner Africa—

Tubo is the finger in Kum.	*Gbala Sara* is the finger in Pika.		*Ozubo* is the finger in Opanda.			
Mo Topo ,, Param.	*Kobo-bui* ,,	Tumbuktu.	*Saba* ,,	Adirar.		
Gbehi ,, Bini.	*Kafo-Gabone* ,,	N'ki.	*Saba* ,,	Beran.		
Igbe ,, Ihewe.	*Kpira-bo* ,,	Egbele.	*Osba* ,,	Wadai.		

The African, *Tch*, with its variant sounds (explained later on) will account for Kep, and Tep being equivalent for the fist and the fingers in Egyptian. *Tef* (Tua) is a name of *Seb*, the Star, and the Divine Father; also of the number 5. These interchange in the names of numbers 5 and 10, as

Tuf, No. 5 in Batta.	*Dsowi*, No. 5 in Pula.		*Gubida*, No. 5 in Biafada.	
Dsif } ,, Bulanda.	*Dsowi* ,,	Goburu.	*Kobeda* ,,	Padsade.
Kif }	*Dsowi* ,,	Kano.	*Khuba* ,,	Absné.
Tsof } ,, Limba.				
Ksof }				

Other African variants for Number 5 corresponding to the Hebrew *Qamz*, a fist, Assyrian *Hamsu*, for number 5, are found in

Gumen, No. 5 in Banyun.   *Hm*, No. 5 in Basa.   *Hm*, No. 5 in Gbe.
Tsamat ,, Baga.   *Hmu* ,, Krebo.   *Mhm* ,, Dewoi.
Semmes ,, Berber.

The Number 10 is—

Zabe Ozabe and *Otabe* in Koro.   *Tsofats* in Baga of Kalum.   *Kepu* in Landoro.
Dsob in Akurakura.   *Kob* and *Kowa* in Ham.   *Igbe* in Egbele.
Dsob in Okam.   *Kof* in Limha.   *Igbe* in Bini.
Tubban in Danakil.   *Gfad* in Bulanda.   *Igbe* in Ihewe.
Tofat in Timne.   *Ukob* in Yasgua.   *Igbe* in Oloma.

These are Inner African.

Number 10 (to carry out the illustration) is—

Tap in Tonkin.   *Sib* in E. Shan.   *Sapulu* in Rotti.
Taap in Cochin China.   *Sip* in Khamti.   *Sapulu* in Manatoto.
Shap in Cantonese.   *Sapula* in Batta.   *Sapulu* in Malay.
Dap in Kambojia.   *Sapulu* in Lubu.   *Kep* in Angami.
Tovo in Japanese.   *Sepulu* in Ulu.   *Kip* in Kirata.
Toverah in Moor.   *Sapulu* in Susak.   *Kep* in Mikir.
Sip in Laos.   *Sapulu* in Sumbawa.   *Kyep* in Mijhu.
Sip in Siamese.   *Sabulai* in Ende.   *Kippio* in Chemmesyan.
Sip in Ahom.   *Sapulu* in Timur.

In the Baniwa and Coretu dialects *Kap*, the hand, is the base of

Nucopi, hand, Maipur.   *Nucabi*, hand, Barree.   *Tchoupumau*, hand, Juri.
Nucapi ,, Isanna.   *Eri-Kiape* ,, Uaenambeu.

This last is founded on the fingers, that is, on the bunch of five.

Tchoupei, fingers, Juri.   *Nu-Capi*, fingers, Uaenambeu.

The Egyptian Kep is a fist, a hand of five. And as the group of five the foot is found under the same name in Hebrew, where the hand and foot are both named *Kaph ;* the same word being applied to branches. This is a type-name for both hand and foot in the African languages. Also,

Tchouoti is the foot in Juri.   *Giapa-muetshu* (literally foot-fingers), the
Giapa ,, ,, Coretu.   toes, Coretu.
  Tchoupomoru, the toes, Juri.

In Sanskrit the 5 appears as *Capata* for the fifth note in music.

Professor Sayce takes the Assyrian name of number 1, *Istin* or *Estin*, to be derived from the root " *es*," to which the t was added, as in the case of the other numerals. M. Bertin compares it with the Hebrew " *Aish*," for the personal one, each one, every one. But *Shá* is the first One in the hieroglyphics, and this is also the Arm. *Shá* is a reduced form of *Shef* and *Kep*, the Arm or Hand. Moreover, this *Sha* is repeated in a type-name for number 6, *the one on the other hand*. *Sha* being the first, as Arm or One Hand, *Sha-Sha* in the duplicative stage of sounds denotes the second or other hand, the first digit on which was the figure of six: *Sha-sha* is expressed by the Hebrew ששׁ, and Shash represents

Sas, No. 6 in Egyptian.	*Shesh,* No, 6 in Duman.	*Szesc,* No. 6 in Sclavonic.
Sisu „ Assyrian.	*Shash* „ Persian.	*Sex* „ Latin.
Shash „ Sanskrit.	*Shash* „ Biluch.	*Size* „ Old English.
Shash „ Brahui.	*Chisa* „ Cochetimi.	*Se* „ Irish.
Skash „ Kashmir.	*Szeszi* „ Lithuanic.	*Sei* „ Basque.
Shesh „ Khurbat.		

Here also the root-word is Inner African. Number 6 being

Eseses in Oloma.	*Aize* in Dahome.	*Esa* in Sobo.
Sises in Kandin.	*Aize* in Hwida.	*Esa* in Egbele.
Soos in Arkiko.	*Aize* in Mahi.	

The name of Number 7, which is

Sibitti in Assyrian,	*Subhat* in Amharic,	*Shebata* in Kaffa,
Sibatta in Gafat,	*Sabata* in Gonga,	*Seb-ti* (5-2) in Egyptian,

appears in the Inner African languages as

Samhoat in N'goala.	*Zimhede* in Nyamban.	*Tsamhodia* in Nyombe.
Sambat in Runda.	*Sambodia* in Mimboma.	*Tsambodia* in Basunde.
Samboade in Kisama.	*Tsamboadi* in Musentandu.	

The Constellation of the Seven Great Stars (Ursa Major) was probably the primordial figure of Seven. Seven was often called the perfect number. Its name, as Hept (Eg.) is also the name for Plenty, a *heap* of food, and good luck. The Seven were the great heap, or cluster of stars, an image of plenty, or *a lot* that revolved together.

The Hottentot *Hongu* the grouped or confederated ones for the number 7, points to the Great Bear as the celestial figure. The Bear also supplied the pointer hand to the Horologe of time in heaven. In fact, as Pythagoras says, the Two Bears were the Two Hands of the Great Mother, who was Kep (the hand) or Kheb in Egypt, and who as *Teb* bears the name of the Finger. The first star of this constellation, *Dubhe,* is *Teb* (Eg.), the finger or pointer. Now with the Kaffirs, pointing with the forefinger of the right hand is synonymous with number 7. In answering the question, "*How much did your master give you?*" they will say, "*U Kombile,*" he gave me seven, literally he pointed with his forefinger. And in describing seven horses they will say, "the horses have pointed" (amahashi *akombile*) that is, there were seven of them.[1] Such a mode of expression is based on finger-counting. The Zulu begins his reckoning with the little finger of his left hand and continues with the thumb on the second hand, so that the forefinger becomes a figure of seven. The verb *Komba,* to point, which denotes the forefinger as the pointer, is founded on the name of the number seven, and the Seven Stars were the primordial Pointers.

It is quite possible, too, that when the North American Indians make the sign of *Good*[2] with the thumb and forefinger of the *right* hand in front of the mouth the other fingers being closed, it is as the

[1] Tylor. [2] Burton.

sign of number 7, the figure of good, luck, plenty, lots of food, in the hieroglyphics.

There is nothing more common than the interchange of the numbers 7 and 10 under the one root-name in the African and other groups of languages. This is on account of the digital origin of numbers and the naming in the stage of gesture-signs. Both hands held up were the first sign of ten, and Seven was indicated by one hand and two digits, or the second digit on the right hand.

Kepti or Kabti in Egyptian denotes two arms, two fists, or two hands. From Kepti we derive Hepti and Sebti, number 7. Kep-ti may be read 5—2, or twice 5, because the ti adds 2, or it may duplicate the hand. These were distinguished by the different gestures.

A perfect parallel to Kepti (or Seb-ti) for either 7 or 10, as hand (Kep) and ti for two, or twice one hand, may be found in the Jower dialect of the Papuan group in which *Rebe* is number 1, *Redoe* is number 2 ; *Brai-a-rebe*, or five-and-one make the number 6; but, *Brai-a-redoe*, actually 5 and 2, *is the name for number Ten*. To make the ten out of *Brai-a-redoe*, or 5—2, the 2 must duplicate the 5 or the hand just as the ti in *Kepti* would have to duplicate the hand to make the value of the number 10 out of a word otherwise signifying 5—2 or number 7.

The general Kamite or Inner African mode of compounding the 7 is by 5 + 2. In the Vei, *Sumfela ;* Gbandi, *Ngofela ;* Mende, Wo-fela, &c., for the number 7, the *fela* denotes Two. *Dsowe*-didi, for number 7 in Goboru and Kano, is 5 + 2. *Tan-na-peli*, is 5 and 2 for 7 in Matatan, and *Tanu-na-Beli* in Kiriman. *Hem*-leso in Krebo is number 7 as 5 + 2. Here the *Sum, Hem,* and *Dsowe* for 5 are identical with the Egyptian *Seb* (5) and Assyrian *Hamsu.*

The Egyptian number 7 as " Sefekh " is found to be written by 5 + 2 in the style of the goddess Sefekh with the seven rays or horns, and this can only be read as Sef, 5, and kh, 2, from khi, the duplicate, the second or two, seven being the second digit on the second hand. The Two Hands of Heaven were the Two Bears. The Bear constellation is Kep, and the two are Kepti. Kep or Keb is the earliest form of Seb (Time, *Xaip* in the Namaqua Hottentot), and she was the Mother of all time, as goddess of the Seven Stars. Sebti becomes Sothis the Manifestor of Time, named from the two hands of time Kep-ti, whence Hepti and Sebti for number 7. The Two Hands turned round and Sebti (Sothis) struck the hour of the year. To this origin in the hand—2, or Kepti—may be traced the type-name for number 7 as :—

Keopits, Witshita.	*Hepti,* Egyptian.	*Heft,* Duman.
Chappo(t), Minetari.	*Hapt,* Biluch.	*Saptan,* Sanskrit.
Sambag, Runda.	*Hapta,* Zend.	*Septem,* Latin.
Shebata, Kaffa.	*Epta,* Greek.	*Efta,* Tater.
Subhat, Amharic.	*Haft,* Brahui.	*Avita,* Koro.
Sate, Hurrur.	*Haft,* Persian.	*Fitu,* Malagasy.
Sabata, Gonga.	*Heft,* Khurbat.	*Vitu,* Fiji.

Whitu, Maori.	*Fito*, Mayorga.	*Pito*, Tagala.
Fitu, Batta.	*Fetto*, Wahitaho.	*Pitu*, Cayagan.
Fitu, Malay.	*Pitu*, Ceram.	*Pitu*, Sasak.
Fiet, Salawatti.	*Pito*, Bissayan.	*Petu, or Pedu*, Savu.
Fitu, Mangarei.	*Pito*, Iloco.	*Pidu*, Bima.

Here it should be borne in mind that numbers 2 and 7 frequently have one name and were determined by the two hands.

Seven is sometimes reckoned as six extended, as in the Aponegicran *Itawĭuna* (from *Itawana*), meaning number 6 drawn out. The Coptic *Sasef* for seven, is from Sas number 6. The British Druids also had a number 7 called Mor Seisor, the Great Six which was a mystical formula.

The Egyptian Ses-sen for number 8, reads 6 + 2. The height was here attained in the Octave, the sign being the third and longest finger (known in Nursery language as "Long Gracious,") on the right, the masculine hand. This was the height of attainment as the repeating number, the same as the first in the scale. In Hottentot, Khaisi for number 8 signifies the "turning number." Eight (Manx Hoght) and height are thus synonymous; and both were represented by the longest finger on the right hand.

The origin and naming of numbers are bound up with the Seven Stars of the Bear. These are dual in the two Bears; one of which represents the Mother, the She-Bear; the other her son or progeny. These were the two hands of Rhea the Genitrix. Rhea is identified with Nupe the Lady of Heaven and Consort of Seb-Kronus. But Typhon (*i.e.* Tep, Teb, Kheb, Kep, or Kefa) was the earlier form of the Genitrix, and Sevekh or Khebekh, her son, was the earlier form of Seb. These two were the two hands of the earliest Horologe, that made their circuit once a year, as Kep the Mother and Kheb (ekh) the Child (or the Seven Companions); Kep is the hand and ti is two or twin; and Kep-ti is both hands or the number 7. The two hands are feminine and masculine as left and right, lower and upper, in Kep and Khebekh (or Kebti, the later Sebti, who became Sut).

From Kepti we derive Hepti (number 7), and Sebti, or Suti. The two hands of Kep are a form of number 10 in language. The Seven Stars identify her name with number 7, and Kep the hand with number 5. She is the figure of number 4, as the Quadruped, and as Apt (variant Fut), the goddess with four aspects representative of the four corners. Number 2 is the same as number 10 in the Two Hands. As Tep (Eg), she is one, the first, by name, in nature or in numbers; and as Teb, she also has the name of the finger.

Another Egyptian name of the finger is *Tekar*. The type-name of Tek or Dek, for number 10 is fixed for ever in the number and the name of the Digits, the original figures used in reckoning. In Egyptian *Tek* is to add, join, and multiply. The sign of this is the Tek Cross, the Polynesian Teka, a Cross, and the Roman figure of *Dec*-em or ten. Thus Tek (Eg.) is to multiply in reckoning ; Tek is the Cross-sign and a figure of Ten ; the reckoning is Digital, and the digit is the Tekar (Eg.) as means of reckoning.

One hieroglyphic of No. 10 is the pair of hands joined together and cut off—one meaning of *Tek* being to amputate or dock. The two fingers stand for two hands, and these, when crossed, make the sign of Tek or 10 (x). In following this Kamite type-name we find that

Tekar, is the Digitus, in Egyptian.   *Tuka-bera*, is the Digitus, in Gbandi.
Toko-jiwo, is the Digitus, in Mende.

The Hand is

Takobero, Baga of Kalum.	*Takha*, Hatigor.	*Tegi*, Tarakai.
Tukui, Gbandi.	*Dak*, Namsang.	*Tag*, Erroob.
Dekunda, Songo.	*Degere*, Gadsaga.	*Iteke*, No. 5, Eregba.
Tekha, Nowgong.	*Dek*, Aino of Kamkatka.	*Taklima*, No. 5, Eskimo, &c.

In the Maori language *Toko* is the prefix to numerals from one (Tahi) to nine (Iwa) and *Tekau* or *Tokau* is No. 10. In the Deoria Chutia language (one of the Naga tongues of India) the numerals are all named with this root as prefix to the word.

Dugsha, One.	*Dugumua*, Five.	*Duguche*, Eight.
Dukuni, Two.	*Duguchu*, Six.	*Duguchuba*, Nine.
Dugda, Three.	*Duguchi*, Seven.	*Dugshe*, Ten.
Duguchi, Four,		

The Numerals of the Nsietshawus or Killamuk language of the Atna group point to the same digital origin by name.

Theike, One.	*Tsukhus*, Five.	*Tukatshi*, Eight.
Tkhlasale, Two.	*Tsulukhatshi*, Six.	*Tkshleio*, Nine.
Tshanat, Three.	*Tutshoos*, Seven.	*Tkhlauhantshs*, Ten.
Tkhlawos, Four.		

Teka (Eg.) to cross and clasp applies equally to the two hands and the ten fingers. Numbers 2 and 10 have the same root-name in the following languages.

The Number 2 is

Tagi in Jaoi.	*Ticknee* in Seneca.	*Dekanee* in Nottaway.
Tech in Kolush of Sitka.	*Tekinu* in Onondago.	*Duke* in Bagwan.
Tuklo in Chocktaw.	*Tekni* in Cayuga.	*Tkhaus* in Piskaws.
Teghia in Oneida.	*Tekninih* in Mohawk.	

The Number 10 is—

Atuk, Mobba.	*Deg* in Welsh.	*Aduk* in Sekumne.
Dekue in Alege.	*Dek* in Cornish.	*Atek* in Unalaska.
Dikui in Kisama.	*Dec* in Breton.	*Tokke* in Lap.
Dokeme in Bagrmi.	*Deich* in Irish.	*Tekau* in Maori.
Dokemy in Begharmi	*Deig* in Scotch.	*Takau* in Tongan.
Degbo in N'ki.	*Feih* in Manks.	*Takakkh* in Ugalents.
Disi in Hottentot.	*Deka* in Greek.	*Tkatz* in Cochetimi.
Tsue in Dsuku.	*Dziesiec* in Sclavonic.	*Tugr*, Set of Ten, in Gothic.
Tacha in Gonga.	*Decem* in Latin.	*Dicker*, Ten Hides, in English.
Tegaun in Tarawan.	*Deszimtis* in Lithuanian.	*Tegotha*, Tenth, in Frisian.
Togaserama in Bishari.		

From this root, Taht as the Reckoner, derives his name of Tekh, and the Goddess of the Months hers of Tekai. *Tekh* (Eg.) the name of the Moon-God and the Calculator, also means the *full;* and in Inner Africa the Full Moon is *Etako* in Wun ; *Etago* in Bidsogo.

The two crossed hands or fingers depict the cross sign of Tek that became the Tau and the letter T which was not, as de Brosses thought, *unconsciously* used to designate fixity, for Teku (Eg.) signifies to make fixed. Another cross, the Tat, is a sign of fixity, and to establish for ever, whilst Teta is the Eternal. Tat is also the hand-type. The Tek Cross X is one figure of 10, founded on the Crossed Tat (or hand) which first signified Ten as the extreme limit, the Infinite or Impassable. It is probable that the origin of the gesture made by clasping the hands in the posture of prayer or beseeching, may be traced to the act of digital reckoning. The Ten of both hands, that is the total,.thus indicated the All. When the Zulus count a hundred the open fingers of both hands are crossed and clasped together at the completion of each 10, as the sign of totality.

So in the clasp of hands in prayer or propitiation, the sign would be one of *tenfold* and *total* submission to the superior power, and therefore the symbol of utter beseeching.

The Hebrew Rabbins speak of the "*primitive existence contained in the letter Jad,*" which is "*unspeakable, incomprehensible, unapproachable,*" because, in reality, it is *related to the most primitive beginnings, the utter simplicity of which supplied the later ineffable mysteries of the mental twilight.* The Jad is the hand, and it has the numeral value of 10, or of two hands, and was therefore made a type of the biune one, applied to Deity.

The two hands (Kepti) clasped together and cut off at the wrists make the hieroglyphic sign of No. 10,. ∩ ; and the most archaic Phœnician or Etruscan form of the letter Jad ∩ is evidently the hieroglyphic Ten ; hence the Jad, called a hand, has the value of two hands, or No. 10.

According to Menasseh Ben Israel the name of *Jah* is not only that of the dual divine essence itself, but it also designated the Aziluthic World, or the World of Emanations which contained the Ten Siphiroth. Jah is the Hebrew form of the Twin IU, AO, or IAU, and the Two-one and Ten are identical in the Kabalist scheme, just as they are in the two hands. Hence the power of the Mystical Jad-sign ot the Two Hands.

Ten was synonymous with the All, the Infinite or *Impassable,* as two had once been in *Neb* (Eg.) for the All. Hor-Apollo makes an uninterpreted allusion [1] to the ten-sign of the clasped fingers. He says "*Seven letters included within two fingers—*ἐν δυσὶ δακτύλοις *symbolize a song* or *Infinite.* It has been suggested by De Pauw that he meant δακτυλίοις, rings, or within a ring. But the reference is to the sign of the two curved hands which were determined by the two

[1] Book ii. 29.

Tebu or fingers ⩄ The figures are seven in number and ten times seven in value. The seven of the song belong to the musical scale. The two fingers denote the 10 of the two hands. Great mysteries lurk in simple signs like these which are the figures of very natural facts.

The sign of 70 is common on the funeral tablets, and is said to indicate the 70 Days of Mourning. Also, the Egyptians sang their lamentations. Seventy then was a sign of the Infinite, reckoned by the seven notes as the All in music, and by the ten of the Two Hands as the Total in reckoning. The Camacan Indians express many, or infinite, by holding out the ten fingers and saying "*Hi.*" This, as Dr. Tylor points out, agrees with the Camé "II," and Cotoxo "*hie-hie,*" "*Euhiahia,*" for Many or Infinite, in the primitive sense. These also agree with the Egyptian *Hihi, Heh* or *Hhu,* for the Infinite, who was of a dual nature, as *Hu,* the Sphinx deity, or the *IU* and *AO. Uwa,* in Xosa Kaffir, signifies an animal uniting both sexes, a hermaphrodite. *IU* (Eg.) is twofold, and the 2 and 10 both meet in the two hands and ten digits. Hence the Iu in Egyptian is number 10 (or io) in common figures. Number 10 is *Hyo* by name in Nutka, and *Hyyu* in the Aht language. The Egyptian U was inherent in the I, and thus we come back to the Hebrew I, or Jad, as the figure of the Infinite. The Coptic letter-sign for number 70 is **O**, the sign of the Infinite, or *Hehu.* Also the numeral value of the Hebrew Ayin is 70, and the oldest form of this letter is O, the figure of Infinity. The O was evolved from the unified Iu, with the Infinite at the numeral value of Seventy instead of Ten, which was worshipped as the god "O" in the Greek Mysteries; whose name is still expressed by the vocative O! of religious aspiration; the God who in Israel was the Deity of the Ten Tribes and seventy divisions which preceded the twelve signs and the seventy-two duo-decans of the zodiac.

Reckoning and making figures with (and of) the hands of course preceded letters, and the ten digits is the number of the earliest signs known to the British Barddas as the Ten *Ystorrinau.* It can be proved to the eye, *even if the mind refuses to take in and utilize the fact* that the Kamite hieroglyphics were extant in these islands, as Boece avers.

The Bobeloth letter, Dabhoith, or D, signifying Wisdom, is a Serpent; and one hieroglyphic T, or Tet, is a Snake, the type of Wisdom. *The Welsh sign of Ng is* ⵖ, *and the Egyptian Ankh is* ⵖ *or* ⵠ. *The round loop of the Egyptian is squared in the Welsh. Also, the Welsh dd sign* △ *is the squared form of* ⌓, *an Egyptian hieroglyphic T, D, or Tet,* a female breast; the English Teat, or Titty.

Among the British signs copied by Ledwick,[1] the R, named *Rat,* is

---

[1] Ledwick, *Antiq. of Ireland,* pl. p. 328.

a squared reverse form of a hieroglyphic R called *Ret*. Also, the British O is called *Or*, and the hieroglyphic *ER* is an oval ◯.

The Barddas tell us that their *Abcedilros*, or Alphabet of Ten Letters was derived from the creative name of *Iau* (later *IO*), called the Younger, or the Manifestor, who, as the *Iu* (Eg.), Manx IE, was the Ever-coming One. This was the youthful manifestor of a Dual Being, who was also the Three-fold One, *i.e.*, the Mother (Ked), Child (Prydhain or Aeddon), and Hu, the pubescent Male; the Dyad in sex, who were triadic in manifestation. Their symbol was the Cyfriu sign /|\ called the "Sacred Symbol of the Unutterable name of God," corresponding to the Hebrew Yad, and the name of Jah.

Now the Kabalist Ten Sephiroth, which are derived from the creative name of Jâh are likewise, as the word shows, a form of the ten letters. Hence they are placed at the head of the thirty letters, which are arranged in rows of ten letters each. The Ten Sephiroth are also traced to a Triad dominating over all, corresponding to the letters Aleph, Beth, and Gimmel, which, by analogy, comprise the whole world, or, as we have seen, the trinity of characters and bi-unity of sexes, in one compound being called Jah, Iu, or Iau, the tri-unity, which is tenfold in the Kabalistic scheme of the Ten Sephiroth, just as it is in the British *Abcedilros* of ten letters, that were all derived from the tri-une I A U.[1] This origin of Ten Letters in the divine name which constitutes the number 10, as I O, was the profound "Secret *from the Age of Ages among the Barddas of the Isle of Britain for the preservation of memorials of country and nation ;*" and this Secret of the Barddas of the past, now penetrated by a bard of the present, is identical with the most hidden wisdom of the Kabalah, when traced back to its phenomenal origin.

The origin is described as being in the "Two Rays," and the "Three Shouts." The Gwyddon, they tell us, looked straight before him along the line of the East. "*Dwyrain,*" *i.e.*, *dwy rain*, is the two rays—the ray of Eilir, and the ray of Elved—which represented the Two Truths of Iu or Iau, the *Triadic* form of the *bi-une One*. Iau is also known as the Yoke. So the Maori Iho (Mangaian IO, the Deity) is the name of the Umbilical Cord, the Yoke of the Mother and Child. Now the Ogham characters consist of the Stroke and Circle, or an IO, the Number 10 in figures. The Ten are digital; ten Branches to the Tree of Knowledge; and the Ogham is based on numerical reckoning of the strokes or digits. The Ten Letters were represented by ten cuttings of wood, and by ten cuttings in the wood of the Gwyddon. These ten cuttings remained a secret with the Barddas when Beli the Great converted or transliterated the ten into letters for all, and added six more, making the number sixteen. The ten originated in the three Shouts or Cyfriu sign, which became the

---

[1] *Epistle of Abulafia in Jellinek's Duswahl kabbalistischer Mystik*, p. 13, part i. Leipzig, 1853.

broad arrow or A 1 at Lloyd's.[1] Thus our A 1, broad arrow, twin rays, or Cyfriu sign /|\ is identical at last with the Egyptian *Au* (a calf of either sex) the AO of the Mexicans and Greeks; the IO of the Mangaians and Maori, and with the I, the one being, two hands and ten digits, which were the first forms of the two and the ten in figures, or in letters.

The Ogham marks are in sets of five—the single stroke, double stroke, three strokes, four strokes, and five strokes. The group of five is the *aieme*, Irish, or *qv* in Welsh. Both *Kef* and *Aem* in Egyptian denote the hand as a fist of five. The Ogham is based on hand-reckoning and on the straight and oblique strokes which turn to either hand; the one that becomes twain in the two rays or two hands. Thus the Ogham is the circle of hand-reckoning, the earliest form of that by which time is still reckoned on the face of the clock. It is from this concrete base that the more abstract *Ghuaim, Guaim,* or Wisdom, through which the Barddas were able to compose, was derived; not *vice versâ*. Finally, as before said, the Cornish *Dek*, Breton *Dec*, and Welsh Deg, for Number 10, repeat the hieroglyphic *Tek*, the sign of which is ×, the figure of 10 or ten (*Tekari*) fingers represented by the double stroke.

The Chinese "Three Lights" are likewise identical in origin and significance with the "Three Shouts" of the British. The radical "Ki" or "Shi" is the sign of the ——— Three Lights, according to Chinese etymologists, and this figure includes the *Triadic* form of the *biune one*. It is also employed to indicate the supernatural or revelation, as was the Cyfriu sign of the Barddas. Moreover, in the Amoy dialect Iu signifies origin, the son and the masculine soul.

This will show that the Kabalists and Athanasius Kircher, who claimed a most ancient origin for these figures and types of the Kabalah were right, and the modernisers of the Kabalah are in a great measure wrong.

The worshippers of Iau (or Hu) were the Iaus or Jews by name, whether in Cornwall, Palestine, China, Egypt, or Mangaia. They must have gone out of Africa when the Number 10 was reckoned on two hands; *the two named IU in Egyptian*, which as two hands are the hieroglyphic 10, the digital sign of the Deity.

The following summaries will show at a glance the relationship of the hand to numbers and naming, and how the 1 and 5, the 2 and 10, may have the same name, for reasons already explained. As numbers and their names originated in the phase of gesture-language it was by gesture-signs that the different values of the same word were determined.

Achup is No. 1 in Panos.	*Kabti* is two arms in Egyptian.	*Kep* is the Hand in Egyptian.
Acap is A (one) in Irish.	*Kabdo* is a pair in Galla.	*Kepu* is No. 10 in Landoro.
Kafto is No. 2 in Mordvin.	*Kif* is No. 5 in Bulanda.	

---

[1] *The Barddas*, pp. 40—52.

Nge is No. 1 in Kakhyen.   *Onka* is Hand in Mandan.
Ankh is to duplicate, also a pair of ears, in Egyptian. *Onge-foula* is No. 10 in Cocos Island.

Tuta is No. 1 in Joboka.   *Tut* or *Tü* is No. 5 in   *Tith* or *Tythe* is a 10th in
Tü is No. 1 in Burmese.   Egyptian.   English.
Tut is Hand in Egyptian.

Rem, Lem, and Lef are interchangeable, and

Alovi is one finger in Hwida.   *Rem* (Variant) is No. 5 in   *Lafa* is No. 10 in Salawatti.
Lof is one hand in Cornish.   Polynesia.

Tep is the first in Egyptian.   *Tabi* is No. 1 in Manyak.   *Table* is a hand in Sunwar.
Teb is a finger   *Tup* is No. 2 in Taraki.   *Tabu* is No. 5 in Kalka.
Taf is No. 1 in Agawmidr.   *Itabu* is a hand in Yala.   *Tovo* is No. 10 in Japanese.

Fito is No. 1 in Japanese.   *Bhit* is hand in Bramhu.   *Pati* is Two Handfuls in Egyptian.
Fitak is No. 2 in Japanese.   *But* is No. 5 in Bagwan.   *Padi* is No. 10 in Telugu.

Irme is No. 1 in Yebu.   *Lima* is the Finger in Port   *Rima* is No. 5 in Polynesia.
Dlem is No. 1 in Nyamban.   Praslin.   *Lime* is No. 5 in Malagasi.
Remn is the Arm in Egyptian.   *Rima* is the Hand in Polynesia.   *Lum* is No. 10 in Dsarawa.

And these types are correlative under one name because of the digital origin in the limb. This base of beginning is well shown in the Celebes Ternati dialect where *Rimoi* is Number 1; *Romo-didi,* Number 2; *Roma-Toha,* Number 5.

The African languages prove the paucity and the persistence of primitive words. One radical does duty for several parts of the body Thus—

Keba is the hand in Kra.   *Gumen* is the hand in Banyun.
Kaffun ,,   ,, Adirar.   *Kamba* ,,   ,, Tumbuktu.
Kaf ,,   ,, Egyptian.   *T'koam* ,,   ,, Korana.
N'kepa ,,   ,, Papiah.

The Arm is

Gobo in Oloma.   *Kova* in Koro.   *Kobeda,* in Padsade.
Gibo in Bayon.   *Kafe* in Gadsaga.   *Sabu,* in Momenya.
Gubu in Boritsu.   *Gubuda* in Biafada.

The Shoulder is—

Kape in Padsade.   *Gaba* in Mandara.   *N'Gamana* in Munio.
Kuban in Filham.   *Kafada* in Kandin.   *N'Gamana* in Kanem.
Gaban in Fulup.   *Gibar* in Boritsu.   *N'Gamana* in N'gura.
Geba in Mano.   *Gema* in Gio.   *Kambo* in Param.
Gba in Gura.   *Gema* in Mu-u.   *Kambo* in Bayon.
Igabo in Sobo.   *Komba* in Pika.   *Kamba* in Momenya.
Gapta in N'godsin.

The Finger is

Kobi-bui in Tumbuktu.   *N'gibo* in Ekamtulufu.   *Saba* in Adirar.
Ozubo in Opanda.   *Osba* in Wadai.   *Saba* in Beran.

That is because the limb or branch of the body was named first, not the particular limb ; and one limb or part of it may bear the type-name in one group of languages, and a different limb in another. This *principle of dispersion* can be followed under the type name of the limb.

The number 5 is

Lime in Malagasi.	*Lima* in Batta dialects.	*Lima* in Sandwich Islands.
Lima in Ende.	*Lema* in Savu.	*Lima* in Rotuma.
Lima in Sasak.	*Lema* in Timur.	*Lima* in Cocos Island.
Lima in Bima.	*Lema* in Manatoto.	*Lima* in Fiji.
Lima in Sumbawa.	*Lam* in Tonquin.	*Rima* in Maori.
Lima in Mangarei.	*Lima* in Ceram.	

because

Liman is the hand in Macassar.			*Lamh* is the hand in Irish.		
Liman	,,	,, Kissa.	*Lamh*	,,	,, Scotch.
Liman	,,	,, Baba.	*Lave*	,,	,, Manx.
Liman	,,	,, Keh Doulan.	*Lof*	,,	,, Cornish.
Liman	,,	,, Buton.	*Alemade*	,,	,, Dumagat.
Liman	,,	,, Solor.	*Rima*	,,	,, Favorlang.
Leima	,,	,, Satawal.	*Rima*	,,	,, Sida.
Lima	,,	,, Fakaofo.	*Rima*	,,	,, Ende.
Lima	,,	,, Malay.	*Rima*	,,	,, Bima.
Lima	,,	,, Wokan.	*Rumcosi*	,,	,, Betoi.
Lima	,,	,, Mandhar.	*Rimani*	,,	,, Saparua.
Lima	,,	,, Bugis.	*Rima*	,,	,, Bauro.

This is an Inner African type-name for the limb, as finger.

Lemi in N'tere.	*Mulembo* in Kanyika.	*Nlembo* in Mimboma.
Olemi in Bumbete.	*Mulembu* in Kisama.	*Nlembo* in Musentandu.
Elambue in Alege.	*Mulempu* in Songo.	*Nlembo* in Nyombe.
Molem in Mutsaya.		

This radical of language had not only passed into the British Isles, but is also found as

Ramo, the finger, Sunda.   *Lima*, the finger, Port Praslin.   *Limak*, the arm, New Ireland.
Lima   ,,   Bati.   *Oulima*   ,,   New Ireland.

The Carib name for 10, or the fingers of both hands, is Chounoucabo-*raim ;* and for 20, or the fingers and toes, it is Chounougouci-*raim.*

The hand leads us to the limb, as arm or shoulder. The Egyptian *Remen* is an arm, the shoulder, to touch the shoulder, a measure, a span, an extent, as far as the limit, which shows the *Remn* or *arm* in relation to measure by the limb; an early mode of determining the *limit.* The Bohemian *Rameno* for the *shoulder*, *arm*, and *branch* retains the full form of *Ermennu* (Eg.) which signifies the shoulder as well as the arm. The Russian *Ramo* is the shoulder, the Latin *Ramus* the branch or arm. *Armus* (Lat.) is the shoulder-joint, particularly of the animal, from which the arm is the branch. The English arm (earm) and *limb* represent the general type.

The *Rim, Lim,* or *Limb* is various. In the Anfue (African) dialect the arm is the *Alome ;* in Takpa the *Lem* is the foot. *Remmu* in the Galla languages is the type-name for number 2, answering to the two arms or Rems. *Baram* is number 2 in Wolof; *Moa-lembo* in Undaza. This name was also applied to the paddle or oar. The hands of Horus are designated his paddles, and the oar is the

Remi, Latin.   *Ramh*, Gaelic.   *Leamh*, Gaelic.
Rem, French Romance.   *Riem*, Dutch.

Following the paddle we have the *helm,* from the same origin.

The African *Remen* or *Lemen* deposits both *Rem* and *Ren* (or Len) hence the interchange, and the hand is

Aranine in Mare.	*Lengye* in Biajuk.	*Lango* in Tibetan.
Renga in Kupuas.	*Lengan* in Menadu.	*Lango* in Serpa.
Rongo in Murung.	*Ranka* in Lithuanic.	*Lang*, No. 5, in Cochin China.

The *Renn* (Eg.) is the child, and the branch or shoot of the tree. *Làn* in Chinese Amoy, is the type-name for branches, as in Renpu (Eg.) for the branch. So in the African Gadsaga the *Lemine* is the boy, the branch. The child is the human branch of the mother (whose type was the tree) and in provincial English is often called a *limb*. With the Kamilaroi people the limbs of a tree include the arm, but the thick branch is a thigh, which points to the genitrix, as the Tree of Life. In Egypt she was *Rennut* by name, the mother of the *Renn* or child.

In the North American sign-language the idea of offspring or *human branches* is pourtrayed by a peculiar gesture which is made by the two hands drawn downward from the *loins* or *reins*, at times with an added illustration of the mother bringing forth or branching in parturition.

Lastly, the *Rima* or five branches of the hand, together with the reckoning of five thereon will explain why *Rim* in Icelandic is a computation, a reckoning; the calendar; why *Riman*, in old English is to number; *Riomh* or *Riamh*, in Irish, *is* numeration, reckoning; and the *Ream* in English is a reckoning of twenty quires of paper.

Here the prototype was the Tree and its limbs; and the Limb and its branches, one body with two limbs, whether these are reckoned as arms or legs, and five branches to each limb; the tree being a primal figure of the mother. And the Tree itself, as the African Cotton-Tree, is

Limi in Bagrmi.	*Limi* in Bornu.	*Limi* in Kandin.
Limi in Housa.	*Limi* in Munio.	*Eram* in Papiah.
Limi in Kadzina.	*Limi* in N'guru.	*Aram* in Param.

This naming of the one that becomes twin is at the very bifurcation of all beginning. When the ear is called *Duas* in Irish and Scotch, that is from its twinship. In Egyptian the ear is named Ankh (as it is in many other languages), and Ankh also means a pair. Kaf and *Kab* are the hand and arm, and *Kab* (Eg.) signifies double; *Kabel*, in Kaffir, to part in two. The knee-pan is a *Kap* in Egyptian and *Cap* English. That also is a dual type. The mouth as the *Gab* or *Chaps* is another, and the twin-type in each case determines the name.

The chief hieroglyphic of the one who divided to produce the Two is the hinder (feminine) thigh, the *Khepsh* type of the genitrix *Khep* or *Kheb;* and in the Inner African languages the thigh as type of her who divides and doubles is named—

Gba in Mano.	*Gbari* in Gbandi.	*Kebel* in Mutsaya.
Gba in Mende.	*Kufa* in Bode.	*Kebele* in Ntere.
Gbara in Toma.	*Kebei* in Nso.	*Kebele* in Mbamba.
Gbara in Landoro.		

The Gba or Khepsh thigh was the *Divider* in parturition. And here we quote a specimen of the beginnings which are so simple as to make the explanation appear incredible, and the too-knowing will be sure to denounce me as over simple.

We read in the *Ritual*, "*I come forth as his child from his sword, accompanied by the Eye of Horus*," *i.e.*, the feminine mirror.[1] Such language is extant in other sacred writings, and has never been interpreted. But how can a child be born from a sword?

In Egyptian the sabre or scimetar is a Khepsh, ⤚ a Sanskrit *Kubja* (Greek Xiphos), a crooked sword, a scimetar—and this has the same name as the hinder thigh, which is represented by the ⌒ hind leg of the hippopotamus, the genitrix of the Typhonians; the one *Khepsh* being *copied from the other*. The hinder thigh is also a type called "*Ur Heka*," the great magic power. This identifies the female sexual part as the great magic power of the primitive mind; the *typical Power before a sword was manufactured to be called a* "*Khepsh*," as a weapon of power. The sword or Khepsh being named from the hinder thigh, these equate, have one name and are equivalent as types. Next, the sword is identical with the dove (the Yoneh), and both are blended in one image under one name, because of the origin in the great magic power or Yoni. In the Hebrew the allusions to the oppressing sword[2] serve to recall the Assyrian emblem of the sword and dove, which were figured in one image.[3] Hence the sword with the divided tail of a bird that was continued in the Greek χελιδών, the sword ending in the bird's tail.

The same symbolism is found in Japan. One of the ancient weapons of the Stone Age is called the stone knife of the green dragon, because the conventional green dragon has a sword at the end of its tail. Thus the hinder part is synonymous with the weapon as it is in the Egyptian *Khepsh*. In accordance with this interchange, the Arabic name of the star Alpha in the dove (Columba) is Fakhz, the thigh.

But this is the important point. *The Khepsh sabre as the weapon used for cutting and dividing was named from the Khepsh thigh because that was the primordial Divider in the body and in giving birth.* Numbers and their names are based on a oneness or a one that divides and duplicates, with the human body and its two arms as chief illustrators in gesture-language. But the same tale is told by every other type-name of this beginning.

The root *Tan, tin,* or *ten* is another of the type-words of numbers. The Egyptian *Ten* to cut off, divide, separate in two halves—ten being the half-moon—shows the reckoning by division. *Ten* also signifies the amount, each and every, that is cut off and reckoned as a total. *Ten* (Eg.) as 10 Kat, is the equivalent of our ten for the

---

[1] Ch. 40.   [2] Jer. xlvi. 16, and l. 16.
[3] *Nimrod*, vol. i. p. 13.

half score. The whole Moon was *Tent* cut in two (English *tined*) to make the fortnight.

The *Tennu* (Eg.) are the Lunar Eclipses which measured time by cutting off the light. *Ten*, Chinese, is to cut in two; *Tanumi*, Maori, to double; English *twain* to be double. Thus twain and ten are identifiable with the aid of the two hands or two legs. The Marquesans reckon their fruit and fish by the *Tauna*, or two-one; they take one in each hand and count by the pair instead of the unit. Their óne is twin[1] as it was in the bifurcation of the beginning. *Ten*, in Egyptian, is a plural for "ye," and "your;" *Tin* is "they" or "them" in the Motor language. This is the most common name for the foot in the Australian dialects, which is—

Tona, Jervis Bay.	*Tina*, Lake Macquarie.	*Dinang*, Wiradurei.
Tina, Peel River.	*Tïnna-mook*, Witouro.	*Dien*, or *Tian*, } King George' Sound.
Tenna, Port Philip.	*Dana*, Muruya.	
Tinna, Adelaide.	*Dina*, Bathurst.	*Dana*, Liverpool.
Tenna, Gulf St. Vincent.	*Dina*, Meidji.	*Idna*, Parnkaïla.
Tinna, Karaula.	*Dinna*, Kamilaroi.	*Dtun*, Aiawong.

This is also found as—

Tin, Laos.	*Ten*, W. Shan.	*Adin*, Guaham.
Tin, Siamese.	*Tin*, E. Shan.	*Tongotra*, Malagasi.
Tin, Ahom.	*Tin*, Khamti.	*Eduon*, Annatom.

It is the type-name also for knee and thigh as—

Toon, Knee, Diegunos.	*Dongo*, Thigh, Fulah.	*Dengalau*, Thigh, Buduma.	
Tungru, Knees, Gúndi.	*Dango* ,, Kano.	*Tanke* ,, Wolof.	
Tanga, Thigh, Zulu Kaffir.	*Itena* ,, Ombay.	*Tangbo* ,, Bulanda.	
Tungei, ,, Musentandu.	*Dangala* ,, Mandara.		

In the Batta dialects *Tangan* is the arm.

Tono, the Hand, Kamkatkan.	*Tangan*, the Hand, Ulu.	*Tangan*, the Hand, Batta.
Tango ,, Malagasi.	*Tangan* ,, Ternati.	*Tangan* ,, Malo.
Donga ,, Furian.	*Tangan* ,, Javanese.	*Tangan* ,, Suntah.
Danicra ,, Cherente.	*Atheng* ,, Borro.	*Tongan* ,, Sow.
Taintu ,, Timbora.	*Otun* ,, Chutia.	*Tong* ,, { Juru Samang.
Tanaraga ,, Mangarei.	*Tangan* ,, Malay.	
Tangan ,, Rejang.		

Hand or foot is an equivalent of number 5 and

Thanu, is No. 5 in the African Makua.	*Tanga*, is No. 5 in Mru.
Tani ,, ,, Fan.	*Tonsa* ,, ,, Tungus.
Tano ,, ,, Swahili.	*Tonga* ,, ,, Yakutsk.
Atton ,, ,, Krepee.	

Tan is the type-name for the number 5 in at least forty of the Inner African languages, and in several of these *Tan* is the full extent of the reckoning. *Tan* is number 10 in Vei, Kono, Mandenga, Toronka, Kankanka, Bambarra, Kabunga, and other of the Inner African dialects, in which the people could count thus far. *Don* and *Ndon* are 10 in Afudu. *Tini* in Fiji is number 10, and the end or finis. In Languedoc *Tanca* means to stop. *Tan* in Zend and *Tena* (Eg.) denote the extent. This extent may be one hand—five; or it may be two hands—ten.

[1] Wilkes, *U.S. Exploring Expedition;* Hale, *Ethnology and Philology*, vol. vi.

Ten, however, has an earlier African form in *Tsen* or *Dsen*, that accounts for both *Ten* and *Sen* as variants of one word, under which name we have the Thigh as

Dsinya, in Kandin.	*Dsiny.t*, in Kano.	*Tsin'a*, in Kadzina.

The female bosom, which divides in two breasts, is

Sin, in Dsalunka.	*Sin*, in Bamharra.	*Siun*, in Mandenga.
Sın, in Kankanka.	*Sin*, in Tene.	*Sundso*, in Kabunga.

The Teeth, that also divide in a double sense, are named

Dz:n, in Tumu.	*Dsina*, in Ntere.	*Dison*, in Baseke.
D suna, in N.ete.	*Dseni*, in Mutsaya.	*Tsino*, in Marawi.
Disonga, in Murundo.	*Edsin*, in Afudu.	*Tsunis*, in Skwali (Atna).
Dzino, in Babuma.		

This type-name, with its variants, is universal as Noun and Verb for that which divides, cuts open, and duplicates. The dividing river may be the *Ticino* in Italy or the *Teign* in England. That which *divides* is fundamental, and the radical *Tes* (Eg.) for the Stone and Stone Knife, whence *Tser* or *Sila*, *Tsen*, *Sen* and *Ten*, may be followed throughout language in relation to the stone, the Weapon (Aitz, Basque), tooth, ivory, the cutter, and cutting; opener and opening, founder and founding. The same word was continued in the Old Algonkin, and other Indian languages of North America as their type-name for Stone.

Assin, is Stone, Ojibwa.	*Assene*, is Stone, Knistinaux.	*Ashenee*, is Stone, Skoffi.
Assin „ Old Algonkin.	*Ashenee* „ Seshatapoosh.	*Asenneh* „ Sauki.

This radical *Dsen* or *Tsen* (whence Sen and Ten), supplies a type-name that runs through all language for things fundamental and foundational. *Sunn*, Assyrian, signifies foundation, or fulcrum. *Sunu* (Eg.) is to found, with various types and modes of founding. One is a stone Statue, another an endless cord twisted into loops without any tie. The types of Foundation are many; the Prototype being one, with variants, and the Name one. In Chinese, another type of *Sin* is the heart; Latin, *Sinu;* French, *Sein.* The heart offers an important ideographic type. In Egyptian the heart as *Mat* and *Hat* is identical with another habitation, the Womb. "*My Heart is my Mother*," says the Osirian in the Ritual. It was a figure of basis, foundation, beginning; abode of life.

In the Imperial Dictionary of Kang-hi, out of 44,500 words, 1,097 are founded on this radical *Sin*, one type of which is the Heart. Thus the Heart may be an ideograph worth 1,097 words. This lands us in the domain of Things, Types, and Ideographs as the earlier stratum of language. Other forms of foundation are seen in *Sende*, Kaffir, a testicle; *Shin*, Hebrew, a tooth; *Sunu* (Gael), a wall; *Son*, a beam or joist; *Son*, Mantshu Tartar, the rafters of the roof; *Sen*, French Romance, a road; *Sanaa*, Arabic, a water-dam; *Tseen*, Chinese, a bank raised against the water. The founder as the Bee is *Soni* in Pika (African); and in Chinese, the foundry, or furnace, is the *Shin*. That which is founded, as Iron, comes under this name in Inner Africa, where

Isen, is Iron, in Eafen.	*Sengo*, is Iron, in Nyombe.
Zengua „ Mimboma.	*Zengo* „ Basunde.

Seng Chinese, is to come into being. *Sono*, Italian, signifies I am; *Sunt*, Rhœtian, I am; and *Sunt* in Latin. The latter is the abstract of *Sunt* (Eg.), to be founded. *Syn*, Welsh, is sense, understanding. *Sin*, Chinese, mind, understanding, and "understanding" shows the passage from the physical to the metaphysical.

Finally we get back to, or primarily we can commence with, the foundation of all in the opening of the Beginning. As aforeshown, the word *Sunn.t* (Eg.), to be founded, denotes the making of a foundation by opening the ground. *Sunn* is to pass; whence *Sunn.t*, the passage, in English the Sea-*Sound;* also the *Snout*, the passage for the breath. Now the ancient British name for Nottingham was *Tyogofawy*,[1] the house of the Cave-dwellers, or the Men who made Holes in the ground. The earlier name of Nottingham is *Snoting-ham;* and *Snot* or *Sunt*, in Egyptian, means to found or establish by opening the ground, which perfectly describes the beginnings of the Troglodytes. Also the *Snood* (Caul) for the hair of the Woman, was a sign of this foundation by opening, at the time of puberty.

The first foundation depended on opening and dividing for the One to become twain, in the way and ways described.

The one that first opened was the Mother, who divided in producing the Child, that opened her, and was then personified as the opener in Mythology; the Sut-Horus or Ptah in Egypt; Chrysoros τὸν ἀνοιγέα in Phœnicia; Samas the Assyrian Heaven-opener, or the God Pundjel of the Australian Blacks, whose name denotes the Opener, and of whom they, the natives, say he has a knife and a Ber-rang, with which he can open anything in such a way that no one can tell how or where the opening was made.[2]

The body divides into arms, breasts, thighs, legs, and becomes twain; and as primitive man began with the body, limbs, members, and gestures, these were his primary means of putting or posing his sense of need, his feelings and thoughts, in visible and imitable attitudes; and it is natural that the most primitive types and type-names should commence with the human body, also that these should be universal. Gesture-signs preceded speech. These were continued in the representation of Numbers and Verbs. The origin of digital reckoning shows us a Way to Words by means of things; the things in this case being mainly limited to the limbs of the human body. This enables us to establish a principle of naming, and prove how a very few words could name many things. For, when language first began, there could have been but few sounds that were combined

---

[1] Asser.   [2] Smyth, *Aborigines of Victoria*, vol. i. p. 424.

to form a few words which became the archetypes of human speech. The Evolutionist alone can comprehend the economy of nature in the commencement. These few Archetypes were of necessity applied to various things, and the process evolved a larger number of homotypes, or variants in things which are found to be interchangeable equivalents under the same name.

The Typology of the Two Truths has now been applied to Numbers, and it has been demonstrated that Number was a prime factor in Naming, which constitutes a link between gesture-signs and the words of later language.

SECTION V.

NATURAL GENESIS AND TYPOLOGY OF PRIMORDIAL ONOMATOPŒIA AND ABORIGINAL AFRICAN SOUNDS.

(Pythagoras taught that "*Number*" was the wisest of all things, and next to that the "*Namer*.")

CONCERNING the *origin of language* it may be briefly affirmed that very little is known, and nothing absolutely established. Also that the help to be derived from mere theorisers on the subject is chiefly negative. Hitherto the "science of language" has been founded, and its ORIGINS have been discussed, without the ideographic symbols and the gesture-signs being ever taken into account.

The Aryanists have laboured to set the great pyramid of language on its apex in Asia, instead of its base in Africa, where we have now to seek for the veriest beginnings. My appeal is made to anthropologists, ethnologists, and evolutionists, not to mere philologists limited to the Aryan area, who, as non-evolutionists, have laid fast hold at the wrong end of things.

The Inner African languages prove that words had earlier forms than those which have become the "roots" of the Aryanists. For example, Max Müller has said that in the word *Asu* (Sansk.), which denotes the vital breath, the original meaning of the root "*As*" has been preserved. "*As*, in order to give rise to such a noun as *Asu*, must have meant to breathe; then to live; then to exist; and it must have passed through all these stages before it could have been used as the abstract auxiliary verb which we find not only in Sanskrit, but in all the Aryan languages. Unless this one derivative, *Asu*, life, had been preserved in Sanskrit, it would have been impossible to guess the original material meaning of the root *As*, to be.[1]" Here the African languages show that *Asu*, to breathe, is *not a primary of speech;* no vowel is *primary in the earliest formation of words.*

In Egyptian *Ses* is to breathe, and in Africa beyond—

Zuzu,	is to breathe,	in Nupe.		*Zuzu*,	is to breathe,	in Basa.
Zuzu	,,	,,	Esitako.	*Yisie*	,,	,,	Kupa.
Zuzu	,,	,,	Gugu.	*Zo*	,,	,,	Ebe.
Zuezui	,,	,,	Param.				

---

[1] *Lectures*, vol. ii. p. 349.

The duplicated sound was first, because, as will be maintained, language originated in the conscious duplication and repetition of sounds. Ses (Eg.) also denotes the brood or breathing mare, a type of the gestator and mother of life, as *Ses*-Mut. And in Inner Africa the mare is named—

Sosa, in Gbese.	*Sosi*, in Hwida.	*Soasi*, in Mahi.
Sosa, in Toma.	*Sousi*, in Dahome.	

Seses, a gnostic form of Tesas (Neith or Isis) is also the Mother of Breath. This is further corroborated by *Ziz* (or Zi) in Assyrian, for the inherent life or soul ; and by *Zuza* in Zulu Kaffir, applied to the breathing life of the unborn child. The Latin *Esse*, to be, has preserved both the s's found in *Ses*, to breathe.

It has been asked, How did *Dā* (Sanskrit) come to mean giving ? Professor Noiré holds that primitive man *accidentally* said "*Dā.*" And there we have a "root" of language! But *Dā* is only a worn-down form of word found in Sanskrit. It is the Egyptian *Tâ*, to give and take ; also a gift. The full hieroglyphic word is *Tat*, and it belongs to the stage of mere duplicated sounds and gesture-signs. It is written with the hand, which is the Tat ideograph ; English *Daddle* for the fist ; the Inner African—

Ntata, the Hand, Meto.	*Ntata*, the Hand, Matatan.	*Tata*, the Hand, Igu.

Long before the abstract idea of giving was conveyed by *Dā* or *Tâ*, the *Tat* was *presented* in gesture-language with the offering, or in the act of offering. The hand, however, is not the only Tat, Tut, or T. Another hieroglyphic, Ta (or Tu), is the female Mamma, ⌒, the English *Teat* and *Titty ;* Welsh, *Did* and *Teth ;* Basque, *Titia ;* Greek, *Titthe ;* Malayan, *Dada*, and Hebrew *Dad*, for the teat or breast. These forms of the name retain the ideographic sound of *T T*. The mammæ sign is the Egyptian feminine article The ; also a name of food, and to drop. "*Tat-tat*" is a sound that may have originated with the child in sucking. It is still made by the nurse when offering the mamma, the primordial giver of food, to the child. Moreover the *Da* personified in Sanskrit is the wife, corresponding to the Egyptian *Tâ*. Language certainly did not originate with the "roots" of the Aryanists, which are the worn-down forms of earlier words. It did not begin with "abstract roots," nor with dictionary words at all, but with things, objects, gesture-signs, and involuntary sounds.

Comparative philology, working with words in their later phase, divorced from *things*, is responsible for the false inference (one amongst many) that until recent times, later than those of the Veda, the Avesta, the Hebrew, and Homeric writings—men were deficient in the perception of colour ; that there was, in fact, a condition of Miopoeia answering to their insanity of Mythopœia. Geiger has even asserted that the language-maker must have been blue-blind. Max Müller

[1] Geiger, *Vorträge zur Entwickelungsgeschichte der Menschheit*, p. 45, 1871.

has affirmed that the blue heaven does not appear in the Veda, the Avesta, or the Old Testament. It is true that language did not commence by *naming those mere appearances* of things in which the comparative mythologists take such inordinate delight; true that colours are among those appearances and qualities, just as white is of wheat—*when ground into flour*. Many early languages have no word for blue as a colour, and yet blue as a thing may be found in them.

The Ja-jow-er-ong dialect of Australia uses the sky itself, "*woorer-woorer*," for blue. That was the thing.

In Maori and Mangaian there may be no name for blue as hue and tint; but this does not show that the people did not know the blue heaven from the white or red heaven when they saw it.

The "*Zulu*" name signifies heaven, as The Blue. Hence, deep water is called *Žulu*. *Zulura*, for the blue thing, literally means *skyishness*.

In Pazand the word *Açma* denotes both stone and heaven, and, as shown by the Minokhird, heaven was identical with precious stone.

The Hebrew heaven is the paved work of sapphire stone beneath the feet of the eternal.[1] *Samu* (Ass.) is both sky and blue.

The Egyptian name for blue is Khesbet; that is, lapis-lazuli.

The Egyptian Heaven was either the Blue Stone, the blue temper-tinted steel, or the blue sea overhead.

The water above is the blue heaven, and in the Ritual the blue called the "Upper Waters" is identified with the blue Woof of Heaven in the worship of *Uat*, Goddess of the Northern Heaven.[2]

If a language does not possess a word for blue as a colour, it may for a blue stone, and certainly will for water.

A lesson in the primitive system of colour-naming may be learned from the Hottentot language in which the word for colour itself is *ïsib*, signifying form, shape, likeness, and appearance. Such a word includes various qualities and properties of things under one name. *Yellow* (Hūni) means the ground-colour, the sandy soil; *Brown* (Gamab) is the vley-colour, *i.e.* the bottom of a dried-up pond; *Red* (Ava) is the blood-colour; *Grey* (Khan) is the colour of the *Bos Elaphus*; *Spotted* (Garu) means the Leopard; *White* is egg-coloured; *Am* for green, originally meant *springing up* and shooting forth like the verdure.[3] Hence when the rainbow is also called *Am* the sense is not limited to the green-colour, because it likewise springs forth spontaneously. This serves to show how the primitive thinkers thought in things when distinguishing properties, qualities, or appearances; how things first suggested the ideas that were afterwards conveyed by words; and how the more abstract forms of phenomena took names in language by means of the concrete,—the unknown being expressed in typology by means of the known.

[1] Ex. xxiv. 10.   [2] Ritual, Ch. 110.   [3] Hahn, *Tsuni Goam*, p. 26.

Power of perceiving qualities and distinguishing things did not depend on the possession of words to express shades of difference. Sweet could be distinguished from bitter when the one was only expressed by the mouth watering, and a smack of gustativeness; the other by spitting with the accompaniment of an interjection of repugnance. So far from "conscious perception being impossible," without a word for each colour, the one word *Uat* (Eg.) for water does duty for several colours, for blue and green water, various paints, plants, and stones. Perception of different colours did not depend on divers words; one served with several determinatives in things. The early men thought in things and images where we think in words, or think we think. Plutarch says, "They that have not learned the *true sense* of words will mistake also in the nature of things."[1] So we may say that those who have not learned the true nature of things will mistake the sense of words.

Professor Sayce holds that there is "*no reason* in the nature of things why the word Book should represent the volume which might just as well be denoted by *Biblion*." But the "nature of things," tells us the Book was the tablet of beech-bark in Britain and the palm (*Buka*) of Taht in Egypt. The Biblion from Bib (Eg.) to roll or be round, had been the roll of papyrus before it was the book. Indeed the oldest words can only tell the most important part of their history when re-related to things. Mere philology can never reach the origins for lack of determinatives.

The Egyptian "Kam" may be quoted to indicate the relationship of words to things. *Kam* signifies black; and Plutarch tells us the Egyptians applied the word to the dark of the eye, the Mirror. The dark was the Mother as reproducer of light. The pupil of the eye reproduces the image. To reproduce is to beget, hence "*Kam*," also meant to form, to create. Here the word branches out in the region of things and modes of action; there being various means of forming and creating. Egypt was literally created by the Nile, and named *Kam, not merely as the Black land!* The sculptor forms and creates the image by carving; and "*Kam*" also signifies to carve. That which is carved may become the "*Kam-hu*" (Eg.) a joint of meat, or the "*Cameo*," a carven image, the root for which word has never been found.[2] The *Word* at first was but a wavering, wandering shadow of *things* which are the determinatives of its meanings that only become finally definite in the ideographical phase which the Aryanists have entirely ignored.

There is no way of attaining the early standpoint and getting back to an origin for words except by learning once more to think in things, images, ideographs, hieroglyphics, and gesture-signs. The

[1] Of Isis and Osiris.
[2] *Cf. Kamut* (Eg.) to carve, or a carving. Lepsius, *Denkmäler*, &c., 48, A. Kam also interchanges with *Kan*, for carving in ivory.

primary modes of expression have now to be sought in their birth-place. In Africa only shall we find the most *rudimentary articulation* of human sounds, which accompanied gesture-signs and preceded verbal speech. The clicks, the formation of words by the duplication of sounds, the original types of expression, must be allowed to have been *evolved* in Africa until it can be shown *how they came there otherwise.* The African dialects, spread over vast spaces of country, point to an original unity in a language which may not be extant for the gram-marian, and certainly will not now be discovered intact by the traveller. The earliest forms can only be found in the primary stratum of lan-guage, that is, in gesture-signs, the primitive modes of articulation, and in aboriginal sounds, although further connecting links of construction may be established, There is of course a kind of grammatical sequence in the order of gesture-signs.

From the present stand-point it would be idle to discuss whether the roots of language were at first verbal or nominal. Where should we begin ? With *which*, or *what* language ? In Maori, the same word at different times assumes the functions of several parts of speech. We also find that in languages like the old Egyptian and Chinese, the same word did duty as noun and verb or other parts of speech ; and one word or sound had to serve at first for various uses, whether these are called the names of things and actions in one aspect, or " parts of speech " in another. Gesture-language shows that verbs as words were the least wanted, and therefore the last named. Verbs would be first *enacted* before they were uttered in what we could recognise as speech. A Cross is the hieroglyphic sign of verbs in general, and the hands were crossed in reckoning ; the sexes crossed ; the sun, moon and stars were observed to cross before there was a verb signifying to Cross. A pair of feet Going is the sign of the transitive verb to Go, and Going pourtrayed in several forms preceded any abstract word for to Go.

So far as gesture-language was primary, the verbs may have been first, but their signification was chiefly conveyed by the action. A *Na-wa-gi-jig's* story, in Ojibwa, told orally and with gesture-signs shows that *Gestures only* were used to indicate the " *old man*," " *many*," " *happening*," " *quickly*," " *hatchet*" (to cut), " *going*," " *starting*," " *wind blowing*," " *ice moving off*," " *to a distance*," " *cutting the ice*," " *it is so thick*," " *number two*," " *tired*," " *by turns*," " *together*," " *twisted three cords*," " *tied three together*," " *threw it out*," " *no go*," " *repeatedly*," " *drifted out*," " *we two*," " *nearly sundown*."

The analysis shows that the speaker who *had words* for his Verbs and Numbers naturally preferred to indicate these by gesture-signs, which were like the actions of an orator only they took the place of the words and made them unnecessary, because they had existed prior to such an application of words.[1] Also the reduction of the noun to

[1] Mallery, *Sign Language*, pp. 519-520.

make the verb might be amply shown as in Tat for the Hand and Tâ to give. So *Paf* or *Bab* (Eg.) denotes *the* Being as the Breath, and *Bâ* is the abstract verb to be, to be a breathing soul. As breathing was observed and breath was named earlier than soul or abstract being, this also shows the Verb is a form of the Noun reduced.

Possibly there is a mode of proving *how* things were named first, when we commence with the most primitive data in the birthplace of words. If we start from Africa, say, with the snake, this may tell us how the noun was extended in the verb stage, by means of the *actions* of the snake. In Egyptian, *Hef* represents an African type-name for the reptile or insect that crawls with the *heave*-motion, as the viper, worm, and caterpillar. These were named in one aspect from their movement, whence *hefu*, or *heft* (Eg.), to crawl by *heaving*; *êfa*, in Welsh, to cause motion or heaving. *But, the snake also sloughed its skin*; hence, *êbu*, in Kaffir, to slough, and *Havel*, English, for the slough. Here "*Hef*" becomes a type-word for things that slough, or *shed*, as well as *heave*; hence, *Avel* for the awn of barley. This process, which is merely hinted at, and which might be followed illimitably, will prove the priority of sounds and names for things, the actions of which were indicated by gesture-signs.

Also certain types of Things equate on account of the unity of origin in the thing itself. Thus the dd (British) and TT or T (Eg.) are signs derived from the female mamma ◠. This becomes our letter D. D is also the *Door*, as Daleth in Hebrew, and the door is another feminine symbol. T or D is the feminine Article (Eg.); the Ru is likewise a female type, the door of life, the mouth of utterance; and *Tr, Dl* or *Dr* furnish the name of the *daleth* and door. Breast and Door, then, become *one in letters because both are interchangeable images of the female sex, and because things preceded signs.*

It may be that the beginning of verbal language with a few simple names for things, sensations and actions is indicated by the mystical value attached in later times to *Names;* their primitive preciousness being reflected in their religious sacredness. The word *Nam* (Eg.), to repeat, direct, and guide, gives a good account of the *Name* and its object. The passage of the Osiris through the underworld is effected by his preserving all the mystical *Names* in memory. Ra has 75 names, Osiris, 153.[1]

Time was when the "Name" was the "Word" and so it remained embalmed in the religious origines when the "Word" (Logos) was the "Name" personified. Names, or substantives, potentially contained all the other parts of speech. These have been continued from the earliest time to the present and remain more or less identifiable according to the principles of naming.

Nor need we marvel that words should retain their identity and likeness in languages the most remote from each other in time and

---

[1] *Rit.* ch. 142.

space, when we find how few they were at first and how faithfully they were preserved.   The earliest races preserved them of necessity. "*Never change barbarous names*," said the Chaldean oracle.[1]   Also, the cry of the Greek writers was for the people to treasure up the "barbarous" or foreign words in their language, although they might not know from whence these had been derived, nor what was their exact import.   When pleading before the tribunal of eternal justice the Osirified deceased declares that among other saving virtues he has *never altered a story in the telling of it.*   And such was the spirit in which the primitive races preserved their knowledge, customs, traditions, *and* words.

But we have to go beyond words to make a beginning at the stage where the act of Sucking might have produced its own self-naming sound in the "*Tt-Tt*" of the suckling.

The earliest Verb would be indicated by the action ; the first Substantive by the sound accompanying the gesture or action.   The gestures must have been simple, self-defining, and the sounds accompanying them would have a natural accord.

Some non-evolutionary writers on language, who, as the Egyptian priest said of the Greeks, wear the *down of juvenility* in their souls, appear to speak as if the origin of language itself depended on "Grimm's Law."   Indeed, one shallow reviewer of the previous volumes of this work thought it sufficient to condemn them if he put forth the foolish falsehood that the author had expressed supreme contempt for "Grimm's Law."

Grimm having pointed out a law of diversity which governs the interchange of certain phonetics his followers have further assumed the non-existence of a law of uniformity in an earlier stratum of language.   But words did not have their beginning in any known form of the Aryan languages, and the proto-Aryan is unknown to them, excepting that which has been created by the Evolutionists of the inner consciousness.

Whilst limiting their comparative diagnosis to this restricted area they confidently affirm that when two words are spelt alike in two different historic languages they cannot be the same ; Grimm's Law forbids.   Further research and a wider application of the comparative process might have taught them that it does nothing of the kind. Indeed, the true moral, the workable and profitable deduction, to be derived from Grimm's Law is that words *do* persist and retain the same signification in spite of, and not in consequence of, the racial or the dialect differences that may be tabulated under that Law.

The followers of Grimm have led men to believe that beyond the little Aryan oasis there is a desert world, trackless, chartless, limitless ; and that none but they could lead in the work of showing the way ; towards which they have not yet advanced the second step.   For

---

[1] Cory, *Anct. Frag.* p. 271.

Grimm's Law has been to them the obliterator of landmarks throughout the range of the pre-historic past. According to the prevailing delusion and the preposterous pretensions of its advocates, it is not only unsound and non-scientific but positively pitiful for any one to compare the words and myths of two different languages which they have not previously proved to be grammatically allied ; this being one of the "*first principles*" of "*Comparative Philology*."

They have come to the conclusion that hardly any relation exists in language between the sound and the sense of words, whereas in the earliest stages both were one ; and now the fundamental sense can only be found in that phase of unity. On the same kind of authority it would be unscientific and absurd to compare the gesture-signs of the North American Indians with those which survive in the Egyptian hieroglyphics until we have first demonstrated the grammatical affinity of the Algonkin and Egyptian languages. Thus stated the theory exposes its own exceeding futility.

In Grimm's Law—to use a very homely metaphor—philologists have found a fork and laid hold of it at the prong-end. The prongs are known to them, but the unity beyond is unknown and denied, because they have not reached the handle.

One writer says the Aryan and Semitic languages may have been originally connected, *but there is no Grimm's Law which will allow us to prove this.* He therefore assumes that connection and relationship can only be demonstrated by unlikeness. For Semitic let us substitute Kamitic, and a comparative vocabulary in these volumes will then show that the word-stock of Egyptian and Sanskrit must have been essentially the same in the proto-Aryan stage.

Pre-historic and pre-Aryan words have remained the same independently of later grammar or phonetic systems. Words coined when we had but ten letters or yet fewer sounds, survive in their primitive forms even when we have twenty-six. Addition did not always involve transliteration or supercession, any more with words than with races ; whereas continual re-beginnings in language and in mythology are assumed by the non-evolutionist interpreters of the past.

But it is only by the aid of what is here designated as " Comparative Typology" that we could ever reach the stages of language in which the unity of origin can be recoverable. Gesture-signs and ideographic symbols alone preserve the early language in visible figures. We are unable to get to the roots of all that has been pictured, printed, or written, except by deciphering the signs made primally by the early man. The latest forms of these have to be traced back to the first before we can know anything of the Origines ; these are the true radicals of language, without which the philologist has no final or adequate determinatives, and hitherto these have been left outside the range of discussion by Grimm, Bopp, Pictet, Müller, Fick, Schleicher, Whitney, and the rest of the Aryan school.

Fuerst is another example of the men of " Letters" as opposed to Ideographs. He asserts and reiterates at every letter that the Hebrew alphabet is not ideographic, and that each name is only employed or intended to represent the initial letter! This is an entire reversal of the fact; but the doctrine is prevalent in current philology, which has ignored the earliest sign-language altogether.

Wherever the ideographic signs of the oldest civilised nations can be compared evidence of the original unity becomes apparent, just as we find it in gesture-language. In fact, the farther we go back the nearer is our approach toward some central unity. From circumference to centre diversity diminishes and dwindles. Finally the most primitive customs, rites and ceremonies are the most universal, and these could not have proceeded from the circumference towards a centre of unity. The unity was first even as the diversity is final.

Grimm's Law does not tell us *why* certain letters are interchangeable in different languages and dialects, so that *Zeus* in Greek represents *Deus* in Latin, and Dyaus in Sanskrit. Neither can any of Grimm's followers. They only affirm that it is so, without knowing the διότι. In Hebrew and Chaldee the T and S are interchangeable. M and N are constantly permutable in language. In English the f and gh interchange, and are equivalents; to such an extent is this carried that the gh is also sounded as f in laugh and cough.

Here the Egyptian hieroglyphics constitute the connecting link between language in Inner Africa and the Aryan phase or status out of it. The origin of Grimm's Law is made manifest in the earliest mode of speech, and the facts are patented, so to say, or stereotyped in the hieroglyphics. These show the Ideographic phase of language which preceded the Alphabetic.

For example, the builders-up of language backwards, who are able to start from a vowel as a "root" (they do so with "i" to go), assume that the word *Mand* in Sanskrit is what they term a *mere strengthening of a root Mad*. The hieroglyphics show that *Mand* and *Mad* (Mat) are identical because an ideographic *Men* preceded and deposited the consonant M; and the sign is readable as a Men (ideographic and early) or a later phonetic M. Beyond Egypt, Man is *Muntu* in Wakamba, and in the neighbouring Wanika he is *Muta;* but the sign of the Idea, Action, or Person depicted by the " *Men*" ideograph is first, the syllabic *Mu* is later, the letter M is last. So in the languages of the Gabun the names for the head run through *Muntue* (in Kisama and Lubalo), *Ntu* (in Nyombe and Musentandu), *Mutu* (in Kanyika and others) and *otu* (in Mbamba). In these the *Ntu* of the same group also implies the form in *Muntu,* which modified into all three.

Grimm's Law is just as applicable to certain Inner African groups of languages as to the Aryan. In the Bantu class the dialect differences and variations in phonology are manifested by the *Mb* of

R 2

Swahili modifying into P in Makua; the Ng (Swahili) into K (Makua). The T (Swahili) is represented by R (in Makua), and the f by K. Ch, hard, and S in Swahili, are represented by *Sh* in Makua; whilst the T of neighbouring tongues is *th* in Makua.[1]

Names were first given with and to ideographic signs. Thus a Tat, Ter, or Tek deposits a phonetic T, and all meet to mingle at last in one letter T which may take the place of a dozen ideographs. Various signs of *Men* are reducible to one phonetic M. -

If we take the *Tes* sign (Tesh, tech or Tek being variants) *this deposits both a T and S in the hieroglyphic* ⟶ and henceforth the T and S go their several ways in forming future words.

An ideographic Hef will deposit both a phonetic H and F. In the hieroglyphics the snake is *Hef* in an ideographic phase. In the phonetic stage the snake supplies the sign of F. The Hef only will account for the Latin *fœmina* being pronounced *hœmina*, as, according to De Roquefort, it was by the ancient Romans, or for similar interchanges of H and F.

The hieroglyphic Mes 𓏪 will account for the Greek Σ being continued as a kind of M = S.

An "original Aryan D" may be represented by L in Greek or Latin simply because there was an ideographic Proto-Aryan Del (its name remains in Delta and Daleth, which describe an ideographic D) or Ter, as in Egyptian; our English door. The Hebrew letters Aleph, Beth, Gimel, Daleth continued that ideographic phase in their names as those of things which are yet identifiable. Here is an illustration.

The hieroglyphic *Ret* 𓎬 a cord used for tethering cattle when grazing, passed into the Hieratic, Phœnician (or Hebraic) and Syriac letters as the Teth, ⟨figures⟩. In Hebrew "*Teth*" signifies something twisted or tied, which the Ret loop explains. In Egyptian this *Ret* deposited a phonetic R. The same sign appears as the R called *Rat* in an Irish alphabet. Thus the ideographic Ret becomes an R in Egyptian and Irish, and a letter T in Phœnician and in other alphabets.

In the inscriptions exhumed by Davis at Carthage, the Phœnician letters *daleth* and *resh* are two slightly varied shapes of the *Ret;* and these are sufficiently like our own figure of four, **4** to show that *it* also is a form of the same original hierogylphic. So the Coptic delta ⲁ and lauda ⲗ, which is R in Bashmuric, are two other variants of the Ret; and delta has the numeral value of 4, in common with the Hebrew Daleth. *Ret* (Eg.) denotes the figure, and one sign of the word is the foot-stool with four steps; another figure of 4. An ideographic RET will further account for the same figure or letter being Ro in Coptic or Greek and D in the Gothic ꝑ. Now the sign

---

[1] Chauncy Maples, and Dr. Bleek.

in the letter stage would determine nothing respecting the origins; we must trace it back to the ideographic *Ret* before we can discuss the origin or unity, and there the Phœnician letter is an Egyptian hieroglyphic which was continued *in the ideographic phase* as the Irish "Rat" or letter R.

The primary form of the sign (as well as of the word) is ideographic. This shows that when certain symbols are found in the *Vei* and *Lolo* hieroglyphics,[1] which are alike to the eye and yet may be different in phonetic value, the bare fact will neither disprove nor determine their unity of origin. That must be sought in their ideographic values. In the process of reduction and distribution an ideographic Del deposits both D and L as phonetics; an ideographic Men deposits both M and N; an ideographic Tek, which is a Cross, both T and χ as two different crosses in the phase of letters; an ideographic Kef both K and F; and so on through all the ideographic signs that passed into separate letters. Just as the ideographic *Pesh* or *Peh*, the rump of Pasht, the Lioness, ⟋⟍ became the Letter *Shin* in Syriac. We have a record of this process preserved in the traditions of the British Barddas, who tell us they began with ten original Ystorrinau, or ideographic signs, which Beli reduced to the value of letters, and then added six others, making sixteen in all.

But *the original unity of various letters in the ideographic phase is afterwards shown by their being equivalent and permutable in later languages*, whether at the beginning or end of a word. Thus *Tset*, the Inner African type-name of the *Hill*, is continued as Tset in Egyptian, where it becomes both Set and *Tet*, as in our Tut Hill. Set and Tet are then interchangeable in the later languages. It is the same with the Tser (צר) Hill, which becomes the Ter (or Tel) and Ser. In the Arabic group the number 8 is both *Temen* and *Seme* in Beran; *Damana* in Wadai; and *Asmanye* in Adirar.

One form of the ideographic *Uts* (Eg.) is a palanquin. The word *Uts* signifies to suspend, support, bear aloft. This is an Ideographic original which will account for the Sanskrit *Ut*, up, upwards; and the Zend *Uz* applied to upholding. It is the same with the equivalent terminals as in *Bit*, Sanskrit, and *Biz* (O. H. G.), to bite, and other instances in which the t or d of one language is represented by s or z in the other. If we take the variant *Tech* this will account for the equivalent terminals t and ch in the English *Pit* and *Pich*, or *Bat* and *Bak*, as variants of one word. An ideographic *Kaf* will account for the interchange of k and f in Swahili and Makua as well as in English. By this process of deriving the consonants singly from the ideographic phase in which they were dual or duplicated, we can prove the proto-Aryan origins to be hieroglyphical and Kamite.

Beyond Egypt the Inner African languages are yet in possession

---

[1] Copied and compared by Dr. Hyde Clarke, *Athenæum*, Sept. 1882.

of certain complex sounds that the European finds impossible or very difficult to reproduce. He can learn to make some of them singly, but cannot *talk* in clicks. Clicks have been detected out of Africa. Three clicks, heard in the Chinook, Texan, and other North American languages are described by Haldeman. Two are found in the language of Guatemala, according to Bleek. Klaproth affirms that clicks occur in Circassian. Whitmee distinguished clicks in some dialects spoken by the Negritos of Melanesia. But Africa is the true land of the Clickers, as the Bushmen, Khoi-Khoi, Kaffirs, Gallas, and others; and *this is the only known country of the Clicking Cynocephalus who was the predecessor of Man*. In addition to the clicks we find such sounds as *Ng, Mb* or *Mf, Gb, Kf, Rl* or *Lr, Dlw, Mhl, Mni,* and Tsh with its variants Tch, Dzh, Th, etc. The nasal Ng bifurcates into N and G. In Fiji the letter Q is sounded Ng. Ng also modifies into Nh and N. Lr is represented by L in one language, and R in another. Captain Burton sometimes renders the same sound by the R that others render by the L. There is no distinction between R and L in the Hieroglyphic ⌒. Hence the necessity of going back to the birthplace of human sounds to reach the radicals of speech. Nothing short of Inner Africa is of primary importance in the origins of Language.

Captain Burton has remarked, that "*The Eafen, or Dahoman, a dialect of the great Yoruba family has, like the Egba or Abeokutan language, a G and a* GB, *the latter at first inaudible to our ears, and difficult to articulate without long practice.*"[1] This *Gb* with its variants, such as *Kf* is one of the radicals of all languages. It might have been the first word formed of two *different* consonants, unless we except the "*Ng*" and *Tesh,* it is so primitive and prevalent. Such an original is still implied, even in English, when the "gh" of "Laugh" is sounded by an "f." The *Mb* (or Mfu) is likewise extant when the ancient Welsh M is sounded V, and the M and V are confused in the cuneiform language. The "*Ng*" persists in the Australian, Maori, Kaffir, and other languages as an Initial Sound, and with us as a terminal. It is represented by the Hebrew Ayin ע, Egyptian NK, and the Hieroglyphic *Ng* of the British Coelbren staves.

Now the names of the Goat and Cow can be traced back to the Inner African stage of pronunciation. The Goat is

Kapros, in Greek.	*Gafr,* in Welsh.	*Khapu,* in Peguan.
Caper, in Latin.	*Gavar,* in Cornish.	*Tkhavi,* in Georgian.
Cabhar, in Irish.	*Gabhar,* in Scotch.	*Abr* (or *Kabr*), in Egyptian.

The accent in âbr denotes an abraded form. This we recover in the Inner African name of the Goat.

Gbarie, Pika.	*Biri-i,* Khoi-Khoi.	*Oboli,* Udso.
Eburi, Matatan.	*Epuri,* Meto.	*Bora,* Mose.
Biri, Ai-Bushman.	*Obori,* Okuloma.	

[1] Captain Burton, *A Mission to Gelele, King of Dahome,* vol. i. p. 36.

Gb and *Km* interchange, and in an earlier stage of articulation the Goat is

Nkombo, in Basunde.	*Kombo*, in Musentandu.	*Kombo*, in Kasands.
Nkombo, in Kabenda.	*Kombo*, in Mutsaya.	*Kombo*, in Nyombe.

The Cow is

Gava, in Sanskrit.	*Govyado*, a Herd of Cows, in Sclavonic.
Gavi, in Gothic.	*Kaûi*, or *Khepsh*, in Egyptian.
Khaboi-kumi, in Indo-Chinese.	*Geûsh*, in Pahlavi.
Chuo (plural *Chuowi*), in High German.	*Gows*, or *Govjado*, in Lettish.
Cow, in English.	

The Sanskrit *Gaus* is said to be from a root *Gam*.
And the Cow is called

Kom, in Karekare.	*Nombe*, in Kanyika.	*Nombe*, in Marawi.
Komo, in Kaffir.	*Nombe*, in Lubalo.	*Nombe*, in Nyamban.
Ngom, in Mutsaya.	*Nompa*, in Runda.	*Enobe*, in Matatan.
Gbami, in Pika.	*Nombe*, in Muntu.	*Enope*, in Meto.
Kebma (Water-cow), in Egyptian.	*Nompe*, in Kiriman.	

The original African form that includes and accounts for the whole of these Variants is found as

Ngompe, in Songo.	*Ngombe*, in N'gola.	*Ngombe*, in Kasands.
Nkombe, in Kisama.	*Ngombe*, in Basunde.	*Ngombe*, in Musentandu.
Nkombe, in Kabenda.	*Ngombe*, in Nyombe.	*Ngombe*, in Mimboma.
Ongombe, in Pangela.		

So is it with the name of the Knee.   This is either

Goab, or *Goam*, in Hottentot.	*Ngbe*, in Gbese.	*Ngumbi*, in Gbandi.
Gbua, in Mano.	*Kembi*, in Soso.	*Ngombi*, in Landoro.

and other African dialects.   But the natives are not *trying to talk Aryan!*

These things were named in the stage of primitive pronunciation, when what we now know as consonants were sounded double as in " NG " for the later N or G, and " *Mb* " for the later M or b, before they had been fully evolved, made out, and discreted into *our* single sounds.

It is at this depth of rootage we have to seek for the reason why M and B, N and G, T and S (or K), K and F, &c., became interchangeable in later language, and we shall find it is because *they are twin from the birth as aboriginal sounds, first uttered by one effort, which were afterwards evolved, divided, and distinguished as two distinct phonetics or letters in later language.*

The process here indicated is that of Nature herself elsewhere, one of dividing, discreting, and specializing on lines of variation from an original form of embryonic unity.

The "origin of language" itself is not a problem to be attacked and solved by philosophical speculations like that of Dr. Noiré. However happy the guess or ingenious the generalisation, it can only be one of the many *may-have-beens* to which there is no end.   To *know* anything with certitude we must go back the way we came, along a track that only the evolutionist is free to pursue and explore.

The formula—"*No reason without speech ; no speech without reason ;*" or "*without language no thought,*" is equal to saying "*without clothes no man.*" We know now that the dumb think,[1] and that man had a gesture-language when he was otherwise dumb.

Darwin's work on the *Expression of the Emotions in Animals and Men*, and Colonel Mallery's *Contributions on the Sign-Language of the North American Indians*, are of more value here than all that has been written on the origin of language by philologists, philosophers, or metaphysicians. Speculations without the primary *data* can establish nothing; and these have never been collected and correlated by those who were evolutionists.

We are now able to affirm on evidence that there have been continuity and development from the first, in accordance with the laws of evolution, and that there was but one beginning for language, mythology, and symbolism, however numerous the missing intermediate forms or widely scattered the nearest links.

Fortunately Nature is very careful of the type when it is once evolved. In truth she seems to stereotype. Nothing is entirely lost or altogether effaced. In various ways we are still the contemporaries of primitive man. The Red Indian and Black African still pound and eat the seeds of grasses for their bread, as did the savage before the cereals were cultivated for corn.

The type of warfare that was founded when the monkeys first threw stones at each other has been continued ever since. It still dominates when the hundred-ton cannons hurl their ponderous shells. So has it been with other types, in gesture-language, in verbal speech and aboriginal sounds, in totemic customs, religious rites and primæval laws. There have been development and extension, but no one can point to entire re-beginnings.

Unity of origin in language was only possible when the human intelligence was too limited to disagree and diverge; and the race was a mental herd making the same signs and sounds for ages on ages, without choice in the matter or desire to differ. The name of the Cock, for example, may be claimed to be self-conferred, and, according to the onomatopœist, was so *given* and might be *given* at any time in any language or land. But this *might be,* this choice in the matter, if extended, would let in a deluge of individual differences which was not possible to a common origin. There could be no consensus of agreement if all mankind set up as conscious language-makers according to the principle of imitation or onomatopœia. *There was but one stage at which the principle could have wrought in the creation of language; that was at the commencement.*

The beginnings were not, as some writers on the subject would have us believe, like mere circles in the water or the air, which give their

[1] "Is Thought Possible without Language?" By Prof. Samuel Porter (of the National Deaf Mute College), *Princeton Review*, January, 1880.

impulsion and pass away. They are registered for us palpably as the rings in the oak, when we can once start from the centre. Many illustrations of this fact will be given, for it is the misfortune of my work that the thesis could not be substantiated or presented without a burdensome mass of verbal details.

Considering that the human form was evolved out of or thrown off from antecedent forms, and that Man commenced as one link of the chain of being prolonged invisibly into the past; it may be assumed that for a vast period of time he was but slightly growing in advance of his immediate predecessors ; and that the means and modes of expression previously extant, were shared by him and continued in his primary stock of sounds. We may be sure there was no such chasm in nature as is perceptible between them now. On looking back we see a great gap or gulf, and are apt to ask where is the bridge? or how did man suddenly leap the gulf? Whereas there was no sudden large leap any more than there was a vast chasm, *at the time*, to be leaped. Fresh points of departure were then so fine as to be imperceptible now.

The cries of animals and birds constitute a limited language. The call of the partridge, the neighing of the horse, the low of the cow, the bleat of the lamb, the bark of the dog, are a current coinage of ascertained value, quotable for ever in their intercourse. These are understood and answered as the language of invitation and defiance, of want (or desire) and warning. That being so the cries are typical, and therefore on their way to becoming recognised as phonetic types. In fact they are recognised by the animals as phonetic types by which passions are expressed in sounds that evoke a kindred or responsive feeling, and this through a considerable range of manifestation. The cry of warning is well known in the rook's caw, the dog's bark, the monkey's chatter, when he utters the signal of danger to his fellows. The *Cebus Azara* of Paraguay is credited with uttering six different sounds, which are said to be capable of exciting corresponding emotions in its fellows of the same species.[1]

At least Man's predecessors uttered a language of warning and want, as the expression of protecting power and the need of protection—the voices of Nurse and Child—in sounds of physical sense that could be transmitted or imitated.

Man's earliest expression of gesture and sound was equally involuntary, or as we say, instinctive, and the first step toward the formulation of language was made when the natural interjections were *consciously repeated* on purpose to arrest attention. *Conscious repetition of the same sound is the first visible phase in the morphology of Words.* We can explain certain evolutionary processes without being able to tell how or why consciousness unfolded, or even what is consciousness.

[1] Faidherbe, *Revue de Linguistique*, 1875.

This, however, applies to the pre-human consciousness as well as to that of Man.

Personally the present writer holds that the main difference betwixt Man and Monkey consists in the growing *rapport* of a more inner relationship of life with the conscious cause and source of life, of which Man himself becomes conscious, more or less, in the upward or inward course of his growth, as the child does of its mother; and that each form of animal life has its own particular relationship to life itself, and carries its own abysmal light in the depths of its darkness, like the miner in the caverns of earth, or the *Pyrosoma* in unfathomed seas.

That, however, is not the side of phenomena or experience with which we are here concerned. Nor would it avail those who do not postulate such a consciousness before or beyond (or *becoming*) the human. But, we have only to start from the mimesis and clicks of the Cynocephalus, and assume a slight increase of imitative power as a result of growth in man, to see how in presence of his deadly enemy the Snake, for example, he might *utter his Sign of Warning in an imitative manner*. As already said, the Cerastes Snake or Puff-Adder became the letter F; which was a Syllabic *Fu* and an Ideographic *Fuf*, our Puff. *Fu* (Eg.) denotes puffing, swelling, dilating, and becoming large, vast, and extended with breath. The Snake distended and "*fu-fu'd*," and thus *made the sound that constitutes its name*. This sound would be repeated as the human note of warning, together with an imitative gesture enacting the Verb, or pourtraying the likeness of the thing signified by the sound, and such a representation made to eye and ear would belong to the very genesis of *gesture-language*. It would commence when the Ape thrust out its mouth, as it does, and fu-fu-ed or blew at the Snake; and when Man imitated this action with intent, the *language consisted in the Man's becoming the living Ideograph of the Snake,*—for this is the fundamental principle of gesture-language; and here we may take a furtive glance and catch a glimpse of Man's likeness to the monkey, just as Harold Transome recognized the likeness of his own face to that of his unknown father reflected sidewise in the mirror.[1] Naturally also when in conflict with each other or with their foes, the nascent race having command of sounds would try to imitate the puffing and hissing of Snakes, the yell of the Gorilla, the roar of the Lion, or the voice of Thunder, and thus turn their own terrors inside out to impose them on the enemy by means of representative noises, which have been more or less continued by the savage races and are still employed by them in battle.

Dogs, horses, and other animals are known to be so affected by fear and terror, also by cold, that their hair will stand erect. Of course terror will turn to cold. This action was involuntary at first, but with the resulting growth of the *arrectores pili* or involuntary muscles,

[1] *Felix Holt*, by George Eliot.

came the means of erecting the hair, bristles or spines at will, with the *intention of striking terror*.

The earliest natural manifestations that were produced independently of the will were afterwards turned to account and reproduced at will, when anger and heat took the place of fear and cold. So would it be with the voluntary production and development of the sounds that were at first involuntary. The earliest vocal signs ever made intentionally must have had a likeness in sound to the thing visibly imaged, in order that the mental link of connection between Eye and Ear might be established ; and the onomatopœtic duplication of sounds would correspond audibly to the objective representation of ideas with gesture-signs. Conscious repetition of the same sound by imitation would constitute the earliest application of mind (or even the sense of want) to the primary matter of language. At this stage the sound of " *Tt-tt* " produced involuntarily by the nursling child, as a need of nature might have served the child of larger growth for thousands of years, as *his sign in sound* for food, eating, hunger, or as the invitation to eat, which is yet made by the nurse to her nursling in its own language, with the reduplicated lingual-dental click.

Voluntary reproduction of the sound first made instinctively and involuntarily would constitute the earliest phase of language. Intentional reduplication which turned the " tut " of the child's smack into " tut-tut-tut " as a sign of the want that created the intent; or the puff-adder's " fuf " into " fuf-fuf-fuf " as a sound of warning would be the first creative act in the morphology of words. But such simple sounds as " tt-tt " " fuf-fuf " " rur-rur " " mam-mam " may have existed and sufficed as the means of audible expression for other thousands of years before two *different consonantal sounds were consciously combined* to form one word.

When the sound of *ka-ka* was added to *fu-fu* and the resulting word *kkf* or *kâf* was evolved, then language in the modern sense was founded. We get the necessary glimpse of this earliest phase in the prevalence of the principle of duplication still manifest in the simplest and oldest of known languages and words.

But one fundamental mistake made in applying the onomatopœtic theory to language, is in supposing the *primitive radicals of language to be words*. Onomatopœists like Canon Farrar and Hensleigh Wedgwood include words containing three different consonants, among those held to be *copied* on this principle. This shows no gauge of the problem, and leaves no room for the human evolution of sounds, without which their value could not have been sufficiently identified. When the magpie, raven, or parrot has had its tongue cut, and been taught to utter two different consonants in one sound, it can speak. But the natural and involuntary sounds are single, or they are not consciously combined ; and these were the only sounds that preceded human speech.

Æons of terrible toil must have been spent in the evolution of the earliest human sounds into a vocal coinage, during which man was getting his lungs inflated and his " tongue cut" for talking ; and when these were at length evolved, they had to be consciously combined and re-combined to form words before language could exist according to the present acceptation of the term.   Sounds like *fu-fu*, *ka-ka*, and *ru-ru* were common to man and animal.   But *no earlier animal than man ever consciously combined two different consonants ;* and language points back to the time when man himself could only produce and duplicate the same sound to form his few words.

We say the clock ticks each time the pendulum crosses ; and it has been assumed that the word *tick* might be *directly derived from the sound.*   But this tick *is a word containing two different consonants,* and not an onomatopœtic sound ; that would be simple, like the nursery *gick-gack*, for the tick tick.   *Tek* in Egyptian is a measure of time, and means to cross as does the pendulum in the tick of time. *Tick* is one with *touch.*   The touch may make a sound or it may not ; the tick or touch of the pulse does not.   Thus the word *tick* is not the mere expression of the sound.

The Shah of Persia laughed at the Tatar arrows that went " *ter-ter.*" Here they seem to make the sound of *ter* or *through* as they tear through the air.   But if the T and R had not already been combined in a word, the arrow would not have said " ter."   The arrow is a *ter* by name.   The hieroglyphic ter is a shoot or *tree*, and the shooting " ter " that pierced through of itself was earlier than shooting with the arrows that were named from the shoot, and had been so named in Inner Africa, where the arrow is called—

Ntere, in Matatan.   *Aturo*, in Anfue.   *Adere*, in Ashanti.

other cutters *through* being—

Dira, the Axe, Biafada.   *Daruma*, the Sword, Landoma. *Terang*, the Knife, Mandenga.
Doro   „   Kasm.   *Deremana*   „   Solima.   *Otalo*, the Spear, Pepul.
Doro   „   Yula.   *Deramai*   „   Kisekise.   *Tiele*, the Axe, Vei.
Darba, the Sword, N'godsin.   *Direndi*, the Knife, Murundo.

In the hieroglyphics the Ram and the Goat are both named " *Ba*," and the onomatopœist would derive the sound of *Ba*, directly from the animal *Ba ;* and if a non-evolutionist *he would not question the capacity of the human being to utter the sound "ba !"* at any stage or time. But this could not be until man had evolved his labials or was able to bring his lips together.   When it was first attempted to teach the Mohawks to pronounce words with P and B in them, they protested that it was too ridiculous to expect people to shut their mouths to speak.   F is the Inner African prototype of P and B.   B and P, says Koelle, are sounded like F, and are only employed in a few languages which possess no real f.[1]   *Fuf-fuf* and *fu-fu* would thus

[1] *Polyglotta Africana*, Preface, p. vi.

precede the p and b of later language. The hieroglyphics show us the *Fa* passing visibly into the *Ba*. Nef or Neb is represented by the snake (Fa), and the Ram (Ba); one sign combines both in a snake with a Ram's head! Read by the Cerastes, this would be *Nef;* by the Ram it would be *Neb*.[1]

In the Mohawk stage of development *homo* could not have imitated the "Ba." *Nor is Ba the earliest form of the name.* Ba is common as a worn down Inner African word. But the Ram is called—

Mba-hina, in Mende.	*Pabea*, in Kasm.	*Fôb*, in Balu.
Pieba, in Koama.	*Pebea*, in Yula.	

The Goat is named—

Febi, in Banyun.	*Mbea*, in Kano.	*Membi*, in Bagba.
Bafui, in Limba.	*Mbê*, in Eafen.	*Mampi* and *Mpi*, in Pati.
Mefi, in Nalu.	*Mbi*, in Bayon.	*Momfu*, in N'goala.
Mbea, in Goburu.		

It seems evident that the Ba or "fa" was only uttered at first by aid of a purchase or leverage on the nasal M or *Um*, hence the well known "*Mfa*" and "*Mba*," *ba* being a final deposit. The Ba (Eg.), is a type of the Breath which is *Paba* or *Pefu*, and these are interchangeable with *Mba* and *Mfu*. It is commonly asserted that the dog says "Bow-wow," but that is a fallacy; no dog ever yet uttered the labial "B." It has also been said that the Egyptians and Chinese called the Cat *Miau*, a name that obviously would never have been applied to the Dog; the *Miau* being so evidently onomatopœtic. Yet *Miau is not limited to the Cat nor is that the earliest form of the word*. *Mmâu* (Eg.), is a type name for the Beast; and this may be the Cat, Lion, or Lynx; the original *Mau* is *Maf* or *Mmafu* (Eg.), (whence Maft) and in Inner Africa the name of the Dog is—

Mfu, in Pati.	*Mfa*, in Babuma.	*Mvi*, in Tumu.
Mfue, in Kum.	*Mpfa*, in Ntere.	*Mpua*, in Melon.
Mfo, in Balu.	*Mfa*, in Murundo.	*Mboa*, in Bumbete.
Mvuo, in Bamom.	*Mfo*, in Dsarawa.	*Mbo*, in Isuwu.
Mvo, in Param.		

and numbers more.

The word relates primarily to opening the mouth, which is named *Mifiou* in Eregba; *Mombo*, in Murundo, a variant of *Mfa;* in the same language, for the dog. The mouth opens and divides in the two jaws when uttering the voice, and this same word is an Inner African type-name for Two, or Twain, as the *Divided One*. The wide-open mouth of the beast is the ideograph of the sound; as it is in *Rur* (Eg.), the name of the hippopotamus, which also means to round out, as did the open mouth of the monster. On the Gold Coast the King's Mouth, or Spokesman, is called his "*Mouf*,"[2] and in English the "Muff" is originally the bad speaker. This will

---

[1] Champollion, *Dictionnaire*, 172.
[2] Captain Burton.

explain why *Mbo* in Bute, and *Mupio*, in Afudu signify the greedy, open-mouthed, and devouring one.

Mve, bloody, Koro.	*Mbwayi*, fierce, ferocious, Swahili.
Mfa ,, Babuma.	*Muwi*, a thief, Ib.
Mbe, bad, evil, N'kele.	*Mayub*, vicious, Hindi.
Mbe, ,, ,, Bambara.	*Mapoya*, a devil, Carib.
Mfu, death, Swahili.	*Miffy*, the devil, English.
Mbi, evil, Zulu.	*Mauvez*, bad, evil, French Romance.
Mofa, mocking grimace, Portuguese.	*Maufez*, demons, French Romance.

The Amakosas applied the same type-name to the gun, which they call "*Umpu.*" This *Um* is designated a prefix, and it is applied to any new word that may be introduced into the Kaffir dialects, but it belongs primarily to a *primitive mode of articulating* sounds; and these sounds were the prefixes in the sense of precursors to all later speech.

The earliest utterance here belongs to the primitive mode of articulating; the type-word includes the *Mau* and *Ba* in one, and they were deposited as two separate names for the Cat and Ram in a later and more distinct stage of utterance. We have to derive the earliest words from the primitive mode of producing sounds, which is more or less extant, for this aboriginal *Mfu* or *Mpu* still survives in our interjectional "*Umph*" as well as in the name of the Dog itself, which is *Amp* in Ostiac and *Emp* in Vogul.

The puff-adder could "*fu-fu*," the birds and frogs could "*ka-ka*," the thunder could Crack-Crack (or "*kak-kak*," as it must have been before the combination of *K* with *Ru*, and is so in the Maori *Ngaeke*), but man alone could combine his nasal and guttural in one sound, as "NG," or turn his "*Um*" and "*Fuff*" into *Mfu;* two of the most important sounds, we may now say words, of the Inner African languages. It is unnecessary then to think of the pre-man as listening round like a modern onomatopœist, or a schoolboy, imitating all he could. Imitation of each other's voices or sounds is very rare in the animal world, the mocking-bird being almost alone.

It is quite probable that no philologist nowadays would be able to make anything verbal out of the earliest articulated sounds that accompanied the gesture-signs of primitive man, such as the Clicks, for example, and yet, as the acorn potentially incloses the future forest, these aboriginal sounds contained the germs of all the vocabularies extant. No natural sound, however, has really been lost in the process of artificial development.

Translators, in trying to catch the exact expression of the "*Oji*" (Ashanti) name, have rendered it by nineteen different variants. The original African articulation here involved may be shown to include the *Ts, Tch, Tsh, Tz, Tk, Th, Ds, Dsh, Dz, Dk, Dj*, and other sounds of some remote original that has descended and been modified on lines of variation. Koelle gives the sound of this *Ds* as that of

Ch in Church, but there are many racial *nuances* in the expression of it. The same variants are to a considerable extent found in Chinese. For instance, the old sounds of *Cha* are *Tsa* and *Dak*, and the variants of *Cha* and *T'ak* are *Dso* at Shangai, *Tsa*, Chifu, and *Tso*, Canton. A variant of *Chi* is *Tszi* or *Dszi*; and *Djak* is a variant of *Choh*, just as it is in the Inner African dialects. In Egyptian it is represented by *Tek*, *Tesh*, or *Tes*. Many of the nineteen variants are extant in European phonetics, such as T, K, S, Sh, Ch, G, J, etc., which answer to the racial or other variations of the African phonology. Now the sound of a sneeze, when consciously copied, takes shape in some such utterance as *Techu* (ch, as in change), or *Teshu*. A child known to Hensleigh Wedgwood called his sister by the name of "*Atchoo*," on account of her sneezing.[1]

The American Indians represent the Sneeze by their "*Haitshu*," *Atchiau*, "*Aichiui*," etc.; and in the Inner African languages, the Sneeze, or to sneeze, is denoted by

Tise, in Bute.	*Tisou*, in Tumbuktu.	*Dsidsi*, in Nupe.
Tiso, in Mandenga.	*Tiso*, in Bagrmi.	*Dsisle*, in Pepel.
Tiso, in Toronka.	*Tisam*, in Dsarawa.	*Dsese*, in Ntere.
Tiso, in Dsalunka.	*Atusaa*, in Kadzina.	*Dsoase*, in Babuma.
Tiso, in Kankanka.	*Ntiso*, in Landoma.	*Sase*, in N'gola.
Tisoa, in Vei.	*Tsatsiso*, in Yala.	*Zezi*, in Dsekiri.
Tiso, in Kisekise.	*Tiesm*, in Timne.	*Sisa*, in Igala.
Tiso, in Mende.	*Dsisin*, in Bulom.	*Esisiuna*, in Aro.
Tise, in Mano.	*Dsisu*, in Bambara.	*Dsuna*, in Momenya.
Tisewo, in Gio.	*Dsia*, in N'ki.	*Siani*, in Krebo.
Tiselu, in Wolof.	*Disa*, in Kambali.	*Sani*, in Gbe.
Tiseou, in Gbese.	*Dsedsie*, in Goali.	*Suana*, in Balu.
Tisou, in Soso.	*Dsedsi*, in Ebe.	

Further, the Nose, the organ of sneezing, is named.

Dsi, in Bayon.	*Iso*, in Oloma.	*Disolu*, in N'gola.
Dsui, in Nso.	*Asot*, in Timne.	*Dizolu*, in Kisama.
Atsi, Param.	*Zakui*, in Saldanha Bay.	*Dshon*, in Akurakua
Adzi, in Pati.	*Tasot*, in Baga.	*Dizunu*, in Songo.
Atse, in Bagba.	*Tasut*, in Landoma.	*Dsenegu*, in Buduma.
Edsu, in Tumu.	*Dzoti*, in Momenya.	*Idsiou*, in Afudu.
Etsoci, in Mbe.	*Diodsu*, in N'kele.	*Esun*, in Okam.
Aesi, in Opanda.	*Dsolu*, in Undaza.	*Ndzon*, in N'ki.
Aseie, in Malali.	*Dizolu*, in Kasands.	*Nidsui*, in Alege.
Isue, in Egbele.	*Dizulu*, in Nyombe.	

The radical *Tes* (or *Tsh*) is employed in the Xosa Kaffir language to express the sound of whispering; *tsu* is to whisper softly. This continues the relationship of sound to breath expressed by the Sneeze.

The same radical that is Inner African for the Nose, the Sneeze and for whispering may be detected in the name of the nose in the North American and other languages, as:—

Tisk, in Hueco.	*Ohtch-yuhsay*, in Tuscarora.	*Dizan*, in Mayoruna.
Idst, in Attakapa.	*Wuschginqual*, in Minsi.	*Tsono*, in Upper Sacramento.
Tzee, in Apatsh.	*Ochali*, in Shawni.	*Tusina*, in Jakon.
Tchaje, in Ottawa.	*Cushush*, in Tekeenika.	*Uchickun*, in Micmac.
Wutch, in Massachusetts.	*Intshiu-ongeu*, in Chimanos.	*Yash*, in Old Algonkin.
Ottschasse, in Potowatami.	*Intshu*, in Guinau.	

[1] *Dictionary of Etymology*, Introd. p. 24.

If the principle of Onomatopœia be admitted at all in the formation of language we may claim that it applies to the natural genesis now suggested for this radical of sound by which the Sneeze named the Nose, or, as it were, supplied the Substantive to the involuntary Verb.

This prolific primate was continued in the Egyptian *Ses* and *Ssen* *i.e. Tses* and *Tssen*, for breathing. *Tes* is the very self. *Ses* is breath; *Sen*, to breathe. *Ziz* (Assyrian) is *inherent motion; Ziz* (Heb.), to flutter; *Ziz*, the Rabbinical Bird of Breath or Soul; *Ziz* (Unakwa), the Nose; *Sisa*, the Soul, Ashanti; *Sus* (Arabic), origin. These are all related, like the Sneeze, to the Soul of Breath.

If we bear in mind the facts that the Breath, SEN (Eg.), is one of the Two Truths of Existence; that *Senesh* (Eg.) means to open, discover, to *open of itself;* that which is self-manifesting, self-revealing, and *Senesh* is the *Sneeze* in English; that the Sneeze is an involuntary emission of Breath in the form of Sound, and the Breath takes voice of itself in the Sneeze, there is nothing incredible in the suggestion that the Sneeze was one of the primæval factors of language.

Sound or Voice was self-revealed in sneezing; whilst the rites and customs of sternutation prove that the Sneeze had a peculiar significance for the primitive Man, and that the character of a discoverer or revealer was assigned to it, or was self-conferred and continued by the self-articulating sound. Thus the Sneeze was one of the *openers*. It opened its passage by means of the Breath (Sen). The Spirit (or Breath) spoke in the Voice of a Sneeze. The Sneeze is expressed by the radical *Tch* or *Dsh*, as natural interjection to which the *nasal* terminal was added for determinative in forming the word *Tchen* or *Dshen*, as the name of that which opens of itself, discloses and makes apparent in Sound. Moreover in Chinese *Tsai* is a particle of exclamation, which, as a word, signifies *beginning*, and *Tsze* or *Tse* is the Self and the likeness of the Self.

The Sneeze translated by a compound *Tenuis-spiritus-lenis* of sound (although the description may be far too fine) would deposit this *Ds, Tz, Tzh, Tch, Tsh,* or *Ch according to the variants of Sneezing and Pronouncing*, on the way to becoming both T and S as does the *Tes* sign in the hieroglyphics. The Hebrew Daleth was sounded " *Ds*" or "DZ." The Hebrew letter צ is likewise a *Tz* pronounced " *Tza*." The same sound survives in the Welsh *Dzh* for J. The Welsh *Tisio* or *Tisho*, to sneeze, is identical with the Inner African. But the word being already extant in the language of the Kymry, when they came, it would not have to be evolved onomatopœtically in Welsh.

Professor Sayce has suggested that language began from the *Sentence* rather than the *Word;* and there is a sense in which this is true; but it was a sentence full of meaning not of syllables, such as can be conveyed by a gesture, a look, or a single sound. The sound of the Sneeze is rendered by the word *Tes* (Eg. Coptic *Djas*) and this word denotes *a whole sentence*, or so many words tied up, a case of words ; and the self-revealing, self-defining, self-naming Sneeze, or the Click, the " Tut-tut," the puffing, or hissing contained a sentence of words in one act, and one self-naming sound.

In attempting to trace (or suggest) the development of pre-human sounds into verbal language it appears to me that one line of variation may be found in *the growth of a conscious manipulation of the Breath.* Conscious manipulation of the Breath lies at the origin of the Hottentot Clicks. Whereas the ordinary sounds of language are now made by the expulsion of the breath, the Clicks are produced on the opposite principle.

The Clickers, *quà* Clickers, do not simply *exhale* their meaning in sound ; they express it by the aid of *inhalation ;* they first lay hold of the air and suck it in to turn it into articulated sound. The Breath is prepensely drawn for the Click to be articulated. They are *Inspirates* instead of *Aspirates.* For instance, we have three Aspirates, a guttural " *ch*," as in the Scotch *Loch ;* the " *H* " aspirate of the English and the aspirated " *P* " (peh) of the Gael. These three may be paralleled by three of the Hottentot clicks out of the four employed by the Namaquas, which are produced by a reversal of the process.

While the anterior part of the tongue is engaged in articulating the Click the throat opens itself to pronounce any letter that may be sounded in combination with the click. In pronouncing the click simply by itself without any supplementary vowel or consonant sound, the breath instead of being thrown out as is usual with other articulations of the voice, is checked or drawn inward, but as soon as it is combined with any other sound it is strongly emitted. It is difficult to speak the Namaqua fluently or intelligibly until the art has been acquired of clicking and aspirating without any perceptible interception of the breath.

We describe the four clicks which are heard in the Namaqua Hottentot by the characters *c, v, q, x.*

C is a dental click ; it is sounded by pressing the tip of the tongue against the front teeth of the upper jaw and then suddenly and forcibly withdrawing it.

V is a palatal click, and is sounded by pressing the tip of the tongue, with as flat a surface as possible, against the termination of the palate at the gums and removing it in the same manner as for *C.*

Q is a cerebral click according to the alphabetical system of Lepsius. It is sounded by curling up the tip of the tongue against the roof of the palate, and withdrawing it in the same manner as during the articulation of the other clicks.

X is either a lateral or a cerebral click ; that is, it may be sounded either by placing the tongue against the side- teeth or by covering it with the whole of the palate and producing the sound as far back in the palate as possible, either at what Lepsius calls the faucal or the guttural point of the palate. European learners almost invariably sound it as a lateral, and hence their articulation is harsh and foreign to the native ear. A Namaqua almost invariably articulates this click as a cerebral.

The Consonants which can be combined with these clicks are *h, k, g, kh, n.*[1]

The Amaxosa Kaffirs employ three clicks which are " represented in writing by our letters C, Q, and X ; the C being sounded by withdrawing the tongue sharply from the front teeth ; the Q by doing the same from the roof of the mouth ; and the X by drawing the breath in a peculiar way between the tongue and the side teeth." [2]

---

[1] Tyndal, *Namaqua Grammar.*   [2] Theal, *Kaffir Folk-lore*

This mode of making the Clicks implies a more conscious manipulation of the Breath for the express purpose of utterance, and shows us the Inhalers of Air and Expellers of Sound as intentionally at work in shaping the result as is the man who in whistling formulates a tune out of Breath, or the player who produces the Vowel-sounds from the Jew's harp.

The first thing that the future speaker had to do was to get his lungs properly developed, by constant inflation, for the utterance of sounds. He was in a condition akin to but probably worse than that of the Congenital Deaf-Mute. We see the experiment of the Dumb acquiring the faculty of Speech going on in our own day, and are shown the processes by which they are taught to articulate. The first lesson is that of blowing or expiration in order that the lungs may be fully expanded, and the child instructed to breathe properly.

Padre Marchio says: " *The breathing of deaf mutes is as a rule short and panting. The lungs have the double office of supplying oxygen to the blood and of furnishing breath—the material of the Voice. The lungs of the Deaf-Mute being used for only one of these purposes, are imperfectly developed, and their functions performed in an abnormal manner. Hence their disposition to pulmonary disease.*"

In the formation of syllables the pupils practise by repeating the same sounds, such as *Pappa, poppo,* etc. The word is formed, if possible, in view of the object, which the Padre calls "Language in presence of the Real."[1]

The Hottentot's inhalation of air to produce the clicks may be compared with the habit of the toad, the puff-adder, and others, of specially inhaling air when angry to inflate and dilate the body and express their feeling in a rushing volume of sound; the early involuntary action being continued and repeated intentionally. But as nothing else in nature is known to produce one consonantal sound by inhalation and another by expulsion of the breath, and as such sounds as "*Mfu*" and "*Nga*" are produced by this double process, which combines a nasal and aspirate in the one case, and a nasal and guttural in the other, these words may possibly show us *Homo* in the position of making a nasal sound whilst drawing in his breath and combining it with a guttural aspirate in the expulsion of his breath, as a continuation of the mode by which he produced his clicks; this would yield compound sounds like *Nga* and *Mfu*. Now, supposing this Mfu (or Mfa) to have been consciously continued as a sound produced by a double action of inhalation and expulsion of the breath, to be afterwards distinguished by the separate sounds of M and B, these would be numerically equal to the singular M and plural B of the numbers in language. Also the nasal is equivalent to *in* and the aspirate to *out*, the Two Truths of the beginning. Moreover, M and N are universally interchangeable. In Maori, as in some of the African dialects, the M,

[1] "Ephphatha," *Macmillan's Magazine,* No. 276, p. 447.

N, and Ng interchange; and if we take the nasal N and guttural Ga in Nga or Ankh, to be the conscious result of the double action, we find the numerical value *was* continued in *Ankh* for the Duplicator, the duplicated, and to duplicate, and in Ankh the pair of Ears, or in Nakh the Testis. In certain Inner African languages the Bull is named from and second to the Cow, as—

Nan, Cow; *Naba*, Bull, in Koama.   *Nåko*, Cow; *Nako-ba*, Bull, in Nupe.
Anoko, Cow; *Anoko-ba*, Bull, in Basa.

Ank, *Nan*, and *N* are interchangeable, and they especially denote the feminine first, the one that duplicates. The Ba is male and secondary. In Egyptian *Nuba* signifies the "All," which was combined in Sut-Nub.

In the chapter on the Two Truths it was shown that Water was the first, Breath the second. Breath, *pef* (Eg.) or *puff*, corresponds by name to No. 2 as *Befe* (Nki). In puffing we have another of the self-naming sounds like the Sneeze. This also is one of the prototypes in primordial onomatopœia. What we term *light* and *lightness* being primarily called *puff* or *pef*, from the Breath, this becomes an archetypal word with several variants in the spelling and many applications of the name. *Pef* will serve as a type-name for all breath-like and light things, elements, characters, qualities, actions, and modes of manifestation in language generally.

Countless light things may be found under this name. *Papapa* in Maori is the calabash, chaff, bran, moss, the shell of an egg. The *Bubu*, Zulu, is a puff or mushroom, also the down-feathers of birds. The *Abebe* in Yoruba is a fan. *Febe*, Zulu, the light person, a harlot. *Bebeza* in Xosa is *fibbing*, or, as the Zulus say, "talking *Wind*"; it may also be called *fabling*. *Babble* is light speech. The Welsh Pabyr is the light thing, both as the rush and the rush candle. The *Puff* is a light tart; the *Bap* a light cake, and *Pap* is light food. *Papa* in Russian is bread. *Bofa*, Brescian, to puff and breathe. In Sanskrit *Phupphu* denotes panting, gasping, puffing; *Pupphula*, wind or flatulency; and *Pupphusa* is a name for the lungs. *Edofofo* in Yoruba denotes effervescence or irritability to such an extent that it means literally a *Liver of Foam*. *Boffy* (Eng.) to swell and puff; *Bof* is a name of quicklime. *Paf* (Eg.) for wind and breath, to fly, be light and puffy, will account for the naming of the thin fluttering tremulous flower, the *Poppy*; French *Papou* or *pabeau*, and for the *Poplar*-tree, Latin *Populus* and German *Pappel*, the tree of light, fluttering, palpitating leaves. This root enters into the names of fluttering wing-like motion as in the Bavarian *Poppeln*, to move to and fro, and *Pfopfern* to palpitate; *poff* (Eng.) to run fast; *popple* to bubble. Yeast dumplings, which are very light, are, in this sense, termed "*Pop-abouts*."

S 2

In Kanuri (Inner African) bellows are the *Bubute*, and in Ife smoke is named *Efifi*. Smoking the *pipe* is accompanied by *puffing*. The *fife*, *pipe*, *pibroch*, and the Algonkin *Pib* are blown with the breath. The *Pub* is a blow-tube used by the Indian bird-hunters of Yucatan ; the *Bobo*, Xosa, a blow-tube. A light leaf called a *Pepe* in Maori is blown to attract birds by imitating their sounds. The act of piping is also called *pepe*. The blown bladder was a kind of *Bauble*. The *pap*, *bubby* and the *bubbly-jock* (turkey-cock) are so named from their swelling-up. Fuf (fâ, Eg.), *Bubi*, in Vei, is to puff or swell in pregnancy ; or to puff and swell the sail. *Beb* (Eg.) is to exhale, as in the bubble. In Zulu *Pupuma* is to boil and bubble ; *Pupu*, Tupi, to boil up ; *Pupu*, Maori, to boil up and bubble. In English *Fob* is froth, *fuf* is to blow ; *Bub*, in Scotch, is a gust of wind. The *Buffie* is a vent-hole in a cask. To *bauffe* is to belch ; *pupa*, Maori, to eructate ; *Pipihi* is wind in Bantik ; *Afufa*, Galla, to blow ; *Fufai*, Magyar, to blow ; *puput*, Malay, and *puba*, Quiché, to blow. *Vivi*, in Vei, is the tornado or hurricane of wind. Also *Vovo* denotes the lungs or lights as one of the blowers. The Toad is the *Bufo* in Latin and *Bufa* in Magyar, as puffer and blower.

Pape or *Ppat* (Eg.) means to fly. The *Ppat* or *Pât* are the flyers as fowls, *Pep* or *Pef* being the breath, wind, a gust of air ; this was the first flyer, the means of flight, and the winged things were named after it. *Pepe* in Maori is the Moth ; *Bebe* in Fiji ; the *Papilio* in Latin is the butterfly. *Ni-pupa*, Makua, is the wing ; *Bubi*, Malay, the feathers ; *pubes* denotes the human feather or hair. *Baba*, in Xosa Kaffir, is to flutter as a bird, whence *Babama*, to swell and flutter in feeling.

The Butterfly was an early type of the Soul of Breath. The Karens of Burmah call a man's soul his " Leip-*pya* " (Leip-*pfa*) or his butterfly, which is supposed to wander away when he is sick, and to need catching or hunting back into his body again. In Xosa Kaffir, *Pupu* is the name of the hairy caterpillar, and *Pupa* is a dream and to dream, which is significant in relation to the soul. *Pabo* (Eg.) is a soul ; *Pepo*, Swahili, a spirit or sprite ; *Phepo* (Inner African), a ghost ; *Popo*, Esthonian ; *Bubus*, Magyar ; *Bobaw*, Limousin ; *Bubach*, Welsh, is a spirit or ghost ; *Pefumlo*, Kaffir, the soul ; *Beba*, Zulu, to inspire the soul ; as in *Pepe* (Eg.) to engender ; soul and breath being synonymous. *Bube* is breath or wind in Galla ; *Pefu* (Xosa) to take breath.

Mi fofi,	is I breathe, in Timbo.			Me fûisafuihe,	is I breathe, in Bute.		
Mi fofi	,,	,,	Salum.	Me pfulu	,,	,,	Mutsaya.
Emi fofta	,,	,,	Kano.	Mu fûtu	,,	,,	Bode.
Me fôtak	,,	,,	Penin.				

This brings us to the human puffer or inspirer of the breath of life, the *Paba* (Eg.) ; *Pabo*, Welsh, as the parent, the *Papa* and Baba of various languages already quoted.

The Mouth as an organ of breathing is the—

Bebe, in Okuloma. *Bebe*, in Udso. *Fôti*, in Limba.
Pfova, is to speak, in Nyombe. *Pobia*, is to speak, in Pangela.

Out of Africa the Mouth is—

Baba, in Malo. *Baba*, in Bissayan. *Fafa*, in Marquesas.
Bubbah, in Sow. *Bibig*, in Tagala. *Fafahi*, in Wokan.
Bubbah, in Suntah. *Vava*, in Malagasi.

The Nose, another organ of Breath, is the—

Bibo, in Ebe. *Pfuna*, in Bulanda. *Opebe*, in Carib.
Epfoa, in Gugu. *Bubuna*, in Dalla. *Aph*, in Hebrew.
Epula, in Matatan.

The Belly, or Navel-type of Breath, in Inner Africa is—

Pop, Ham. *Efu*, Igala. *Apfok*, Param.
Pobob, Pepel. *Evu*, Sobo. *Pfumu*, Musentandu.
Pipai, Kanyop. *Pfam*, Balu. *Pfumu*, Nyombe.
Pfuru, Mano. *Apfom*, Papiah. *Fubum*, Mbe.
Ofofoni, Anfue.

Fuba, the bosom in Zulu, and *Vovo*, in Vei, for the Lights or Lungs, identify other of the puffers or breathers by name.

The " Bubby " or female Breast is a type of swelling and dilating with life ; this is named the—

Bobei, in N'ki. *Ebe*, in Esitako. *Fafa*, in Tumbuktu.
Bebe, in Gugu. *Pebr*, in Padsade. *Efie* and *Evie*, in Sobo.
Bebe, in Puka. *Ube*, in Yasgua. *Fufou*, in Doai.
Bewe, in Musu.

With several other Inner African variants.

The Breather or Puffer as the Frog is the—

Fabu, in Kano. *Oafob*, in Yasgua. *Efol*, in Filham.
Faburu, in Salum. *Mpfuie*, in Bute. *Obopal*, in Bola.
Faburu, in Goburu. *Afôdo*, Legba.

A prominent type of the light aerial thing is the Butterfly, the *Bebe* in Fiji, and *Pepe* in Maori, *Papillon* in French. This in Inner Africa is the—

Pepeli, in Undaza. *Papatane*, in Nyamban. *Sibebe*, in Opanda.
Ipepe, in Yala. *Napapa*, in Kupa. *Mafefirin*, in Nalu.
Bifefeg, in Anan. *Dopopehe*, in Puka. *Gbabaliho*, in Anfue.
Efafareg, in Penin. *Numpapa*, in Basa. *Alan-bebe*, in Yagba.
Avievie, in Egbele. *Kumpapa*, in Ebe. *Efuranfu*, in Mbofon.
Ube, in Dsuku. *Flé-biba*, in Ibu. *Epfurunganga*, in Orungu.

The Spider is an Inner African type on account of its light suspended filmy web ; this is the—

Bubi, in Basunde. *Diboba*, in N'gola. *Libobu*, in Baseke.
Bube, in Mimboma. *Libobi*, in Kasands. *Ebobulu*, in Undaza.
Ibubu, in Kabenda. *Libuba*, in Nyombe. *Pfurubata*, in Okam.

Applied to Light itself, or *Pef* (Eg.) as the rising dilating day, the Inner African languages show—

Efifi, for Day, in Akurakura. *Ofofa*, New Moon, in Yasgua.
Efifie „ Abadsa. *Ofe-ofefa* „ Akurakura.
Efifi „ Mbofia. *Afafion* „ Anan.
Ufo and *Uvo* „ Sobo. *Oyonipepe* „ Yala.
Ipehe „ Puka. *Nafafu* „ Baga.
Mpfusin „ Bute. *Nofafu* „ Timne.

Puf, the light, is a chief type-name for *White*, as the light, in Inner Africa.

Fefe,	White,	Dsekiri.	*O fufu*,	White,	Ife.	*Apowa*, White, Melon.	
Afu	,,	Igala.	*O fufu*	,,	Ondo.	*Mpupa* ⎫	
Fufuo	,,	Ashanti.	*Ififi* ⎫			*Apup* ⎬ ,, N'goten.	
Fifu	,,	Egba.	*Ifob* ⎭ ,,		Balu.	*Ka-pup* ,, Mfut.	
Fufu	,,	Yagba.	*Afufu*	,,	N'goala.	*Bubu* ,, Ebe.	
Fufu	,,	Eki.	*Efufu*	,,	Param.	*Bubuli* ,, Goali.	
O fifu	,,	Ota.	*Efufaka*	,,	Murundo.	*Efifie*, Day, Abadsa.	
O fufu	,,	Idsesa.	*Pfu*	,,	Undaza.	*Efifi* ,, Akurakura.	
Ofufu ⎫			*Popo*	,,	Tiwi.	*Efifi* ,, Mbofia.	
Ofu ⎬ ,,		Dsumu.	*Epupa*	,,	Baseke.	*Ufo* ⎫	
O fufu	,,	Yoruba.	*Apuwa*	,,	N'halemoe.	*Uvo* ⎬ ,, Sobo.[1]	
O fufu	,,	Oworo.					

(*Bup*-al, is Pipe-clay in the Ja-jow-er-ong dialect, Australia.)

It is applied to the White Man as

Babo and *Obabo*, in Banyun.	*Nambabu*, in Bola.	*Tubabo*, in Kabunga.
Za-Bubulie, in Goali (Bubuli being white).	*Nimbabu*, in Pepel.	*Tibabu*, in Toronka.
	Urubabu, in Padsade.	*Tibabu*, in Dsalunka.
Nababo, in Kanyop.	*Tibabu*, in Mandenga.	*Tibawu*, in Bambara.

In a large number of other African languages Babu is reduced to Obu, or some modified form. This is one of several type-words that will show us why we should go to Inner Africa for the birthplace of Roots, Names, Words, Sounds, and therefore of Speech. The true roots show that the duplication of the consonants was primary, and the single consonant, with the accented vowel as in *på*, is a reduced form. In Egyptian *Pepe*, whence *Ppat*, to fly, wears down to *åp* and *på*, to fly, also for the fly and beetle. But *pepe* or *faf* is primary. With the B sound instead of P we have the full form of Pap, to fly, in the Leicestershire " Biblin," for a young bird nearly fledged.

The archetype here is the Breath, Wind, Air, or Soul, which correlates with the other types of light and lightness that come under the prototypal name, and shows at the same time why the Butterfly and Moth are called Souls, and why a man's Soul should be called his Butterfly, on account of the system of homotypes and the naming of many things in accordance with the archetypal idea. The Mantis, Ntane, in Zulu, is literally the *Child of Heaven*, *i.e.* as one of the winged things of the air. *Ntanta* in Xosa means to float or swim.

In Inner Africa the Calabash is equivalent to our *Puff* by name. It is the

Pepe, in Mampu,	*Apepe*, in Timne,	*Effue*, in Gugu,
Pepe, in Bulom,	*Bapa*, in Okuloma,	*Ibiba*, in Anan,
Apepe, in Baga,		

as the round, dilating, light kind of thing. This too was a type of the Soul, as well as Bird and Butterfly, and when the African Mother begins to dilate with the forthcoming life she carries a Calabash in her arms as a token of the *Pupa* (chrysalis) ; or nurses one after her

---

[1] To this rootage the writer would trace the Egyptian word *åb*, white, which is an earlier *fab*. Also the Bethuck, *Wobee* ; Cree, *Wabisca* ; Ojibwa, *Wawbishkaw* ; Old Algonkin, *Wabi* ; Micmac, *Wabeck* ; Sheshatapoosh, *Wahpou* ; Passamaguoddy, *Wapio*, the type-name for white.

child's death, as her puppet, the type of her lost little one ; and this Pepe, Bebe, or Babe, was continued by name in the round 'Bubu-beads, nine of which were worn in the collar of Isis during gestation. The Babe, Pupa, and Puppet, are three of the homotypes by name.[1]

In Italian the Pupa or Puppa is the child's baby or puppet, the Pup or Puppy, as little one ; English Poppet a puppet, idol, darling. The Dutch Pop is the cocoon or case of the caterpillar, and also denotes the puppet, doll, and baby.

The African languages show us the stage at which the whole of the Light things and things of Light could be indicated by one word or the sound of the breath expelled in a puff to accompany the ideographic gesture-signs which delineated the things or thoughts intended. The words are all correlative according to one type, and a principle previously identified with the second of Two Truths. Nor can there be any difficulty in connecting an archetypal idea of, Pef or fuf with its expression in sound. The human being at any stage eructated, panted, and broke wind. The wind itself as puf made the sound of puf as it puffed. But the serpent-type impinges more definitely than these, and its fu-fu-ing was perhaps more likely to evoke the consciousness of a connection between the thing and sound of puff. The serpent or snake in Toda is the Pab, pavu in old Cana-rese. We also have the name in the Puff-adder. In Wadai it is Debib ; in Biafada Wab ; In N'ki, éfi ; in Koro, Bûa. But in Inner Africa the name was generally worn down to Ewa, Iwa, Ewo, or Uwa, from Fufa. The Egyptians continued it under two names. Thus the serpent Bâta, the soul of the earth, is from a reduced form, like the Zulu Fûta, to puff, blow, breathe venom, as the snake. But the hieroglyphic puff-adder is the Cerastes snake. This was an

---

[1] It was suggested at an earlier stage that the name of the butterfly might be derived from Put (Eg.), the type, and ter, entire or perfect ; but the writer is now convinced that butterfly is a corrupt form of Boder-fly, or the French Bouter, to bud or put forth, as the tree does in spring. Bud or bode is our representative of put (Eg.). Bode is a name of the Beetle, as the Sharn-bode for the Dung-beetle, and the Wool-bode for the hairy caterpillar. This Bode is the probable original for the Boder-fly, whence the Butter-fly. BODE means living, a Message, an Omen ; Boded is fated ; the Boder, a Messenger, equivalent to Putar (Eg.) to show, discover, explain, reveal. The Butterfly, as a messenger of time, was a type of transformation, an image of the Soul, a Boder or foreboder of the future life. The Boder is equivalent to Beetle. In Devon the Black Beetle is called a Bete. In Egypt the Beetle was a type of Putah, the opener ; puth meaning to open. We have the Pote, as an instrument for opening, still made use of by thatchers. Also the Chicken is called a Beedy. The Tadpole, another type of transformation, is a Pode, whence the Puddock or Frog. The Bete, Pode, Bode, and Boder-fly, were Messengers to man of a life beyond the present tadpole or chrysalis condition, hence the Moths and Butterflies were called Souls, and the Lady-bird (i.e. Bode) is a form of the living, foretelling, and pre-figuring bode or Put (Eg.).

A lowly form of the Bode survives in the Louse called Biddy, and if one is found on clean linen it is a sure messenger of sickness or death in the family. Thus, by means of the Types, we hope to get back to the mental region of the Thinkers in Things, and attain a foothold beyond that of the Philosophizers in Words. The Irish divinity called the Crom Cruach, said to signify the "Bloody Maggot," was probably connected with this type. Crom, i.e. Crobh, is a form of the Grub that transforms into the Boderfly.

ideographic *fuf;* a syllabic *Fu* and their sole phonetic *F* which became the Phœnician, Greek, and English letter F.

The snake was a type of speech, and " I speak " is " I puff," in the Inner African.

I *Fof*, in Timne.   Nda *Pobia*, in Pangela.   *Pfova*, in Nyombe.
A *Fò*, in Bulom.

In the present instance the links are all complete from the first archetypal idea, through the various Homotypes and correlates, to the final phonetic in the snake as the palpable image of the sound and visible sign of " *fufu,*" or puffing ; and as an expression beginning with a mere utterance of the wind and of breath *Pef* (Eg.), *puff*, *fuff*, or *fufu*, we have in this one word or sound the interjection, the verb and adverb, substantive and adjective of later language, these parts of speech being really *contained in the nature of phenomena and modes of manifestation*. Breath or breathing anger was also represented by the Great Ape as one of the Seven Elementary Types in Egypt.

We have now to make what will look like a wide digression. The Mother and Water have been compared under one name (Momo) ; but the old Mother, the Great or Grandmother, has also the same Inner African type-name as Darkness.   She is

Koko,	Grandmother,	Ebe.	*Koku*,	Grandmother,	Pangela.
Kaga	,,	Kanuri.	*Kukuyamhetu* ,,		Songo.
Kaka	,,	Karekare.	*Kogwan*	,,	Nyamban.
Kaka	,,	N'godsin.	*Kaka*	,,	Kandin.
Kaka	,,	Doai.	*Kaka-woi*	,,	Tumbuktu.
Kaka	,,	Basa.	*Kaka*	,,	Housa.
Kaka	,,	Kabenda.	*Kaka*	,,	Kadzina.
N'kaga	,,	Mbamba.	*Okoku*	,,	Yala.
Kaka	,,	Kanyika.	*Kaka*	,,	Kambali
Kaka	,,	Mutsaya.	*Kogo*	,,	Undaza.
Kaga	,,	Babuma.	*N'kikula-Nana*		Ekamtulufu.
Kugu	,,	Kasands.	*N'kaka-Mama*		Mimboma.

The last but one contains a type-name (*Nana*) which permutes in these languages with the *Mama*.   The last is equivalent to the *Mama* Cocha of the Peruvians, who was worshipped as the Mother-Sea or genitrix of the water, like Tiamat and Typhon.   Very probably however the type-names of the Mother as *Kaka* and *Nana* were both deposits from the Inner African primitive " *Nga-Nga.*"   But *Kaka* as the old first one, furnishes a type-name for No. 1, which is

Q'kui, or *Q'qui*, in Hottentot.	*Quigne*, in Araucanan.	*Atta-shek*, in Tshuktshi Nos.
Akakilenyi, in Bambarra.	*Kuc*, or *Huc*, in Quichua.	*Atta-zhhk*, in Eskimo.
Kokka, in Adampi.	*Chassah*, in Arapaho.	*Yoko*, in Isuwu.
Chig, in Tibetan.	*Chas*, in Lifu.	*Yik*, in Canton.
Chik, in Hor.	*Cheos*, in Hueco.	*Yek*, in Tater.
Kaak, in Chemmesyan.	*Tchika*, Fenua and Galaio, New	*Yak*, in Deer.
Gikk, in Gipsy of Norway.	Caledonia.	*Yak*, in Persian.
Caca, in Tagal.	*Dysyk*, in Kamkatkan.	*Yak*, in Biluch.
Meea-chchee, in Omaha.	*Dschyk*, in Tanguhti.	*Yek*, in Pakhya.
Jung-Kikkh, in Winebago.	*Tsikai*, in Mallicollo.	*Yks*, in Fan.
Pey-Gik, in Old Algonkin.	*Atuu-chik*, in Kuskutshewak.	*Yks*, in Esthonian.
Quen-Chique, in Bayano.	*Atton-sck*, in Labrador.	*Juksy*, in Karelian.

Juksi, in Olonets.
Yaguit, in Vilela.
Wakol, in Wiradurei.
Wakol, in Lake Macquarie.
Wikte, in Sekumne.
Ikht, in Watlala.
Ektai, in Kirata.
Akt, in Lap.
Akhad, in Arabic.
Keddy, in Begharmi.
Akhet, in Khari.
Kadu, in Pwo.
Kĕta, in Buduma.
Gŭdio, in Doai.
Kĕde, in Bagrimi.
Kado, in Afudu.
Kŭdem, in Legba.
Kŭdum, in Kaure.
Kŭdom, in Kiamba.
Ogba, in Egbele.

Ogu, in Oloma.
Guih, in Tesuque.
Chhi, in Newar.
Kahi, in Sandwich Islands.
Ka, in Sunwar.
Cha, in Tablung.
Ogy, in Ostiak.
Egy, in Magyar.
Ikko, in Gonga.
Ikka, in Kaffir.
Eko, in Ashanti.
Gô, in Timbo.
Gôo, in Goburo.
Gŏo, in Kano.
Eôko, in Murundo.
Ako, in Abor.
Eking, in Tayung.
Ek, in Kurbat.
Ek, in Duman.

Ek, in Hindi.
Ek, in Darahi.
Ek, in Kuswar.
Ek, in Kooch.
Ak, in Gadi.
Eko, in Uriya.
Ak, in Kashmir.
Ek, in Singhalese.
Ek, in Shina.
Ik, in Tirhai.
Eka, in Sanskrit.
Yo, in Western Pushtu.
Aoh, in Keltic.
Owe, in Caribisi.
Ai (First), in Siamese.
I, in Arniya.
I, in Kashkari.
I, in Lughman.
I, in Pashai.

The I one ; the A I, the *Ego* and *Ich*, are deposits from an original *Kak, Ka-ka*, or *Nga-Nga*, no initial vowel being a primary in very ancient language.

Also as the Numbers one and five both meet in the hand, it follows that the Number 5 will be found to range under a type-name of Number I. Thus Number 5 is

Kakhoo, in Mandan Indian.
Chichhocat, in Crow.
Huch, in Yangaro.
Chak, in Joboka.
Chahgkie, in Creek.

Gag-em, in Inbazk.
Geigyan, in Assan.
Hkagae, in Kamacintzi.
Kega, in Kot.
Cuig, in Irish.

Cuig, in Scotch.
Queig, in Manks.
Wuku, in Gyami.
Huka, in Gonga.
Huka, in Kaffa.

In English to be left-handed is to be *Keck*-handed, *Gauk*-handed, or *Gawk*-handed. This is the French *Gauche*, for the left. And in the Inner African languages the *left*, inner, or female hand is

Koko, in Bidsogo.
An-koko, in Wun.
Ekaka, in Undaza.
Kekai, in Ntere.

Kekai, in Mutsaya.
Eke, in Babuma.
Yekui, in Soso.

Ngeya, in Landoro.
Lekaka, in Orungu.
Yonko kake, in Limba.

Now that which was first in phenomena became the negative to that which was second, or following, in the naming. Darkness was the first, and it is the negation of Light. Water was first, and it is negative in relation to Breath. The left hand was first reckoned on, and it is the negative hand. The Mother was first, and she becomes secondary to the Male. The hinder part was first, as place of birth applied to the Female and to the North, which is negative to the South, as front.

The earliest races like the Kamilaroi tribes of Australia, are the " *Noes*," because they date from the female first. *Coca* means " *No* " in the language of the Tapuya tribe of Brazil, and their name of the *Coca-Tapuya* signifies the No-people, or those who date from the Mother, the Water, the Negation, the Darkness which they came out of, just as *Enti* (Eg.) for primal existence means " out of.".

Thus the *Mama, Mumu,* or *Momo* name was applied to negative or inarticulate speech ; to Mumming, to Silence, and the Dead ; *Mum,* English, to be silent or to make indistinct sounds instead of speaking ; *Mamelen,* to mutter ; *Momata,* Zulu, to just move the mouth or lips ; *Omumo,* Tahitian, to murmur ; *Mueô,* Greek, to initiate into the mysteries ; *Momo,* Tahitian, to be silent ; *Mem,* Quichua, to be mute ; *Mumu,* Vei, to be deaf and dumb ; *Imamu,* Mpongwe, to be dumb. The *Mum* in Egyptian is the dead, the Mummy, the negative image of life, and the *Mam,* or *Mamsie* (a Scotch tumulus), was the burial-place of the *Mum,* the silent dead.[1]

This shows how that which was primary in time became subsidiary, secondary, or negative in status. Further it has to be seen how Darkness was the first devourer, adversary, opponent, recognised, typified as the *Akhakh,* or *Nakak* monster. *Kak* (Eg.), *Gig* (Akkadian) is Darkness, the Shadow of the Night, a name of the Black One, and Inner Africa is the primæval home of the Kakodæmon who, as *Kakios,* was the stealer of the cows which he had dragged into his cave, when Hercules forced his way into the monster's den and, in spite of the flames and smoke which Kakios vomited, overcame him and rescued the cattle and recovered the rest of the stolen treasures.

The AKHAKH monster is the Devil of Darkness typified, and

Gigilen, is the Devil, in Dsarawa.		*Kıkia,* is the Devil, in Kasm.		
Kogwu	,, ,, Gurma.	*Igue*	,, ,,	Isoama.
Kekuru	,, ,, Guresa.	*Gwigwiou*	,, ,,	Doai.

Another form of the Devourer is the Alligator (or Crocodile). This is the

Egugu, in Ondo.	*Agiyi,* in Isiele.	*Nyakok,* in Kiriman.
Agogu, in Egbira-Hima.	*Akúi,* in Mbofia.	*Akako,* Hippopotamus in Aku—

and other dialects.

The Scorpion, another type, is the

Kak, in Mfut.	*Ngéo,* in Baseke.	*Nkûe,* in Bagba.
Akeke, in Yoruba.	*Nakale,* in Ebe.	*Ngekoa,* in Landoro.
Gigaya, in Krebo, &c.		

Also

Khai-khai, is to darken, in Namaqua.		*Gije,* is Night, in Osmanli.		
Okuku, is Night, in Aku.		*Kaak*	,,	Kenay.
Kigi	,, Tumbuktu.	*Kwaiekh*	,,	Kowelitsk.
Okiki	,, Abadsa.	*Kaehe*	,,	Jakon.
Uchochilo	,, Makua.	*Coucoui*	,,	Blackfoot.
Kak ⎫	,, Egyptian.	*Oche*	,,	Crow Indian.
Ukhakh, ⎭		*Weechawa*	,,	Catawba.
Agi	,, Koro.	*Gaù*	,,	Basque.
Gig	,, Akkadian.			

---

[1] "*Mum.*" There is a drink called Mum, or Mum-beer, in England ; a non-spirituous liquor. This sense of spiritless is also found in the German *Memme,* for a coward.

Night and Black are likewise synonymous, and

Kugbeto, is Black in Legba.
Kegbado „ Kiamba.
Kugbadyo „ Kaure.
Gwigwe „ Ihewe.
Koko, Black Monkey, in Kisama.
Kaka { Black Hole of the under-world, } in Fijian.
Cockmun, is Black Fish, in Victoria (Aust.).
Chuch, is Black Ant, in Harari.
Akahha, is Black, in Maya.
Nikuku, is the Crow, Makua.
Kak „ Toda.
Kaka „ Sanskrit.
Waugh, is the Raven or Crow, Yarra (Aust.).

Kakola, is Black Poison (*Coculus indicus*), Sanskrit. Also one of the hells.
Cacis, is Black Current, in French.
Caoch, is Blind, Void, Empty, in Gaelic.
Uchukula, is to fear, in Makua.
Chouk „ Walach.
Houge, is to feel horror and shrink from the Darkness, in English.
Cocgio, is to delude and trick, Kymric.
Kake, is to steal, in Vei.
Kike, is to sleep, in Vei.
Ukhakh, is to watch, in Egyptian.
Gacha, is a watch, or Sentinel, in Languedoc.
A-kucha, is Morning, in Ude.

These are all related to the Night and Darkness.

This name for Darkness, the Shadow and Blackness, is also applied to Coal as the Inner African type-name for the Black thing.

Geki, is Coal, in Papiah.
Kikemu „ Bayon.

Kakue, is Coal, in Wun.
Kokatera „ Koro.

Igoigo, is Smoke, in Bini.
Egoigo „ Ihewe.

The same radical supplies the name for the *Gigim* (Akkad.) the night fiends, and for the giant as the *Gigas*. Another form of the Typhonian monster in Africa is the moving desert sand. This comes under the same type-name, it is—

Gagei and *Gagiwag,* in N'godsin.
Kekulu, in Kono.
Chicana, or *Dsikana,* in Nupe.

Kigen, in Bode.
Nyek, in Hwida.
Nyeke, in Dahome.

Nyieke, in Mahi.
Cooach, in Victoria, Aust.

Various other co-types of the inimical and opposing condition or thing might be adduced under the one word, as—

Cac, Evil, Irish.
Kakos, Vile, Bad, Greek.
Kaki, a Wicked Man, Mantshu Tarter.
Gygu, Grim-looking, Welsh.
Chukia, to abhor, Swahili.
Chakha-chakhi, Discord, Hindu.
Chukki, Fraud, Deceit, Hindu.
Cog, and *Gag,* to lie, English.
Cacaphone { a Bad, False, Discordant Note, } French.

Kahaki, To carry off by stealth, Maori.
Gaga, Poisonous, Fijian.
Keke, Disease, Fijian.
Kacchu, Itch, Scab, Sanskrit.
Chakawi, Ringworm, Hindu.
Ququ, Stench, Fætor, Zulu.
Caci, to starve, Quichua.
Ghyuch, Death, Turkish.

All that is inimical, bad, dark, opposite or appalling in phenomena may be found under this name. Hence that which is bitter is—

Gaga, Fijian.
Khika, East Nepaul.
Khaco, Magar.

Khako, Tibetan.
Khakha, Dhimal.

Gakha, Bodo.
Haikia, Finnic.

Now, the first teacher of the Adult was Terror, and the earliest pupil was Fear. This teacher became *Kak* (Eg.) the God of Darkness, born of the Dark and named from it; the Black Fetish, known to various languages by this name. *Kuku* or *Ocucu* is the Black Spirit of many African tribes. This was *Ukko,* the Finnic god of fire and darkness, whose voice is the thunder. Fire or lightning is *Kako* in Kaffa; *Caigha,* Namaqua Hottentot; *Koko,* Legba; *Chek,* Uraon; *Chaki,* Paioconeca; *Kakk,* Maya and many more. *Chaka,* the "fire-brand" was the name of Cetchwayo's uncle. *Uchacha,* in Makua, is savage, fierce, furious. The Finns call a thunderstorm an *Ukko* or *Ukkonen*, just as the Inner Africans called it a *Kaka* or *Kak-Kak* by imitating the sound with a very guttural voice. The noise of cracking is represented in the Galla language by *Cakak*, the C standing for a click of the tongue, and *Cakak Djeda* to say *Kak* is to crack; *Kek* (Eg.), *Khakha*, Ude, to break.

Heigh-heigh is a sound of astonishment made with protruded lips by the Negroes on the West Coast of Africa, when it thunders. *Kakulo*, Zulu, signifies greatly, hugely monstrous.

In the Maori *Ngaeke* denotes the sound of cracking, splitting, and rending, which applies to thunder. And in Quichua the lightning spark is *Ccachachacha*; whilst *CCacniy* is thunder, and a *CCaccaccahay* is a thunderstorm. The Thunderer was personified by the Sioux as the giant, *Haokah*. *Hoa-Haka-nana-Ia*, was a Polynesian form of the giant or thunderer. And as Kak, or *Ukko*, the black god of darkness, the Thunderer, the vast voice in Heaven (which was also represented by the *Chachal* or Jackal) is one of the Seven Elementary Powers that were typified and brought on as gods, there would be nothing improbable in suggesting that the earliest *formulation* of the Onomatopœtic *Kak Kak* or *Kaka* may have been in imitation of the voice of darkness (Kak) and lightning, the Thunder. There are various *Kak-ers* and acts, or modes of Kaking or Kâ-ing, but thunder was loudest and most impressive, and *this was one of the Seven types that were divinised* as children of the most ancient genitrix.

The Dark was the great first obstruction and visible form of Negation. The Serpent of Darkness coiled and contracted round, restrained, hindered, imprisoned, constricted and throttled, and—

Cuch, is a contraction, in Welsh.
Chhuko, to grasp, in Vayu.
Cuig, a circle, round, in Irish.
Chug, a ring, in Arabic.
Khakh, a collar, in Egyptian.
Coko, is to tie, fasten round, in Fiji.
Cacht, is a straight, narrow, confined place, in Irish.
Chhek, is to constrict, tie a slip-knot, in Amoy.

Cagg, or *Gag*, is to bind, in English.
Gaga, prisoners, in Fiji.
Gak, is a prison, in Amoy.
Kakoi, to enclose, shut in, bind round, in Japanese.
Kuku, is to hold, constrain, in Fiji.
Kek, is negation, no, not, in English Gipsy.
Kek, is boundary, in Eskimo.
Kakhya, an enclosure, Sanskrit.

Kak as the Darkness and the Devourer is that which obstructs and stops or *chokes*, and—

Cegio, is to choke, in Welsh.
Choke, is to put a stop to in English.
Xaxa, is to obstruct, in Xosa.
Xaxe, is an obstruction, that which checks and impedes, in Xosa.

Ciko, is a woman's word for a stopper, in Zulu.
Choc, is movement brought to an abrupt stop, in French.
Coccare, is to move with a click of concussion, in Italian.

This sound of concussion is represented by *Khekh* (Eg.) to repulse, return (as in sound), Welsh *Cicio*, to *kick*. *Gike* and *Chick* in English, are to click, crack, or creak. It is the noise of striking, as was the voice of thunder. That which is struck *Khekh's* back again. *Choc* in

French, *Chack* in Scotch, and *Kakka*, Norse, for striking together, denote the *check*, *shock*, or *Khekh* of concussion, the *voice of the blow*. Whaka-*Kiki* (Maori) to make *Kiki*, is to incite, instigate, urge on as is done with the click and whip, the Egyptian *Khi-Khi*, in which the sound names its producer as the Whip.

The acts of *chuckling, giggling, kicking* (or other mode of contact) are self-named by this word or sound. The monkey and the rabbit strike the earth with the foot and produce a *Kick*-sound. With the rabbit this is a signal that is understood, and constitutes a call to come out. It is used both in courting and as a challenge to fight. Sheep also stamp on the ground furiously when a fight is going on, and the kick and Khekh-sound are synonymous. Here the *Khekh* reaches back to the gesture-language of animals.

The West Indian negroes make a rattle with seeds placed in a dried bladder. This is called a *Chack-Chack*. So the Inner African natural rattle, the Calabash, is named the—

Koko, in Akua.	*Gukonje*, in Banyun.	*Uko*, in Bini.
Kika, in Marawi.	*Kagudu*, in Bidsogo.	*Kiki*, is a gourd, in Egyptian.
Kekanda, in Bola.	*Yika*, in Kiamba.	

This is the *Koku*, in Bribri, Costa Rica.

There are various self-named *Kak-ers*.

Captain Burton, speaking of the African dialects, has remarked that " *The childish form of human language delights in imitative words, as Koklo, a Cackler, or fowl.*" [1] Because they have retained the primitive childishness.

The Cock, or Cackler, undoubtedly named itself in Africa. It is the

Okoko, in Abadsa.	*Kugei*, in Buduma.	*Akukoro*, in Basa.
Okokoko, in Mbofia.	*Akiko*, in Idsesa.	*Akika*, in Anan.
Okokulo, in Opanda.	*Akuok*, in Yoruba.	*Ekuok*, in Yasgua.
Okokuro, in Igu.	*Akiko*, in Yagba.	*Kogurot*, in Bulanda.
Koko, in Kra.	*Akiko*, in Ekî.	*Kokunini*, in Ashanti.
Kokulosu, in Adampe.	*Akiko*, in Dsumu.	*Kororok*, in Penin.
Kokulotsu, in Anfue.	*Akiko*, in Oworo.	*Nkek*, in Pati.
Kokulosu, in Hwida.	*Akiko*, in Dsebu.	*Kikowa*, in N'goala.
Kokulozu, in Dahome.	*Akiko*, in Ife.	*Nuan-kog*, in Mbofon.
Kokulo-su, in Mahi.	*Akiko*, in Ondo.	*Ndum-kog*, in Eafen.
Kokoro, in Egbira-Hima.	*Akeko*, in Dsekiri.	

This is also the name of the Hen, as

Ogok, in Bola.	*Kokuro*, in Gurma.	*Kugui*, in Kanuri.
Ugok, in Sarar.	*Okoko*, in Isoama.	*N'kok*, in Ekamtulufu.
Ogoka, in Pepel.	*Okoko*, in Isiele.	*N'kog*, in Udom.
Ugog, in Kanyop.	*Okoko*, in Abadsa.	*N'kog*, in Mbofon.
Kokulo, in Adampe.	*Okuko*, in Aro.	*N'kog*, in Eafen.
Kokulo, in Anfue.	*Okoko*, in Mbofia.	*Kuku*, in Xosa.
Kokulo, in Hwida.	*Okoko*, in Bini.	*N'kuku*, in Marawi.
Kokuro, in Dahome.	*Okoko*, in Ihewe.	*Koku*, in Nyamban.
Kokulo, in Mahi.	*Kaguiou*, in Buduma.	*Kugala*, in Mandara.

Koki, in Maori, is to " *Sing early in the morning*," as did the Cackler. This applies to both Cock and Hen, but the likelihood is that the

[1] Dahome, vol. ii. p. 76.

Hen was named first, or rather imitated first, because her clucking announced that she had laid the Egg.   Hence the Egg has the same name ; this is

Koko, in Basque.	*Kuko*, in Magyar.	*Goggy*, in Craven, Yorks.
Coco, in Old French.	*Kek*, in Tablung Naga.	*Gagkelein*, in Bavarian.
Cucco, in Italian.		

The Egg has the same name as the Fowl in Inner Africa, but chiefly in words more reduced.

N'keke, in Bidsogo.	*Eke*, in Ihewe.	*Agoci*, in N'godsin.
N'kege, in Wun.	*Akua*, in Isoama.	*Gôai*, in Doai.
Kogba, in Koro.	*Akua*, in Abadsa.	*Eko*, in Orungu.
Ege, in Afudu.	*Akua*, in Aro.	*Ekie*, in N'goten.
Eze, in Igala.	*Ikôho*, in Sobo.	*Eki*, in Melon.
Ekua, in Isiele.	*Agie*, in Igu.	*Aki*, in N'halmoe—
Ekua, in Mbofia.		

and various other abraded forms.   Here it is obvious the cry was repeated as the name for the Egg, or Goggy, because the idea of food would be a primary.   *Kaka* (Eg.) means to eat and masticate.   The *Gege*, in Zulu, is a Devourer, a greedy-guts.

The " Xoxo," or Koko, in Xosa Kaffir is a large Frog or Toad. The name expresses the croaking of the frog or frogs.   " I *Xoxa* " is a confused, general, or frog-like conversation.

Quack is the language of the Duck.

Kao-kao, of the goose, Chinese.	*Akoka* „ Iho.	
Kak, the goose of Seb, Egyptian.	*Kuku* „ Zulu,	
Kaka, to cackle, Egyptian.	*Ku-kuk* „ - Malay.	
Keke, to quack, Maori.	*Kokoratz*, to cluck as a hen, Basque.	
Gagkezeu, to cough, also cluck like a hen, Bavarian.	*Kokot*, clucking of a hen, Servian.	
Kuk-ko, to crow, Fin.	*Kakulla*, to cackle, Turkish.	
Kukuta „ Sanskrit.	Κακκάζειν „ Greek.	
Koklo, to crow, Yoruba.	*Kakaloti*, to chatter, Lithuanic.	
	Kukku-Vach, a deer, Sanskrit.	

A radical like this *Kaka* keeps its primitive status in later language, and tells of its lowly origin in various ways.

Cach is a primitive form of *utterance* in provincial English, as is *Kak*aista, to vomit or evacuate, in Finnic ; *Kika*, Zulu, a discharge ; utterance being manifold.

The Maori have a chorus in which they imitate the " *Akh-Akh* " or " *Kak-kak* " of the carpenter at work.   The Egyptian, *Kah-akk* ; Coptic, ⲕⲉⲅ-ⲕⲉⲅ ; Xosa, *Ceketa*, mean to work as a carpenter.

Akah (Eg.) is the Axe or Adze—the first form of which is the Thunder-Axe.

Ako-Ako, Maori, is the voice of splitting open.

Chazha in the Aino dialect is to saw ; *Chhak*, Chinese, to work with a chisel.

The Australian Aborigines have a sort of old women's chorus or friendly salutation consisting of a " *Kaw-kaw-kah-kah-kaw*."   This is consecrated to those who are the " *Kakas*," or old women, as grandmothers, in the Inner African languages.

Kiuka, Australian, is to laugh.

Kaka-kaka is to keep on laughing loud, Dayak.

Gigiteka, to giggle, Galla.

Gigiteka, to shake with laughter, Xosa.

Gig, giggle, and *giglet* are forms of the same onomatopœtic original.

Akhekh, in Egyptian, signifies to articulate, and the earliest articulation was expressed by this name.

Chacambi, in Mantshu, is to talk in such an obscure way as not to be understood.

Gigken, in Bavarian, and *Kūj*, in Sanskrit, mean to make inarticulate sounds.

Gag, in English and other languages, denotes inarticulate noises made in trying to speak. To utter or gabble is

Gagei, in Breton.
Gigagen, to bray as an ass, Swedish.
Gagach, stuttering, Gaelic.
Gaggen, incoherent speech, indistinct articulation, Swiss.
Gaggyn, to strain by the throat in guttural utterance, Prom. Parvulorum.
Kakkaset, stutter and stammer, Lap.
Koegalema, stutter, Esthonian.
Kikna, gasp or choke, Swedish.
Chichila, voice of boiling water according to certain Buddhist mysteries.
Keku, speech, Maori.
Kaka, to say, Akkadian.
Kiko, oratory and eloquence, Xosa.
Kuoku, to speak, Isiele.

Ekuka, to speak, Aro.
Ekuoku „ Abadsa.
Ekuoku „ Mbofia.
Chich, voice of grief, lamentation, Irish.
Kagh, voice of mourning, Persian.
Kokuo, wail and cry, Greek.
Keke, be beside oneself with grief, Maori.
Kuk, loud lamentation, Hindustani.
Kukli, howl and cry, Lithuanic.
Gagga, to mock, Icelandic.
Goic, scoff and taunt, Irish.
Geck, derision, English.
Kekas, abuse, Greek.
K'ok, to cough, Chinese.
Keiche „ German.
Khakh, to clear the throat, Amoy.

Now, if the Ape-Man could not chuckle or giggle he was compelled to *Cough*, i.e., *Khekh*, and so produce this prototypal sound in the involuntary stage. Moreover, we find the *Cough* was included with the Sneeze as a sign of spirit-presence. This may be seen in Sir Thomas Brown's version of the story about the King of Monomotapa, in *Vulgar Errors*. The Cough is still employed like the "Hem" to call attention without using words. "I *coughed* to call his attention," said a Coast-guard in a recent law case. The name of the Cough is identical with that of the Gullet, which is

Khekh, Egyptian.   *Ceg*, throat, Welsh.   *Goggle*, to swallow, English.
Koki, throat, Maori.   *Geagl* (whence gullet), English.

This is Inner African, where

N'kog is the Gullet, Bola.   *Okokuturi*, the Gullet, Egbele.   *Khekh*, the Gullet, Egyptian.
Guegue „ Ashanti.   *Ekogwe* „ Igu.   *Uge* „ Dsebu.
Gegolwe „ Bulanda.   *N'gogulo* „ Kanuri.   *Kogbe*, the Throat, Koro.
Ekoka „ Adampe.   *N'gaguldo* „ Kanem.   *Kokore* „ Mose.
Ugogo „ Ondo.   *Okokuro* „ Okam.   *Okuku*, the Mouth, Aku.
Kokorawo „ Mese.

The *Cough* itself is Inner African under this name, as the

Kuoka, in Yala.   *Kokuara*, in Aro.   *Kuekuei*, in Param.
Kuko, in Igala.   *Akukuara*, in Mbofia.   *Kokule*, in Kra—
Kokuara, in Isiele.   *Gegesla*, in Doai.

with the worn-down forms, *Wuko*, (Aku dialects), *Ŭko*, *Kuê*, and others.

The *Cough* issued from the Throat, and has the same name. It was the spontaneous utterance of *obstruction, constriction*, and *choking*. Here we find a natural genesis for the sound that was produced involuntarily, but which is continued in language as the type-word for all forms of obstruction or repulsion and their involuntary voice.

In accordance with *Kaka* being the type-name for that which was first as Darkness, or the Old Mother (*Koka*, in Maori; *Caca*, Japanese), and for the Number 1 we may look on this as a primordial word.

The language of "*Kak*," so to speak—for the time was when a very few sounds constituted the sum-total of human utterance—is yet extant in the guttural *Ka-ka*-ing of the Australians at the southern side of the world, and at the other in the "*Ugh*," or "*Ugga*" of the north; the *Caca* of the English nursery; Finnic, ââkka; French, *Caca;* Mantshu, *Kaka;* English, *Gag*. "*Kaka*" might be still further followed.

Kâkâ (Eg.) is to eat, masticate, swallow, or devour (English, *Chew-chew*); and *Kak* denotes the Devourer in various forms and languages. Ugede describes a Greenland woman as expressing her sense of supreme pleasure by drawing in a very long breath of air and ending at the bottom of her throat with a great guttural smack of satisfaction (*cf.* the Egyptian *Smakhakh*, to rejoice), as the primitive Click, or "*Kak*" of gustative delight. This action and sound correspond to the Quichua *Ccochuy* for pleasure, and the interjection of pleasure called "*Ha-chach-allay;*" the Maori *Koa-Koa*, to be joyful, and the Gippsland *Koki*, a sound (smack) of pleasure.

The language of "*Kaka*" includes the kiss; Sanskrit, *Kuch;* Gothic, *Kukian;* German, *Küssen;* English, *Kiss*. The kiss utters the sound of contact; the *Click or Cluck of the Copula*.

Cache, to go, English.	*Jeka*, to strike home, Zulu.
Kuug, to go together, Chinese.	*Kuc*, to connect, mix, go, *sound*, Sanskrit.
Kokku, copulatio, Tamul.	*Cic*, movement in concert, Welsh.
K.ka ” Zulu.	*Kiss*, concussion with sound, English.

It is noticeable that *Pkhkha* (Eg.), to stretch and divide, has the sign 𝕜 ꜣ for determinative, which supplies the Khetan, Etruscan, Umbrian, and other forms of the 𝕜 or letter K. The hieroglyphic *shows* the sign of *breaking* in two, which the K or KK *conveys in sound to the ear*. Thus the visible action becomes audible, and the word *pkhkh* or *fekh* (Eg.), to break open,—which may apply to various modes—is the *vach* or *voice* of the self-naming action. With this we might compare the stories told of Kak or Ukko, the Thunderer, and his mode of *Khak*-ing.[1]

Nga is the earlier form of Ka, and *Nga-Nga* of Ka-Ka. Thus the

---

[1] Thunder in Finnic is also called *Jymj; Jym*, Zyranian; *Jom*, Mordvin; *Juma*, Tsherimis. This is *Jum* in English for knocking; and *Jumme* is *Futuere*. The Voice of Thunder was a supreme expression of power.

Click and Crack is *Ngaeke* in Maori, and the "Ka-ka" of the Australian natives is also "Nga-Nga." With both, "Nga" denotes *fetching* breath. In Gipps Land "Nga-anga" is breath, and to breathe *Nga-a-a-a-h*, with the H strongly aspirated, is a cry of the Australian Aborigines, used to arrest attention. "*Ng-ng-ng-ng*" is a sort of prolonged grunting, expressive of satisfaction and pleasure. Possibly the Goddess Vach would have to be consulted in her mystical *Oraculum* for the most primitive human phase of the *kk*. *ñk* or *k*-sound, which became lingual in *nga-nga* and *kaka*.

In the *Kk*, or Click, whether sounded with a nasal utterance or not, we find another radical by which some human action first named itself in making the involuntary sound, whether in eating, coughing, or the click of copula or contact ; another utterance of an act of nature, like the "Tut-tut" of sucking ; or the "Fuf-fuf" of blowing with the breath, and the "Tishu-tishu" of sneezing.

R was called the Dog's Letter (*litera canina*) by the Romans, and is referred to as such by the Elizabethan dramatists. The dog makes the sound or *R-r-r-r* when snarling and showing its teeth, or open mouth. *Ari*, Fin, *Hirrio*, Latin, is to snarl like a dog. *Herr, Hyrr*, Welsh, is to incite a dog in its own language. In the hieroglyphics the mouth ⬯ is the Ru or Lu sign, and in the Inner African languages the Mouth, Tongue, and Throat are named from this radical in the duplicative stage. For example,

Luru, the Throat, Legba.	*Olulo*, the Gullet, Isoama.	*Torolo*, the Gullet, Babuma.
Leor ,, Dselana.	*Lilon* ,, Bayon.	*Ularua* ⎫ ,, Mandara.
Ulolo ,, Basa.	*Lelon* ,, Momenya.	*Ule* ⎬

The Ululant type of words found in Irish, Latin, and Greek, the Polynesian *Lololoa;* Zulu, *Halala;* Dacotah, *Hi-le-li-lah;* *Allelu, Lullaby*, and many others may here be recognized.

The Tongue also is named,

Liliwi, in Ekamtulufu.	*Lilim*, in Mutsaya.	*Orlala*, in Ukuafi.
Leliwi, in Udom.	*Lilime*, in Muntu.	*Rale*, or *Ale*, in Igu & Opanda.
Lil, or *Ile*, in Isoama, Isiele,	*Lirume*, in Marawi.	*Halla*, in Fazogla.
Abadsa, Aro, Mbofia.	*Lelimi*, in Undaza.	*Lilla*, in Accrah.
Lelim, in Babuma.	*Irale*, in Egbira-Himi.	*Lilla*, in Adampe.

In Sanskrit *Lal* means playing with the tongue, to loll it, move hither and thither, to dart it forth amorously, fiercely or savagely.

Llaana is the Tongue ; *Lalantika*, a Lizard, or Chameleon ; *Lela-yamana*, one of the Seven Tongues of Fire ; *Lalat* is the Dog. *Lill*, in English, is to loll out the tongue which is called a *Lolliker*. *Rara*, in Maori, is to make a continual sound, to *roar ; Riro* is the Intensive form. *Riri* denotes anger, to be angry, hence to *roar. Rorea* is the rearing roaring Bore, or high tide. *Ruru* is to shake and quake. Ru is the earthquake.

Lila, to lament and mourn, Xosa.	*Lolo*, to lull asleep, Ude.
Lloliaw, prattle to a child, Kymric.	*Lellen*, to tattle, Dutch.
Lalle, babble to a child, Danish.	*Lalein*, to speak, German.

Rire, in French, is the Laugh, or to laugh; and this is Inner African, as

Rere,	Laugh, Gbese.	*Reri*,.	Laugh, Yagba.	*Lela*,	Laugh, N'gola.
Reri	„ Aku.	*Lori*	„ Eki.	*Elela*	„ Lubalo.
Reri	„ Egba.	*Rari*	„ Dsumu.	*Lela*	„ Songo.
Reli	„ Yoruba.	*Reri*	„ Ife.		

Many kinds of *utterance* are called by variants of one name, which, in this case, is extended even to writing in the Assyrian *Rilu*. Earlier than the verb forms were the names of the organ as Tongue and Gullet in Africa. Also to "Tongue" in gesture-language was prior to verbal speech.

Protruding and lolling out the tongue is employed as a universal sign of repulsion, contempt, or hatred. Dr. Tylor says he is not clear why this should be so.[1] But it is simply a case of reversion to an earlier type of expression. Signs were made with the tongue in gesture-language before the time of verbal speech. The tongue was used according to the feeling which sought expression by that member. The Australian expresses "No" by throwing back the head, and *thrusting out the tongue*. Negation is one form of repelling, and the earliest mode of repulsing is reverted to as most repellent and effective. That which served to typify when there were no other means of expression still serves as symbol for that which transcends all verbal expression, and when the choke of feeling is too strong for words, the tendency is to take to gesture-language and enact it whether by thrusting out the tongue, the foot, or the fist.

The loud-crier, the *Roarer*, the rapacious beast, is a "*Ruru*" in Sanskrit. The dog also is a *Ruru;* and this is a name of one of the *Seven* Rishis, who correspond to the *Seven Taas* (Eg.), *Seven* tongues of speech, *Seven* notes in music, *Seven* vowels, and therefore *Seven* primitive sounds, out of which the vowels were finally evolved. The Sanskrit *Ril* is to roar, howl, bellow, yelp, bray, shriek, shout, wail. *Roruya*, to howl or roar very much, and *Roroti*, to yell and roar and bellow loudly, are intensive forms of what is considered the root. But the intensive was primary at an earlier stage; the earliest words being made by duplication of the same sound. This is shown by *Rū*, as in the Latin *Rū*-mour, which indicates the full value to be *Rru* (Rr), as it is in the hieroglyphics.

The dog is *one* of the animals that utter the "*Rer-Rer*," which deposited the letter *r* in language. But a far more potent claimant for the *r* or "*Rur*" sound is the hippopotamus. This is named "Rur," or, with the feminine terminal, Rurit. Rur is written ⋛, or double-mouth. The horizon is likewise the *Ruru*, or dual mouth. The female was a *Ruru*, or double mouth, as the Lioness-Goddess Pehti, one of the *Roarers*. If we apply this to the roar of the hippopotamus, she is the double-mouth of sound. *Raro*, in Maori, is the north, the mouth of the abyss, and Rurit typified that mouth (or

[1] Tylor, *Early History*, p. 52.

uterus) as Goddess of the North, the Roarer who came up from the waters. She is usually pourtrayed with the tongue lolling out of her mouth. Her name of Tep is also that of the tongue, and she is designated the "*Living Word*," because she was the first Utterer-forth in heaven above and the abyss beneath. And the roar she made with her vast mouth reverberated for ever through all the realms of human speech. The dog (or jackal) was her son, and he too *rurs* out her special letter, the phonetic *R*, the mystical Sanskrit *Lri*, which, according to Monier Williams, is one of those things that "*have apparently no signification.*" But, if they had not, we may be sure they would not have been so faithfully preserved.

The Maoris attribute the gift of language to the Old Mother, *Wha-Ruri*, or *Whu-Ruruhi*, whose name denotes the old woman that revealed or disclosed; and her name also corresponds to that of *Ruri*(t), or *Urt*, in Egypt; *Lri*, in India, and *Rî* (Ishtar) in Akkad., the Old First Mother of all things, including language.

The sounds of "*Kak-kak*," "*Fuf-fuf*," "*Tut-tut*," "*Rur-rur*," "*Tshu-Tshu*," "*Nen-nen*," were rudimentary gutturals, aspirates, linguals, dentals, palatals, and nasals, from the first, produced by the gullet, lips, tongue, teeth, and nose; and these "parts of speech" would be first distinguished by the organ of utterance. This is shown by gesture-language, when the tongue is touched as a sign of taste or distaste, and the nose as the sign of smell. The organs can be more or less identified with their especial sounds. There are Seven, as the gullet (gutturals), tongue (linguals), palate (palatals), teeth (dentals), lips (labials), nose (nasals), and breath (aspirates), the names of which were self-conferred by the nature of their action. Thus the Throat was the *Kak*-er; the Nose, Smeller; the Mouth, Puffer; the Tongue, Taster, from the first, and the gesture is the visible link between the organ and the name of the particular sound which it produced. The *Tooth* has the same name in English that language, utterance, tongue, the Utterer, have in the Egyptian *Tut*.

The various members of the human body extant as hieroglyphic signs are so many illustrations of gesture-language which show us how the primitive man drew on and from himself. The human body supplied the following syllabics and phonetics to the Egyptian signs:

Api or *A*, the head.
At and *Ankh*, the ear.
Ar and *An*, the eye.
Bah, the phallus.
Ba, the soul of breath.
Bu, the leg.
Her or *H*, the human face.
Hem or *H*, the *mons veneris*.
Hu, the tooth-sign of the adult.
Hu, the tongue.
Hat, the heart, abode of life.
Kha, vagina sign.

Ka, two arms uplifted.
Ka, a knee-cap.
Kaf, *Fa*, or *A*, the single arm.
Mat or *M*, phallus.
Ma, an eye.
Nen or *N*, a pair of arms held down.
Ru, the mouth.
Tebu, a finger.
Tet or *T*, female breast.
Tat, phallus.
Tut, a hand.

In the hieroglyphics the Nostrils are named *Sherui*. *Sher* is to breathe, and to breathe is synonymous with joy and to rejoice (*Sheri*). *Sher-Sher*, or breathe-breathe, is the plural for joys. Fû (fut) signifies dilation and dilatation; *Fu* being ardour; *Fua*, life. These are likewise related to the breath. *Fu* is especially indicative of a bad smell, of ordure and impurity (futi), which therefore may be held to account for one type-name of the Nose. This, in Africa, is—

Efu, in Yasgua.	*Epofa*, in Gugu.	*Pfuna*, in Bulanda.
Pua, in Swahili.	*Ebua*, in Puka.	*Puno*, in Kiriman.
Aifoa, in Esitako.	*Ipula*, in Meto.	*Puno*, in Marawi.
Eboa, in Musu.	*Bibo*, in Ebe.	

Out of Africa the Nose is named—

Pahoo, Mandan.	*Fuiya*, in Chanta.	*Evi*, in Sapiboconi.
Pau, in Osage.	*Puiya*, in Kaikha.	*Pi*, in Mandarin.
Pah-hah, in Winebago.	*Phiya*, in Kamas.	*Pi*, in Canton.
Pah, in Omaha.	*Puiyea*, in Tawgi.	*Pi-chi*, in Cape York.
Apah, in Minetari.	*Puiyea*, in Yurak.	*Pi-chi*, in Massied.
Peh, in Tsherkess.		

The Tongue is the hieroglyphic symbol of Taste. But it is equally the organ of distaste, and in Sanskrit, " *Thut*," which corresponds to *Tut* (Eg.) for the Tongue, means to spit; and *the word represents the sound made in spitting*. *Tutua*, in Tahitian, also signifies to spit. Spitting or " *Thut* "-ing is an involuntary mode of expression that was continued from the pre-human stage, as an *intended* utterance. Spitting is a universal mode of expressing disgust, repulsion, and repugnance. Leichardt describes the native Australians as interrupting their speeches by spitting and uttering a *pooh-poohing* sort of noise, apparently denoting disgust. With the Malays of Malacca the expression of disgust " *answers to spitting from the mouth*." [1] Spitting was a Greek sign of aversion and contempt, and to spit was to condemn. [2] In Lincolnshire the people believe in a ghost or sprite known as the " *Spittal Hill Tut !* " The Muzunga exclaims " *Tuh-Tuh*," and spits with disgust on the ground. [3] *Tuh*, like Tut, in Egyptian, signifies to tell; it also denotes an evil or bad kind of speech; and spitting was a mode of telling their disgust. *Tutu* and *Tuh-tuh* are in the duplicative stage. In *Tuf* (Eg.) to spit, the Galla *Tufa*, English *Tuff*, Chilian *Tuventun*, to make *Tuv*, or to spit, the *Tut* is worn down and recombined with another consonant. The English exclamation of disgust used for repudiating or rebuking, as " *Tut-tut*," answers to the spitting of the less civilized, and it *re-translates the act into that verbal sound which was first derived from the act*.

Tut, or *Thut*, to spit, then, is a most primitive mode of utterance; the lowly status of which is reflected in later language under the same type-word as *Tad*, English, excrement; *Tutae*, Maori, dung. In vulgar English a more excrementitious exclamation takes the

[1] Darwin, *Emotions*, ch. ii.　　　[2] *Scholiast*, Sophocles, *Antigone*, v. 666.
[3] Burton, *Lake Regions*, vol. ii. p. 246.

place of "*tut*." The lowly status of Tut (Eg.) for speech or utterance is continued in—

Titi, to stammer, Egyptian.
Teet, and *Tatel*, to stammer, English.
Totario, to stammer, Portuguese.
Tottern, to stammer, German.
Tot, to mutter, murmur, or whisper, Norse.

Totte, to whisper, English.
Toot, to whine and cry, Ib.
Teet, the least little word or sound, Ib.
Titter, suppressed laughter, Ib.

Tetea, in Maori, is to strike the teeth. *Tatu*, to strike home, reach bottom. *Dudu*, Assyrian, and *Tata*, Egyptian, are to go rapidly, as the tongue may be moved in making the sound of "Tut-tut-tut." *Tata* in Zulu expresses the impatience of desire.

Impatience is also expressed in nursery language by the "*tut-tut*" of the tongue producing a click.[1]

The element of negation finally expressed in one form by the letter N, may have originated in repelling a nasty smell by inhalation with the nasal sound and expulsion with the guttural which formed the primate Nka, that deposited an N or K. The N is a Nun in the hieroglyphics and Nin in Hebrew. These represent an African type-name for the Nose itself, which is

Nini, in Okuloma.   *Nnui*, in Eafen.   *Nuhutu*, in Bushman.
Nine, in Udso.

This is the name of the Nose in the Lap and Finnic languages, as

Njuone, in Lap.   *Ninna*, in Esthonian.   *Nena*, in Karelian.
Nyena, in Fin.   *Nena*, in Vod.   *Nena*, in Olonets—

and also occurs as

Unan, in Willamet.

Water, however, is a type of Negation, and the first of the "Two Truths," corresponding to the Mother and Night; *Nun* (Eg.) is the primordial water, also the Inundation; and in Chinese *Non* means *the sound of water among stones, signifying Anger.* Here the *Nun*, or *Nnu* our No, is the voice of water; and running water is the ideograph of negation, of No and Not. An Esthonian legend tells how language was derived from the sounds uttered by the boiling and bubbling of water.

These primitive radicals or aboriginal sounds are in the ideographic stage which preceded the syllabic and phonetic phases, and which alone reaches the point where the bridge has to be built that will connect the earliest imitation and utterance of sounds with formulated words.

If some Seven such can be identified and are found to be universal they will give an intelligible account of the origin of language in the

---

[1] One of the most curious relations to language as Tut (Eg.) is illustrated by the Dæmon *Tutivillus* who is supposed to collect *all the Words that are indistinctly uttered* by the priests in the performance of religious services. These abortions of speech he carries off to Hell, which is also the *Tut* by name in Egyptian.—*Townley Mysteries*, pp. 310–319; *Piers Ploughman*, p. 547.

primordial Onomatopœia. The "*Kak-kak*" is still continued in the click stage of sounds as well as in the cough by the vulgar with occult significance; the *fufu*-ing or *fuffing* with the breath, in snake-like inflation and figure of repulsion, survives in the various modes of *Pu-pu-ing* or *Pooh-pooh-ing*, including the action whereby the feeling is uttered or evacuated in spitting out the sound. When a child is called the "spit of his father," it is in the language of evacuation. *Spit* is a name for spawn.

The *rer-ring*, *arre-arre*-ing, hullilooing still exists in the frequentative "*Ara-arai*" of the Maori, or the "*Arree-arree*" of the Pelew Islanders; Æthiopic "*Hur-hur;*" the Norse, "*Hurrar;*" Hebrew, "*Allelujah;*" Red Indian, "*Ha-le-lu;*" Tibetan, "*Alala;*" Inner African, "*Lulliloo;*" Coptic, "*Heloli;*" Irish, "*Hooroo;*" English, "*Hey-loly,*" and "*Hurrah.*"

The "*Mum-Mum,*" although not among the earliest sounds as a labial may have been as a nasal; this was continued as a Mystery in Mum-ming. The nasal of Negation has become the universal No, Na, Nen, or None; and the name of the Ninny.

Like the primitive customs and weapons, the Totemic and mythical types, words and sounds show the same survival of the past in the present, and add their evidence for unity of origin and the truth of the doctrine of Development.

Articulate utterance in Man was preceded by the semi-articulate, and non-articulate; by clicks and puffs; guttural and nasal sounds; by mere audible and visible signs, all of which were pre-verbal. Yet such sounds must have been definite enough to express definite ideas before words existed, because they continue to do so after language is perfected. And when later language fails to utter the passion we still revert to our primitives of expression. The full heart that silently overflows in tears; the sigh of love; the moan of misery; the snarl that lifts the lip all a-quiver to show the *Canine* tooth; the laugh of delight, the click of the wanton,[1] are more eloquent and make a profounder appeal even than verbal utterance. These are as intensely concentrative in act as language is widely expansive in words. The impatient one has recourse to his "Tut-tut," for "don't tell me," and the nurse to *her* "tut-tut," for "so nice," by which she makes the child's mouth water. One "pahs," and another "pooh-poohs," with disgust; the vulgar thrust out the tongue or tell you something or other is not to be *sneezed* at; the *he* at the street corner *hems*, or makes his guttural click to the *she* who passes by; or the savage within breaks out still more ignobly and nature is hurled back on a return tide of reversion to the manners of the remotest past.[2] These

---

[1] *Cf. Khygge*, or *Caige*, Scotch, to wax wanton.
[2] Sign-language still survives amongst us in gestures that correspond to the nature of primitive sounds, as in "*Geasoning,*" which has persisted from the time when

show the predecessor and the creator of verbal language in the position of being still independent of words, as he was before they were fashioned.

We find that there is a stage even in verbal language, in which doing and saying are one, and both are expressed by the same sound or word. Following this clue to the end or rather to the beginning, we see that *certain natural actions include both the act and sound, the later verb and noun in one ; the involuntary sound being spontaneously produced in and with or by the action*, and this sound it is suggested was repeated voluntarily and duplicated to form the earliest vocal sign preceding words—repetition being the primary mode of consciously employing sounds which had been involuntarily evolved in the natural act, to become the recognized voice of each special sensation and finally of ideas.

Man had no need to *derive* the sounds of sneezing (Tsh), coughing, or clicking in eating and swallowing (gustative Kak-Kak—Kâ-Kâ (Eg.) to chew and masticate) or the click of personal contact ; of panting or puffing with the breath (fufu), of sucking or spitting (Tut) from external nature by consciously imitating the animals, as these sounds were uttered in the acts in however rudimentary a manner, to be evolved into voice, and perfected by intentional and continual repetition. Such sounds would be consciously repeated for use as an accompaniment to the gesture-signs, until the primary elements of language, the mere voice of evacuation, could be applied to the things of external nature, which uttered similar sounds, *as their names*, such as " Kak-Kak," for the thunder ; " fuff-fuff " for the wind, breath, soul, or snake ; " rur-rur," the roarer ; only Seven of which are required for language in general.

Primitive onomatopœia would consist *in the conscious reproduction of sounds native to man, rather than in imitation of sounds external to*

pubescence was synonymous with being *open* and unprohibited. In one form to *Geason* is to just open the lips and show the teeth. This may be with the feeling of anger, scorn, derision, provocation, bantering, or attracting. It is a mode of inciting, from whatever motives. The Gaelic *Geason* also signifies to charm, allure, and enchant. This shows the aim (guess) of the gesture (or gest) that disclosed the mouthful of teeth in which the African women file their opening ; the " Gat-teeth " in England. Geasoning, or gestening, once indicated lodging and entertainment for the guest who was thus invited. *Geasoning* was also continued in the dance,—the *Cheza* in Kisawahili, *Khez*, Persian, a sort of *Can-Can*, and a primitive form of feminine Geasoning. In Egyptian *Kes-Kes* is to dance, incline towards, entreat in an abject or degrading manner—as it came to be considered. The *Geasoning* dance also survived to a late period in England, as is shown by the old tune "*Dargison.*"[1] This, according to the name, was intended to provoke desire. *Geasoning* is yet continued by our " noble barbarians " in the " full dress " of the female that advertises the prominent or padded mammæ, which are not always intended for the natural use as they were with the ignoble barbarians. The female still " comes out " to show that she is " open " and free to *Geason*. Indeed, it looks as though the fashion in feminine dress was one never-ceasing wriggle to get back without going back to the most primitive phases of natural Geasoning.

---

[1] *Book of Beginnings*, vol. i. p. 161.

himself; and these involuntary and interjectional sounds are universal; they still preserve their primitive nature or status. Also the duplicated sounds remain to the end as from the first. We can no more wrench language out of the mould of the beginnings than we can jump off our own shadow whilst standing in the sun.

Words founded on the mere repetition and duplication of a sound constitute a common universal property in mimetic expression. But these are by no means an inorganic substratum of language. The moment that a sound was consciously repeated to produce the word "fufu" or "Kaka," etc., it partook of an organic nature and was separated from chaos for ever.

The nursery words of our race to-day are survivals from the infancy of speech. In them the onomatopœia of the commencement persists, however limited or overlaid by the growths and accretions of later language. They took too long a time, and cost too prolonged an effort to get evolved, for them ever to be let go again or altogether lost. They have not suffered change by reduction into roots for regenesis in later words. They are like the oldest order of fish, which did not become reptilia themselves, and yet were the progenitors of reptiles that finally attained wings.

None but the evolutionist can have any approximate idea of the slow processes by which the amazing phenomenon, language, must have wormed its way to the surface from the ungaugeable depth of the past; or of the long procession of series and sequence up to the present time.

It seems to me that we only reach the beginnings where we see that it could not have been otherwise, and where the initial phase would be as practicable, on the same visible grounds, if we could begin again to-day, as it was in the remotest bygone age.

The solution of the problem demands that it should be explained by conditions which are still present, and universal as the human race. The origins now presented conform to these conditions; and the interjectional sounds yet extant as the involuntary voice of natural acts can be cited as living witnesses.

The theory here propounded is that the primary elements of language originated in the involuntary utterance of natural sounds; when the utterance was the mere voice (Vach) of evacuation and sensation. That these sounds were continued by the dawning consciousness now known as human and repeated as signs of want and warning, desire and satisfaction, fear and anger, pain and pleasure, their current value being recognised by force of repetition, accompanied, as they were, by determinative gesture signs; that the first words were coined by repetition of a sound; that the sound-stuff of all speech existed in the embryonic *Tch* (*Dzh* or other variants) of the sneeze; the *fufu* of puffing out the breath; the hiss; the nasal negative; the *tut-tut* of sucking; the click of contact; the *kak-kak* of eating, and *rur-rur* of the roarers; that we do not reach back to an original "root" of language short of a word the earliest form of which could be sounded by a click, a puff of breath, a sneeze, etc.; which word could be coined to-day (as ever) by reduplication of the first natural sound or its modern equivalent.

Thus primitive language is considered to have been evolved by a series of self-naming acts and involuntary sounds; and may be described as the earliest mode of consciously *Puffing, Kakking, No-No-ing, Rur-rur-ing, Tut-tut-ing, Tshu-Tshu-ing, Mam-mam-ing* by means of aboriginal sounds belonging to the primordial onomatopœia.

The second phase of sounds and of conscious duplication to produce the earliest words is yet traceable by means of the Negro, Maori, and other pre-historic languages. In Chinese the *oldest Sounds* of *Ang* and *ong* were *Ngang* and *Ngong*, as they are in the Australian and African dialects.

In Egyptian *Mâ-Mâ*, to bear, as the Mother, implies the form of *Mam-mam;* and *pâ-pâ*, to produce (as the Mother), implies a prior *Paf paf*, which becomes *pâ-pâ*, which becomes *Pepe*, to engender, as the Male, and passes into *Pâ* and *Bât* for the Father. The process of development is made visible in the hieroglyphics. For example, from Puf to blow, the Blowers were named, first by direct representation of the sound, and afterwards by the reduction and combination of the sound. Puff being reduced to the syllable Pu, the article *Tu* (Eg.) for The is prefixed and the word *Tupu* is formed. *Tupu* (Eg.) means to breathe and blow, and it is the name of the buffalo and others of the blowers. But the original puffer remains in the name of the *Buffalo*, and the *Bufo*. The letter V that turns into U, illustrates the process by which *Pf* was modified into *Pû*. When the reduced Puf is combined with the sign or letter T, as a suffix, the result is the word (with variants) *Put, Fut*, or *But*, the type-name in Egyptian, Chinese, Akkadian, English, Sanskrit, and many other languages, for that which opens, duplicates and becomes "*Both.*" Thus *Puth* (Eg.) is to open the mouth; the Hebrew *Puth* or opening also applied to the female genitals. The Mouth is opened by the Breath, Pef in Egyptian; Puff in English. The opening of the Mouth divides into duality.

The Male likewise is opened, to enter his *second* phase at the time of Puberty; and *papoi* in Coptic denotes duplication. He becomes the *Papa* (Pepe, Eg., to engender) the Pubescent male. "Papa" reduced and reconstructed with the T terminal passes into the word *Pat;* Sanskrit, *Pati*, the Husband; Greek, *Phator*, the Engenderer; Australian, *Pyte* and *Bait*, the Father; Malay, *Butu*, the Virile one; Irish, *Bud*, the Virile member; English, *Fude*, the Man; Egyptian, *Bat*, the Father.

---

[1] *Pati*. The Sanskritists would render *Pati* as the Strong. But that is in the abstract and vague stage of the word. The original meaning is male potency, or pudency. The root *Pâ*, an earlier *Pfa* in Egyptian, denotes the masculine species;

The second and dual stage is denoted by the T being a plural sign which in the Hieroglyphics is the hand or a female breast, *one of two* in either case ; and therefore a duplicative type that figures duality to the Eye instead of representing it to the Ear, as was done in the stage of *Papa* and *Mama*. It appears to me that this process might be applied until the later words in general were traced back to the primary duplicated sounds.

The results of this reduction and recombination may be formulated or illustrated thus:—*Fuff-fuff—Fufu—Fu—F—Fut; Kak-kak— Kaka—Ka—K—Kat; Mum-mum—Muma—Mu—M—Mut; Na-na* or *Neh-neh—Na—N—Nat; Rur-rur—Ruru—Ru—R—Rut.* The vowel sounds together with the prefixes and suffixes of course may vary indefinitely. The Syllabics Fu, Ka, Mu, Nu, Ru, and lastly the Phonetics F, K, M, N, R, become the bases for many future combinations of letter sounds in the morphology of later words.

The hieroglyphics show the *visible sign* of duplication in the act of superseding that of *audible repetition* in such words as—

Mama, or *Mat*, Mother.   *Seb-Seb*, or *Sebti*, encase or enclose.
Papa, or *Bat*, Father.   *Khi-Khi*, or *Khet*, to go.
Peh-Peh, or *Pehti*, the double force.   *Mum*, or *Mut*, the dead.
Pepe, or *Pat*, to fly.

Here, then, to recur to our image of evolution, the primitive fish that wriggled blindly as a simple Sandworm, took to its legs as a Reptile and walked off along the ways of manifold transformation, until it became a winged word; winged, bird-like, for unfollowable flight—that is, unfollowable here—although it seems to me that all words might be followed from their natural genesis. For *just as the interjections survive, so do the original words formed by duplication of the same sound still exist after the reduction and re-application in later forms.* Thus *Shash*, No. 6, becomes *Shat* in Sanskrit ; *pap*, or *fap*, in Old Chinese becomes *fât* in Cantonese. So *Kak* precedes *Kât* (from Kakt)[1] just as *Pat* (Eg.) comes from *Ppat* and both from Papa in Egyptian ; so that Papa and Father, Bat (Eg.), are identical at root.

The number Four is *Fut* in Egyptian ; *Fudu* in Bode, Hausa, and other African languages ; but it is

Piffat, in Guebe (Port Dory).   *Effat*, in Malagasi.   *Mpat*, in Sasak.
Pobits, in Yengen.

Fûdu was originally *ffdu*, from Fuf ; and the double consonant explains why *Pip*-ing is number Four in Cayus ; *Pev*-ar in Breton ; and

article or member. The Pat, or Bat, is simply the progenitor, as the inspirer of the Ba (Breath or Soul), with the Bahu. So the Male as " *Sesmu* " (Eg.) is the breather of the Mother. Also *Patni*, for the Mistress, is the property and possession, the one " belonging to," as the Egyptian " *Patni*."

[1] Williams, *Syllabic Dictionary*, intro. p. 29 ; also Edkins.

why *fob*-ble in English means quadruple. In these the *duplicative. phase of sound has survived.* So

Meme, is the Mouth, in Mandara.	*Mimia*, is the Tongue, in New Hebrides.	
Mombo ,, ,, Murundo.	*Mamalo* ,, ,, Papuan.	
Mamadthun ,, Bethuck.	*Mamana* ,, ,, Tasmanian.	
Mme, is the Tongue, in Grebo.		

whilst

Mut, is the Mouth, in Egyptian.	*Mits*, is the Tongue, in Andi.
Mot, is the Tongue, in Tshetsh.	*Mot*, is the Word, in French.
Motte ,, ,, Ingush.	*Mut* (Eg.), is formed from *Mumu*, as Mû
Mets ,, ,, Dido.	with the feminine terminal.
Maats ,, ,, Tshari.	

The Inner African *Mfu* for the Dog or typical Beast is represented by *Mâf-t*, the Lynx or other Beast, also the skin in Egyptian. *Mfu* becomes *Mâu* and the terminal T is added. Thus in Inner Africa the Cat is named

Muti, in Gurma.	*Medsa-ku*, in Dsuku.	*Omati*, in Yasgua.

In this form it passed into Europe as *Muti*, Fin., a cover of reindeer skin, a hairy shoe or glove; *Mudda*, Lap, (Norse, *Muda*), a cloak of reindeer skin; *Mutau*, Gaelic, a muff, a thick glove of skin; *Miton*, French, the cat, as well as the fur-skin; *Mudel*, Bavarian, the cat, cat-skin or fur. But the word *Muff* or *Muffet* survives in the stage of *Mfu* and *Maft* (Eg.), a kind of anklet worn by the Egyptians. Also the Inner African *Mfu* or *Mpu* remained the dog's name in the Vogul *Emp* and Ostiac *Amp*.

Such words then as *Mama, Fu-Fu, Papa, Kaka, Ruru, Tutu,* and the rest of these primordial duplicates did not pass away because the reduced *Mâ, Pâ, Kâ, Rû,* and *Tû* were re-combined as roots in the Aryan stage, and it is a blabbing folly to talk of the sterility of these radicals, which were formed in the duplicative phase of sounds, after all language has been developed from them.

Also the original duplicate is continued in the *Pp*, the *Tt*, the *Rr*, the *Khkh*, the *Nn*, of the Hieroglyphics; the double Ff, double Ll; and double *Dd* of the Welsh, and the *Lri* of the Sanskrit signs. Furthermore *the duality once signified by repetition of the sound, was also continued to the eye in the figures of certain letters which represent the duplicated sounds.* The letter B is a double P, it is a figure of Two in Coptic, Hebrew, Pahlavi, and other languages, and this continues the duplicate Ff or Pp. The T is double in the Hieroglyphic ▭ in the hand and the female breast. This duality is figured in the Cross Θ, Tau, or T which is equivalent to Tta, *i.e. Theta* in Greek, and by the T being a plural terminal. It is the same with the χ or K. This was the principle of our letter formation, visible in the V and Y,

and continued even in the double-looped *f*, and the Twy-formed *L*,

S, or Z. The principle is carried out to the dotting of the i, which is dual in the Hieroglyphics as $\big|\big|$; where the u is inherent in the I, and IU signifies the dual or Twin One ; also to come and go.

The written æ is an IO united in one letter, and with the 0 itself duality attains unity at last in the primordial figure originally imaged by the Ru   of the beginning, the nought in one sense but the true Alpha and Omega, the sign of the genitrix, who was the mouth that emaned the Word at first.

Thus the *letter* still remains an ideograph of that duality which was previously expressed by the duplication of the sound. This is the final answer to the Aryanists who start with "Pa," "Ma," and "Ta" as the roots of language and consider duplication the later stage. For us, duplication was first in language, and is final in the dual forms of letters, howsoever it may be at the starting point in Sanskrit.

The clicking Kaf or cynocephalus of Inner Africa preceded the clicking Kaffir,[1] Hottentot, and Bushman. On the monuments this animal images speech, the word, the voice, as a type of Taht-Aan in the Lunar Mythos, and Shu the God of Breath in the stellar phase ; also Hapi, who represents the breathing quarter in the East, as one of Four of the Seven Elementaries.

"To symbolise speech," says Hor-Apollo[2] " the Egyptians depict a

---

[1] "*Kaffir.*" Captain Burton has questioned my derivation of the "Kaffir" name from "Kaf," and called my attention to the Arabic Kâfir. Mr. Theal also says the Kaffirs cannot even pronounce the name because the sound of R is wanting in their language. But this is not merely a question of R or L. I had previously tested my conclusion and rejected the Arabic Kâfir ; words do not begin where we first meet with them, and the Arabic Kâfir for the Infidel is not a primary meaning of the word. Not even in Arabic. The early Arabian etymologists knew the word had only acquired that meaning through Islamism, and that it had the prior signification of the Coverer, or darkness. Old poets call night the Kâfir, because it covers with darkness, and is the Black. The physical complexion was first, and this is applied from that of the black man. So in the Resurrection, according to the Korân, the Kâfirs are to come out of the earth all black in the face. The accented â indicates an earlier consonant, and points to the root Kak, which means black in Egyptian and other languages. So much for the Arabic. On turning to the African languages we find that *Kaf* is the black apē (Egyptian) ; *Akafi*, the black man (*cf.* Cuffey, the Nigger), Bambara ; *Ckhip*, the black rhinoceros, Namaqua ; *Kabilo*, the black man, Bidsogo ; *Ogabu*, the black man, Kamuka ; *Gbei*, black, Dewoi ; *Gberi*, black, Gbe ; *Gbalwi*, black, Salum ; *Kupirira*, black, Muntu ; *Guafili*, night, Boko. There is no chance whatever of these having derived their type-name for the Black from the Arabic Kâfir. Dr. Koelle says the Phula people call the Hams *Kaffiri;* and language shows that "Ham" and "Kaf" are identical at root. If man and speech began with the black race, language will be sure to show it, without man having first or directly dubbed himself the black. In Bambarra *Akafi* is the Negro, and the word for Beginning is *Kafulo.* Black is synonymous with first as *Kak*, whence Kâ and *Kaf*, later âf, âp, and âu. Further, in the Natal Zulu, the name for sorcery, charms, or enchantment, is *Kafula.* So, in the Xosa Kaffir, Isi *Kafulo* denotes a charm or sorcery, black magic. This is the far likelier original of the Muhammedan Kâfir applied to the sorcerers with the r instead of the l terminal. The Inner African Kaf for the black remains, and from this I derived the name of the Kaffirs and of the Au-ruti (Af-ruti or Kaf-ruti) who went down into the valley of the Nile.—*Book of Beginnings*, vol. i. pp. 28, 29.

[2] Book I. 27.

tongue and a hand beneath." These in the later stage were made human. The first hand and tongue was the Kaf-Monkey, whose name is yet followable through universal language as the type-name for both tongue and hand. This has been shown by the names of the hand. Tongue and Mouth are synonymous, and these take their names from the Kaf-type, or have the same name, as—

Gab, the Mouth, English.			*Egbe,* the Mouth, Puka.		*Kababon,* the Tongue, N'ki.	
Gob, a Beak, Gaelic.			*Oyaf* „ Bishari.		*Jivha* „ Sanskrit.	
Geba, the Mouth, Sclavonic.			*Aof* „ Adaiel.		*Jivha* „ Pali.	
Kiffe, the Jaw, Pl. Dutch.			*Af* „ Faslaha.		*Jivha* „ Kooch.	
Kapiour, the Mouth, Guebé.			*Af* „ Arkiko.		*Jhibh* „ Siraiki.	
Chabui „ Tshampa.			*Aj* „ Amharic.		*Jibho* „ Uriya.	
Zuba „ Pushtu.			*Afa* „ Danakil.		*Jubh* „ Gujerati.	
Zuvar „ Tshuash.			*Affan* „ Galla.		*Jibh* „ Hindustan.	
Yubotarri „ Accaway.			*Gbe,* the Throat, Mano.		*Jib* „ Mahratta.	
Yefiri „ Pianoghotto.			*Gefe,* { the Throat and Gullet } Oloma.		*Cubhas,* a word, Irish.	
Yip „ Korean.					*Chava,* to say, Hebrew.	
Hube „ Talatui.			*Ggbe* „ Opanda.		*Qabah* „ Assyrian.	
Ap „ Palaik.			*Ogbe* „ { Egbira- Hima. }		*Chwed* „ Welsh.	
Aboa „ Basque.					*Cedeach* „ Irish.	
Egbe „ Gugu.						

The *Kaf* was continued in Britain as a type of this primitive *talker,* chatterer, or clicker among animals in such words as *Chaff,* to chirp and chatter; *Caffle,* to cavil; *Chafty,* talkative; *Chavish,* confused chattering of birds; *Chaffinch,* the cheeper or chatterer, opposed to the singer; Gaffle, Gabble, Gobble, Gabber, Gibber, Gibe, or Kibe. *Chaf* modifies into *Jaw* and *Caw*—the Jack-daw being a *Caw-daw.* To *Caw* is to cry or call as Daws, Rooks, and *Jays. Gaowe* is to jaw or chide.

From *Kaf,* later *Gab,* the mouth, the utterer, came the names of *Jaw* and *Jole* or *Chowl,* earlier *Chavel.* In Low Dutch *Kiffe* is the jaw, and *Keffen* means to yelp. In the Walloon *Chawer* is to cheep and *Chaweter* is to chatter. Thus the status of the earliest type of language is still preserved, and the *Kaf* name continued in the *Cheep-cheep* of the finch, the *Caw-caw* of the chuff, the *Gibbering* of the monkey, the *Gobble-gobble* of the turkey, the wide-mouthed bay of old *Chowler,* the *Gabble* of the foolish, the *Gibe* of the face-maker, who still imitates the ape and makes his *jape* (*cf.* Swed. *Gipa,* to wry the mouth and make a grimace); which still testify in *their* status to the lowly beginning with the *Kaf* (Ape) as a primordial speaker. Also, the ape in the monuments is not only a personification of "hand conversation," and of speech, he is also the *Bard,* the *Singer* of the gods. Evidently the singing ape had not escaped the attention of the Kamites. Moreover, the Kaf as singer is earlier than the speaker as Taht-Aan, the tongue, mouth or speech of the gods. *Kä* is to sing, as well as to say, and the singer as the first proclaimer is in keeping with the order of the facts suggested by Darwin. The ape was brought on as the singer, poet, hailer or howler of the gods whom it salutes with up-raised hands because it hailed the New Moon and howled in the darkness at the absence of its light. Darwin inferred that the nearer progenitors of man probably uttered musical tones before they had acquired the power of articulate speech.[1] It is historically certain that tones were most important if not absolutely primary in language. This is shown by the mere vowel-change which is sufficient to distinguish the two sexes.

The Hottentot has three tones that give three meanings to one word, according to the intonation. Captain Burton points out that the Yoruban languages, like the Chinese, depend on accents and tone-variations to differentiate the meanings of the same words. These "*delicacies of intonation are inherent in monosyllabic tongues.*"[2] They are inherent in the most primitive pronunciation, and the Chinese show one form of an elaborate system. The Gibbon's scale contains the system that was established in music. It preceded, and may therefore be claimed as the originator of that which was perfected by man. Lower than the ape as the evolver of the octave and admirer of the moon, the follower of the ape could not have begun in music. And here is the connecting link in tone-language, which language was afterwards used as a vehicle of words whether in the Inner African tones, or in the Chinese tonic system, or in modern music. The number of tones in the musical scale is Seven, the eighth being a repetition of the first. These had been rudely rendered by the ape. Seven may be accepted as the total number of primary sounds in the alphabet. All the remainder were evolved from these. The number of forces, powers, gods, produced by the Mother nature, is Seven. The Egyptians have the Seven *Taas* called Gods of the Word or Speech ; Seven personified forms of utterance.

Brugsch has attributed the meaning of Sage to the word *Taas* (or Djas), which is analogous to the Coptic *jas* or *gis*, and the Chinese *Tze* for the Teacher. The Taas are thus the Seven Sages. In the *Memoria Technica* of the Hindu sages, the Sage, or Vowel, stands for number 7, there being Seven Sages and Seven Vowels.

The Seven Sages also appear in Greece. These, then, are related to the vowel that takes Seven forms of utterance. The utterance of the Seven Vowels was one of the mysteries in Egypt as in India. Savery, in his *Letters*,[3] says that in the Temple of Abydos the priest repeated the Seven Vowels in the form of hymns, and that musicians were not allowed to enter the building during the performance. Like the Gibbon they were practising their scales, but not in tones only. The tones conveyed the *Seven forms of breathen utterance*, the latest product of language, known to us as the Seven Vowels. The Seven Vowels were known and are acknowleged to be a sevenfold form of a dual one which was the Iu (Eg.) or Ao of the beginning, and the O, or Omega, in the end ; the Au (Eg.) that signified Was, Is, and To Be.

[1] *Expression of the Emotions*, ch. 4.
[2] Burton, *Dahome*, vol. ii. p. 76, note.			P. 566.

When personified this Biune One with the Triune character became the God of the Seven Spirits, which were Seven Breaths, and these made up the ten-total as in the Ten Sephiroth of the Kabalah and the ten letters of the British *IAU*. Iao-Sabaoth was a form of this combination of the Threefold One with the Sevenfold manifestation.

Sevekh (Eg.), whose name reads number 7, was another divinity of the same type.

Sut-Nub-ti was likewise a form of this compound nature. Nub signifies the All, that is the plural expressed by Three; and Sut (Seb-ti) is number 7.

Sut-Nub was continued by the Gnostics, and his name of Iu or Iao, was kabalistically expressed, and probably sung to scale by the Seven forms of the same vowel, as ΑЄΗΙΟΥⲰ, which are found on the rays of the lion's crown of an Agathodæmon or Chnuphis serpent.[1]

Nef (or Nub) signifies the breath or spirit, and this was the Good Spirit with Seven rays or emanations, which represented the Seven Spirits whose physical origin has yet to be traced. These Seven agree with other forms of the type brought on from the beginnings of the Kamite typology. Spirits were breaths at first, and the vowels are breaths. Thus the Seven forms of breathen utterance, the Seven Vowels, represent the Seven Spirits of the Triune Nature.

The Chant of the Seven Vowels was apparently practised by the natives of the Friendly Isles, who intone a solemn dirge at the funeral of their chiefs. So ancient is it as to be no longer intelligible, but its refrain consists of a wail expressed by a series of vowels rendered by Lang as O I A O O E.[2]

The North American Indians heard by Adair were probably calling on the name of the Triune Iao, which was more fully expressed by the Seven Vowels.

Amongst their funeral rites and ceremonies the Todas perform a circular dance, in which the men by *three and three* perambulate round and round like spokes in a wheel, all exclaiming "*A U!*" "*AU!!*" in time with their steps. This likewise presents a form of the divine triad.

Hymns were addressed to a god, "*Who*," by the Hindus, and called the "*Whoish*" hymns. This mystical name is resolved by Max Müller into a mere interrogative pronoun. But there is nothing more certain or more pathetic than that God was sought for under this name of "*Who*," the Unknown.

The Abipones expressed the name of some deity by their interrogation "Who?"

The Hebrew name of the Very One God Alhu, אלה, is a form of the Who, the interrogative pronoun; the *Who* (אלה, as unknown subject) of the Kabalah. This is the Egyptian deity, *Hhu*, or *Huh*, whose

[1] King's *Gnostic Gems*, p. 74.
[2] Lang, *Origin and Migration of the Polynesians*.

name signifies to seek and search after, or, as we have it, to *woo*. One mode of seeking and inquiry was by singing the name with Seven Vowel-sounds. These the translators of the Hebrew Scriptures have contrived to make permanent in the name of *IEHOVAH*.

This compound deïty, as Iao-Sabaoth, was finally the God of the Seven Planets. Each of these was represented by a Vowel and each Vowel dedicated to one particular day of the week. So, in the Seven notes of the scale, and the orbit lines of the Planets—

Si	was assigned to the		Moon.
Ut	,,	,,	Mercury.
Re	,,	,,	Venus.
Mi	,,	,,	Sun.
Fa	,,	,,	Mars.
Sol	,,	,,	Jupiter.
La	,,	,,	Saturn—

n making the music of the spheres.[1]

The seven vowels, to take them as they are printed by Bunsen[2] A E Ê I O Ô U, though not a perfect form, were all contained potentially in the A I U, which in Egyptian and Coptic resolve into Iu, Ei, or an I with the U inherent. Iu signifies to come and go, but it also denotes duality, to be twin or two. The Arabic and Syriac Alif is likewise figured double. The hieroglyphic *Calf*, which became the Phœnician and Hebrew Aleph, the Steer, was a dual image, because a calf is of either sex. The Hebrew Jad ', or I, is a hand that has the numeral value of 10. The one vowel, therefore, whether represented by A, I, or U, was a diphthong that bifurcated and became sevenfold in the vowel sounds.

Now the hand as *Kaf* or *Kab* signifies to be double and to duplicate, as does the calf in its two sexes. The *Ka* visibly modifies into *da*, and the *fu* (or *bu*) into U, and thus *Kaf* became *Kau* and *Au* for Cow and Calf; and *Au* or *Iu* are the dual source of the seven vowels. Moreover, the Nose of the Calf is the ideograph of Breath, and the Egyptian deity is pourtrayed as the Calf-headed *Au*, or the *Iau*, from whose name we derive the seven vowels, and from which the Hebrew Kabalists derived their ten sephiroth and ten vowels, and the British their ten primordial letters. Finally, then, the A, as representative of the sounds that were the last evolved in language, is now for ever first as the letter-sign of the *one* that duplicated (who was the Mother), whilst the letter B (with the leg-sign) remains the sign of the duplicated one, the child of either sex, which, as male, triplicated at puberty.

The *a* is a kind of Io in our written letter, but in the A it is triadic, as is the Hebrew Aleph, א; and the triad of *IA U*, was symbolized by this one letter. A story told in the Arabic Gospel of the Infancy, connects the Child-Christ, when he was about twelve years of age, with the letter Aleph. There was a teacher of boys

---

[1] Dupuis, Tom. i. p.-75, who cites authorities.
Egypt's Place, vol. v. p. 747.

at Jerusalem named Zacchæus, to whom the Child was sent for the purpose of learning his letters. The master wrote out the alphabet, and bade the Boy say "Aleph," and when he had done so, the master ordered him to say "Beth." Whereupon the Child demanded to know the nature and meaning of the Aleph first. The master could not tell him, therefore the Child made known to him the *gnosis* of the letter Alpha, and the rest of the alphabet. In the Gospel of Thomas the Child says, "*Hear me, doctor; understand the first letter.*" And He points out that the *one* letter is "*three-fold and doubly mingling*," and thus is a figure of the Trinity in bi-unity, as expounded by the Kabalah.[1] The Child, no doubt, expounded His own nature as the mythical IU who, as the Child, was the Iusu (or Jesus), Iu-em-hept in Egypt, the Son of Iu-sû-as, and the god Tum.

The Jew's harp remains a symbol of the divinity whose name it bears. It is *one* as a total figure; *dual* as the Io of the male and female, or of the Number 10; and *triadic* in its shape, which answers to the trinity of *Iao*. The correct way of playing this instrument is by producing various vowel sounds, and it is a fact that its tongue can be made to utter the seven variations of the vowel, according as the player consciously shapes his mouth, without the aid of the human voice. Thus breath is turned into seven sounds by the tongue of the *Iao*, as it was in playing the flute, which has the name of Sebti (7) or Sut; and also in blowing the Seven-fold pipe of Pan. It is no marvel, then, that the Jew's harp should retain the name of the *Iu*, *Io*, *Iao*, or Jah, the God of the Jews.

The Typical Prayer uttered in the Seven Vowel Sounds may have been the model of the Prayer on the Mount, in which the sum of all seeking and request is supposed to be divinely expressed by an invocation comprising seven petitions in one prayer.

The Egyptian chant of the Seven Vowels of the ineffable name, which *might be breathen or intoned, although it must not be spoken as a word,* was the probable origin of the Seven-fold Litany, or *Litania Septemplex* associated with the name of Pope Gregory the Great. In the year 590, when Rome was afflicted with .pestilence, Gregory ordered a public supplication to God, and the people were commanded to assemble at day-break in *Seven* different companies, arranged according to their ages, sexes and stations, and walk in Seven different processions reciting the Seven-fold Litany and other forms of prayer intoned. They carried with them, by express command of Gregory, an image of the Virgin, the latest form of the Lady enthroned on the Seven Hills, who had been the Mother of the Seven when these were but Seven Elementaries in Chaos.[2]

The typical Seven were further continued by the mediæval Church in its Matins, Prime, Tierce, Text, Nones, Vespers, and Complines, as

---

[1] Arabic Gospel, ch. xlviii. Gospel of Thomas, ch. vi.
[2] Baronius, *Annales*, 590, tom. 8, p. 6.

the Seven times for daily praise. These seven canonical hours, however, had been devoted by decree of Pope Urban II. to singing the
praise of the Virgin Mother, who was the original author and inspirer
of breath.

The Gnostic Marcus held that Seven Elements composed, and
Seven Powers expressed, the "Word," which could be uttered in
an "O!"[1]

Lastly, the Coptic ω or Ō summed up the power of the seven
vowels, and represented the value of No. 8 in hundreds. Here the
Ogdoad was complete in the O as a final vowel sound, and a sign of
the God who was worshipped as the Ō in the Mysteries; the Ō or
A O of the Greek Iconography.

Thus we have the Ape in the beginning evolving his scale of Seven
Tones. The Ape, or Kaf, is the hieroglyphic type of speech, singing,
worship, and breath; Shu, the Kaf-headed, being a god of breath.
This god of breath, as Nef, is the Agathodæmon or Chnuphis, the
IAO who has the Seven-Vowelled name which was intoned by the
priests of Abydos when they employed the Seven breathen Sounds
or Vowels in their worship of the god of breath. And in the end
the Seven-fold Litany was treasured up amongst the relics of the
past in the religious Ritual of Rome.

The black Kaf Ape, preceded the black Kaffir (or Akafi) as clicker
and master of a scale of sounds. The living clickers prove that the
breath was inhaled to articulate the sound. This shows the one act
of a dual nature, which was represented by a dual sound; the air
being indrawn with a nasal noise and expelled in a guttural click.
The double action and dual sound contain the negative and affirmative, the No and Yes, the Two Truths or one and two of all beginning.
Represented by the sound "Nkakh," or " Nga," the duality becomes
audible in a word that signified duplication as the name for the twin-
member, the ear, hand, testis, eye, nose, or mouth, in the oldest
languages. These languages also show the priority of words that
were formed of merely duplicated sounds as the basis of speech.
The Egyptian hieroglyphics exhibit the process by which the
mimetic duplicates of sound were reduced for re-combination with
others to form words from two different consonants, and thus extend their range indefinitely. The hieroglyphics likewise show the
process whereby the ideographic signs and gestures that accompanied sounds in the ideographic phase were divided and reduced to
the letter-values, and thus account for that equivalence and interchange which are found in all later language.

The clickers inhaled the air to articulate their sounds, and the
utterers of the Seven-Vowelled chant exhaled their soul or breath
toward heaven, the height being scaled and the summit of religious
aspiration very literally attained by the ascent of the Seven Vowels,

[1] Irenæus, B. i. ch. xiv. 8.

and the breathen utterance of the letters composing the ineffable Name that was *noted* on the Planetary orbit-lines of the celestial scale.

Thus the Seven Vowels were *consciously evolved, discreted, and deposited from Seven Consonants, in which the Vowels had been inherent in the syllabic form ; the syllabics being a previous deposit from words formed by repetition of the same sound in the ideographic stage of expression ; these words having been created by the conscious utterance and duplication of natural and involuntary sounds.*

The Alphabet is still reducible to some Seven original types, and this Seven corresponds to all the other typical Sevens: the Seven Tongues of Fire ; Seven Taas, or Gods of the Word ; Seven Rishis ; Seven Notes in Music ; Seven Elements ; Seven Senses ; Seven Sciences ; Seven Elementary Powers or Spirits ; the Seven Stars of the Greater and Lesser Bears ; the Seven Planets, and Seven Days of the Week.

As the result of the foregoing research, my conclusion on the whole matter is, that the origin of language resolves itself into the production of some Seven primary sounds in an early phase of articulation, and that the fundamental facts are registered in language and typology where they have been stereotyped by man with no more choice in the matter than the mirror has in its faithful reflection of forms, except in the conscious care with which he repeated and tried to preserve the primæval tradition in ever-living memory.

SECTION VI.

NATURAL GENESIS AND TYPOLOGY OF THE MYTHICAL SERPENT OR DRAGON AND OTHER ELEMENTARIES.

"The object of our inquiry is no trivial thing; it is a diversified and complicated one. This is a various and most questionable animal, one not to be caught, as it were, with the left hand."—Plato.

THE *Serpent* is one of those few great primitive types that constitute the earliest objective castings of human thought when it groped in the underground condition of its far-off past, which may be compared with that of the earth-worms throwing up the first castings of vegetable mould for the use of the farthest future. It was primordial, and it is universal. The dominion of the Serpent has been wide-spread as that of night, from the most known to the remotest parts of the earth. The symbol has literally realized that Serpent in the mythologies which is depicted as circling about the world and clasping the whole wide round in one embrace.

The Serpent-type has been venerated in lands where the Serpent itself does not exist. It was the representative of renewed life or immortality in the Rites of Sabazios and on the doors of the Chambers of the Dead in the Egyptian and Chaldean tombs, and it is yet a symbol of eternity in the bracelet on an Englishwoman's arm. It is represented in the finger-ring, and coils about the walking-stick as it did around the tree of mythology. It is the great Dragon of the Celestial Empire, the Long Serpent of the old Norse Sea-Kings, the Lambton Worm, the Dragon of St. George on our own public-house signboards, and old English penny-pieces. There are still no less than 700 Serpent Temples in Cashmere alone. It is only a few years since that buildings dedicated and devoted to its rites were found in *Cambodia*, surpassing in size the cathedrals of York or Amiens, and in grandeur the temples of Greece and Rome.[1] It is not my province however to expatiate on the "Worship" of the Serpent, but to explain the origin and development of this universal type, as an ideograph that guides us round the world.

[1] Mouhot.

The "*Way of a Serpent*," and the workmanship, are among the most amazing in all nature. It has no hands, and yet can climb trees to catch the agile monkey. It has no fins, but can outswim the fish; no legs, yet the human foot cannot match it in fleetness. Death is in its coil even for the bird on the wing, which the springing reptile snatches out of its own element. The Serpent slays with a dexterity that human destroyers might look upon as divine.

One of the most arresting sights is to see this limbless creature turn its coils into a hand to grasp its prey, and lift it to the deadly mouth. The serpent in the pangs of sloughing is a phenomenon once witnessed never to be forgotten. There is a startling fascination in the sight of that image of self-emanation proceeding from itself, the young, repristinated, larger life issuing of itself from the mask of its old dead self like a spiritual body coming forth from the natural body, the unparalleled type of self-emanation, of transformation, of a resurrection to new life, of "*Time, or Renewal coming of Itself.*"[1]

The Serpent has the same name at root in several groups of languages.

Nâga, in Sanskrit.   *Nachash*, in Hebrew.   *Snake*, in English.
Neke, and *Nakahi*, in Maori.   *Naya*, in Arabic.

This name is pre-eminently Inner African.

The Serpent is the

Nyok, in Kanyika.	*Nyoka*, in Nyombe.	*Nyoka*, in Kisama.
Nyoka, in Kabenda.	*Nioka*, in Basunde.	*Nyoka*, in Nyamban.
Nyoka, in Mimboma.	*Nyoka*, in N'gola.	*Noga*, in Basuto.
Nyoka, in Musentandu.	*Nyoka*, in Lubalo.	*Nyoke*, in Swahili.
Nyoga, in Kasands.	*Nyoka*, in Songo.	

With modifications such as

Nyush, in Guresa.   *Nyos*, in Legba.   *Nyowe*, in Baseke, &c.

The Y in these names is not primary, but represents an earlier sound. Thus *Nyoke* is *Ngoke*, the Kamite *N* being *Ng*, and this form has been preserved in the hieroglyphics where *Nkaka* interchanges with *Kaka*, and obviously continues the African *Nk* or *Ng* sound. *Nkaka* then abrades into *Naka* (Eg.), *Nâga*, Sanskrit, on the one hand, and into *Kak*, *Hak*, and *Hag* on the other, and *both are found united in the African original*. In the Hymn to Amen-Ra the Sun-God is said to send his arrows against the Evil Serpent *Naka*, to consume him.[2] Here the typical Serpent or devouring Monster is the *Naka* or *Nâga* by name. *Nakak* (Eg.) also denotes *the Curse*, or Accursed, with the Typhonian Devourer, the *Crocodile-Dragon*, for determinative. *Naka*, to delude, be false, has the Dragon or Apap Monster, the piercing Serpent of Evil, for its Determinative. Now the *primal monster was the Shadow of Darkness*. The first type of this is the *Nâka*, *Nakak*, or *Akhekh*. In Egyptian

[1] *Ritual.*   [2] *Records*, vol. ii. p. 131.

the Shadow of Night, the Darkness, is called *Kak*, *Akhekh*, and *Uklâ;* and the Mythical Monster has the same name in the *Akhekh* Serpent, or Gryphon, the type of evil being primarily identical with Darkness. This old Serpent is depicted as the *Crooked* Akhekh, and in some of the non-Aryan languages of India the word supplied a type-name for the *Crooked* things as

Gokke, in Badaga.	*Kokki*, in Irular.	*Kochamocha*, in Kol.
Gogu, in Newar.	*Kakroi*, in Garo.	*Kok*, in Burman.
Kyoke, in Dhimal.	*Kok-lok*, in Serpa.	

This name of the *Crooked* One is African, as O *kako* in Idsesa ; O *kako*, Yagba; *Wogu*, Kiamba, &c.

Darkness was the Shadow that stole his Substance, destroyed the foothold, and deluded the eyesight of the primitive Man. Hence the Monster in mythology. Hence also the Night and the Naga or Nakak, the devourer, are synonymous. The name of Night, is likewise Inner African, under the *Naga*-name.

Nak, or *Nakta*, is the Night in Sanskrit.	*Nakti-s*, in Lithuanic.	*Nacht*, in German.
Nochd, in Irish.	*Nocyi*, in Russian.	*Noshti*, in Sclavonic.
Nox, in Latin.		

and

Nkó, is Night, in N'goten.	*Enokon*, is Night, in Ekamtulufu.	
Nkô ,, Melon.	*Yungo* ,, Mose.	
Enukon ,, Mbofon.	*Nyaka*, is Black, or Night, in Mbofon.	

Nakak, *Akhekh*, and *Kak*, are names then of the mythical Monster the Dark, the Blackness, the devouring Dragon, *Kok* is the name of the Dragon in Amoy. The Dragon-Constellation is called *Kok-Sing*. The Cockatrice is a mythical Serpent. Also, the English Dragon-fly, called a *Coach*-horse, is a form of the *Akhekh* (Eg.), or Winged Dragon, by name, and our *Cock*-roach is the night-walking Beetle. The Assyrian Vampire is called the *Akhkh-aru*, in the shape of which the Dead are supposed to rise up and attack the living. The *Yaksha*, or *Jaksha* (Sans.), is the Devourer. A *Gege* in Zulu is a Devourer. The *Ôgre* is a mythical monster, the Devourer. The Fijian *Kaka* is the Mouth of Hades, the Swallowing Throat of the Underworld. The Kamkadal Evil Spirit is a Water-Dragon called Mit-*gak*. *Kikymora* is the Sclavonic God of Night ; *Eyak* is the Koniaga Evil Spirit; *Aka*, a Japanese Evil Spirit. The *Yaga* Baba of the Russian folk tales is identical with the Typhon of Darkness. *Jugah* Pennu is the Khond Goddess of Small-Pox. *Jaca* is the Devil in Singhalese mythology ; *Akea*, the first ruler of Hawaii (Savaiki) now rules over the land of Darkness and the Dead. *Agoye* is the Black God of Hwida. Many more deities or Devils of Darkness may be traced under the variants of this type-name for Blackness, Crooked-ness, and other forms of the adversary. The Akhekh Serpent is Inner African by name. In the Makua dialect *Ikuka* is the great Python. Dr. McLeod says that in Dahome the Python has been found from thirty to thirty-six feet long, and of proportionate girth.

Here then is the natural type of the Akhekh (or Nakak) of Darkness in the shape of an enormous serpent. In the solar stage of the mythos, when the sun passes down through the underworld, the *Akhekh* of Darkness lies in wait to swallow or pierce the god as he goes along, or it rises up and tries to overturn the solar boat. "*I pass from earth to heaven, I grow like Akheku,*" [1] says the Osirified, using an image drawn from the sudden and huge up-rising of the Gloom as the Devourer. The assistants and co-conspirators of this deluding Monster of the Dark are called the *Sami*. *Smi* says Plutarch is Typhon. Here again *Sami* in Egyptian is the name of *total Darkness*. In the Fijian mythology we find the same opponent of the soul and the light who was at first the actual darkness. In passing through the underworld, the ghost of each dead warrior must fight with *Samu* and his company. If he is brave enough to conquer he will cross into Paradise, but if beaten he will be devoured by the terrible *Samu* and his brethren, just as it is in the Ritual. In Sanskrit *Samani*-Shada is a Demon of the Dark ; *Summani*, in Latin, is a name of Pluto, as King of Hell. The *Saman*, in Fanti (African), is a Ghost, Demon, or Devil. The *Sami* are also extant as the "*Cemis*" of the West Indians, Caribs, and other tribes, who regard them as the evil authors of every calamity that afflicts the human race.[2] The Monster Yaga-Baba of the Russian folk-tales, who bears the name of Typhon, or "Baba the Beast," has, for one of her types, the snake *Zmei*,[3] which is identical with the Egyptian *Smi*, or *Sami*, the Conspirator, the Dark Deluder. *Sami*, total darkness, has an earlier form (or variant) in *Kami*, the Black; and the Basuto *Sami* is *Kamm*-appa, the wide-mouthed, throttling, and devouring Monster, who was conquered by Litaolane, the local "St. George." [4] The *Apap* (Greek Apophis) is another form of the Serpent of Darkness, the deluding and devouring Monster. The Apap reappears in the Assyrian *âbu*, the Hebrew pythonic אוב, a name of the Monster who is the "Enemy of the Gods." The *Apap* is apparently the Inner African Rock-Snake, not a native of Egypt itself, so large as to be like the *Boa*. Its name signifies that which rises up tall, vast, *gigantic*, as did the Darkness in its most appalling shape.

The Platonist Damascius reports that the Egyptians began with Darkness as the first principle of all things, the unknown, incomprehensible, inconceivable Darkness, from which the Light was emaned. But the primæval Darkness was not that of Orpheus and the Platonists which was dark with excess of light. They came in the course of time to say there were two kinds of darkness, the one being below and the other beyond the light. That was afterthought. The Esoteric is the latest and not the primary interpretation of phenomena ; and a great deal of the error extant is the result of thus surreptitiously

[1] *Ritual*, ch. 98.   [2] Robertson's *America*, b. iv. p. 124.
[3] Ralston.   [4] *Book of Beginnings*, vol. ii. p. 649.

imposing the later thought upon the aboriginal imagery. Darkness was the first Revealer of Light in the stars, and therefore a form of the genitrix, the Mother (Mut) who is called Mistress of Darkness and the Bringer-forth of Light. In the last of the Izdubar Legends the Mother of all as Ishtar is " *She who is Darkness ; She who is Darkness, the Mother, the emaner of the Dawn ; She is Darkness.*" The Mexican genitrix, Cihuacohuatl is the female Serpent who gave birth to Light, and is the mother of the Twins, Light and Darkness. The " *Wisdom*" of Solomon [1] is a personified phase of primordial Darkness. " *She is more beautiful than the sun, and above all the order of the stars. Being compared with Light she is found before it*"—the analogue of Plutarch's saying, " *Darkness* is older than Light." We read in the Ritual [2] " *the Æon or age* (Heh) *is the day, Eternity is the Night.*" In the beginning of time say the New Zealanders was *Te-po.*[3] *Te* is *the*, and PO is Darkness, Night, or Hades. The same PO as the point of beginning with Darkness is the Mangaian night; Po being the equivalent of Avakai or Savakai, the birthplace. After *Te-po*, the Darkness, came *Te-ao.* *Ao* (Maori) is to become Light.

The first conditions of existence observed by the primitive men were precisely those that were first observable. These were the Dark and the Day, which followed each other in ceaseless alternation. In the beginning was the impenetrable obscurity of primæval Darkness. The universal exclamation of mythology as its first word is " *There was Darkness.*" All was Darkness at first and the All was the Darkness. Primitive man came out of the night with his mind as deeply impressed and indelibly dyed as was his body with its natural blackness, because the influence of night was the first to be consciously reflected, the first that arrested attention and lifted the look upward when he was going mentally on all-fours.

A Maori tradition describes the first children of Earth as " *ever thinking what might be the difference between Light and Darkness.*"[4] That contains a true record of what must have been a primal subject of thought. Also it does not represent them as dreading the dark or cowering from it in caves, but as marvelling over the alternation of phenomena. It would be a mistake to picture the primitive man as the prone coward of subjectivity. The ancient races that survive to-day and are mortally afraid of the gloom are not likely to represent the earliest man who had not yet peopled the darkness with his Terrors. These take a spiritual shape, and the very animals that the savage most fears are dreaded most in a *ghostly* form. Ideas make all the difference. Fear of the dark with children is frequently cultivated, where it is not inherited. We see what plucky little pigmies they were in the valley of the Thames at the time of the Palæolithic Age, who with their rude weapons attacked and triumphed

[1] Ch. vii. 29.   [2] Ch. xvii.
[3] Shortland, *Traditions*, p. 55.   [4] Grey, *Polynesian Mythology.*

over the mightiest monsters of the animal kingdom, like the tiny cock-boats of English ships swarming round and conquering the large galleons of the Spanish Armada.

Darkness, however, was the first Devil, Satan, or *Adversary* discovered, because it presented the primordial form of *obstruction*, whether to the light or to the human being. Darkness was the earliest monster personified in the image of ugliness, because the light was pleasant. Moreover, Darkness, not Light, made the first appeal to consciousness in feeling, and perception in thought. This, too, is on record. The primitive myths all date from the Darkness. The starting-point is on the night side of phenomena. Hence the earliest reckoning of time was by nights not by days. So many Darks were counted rather than so many Dawns. The Dark presented the barrier that was tangible to the nascent consciousness. The *Going* of the light preceded the sense of its *Coming*, and the *Coming* of Darkness was the shape in which the going of light was earliest apprehended. The coming of darkness is felt by certain gregarious animals, including sheep, which in hill-countries show an instinct for taking to the higher grounds after sunset, as if conscious that the deluge of the dark is rising round them. In the Akkadian legend the Seven Devils, or bad spirits, who bring blackness from the abyss are said to be born in the Mountains of Sunset. In Africa the advance of night is sudden. There, if anywhere, "at one stride comes the dark." You watch the sun drop down, and darkness is behind you. The "*Jaws of Darkness*" have supplied a figure of speech for us, but there they *are* in reality. They close upon you as if to devour their prey, subtly, swiftly, silently. What but the serpent with its gliding stealth and instantaneous spring could be adopted as a first fit type of the Darkness of night? Hor-Apollo says the Egyptians represent the Mouth by a serpent, "*because the Serpent is powerful in no other of its members except the mouth alone.*" The serpent is all mouth, and both as the "*Ru*" and the "*Tet*" it has the name of *Mouth* in Egyptian. In the Inner African languages the Mouth and the Serpent are frequently synonymous. The Jaws of Darkness are thus an equivalent for the Serpent or Dragon. The Serpent, it may be inferred, was one of the first external figures taken by death. It brought death into the world. If the dark cloud lightened with death it was the Serpent. If the water drowned it was the Serpent or Dragon that lay lurking there to put out the light of life as the Apophis, Akhekh, Nakak, Naga, Nocka, Nickur or Nekiru (a devil in the African Yula language), and Nick, the "Old Nick," the evil being, or the "Raw-head-and-bloody-bones," our English Red Typhon. One form of the Serpent running, or rather zig-zagging, through the mythological maze is the *zig-zag* of the lightning. The Algonkins were asked by Father Buteux who was among them in 1637 as a Missionary what they thought of the nature of lightning. They replied that it was an immense serpent that the

Manitu, their great spirit, was vomiting forth. " *You can see the twists and folds that he leaves on the trees where he strikes, and underneath such we have often found snakes.*" When lightning enters sand it will fuse and convert it into a solid tube of serpentine shape, which is sometimes called a thunderbolt.

The Chinese believe in an elemental Dragon of enormous strength and sovereign power which is in Heaven, in the air, in the waters, and on the mountains. The Caribs speak of the god of the Thunder storm as a great Serpent or Dragon dwelling in the fruit-forests. The Shawnees called the Thunder the hissing of the great Snake. And Totlec, the Aztec God of Thunder, was represented with *a Golden Serpent in his Hand.* Here the lightnings are identified with serpents because the serpent in the earliest coinage of human expression was a type of the Lightning. The serpent having made its mark on the mind of man by the exercise of its fatal force became an ideograph of Death. The Serpent utters a hiss, so do the Lightnings. The serpent's hiss supplied a definite sound that was for ever connected with a distinct idea. This idea, this sound would serve to express Lightning and its fatal flash, and thus both Lightning and Serpent came under one type and could be expressed by the same noise. The Thunder is said in an American myth to be the *hissing of a fiery flying serpent,* in accordance with the mode of interpreting the unknown by means of the known ; and the lightning-flash is depicted as the Spit-fire with the head of a serpent in some figures found on the walls of an Estufa in Pueblo de Jemez, New Mexico.[1] The Lightning-dart of the darkness is the forked tongue and sting of the Serpent. The first of the Seven Akkadian evil powers is the Scorpion, or the sting-bearer of Heaven, and therefore representative of an elemental force, apparently that of sunstroke.

The Hiss of the Serpent or the Puff of the Adder is but magnified in such a title as the " *Wind of nine Snakes*"; a Miztec mythical name. In a Kaffir folk-tale when the Chief comes home the sound of a great wind is heard. " *That wind was his coming, and he was a big Snake with five heads.*"[2] In these we see the Serpent type applied to the wind. Thus we watch the unknown taking shape in images of the known. The Lightning as unknown subject could be represented by the Serpent as object; the voice and sting of the unknown by the hiss and sting of the known. We have this postulate more directly illustrated by the Lightning as unknown subject with the Thunder-stone or Aerolith as a Fetish image of the power that flashed and fled ; for what the flash revealed besides itself was the thunder-stone.

In man's state of mental darkness the serpent-image of the destroyer and of the darkness of death had made its mark on the human being

---

[1] Mallery, *Sign Language,* fig. 188.   [2] Theal, *Kaffir Folk-lore,* p. 51.

and its deadly folds had imprinted on the race the figure of the darkness coiling round by night with death lurking in its embrace. The serpent drew its own symbol in the mind like its own circle on the body of man, and this is what man tells us when he in turn had learnt to draw the serpent-symbol. As man was a dweller in caves and trees his most mortal foe was the serpent, the forked tongue of the Darkness that darted death ; and what form so fit as this to image the appalling power whose habitation was Blackness and whose voice was Thunder, and who, when angry, would look out with eyes of lightning and shoot forth the forked blue flashes that could lick up forests with their tongues of fire and the lives of men like leaves? The fearful fascination and appalling magnetic power of certain snakes over man, bird and beast has often been described. The Serpent is the Mesmerist and Magician of the animal world, who evoked the earliest idea of magic power. A deluding snake in the Ritual is called the *Ru-hak*, the reptile which makes use of this magic power (hak) to draw the victim towards his mouth. " Go back Ruhak ! fascinating or *striking* cold with the eyes,"[1] exclaims the contending spirit. *Ra* the sun-god, in his old age or decaying force, speaks of the evil serpents as the subtle enchanters who have enchanted him beyond the power of his own self-preservation, so that he needs to be sustained against them. In the " *Avesta* " the " *look* " of the mythical serpent is synonymous with deadliest opposition. The good god Ahura-Mazda says, " when I created this beautiful, brilliant, admirable abode, (the Earthly Paradise) then the Serpent (Anra-Mainyus) *looked* at (that is opposed) me."[2] " *Charming* " was the great mode of exhibiting power. " These are the gods who *charm* for Har-Khuti in Amenti. They, the Masters of their Nets, *charm* those who are in the Nets."[3] Those who are in this scene walk before Ra, they *Charm* Apap for him. They say, " *Oh! Impious Apap! Thou art charmed by us through the means of what is in our hands !* " The first star in Ophiuchus is known in Arabic as *Ras-al-Hawwa* the head of the " Serpent-Charmer " not merely the Serpent-Holder.

The influence of the Serpent over the mind of primitive man can never be understood apart from the abnormal conditions of what are termed Mesmerism and Mediumship. The present writer has had a personal and profound experience of the abnormal in nature, as manifested by one of the most marvellous Sensitives ever known. This face to face familiarity with the mysteries of its phenomena enabled him to apprehend the part played by the Serpent as the Mesmerizer (Charmer) in the mysteries of the past. The disk of the Mesmerist and the look of the human eyes have no such power in inducing the comatose and trance conditions as the gaze of the Serpent ! The Africans tell of women being "possessed," seized

[1] *Ritual*, ch. cl.   [2] *Vendidad, Fargard* 22, lines 3, 4, 5, and 24.
[3] *Book of the Hades*, 9th division.

with hysteria, and made insane by contact with the Serpent. That is, the Serpent by the fear of its touch and fascination of its look, produced the abnormal phase, in which the Medium raved, and talked eloquently, or was divinely inspired by the Serpent, as the phenomena were interpreted. In this way the Sensitives were put to the test, and the Serpent chose its own human oracle. Those who were found to be greatly affected by the Serpent were selected to become Fetish Women, Pythonesses, or Priestesses. They were secluded in training hospitals, and prepared to become the oracles of the Serpent-wisdom, and mouth-pieces of Supernatural utterance.[1] This was in Africa, the dark birth-place of that *Obeah* Cult which survives wherever the black race migrated. The stupor caused by the Serpent's sorcery inspired a primary form of religious awe; and the abnormal effects produced upon the *Sensitives* were attributed to supernatural power possessed by the Serpent. We see that Serpents were employed in the cave of Trophonius for that purpose. It is said that no one ever came out of the cave smiling, because of the stupor occasioned by the Serpents.[2]

In many parts of Africa, as on the Guinea coast, and elsewhere, the Serpent oracle was a common institution. The reptile was kept in a small hut by an old woman who fed it, and who gave forth the answers when her oracle was consulted. She was the Pythoness, the Medium of Spirit communication. The feminine origin of the Priesthood is also indicated by the *Danhgbwe-No* or Fetish Priests of Hwida, whose names signify the *Mothers of the Serpent*.[3] The tongue of the serpent is known to be a very peculiar organ of touch. This was employed in the Mesmeric Mysteries like those of Samothrace in which Olympia was such an inspired Ophite; one that loved

> "To dally with the crested worm,
> To stroke his azure neck, and to receive
> The lambent homage of his arrowy tongue,"

which was at times made use of to produce ecstasy and trance. A snake called Ganin-Gub by the Hottentots is also said to have genitals and to seek to have connection with women *while they are sleeping*.[4] The statement, however, may be typical of the Coma that COULD BE induced by the Serpent's look, and likewise by the dart of its tongue.

The earliest Medicine was a *Mental* influence. This was exerted by the Serpent over Man and imitated by him according to the laws of Animal Magnetism. In a trial of power between two rival Medicine Men belonging to two tribes of Red Indians, the contest was con-

[1] Des Marchais, *Voyages* (1725), vol. ii. p. 135.
[2] Bulenger, de Orac, *apud* Gronovius, 17, 44. Salverte, *Des Sciences Occultes*, p. 282.
[3] Burton, *Dahome*.
[4] Hahn, *Tsuni-Goam*, p. 81.

ducted on "*principles of Animal Magnetism.*" It lasted a long while, until one of them concentrated all his force, or "*gathered his Medicine,*" and commanded his opponent to die. Whereupon he died on the spot.[1]

Belief in such a power furnished one important element of the "Medicine," just as does a belief in the sanative virtue of vaccine, "tar-water and the Trinity," or any other nostrum. The root of the *Abus* shrub is used by the Hottentots as a deadly charm. It is pounded and put into milk, when it is supposed to cause the death of the person who drinks it; and *yet the root is not poisonous at all.* But it has become a type.[2] Belief is a medicine that *does* work wonders whether for good or evil.

To *Charm* became a supreme manipulation of mental or spiritual power when this was exercised *over the Serpent and all that it represented,* because it had been exercised over Man by the Serpent. Thus when death is imaged as the Serpent with the magical influence, this may explain the persistent notion of the primitive races that death is not the result of various "natural causes," but is the effect of magic, sorcery, and witchcraft. The idea of death has not yet passed out of the first stage, where it was identified with the occult potency of the Serpent's sorcery. The Enchanter as the Serpent-type of death is now represented by an Enchanter who is assumed to have bewitched the victims to their death. The only question being *who* is this son or daughter of the Snake, this devil working darkly? Both Wallace and Stevenson testify that in South America one or more diviners are consulted on the death of an individual, and these generally name the Enchanter who is as generally sacrificed.

The Africans and Australians share the same belief, and grope mentally in the same shadow of the ancient darkness. Also, according to Huc, certain Buddhists attribute all diseases to evil spirits. This is the doctrine of the Avesta which begins with the *Elemental Darkness,* as twin with the Light, and develops it into the *Dark Mind* who produces the Serpent and all kinds of disease prepensely. The Lizard takes the place of the Serpent-type in New Zealand, where the natives assert that sickness is "*brought on by the Atua who, when angry, comes in the form of a Lizard, enters their inside, and preys upon their vitals till they die.*"[3] Hence the need of appeasing the Atua and giving it what it likes; all curative medicine being resolved into that! Hence, also the necessity of opposing sorcery with sorcery, magic, incantations, and potent charms, and meeting abnormal effects with the abnormal powers of the primitive Medicine-men, and Serpent-charmers.[4]

[1] John Mason Browne, *Atlantic Monthly,* July, 1866.
[2] Hahn, *Tsuni-Goam,* p. 83.
[3] YATE, *New Zealand,* p. 141.
[4] An eminent naturalist has confessed to the present writer that he takes no interest in mythology. And no wonder, from the non-naturalistic treatment that it has received. Yet mythology is a most ancient record of natural facts; this type of a

Mr. E. S. Parker's pamphlet, on the Aborigines of Australia, contains a curious statement respecting the "*Myndie*." He says,—

"In the latter end of the year 1840 the Aborigines of all the neighbouring districts were in a fearful state of excitement owing to the capture and imprisonment of some hundreds of their number. Two died on the spot and several sickly people, eventually, from fright. Some of the natives told me confidentially that destruction was coming upon the white population, even those who were friendly ; as it was known that secret incantations were being practised with this object. The effects were graphically described as producing dreadful sores, dysentery, blindness, and death. The Myndie was to come! At the time I did not much regard the prediction, but afterwards ascertaining that the scars of the small-pox were termed 'lillipook Myndie' (the scales of the Myndie), and the plague itself, which was to come in the dust, as *Monola Myndie*, the dust of the Myndie, I was able to identify the threatened agent as small-pox, about the ravages of which there are traditions among the natives of the interior. It is thought to be in the power of the large serpent Myndie to send forth this plague in answer to the appeal of those who seek the destruction of a foe (that is the sorcerers and charmers). The natives of Melbourne say the *Myndie* is a great snake, very long, thick and powerful, under the dominion of Pund-jel ; and when commanded by him, Myndie will destroy black people young or old. He can do nothing of himself, and must first receive orders from Pund-jel. He knows all tribes and they all know him, and when a tribe is very wicked, or when a tribe fails to overtake and kill wild black fellows, then Pund-jel makes Myndie give them diseases or kill them. Myndie isn't quite snake-like, having a large head, and when he hisses or ejects poison his tongue appears, which has three points. He lives in a country called Lill-go-ner, to the N.W. of Melbourne, near a mountain named Bu-ker-bun-nel, and he drinks from only one creek named Neel-cun-nun. The ground round about this spot is very hard—no rain can penetrate it; and it is covered with hard substances, small and white like hail. Death and disease are given to any blacks who venture near this ground. Myndie can extend or contract his dimensions when ordered by Pund-jel; he can hold on to a branch like a ring-tail opossum, and stretch his body across a great forest so as to reach any tribe. Myndie has several little creatures of his own kind, which he sends out to carry diseases and affliction among those tribes who have not acted well in war or peace ; these creatures are troublesome, but not so dreaded as a visit from Myndie himself—from whom no one can escape. All plagues are caused by Myndie or his little ones ; and when he is known to be in any place the blacks run for their lives—they don't stop to take their weapons, or bags, or rugs— not even to bury their dead, but set the bush on fire and run as fast as they can. Some, as they run, are afflicted by Myndie ; and becoming sick lie down and die; some try to rise, but fall down again, but those who can run swiftly and escape are always quite well and never suffer from sickness."[1]

In the Inner African languages, Blackness is *Mindi* in Kiniam-wezi ; *Maundi* in Gindo ; *Muindo* in Diwala ; *Moindo* in Isuwu ; and in Egyptian *Menat* is death. The Hurons likewise held that disease and death were caused by a monstrous serpent that lived under the earth.[2] The Chinese have a sort of serpent known as the *Min*.

According to the present derivation from the Kamite origines the *Myndie* serpent of the Australian Blacks is identical with the *Mehnti* serpent of the Egyptian Ritual, the name of which signifies "*the Snake from what is in the Abyss*," the Meh of the North. Death, Darkness, Disease, were in the Abyss which lay between the

lizard that is poisonous and deadly, like the serpent, being one. The existence of such a lizard was denied, because unknown to science. But it had been preserved as one of the mythical types, and the other day the venomous creature was re-discovered.

[1] SMYTH, *Aborigines of Victoria*, vol. i. p. 444.
[2] RAGUENEAU, *Relation des Hurons*, p. 75.

West and East, and we learn that all the evils that have ever afflicted the blacks of the southern and south-eastern tribes of Australia have come, they believe, from the north north-west. The Myndie was dominated by the power of the God Pund-jel, and in the Ritual the Mehnti draws the Boat of the Sun, to which its tail is securely attached.

Disease being typified by the Serpent of Evil, any power over disease was described as influence over the Serpent. The Healer, Doctor, Medicine-man, Magician or Manitu was a charmer of the Serpent. "*Who is the Manitu?*" is asked in an Algonkin Chant, and the reply is, "*He that goes with the Serpent;*" that was the conqueror who could charm the Serpent into subjection; magic being the earliest Medicine and the first healing, a mental operation supplemented by fetish images, and lastly by drugs. The Medicine-man, as the *Manitu*, is the Charmer of the Serpent of evil or disease. The root of this name is widespread. *Mana*, Maori, is magic influence and power. In Irish, *Manadh* is magic, incantation; *Mantra*, Vedic for magic incantation; *Moniti*, Lithuanian, incantations; *Manthra*, Pahlavi, magic incantation against disease. It denotes the primary form of *Mind*. The Blacks of Australia have their *Manitu* in *Min-nie Brum-brum*, who is able to arrest and pull back the Myndie with a wave of his hand or a movement of his finger; but none know his secret, no one can arrest Myndie but Min-nie Brum-brum. A family named *Min-nie Brum-brum* was the only one that ever set foot on Myndie's territory. Mr. Thomas says, "A sorcerer, celebrated as a man possessing great power, a very old black, and a member of the same tribe as *Min-nie Brum-brum*, was a prisoner in the Melbourne gaol many years ago for having committed some depredations on the flocks of the settlers. The news of his arrest was carried to tribes far and near even to 200 miles off. Telegraph fires were lighted. Messengers from seven tribes were sent to my blacks, who importuned me to set free the black stranger. Finding I would not they urged me and all the settlers to leave the district and go to Van Dieman's Land or Sydney. Some hundreds of blacks were in Melbourne when the old man was imprisoned, and they all fled in terror fearing he would move Pund-jel to let *Myndie* loose, who they believed would spare no one—and, what is more, they did not return until the prisoner was set free, some months after." [1]

In Egypt, Taht was the divine doctor, the God of Physicians, and his medicine is magic. The Stele of Metternich informs us that Taht has *magical words to bewitch poison and prevent it from doing serious injury, and by his words he bewitched the Apap Serpent and all the evil enemies that for ever fight against Ra.* The same power is assigned to Horus the healer or saviour of souls, when he is depicted in the act of

---

[1] SMYTH, *Aborigines of Victoria*, from MS. of the late William Thomas.

holding the Serpent, Scorpion, and other Typhonian types of evil, helpless and harmless through the power of his charming.[1]

Here we can further see how AGE itself became identified with sorcery, because the Aged and the Wise were synonymous. In Egyptian, Aak the Aged Man, and Aak the Mage or Magician are identical. The Aged were the wiseacres, wizards, and witches. Hence the Hottentot tribes used to leave their old people behind to die the "devil's death" and be devoured by vultures, because being aged they were all the greater sorcerers, and the awe-stricken tribe were so fearful of witchcraft, that friends dared not keep their own relations alive.[2] So, in Europe, old women were naturally considered to be witches, and were persecuted accordingly. The Amazulus generally regard the grandfathers as the dead;[3] and in Egyptian the *Akh* is the Dead, the Manes as well as the Aged one, or the Mage. These three are one by name. Moreover, the *Akhekh* becomes our *Hag* for the snake and the old witch, Russian *Hexe*, Polish *Yega*, the sorceress or fiend. The Egyptian form of the word as *Hekau* means magic and to charm. The same word signifies a net, snares, and the serpent is the ensnarer as the magnetiser and lier-in-wait. It is likewise the name for intoxicating drinks in which the enchanter lurked. *Hekau* is Beer, containing the alcoholic *Spirits*, and in Chinese, *Hak* is a name for distilling spirits. This also was a mode of magic. *Hekau* for Magic is the name of Thought. So *Hugi*, according to the Prose Edda is Thought in person. The "Serpent-charmer" who was primally the Serpent itself, made so early an appeal to thought by means of its magic power, that Thought, Mind, and Magic, were named after it, and this will help to explain why the Serpent became a type of Wisdom, Knowledge, occult influence, the Wise *Hag*, *Yaga*, or *Khekh*, synonymous with the Wise Woman or Wise Man. Though not particularly profound, yet it was the first *Thinker* or Magician to the primitive sense, on account of its deluding and eluding subtlety. The Hottentots still believe that a particular Snake, the Dassies-Adder, can detect the criminal among hundreds of people and kill him unerringly, without turning its avenging ire on the innocent.[4] Amongst the types of the "Elementaries" perceived as active forces of the material universe, the Serpent naturally rose to supremacy as very crest of crests on account of its subtle craft and glozing guile. The Hippopotamus and Crocodile were wider-mouthed, but manifested no such commanding cunning as the Serpent with its secret sorcery. Hence, in Egypt, it became the one universal symbol of the Gods. This beginning with the Darkness, symbolised as the deluding and

[1] "And he said unto them, I beheld Satan as lightning fall from heaven. Behold, I give unto you power to tread on Serpents and Scorpions, and over all the power of the enemy."—Luke x. 18, 19.

[2] Hahn, *Tsuni-Goam*, p. 74.   [3] *Ibid.* p. 86.

[4] *Ibid.* p. 108.

devouring reptile, will likewise account for the common notion of primitive races, that Spirits or Divinities are Demons in the bad Sense, and naturally evil, like the bad Spirit of the Eclipse, who mischievously intercepts the light intended to be shed on the earth and its inhabitants.[1] This is particularly shown by the North Australian Aborigines, who will not go near to human graves by night, but when compelled to pass them they always carry a fire-stick to keep off *the Spirit of Darkness*.[2] *The Beginning was not with the Spirits of the Dead, but with the inimical in external nature,* and this mould continued to shape their later thought. The first Monster was the Darkness solidified (so to say) as that which checked, Egyptian *Khekht;* Amoy *Kek;* repelled, repulsed, and turned back. *The type of this was that which did the same, whether as the Serpent, Crocodile, Alligator, Scorpion, or other Turner-back.* The Darkness as the enemy of Light was naturally represented by the greatest enemy of man. In the recurring phenomena of the Lunar Eclipses, the Dragon of the dark took form in space as the visible opponent of the Lunar Light. In Egyptian, Lunar Eclipses are named *Tennu* or *Tannu*. *Tan* signifies to rise up in revolt and to cut off. The Tan of the Eclipse rose up in revolt and cut off the light. The *Tan* is a well-known typical Monster in the Hebrew writings. One form of it is the Dragon of the deep. *Tan* is an Egyptian name for the Water-Worm (Tanmu) the Destroyer in the Waters, and in Hebrew the *Tannin* may be the Crocodile, a Sea-snake, the Monster of the Mythos or the Dragon of Eclipse. The Hebrew Levia-*than* is the Mythical Monster of the Waters, the DEN-dayan of the Book of Enoch. This name, like that of the *Khekh*, is world-wide, as is the type. In Arabic the *Tannin* is the Serpent. The *Tan*iwha of the Maori are huge Mythical Monsters, of reptile or dragon-shape, who seize and swallow people in deep waters. They lurk in the *bend* of the river, like the Egyptian Dragon in the *bend of the great Void*. That was where the starry procession dipped down below the horizon. The *Tan* is Inner African also as the *Danh* Serpent of Dahome the Great Divinity of the Pantheon. This Serpent or Snake takes two forms, as the Serpent of Earth, the *Danh*-Gbwe, and the Serpent of Heaven, in strict keeping with the dual Serpent and the Twin Truths of Egypt. The Serpent of Earth is first. The Serpent of Heaven is simply called the *Danh*. This is the Rainbow. Danh makes the *Popo* Beads, and showers wealth on men. He is represented as a Horned Snake made of clay and coiled up in a Calabash.[3]

Duno, is the Serpent, in Kasm.			*Dom*, is the Serpent, in Kiamba.		
Dunu	,,	,, Yula.	*Tum*	,,	,, Legba.
Danawe	,,	,, Udso.	*Dom*	,,	,, Kaure.
Dem	,,	,, Koama.			

[1] *Archæol. Americana*, vol. i. p. 351.
[2] Keppel, *Visit to the Indian Archipelago*, vol ii. p. 182.
[3] Burton, *Dahome*, vol. ii. p. 148.

We shall find the Serpent and Rainbow are equivalents elsewhere.

The Scorpion is named *Yatan* in Mampa.

Ndengei is a Fijian Serpent-deity, who is pourtrayed with a serpent's head and body, and who dwells in darkness where he does nothing but crouch in his cave and devour his food. Our own *Thunder* when personified is a form of the *Tan*. The German Sa*tan* was at one time represented by the *red-bearded* Thunder. Sut Typhon was of a red complexion, and this one of the two proper hues was retained in the beard of Thunder and of the Giants, who were images of the *Akhekh*, the gigantic, the monster. Indeed, *Thunder* was one of the giants slain by Jack the Giant-Killer, who cut the ropes that suspended the drawbridge, and when the giant tried to cross he fell. In a later phase the *Thunder* was represented by the Thunderer as *Don*-ner. In English heraldry *Tenny* denotes the dragon's head ; the swallower during an eclipse. One primitive and universal idea was that in its period of eclipse the orb of the moon or sun was being seized, gripped, pinched, choked or swallowed by the monster of darkness. The Tahitians say of the Moon under an eclipse she is *Natua* (Maori *Nati*, to pinch, constrict, throttle), that is, pinched and strangled, showing the idea of the serpent or dragon, the Ahi or throttling serpent. The Caribs held that the demon Mabaya, the enemy of Light was devouring the Moon or the Sun. The Chinese of Kiatka said that eclipses were caused by the Evil Spirit placing its dark hand on the face of the Moon. *Knowing the Monster's mealtime* was the Siamese equivalent for knowing how large an eclipse was about to occur. Sometimes the Swallower was the *Jaguar;* at others, the Dog ; at others, the Wolf of Darkness. When the Sun was eclipsed the Tupis said the "*Jaguar has eaten the Sun.*" "*God guard the Moon from the Wolves,*" became a French proverb. "*My God! how she suffers!*" exclaimed a crowd of French country-folk during an eclipse of the Moon, believing that she was falling a prey to the monster who sought to devour her. To all appearance it was a lunar eclipse that so terrified the Lybians in the time of Neb-Ka the first king of the Third Dynasty, that they once more submitted to the rule of Egypt, against which they had risen in revolt. When an eclipse of the Moon occurs, the Hottentots who are out on an expedition of war or hunting will return home saying, "*We are overpowered by Gauna,*"[1] the dark and evil opponent. The Finns and Laps say the Moon is being eaten, and the primitive conception was preserved by the Mexicans when they also spoke of the Sun or Moon being eaten or swallowed, although they had attained exact knowledge of the cause of eclipses. In an allegorical dance the Mexican priests represented the Sun as being devoured by the Moon.[2] The Moon in the dragon's mouth was likewise an emblem of eclipse in the old British calendars.

[1] Hahn, *Tsuni-Goam*, p. 89.   [2] Humboldt, *Vues*, pl. 56.

This, with so many other mythical types, survived in the Christian Iconography. In the Church of Our Lady of Halle, the Devil or Dragon is depicted as endeavouring to swallow the Bible, which is upborne on the back of an Eagle, the soaring Bird of Light. The Greek *Gorgô*, the Swallower or Devourer, imaged with the Mouth wide open was a continuation of the Akhekh dragon, and the Nakak crocodile, both of which were pourtrayed with the wide-open Mouth, the throttler with its throat. *Gorgeo Negro* or Black Throat was an epithet of the Monster hurled at the Huguenot by the French Catholic. The *Gorgeo* or *Gorge* was personified in the *Gorgô*. And—

N'gorgu, is the Gullet, in Mbarike.	*Gorokub*, is the Gullet, in Buduma.
N'gungulsio ,, ,, N'godsin.	*Gargant* ,, ,, Banyun.
N'koriyon ,, ,, Param.	

The *Gorgon* as Swallower is the—

Karku, an Alligator, in Barba.	*Kurguli*, the Lion, in Kanuri.
Koleko, the Lion, in Dsebu.	*Kurgoali* ,, ,, Kanem.
Koriko ,, ,, Idsesa.	*Gaire* ,, ,, Wolof.
Kurguli ,, ,, Buduma.	

The Gorgon's head was a common type of the grave, or the devouring dark of death, on Etruscan temple-tombs. The first Gorgon would be the Darkness when the livid gleams with petrifying stare made visible a face of ghastly gloom, that looked and lightened, and some victim fell stone-dead, or was turned to stone. The face of Darkness in the orb of the Moon was a projected shadow of the monster of eclipse, the Gorgon. Epigenes of Sikyôn, the most ancient writer of tragedy, in his lost work on the poetry of Orpheus, said the Theologer called the Moon Gorgonian *because of the face in it*.[1] Plutarch quotes Homer as saying that in eclipses the faces of men were *seized upon by Darkness*. He also intimates that evil spirits were daunted and driven away from the lunar paradise by the awful face seen within the orb.[2] When the shadow of the black Aharman was cast over the world, and was beaten back again by the good Spirit of Light, it is said, "*Many dark forms with the face and curls of Azi Dahaka* (the Serpent of Evil) *suffered punishment*."[3] The Dragon or Devil of darkness did not originate in the mere form and look of a "*Cloud that is Dragonish*," nor in a cloud that is supposed to imprison the rain. The blacker the cloud the more certain is it *not* to withhold the rain. These types did not originate in any such child's play with phenomena as the Aryanists have assumed. The struggle of Indra and Vritra, the Devil of darkness, the constant theme of the Vedic poets, is identical with that of the Sun and Apophis, or in the later rendering of Horus and Typhon, in the Ritual. The Vedic *Vritra* is the old Dragon-type of physical phenomena, the Coiler round the Light, no matter whether the light be Stellar, Lunar, or Solar. Indra

---

[1] Suidas, in voc. *Thespis*, Clem. Alex. strom. 5—8.
[2] Plutarch's *Moralia*. " The face appearing in the orb of the Moon."
[3] *Zad-Sparam*, ch. ii. 10.

is a form of the Solar God, whose birthplace is the spot where Vritra lies dead. Vritra is the Coiler round who envelopes and hides the light. *Vri*, to unfold, represents *Pri* (Eg.) to come out, to wrap round; *Prt* answers to *Vrit* (Sans.) and *Varto* (Lat.) to turn in a *reverse* way; but Vritra is also a form of the "Crooked" Serpent of Lightning that never goes straight, like the Hottentot Gama-Gorib, the zig-zagger. In a Karen myth *Ta Ywa* was born as a very little child who went to the Sun to be made to grow. The Sun blew him up until his head reached the sky. He went forth and travelled over all the earth. Then he was swallowed by a great snake. This was cut open, whereupon *Ta Ywa* issued forth to a new life.[1] The Myth evidently relates to the Light of day being swallowed up by the dark typified as the Akhekh serpent. In this the Day-light is treated as a child of the Sun.[2] When an eclipse of the Moon occurs the Akkadian Legends describe the Dragon with the Seven heads, or the Seven Evil Spirits, as rushing on the Lunar orb with intent to destroy its light. With terror the gods behold their lamp going out in Heaven. Bel saw the eclipse of the Moon-God and sent Nebo (Nusku) his messenger to Hea for advice. Hea called his son Merodach, and said, "*Lo, my Son, the light of the Sky, even the Moon-God is grievously darkened in heaven, and, in eclipse, from heaven is vanishing. Those Seven wicked gods, the Serpents of Death, who fear not*," were waging war on the Moon.[3] Merodach overthrows the Seven Powers of Darkness. The Gods do all they can to help the Moon in eclipse, as did their human imitators in all lands, who howled and threatened, and clenched their fists, threw stones or shot their poisoned arrows at the gruesome shadow of danger that turned the Moon to blood, laid the dark hand upon her face or covered earth with the drear dun hues of the solar eclipse. In this representation the Dragon-Slayer is the Solar Hero; but the Solar God, as conqueror of the Evil Power, typified by the Serpent, implies the latest form of the Myth. The Moon that shone by night was an earlier opponent of the Darkness than the Sun, and the earlier Dragon Slayer was Lunar. In the Moon-Myth we find Khunsu the youthful god of the Moon, is especially personified as the Giant-killer, and therefore the con-tender with the Apap *by night* as the Visible Luni-Solar Hercules. But the Lunar Mythos was extant long before the Moon was known to derive its light from the Sun, or the Sun was pourtrayed as descending into the underworld, to fight the Devouring Dragon of Darkness. Thus, when Typhon tore the body of Osiris into 14 parts,

---

[1] *Ta Ywa* places the god *Shieoo* under the earth to support it, and whenever he moves there is an earthquake. *Shieoo* corresponds to the Egyptian Shu, who is the supporter of the nocturnal heaven.
[2] Mason, *Journal of the As. Society*, Bengal, 1865.
[3] Sayce, *Bab. Lit.* 35.

the conflict was between the dark power and the lunar light, during the waning half of the Moon.   One character of Osiris is that of the Lord of Light in the Moon, the reflector of the Solar light.   The fourteen parts are the fourteen days or nights from Full to New Moon, the " obscure half," during which the Dragon of Darkness was dominant.   Hence the type of a *feminine* Dragon-slayer.   In various versions it is the *Woman*, and not her Son, that crushes the Serpent's head.

The Australian blacks tell of a mysterious creature, the Nar-gun, a cave-dweller that inhabits certain places in the bush, especially the Valley of the Mitchell in Gippsland.   He has many caves, and if any one should incautiously approach too near one of these, he is dragged in by Nar-gun and seen no more.   If a spear is thrown at Nar-gun, the spear returns to the thrower and wounds him.   Nar-gun cannot be killed.   He dwells in a cave at Lake Tyers.   *A native woman once fought Nar-gun at this cave*, but nobody knows how the battle ended.[1]

In the Chippewa tale of the " Little Monedo " it is related that there was a tiny boy, who grew no bigger with years, but who was mighty powerful and performed marvellous feats.   One day he waded into the lake and shouted, " You of the red fins come and swallow me."   Here it may be remarked that red fins, or the red, *i.e.*, Typhonian fish, appears in the Egyptian Magic Papyrus.[2]   The fish came and swallowed him.   But seeing his sister standing in despair on the shore, he called to her, and she tied an old mocassin to one end of a string, the other to a tree and threw the shoe into the water.   " What is that floating on the water?" asked the monster.   The boy said to the fish, " Go take hold of it, and swallow it as fast as you can."   The fish darted towards the old shoe, and swallowed it ; the boy-man laughed to himself, but said nothing till the fish was fairly caught, and then he took hold of the line and hauled himself to shore.   When the sister began to cut the fish open she heard her brother's voice from inside the fish, calling to her to let him out, so she made a hole, and he crept through, and told her to cut up the fish and dry it, for it would last them a long while for food.[3]

On the monuments it is the genitrix herself in the character of Isis-Serk, who is placed in command over the Apap Dragon by night, and when he is seen fettered and fast bound, the end of the cord or

[1] Smyth, *Aborigines of Victoria*, vol. i. p. 456.
[2] *Records*, vol. x. p. 145.
[3] Tylor, *Early History of Mankind*, p. 343.   This is a form of the Mythical Jonah, whose phenomenal origin was the Sun, or Fire, that was carried across the Waters by the Fish, probably *Piscis Australis*, which marked the passage of the sunken Sun.   A writer in the *Dictionary of the Bible* (Article, Jonah) remarks with much simplicity—" We feel ourselves precluded from any doubt of the reality of the transactions recorded in this book (Jonah) by the s:mplicity of the language itself, and by the thought that one might as well doubt all other miracles in Scripture as doubt these."   Oh ! *Sancta Simplicitas!*

chain is held in her hands. The genitrix also triumphed over the Darkness, as the "*Woman*" of the Moon who "*guards the forepart of the orb at the paths of total darkness.*" She boasts that the Twin Lion-gods are in her belly, and says she has deprived the darkness of its power. "*I am the Woman, an orb of light in the darkness. I have brought my orb to the darkness, it is changed into light. I overthrow the extinguishers of flame! I have stood! The Fiends have hidden their faces. I have prepared Taht* (the young Moon-god) *at the gate of the Moon.*"[1] In a Chinese Myth the Dragon devours Nine Maidens consecutively. Then *Kî*, the daughter of *Li Tau*, volunteered to go to the monster's cave. She took a sword and a dog that would bite snakes; and placed rice and honey at the mouth of the monster's den. At nightfall out came the Dragon with its head as big as a rice-rick, and its eyes like mirrors, two feet across. The mess attracted it; the dog attacked it in front and *Kî* hacked at it behind until it was mortally wounded. *Kî* then entered the cave and recovered the skeletons of the Nine Maidens whose fate she bewailed, and then she leisurely returned home.[2] The Prince of Yueh on hearing of her exploit, raised her to become his queen. This is a Lunar form of the Mythos in which the Woman spears the Serpent's head, instead of Horus, her son and seed. *Kî* and her dog answer to Isis and her dog in the under-world; and in relation to the Dragon of Eclipse, the Nine Maidens may possibly represent the Nine previous Moons; the Tenth the genitrix, as the bringer-forth of the young Sun-god at the time of the Spring Equinox (Nine Months from the Summer Solstice), when the Moon in her travail wrestled with the Dragon of Eclipse, and this time conquered for the year; or the Nine Months reckoned from the Harvest Moon of the Autumn Equinox to Mesore (Egyptian), the Month of re-birth at the Summer Solstice. It is noticeable that the Marquesans had a Year which was reckoned as Ten Moons, and that in Egypt the Year consisted of Ten Moons, or Nine Solar Months, with an Inundation (which was the Child of Isis), that flowed during Three Months.

There was a stone in the north end of the Parish of Strathmartin, Forfar, called Martin's stone. Tradition affirmed that this was erected on the spot where a Dragon had devoured Nine Maidens, who had gone out on a Sunday evening one after the other to fetch water from the well or spring. The Dragon was said to have been killed by Martin.[3] At Lambton Hall the *Worm*[4] was reputed to drink the Milk of Nine Cows, which correspond to the Nine Maidens or Moons.

[1] *Rit.* ch. lxxx. Birch.
[2] *A Chinese Story.* Notes and Queries, vol. i. p. 148.
[3] Brand, *Midsummer Eve.*
[4] *The "Worm"* was the Dragon in Britain. The Worm is the *Krimi* in Sanskrit; *Kirm*, Hindustani; *Kirmele*, Lithuanic; *Cruimh*, Irish; and in Inner Africa the Alligator is the *Karam* in Kanuri; *Karam* in Munio; *Karam* in N'guru; *Karam* in Kanem; the animal being a real Dragon of the waters.

In one Myth the Light is rescued by the Sun-god, and in the other it is re-born of the genitrix. The "Woman" in the Ritual boasts that she has "*made the Eye of Horus, when it was not coming at the fifteenth of the Month.*" The Eye was the Mirror or Reflector, and the Full Moon was an Eye of Sight that *reflected the Sun.* This was in connection with the origin of the so-called "Eye-goddesses" in Egypt, such as Tef-nut who is named from Tef, the pupil of the eye.

The imagery pourtrayed in the planisphere shows the Woman as the bruiser of the Serpent. On Christmas Day when the Christ, the Buddha, or Mithras was born, the birth-day of the Sun in the Winter Solstice, the constellation of the Virgin arose upon the horizon ; she was represented as holding the new-born child in her arms, and being pursued by the Serpent which opened its mouth just beneath her in the position of being trodden under-foot. The symbolism was applied to Isis and Horus in Egypt ; to Maya and Buddha in India and China ; to the Woman and Child in Revelation, to Mary an Jesus in Rome ; and is still to be read in the signs of heaven, where it is old enough to prove a unity of origin for the several myths.

Alexander Henry in his travels among the North American Indians, relates that when the Mother was travailing sorely in the pangs of labour, like the Woman in Revelation, or the Mother-Moon in Eclipse, and the Midwives grew fearful lest the Child should be born dead, they hastened to catch and kill a Serpent and gave the Woman its blood to drink.[1] Here the origin of the Serpent-type alone will enable us to interpret the custom. The Dragon of Darkness had to be *cut in two* at the crossing for the orb to pass through or the light to be re-born. In Kanuri, "*Dinia fatsar kamtsi,*" for the Day dawns, signifies the Day has cut through. The Solar conqueror, as Horus the cutter-through, is pourtrayed as the wearer of the Serpent's skin for the trophy of his triumph. So in the Algonkin Myth, Michabo, the Solar god, is represented in conflict with the Prince of Serpents who dwells in a deep lake ; he destroys the reptile with his dazzling dart, and clothes himself in the skin of his fallen foe.[2] It was at one time common in England for people to believe that the skin of a snake bound round a woman in travail would ease her labour pains.[3] The Serpent that was slain was the Dragon of darkness, which became the Serpent of Life and Healing *as a type of sacrifice* when

[1] *Travels,* p. 117.
[2] Brinton, *M. N. A.* p. 116.
[3] The Egyptian Magical Texts show that hair, feathers, the serpent's skin, and the "*blood of the mystic eye*" were used as charms of protecting or destroying power. "*Shu takes the shape of an Eagle's wing.*" "*A lock of hair is made to strangle the soul*" of an enemy. Shu prevails by carrying the "*hair of a cow*" the hood of a serpent, and the "*blood of the mystic eye*' The latter denotes what is known amongst certain of our peasantry as "*Dragon's Blood,*" (not the chemical compound used as a kind of *size*) which is employed as a potent love-charm or philtre according to instructions still or lately given by the *Wise Woman.*— *Records of the Past,* vol. vi. pp. 119-120.

the Serpent that was severed at the Crossing was "offered up" on the Cross.

Mr. Ruskin speaks of the "*True Worship*," which "*may have taken a dark form when associated with the Draconian one.*" He assumes some "*primæval revelation*" vouchsafed to a chosen people from the truth of which men lapsed into error; but the Dragon is part and parcel of all the primæval revelation there ever was; the Draconian was the first as the Dragon at the Polar centre still bears witness, and it was the fetishism of the dark because it was primæval. There has been a mental evolution corresponding to the physical, and Mythology retains the means of tracing the progress from the vague darkness through the Stellar, Lunar, and Solar phases of thought into the later light of Day.

When Sanchoniathon says the First Men "*consecrated the Plants of the Earth, and judged them gods, and worshipped the things upon which they themselves lived*, and to which they made libations and sacrifices," [1] his statement is made according to the later thought and mode of expression. "*Consecration*," "*Gods*," "*Worship*," must have been very remote from the minds of the *First Men*.

Augustine has remarked of Hermes Trismegistus, that he affirms the visible and tangible images to be as it were the "*bodies of gods,*" because there are within them various invited spirits. By a "*certain art*" these invisible spirits are made visible in a vesture of corporeal matter. "*This is what he calls making gods.*"[2] Hermes was the great Hieroglyphist of Tradition, the supposed Inventor of Types, and of Typology; the earliest mode of representing things, or making gods. We are now in a position to prove that the earliest "gods" were "elementary powers" which were directly apprehended at first; and to show how they were represented by natural types, in short, how the first gods grew. The Egyptian divinities, as the *Nenu*, of which there is a figure of 8,[3] are only the *types*, or representatives, the fetish-images of powers considered to be superior to man.

It has been assumed that the early Man projected his own spirit upon external nature as the mirror which returned the shadow of himself. But if so, the earliest personifications of natural forces ought to have been in his own likeness, whereas the Devil or Divinity in the human form does not belong to the primary Mythical formation. Powers beyond human were recognized in external nature,—furies of force in whose presence man was but an image of helplessness altogether inadequate to express them. The powers were super-human; their likenesses are pre-human, and with the human advance the types were humanized. We see the Beast transfiguring into the Beauty, when the Mother Nature, who was once a Dragon, a Lioness, a Hippopotamus, a Milch-Cow, a Serpent, changes into

---

[1] Eusebius, *Præp. Evang.* i. 10.   [2] Augustinus, *De Civ. Dei*, 8—23.
                        [3] *B. B.* vol. ii. p. 140.

Uati, Hathor, Neith, or Rennut, as the Goddess who wears the shape of Woman. It is another mistake to imagine that primitive Man began personifying, and, so to say, *entifying* the elements by *conceiving* the *eidolon* of Fire, Wind, or Water. Typology proves that he *did not personify, as his mode of representation.* His process was mainly that of objective comparison. He represented one thing by another ; the invisible force by a corresponding type of power.

The process of representation was that which the logician terms in another application of the words, the "*substitution of similars.*" For instance, having no name for the moon, he saw it as the eye of the dark, and called it the Cat, earlier Lynx or Lioness, whose golden eyes were luminous by night This was in the natural phase ; but the image still served for typifying, when it was known that the Moon was only a reflector of the solar light, because the eye is a mirror. Hence, the Lunar Cat-headed, or Lioness-headed Goddess, became the Eye of the Sun.[1] The primitive man did not animate the darkness or the water with any abstract spirit of destruction. But he realized the less definite Swallower in the most definite form of the Dragon, because he was compelled to think in things. He did not know how the Earth gulped down the stars, or the Water devoured the life, but he adopted the Crocodile and Hippopotamus as forms most palpable. Earth was the visible *cause* of darkness, and therefore it was represented by the Crocodile that swallowed the lights as they went down in the darkness. The Serpent was that which darted death, so was the Lightning. The Hippopotamus was the power of the Deluge broken out of bounds ; the howling wind was the Great Ape in its wrath ; the fire was the flaming Yellow Lion or the Golden Bird that soared aloft fearlessly in the flames of the Sun.

This mode of expressing phenomena was the origin of the primordial types which were continued as mythical, Totemic, divine, and thus we are enabled to see that *typology and mythology are twin from the birth and one in their fundamental rootage.* Primitive men were forced to typify in order that they might know by name these Elemental Energies and non-intellectual Powers, even as they represented their own Totems, and named themselves by means of the animals.

According to the laws of evolution, cognition of the unapparent power as cause of phenomena must have belonged to the latest perception, not the primary ; and it is an axiom of the present work that religious feeling originated in awe and admiration of powers superior to those possessed by the human being, but that the nearest and most apparent were the earliest. The first so-called deities of primitive man may be named Weather-gods. The god and the weather, the

---

[1] The Cat—as *Peht* or *Buto* in Egyptian ; *Pâtu*, Mandara ; *Patu*, N'godsin ; *Budi* in Mimboma ; *Poti*, Maori ; *Bede*, Australian ; *Footie*, Shetland—also brought on the name of the Lioness, which was *Pekht* in Egyptian, the earlier form of the word.

wind and the rain, are often synonymous among the African races. The "*Yongmaa*" of the Akra people is either the Rain or the God. The Divinity, the Heaven, and the Cloud, are synonymous among the Makuas. Rain-Giver is a common African name for the Power above. The savage may have advanced somewhat beyond the elemental stage, but the elements made the primary appeal. Air was the god *Hurakan*, pourtrayed under that name by the Quichés. Certain forces of nature were represented, but not personated, and their representatives became the earliest types of the particular powers. They were not personified in the human likeness ; neither were they of any sex. The Elements are of no sex ; neither were the elementary types, or primordial gods. The seven "*Elementaries*" in Akkad are so far impersonal powers that they are *sexless ; "female they are not, male they are not*" (Akkadian) ; or "*male they are not, female they are not*" (Assyrian). The producer as female is the only one whose sex is determined, and she is the Dragon-horse. The Sun or Moon considered as the masculine in one language and feminine in another, is a result of this indefinite and impersonal beginning with the neuter type which could and did become both male and·female in mythology and language, because it was neither in itself at first. The most perplexing elements of mythology and language originate in this the primary stage of typology, the elementary and elemental. When among the blacks of Australia men are named Wind, Thunder, Hail, Fire, the custom reaches back to this beginning.

The primary gods of Egypt are eight in number. They were gods in space who ruled over Chaos, or failed to rule it, *before the cycles of Time commenced*. According to Herodotus the Eight gods were extant for 17,000 years before the reign of Amasis.[1] These were the eight, however, who existed when Taht had superseded Sut; not the original Eight Elementaries. As before said, the eight gods of the beginning, who consist of the Great Mother and her Seven Children, afford one of the test-types for the unity of origin in mythology. They are found in the British Arthur and his Seven Companions in the Ark. They are found also as the Eight Great Gods of Gaul, and the eight who were represented by the Eight Great Pillars in the Temple on the Island of Fortuna.[2] The Japanese Great Mother, Quanwon, and the seven Shintu Gods also form an Ogdoad; they are sometimes represented by an eight-headed figure. The Maori mythology likewise commences with Eight Elementary Powers, personified as—

Papa (Earth), the Mother who is the foundation of all.
Rangi (Heaven), called the Father.
Tane-Mahuta, Father of forests.
Tangaroa, Father of fish and reptiles.

Haumia-Tikitiki, Father of wild-growing food.
Rongo-ma-tane, Father of cultivated food.
Tu-Matauenga, Father of fierce men.
Tawhiri-ma-tea, Father of winds and storms.

---

[1] Book ii. 43.			[2] *Book of Beginnings*, vol. ii. p. 560.

These are the Genitrix and the Seven Pitris, or Fathers, who were born as her Seven Sons.

In the account of creation inscribed on the Bark Record of the Lenape Indians, the primal power (or powers) rises from the waters eight-rayed. *This precedes and does not represent the Sun.*[1] The number likewise agrees with the Quiché creative powers, who are described as eight in number. These, however, are called half male and half female. The Quiché legends, which tell of the struggles between the rulers of the upper and nether realms, also relate that in Xibalba, the realm of disappearing, the rulers or lords are " *One Death and the Seven Deaths.*" The One and the Seven, just as we find them in the Dragon and her Seven-fold progeny, in Sut Typhon (or the Eight Gods), and in the Divinity of the Templars, *Mete,* whose " *root is One and Seven.*" Ximenes says of these eight reduced deities who had been superseded, as in Akkad and Egypt, " *In the old times they did not have much power, they were the annoyers and opposers of men, and in truth they were not regarded as gods. But when they appeared it was terrible. They were of evil, they were owls, things of darkness, fomenting trouble and discord.*"[2] It was in the *old times,* however, that the Eight had all power, and only in later times were they relegated to their native hell as the Devils of Theology.

In the Latita-Vistara[3] eight heavenly beings are enumerated as *the* Gods or Devas. These are the *Nagas, Yakshas, Gandharvas, Asuras, Garudas, Kinnaras,* and *Mahôrgas,* which are submerged like the ruins of Yucatan beneath whole forests of aftergrowth; but they correspond fundamentally to the Eight Elementaries of Egypt, and can be recovered by the comparative process, because in them the earliest types are retained.

The Vedic Aditi is a form of the primordial genitrix, called in the vague stage of thought the *boundless,* the INFINITE. She also preceded Time and the established order of things that followed Chaos. The infinite *Aditi* is really the non-established, the unopened, or undivided. She has seven sons called the Seven Adityas. The Eight —the genitrix and her seven-fold progeny—when compared with the Egyptian Eight, will be found like them to be the gods of chaos, who existed as *Elementaries* before the creation of Time. The Elementaries of Egypt are likewise represented by the Asuras in India. The Mahābhārata[4] says that in the battle which they fought with each other, the Asuras were the elder brothers and the gods the younger. The gods were of the same parentage as the Asuras, but from a footing of equality they became superior to them.[5] The Asuras were primarily the product of an earlier phase of thought, and were afterwards considered non-spiritual on account of their physical and

---

[1] W. W. Beach, *Indian Miscellany,* p. 21.
[2] Ximenes, *Or. de los Indios de Guatemala,* p. 76 ; cited by Brinton, p. 64.
[3] Foucaux, p. 250, *et passim.*   [4] S'Antip, 1184.   [5] Muir, *Sans. Texts,* v. 15.

material origin. It is the same with the *inferior* and *superior* Hebdomads of the Gnostics.

The Seven who are the Evil Progeny of Tiamat in Akkad, the Seven-headed Thunderbolt, and the Seven-headed Serpent, are also the Seven-fold Storm-wind as one of the Tempest-types of fatal force. They are said to rush from the four cardinal points; they swoop down like a violent tempest in heaven and earth; they are the destroying Tempests, the fiends of storm *on their way to becoming the Maruts of the Indian mythology*, who are Seven at first, corresponding to the Seven in Akkad. They are described as the "Seven with spears." The embryo of the genitrix Aditi was divided into seven parts, and from these sprang the Maruts of the Vedas. As the story is told by Sāyana, the Embryotic Seven were born of Diti, the Divider.[1] In India the Seven were developed into Seven Troops of the Maruts, but they had the same sole origin in nature, and in the typology. It was they who "*stretched out all the terrestial regions and the luminaries of the sky*"; they who "*divided and held the Two Worlds apart.*" The Maruts have the same development from the status of evil destroyers who become supporters of the good god. They fight on the side of Indra just as the Seven Spirits of the Great Bear become the supporters of Osiris. They are likewise particularly associated with the Seven Rishis of the Great Bear. Seven Elements were identified with these Seven Elementaries or later spirits; also Seven Properties in Nature, such as Matter, Cohesion, Fluxion, Coagulation, Accumulation, Station, and Division.

And although the present writer is unable to fathom or follow the subject in India, he is satisfied that a mass of mysticism in Buddhism is the result of this beginning with the Elementaries. For example, *A-Kāsa* is called the Fifth Element, the subtle ethereal fluid, which is the *vehicle of sound*, and the peculiar vehicle of life. Then it becomes the Creator (Brahma or other god) identical with Ether. As *Kāsa* (Sans.) is the becoming visible or apparent, *A-Kāsa* is the invisible or unapparent. But in this Elemental stage the unapparent is not God; it is only atmospherical. Ether is represented by the Cone as the fifth sign in the diagram, in which the square signifies earth; the circle, Water (heaven as the water above); the pyramid or triangle, Fire; the cresent, Air, and the cone, Ether, which as fifth was once the *quint*essence of the elements. The full number of these is Seven in India, Egypt, Britain, and other countries. The Seven Elements from which came the Seven Spirits of mythology, are identified by the British Barddas, as Earth, Water, Fire, Air, Ether (or Vapour), Blossom (the Seminal principle) and the Wind of Purposes (or the Ghost). A sixth element was identified by the Hindus with Bala-rama the representative of

[1] Sayana on *Rig. Veda*, 8, 28, 5. Muir, *Sanskrit Texts*, vol. iv. p. 256; vol. v. 147.

masculine virility.   Bala denotes force considered as a sixth form or mode of manifestation.   It is the innate strength of the male, the semen virile.   This is the sixth element, the fructifying principle of the Druids named blossom.   The seventh was the soul and summit of the rest.   Elementary types (or gods) were founded on the Elements, and they are symbols of the elements which were typified.

It was argued in a preceding volume that the Jehovah-Elohim of Genesis comprised the same pleroma of Eight gods.   This is corroborated by the Gnostic Pleroma of the Eight, consisting of Sophia the genitrix and her Seven sons, who are named—

1. Ialdabaoth, Lord God of the Fathers (Pitris).
2. Iao, Javeh.
3. Sabaoth, Hosts.
4. Adoneus, Lord.
5. Eloeus, God.
6. Oreus, Light.
7. Astanpheus, Crown.

And this Pleroma of Eight is acknowledged by the Kabalists as constituting the totality of אהיה,[1] the Existent,[2] also termed *Chivth* (חיות), which may be rendered by Circle or Pleroma.   The Eight are likewise Phœnician, as Sydik and the Seven Kabiri, although the father (Sydik) has been elevated to the place of the genitrix, in accordance with the later thought; as it was with Ptah and his Seven Assistant Gods, or the Phœnician Illus and his auxiliaries, the Elohim.

There are Seven Spirits called Archangels in the Parsee Scriptures, who have severally the charge over man, animals, fire, metal, earth, water and plants.[3]   But the Amshaspands are the primary form of the Persian Seven.

The primæval progeny of the genitrix also survived as the Seven Governors in the Divine Pymander where they are said [4] to be both male and female in one, whereas the Akkadian Seven are neither male nor female, because the types had not then bifurcated into sexes.   The illuminatist, Jacob Böhme, will show us how the ancient genitrix and her seven elementaries were continued in the teachings of the mysteries with a more abstract rendering of the Gnosis or Kabalah.   He says, of the Seven primary or "Fountain Spirits," and the feminine producer, "We find seven especial properties in nature whereby this only Mother works all things" (to wit, *desire* which is astringent, *bitterness*, cause of all motion, *anguish*, cause of all sensibility, *fire, light, sound*, and *substantiality*); "whatever the six forms are spiritually that the seventh is essentially" . . . "These are the seven forms of the Mother of all Beings, from whence all that is in this world is generated."[5]   Which proves the survival and continuation

[1] Ex. iii. 4.
[2] Ginsburg, *The Kabalah*, p. 11.
[3] *Shayast La-Shayast*, ch. xiii. 14 ; ch. xv. 5.
[4] *Hermes Trismegistus*, b. ii.
[5] *Signatura Rerum*, ch. xiv. pars. 10, 14, 15.

of the primitive thought and typology in the theosophy of European mystics. When the male creator takes the place of the Mother in Egypt the Seven are described as the Seven souls of the God Ra or Osiris. So in Böhme's theosophy, "The Creator hath, in the body of this world, generated himself as it were *creaturely* in his qualifying or Fountain Spirits, and all the stars are nothing else but God's powers, and the whole body of this world consisteth in the seven qualifying or fountain spirits."[1] Man was created by, or in accordance with, these Seven, "*therefore* man's life hath such a beginning and rising up as was that of the planets and stars."[2] "But that there are so many stars, of so manifold different effects and operations, is from the infiniteness that is in the efficiency of the Seven Spirits of God in one another, which generate themselves infinitely,"[3] and "man's property lieth in sundry *degrees*, according to the inward and outward heavens, viz., according to the Divine manifestation, through the seven properties of Nature."[4]

The student of Böhme's books finds much in them concerning these Seven "Fountain Spirits," and primary powers, treated as seven properties of Nature in the alchemistic and astrological phase of the mediæval mysteries. These Seven revolve wheel-like in their workings with fire (that is the Har-Sun or Solar Soul) in the centre of all,[5] and their wrestle for supremacy is the working of generation or creation. The followers of Böhme look on such matter as the divine revelation of his inspired Seership. They know nothing of the natural genesis, the history and persistence of the "Wisdom" of the past (or of the broken links), and are unable to recognise the physical features of the ancient "Seven Spirits," beneath their modern metaphysical or alchemist mask. A second connecting link between the theosophy of Böhme and the physical origines of Egyptian thought, is extant in the fragments of *Hermes Trismegistus*. No matter whether these teachings are called Illuminatist, Buddhist, Kabalist, Gnostic, Masonic, or Christian, the elemental types can only be truly known in their beginnings. When the prophets or visionary showmen of cloudland come to us claiming original inspiration and utter something new, we judge of its value by what it is in itself. But if we find they bring us the ancient matter which they cannot account for, and we can, it is natural that we should judge it by the primary significations rather than the latest pretensions. It is useless for us to read our later thought into the earliest types of expression and then say the ancients meant that! Subtilized interpretations which have become doctrines and dogmas in theosophy have now to be tested by their genesis in physical phenomena, in order that we may explode their false pretensions to supernatural origin or superhuman knowledge. As

[1] *Aurora*, ch. xxiv. p. 27.   [2] *Ibid.*, ch. xxiv. par. 39.
[2] *Ibid.*, ch. xxiv. par. 28.   [4] *Mysterium Magnum*, ch. xvi. par. 15.
[5] *Aurora*, ch. xxvi. 48, 49.

Elementals the Seven (with the Mother, Eight) were not *Intelligencers* to men ; they were seven overpowering, overwhelming forces recognized in the dragon, the scorpion, the leopard, or lion, the lightning, the hurricane and their kindred agents of violence, destruction, deluges, diseases, and death, who were the born children of the darkness, external *and internal*. The types themselves suffice to demonstrate the fact that they do not represent any personal beings conceived behind phenomena, and causing the on-goings amid which man found himself to be going on. The Serpent emaning itself from its own mouth images no personality but a condition of being, perceived by man, an existence for ever self-emaning and self-renewing which the Egyptians termed " *Renewal, coming of itself.*"

Primitive Man did not begin with concepts of cause beyond the visible phenomena. He did not postulate a Devil that made the darkness. Darkness from the depth was the Devil. And the darkness brought forth its brood of baleful beings, inimical to him. As the female was the obvious bringer to birth it followed that nature or space or the abyss of night should be first represented as the genitrix. In Egypt this abyss, the source of all things, also called the hole of the snake, serpent or dragon, is the Tepht ; *Tepht* modifies into *Tet* (Eg.), the English *Depth ;* Welsh *Dyved ;* Cornish *Defyth*, for a desert, wilderness, and the *Toyt*, as the Shetlanders call their mystical sea, with the same meaning. These are Inner African names for the abyss of darkness, the night.

Defid,	Night,	N'godsin.	*Tétan*,	Night,	Bagbalan.	*Dûdu*,	Black,	Eki.
Dʒfid	„	Doai.	*Otttan*	„	Mbarike.	*Dûdu*	„	Dsumu.
Itoafiu	„	Mhe.	*Dûdu*,	Black,	Egba.	*Dûdu*	„	Ife.
Têto	„	Kum.	*Dûdu*	„	Yagba.	*Dîdu*	„	Dsekiri.
Têtan	„	Koama.	*Dûdu*	„	Yoruba.	*Didi*	„	Ebe, &c.

The Egyptian *Tepht* is one with the *Tavthe* of the Babylonian cosmogony. *Tiamat* and *Tavthe* are the same name by interchange of m and v, and the *Tavthe*, as place, is the abyss of source, the hole of the dragon. *Tavthe* personified is the Mother of the Gods. Tiamat personified is the dragon, Mother of seven wicked spirits. This was the Egyptian *Tep*, *Teb*, or Typhon, one of whose types was the crocodile, *Sevekh*, the dragon of the deep. It was a dragon from the deep that first taught Fo-hi the distinction of sexes, as it is stated in the Chinese sacred books. The Hottentot snake called the Gâbeb, or *the one which lives in a hole*, is likewise the typical snake of the abyss. It is the snake supposed to dwell in every fountain of the land, and if it be killed the fountain will dry up.[1] This FLOW-ER forth identified with the

[1] Hahn, p. 77. Dr. Hahn, explains that in Khoi-Khoi, *Au*, is a root, meaning to flow, or bleed, from which he derives *Aub*, the Snake. and *Aus*, a Fountain. Then the Khoi-Khoi forgot this original signification and " Mythology got hold of Aub and Aus, and made sure that in every fountain lived a snake," p. 79. This is the Müllerite interpretation of Mythology as a disease of language, and a misapprehension of the meaning of their own words made by all the people of the past. The motion of the Serpent made it a type of that which *flows*—water flows,

issuing water of source is one with the dragon Tiamat, or Typhon, but it has not yet passed out of the serpent phase into that of the genitrix of the abyss. In Egyptian, however, the *beb* is the hole of the abyss and *Kebeb* signifies the source.[1]

At the spot in Syria where Typhon went underground the river Orontes had its origin. In German folk-tales, when Winkleried kills the dragon, a rivulet issues out of its hole. When the swollen torrents rush down from the Swiss mountains after a thunderstorm, the people say the dragon has come out. This identification of the dragon with the water shows the beginning with the water-flood as the destroyer! The water comes out of the abyss, the Tepht (Eg.), which is the " Hole of the Snake." Thus the beginning with the dragon or serpent of source in the abyss is common to Akkad, China, Shetland, Egypt and Inner Africa. The serpent and dragon became interchangeable as types, but they can be distinguished from each other.

Professor Fraas of Stuttgart has reconstructed the Swabian Lindwurm for the Natural History Museum of that capital. This dragon combined the bird, lizard, kangaroo, and pachyderm; and could fly, crawl, leap, and swim. It is very curious for these Four are a form of the Hawk (bird), Crocodile (lizard), Ape (kangaroo), and Hippopotamus (pachyderm), which represented the Four elements and Four quarters, and the four (with variants) were compounded in Typhon the mythical dragon. The Monster of the abyss in the beginning, the crocodile or dragon of the west, that swallowed the setting stars, was preserved in the eschatological phase as the devourer of the souls of the damned.

The Egyptians had their museum of monsters in the underworld of the dead. Here the primitive types of destroying power served as imagery in the eschatological stage, where they were intended to strike terror as they had done on earth. This may be gathered from the following text, " Greatest of spirits, red-haired Monster, coming from the night, correcting the wicked by creation of reptiles."[2] Amt, the devourer in the Hades is depicted with the *head of the crocodile*, the fore part of the lioness, the hind quarters of the hippopotamus. The ancient genitrix of the abyss was thus turned into the evil Typhon of the Egyptian hell. Another compounded monster, the *Sesh-Sesh* dragon, is a *crocodile* in front and a serpent behind. The crocodile is the dragon of the waters. In Revelation, when the young solar god is born, the dragon is described as emaning a flood from its mouth; that is equivalent to the end of a period called the deluge. *Hydra*, the sign of the inundation in Egypt, will also

---

blood flows—here we shall find the *flowing* Serpent in a mystical sense—and the Serpent flows along the ground. When the fount dries up the typical Serpent ceases to flow, and is said to be found in the fountain dead. This is according to a mode of typology, not a disease of language. Cf. the מקור דמים or fountain of blood for the feminine pudenda, Lev. xii. 7, which is likewise the Tepht of the snake.

[1] Pierret, *Vocab.*   [2] *Rit.* Ch. cxlvi.

explain why the serpent or dragon is the symbol of the flood. Also the red dragon of fire or lightning will account for the alternative type of an ending in a conflagration.

In times of drought the Chinese beseech the dragon of rain for wet weather. They affix on the houses pieces of paper containing prayers and also the likeness of the dragon of rain. Images of the dragon are carried in procession, and if no rain follows the dragon is smashed[1] into small pieces. The symbolical dragon is somewhat of a. crocodile with wings, and the crocodile was a type of Typhon, the genitrix of the Seven Stars. Sevekh, the crocodile, is the capturer. This image of the genitrix was continued in Sevekh, her son. The crocodile was a type of darkness, even to the tip of its tail, which is a sign for black. Therefore it is feasible that the mythical dragon of the abyss, the waters of source, was *founded on the crocodile*, if not on the geological dragon. There was a great fish which the Greeks called "Dracon," and the crocodile is the fish and dragon under one type.

We find another reason why the crocodile should have been the natural prototype of the mythical dragon with the lidless eyes. Plutarch tells us one of the Egyptian reports was that the crocodile *" is the sole animal living in water that hath his eyesight covered over with a thin transparent film which descends from his forehead, so. that he sees without himself being seen by others, in which he agrees with the First God."*[2] The crocodile was a type of the first goddess, Typhon. And if there be a *first god* in Egyptian mythology it is *Sevekh*, her son, who bore her image as the Crocodile. That is Sevekh (or Khebek, whence Kek) was *the* one of the Seven (the Eight with the Mother included) who was elevated to the primacy in the oldest, the Typhonian, Cult, as Sevekh Kronus the earlier form of Seb Kronus.

Assuredly no apter image of the jaws of darkness, as the earth or grave, silent, wide open, and waiting to devour, could have been adopted than this figure of the tongueless Crocodile to form a basis for the mythical Dragon. Darkness being the first producer personified as the Dragon or the Genitrix, and the earliest modes of phenomena that most impinged on primitive man being inimical and opposed to him and therefore Evil, the first Adversary as the Dragon of Darkness was *accredited with a progeny of adversaries*. These were reckoned as Seven in number; the Genitrix herself being either the First or the Eighth. From these we shall derive the Dragon with Seven Heads.

The Egyptian mythology begins with the Eight Gods that ruled in Am-Smen, the Place of Preparation or of Chaos. Their domain was the timeless Night which preceded the reign of Order and the dawn of day. Egyptologists term them " *Elementaries,*" *faute de mieux.* They are looked upon as elementary forces of nature personified as

---

[1] Huc and Gabet.   [2] *Of Isis and Osiris.*

Gods; or, rather, some French Egyptologists,[1] who are not Evolutionists, look on these primordial figures as mere types that were *adopted by the Egyptians* to express the various attributes of *the one God*.

The allusions to these "Gods" of the Beginning are obscure and obscured; but they were the *birth of Chaos*, they were *primary*, and they were *Typhonian*. They are denounced as the *Betsh*, the Children of Revolt and of Inertness, corresponding in the latter phase to what Taliesin terms the "Sluggish Animals of Satan." The same place of birth and rebirth in the Ritual is called *Smen*, the place of the Eight, in the Stellar phase; *Hermopolis* or Sesennu in the Lunar, and *Annu* (Heliopolis) in the Solar Myth, in accordance with the order of development from the Elementary stage. The Eight then are composed of the genitrix Typhon and her brood of Seven. These re-appear in Akkad and Assyria as the Dragon *Tiamat* and the Seven Children of Revolt, the Seven Wicked Spirits that constitute the Seven Heads of the Dragon of Eclipse, or the Devouring Dark. *The first* is a Scorpion, or the Sting-bearer of Heaven, *the second* is the Thunderbolt, *the third* a Leopard or Hyena, *the fourth* a Serpent, *the fifth* a raging Lion, *the sixth* a rebellious Giant who submits neither to god nor king, *the seventh* the Messenger of the fatal Wind. The scorpion, serpent, leopard, thunderbolt and typhoon are sufficient to prove the representation of those powers that were adverse to man. That the Serpent was his mortal enemy—whence he became a supreme type of his immortal enemy—that the Scorpion stung, whether called the scorpion of the dark or of fire, or the Stingray of the sun, that the Thunderbolt carried death in its stroke, and the burning breath of the Typhoon or Simoom was fatal, were among the simplest, most fundamental facts in nature. And of such were the seven-fold progeny of the Dragon of Darkness. The Seven appear in the Egyptian Ritual, where two lists of their different names are given. In one they are called, *Het-Het; Ket-Ket; The Bull, who never made smoke to dwell in his flames; Going eating his hour; Red Eyes; Follower of the House of Ans; Hissing to come forth and turn back, seeing at night and bringing by day.*[2] These may be paralleled with the Akkadian Seven, thus:

AKKADIAN SEVEN.	EGYPTIAN SEVEN.
1. The Scorpion or sting-bearer of heaven.	1. Het-Het.
2. The Thunder-bolt.	2. Ket-Ket.
3. A Leopard or Hyena.	3. The Bull (or Beast) who never made smoke to dwell in his flame.
4. A Serpent.	4. Going eating his hour.
5. A raging Lion.	5. Red eyes.
6. A rebellious Giant.	6. Follower of the House of Ans.
7. The Messenger of the fatal Wind.	7. Hissing to come forth and turn back; seeing by night and bringing by day.

---

[1] Champollion-Figeac, Chabas, Pierret, Lenormant, and others.
[2] *Ritual*, ch. xvii.

The first is *Het-het*, and *Hetet* is the Scorpion. HET means to afflict and injure. *Kheti* is the Serpent of fire. In the Inner African languages the Scorpion is

Hudu, in Biafada.	*Kutu*, in Musentandu.	*Nkutu*, in Mimboma.
Kutu, in Nyombe.	*Kutu*, in Basunde.	

Ket (Eg.) signifies to shake or quake, and the duplicate *Ket-Ket* would be to shake very much, as does the Thunder. "*Going eating his hour*"[1] is the Serpent, which became the type of Time eating its own body. "Red-Eyes" renders the rage of the Lion. The rebellious Giant is likewise a perfect parallel to *Hapi*, the Giant Ape, one with *Kapi*, or Shu, the Egyptian Nimrod.

Now, if we take the so-called "Four Elements" of Fire, Water, Earth and Air, *which are inseparable from four of these Seven Elementary Types* that became the Gods of the four quarters, and try to realise the earliest perception and configuration of these as governing powers, we must not think of the *Har* Sun typified by the Solar Hawk, the glorious God of later times—but the *Har* Fire, the hell of fire, the consuming element, the devouring fire, and we have the Solar Serpent or Stinger in its elemental phase. The sun in inner Africa was looked upon as a source of torment. Sir Samuel Baker affirms that the rising of the sun is always dreaded in Central Africa and the "*Sun is regarded as the common enemy.*"[2] This corroborates the statement of Herodotus respecting the Atlantes of interior Africa, who regularly "*Cursed the Sun at his rising, and abused him with shameful epithets for afflicting them and their land with his blasting heat.*" Even by night the air is often like a heated oven.

When a Christian missionary was expatiating on the attributes and the goodness of his God to the Liryas, a central African tribe, they refused to allow the goodness. On the contrary, they said He must be very angry and wicked for He sends death and the sun that scorches up our crops. "*Scarcely is one sun dead in the west in the evening than there grows up out of the earth next morning another which is no better.*"[3]

All who attempt to interpret the ancient thought without the doctrine of development have now to reckon with evolution and go back to begin again. This beginning in physical phenomena was continued in the eschatological phase by the Egyptians who held that all evil proceeded from the place of sunrise, and all good, healing and life came from the land of the setting sun. The Lion, another symbol of fire and one of the *Elementaries*, was a type of terror. To signify the *Terrible*, says Hor-Apollo, the Egyptians make use of the lion because this animal, being most powerful, terrifies all who behold it.[4]

---

[1] Hor-Apollo, b. iv. 2. See also the *Book of Hades.*
[2] Albert Nyanza, vol. i. p. 144; Herod. b. 2. p. 216; b. iv. 184.
[3] Sepp, *Jerusalem und das Heilige Land*, ii. p. 687.   B. i. 20.

The serpent-goddess *Heh* especially represents the Element of Fire . that was first signified by the lightning of the serpent's sting. But the serpent itself was recognised before a goddess of fire or heat was personified. She is called the Maker of Invisible Existence Apparent. But it was the Serpent itself that first revealed and made manifest in pain and death the fiery power that existed invisibly. They did not *begin* with a goddess behind phenomena who made use of a serpent to bite, and thus revealed *her* invisible presence. That may be the non-evolutionist view, but is an utter reversal of the actual process. Primitive men commenced with phenomena themselves, and not with the postulate of powers beyond *their* powers. This is provable. Physical and mental evolution corroborate each other according to the doctrine of development. Trees, stocks, and stones preceded the human-shaped images of the divinities. Primitive men were not carvers and sculptors, and the early temples were without statues. And just as the shapeless stone preceded the statue, so did these elementary powers evoke recognition and fear, the earliest form of a religious feeling before man had any idea of A God. Heat or fire was expressed by means of types. The fury of the Solar fire suggested the Fang and the Sting. The name of the *Sirocco*, the very breath of fire, identifies itself with *Serk* (Eg.), the name of the *Scorpion*, which further shows the hard form of *Serf* (Eg.), the blast, a burning breath.

If the early men had commenced with a Concept of Cause behind phenomena, *they would never have personified it as female at all.* This Mould of Creation, or rather of Evolution, was only possible because they began with the simplest observation of natural phenomena. *If they had conceived a God it would assuredly have been in their own* image, not in that of womankind, whether typified by the dragon, serpent, water-horse, or cow. That African furnace of fiery heat did not offer much incentive to the so-called "*Solar Worship !*" On the contrary, in thirty-six African languages the name for Hell is the same as for fire, and fire is frequently synonymous with the Sun, as in the type-names *furo, Mu,* and *Har, ôro* or *Ala.* The Sun is

Horu, in Idsesa.	*Oru*, in Yoruba.	*Oru*, in Yagba.
	Har, in Wadai.	

This being a synonym for fire and Hell, will show us how and *where* the Solar *Horus* began as one of the Elementals who were considered to be the foremost enemies of man. The Sun was the physical fount of theological Hell-fire. The name of Hell, in Yagba, signifies the "*Heaven of Ashes*," and Heaven was often looked on as a Hell of fire. *Thus Har* (Horus) *the later Solar God, was one of the Seven Elementaries as the terror of fire,* and the word *Har* (Eg.) signifies terror, to terrify, as did the zig-zag lightning and the deadly sting-ray of the Sun. *Har* then was a primary power born of the

Hell of Inner African Heat, who became the Sun-God Har, or Horus, in the Egyptian mythology.

What was the Earth to the primitive perception ? Another form of the Devourer and Swallower of the light and the lights as they went down from heaven. The Egyptians denote eating, says Hor-Apollo, by pourtraying a crocodile with his mouth open.[1] The Stars are represented as being swallowed by the Crocodile of the West. This was the Crocodile of Earth, the Swallower, when it was not known that the earth was a rotating globe. The crocodile is *Sevekh*, the Capturer. Sevekh signifies to noose, catch, the place of execution. Sevekh was the Terror of Earth, and another of our *Elementaries*. The Element of Air was potential death before it could be recognised as the breath of life. The burning blast, the simoom or typhoon, first made itself felt and acknowledged, in such forms as the African hurricane, known as the terrific *Kamsin*, which stirs the desert to its depths, sets its surface moving in a vast suffocating, overwhelming storm of sand, and mixes up the elements of wind and water, fire and dust, in a chaos of confusion that blots out heaven for the time being and seems to blind the sun. This was the Air in motion, personated by Hurakan, the Quiché deity. The rudest awakeners appealed to the dawning consciousness of man, not the gentle breeze and genial warmth, not the fertile fruitful earth and fostering dews of heaven ; not the light but the lightnings ; not the voice of birds and murmuring of rippling waters, but thunders, the voice of tempests, and the roar of devouring beasts.

One of the *Elementaries* is the Monkey-God, the Kaf, or Kânt. As *Hapi* he is one of the Four Genii, and Hapi is the earlier Kafi, the Giant-Ape, a type of Shu. Shu, as a god, is a representative of Wind (later Breath and Soul), and Wind, in its fury, is the Typhonian tempest. This type of the Kaf-Monkey is the personification of anger or fury in the hieroglyphics, and the *Kafau* are the Typhonian Desolators by name. Water was not *first* appreciated as one of the two Elements of life. On the contrary, it was that which devoured in drowning, and swallowed up life like the hippopotamus. Hence the hippopotamus that could crush a canoe in its ponderous jaws was *the typical terror of the Waters*, and yet a form of the Bringer-forth from the Waters, the Dragon of the Abyss, the Mother of the Seven. Water was that which broke forth wide-mouthed as the Dragon of the Deluge. The indefinite beginnings of Mythology are defined enough in physical phenomena like those in which the working types originated as representatives of the seven primary forces of the Mother Nature. We can also perceive how some of these *Elementaries* found a representative *Voice* for their power. The great Ape is such a howler that it was continued as a Voice of the Unknown, a speaker for the gods of later times. So that the Image of Anger, which chattered or howled

[1] B. ii. 8o.

furiously, represented in visible form the passion swelling in the
throat of destroying Power and the howling of the Hurricane. The
Kaf-Ape was the animal type of the Breathing Power when it was a
fiend of the storm, the Element that was the origin of the God of
Breath or Soul, as Kafi-Shu.

The fire of the sun in Inner Africa found fitting voice in the Lion,
with its yell of rage, awful as if the sky had gaped audibly, and the
solar furnace was heard to roar. Wind and heat were ungraspable,
ungaugeable, inexpressible, thence the need of the Ape and Lion as
sensible equivalents; hence, too, the origin of that typology which
preceded verbal speech. The Lion is another of the Four chief
elementary types. One of the first voices of Darkness, or the Unknown, that arrested attention and awakened terror would be Thunder.
It has been said that Thunder was the primordial divinity. Undoubtedly it was the voice of one of the earliest *Elementaries* or
powers recognized in external nature. Hor-Apollo says, " *When the
Egyptians would symbolize a voice from a distance, which is called by
them Ouaie, they pourtray the voice, i.e., Thunder, than which nothing
utters a greater or more powerful voice.*" [1] In the Magic Papyrus the
" *Bad Dog*" is addressed thus : " *Up, bad dog ! be thy face the gaping
sky ! Usaf-Hu thy howling.*" That is, Be thy howling Thundrous.[2]
The Thunder would be the Dog, Jackal, or Wolf of howling Darkness, the voice afar off. Captain Beechy describes the " *sudden burst
of the answering long-protracted scream*" of a pack of jackals " *succeed-
ing immediately to the opening note*" as being " *scarcely less impressing
than the roll of the Thunder-clap immediately after the flash of
lightning.*" So thought the early men who made the Jackal a typical
announcer, a voice of darkness, of prophecy in heaven, that foretold
the coming night and the inundation in the distance. The Jackal,
or Dog, is also one of the seven types, which were continued when the
Elementaries had passed into the Star-Gods of Time.

A divinity like Baal-zebub was a devil from the first; a devil in
physical phenomena before he became the Satan in a later sense. He
is called " God of Flies." But the *Zebub* Fly makes the name more
special, and shows the Inner African origin. The *Zebub* is described
by the Rabbins as a fly that stings to madness. It is one of the chief
plagues of the stinging things produced by nature when *in heat* at the
time of her midsummer madness, that settle on man and beast like
showers of fire, or darts of death, or serpents of the air. Bruce gives
us a striking account of the Æthiopian and Abyssinian Fly, called the
Zimb, which is a frightful scourge. As soon as the Zimb appear, and
their buzzing is heard, he says the cattle forsake their food and fly,
until they drop at last and die of fright and fatigue. The natives are

[1] B. i. 29.
[2] Rendered " tremendous " by M. Chabas (*Records of the Past,* vol. x. p. 156), who
did not compare Hor-Apollo's explanation.

compelled to quit the "*black earth*," and take refuge on the sands of Atbara, and there remain until the plague has past. The elephant, rhinoceros, and hippopotamus are forced to roll themselves in mud to coat their hides with an armour that will resist the stings.[1] The *Zimb* is identical with the Hebrew *Zebub*, the m in one word interchanging with b in the other. In their translations the Arabs rendered *Zebub* by the *Zimb*. So in Assyrian the word *Zumbi* appears as a variant of Zebub. In the Deluge Tablet, when the sacrifice is offered, it is said, the gods swarmed over the sacrifices like *Zumbi*, to *devour* the offerings. In which the *Zimb*, or *Zebub*, is thus cited as the typical Devourer. This is the Fly mentioned by Isaiah, "*And it shall come to pass in that day that the Lord shall hiss for the Zebub that is in the uttermost part of the rivers of Egypt.*"[2] It is the *Zebub* of Death.[3] In the Inner African languages the *Zimb* is synonymous with the Devil and Hell. *Nsumbi* is the Devil in Kasands; *Ndsumbi* is the Devil in Undaza; *Ndsombau* is Hell in Bumbete; *Zume* is Hell in Dahome; *Ozohim* is Hell in Igu; *Simo* is Hell in Nalu. The *Sami* (Eg.) are the typhonian Devourers, the Devils that swarm and buzz and torture, like the *Zimb* (flies) in the Egyptian Hells. The Hebrew *Tsamim* are the Devourers,[4] and the *Zamzummim*[5] are the mythical giants. The *Zimwi* in Swahili is an ogre, ghoul, or other evil being said to devour men. The *Zimu* in Zulu-Kaffir are cannibals believed to live in the far North, as a race of long-haired people. The *Sami* buzz and sting as spiritual beings in the Hells of the Damned because the *Zimb* first made hell upon earth in Africa; and in Baal-zebub (or Bar-Typhon) we find the devil-type on its way to divinity.

Monumental Egypt can tell comparatively little of the vague period. The Shadow of Darkness and the terror of the physical Typhon had passed away when her monumental record comes into view. The prior phases of feeling and thought are only reflected for us in the types with which she speaks to us of the remoter past. Her Eight Elementaries born of chaos, as the genitrix and her Seven-fold brood of nature-powers, were superseded as the Children of Inertness, the Demons of Revolt, or, rather, their types were transformed into the *Vahans* of later ideas. But outside of Egypt, all round the world, we find races still under the shadow of the early darkness, who yet utter the fears of the human childhood, for whom the *Akhekh* is a real terror, and not a type to interpret. We see by the old *Ukko* of the Fins how the *Akhekh* or Dragon of Darkness would pass into a God of Thunder and Lightning. So closely is *Ukko*, the *old one* associated with thunder and lightning, that the Fins call a thunderstorm "an *Ukko*," and when it lightens they exclaim "*That is Ukko*, there he is striking fire."[6] This god in Egypt was Kak, or Khebekh whence

[1] Bruce, *Travels*, vol. i. 5; vol. v. 191.   [2] Ch. vii. 18.   [3] Eccl. x. 1.
[4] Job xviii. 9.   [5] Deut. ii. 20.   [6] Castrén, *Finn Myth*, p. 39.

Sevekh, the Crocodile of Darkness, and under the name of Sevekh, he can be recognized in the Carib deity *Savacou*, a god of the dark, the Lord of Thunder and Lightning and Hurricanes; the very Typhon in a masculine form. He blows fire through his tube, and that is lightning; he sends the great rain, and is thus identified with the Dragon of the Waters. *Savacou* was said to have been *one of those men who are now stars*.[1] Darkness and its divinity were forms of the typical "*Old One*," as in *Ukko*, and in the Inner African languages the "*Old One*" is

Kokohe, in Puka.	*Ekui*, in Eafen.	(Wa) *Kuka*, in Lubalo.
Okok, in Konguan.	*N'kokun*, in Mbofon.	(Wa) *Kuka*, in Songo.
(U) *Kug*, in Yasgua.	(O) *Gugu*, in Igu.	(Dsa) *Koka*, in Kisama.
Akuku, in Kupa.	(Wa) *Gugu*, in Kasands.	(Wa) *Kuku*, in Nupe.
(U) *Akuku*, in Basa.	*Keokolo*, in N'goala.	(Wa) *Kuku*, in Esitako.

The Yorubans have a God of Thunder named Shango, whom they call the Stone-thrower (Dzakuta), who casts the thunder-hatchets down from heaven.[2] Now, as Darkness was the primal producer or parent, the first voice with which she spoke to man was thunder. Out of that darkness leaped the lightning, and the lightning was thought to deposit the thunder-axe, bolt, or stone from heaven, the cloud-cleaver and Celestial *Celt*, which preceded and possibly *suggested* the manufactured weapon. For the Celt adze (named Anup) is the Nuter-sign of divinity, and this came from heaven as lightning born of darkness. Such was the kind of *revelation* made by external nature to primitive man. The stone-axe gave him supremacy on earth, and that weapon was first hurled at him hot and hissing from the thunder-clouds of heaven. An instance of a thunder-stone having been found on the spot where the lightning had struck has been given in the "*Reliquary.*"[3] The peculiar smell of it when broken showed that it was lightning-born. *This was a form of the Axe which the Great Mother gives birth to in various American Myths as her First Child.* In Egypt it is identified with Sut-Anup. *Sut* also signifies the fire-stone. Anup is a name of the *Celt*-axe. Anup was the Jackal or Fox, and the Japanese still consider the *Celt*-stones, which they find, to be weapons of an evil spirit, whose type is the Fox; this, therefore, was Sut-Anup, one of the *Elementaries*, the Jackal (Fox or Wolf) of Darkness. "*Stone-Head*" is the name of the Serpent that guards the sixth of the Seven Halls of Osiris.[4] The huge Akkadian Serpent with Seven heads is the Thunderbolt of Seven Heads in the Hymns.[5] When the Serpent-Lightning darted out of the cloud it buried itself in the earth, leaving its stone head in the aerolith or smelted sand, the Thunder-hatchet, *the ideographic Nuter that was continued as a type of the primordial Power which dwelt in darkness and manifested itself by*

[1] De la Borde, *Caraibes*, p. 530.
[2] Bowen, *Yoruba Lang*, p. 16; Burton, *Dahome*, vol ii. p. 142; Smithsonian Contr. vol. i.
[3] F. C. Lukis, vol. viii. p. 208.   [4] *Ritual*, ch. cxliv.   [5] *Rec.* iii. 128.

death and destruction as one of the Elementaries.   In the Inner
African languages the Stone and Iron are named *Tan* like the Dragon,
the Serpent, the Cutter or Destroyer.   It is difficult, says Dr. Arthur
Mitchel, to see why to nearly all the cultured nations of Western
Europe a stone-celt becomes a Thunderbolt, and a flint arrow-head an
Elf Dart ; and why these relics of a complete or comparative barbarism
should be venerated in the midst of civilized and cultivated people.[1]
The reason is *because they* ARE *the* typical *Thunderbolt continued ;
the Divine Thunder-axe repeated by human workmanship.* " Cut (or
engraved) stones " is the Nicaraguan name for the images of Mixcoatl,
the *Cloud-Serpent ;* an evident allusion to the products of thunder.
The cut or engraved stone becomes the Egyptian Kart and British
Celt of the Neolithic age.   The Guaranis of Brazil name the Celt or
stone-axe *Korisko,* which means lightning.   The Pueblo Indians go
out to look for the *Celts* after a thunder-storm.   The shooting star is
likewise identified with the aerolith by the modern Greeks, who call
the Celt-stones and star-hatchets, ἀστροπελέκια.[2]   Pelekys was a title
of Dionysus as Lord of the Thunder-stone-axe.   Pliny reports that
stones which had fallen from heaven were invoked by the Romans
for success in war.[3]   The Africans about Axim, on the Gold Coast,
still call the Lightning-stone, or that which passes for it, by the name
of *Lebonua,* the Axe.[4]

Of course one original type of the Lightning-stone is represented
by various kinds of stones that may be adopted as charms, fetishes,
or medicine.   The thunder-bolt, which was first of all a stone,
remained a well-known type of primordial divinity, *that is of destroying power.*   When the Japanese preserve the Celt-stone or Fox-hatchet
in their temples as relics of their divine ancestors, the *Kami,* the act
identifies these with the elementary gods, the chief of whom was the
power that lightened and thundered and hurled the bolt from out
the black cloud.

The Thunder-axe being the form in which the lightning quenched
itself in the earth ; this may possibly account for the superstition
against cutting wood with an axe near the fire for fear of *cutting
off the head of the fire.*   This is held by the Sioux Indians, the
Tatar and other races.   The first stone-axe was the head of fire,
which may, have suggested the Arrow-head, and the superstition
appears to recognize this origin of the Fire-axe.

The Akhekh Gryphon is a Dragon with wings.   Wings and feathers
furnish a type of fire in the later Solar Bird.   But the Winged Lightning
was first, and this suggested the well-known winged Dragon, or Bird
of Thunder.   The Bird-Dragon was a common Chimera of the middle
ages.   A French Swan-Dragon unites the Bird's head and Serpent's

---

[1] *Past in the Present,* p. 22.
[2] Hyde Clarke, *Prehistoric Names of Weapons,* p. 148.
[3] Pliny, *H. N.* 37.   [4] Captain Burton.

tail. The typical Monster on the Scottish stones is sometimes Bird-headed. According to Philo-Byblius [1] Epeis had translated an Egyptian work into Greek in which it was asserted that the first Divine nature was the Serpent metamorphosed into a Hawk. This created Light by opening its eyes and Darkness by shutting them. It took feathers *or flame* to fly with, and the Dragon, Darkness, took wings of flame when it lightened ; these were added to form the feathered Serpent and fiery dragon to express motion in the air. The *Tupan* of the Tupi Tribes of Brazil is the Typhon of Egypt by name, and Typhon is the Akhekh dragon. Tupan is the Thunderer and Lightener which rears its dragon-shape of Darkness, flaps its wings, thunders, and flashes with infernal light. The Zulus of Natal have been known to buy peacocks' feathers at a very high price because they identified them as belonging to the Bird of Thunder. That is the hieroglyphic peacock-headed Akhekh or Gryphon of Darkness.[2]

The Hebrew Thunder-god, the male divinity, is the same *Kak* or *Iach*, who was *continued from the Dark into the Stellar phase, thence into the Solar as the Sun of the Night*. He also rode upon a Bird of Thunder. He "*thundered in the Heavens*" and "*rode upon a Cherub and did fly*." He "*made darkness his secret place ; smoke issued from his nostrils and devouring fire out of his mouth. Darkness was under his feet and he hurtled stones and coals of fire*."[3] He is called "Light-ning-sender." It is the same God of Thunder, the stone-caster, flying all abroad on his bird, as that of the Yorubans and Central American Indians, the same as Hurakan with his bird Voc. The Mandans attribute the thunder and lightning to a vast and awful Bird of Heaven, which is either the Manitu himself, or his messenger. The Dacotahs are said to explain thunder as the sound of the cloud-bird flapping its wings.

By degrees, however, the aspect of the Elementaries was modified as the face of Nature became less terrible. This can be traced. Hurakan (our Hurricane) is the name of the Quiché primordial

---

[1] Philo-Byblius, *apud*, Euseb. *Præp. Evangel*, i. c. x. p. 44.
[2] One form of the Egyptian *Akhekh* is a gryphon with the winged body of a beast, the tail of a serpent and head of a peacock. This is the Winged Dragon, which became the Mythical *Cockatrice*, a compound monster having the head of a cock, the wings of a fowl, and the tail of a serpent or dragon. It was said to be so named because of its origin from the egg of a cock hatched by a serpent. From this comes the cock's egg of our Mythology. It was the egg of the *Akhekh*, serpent, or dragon, and allowing for the *Peacock* instead of the *Cock*, the *Akhekh* sign survives as the *Cockatrice*. The bird-headed, serpent-tailed Akhekh appears in India as the figure of Viratarupa, the universal-monarch-form, with a human hand for one fore-foot, the elephant's foot for another, the two hind feet being those of the tiger and horse.[1] This bird-headed and serpent-tailed *Akhekh* was continued into the Christian Iconography. A picture of the Temptation of Christ, from a French miniature of the twelfth century, shows Satan as a survival of the Akhekh Gryphon, with the head of a *Cock*atoo instead of the Peacock, and a serpent for his tail.[2] The Peacock as a bird of ill-omen in England still suffers for its symbolical character.
[3] Ps. xviii.

---

[1] Moor, *Hindu Pantheon*, pl. 93.　　　[2] Didron, fig. 70.

power. *Hurakan* in Quiché means a stream of water that pours straight down. In the hieroglyphics (Eg.), *Hura* is Heaven, over, above. *Khan* is the Typhonian Tempest with the determinative of water pouring straight down from Heaven, and Khan is water. Typhon and Typhoon are identical. Hushtoli, the Storm-wind, was the original Choctaw word for Deity. "Mixcohuatl" the "Cloud Serpent," a chief or the chief of Mexican gods, bears the name of the tropical whirlwind. Such representation was primal and the later God of Air and Breath was a modification of the demon in his first fierce phase of the terrible tornado. Lightning, with its crooked fires, world-shaking voice, and dart of death, made its first appeal to fear. In a Hottentot Hymn of Thunder we read

> " Son of the Thundercloud:
> Thou brave loud-speaking Guru!
> Talk softly, please,
> For I have no guilt!
> Leave me alone!
> I have become quite weak with terror,
> Thou, O Guru!
> Son of the Thundercloud!"[1]

By degrees it was answered with defiance. The Namaquas still shoot their poisoned arrows at the Lightning and bid it begone. The Khoi-Khoi and the Damaras are reported to curse the Thunder, and to shoot their arrows at the Lightning, dart for dart. So the black Tatar tribe of the Urjangkut were in the habit of threatening the Thunder and trying to scare off the Lightning.[2] Lastly, it was observed that Thunder was the especial announcer of Rain, and the beneficence of this deadly power was recognised. The Hottentots think that its downpour of deluging water has a fertilizing effect on the female. In accordance with which idea it is the custom for the girls, after the festival and rites of their coming of age have been celebrated, to run about quite naked in the first *thunder-storm* that follows. This wash of rain over the whole body is held to make them fruitful and to ensure lusty children. The Hottentot custom shows the baptism of Fire and Water as a rite of generation and fertilization. The Lightning represents the fire that vivifies and the Thunder-Rain—which some Africans call a "He-Rain"—the Water of Life. English boys have a game called "Running through Fire and Water" in which the runner is beaten and buffeted as he hurries down their ranks. Here, then we can trace another of the "Elementaries" (if not two—fire and water) passing from the first stage of destroying power into that of the fertilizing and beneficent influences or Gods. The Crocodile, Sevekh the Capturer, becomes a type of tractability in Egypt, and is considered the purifier of the sacred

[1] Hahn, *Tsuni-Goam*, p. 59. *Guru*, is Thunder. *cf.* Kheru (Eg.), a voice, to utter.

[2] A. Bastian, *Zeit. für Ethnologie*, p. 380. 1872.

Nile. The howling Jackal (Sut-Anup) typifies the messenger Mercury, the prophet of the Dog-star and Inundation; of Sunset and Sunrise. The Ape-image of Ire and Choler serves as a type of Shu, the God of Breath.

A great mass of the primitive Mythology remained in the vague and elementary condition in which the principal figures are powers of the Earth and Heaven, Wind, Water, Fire, and Thunder, Scorpion, Lion and Serpent. But, in Africa these became definite in their Egyptian Types, by means of which we can follow their development from the elementaries of Chaos and Space into Celestial Intelligencers; the tellers and fore-tellers of time and season to men; the Divinities of the later Pantheon. The primary Seven (or Eight) were continued as Types of Power and adapted to convey other ideas until at length they attained the status of Gods in relation to the celestial phenomena in the sphere of *Time*, where " *The Gods were seen in their ideas of the stars, with all their signs, and the Stars were numbered with all the gods in them.*" [1] Seb, the Star, is the sign of god as well as the Soul or Spirit. So the idea of god expressed by the Assyrian word *Ilu* was originally represented by the sign of a star. The star is also the symbol of Seba for worship and adoration. In this phase the gods (or types) became Kronian; the Ili, Ali, or Elohim, who were the auxiliaries of Kronus.

Damascius in his "Primitive Principles" says, " *The Magi and the whole Aryan nation* (or the Medes) *consider, as Eudemos writes, some* SPACE *and others* TIME *as the universal cause out of which the Good God as well as the evil spirit were separated; or as others assert, Light and Darkness, before these two spirits arose.*" [2] These "two spirits" being the Ahura-Mazda and Angro-Mainyus of the Avesta.

Plutarch fears that if he unfolded the secrets of certain constellations it would be declaring war *against length of time.*[3] The Serpent called " *Going eating his hour*" (one of the Elementaries) was a sort of time-symbol, but the first perception of time was that of mere lapse and "renewal, coming of itself," when there were no means of *measuring* its periodic return. " *They* (the human race) *had no certain sign for Winter, for the flowery Spring, or fruitful Summer, but did everything hap-hazard, or without judgment, until I showed them the risings of the stars and their settings.*" [4] *The Divinities proper, then, were born in the second stage as keepers or tellers of Time and Season.* The Elementaries, or brute forces of Nature, may be said to have obtained their Souls in the Stars. Hence, as Plutarch says, the Dog-star is the Soul of Isis; Orion is the Soul of Horus; and the Bear is the Soul of Typhon,—Soul and Star being synonymous in the Egyptian word Seb. In this way the seven

[1] Hermes Trismegistus, b. iii. 6.   [2] Haug, *Essays.* p. 12. West.
[3] *Of Isis and Osiris.*   [4] Æschylus, *Prometheus Bound,* 454—7.

non-intelligent powers, monsters, giants, blind adversaries, became intelligent Spirits, or Starry Souls, as tellers of time. Much of the mythology of the savage races has survived from the first vague stage. But even with these, as in Inner Africa and Australia, the star-gods are the messengers of periodic time, and intelligencers to men, according to their risings and settings. The genesis of the first gods that were endowed with intelligence as the tellers of time, because they represented its various cycles, is illustrated by a magical text in which they are threatened with dissolution if they do not perform what the invoker wishes. "*You shall be undone, you cycle of gods! There shall no longer be any earth; there shall no longer be the five supplementary days of the year.*" Thus, if time is no longer kept there will be an end to the gods born of cycles.[1] The Elementaries had warred and contended in space as representatives of the evils found in phenomena *before Time existed, and it was the bringing of certain symbols out of Space into Time that caused them to be transformed from types of Evil into images of Good*, or *separated* and distinguished as good and bad. The first Serpent or Dragon was altogether Evil, but by degrees it became an emblem of Good. This may have partly arisen from the discovery that some snakes are harmless. According to Clot Bey the supreme type of the Good Serpent in Egypt, the Royal Uræus, is not poisonous. The Zulus have two familiar spirits each, a good and a bad one, which are represented by two different snakes, one being harmless. The Serpent in Egypt, Chaldea, India, America, and Europe, is the Good Spirit generally; the Agathodæmon. Therefore the type appears to have passed out of the phase of the terrible at the time of the various migrations. Hence we meet with both but chiefly with the good dæmon. The serpent became pre-eminent as a type of time in many phases. Time was the foundation of an established order of things, and Time, as *Seb*, is identical by name with the Serpent. The Australian Aborigines have traditions of a gigantic Serpent that created the world by a blow with its tail.[2] That is a fading reflection of the serpent with the tail in its mouth. By bringing the head and tail together the circle-symbol was shaped which denoted endless continuity. The Australians make the meeting-point a blow. Seb, the name of time, means a turn, a revolution, and the turn of the serpent round the pole and the return of Hydra denoted a year, the same as if it were reckoned by the Great Bear and the heliacal rising of Sothis. This revolution was represented by the Serpent's Egg. The Serpent lays eggs and coils itself round them for incubation, therefore the Serpent was made a type of the gestator, as it coiled about the Egg. But this is not the most recondite form of the Serpent's Egg. The god Ptah as the figurer of a cycle of time is said to *make the Egg of*

[1] Renouf, *Hibbert Lectures*, p. 212.
[2] Ferguson, *Tree and Serpent Worship*, Introd. p. 54.

the Sun and Moon. That is by representing the Soli-lunar revolution. The Egg was then the solid figure of a circle of time. Thus when the Serpent (Draconis) turned once round the Pole-star or revolved on its Eye, it was fabled to have laid an Egg, the Egg of the primary year in Heaven. This was the egg emaned from the mouth of the serpent, as Ptah was said to have been from the mouth of Khnef, one of whose types is the serpent; the mystical egg of the Druids which the serpent is said to evolve at a particular moment on one night of the year. The Egg of the Serpent was a year; an *Egg* and an *Age* are thus synonymous, and this type of a year is extant in the Egg of Easter. A serpent emaning an egg from its mouth was figured by the Mound-Builders as one of their vast *Relievos* in Adams County, Ohio. It is over 1,000 feet in length with an oval, egg-like figure within the open mouth.[1] Mr. Phryne claims to have traced a similar design in an earthwork found in Argyllshire.

Popular belief preserves many of the precious relics of the past, but they are of a strange fashion now and need re-setting. One of these may be found in an Egyptian Calendar for the year 1295 A.H., or 1878 A.D., published in Alexandria. In this the reader is told that on December 19th, "*Serpents become blind,*" and on March 24th, they "*open their eyes.*"[2] For serpents we have to read the Serpent of the Year, the dual symbol of the Two Truths of Periodicity which were represented by the nine months of gestation, and the three months of the inundation; or by the serpent seeing during nine months and being blind the other three. The month Mesore (the re-birth of the River) is found typified by Horus the Elder with a snake in his hand. The inundation was also called the *Burial of the Serpent.* The blind serpent is the sloughing serpent. During the change of its skin, the serpent may be said to go blind. English readers will remember the story of the great boa "Bess," of the London Zoological Society's Gardens who was so nearly blind in her period of sloughing that she swallowed a blanket, which caused her death.

The sloughing and blindness of the serpent is here represented by the Sun in the Three Water Signs. The length of time assigned to this phase is exactly three months plus the five black or negative days of the intercalary period of the Epagomenæ; and these negative days are rightly added to the phase of negation. This Serpent of the Year that sees during nine months and is blind during three would, in folk-lore, take the form of the Serpent-King's Daughter, who had a nine-headed Nâga appearing from the back of her neck, and when her husband cut it off she was blind.[3] The Serpent is a type of Two Times, Two Phases, Two Elements, the Two Truths on account of its sloughing. Also, the Quiché name for lightning is *Cak-ul-ha,* that is, fire coming from water, and the serpent of both fire and water is *one*

[1] Baldwin, *Ancient America*, p. 29, fig. 9.   [2] A. Moures, p. 24.
[3] *Voyage de* Hiouen-Thsang, ii. 141.

in the Serpent of lightning, a production of Two Elements. The primitive observers must have seen with much satisfaction that serpents and snakes had the habit of eating themselves—or rather each other. The royal Basilisk of Egypt has a reputation for devouring snakes. Hor-Apollo says of the serpent, "*Moreover it every year puts off its old age with its skin, as in the Universe the Annual Period effects a corresponding change, and becomes renovated. And the making use of its own body for food implies that all things, whatsoever that are generated by Divine Providence in the world, undergo a corruption into it again.*"[1] The self-eating and self-renewal of the serpent made it the most perfect image of Time (Kronus), who was fabled to devour his own children by eating them.

The Great Serpent called the Devourer with the coils is depicted with twelve human heads on his back. He is borne on twelve forked sticks and twelve stars denote the twelve hours of darkness which the monster typifies. This Serpent of Night is called "*The Serpent that begets twelve little ones to eat by the hours.*"[2] And on a limestone tablet in the British Museum there is a bas-relief of a large serpent and twelve small ones which shows the generation of the twelve hours of night.

Ra says "*Listen, Hours! I call you to eat (make) your repast. Rise, Reptile! Live on what comes forth from it. Your office* (that of the Hours) *is to eat what the Snake brings forth, and to destroy what comes forth from it.*[3] The Serpent of Night with twelve heads for the twelve hours of darkness appears in a Russian Myth as the twelve-headed Snake, "Usuinya," which steals the golden apples from the King's garden, and is slain by Ivan the Prince, the Young Solar Hero, or Horus who was with the twelve-headed serpent all through the night. Here, the Golden Apples represent the light, the fruit of the Sun, and the Snake is the evil devourer, not the good guardian of the Garden or Tree. The Myth of a Deity who swallows his own children is found amongst the Bushmen, Zulus, and the Blacks of Australia. In one of the African versions the God or Being who swallows his Daughter is the divinity of the Planet Jupiter, which will be identified as that of Seb-Kronus. Time eating his progeny was represented by the Egyptian Observer of the hours. Hor-Apollo tells us that in signifying an Horoscopus the Egyptians delineated a Man "*eating the Hours. Not that a man eats the hours, for that is impossible, but because food is prepared for men according to the hours.*"[4] The Horoscopus was an image of Kronus eating his Children, the Hours, Days, Weeks, and Years. The same mode of measuring time survives in England where the Law students still continue to "*eat

---

[1] Book i. 2.
[2] *Book of Hades; Records*, vol. x. p. 101.
[3] *Ibid.* p. 103. Duemichen. *Tempelin-schriften*, i. 24. Lepsius, *Aelteste Texte des Todtenbuchs*, 13. Champollion, *Monts.* pl. 123. [4] B. i. 42.

their terms." The numbers of these is that of the Decans and Duodecans. *Thirty-six* dinners are eaten by a man who has a degree and *seventy-two* by him who has not. The Inner African (Yoruban) formula for may you live long, or enjoy long life, is, " *May you eat Old Age!*"

In the story of the Wolf and Seven little Kids, found in Grimm's *Tales*, the Wolf swallows six of the family, and the Seventh conceals itself in the clock-case. But he has swallowed them whole, and they are still alive within him, and whilst he is sleeping the mother of the Goats rips open the monster's hairy coat and lets out her little ones. Then they fill his belly with stones and sew him up again. The little Goats are the Seven Days of the Week, identified with time by means of the clock-case. But, according to the present interpretation, the type was derived from the Seven Stars of the first time, the Seven of the Bear who, with their Mother, the genitrix, were the Eight Gods of the Beginning and the creators of time. The Wolf is a type of *Seb*, and bears his name in Egyptian, he *is* Seb, a planetary form of Kronus.

In the present stage of language we have a separate word for almost every shade of meaning. Some words will do double duty, but scarcely need to be called upon. At an earlier stage one word or sound had to express divers ideas, and that is still the status of many words found scattered in language generally. But a type like this of the serpent was made use of to express many various ideas. When we use the word serpent directly, it has only one meaning. It has a second when we use it figuratively. Language, however, was all figure at first, and there were very few of these figures or types to express the sum-total of ideas or intentions. Of these the Serpent was the most primal and important. It was in itself an archetypal polyglot. Every Serpent set in heaven represented a different idea, chiefly relating to time and season. The Four Elements had each their Serpent. *Bata* is the Soul of the Earth ; *Heh* and *Kheti* are Serpents of Fire. *Nef* represents Breath, *Hydra*, Water. One Serpent typified Matter ; another, the Hawk-headed, a Soul. The dual phase of feminine periodicity was usually signified by the Double-headed Serpent, or the Two Serpents. " *Paint Two Snakes,*" says Perseus, " *the place is then sacred."* In Egypt, the Double Uræi constituted the Sacred Crown of Maternity. The Two Truths of the Motherhood, that of feminine pubescence and gestation, were signified by the Two Serpents, or the double one. It is a habit of the serpent to roll itself round and form a spiral heap with its head atop. The serpent built the primal pyramid with its eggs, and then coiled round the conical pile to hatch them. That was a sight never to be forgotten. Hence the Serpent was also a type of the gestator, as in Rennut, the Goddess of gestation, who coils in the shape of a serpent about the unborn child. She is a Serpent first and a Woman afterwards. In some representations she is both, therefore the Mythical Serpent-Woman. As such, she is the Goddess-serpent of goodness, who is depicted, amongst other forms, as a Serpent below with a Woman's head and bust above. In her Serpent-shape she coils about the shrine of Breath in ten loops. These form a figure of 10, denoting the Ten Moons of gestation.[1]

The Serpent-Woman, as genitrix of the human race, is to be met with under various names. According to Tanner's narrative, the Grandmother of Mankind, *me suk-kum me go kwa*, was represented indifferently by an Old Woman and a Serpent. The Mexicans gave the Serpent-form to the Mother of the human race, one reason for this being that in their annals the first woman whose name was translated by the old Spanish writers, "*the Woman of our flesh*," is always represented as accompanied by an enormous male Serpent, and in the Mexican mythology *Cihuacoatl*, the Goddess-parent of primitive man, was also called the Serpent-Woman. The Rabbi Moses affirms that the name of *Ihvh* has the meaning of half-serpent, half-human. In the previous volume it was shown that *Ihvh* (Jehovah) was the Egyptian genitrix named *Kepu* or *Kefa*, and is identical with Chavvah or Eve, who is identified by the Rabbins with the Serpent-Woman. *Kefa* is also pourtrayed as the Goddess of gestation with the serpent on her head.

When Ahura-Mazda formed the Garden of Delight, the Eden of the Avesta, the first thing created in opposition by the Dark Mind was the *flowing* Serpent (*Azhim raoidhitem*). This is the Serpent in Paradise which is represented as tempting the Woman to sin. Its original nature is shown by that epithet of flowing or running. This was thought by Haug to refer to the ejection of venom. Others have turned the Serpent into *Rain*. It is the exact equivalent of that menstruation with which the Dark Mind opposes the Good Creation in the same Fargard.[2] This Serpent typified the "*Moist Substance*," or primæval matter of the Ophites, that which was so often fabled to be eaten in order that spirit might become *fleshed* and embodied. It *was* the Serpent of Rain, of Wet, in the occult sense, as the alternating type was the Serpent of Heat, Fire, Spirit, or the Head of the Hawk.

This was the Dragon that taught Fohi *how* the sexes were divided. The Lizard interchanges with the Dragon or Serpent, and the Tasmanians have a legend of a lizard which *divided the sexes*. It is related or referred to by the Lubras with much significance and merriment.[3] The Australians credit the lizard with being the discoverer of marriage. That is, the Lizard, like the Serpent, was the type of feminine pubescence. In one Australian myth a Snake is said to sever the Tree of Life, so that it could walk off in human fashion as the male and female. In this the Snake is the divider, because

[1] Hay *Collection*.   [2] V. 17.   [3] Bonwick, *Tasmanians*, p. 189.

it was a type of menstruation. The Lizard, in Maori, is the *Moke*. *Moke* signifies to be separated, set apart (during the period). *Moku* is the first person singular, the individual discreted by the *Moke*, which divided sex at first. *Moko*, the Lizard, is also the name of tattoo marks, and the lizard is an Egyptian ideograph of multiplying and fertility. This co-type of the Serpent is also found among the Semites as the mythical Lizard Tzab. Vast length of life is attributed to it in the Arab proverbs, and its cunning or wisdom is frequently referred to. As Seb (Eg.) for the reptile, it has the name of Time. The Gnostic Ophites knew the reason why they honoured the serpent. It was because the primal pair derived from it a knowledge of the mysteries.[1] It was a symbol of that which divided the sexes, as the lizard was with the Tasmanians.

Casalis, in his book on the Basutos,[2] speaking of their mysteries and the rites performed at the time of young-woman-making, says that " *Girls from twelve to thirteen years of age are also subjected to a rite, to which certain tribes give the name of circumcision, but which more resembles baptism. They are committed to the charge of certain matrons, whose duty it is to watch over them for several months ; these women first lead them to a neighbouring stream, and then into the water, and sprinkle them. They then hide them separately in the turns and bends of the river, and, telling them to cover their heads, inform them that* THEY WILL BE VISITED BY A LARGE SERPENT. *Thus these poor daughters of Eve have not forgotten the form taken by the arch enemy to deceive their mother. Their limbs are then plastered over with white clay, and over the face is put a little straw mask, an emblem of the modesty which must henceforward rule their actions. Covered with this veil, and singing melancholy airs, they daily follow each other in procession to the fields, in order to become accustomed to the labours of agriculture, which, in that country, devolve especially on their sex ; in the evening they bring back a small fagot of wood. Neither blows nor hard treatment are spared in the vain hope of better fitting them for the accomplishment of the duties of life. They frequently indulge in grotesque dances, and at those times wear, as a sort of petticoat, long bands composed of a series of rushes artistically strung together. The natives probably find that the rattling of this fantastic costume forms no disagreeable accompaniment to the songs and clapping of hands in which they indulge.*"

The Serpent is here the type of the period which arrives with feminine puberty, and is the teacher still of the human nakedness. Hence the symbolical petticoat made of rushes. The clay and the mask signify the transformation into womanhood, the slough of the Snake being typically turned into a garment.

One of the Rabbins relates that when the old Serpent shed his

[1] Epiphanius, *Adv. Hæres*, 37.
[2] P. 268.

skin presently after the fall of man, the Creator made a garment of it to clothe Adam and Eve.

The Kaffir story of the girl who disregarded the custom of *Ntonjane* shows the serpent in relation to the pubescent period. When the girl came of age, instead of remaining the customary twelve days in seclusion, she was tempted by her companions to go with them and bathe in a stream. As they came out of the water they saw a snake, near their clothes, covered with black blotches. This the girl made a mock of, and scoffed at it, whereupon it grew angry and would not restore her mantle, but bit her and caused her to become of the same hideous colour as itself. She was cured and made beautiful as at first by being washed white with milk.[1] The riddle is easy to read, according to the typology of the Two Truths. The fountain of milk was the sign of Motherhood, a natural prototype of the White Crown, which was the symbol of the Second Truth or Time.

The Serpent's visit is responsible for various stories like the following: The wife of Publius Scipio was *barren for many years*, until she despaired of issue. One night when her husband was absent she found a large serpent in his place, and the soothsayers informed her that she would bear a child. A few days after she showed signs of conception, and in ten months (lunar) gave birth to the Conqueror of Carthage.[2]

The Serpent which determines the chastity of Priestesses, as in the Temple of Lanuvium,[3] sixteen miles south of Rome, was that which proved they had not entered the period of gestation or earned the right to wear the double Uræus of the *Maternal* Crown. In short, they were not pregnant, and therefore not disqualified to serve as chaste virgins; this fact being revealed by the mystical Serpent.

The Serpent type of periodicity in its most hidden mystery and meaning may be seen in the Hindu sculptures. In these the Nâga is pourtrayed at the back of the human figures, with its hooded crest over-topping and overlooking the human head. Sometimes it is single, at others the serpent has five heads. In one of these pictures the back of the body is turned towards the spectator, and the Nâga Snake, single-headed, is *visibly proceeding out of the human body*. The serpent's head towers over the human, and its tail is in the place of the Two Truths in their most secret significance, and of the dual phase of feminine periodicity.[4] The Serpent thus issuing, if five-headed, would denote the five days' flow; if nine-headed, the nine solar months of gestation; if ten-headed, the ten lunar or menstrual periods that make the nine solar months. In this picture the Serpent is finally unwound to its last hiding-place, with the tail in the human *tepht* (Eg.), the hole of the Snake, the *ru* (Eg.) of life, the abyss of

[1] Theal, *Kaffir Folk-tales*, p. 64. [2] Aulus Gellius, lib. vii. cap. i.
[3] Ælian, *Varia Historia*, ix. 16.
[4] Ferguson, *Tree and Serpent Worship*, pl. 24, fig. 2, from Sanchi.

source, which was personified as Tep or Typhon, and reproduced by name in the Pueblo Ar-*tufa*. In the Mysteries, the Snake's hole and circle was the place of transformation. The Initiates went through the passage and the process of the sloughing snake, the *Hefa* (Eg.), and cried *Eva*, and were called the *Hivim*. *Votan*, as related by Brasseur de Bourbourg, tells how he, the son of the Snake, entered

 a subterranean passage that ran to the very roots of heaven. This was "*un ahugero de colubra*," or Snake's hole. The Snake's hole or circle, represented by the coiling snake, was the *Kuklos anakhes* of the Egyptian Mysteries called the Circle of Necessity and the inevitable circle. This circle of the transformation of the snake was the period of gestation, and the Hindu sculpture re-unites the serpent with the human origines. The sloughing of the serpent was performed in the stripping naked of the devotees to be clothed anew. Proclus states that in the most holy mysteries the mystæ were divested of their garments to participate in a divine nature.[1] The new robe was the garment of salvation, and it was accounted sacred to the last, never to be cast off till worn out; and if possible the mystæ were buried in this raiment in which they had been divinely invested when their life was serpent-like renewed. The serpent was the great emblem of Mystery in the Mysteries, and this picture will show us one reason why. It was adopted as a type of feminine pubescence on account of its sloughing and self-renewal, and the symbol of re-clothing and re-birth in the Mysteries was its final phase.

On the sarcophagus of Seti I. there is a picture of the serpent borne by nine gods in a line reaching from head to tail. This serpent of nine is *Nenuti*, the cord, in which the elect souls, the *re-born*, are bound up for ever, and saved in the fields of heaven. The number is ideographic, and it makes the cord analogous to the collar with nine beads denoting child-birth.

When the *Nachash* (or Tannim) was lifted up as the Saviour on the Cross, whether by the Hebrews in the wilderness or the Mexicans in their sacred processions, the Dragon of Darkness had passed out of its primal phase and become the Good Dæmon, which was looked up to in the Temple of the Jews until the image was cast out by Hezekiah. The Pueblos still hold in reverence the Great Snake to whom Montezuma, Moses-like, commanded them to look for life.[2] The Dragon retained its character of Good Dæmon with the Chinese, leaving the Serpent to bear the curse of the Eschatological change. Chinese Genii, when their earthly work is done, still

---

[1] Taylor's *Jamblicus*, note, p. 148.   [2] Bancroft, v. iii: 173.

ride to Heaven on the Dragon's back.[1] With the Japanese likewise, the Dragon is reverenced as an Agatho-Dæmon. Saturn also was designated the " Dragon of Life." The Good Dragon or worm was worshipped at Poictiers, as an Agathodæmon, under the name of the " Good St. Vermine."[2] This change may be traced to two causes : one of these being the modification of ideas concerning phenomena, as Man himself began to slough off his original darkness. As an illustration of this change, we may quote the Assyrian *Atalu*, which is the name for Eclipse; a reduced form of the Akkadian *An-talu* for heaven-darkness.

In Egyptian *Atalu* denotes something that is unreal, fantastic, and a sham. The Akhekh Dragon of Darkness and Eclipse is the determinative. This once typified the devouring Monster of the Dark, whose coming was looked upon with awe. But the *talu* or darkness that stole, swallowed and ran off with the Moon, was discovered to be only a shadow after all, hence *Atalu* the fantastic, the sham, the unreal. The *Deluder* of the early time, whether as the Shadow of Night or eclipse, is now known to be a delusion. Having passed through them so often with impunity, men find out the hollowness of their bugbears and bogies. At first when the Sun and Moon went down they were swallowed by the devouring Darkness. The time came when it was known that the *same* Sun and Moon were reborn of the Darkness, and thus men began to *see through it*. We find in the Eireks-Saga (3 and 4) that when Eirek journeyed toward Heaven he came to a bridge of stone that was guarded by a Dragon whose jaws he boldly entered ; whereupon he found himself in Paradise. He had passed through Death typified by the Dragon of Darkness. So was it with the Darkness of Eclipse.

We see that when men discovered their fears of the Darkness were vain the old *Kak* was turned into a laughing-stock. The *Khakh* in Egyptian is the old man, the fool, the blind. The *Kaka* in Sanskrit is a cripple. This is the Scottish " *Chache-blind-man*," who cannot catch anybody in his darkness ; the Welsh *Cachgi*, for the fool and coward ; the *Gec* and *Gouk*, who are made fools of on Old Fool's Day. The *Kak* (Darkness) being thrown off like a Night Mare, the French *cauchemar ;* it was made fun of in various pastimes, such as Blind-Man's-Buff, and sending the *Gouk* on the Fool's errand. The deposed potentate was looked upon as the literally " damned Fool." It was the humour of the young World in the spring-time of the year to laugh at the old *Kak* or *Age*, or the cast-off darkness of winter, and make mocking grimaces behind its back and dramatize its impotency. The *Jack*-o'-Lent was one form of the old *Kak*. In Franconia the Puppet that was pelted was an image called " *the Death*," and the sport was the " *Expulsion of Death*."[3]

[1] Dennys, p. 81.　　　　[2] *Society of the Antiquaries of France*, v. i. p. 464.
[3] Brand, *Mid-Lent Sunday*.

The second cause of the change was in the translation of the elementary types out of mere Space into *Time* where they became *intelligencers* to men. The Hurons called the Evil Principle the Grand-Mother of the Good.[1] She is identical with Typhon and Tiamat the Dragon. This old Dragon of Darkness and Mother of the brood of Evil in the Abyss, the representative of discord, disorder, or chaos, was transformed into the Goddess of the Great Bear, and turned into the primordial type of time above as the "Mother of the revolutions." In this process the Dragon changed colour. The Akhekh monster was black. The Beast with the Seven heads, in Revelation, is the Red Dragon. So in Egypt Typhon was said to be of a red complexion. It was the Ruddy Dragon of the Pharaon on the British standard. The Red Dragon that was likewise pourtrayed on the Roman standard, which Ammianus Marcellinus calls the *Purpureum Signum Draconis*.[2] In like manner the earliest nocturnal Sun was black, the later, as Atum, was Red. The one had the hue of the black race ; the other of the red Adam.

One of the inscriptions which may be termed the "*New Creation by Ra*," actually shows us the Scene of Conversion. In this the old serpents, who were the Enchanters, Deluders of Chaos, "*perverted through their Intelligence*," are turned into the serpents of Seb (Kronus), who is commanded to see that they DO keep time henceforth as *true* intelligencers to men.[3] *Time* was the antithesis of disorder, falsehood, and dissolution. The Osirian in the other world rejoices that there is *Time in his body ;*[4] as the opposite of negation, non-existence, and return to the elementary condition of chaos. In the Bundahish the Dark Spirit meets and joins hands with the Bright Spirit in the *Twilight*, and thus becomes a co-creator of Time in the round of Night and Day. The Serpent of Darkness that lies in the "*Bend of the Great Void*," the Solar North, was a part of the circle of time in which the dark of night is as necessary as the light of day. Hence the Apophis, though wounded and maimed, overcome and fettered fast to the bottom, could never be destroyed. This is the Midgard Serpent which Thor fished for and nearly broke in two as he lifted one part of it so high aloft ; the coiler round and encompasser of the earth, but only just long enough to make ends meet with the touch of head and tail. This being the primal form of the Serpent it will naturally come to an end in the final destruction at the last day, when the deluder and devourer of the dark will not be resuscitated in the world of universal and eternal light, where *Time shall be no more*.

In a Buddhist account of Indra, the God is represented as pursuing the Monster *Râhu* with his Thunder-bolt and ripping open his belly so that the heavenly bodies may pass through whenever he swallows

[1] Waitz, *Anthropologie*, vol. iii. p. 183. [2] Lib. 16. c. 12.
[3] *Records*, vol. vi. p. 110. [4] *Rit.* ch. lxxxiv.

them. This same Monster of Darkness or Dragon of Eclipse was depicted as being cut in two halves by Indra, *and the head and tail of the dissevered devourer were then set in Heaven as time-symbols to represent the ascending and descending Nodes of the Moon on which the lunar eclipses depend.* Drummond observes that from the most remote antiquity the two points at which the ecliptic and the Moon's orbit intersect each other, were called the "head and tail of the Dragon."[1] The Hindus tell the tale of the Monster *Râhu* (our Dragon of Darkness and Eclipse), who smuggled himself into the presence of the Gods of Light and drank the Amrit-juice of immortal life. He was cut in two but could not be destroyed by Indra, *and the two halves were set as signs in Heaven at the place of the lunar eclipses.* Three months were assigned to the blind Serpent, likewise to the Dragon in the Abyss of the Waters, our Winter, and at the end of that time it was cut in two by the Young Solar God, or by the Goddess who annually reproduced the light in the Lunar Mythos; the two halves being figured in heaven as a type of time at the place of division, the Equinox.

Another form of the divided monster is extant in the Chinese "*bob-tailed Dragon*," that now represents the Typhonian idea, and is connected with typhoons and storms. "*The Bobtail Dragon is passing,*" say the Cantonese when a violent tempest goes overhead. This head and tail of the divided Dragon appear in a Tongan Myth. The Divinity or Demon *Hikuleo* (*Hiku* is the tail of a reptile) is said to dwell in the land of Bulotu, far out in the Western Sea, where the Egyptians have placed Typhon the serpent-tailed[2] in the sign of Scorpio. When *Hikuleo* goes away on his journeys he is said to leave his tail behind to watch over Bulotu, so that he is aware of all that goes on in his absence. Typhon placed at the Western equinox has his tail in the under-world and his head in the upper. *Hikuleo used to be dominant but* (like the Hebrew Deity) *he carried off the first born sons of the chief Tongan families so fast that the Gods of Light Maui and Tangaloa had to interfere. Hikuleo* was treated precisely in the same manner as the *Akhekh* Dragon in the Ritual. Tangaloa and Maui seized *Hikuleo* and fastened him down with a strong chain, one end of which was attached to heaven, the other to earth.[3] This is a form of the *Akhekh* Dragon of Darkness to whom the best and dearest of human beings were offered up in sacrifice of old, and the fastening down of *Hikuleo* by Maui and Tangaloa agrees with the chaining of the Akhekh Dragon to the bottom of the lake of Darkness, by the Sun-God, when the Hero of Light was personified as an opposing power, the eternal conqueror who cut the Dragon of Darkness through and through, and thus deposited the typical two halves in heaven as *Caput* and *Cauda Draconis.*

[1] *Œdipus Judaicus*, p. 73.   [2] See plate, *Book of Beginnings*, vol. ii.
[3] Tylor, *Prim. Culture*, v. ii. p. 281.

The head and tail of the Dragon which represented the ascending and descending Nodes of the Moon are also imaged as the Two Serpents that were strangled by the infant Hercules as soon as he was born. His Nest or Cradle (the Egyptian *Apt*) was denoted by the twining Serpents of the Caduceus, the head and tail of which were called the points of the ecliptic In like manner the Dragon of Night or devouring Crocodile of the West and of Earth, that once merely opened its jaws of darkness and swallowed the stars, was turned to account as a starry type of periodic time. In an ancient Egyptian planisphere the Crocodile sign appears at the place of the autumn equinox, close to the Scorpion,[1] lying across Six Decans of the Zodiac. There the same type that once symbolled the swallowing Earth in the West takes its starry shape in heaven. Thus we find a form of the Dragon stationed at the point of both equinoxes. Now the Jews have a Devil or Devouring demon "*Ketef*," the terror of the Chamber, whose name is derived from *Ketf*, to cut and split. *Ketef* rules between the dark and day, and he is the symbol of a division of the year and divides its course into two. His reign is between June 17 and July 9, the time of the summer solstice.[2] *Ketfi* (Eg.) is the snake, a reptile, a form of the Monster. The Egyptian reptile serves to identify the *Ketef* with the Hindu *Ketu* (the Demon Sainhikeya) the Dragon's tail personified. Here we have the Dragon at the place where the Egyptian year commenced at the time of the Summer Solstice with the rise of the Inundation. At that point in the planisphere the Kamites had figured the Dragon of the Waters as the Constellation *Hydra*. Now, if we take our stand with the earliest observers of the heavens, say, in Equatorial Africa, the first fact revealed by the darkness is that the whole starry vast above is slowly crawling round and round in one general movement like a serpent. Hence the Egyptians represented the Universe as a serpent with variegated scales, which denoted the stars.[3] The motion of the setting and rising stars heaving, as it were, along the horizon, increased the likeness to the serpent's motion. Also, when above, it was the Serpent of Air and Fire, and below the Serpent of Water and Earth ; and so we have a Serpent of the Two primary elements of life, Air and Water, and of the Four elements to which the Serpent is afterwards related. Thus, we see the Egg of the Year being emaned by Two Serpents, which shows the cycle of two halves, whether reckoned by the two Solstices (Draconis and Hydra) or by the double Serpent of the Equinox. Closer looking would reveal the fact that there were *Two turning points at the Poles which are seen low down on the horizon North and South.*

Mr. Procter has remarked, that when the North Pole Star was *Alpha Draconis*, the Southern was most probably the Star *Eta Hydri*

---

[1] Drummond, after Kircher, *Œdipus Judaicus*, pl. 2.
[2] Eisenmenger, vol. ii. p. 435.   [3] Hor-Apollo, b. i. 2.

and certain to have been in the Constellation Hydra. On this dual pivot of the Dragon the starry heavens revolved. Such would be the first fact observable, therefore the first fact observed and registered in the double Dragon. In accordance with exactly such a beginning we find in a Miztec Myth that the commencement of creation was with *Two Snakes;* the Lion-Snake and the Tiger-Snake. These two gods were the origin of all the gods. When these two gods became visible in the world, they made, in their knowledge and omnipotence, *a great Rock, upon which they built a very sumptuous palace,* a masterpiece of skill, in which they made their abode upon earth. On the highest part of this building there was an *axe of copper,* the edge being uppermost, and *on this axe the heavens rested.* This rock and the palace of the gods were on a mountain in the neighbourhood of the town of Apoala, in the province of Mizteca Alta. The Rock was called the *Place of Heaven;* there the gods first abode on earth, living many years in great rest and content, as in a happy and delicious land, though the world still lay in obscurity and darkness.[1] The Mythical Rock or Mount will be described hereafter; but it has been suggested in a previous volume that the serpent and Z-sign on the Scottish stones were figures of the Solstices united with the Mount of the Equinoxes; and this is confirmed by the double Dragon or Serpent of the North and South.[2]

It must not be supposed that a Science of Astronomy was made out by primitive man, or that the earliest observations of the stars *could not* have been made in Equatorial or Tropical regions, because the Southern Heavens are comparatively vacant, and have but few humanly-figured constellations. The first observers looking to the Southern Hemisphere were *not Astronomers,* nor was Astronomy *invented,* or the star-groups composed straight off any more than the hieroglyphics or the alphabet. The present writer once heard a clever person say in public, "*I wish I knew the Man who* INVENTED *the Alphabet.*" In course of time the doctrine of Evolution will banish all such non-comprehensive notions of the past, and its slow castings and deposits of the human progress. The paucity of ancient constellations around the Southern Pole would be an inevitable result of the *few observations that were made at first,* which were increased as the observers came farther north into Æthiopia on their way towards Egypt. This offers good evidence that the beginnings were Equatorial or Tropical, and that the Northern Heaven was crowded only as the observations increased in the course of ages by a people looking northward, who first named Khepsh (Kush or Habesh) as their North. Enough that the encircling Serpent, the symbol of eternal going round, is figured at both Poles, the two centres of the total starry revolution. That these two polar pivots were connected as the two fixed points about which the serpent coiled,

[1] Bancroft, vol. iii. p. 70.   [2] *Book of Beginnings,* vol. i. p. 423.

is doubly *shown by the Two separate Serpents being twinned as a figure of the Equinoxes, and the Dragon of Darkness severed in twain at one of these places to represent the Lunar Nodes.* Herschel, speaking of the Egyptian Planisphere, said the heavens were scribbled over with interminable snakes. These resolve, however, into the Two of the Beginning, *Hydra* South and *Draconis* North, and the two are the one type in two aspects. Hydra is the Serpent of wet, of moisture, the first element of life; the Dragon of the North, the winged Dragon, the fiery Dragon, the original of all the dragons of flame and drakes of fire, was the symbol of the second element of life, the breath, heat or fire that vivifies. This double Dragon of water and fire still survives in the "Green Dragon" (water) and the "Red Dragon" (fire) of our public house signs. In the Ritual the Four Quarters are associated with the Serpent of Seven heads. "*I am the Four Quarters, the first of the Seven Uræi in their transformations in the West. The Great one shining with his body as a God is Sut.*"[1] The Seven *Uræi* of the West answer to the Seven-headed Serpent or Dragon. In this passage *Sut* is not the evil one, and the seven *Uræi* are typical of life, not of death. A Serpent with four heads and one with four wings are found to stand for the Egyptian four corners of the earth. A Serpent *Apta*, whose name denotes the corner or end of the world, is depicted with four mystic figures joined to it, this means the Serpent of the four corners.[2] The Serpent *Hapu* is four-headed, and Hapu also denotes the corners and the secret places. The Great Temple of Mexico, according to Acosta, was built of large stones, after the pattern of snakes tied one to another, and was called Coatepautli, the Snake-Circuit.[3] The four cardinal points were also indicated by the Mexicans, with four knots twisted in a Serpent that formed the circumference.[4] In like manner the vast Seven-headed Nagas formed the circuit of the Temple of Nagkon-Wat. "*Every angle of every roof is adorned with a grim Seven-headed serpent*" with the crest feathered; and "*every entablature is adorned with a continuous row of these Seven-headed Deities.*"[5]

The constellation *Hydra*, the Dragon of the Waters, offers another perfect illustration of the *transference of a type out of the Vague Stage of Mythology into its Definite phase of time.* In Egypt the *heliacal*

---

[1] Ch. lxxxiii. [2] *Sarcophagus of Seti* 1st.
[3] *Natural and Moral History of the Indies*, p. 361.
[4] Clavigero, vol. i. p. 296.
[5] Ferguson, *Tree and Serpent Worship*, Introd. p. 48. As the present writer maintains the thesis of the Inner African origines, it may be pointed out that this Temple of the Seven-headed Serpent is in *Cambodia*, to the north of the sacred "Sweet-water"; that the Seven-headed Dragon will be found in the northern heaven, and that in the Inner African languages the name for Seven is—

Sambodia, in Mimboma,   *Tsamboadi*, in Musentandu,   *Sambat*, in Runda,
Tsambodia, in Nyombe,   *Samboade*, in Kisama,   *Sambids*, in Kanyika, &c.
Tsambodia, in Basunde,

rising of Hydra announced the very beginning of the Inundation. Theon was right in reporting that the constellation Hydra was so directly connected with the Nile that it *bore even the name of the deluge*. Hi, or Hiu (Eg.), signifies to inundate. In the Vague Stage the Dragon is the dark concealer of treasures, water included. In the Veda the Dragon of Darkness is the typical keeper and restrainer of the Waters. In Egypt, and still further inland, the Dragon in its starry stage became a time-keeper that announced when the Waters were let loose, and the downward flow began. In the Vague Stage the Coming Light would put the Dragon Darkness to flight. In the Definite stage of Time, the Dragon has its starry Type also, in which it rises *before the Sun*, and when the old Evil Dragon was fabled to flee in the presence of the Day-god, the Good Dragon as the starry Hydra rose up to announce the setting free of the Waters as the friend of Man. But the Dragon that kept the Wealth of Waters concealed was primary, and these were set free at Midsummer, at which time the people of various lands celebrated the victory over the Evil Dragon of the Waters. "It was the custom at Burford within living memory," says Dr. Plott, to "make a Dragon and convey it up and down the town in triumph along with a Giant on Midsummer's Eve."[1] Midsummer Eve's celebration of the defeat of the Dragon was continued at Chester till a late period. The "Beasts" were destroyed during the Commonwealth but were very literally *renewed* with the restoration of Charles II. as the ancient models had been broken.[2] This festival in Britain belonged to the Worship of the starry Baal, and the re-beginning of a Solstitial Year; that of the Inundation in Egypt. This was the day on which the spell was broken, when the mountains opened and the captive White Women, Maidens, Princesses, the Waters, Cows, and other kinds of treasure were once more wrested from the vanquished Dragon.

At last the "Elementaries" and primitive types in what may be termed the Cult of Darkness became the Servants of the God of Light in the Solar Mythos; and they who once warred in fierce opposition to Man as the Seven Adversaries, now fight for Ra against the Darkness and every phase of Evil. The ancient genitrix, Typhon, who brought forth her brood of Chaos in the Abyss, brings forth the young Sun-god. The Lioness spends her fiery fury against the Wicked. The Scorpion stings *on behalf* of Gods and men. *Serk*, the Scorpion Goddess, is the Guardian of the Sun, and Keeper of the chained Apophis. So it is said of the Scorpion-Men in the Akkadian Myth of Izdubar, "*At the rising of the Sun and the setting they guard the Sun*."[3] The Lion and Scorpion occupy two of the four corners in their starry shape. "*I have come*," says the Osirian, "*like the Sun*

[1] *History of Oxfordshire*, p. 349. Brand, *Midsummer Eve*.
[2] *Every Day Book*, vol. i. p. 834.
[3] Smith, *Chaldean Account of Genesis*, p. 259.

through the gate of the Sun-goer, otherwise called the Scorpion," [1] recognizing the Scorpion as the sign of Sunset or Autumn Equinox. The Ape and Jackal are the guides of the Sun on its two roads.

The Serpent-symbol of destroying power is elevated to be worn on the frontlets of the Gods, where the most deadly becomes the most divine. It is said of each Serpent emitting balls of fire in the Hades, *"Its flame is for Ra."* Its fatal defiance was now on the side of the Gods. The fire-breathing serpents of the Egyptian Phlegethon darting death are the guardians and keepers of the gates of heaven.[2] In this process of transformation Seven of the *Elementaries* whose titles identify them with the Seven Wicked Spirits of the Akkadian Hymns, appear in the Egyptian Ritual as the *Seven Spirits associated with the great Bear*, that is, the constellation of Typhon, the genitrix who had been the Dragon, Crocodile, or Hippopotamus of the Abyss.

Here they have been promoted from the Elementary phase to become the *"Seven Great Spirits in the service of their Lord,"* and the Seven. Spirits of the Solar Ra. These Seven then in the course of evolution have become Spirits, Genii, or Gods, as the servants of Osiris or Ra, the later God; just as the Seven Amshaspands became the Seven Spirits of Ahura-Mazda in Persia, and the Seven Spirits were considered to be the Seven Manifestors of Agni in India. This shows a re-adaptation and extension of the type from the primordial idea of the Seven evil or inimical influences to that of the Seven starry Spirits, Seven Chieftains, of whom it is said, *" These same are behind the constellation of the Thigh, Ursa Major, of the Northern Heaven."* They are now called the *"followers of Osiris"* who *"burn the wicked souls of his enemies,"* the *"givers of blows for sins."* [3] *"* These Seven Spirits are *Amset, Hapi, Tuautmutf, Kabhsenuf, Maaentefef, Karbukef,* and *Har-Khent-Skhem.*[4] Four of them are the established Genii of the Four Quarters, and all Seven were appointed as chieftains of Seven different constellations, and, finally, the Seven Planets, as we shall find them in the Bundahish; although the whole Seven are not always so well defined as the Four.

Kefa, the Beast in the Abyss, became the Goddess of the Great Bear and Mother of the revolutions or cycles of Time. Sevekh did duty as her Dog (Lesser Bear, or Dragon). Anup, the Jackal, was developed into Sut-Mercury, the announcer of the Inundation and the guide of the Sun and Souls through the under-world. The Ape became Kafi-Shu, the God of Breath and Soul, to each of whom a constellation was assigned, beginning with the Four Quarters.

In the *" Chapter of stopping the Crocodiles"* which come to take the mind of a Spirit from him (presence of mind) in Hades, the Swallowers

[1] *Ritual*, ch. cxlvii. 15th gate. [2] Tomb of Seti 1st at Bab-el-Muluk.
[3] *Ritual*, ch. xvii. [4] *Ibid.*, ch. xvii.

are *Eight* in number ; and in the 17th Chapter [1] the Seven Spirits, or
Genii, who are stationed behind the constellation of Ursa Major in the
Northern Heaven, are called the Crocodiles.   According to my
interpretation we have to look on the Seven Stars of the Lesser Bear
as representative of these elementary gods, who were Seven as the
heads of the Dragon, but who were also one as a constellation repre-
sented by Sevekh.   For example, at the centre of the zodiac of
Denderah we see the Hippopotamus and the Dog, Jackal, or Fox.
These two were a form of Sut-Typhon.   "The Little Bear," says
Dupuis, "was also known as the Fox."   The Egyptian Fox was the
Fenekh-type of Sut, the Fox-dog.   Thus the Two Bears represent
the Mother and Son at the centre of all.   In Cicero's *Aratus* the
"Little Bear" is called *Cynosura*, not from the Dog's Tail, but as the
Dog of the hinder part, North, and the opposite to Sothis, the Dog of
the front or South.   The Dog, Wolf, or Jackal, is the Seb that stands
opposite the Great Bear.   Moreover, the Arabs call the Star *Alpha* in
Draco, the Wolf (Dzib), or Jackal, as well as *Thuban*, the Dragon.
Thus the Wolf, Seb (Eg.), and the Dragon meet in one constellation,
and Sevekh, whose name signifies No. 7, is the Son of Typhon, and
his type is the Crocodile or Dragon.   Now Mr. Proctor, the astronomer,
considers the Lesser Bear to have once been a portion of the Dragon
which has been made a separate constellation.   This view is corroborated by the Mythos; by the figure of the Polar Dragon,[2] and the type
of the Seven-headed Dragon when this is interpreted by the Crocodile.
The Crocodile was one form of the old genitrix, and the Eight
Crocodiles represent her and her Seven-fold progeny.

In the Book of Enoch Leviathan (the Arabic Tannim for Draco)
is called a female monster, and Behemoth is a Male, whereas the
Egyptian Bekhmut is the Great Bear (Hippopotamus).   But, in spite
of any shifting, the double type of Sut-Typhon remains in the Great
Bear and the Seven-headed Dragon.   Proclus (second book of his
Commentary on Euclid) says "the Pole of the World is called by the
Pythagoreans the Soul of Rhea."   This was Rerit or Typhon in
Egypt.   Here, then, in the Seven-headed Dragon of the Pole we have
the Tan of Darkness and Eclipse with Seven Stars for its heads
called Seven Crowns in Revelation, taking a starry shape by Night in
what was assuredly one of the first figures set in Heaven.   One
group of Seven Stars represents the Mother, and one her Son, or her
Seven-fold progeny, as the Seven-headed Dragon.

In "Old Deccan Days" [3] the narrator says : "*All the Cobras in my
grandmother's stories were Seven-headed.   This puzzled us children, and
we used to say to her, 'Granny, are there any Seven-headed Cobras
now ? for all the Cobras we see that the conjurors bring round have
only one head each.'   To which she used to answer, 'No, of course there
are no Seven-headed Cobras now, that world is gone.   But you see*

[1] Ch. xxxii.   [2] See Plate in this Vol.   [3] P. 27.

each Cobra has a hood of skin, that is the remains of another head.'
Although we often looked for Seven-headed Cobras we never could find
any of them."

In Sanskrit the *Naga* Snake is synonymous with the mystical
Number Seven. There is no Seven-headed serpent in Nature, but
there is a Polar Dragon whose coilings round and round on itself,
when *a*-Draconis was the Pole-Star, were made at the pivotal
Centre of Motion in the Planisphere, and with the Lesser Bear
for its Seven heads we can identify the Seven-headed Dragon of
the Mythos.

The natural genesis of the Seven-headed Cobra, Naga, Dragon,
Crocodile, or Akhekh has (together with other Elementaries) now
been traced from its birth in mere Darkness to the transformation
into a Constellation with Seven Stars for its heads. And this process
of evolution will further explain *the reversion of the Starry Dragon in
its fall to the black lurid monster of the beginning, the Akhekh Dragon
of the Deep*.

The *Sesha-Naga* of India begins in the Dragon of Darkness. Its
black body and black tongue especially tell of the *Akhekh* of Night.
But it is clothed with Jewels, as heaven is with Stars, one of which
is larger and more lustrous than all the rest, as if it might represent
the Pole-Star *Alpha Draconis*. The Black Jaga-Naut is sometimes
depicted in the form of the Seven-headed Serpent. *Sesha* has Seven
heads which identify it with the Dragon of the Seven Stars. It is
also the Seven-headed serpent of Eternity. As Ananta it typifies
the Vague Infinite. Its Jewels are the Variegated Scales which
bespangle the Egyptian Symbol of the Infinite or the serpentining Universe. The Dragon that was cast out of Heaven had
been the base of all beginning, and in India it was continued
as a foundation of the later Solar Creation. The Serpent with
Seven heads forms the support of Vishnu in the Abyss of the
Waters when he dreams or muses in the Intervals of Creation, with
the lotus springing from his Navel, and Brahma issuing forth to effect
his Thought anew.[1] In this picture the Seven-headed Sesha is a
figure of Mythology akin to those Dragons of the fore-world which
preceded the Earth of Man ; it represents the pre-solar Creation, now
sunken below the Waters ; the leavings, remains, residue of the
remotest past. *Sesha* signifies that *which has been rejected, cast, or left
out*, as was the bygone Dragon of Earth and of Heaven, buried as the
forgotten foundations of later worlds.

The Great Bear, the Constellation of Typhon, still continues the
name of *Tep* or *Teb* (Eg.) in the Star *Dubhe*. In like manner the
Arabs have preserved the Typhonian character of *Draconis* in calling
the old Pole-star *Thuban* or *Al-Thuban* the Dragon ; the Carib *Tupan*,
the god of Darkness and Thunder. This name further identifies the

[1] Moor, *Hindu Pantheon*, pl. 7.

Star and Constellation with Sut-Typhon depicted at the centre of the Planisphere.

Not by chance nor without meaning was the Great Pyramid of Gizeh built with its Northern shaft pointing like a telescopic tube to focus the star *a Draconis*, either at the time of its coming round again or with the knowledge of its return to that point where it would be once more the polar pivot of starry motion.

There is an occult connection suggested by the monuments between the Star Sothis, the Dog, and the Star of some end of things called the final Judgment. It is a star high up in Heaven only shown by its descending rays. The Judge is represented seated on his lofty throne, and this star in the Apex of Heaven is the Star of Judgment, or, when interpreted, of the great Time-Cycle. That was the Pole-Star, which, as the Eye of the Dragon, was *a Draconis*.

One type of the Typhonian genitrix, the Goddess of the Great Bear, is the *Rhinoceros Rerit* (Eg.) the *Unicorn*, and it has now to be shown that the Unicorn was a form of the mythical Dragon. Horn is a primæval type of foundation and of duration. The earliest weapons and implements were fashioned ready to hand as horns, tusks, and teeth. The supreme value set upon horn can be estimated by its adoption as the symbol of supremacy. The Horn of the Rhinoceros, a Type of Typhon, is an Inner African Sceptre of Sovereignty. "*Beings prevailing by the hardness belonging to their head*" (such as was symbolled by Horn and Beak) are spoken of in the Ritual.[1]

The Equator as *Apta* (Eg.) is the *Horn-point* of the World. This was a typical expression for the highest point, at the end or in the beginning. "The Horn" was likewise a typical point in the Babylonian Astronomy. Thus "*a dark Cloud covered the Horn*" "*owing to rain the horn was not visible.*" Venus in the Ascendant is said to be "*on the Horn.*"[2]

If we apply this *Horn-point* to the Northern Heaven the pole IS the horn-point in the Planisphere. Thus the Horn and the pivot on which all turned round are identical at the pole. THERE, the Horn of Sut-Typhon typified the primæval pillar of the heavens, the foundation and support of all, at the centre of all; and it is there we have to look for the origin of the mythical Unicorn.

It has been argued by some that the Unicorn is a Lunar emblem. But, the genesis of these types is always found to be in accordance with natural fact; it is only false theory that needs to twist the Moon's Two Horns into one. True, the Moon is renewed *from the Horn* or horned phase, but the type did not originate with the Moon, nor is it limited to the Moon. The Moon was double-horned in the past, as now, and cannot be the Unicorn.

The Unicorn is found on the Monuments with the Single Horn in

---

[1] Ch. lxxxiv.   [2] *Trans. Soc. Bib. Arch.* vol. iii. 199, 226, 297.

front, and the tail of the Typhonian animal behind, as an image of the dual Sut-Typhon, who is continually identified with the Horn and its hardness. In the Ritual Sut is called a Deity who has power over the head to confer hardness for resisting blows on the day of cutting off heads.[1] As an animal the Rhinoceros was the true Unicorn; the African species described by Pausanias as the Æthiopian Bull, which they call Nose-horn (Ῥινόκερως).[2] This is the Egyptian *Rumakh* (and Rerit) a type of Typhon as the Great Bear. The *Rumakh* or *Remakh*, the Single-horned, apparently supplied the "*lem*" of our di-lemma, which denotes the double-horn. Typhon is not only represented as Nosehorn, for she has a *phallus* for her Nose-horn, which is identical with the *pole*.[3]

· The Unicorn as a Rhinoceros, or Water-horse, also accounts for the fabulous animal of Heraldry being a Horse with the horn of the sword-fish stuck in its forehead to *indicate the water-type of horse*. This was the way in which the prototypes were continued where the original animal did not exist.

Typhon in Egypt and Tiamat in Akkad represented the foundation of all things in the Abyss of Darkness and the Water of the Beginning. In a scene depicted on a Babylonian cylinder the conflict of Bel and the Dragon of Chaos is the subject and Tiamat is pourtrayed as a Chimera with a Beak, Crest, and Wings, and a SINGLE HORN. She reappears as one of the Wicked Spirits that war against the Moon, with the same *Single Horn*. The Unicorn was therefore the type of Tiamat as it is of Typhon.[4]

Layard copied an Assyrian scene which shows a worshipper adoring a winged Unicorn-Bull. These are accompanied by the Sun radiate, the Moon Crescent, and the *Seven Stars;* not the Seven Planets or there would be nine. When they meant the Planets they figured five stars, not seven.[5] The Seven Stars we claim as the Constellation *Haptoring*, so prominent in the Bundahish and other Persian Scriptures; but totally unrecognised by writers on Mythology.[6]

A representation found at Pterion, in Asia Minor, shows a Goddess supposed to be Anaitis, standing on the back of a Leopard-like animal holding in her hand a crescent-crowned staff. She is accompanied by the *Unicorn*, and has an attendant who stands on the back of a Dog.[7] Here the Unicorn typifies the primordial genitrix, and the Dog, her Son.

The Rhinoceros or Great Bear is the Unicorn North, but this had two characters—North and South; the North being the hind part, the South the fore part of the heaven. These two agree with the dual type of Sut-Typhon as the Unicorn; the only one ever "*endowed*

[1] Ch. l.   [2] Pausanias, 9, 21, 2.   [3] Birch, *Gallery.*
[4] Smith, *Chaldean Account*, pp. 101, 109.   [5] Porter, R. K. vol. ii. pl. 80.
[6] King, *Gnostic Remains*, v. ii. pl. I. fig. I.
[7] Waring, *Ceramic Art in Remote Ages*, pl. 39, fig. 16.

with a wonderful Horn which it would sometimes turn to the left and right, at others raise and then again depress." [1]

Because the Horn was an emblem of foundation and duration, and the Unicorn was placed at the centre of the northern Heaven as a support, the heraldic Unicorn remained the typical supporter in coats of arms. The fact is that both the Unicorn and Lion were represented by the old Typhon at the Polar centre, for these are two of her types. She *was* the Unicorn in front and the Lion in her lower part; she is also pourtrayed with the head of a lion.[2] Consequently the national arms of England contain a copy of the earliest figures set in Heaven by the Kamite typologists. Moreover the ancient " Horn-Book " was ornamented with a rude drawing of St. George and the Dragon, which as Tiamat and Typhon first wore the horn. The Horn-Book or " A.B.C." thus contained the A.B.C. of the Book of Beginnings. One, mode of representing the central support was by means of the Unicorn pourtrayed with its horn struck into, or pointing to, a tree. The Tree signifies the Pole ; the Celestial Roof-Tree. The author of the " *Great Dionysiak Myth* " has well shown how common in symbolism is the " Unicorn and Tree." [3] The Tree which was guarded by the Dragon in one form of the Mythos is supported by the Unicorn in the other. No better illustration can be found in Egypt, Assyria, or Greece than the one on the Horn of *Ulf* which he has copied. The Unicorn is depicted with a bird-headed serpent for its tail ; this identifies it with the Dragon, the Akhekh of darkness, and with Tiamat who has a beak, wings, and a single horn. The Horn of the animal is thrust into the Tree. The Dog appears beneath the Unicorn. By the Tree we identify *the Pole of the Heaven ;* the Dog is one with the Lesser Bear. This being the child of Typhon, the Unicorn represents the genitrix herself with her dog in position as first guide and announcer in heaven.

The Unicorn has but one large round Eye, corresponding to its single horn. This prominent single Eye of the Unicorn *regardant* is as common as the Horn and the Tree. It is the Eye of the picture that turns on the gazer in all directions ; the Eye of Heaven at the centre of all. It is the Pole-star in the Dragon or the Bear, according to the period. We are expressly told that in figuring the serpent Circle with the tail of the reptile in its mouth the Egyptians made the inner Eye very conspicuous at the juncture and centre of the coil. It was essential to the symbol of the coiled-up snake, says Philo, that the eye should be visible inside the Circle. This figure was represented in the Planisphere, at the centre of all, by the Seven-headed dragon turning round on its inner Eye, fixed as the polar pivot of the starry revolutions.

[1] *Penny Cyclopædia*, " Unicorn."
[2] Pierret, *Panthéon Égyptien*, figure on p. 37.
[3] Robert Brown, Junior, *The Unicorn ; a Mythological Investigation.*

The typology of the Tree has yet to be traced and interpreted. Here it is affirmed that the Mythical Tree, like the Pillar and the Mount, is a *type of the celestial Pole.* Lucian asserts that a virgin delivered the oracle at Delphi (whence the symbolic Constellation *Virgo*), and a dragon spoke from under the Tripod *because of the Constellation Draco among the stars.*[1] The Tripod was also a form of the Tree. The Tree with Seven Branches appears as the Tree of Knowledge on the cylinders[2] accompanied by the Sun, Moon, and Seven Stars. This is the Tree of the Serpent and the Pair, male and female, as in the Book of Genesis.

The Assyrian Asherah-tree or grove is based on a central pillar or Tree with *Seven heads or hoods of a conventionalised Nâga-snake,* which identifies it with the Seven-headed Nâga and the Seven-headed Dragon of the Pole. In the Nâga sculptures the Tree of the Mount (or Pole) is identified at the bottom by one tree, and at the top by another, and between the two there is *a kind of ladder with a series of steps or stairs which ascend the tree in place of a stem.* These denote the Tree of the Ascent, Mount, or Height,[3] now to be considered as representing the Pole.

In the Avesta the Star-Serpent is said to make a road between the sky (heaven) and earth. One type of this Road was the Mount; another the Tree. These offered physical foothold and tangible means of ascent, and were applied on a vast scale. The primitive man climbed the tree in thought to attain the summit, just as Jack mounted the bean-stalk. The Tree of the Pole is extant in Celebes, where the natives believe that the world is supported by the Hog, and that earthquakes are caused when the Hog rubs itself against the Tree.[4] The Hog (Rerit) was an Egyptian form of the Typhonian genitrix, who, as the Great Bear, revolved about the Pole (Tree), and is here said to rub up against it.

At Ephesus they showed the Olive and Cypress Grove of *Leto,* and in it the Tree of Life, to which the Great Mother clung in bringing forth her twin-born progeny. There also was the Mount on which Hermes announced the birth of her twins, Diana and Apollo.[5] The imagery is at root the same as the Hog rubbing against the Tree of the Pole. The Tree which the earliest people leaned against for mental support, and hung their signs of beseeching and tokens of gratitude upon, and garlanded with the flowers of spring, and fruits of harvest, or set alight with candles in imitation of the starry fires, was the Tree of Heaven, and it was the Tree of Heaven figuratively, because of the celestial Pole at the fixed centre, on which their eyes

---

[1] Lucian, *De Astrologia,* p. 544.
[2] Lajard, *Culte de Mithra,* pl. 6, fig. 4; pl. 30, fig. 7 ; pl. 39. fig. 8.
[3] Ferguson, *Tree and Serpent Worship,* pl. 27.
[4] *Journal Ind. Archip.* ii. 837.
[5] Strabo, xiv. p. 947 ; Tacitus, *Ann.* iii. 61.

first rested to be followed by their thoughts; and by that Tree, as up the Mount of the North, they first ascended heavenward. The Dragon revolving round the Pole supplied the natural genesis of the Serpent coiling and twining round the Tree. The Serpent and Tree are twin, and inseparable. *There is a Serpent in the Tree, an ugly beast without failings.*[1] The Serpent in the Fruit-Tree is common in the Greek drawings. It has been found in Indian caves and Abyssinian temples. The Serpent twined around a tree with fruit-bearing boughs is sometimes painted on Egyptian sarcophagi. So on the coins of Tyre we see the Serpent coiled about the Tree that is in fruit. At other times the Tree with the Serpent round it is but a bare stock or log, like the Yule-log of Christmas. The Caribees of Central America were found worshipping the fruit-bearing Tree with the Serpent dwelling in its branches. The earliest races, the African, still think some of the earliest thoughts of the human mind, still retain the most primitive types of expression, and with them the Tree and Serpent keep their primal place. The first divinity in the Dahoman Pantheon is the Serpent in its two charac-ters. The next is the Tree, represented by the bombax or cotton tree.[2] The third is Water. Bosman found the three chief types, divinities, or fetishes, worshipped by the Guinea negroes, were the Serpent, the Tree, and the Water.[3]

We are sometimes told that this or the other race of people have no mythology, no gods or goddesses, because their typology remains in the elementary phase, in which the Water (heaven), the Tree, the Serpent, or other powers were un-personified, and yet were repre-sentative, as in the primary phase of typology. Bruce describes the Shangallas as worshippers of the Serpent, the Tree, the Moon, Planets, and Stars.[4] Here the Tree and Serpent are identified with the Stars. We shall find no simpler form of the beginnings that dawned out of the darkness. The Water was the firmament at first. In this blue Water above, the Tree of Life was figured at the point of commence-ment, and round the Tree the starry Serpent or Dragon twined with its Seven heads, or the Crocodile Typhon revolved with her Seven Crocodiles of the Lesser Bear; the Seven heads of the Dragon. The Great Fetish or Idol of Hwida, called "*Agoye*," is pourtrayed with the *Double Serpent* and *Seven* Lizards issuing from its head. One of the Seven is in the centre climbing the Pole or summit, represented by a dart. The new moon shows the celestial nature of the imagery. The Largest Lizard (or Dragon) is revolving round the Pole. This Great Lizard and the Seven smaller ones answer perfectly to the genitrix of the Seven Stars and her Seven-fold progeny (or the Seven-headed Dragon), who appear as the Eight Crocodiles in the region of the Great Bear.

[1] *Origo Mundi*, p. 797.
[2] Burton, *Dahome*, v. ii. p. 140.
[3] Bosman, *Pinkerton's Voyages*, vol. xvi. p. 494.
[4] *Travels*, vol. iv. p. 344.

An exhaustive investigation shows that these figures of the Serpent, Dragon, or Lizard, are derivable from one common type, which served as foundation for them all. Not only is the type sole in its origin, but the Mount of the North and the celestial Tree are the same, as

surely as the North Pole is single and there alone can be seen the twin Constellations of the Seven Stars, which Pythagoras called the " *Two Hands of Rhea.*" Philo-Judæus says, " *Of the flaming sword turning every way, it may be understood to signify the perpetual motion of the cherubim.*" Clemens also observes of these, " *There are those golden images. Each of them has six wings; whether they typify the Two Bears, as some will have it, or, which is better, the Two Hemispheres.*"[1] In the Book of Genesis the Two Cherubim were placed to cover or guard the Tree of Life. Ezekiel describes the Griffin or Dragon as the Covering Cherub on the holy mountain of God, that moved amid the stones of fire as a personification of Phœnicia; that is, Kefa (Eg.) in the North, the hinder part of heaven. " *Thou art the anointed Cherub that covereth, and I have set thee. Thou wast upon the holy mountain of God; thou hast walked up and down in the midst of the stones of fire;*" that is, the starry constellations called precious stones. " *I will destroy thee, O Covering Cherub from the midst of the stones of fire.*"[2]

Ashtaroth was the Goddess of the Sidonians, and she is pourtrayed on the coins, with her Seven Stars, and with the horns of the Cow. As-Ta-Urt (Eg.) is the Water-Cow, the Isis-Taurt of the Great Bear, who also has the Cow's horns on the Hippopotamus body; Ta-Urt, the Water-horse, became As-Ta-Urt in the Cow character. On the Assyrian cylinders the Two Cherubim appear in the shape of Two Gryphons. Upon other cylinders the Tree of Life is planted between Two Unicorns. These, therefore, are identical with the Two Gryphons and the Two Cherubim of the Hebrew Genesis, the Two Bears, Sut-Typhon or Astarte and Sutekh.[3] These are pourtrayed standing on either side of the Tree of Life in the act of covering, guarding, and protecting it. The Tree is of the conventionalized Palm type. This Archaic Tree is common, and it points to the original home of the Palm. The Burmese have an enormous pair of Griffins, one of which is *pourtrayed with the horn of the Rhinoceros on its nose,* the other without. Their fore-feet are elevated on a lofty pedestal.[4]

---

[1] Strom. v.　　　　　　　　　[2] Ez. xxviii. 14, 16.
[3] King, *Ancient Gnostic Remains,* vol. ii. pl. 1. figs. 1 and 7.
[4] Brown, *The Great Dionysiak Myth,* vol. i. p. 336, plate.

Two powers of evil or deposed divinities were known to the Californian Indians near Trinity River as *Omaha* and *Makalay*. The first of these had the shape of a bear ; the second is a fiend who has a single horn, like a unicorn.[1] In the Egyptian Magic Papyrus *Makai*, the Crocodile, is a son of Typhon,[2] whose starry type is the Great Bear ; and the Bear and Unicorn correspond to the Two Constellations of the Pole or Tree. Gryphon, Griffin, Hippo*grif*, Harpy, or Cherub, are all explained by the Egyptian *Kerub*, a primordial type, or a model figure. "My *original* country," sings Taliesin, "is the region of Cherubim ;[3] the *fons et origo* and the place of repose at the centre of all. In the Naga sculptures of India Two Griffins or Garuda-like Gryphons, called Kinnaras, are sometimes pourtrayed on each side of the Naga-Tree,[4] corresponding to the Two Cherubim and the Two Griffins, or the Two Unicorns. The double Dragon or Gryphon also supports the Tree of the Cross on the sculptured stones of Scotland.[5] The Tree, which was that of Knowledge, was identified by the Druids with the Ogham Pillar, and every science was considered to have emanated from this Tree or Pillar.[6] The Irish had the Tree of Knowledge as the Vine or Fin, called the *Fegee Fin*. *Fegee* denotes the branching or branchy, like the Egyptian Fekh or Pekha for divisions. This Vine was an Ogham, consisting of five circles instead of one. The five-branched vine was an equivalent for the hand or five digits of the Ogham reckoning. It is commonly supposed that our Oghams are not much older than the present era, but they were the direct representatives of gesture-language which continued digital counting into the domain of letters, the very link betwixt figures and phonetics as well as between the Pillar and the Tree. The Red Dragon of the Pole was the Red Dragon ON the Pole, Tree, or Stauros of the British standard, as it was in Mexico and "in the Wilderness." "*Swiftly moving in the course of the sky, in circles, in uneven numbers, Druids and Bards unite in celebrating the Dragon.*"[7] The Dragon was the leader in the mystic dance, as it was in heaven when *a Draconis* was the Pole-star.

The Dragon, in Welsh, denotes the Leader. Uthyr Pendragon, called the father of Arthur, son of Arth, the Great Bear, was the Supreme Leader, as the Dragon was in Heaven. Another title of the Dragon Chief of the World is *Menwyd*, who is accredited with fabricating the Arkite means of traversing "the Abyss by *serpents joined together*," *i.e.* by cycles of time. The chief dragon, Menwyd, answers to the Great Serpent of the Abyss, the *Mehnut*, which has already been compared to the Australian *Myndie*. The word δράκων (Dragon) denotes the keen-eyed Seer. *Dreg*, in English,

---

[1] Bancroft, vol. iii. p. 176.   [2] *Records*, vol. x. p. 154.
[3] Hanes Taliesin in Gunn's *Nennius*, p. 41.   [4] Ferguson, pl. 24, fig. 2.
[5] Stuart, vol. ii. pl. 79.   [6] Vallancy, *Vind.* p. 86—94.
[7] *Cynddelw : poem addressed to Owen Cyveiliawg.*

means subtle, crafty; Magical Art is *Dreg* (or Dry), Craft; Gaelic *Draoi*, for the magician or sorcerer. The *Druic*, in Cornish, is the Dragon, and this was a form of the Druid as the Wise Seer, the *Draco*. The root has many meanings all circling about their source in the Serpent.

The Barddas describe the Dragon as pursuing Keridwen the Fair around the stones of Kaer-Sidi. So Draconis would pursue the Great Bear (Arth), around the Pole or Mount, as it was figured, and this was the constellation of the Great Mother of the Revolutions, the Draconian Mother of the Dragon-progeny. The Dragon in the "*Pool of Pant*," is one with our Lambton Worm in the Well. The heir of Lambton was fishing when he caught the worm on his hook, and in disgust flung it into a well hard by, still called the Worm Well. It resembled an eft. In the well the worm grew and grew until it grew out of it. It left the well, and by day it lay coiled around a rock in the middle of a stream, and at night it twisted itself around a neighbouring hill. And it grew and it grew until it could clasp the hill three times round. In like manner the Worm of Linton, which was slain by the Laird of Lariston, coiled and contracted itself so tightly round the hill as to leave the marks in spiral impressions. Both the Hill and the Coiling Snake appear in the Ritual. "*Oh the very tall hill in Hades! The heaven rests upon it. There is a snake on it, Sati is his name. He is about seventy cubits in his coil.*"[1] The Serpent Sati, or Bata, on the High Hill of Heaven, is called "*the Serpent of Millions of Years; millions of years in length in the quarter of the region of the Great Winds* (the north and) *the Pool of Millions of years. All the other gods return to all* (their) *places. Millions of years are following to him.*"[2]

This serpent is represented as coiling round and enveloping the Hill, or Mount of the North. It is the hill of the *Bat*, or cavern toward the east; and Sebek (the crocodile-dragon, whose name is Seven) is said to be on the hill as Lord of the Bat! "*Sebek is on the hill in his temple upon the edge.*"[3] Sebek having been the ancient "Star-God" of darkness, who was turned into a later solar god. Taking the crocodile as the natural image of the Seven-headed Dragon of the Mythos, we here find the beast with its temple on the mount that supports the heaven, primally the Mount of the Pole and of the first Circle of Time. This hill or mound, which stands for the Mount of the North, of the Seven Stars and the Dragon, was the Sacred Mound of the British Bards, one of whom invokes "*Hu* with expanded wings," and says, "*My voice has recited the death-song where the mound, representing the world, is constructed of stone-work.*" This was at the "*Solemn festivity round Two Lakes* (the Two Waters), where the Sanctuary is earnestly invoking the gliding King before whom the fair one retreats upon the veil that covers the huge stones,

---

[1] *Ritual,* ch. cl.   [2] *Ibid.* ch. cxxxi. Birch.   [3] *Ibid.* ch. cviii.

whilst the Dragon moves round over the places which contain vessels of the drink-offering,"[1] in which description we find the "Mountain of the World" and the Twin Lakes.[2] It is an artificial mound, as is that of Silbury Hill. The starry Dragon moving round the mount was *Draconis* serpentining round the Celestial Pole. The Mount was intended by the mound of stone or earth on the top of which the dragon-flag, the magical *magnum sublatum*, was unfolded by the Druids with the figure of the great red dragon on it, the type of a deity that preceded Hu, the Solar God.

Silbury Hill is a stupendous cone containing 13,558,809 feet of earth. Sir R. C. Hoare says: "*This artificial hill covers the space of five acres and thirty-four perches of land.*" It measures 2,027 feet round its base, runs up 170 feet perpendicularly, and the top is 165 feet in diameter, which, according to Stukeley's measurement, is the exact diameter of Stonehenge. North-east of Avebury is the "Hakpen" Hill, a natural mound, or head of the Dragon. Still north of Silbury Hill is the artificial Dragon (or Serpent) the figure of which, as copied by Stukeley, Duke, and others, corresponds exactly to the Dragon of the Pole in an Egyptian Planisphere;[3] and it has now to be suggested that this lofty mound, with its serpent or dragon, is another image of the Celestial Mount of the Pole *The Mythical mount was the initial point of the geocentric system of astronomy, the earth-centre of motion before it was known that the earth itself was a rotating and revolving globe.* Colonel Drax, who very carefully opened Silbury Hill under the direction of the Duke of Northumberland with a company of Cornish miners, *found some remains of oak wood in the earth, and he fancied the mound might have been raised over a Druidic oak-tree.*[4] The author of *Druidical Temples of the County of Wilts* considered the bits of oak discovered were the remains of one entire bole or log, and he tells us, from his own observations, that heart of oak immured in chalk is almost imperishable.[5] The Temple of "*the Great Tree*" was a very ancient institution that had been continued in Babylon from time immemorial, and the Tree and Mount are identical as figures of the Pole.[6] The evidence all points to Silbury as being the Mound of the Tree or Pole. The name of Sil agrees with the Egyptian Ser or Tzer, *which was the typical Hill of the Horizon especially designated the Ser (or Sel) as the Bury, or the "Burial Place."* Thus the mythical Tzer Hill was the

[1] *Marwnad Uthyr Pendragon*, Davies, p. 557.
[2] So, in the Chinese Bamboo Books it is said of the genitrix *K'ing-too*, that whenever she looked into any of the three Ho there was to be seen a dragon following her. One morning the dragon came with a picture and a writing, the substance of which was, "*The Red one has received favour of Heaven.*" The red dragon having made K'ing-too pregnant, she gave birth to the yellow-pupilled Yaou, who corresponds to the British god Hu.—Legge, *Chinese Classics*, vol. iii. part 1, p. 112.
[3] See plate in this vol. [4] Douglas, *Nenia Britannica*, p. 161.
[5] Duke, *Druidical Temples*, p. 42.
[6] Inscrip. of Nabonidus, *Records*, vol. v. p. 143.

Egyptian Silbury, the Mount of the burial place which may have surrounded the pile as the graveyard does the church.

A serpentine earthwork near St. Peter's River, Iowa, is a conical and truncated mound 60 feet in diameter at the base, and 18 feet high, erected on a raised platform or bottom. *It is surrounded by a circle 365 feet in circumference.* Round this circle there is an embankment in a triple coil 2,310 feet in length. This is in the shape of a serpent of eighteen feet diameter at the centre, and diminishing proportionately at the head and tail.[1] The Mexicans carved the feathered rattle-snake encircling a column of basalt in ascending spirals.[2] About this Mount or mound, Tree or Pole, the Dragon or Serpent coiled and kept eternal watch around. As the Seven-headed revolver about the Pole-Star which was its own Eye, it was the good Dragon. Hesiod describes the terrible Serpent that watches the all-golden apples lying in a cavern of the dark earth at its furthest extremity. This was the Dragon watching in the Northern Heaven. The serpent twining round and guarding the apple-tree of the Hesperides is pourtrayed on a Greek vase in the British Museum.[3]

The guardianship of the Dragon or Serpent was so ancient in Egypt that the fire-breathing Uræi which protect the pylons of Paradise were almost as common as the Greek "border-pattern" is now. It is the main object of my work to trace these types from first to last, though the end of some of them will seem ludicrous. But the Dragon that guarded the golden apples of the Hesperides and turned Tempter instead of protecting the tree in Eden, the Dragon that fulminates fire to defend the portals and fruit-tree of Heaven in the Monuments, survives in the English Snap-Dragon. *Snab* (Eg.) is fire (German, schnapps, spirit), and the Snab-Dragon is the fire-Dragon or Dragon of spirit-fire, from whom the forbidden fruit continues to be filched at Christmas in the shape of raisins soaked in a flaming phlegethon of burning gin.

According to all primitive traditions the Dragon and Griffin were the appointed keepers of the hidden treasures on the Mountain of the Gods; the Mount that interchanges with the Tree. The hyperborean legends tell of the Griffins that guard the Gold. The Dragon of Darkness is described as gloating with lidless eye over its treasury of starry gems and other precious things. These were seen to peep and peer out of the gloom with their live sparkles of lustre at night. And when gold was discovered and made use of, the wealth of stars or sunlight eclipsed by the Dragon would be described as golden. In the same way Heaven was a place of precious stones, and these were in the keeping of the Dragon of

---

[1] Squier, *Serpent Symbol*, fig. 29.   [2] Squier, fig. 52.   [3] Sharpe.

Darkness, under its open-eyed starry type, which had superseded the blind monster of chaos.

In many lands the Serpent has been looked upon as the curator of supernatural treasures of knowledge and the type or medium of communicating wisdom more than mortal. So much so, that one mode of obtaining this was to eat the serpent, or a part of it, and drink the dragon's blood. Philostratus in his life of Apollonius of Tyana asserts that the natives of Hindustan and Arabia ate the heart and liver of serpents for the purpose of acquiring a knowledge of the language and thoughts of animals.[1] So, when Sigurd the Solar Hero was roasting the heart of the Dragon Fafnir, he tried it with his finger to see if it was done, then he put his finger into his mouth and accidentally tasted the blood of the Dragon. Whereupon his eyes and his ears were opened and he understood what the birds sang and the swallows chattered to each other. "*There thou sittest, Sigurd, roasting Fafnir's heart; eat it thyself and become the wisest of men.*" The temptation of Eve is here repeated by the swallows in place of the Serpent! Then Sigurd ate the heart and became a god in power, the most famous of men, learned in all runes, the master of magical arts. A version of the Kamite original of these stories is found in the *Tale of Setnau*.[2] In this there is a precious book of wisdom spoken of, which was written by the hand of Taht himself. It contained the divine mysteries and charms so potent that if two pages of it, those on the back, were recited they would charm heaven and earth, the abyss, the mountain, and the seas. "*Thou shalt know what relates to the birds of the sky and the reptiles, and all that is said by them. The divine power will raise the fishes to the surface of the water. If thou readest the second page it will happen that if thou art in the Amenti thou wilt have power to resume the form which thou hadst on earth.*" This marvellous book had been placed in *a box of iron, inside a box of brass, inside a box of bronze, inside a box of ebony and ivory, inside a box of silver, inside a box of gold*, and concealed in the middle of the river of Coptos. Iron, brass, bronze, ebony, ivory, silver and gold make up the symbolical number Seven, equivalent to the Seven coils of Fafnir the Dragon. Also, there was a live serpent shut up in the box guarding this treasury of learning. The hero finds the box and has to kill the serpent. Having a knife with him he slew it, but it came to life again and again, and all he could do was to cut it in two and *place sand between the two parts so that the serpent could not join together again or resume its former shape.* So, in one of the Norse tales a troll who has carried off the princess is killed, together with his companions, by *one grain of sand* which is

<hr/>

[1] Philostratus, *De Vita Apollonii*, lib. i. c. xiv. When vaccination was first introduced into India, the country-folk held that those who were vaccinated partook of the nature of the cow (Vach), and were more cowardly than other people.

[2] *Records of the Past*, vol. iv. 133.

found beneath the *ninth* tongue in the *ninth* head of a certain dead dragon.[1]   Then the hero reached the writing and read ; he charmed the heaven, earth, abyss, the mountains and the seas.   He understood what related to (or was said by) the birds of the sky, to the fishes of the sea, and to the four-footed beasts of the mountain.   It was spoken in it of them all.   A copy of this magical manuscript was made by the brother of the finder, who wrote down every word, then *dissolved the papyrus in water and drank it, whereupon he knew all that it contained.*

The Serpent is identified by Taht as the guardian who watched over his treasures.   He says to Ra, "*Know that my Law and my Science are with Ptha-nefer-Ka : he hath gone into my dwelling.*   He hath taken *my box beneath my* . . . (lacuna).   *He hath slain my guardian serpent that watched over it.*"   The Serpent is here the Warder of Letters and the Types of Taht.   The Revolution of the Dragon and Great Bear about the Pole constituted the first cycle or year of time, and *thus the Serpent or Dragon became the author of knowledge and the type of wisdom as the starry Intelligencer to men,* the sign of the solstices and equinoxes, the indicator and guide of the recurring seasons.   Gradually the starry Heavens were filled with the earliest hieroglyphics and became a vast volume of hidden knowledge, which the Dragon circling at the northern centre was fabled to possess and to pore upon in secret with its lidless eye.   The knowledge was also the fruit upon the Tree that he protected.   And from this genesis arose the Dragon's mythical love of letters in the later legendary lore.

The Serpent-Type has three phases.   At first it was the representative of physical evil in nature, as the mortal enemy of man, the dart of lightning, the sun-stroke, the sting of death.   As such it was the *Kakodæmon,* the Bad Black Serpent, the Evil One of external phenomena.   Next it was made a type of Time, periodic renewal, eternal circulation, life, salvation, immortality.   This was the *Agathodæmon,* or the Good Serpent.   In its third phase the type of Evil in the physical domain was reproduced as the Evil One, the Dragon, the Devil in the moral or spiritual sphere.   In this the Eschatological stage, the ancient Dragon Typhon who had been the Nurse of Souls in the present life was turned into their devourer in the future state.   Her son, Sut or Sevekh, is identified with the Apophis Monster, the Akhekh of darkness, and changed into. the personal Satan of theology, who had that origin and was " revealed " in no other way.   Sut was formerly the divine Messenger, the earliest Mercury, the character afterwards assigned to the Moon-God, Taht.   He is termed the Great Warrior, and *the God who watches always ; the Good God, the Star of the Two Worlds.*   At Thebes he was pourtrayed as *the Enemy of Apophis, instead of Apophis the Enemy.*   Sevekh

[1] Asbjornsen, new series, "No. 70, p. 39.

appears in the Solar Bark piercing the Apophis with a double-pronged spear, and is called the God who strikes down the Apophis in the fore-part of the Bark of the Sun.[1] These are two names and types of the son of Typhon. When the Draconian Cult was superseded by the Osirian in Egypt, the ancient Mother and her Son (or the Seven) were cast out and re-clothed in the original imagery of Evil, as the Viper Sut, and the Dragon Typhon. There was war in heaven, and the myth of the cast-out Dragon is common to Egypt, Britain, and Babylon. In this later phase it does not imply that either Babylon or Britain derived it from Egypt ready-made; but that the same phenomena were interpreted according to the mythical mode, in accordance with the Gnosis *which was previously a common possession*. The Seven-headed Dragon of Darkness *had been cast out before the Dispersion*, and when the stellar Dragon was found to be playing false as a type of Time because the earth's axis changed in the course of precession, and pointed to a different star as the pivot of its revolution on which all turned, there was a re-application of the typical casting-out of the starry Dragon. The old Dragon of Darkness was self-condemned and self-dethroned. Typhon was thrust out of Egypt by the Osirians; but was changed into a solar God, as Sebek-Ra, by those who continued true to the most ancient Cult. The Dragon tyranny was overthrown by Hu, the Sun-God in Britain, and Arthur—like Sevekh (Khevek or Kek), the old God of Darkness, who was turned into a God of Light—was changed from a Star-God into the Sun-God. HU was celebrated as the deity that put an end to the *Tyranny of the Dragon;* we also hear of the *"Deluge that afflicted the intrepid Dragon."*[2] A Deluge will be shown to be the end of an Æon, cycle, creation, or period of time, which in typical language was called the end of a World. The Dragon was the acknowledged chief of that world in Britain, as the Seven-headed Nâga was in India; as the Seven-headed Dragon was in Akkad; and as it is in Egypt, where the Crocodile-Dragon Sevekh has the name of Number 7. This is represented in the Welsh writings by the passing away of the kingdom of the North when its name of "Y Gogledd" was transferred to Gwynedd the White; and the Dragon was then buried as the Palladium of a new metropolis. So Sesha, in India, is the Seven-headed Dragon as the foundation and support of the new creation rising from the waters of the Deluge.

In the story of "Bel and the Dragon," cut off from the end of the Book of Daniel, the Dragon was the Brazen Serpent, the *Nachash.* *"The King said unto Daniel, Wilt thou also say that this is (merely) of Brass?"*[3] The Nachash, as before suggested, was the *Naka* Serpent on the Ash (Eg.) Tree of Life, the Stauros or Cross being another form of the Tree; and the *Nachushtan* of Israel's worship was the Tan

---

[1] Rosellini, *Mont. da C.* xlvi. [2] *Welsh Archæology,* p. 202.
[3] Verse xxiv.

(Leviathan), or Dragon of the Pole, which was depicted as the Serpent on a pole, cross, or tree, or as we have it still, the Cross-tree at the mast-head, where the flag or pennon flies. It was *not* merely Brass, but a magnificent emblem, full of meaning for those who could read the primordial figures and types. Daniel's manner of killing the Dragon with pitch and fat is exactly the same as that adopted by an English hero, who killed the Worm, only the Hebrew writer has failed to set fire to the pitch. This tends to identify Daniel with the Solar God who slew and succeeded the Dragon. The same overthrow of the Dragon by the Sun-God is one of the most ancient traditions of, Greece. Apollo destroyed the Dragon and took his place as Guardian and Inspirer of the Oracle.[1] In all these instances it was the final overthrow; not the daily or yearly triumph of the Solar God, as it was in the earliest and vague stage of the mythic conflict, but a total change in which the divinity of Light superseded the Dragon of Darkness altogether. In Babylon Bel (the Akkadian Bil-ge) became a Solar God and overthrew the Dragon. In Revelation *"there was war in heaven." " Michael* (Makha-El, or Har-Makhu), *and his angels going forth to war with the Dragon, and the Dragon warred and his angels; and they prevailed not, neither was their place found any more in heaven. And the great Dragon was cast down to the earth, and his angels were cast down with him. And I heard a great voice in heaven saying, ' Now has come the salvation and the power and the king-dom of our God, and the authority of His Christ: for the Accuser of our Brethren is cast down, which accuseth them before our God day and night.' And they overcame him because of the blood of the Lamb."* [2] Or because the Sun had entered the sign of the Lamb. This is not a description of the Dragon as the cause of the Annual Eclipse. It is the personification of Sut-Typhon as the Dragon or Draconis of the Pole-Star. The great celestial Apostate is absolutely identified as the Polar Dragon by the Seventy, who render the " Crooked Serpent " as the Δράκοντα τὸν ἀποστατὴν. " By his hand he hath slain the Apostate Dragon." [3] The Apostasy consisted in its falling away from the True Pole of the Heaven when the earth's axis changed in the course of precession. Moreover, the supremacy of the Dragon as the watcher and guardian of the Tree of Know-ledge, or the Pole, is *especially connected with the sun in the sign of the Bull;* and about the time of the sun's entrance into the sign of the Ram, the Crocodile God of Darkness (Khevekh) was turned into Sebek-Ra, wearing the head of a Ram with the erect Serpent. The Sebek-Hepts of Egypt considered the Ram to be a Lamb, a biune type of either sex. In the Persian planisphere the Ram figures as a Lamb. This is the Lamb in the Book of Revelation. Hence the great change resulting from the shifting of the Pole-star coincides roughly with the sun's entrance into the sign of the Lamb when

---

[1] Hyginus, *Fab.* 140.   [2] Rev. xii. 7—11   [3] Job xxvi. 13.

there was war in heaven, and the dragon was cast out. The writer of Revelation reproduced the matter from the Parsee scriptures or Mithraic writings, but the original mythos is Egyptian. Sut-Typhon the cast-out Satan of Egypt, had been degraded into the Apophis type of darkness as the Accuser of Souls in the Hades, and it is again and again proclaimed in the Ritual that the " Accuser Sut " is overthrown. " *The Apophis and Accusers of the Sun fall overthrown.*" " *Overthrown is the advance of the Apophis.*" " *The tongue that is greater than the envious tongue of a Scorpion has failed in its power for ever.*" " *The Great Apophis and the Accusers of the Sun have been judged by Akar.*" [1] This will be found *en bloc* in the Book of Revelation.[2] " *Another beast*" succeeds the casting out of the Dragon with Seven Heads and Ten Horns (these will be identified hereafter). " *And I saw another Beast coming up out of the earth, and he had two Horns like unto a Lamb* (the Ram), *and he spake as a Dragon. And he exerciseth all the authority of the first Beast in his sight, and he maketh the earth and them that dwell therein to worship the first Beast.*" " *He that hath understanding let him count the number of the Beast ; for it is the number of a Man: and his number is Six-Hundred-and-Sixty-Six.*" [4] Now, in the original mythos, there are in fact three forms of the Dragon or Beast. The first of all is the genitrix Typhon of the Seven Stars. The second is her son Sevekh, the Dragon or Crocodile, also of the Seven Stars and of the Seventh Planet, Saturn. The third is the same Dragon (Beast) in his final character, as Sebek-Ra, the Solar God of the Typhonians, who was worshipped especially at Ombos and Selseleh in Egypt. The Dragon and Ram were both united in him whether we take the Serpent or Crocodile for the typical Dragon. The Star-God Sevekh was continued as the Sun-God Sebek ; even the mode of spelling his name was changed. Sevekh reads number 7, but Sebek *may* have been read number 6 as Seb is number 5, and k ⟅ signifies one more. This change could scarcely have been unintentional. Sevekh, the son of Typhon, was degraded by the Osirians in Egypt, and turned into an eschatological image of the Evil One. The Crocodile was hurled into Hades, where he is a follower of the Apap of Darkness, and is blended with it under a type called the *Shes-shes,* or *Sessi,* to whom it is said by the defenders of Ra, " *Thou art destroyed, crushed, punished (Serpent) Sessi.*" [5] This Beast is a Dragon-like Crocodile with the Apap for its tail, and as the Crocodile is Sevekh this Typhonian Monster is a form of the Dragon that was cast out of heaven. The Apap identifies it with the Dragon of Darkness, and the Crocodile shows the original type of the mythical Dragon, Sevekh of the Seven Stars. Again, we have the Beast whose name was number 7 turned

[1] Ch. xxxix.
[2] Ch. xii.
[3] Ch. xiii. 11, 12.
[4] Ch. xiii. 18.
[5] *Book of Hades. Records,* v. x. pp. 130, 133.

into a possible figure of six. For Ses (Eg.) is the number 6, and he is called *Sessi*. According to Jamblichus, 60 was the number of the Crocodile.[1] This seems a strange statement to Egyptologists, who would reply that Sevekh is the Crocodile, and it has the name of number 7. But the "Wisdom" of Egypt has not yet been fathomed by mere transcription of the hieroglyphic language. Plutarch also tells us that the Crocodile lays *sixty* eggs, is *sixty* days in hatching them, and lives *sixty* years, this being the first or foremost measure employed by the Egyptian astronomers. When Sevekh of the Seven Stars became the Crocodile Solar God, he was forthwith associated with the number *six, as the number of the four corners, and the Nadir and Zenith*. Like Anu, the Babylonian Heaven-God, he was the *one-six*, on this cubic foundation. Moreover, in his change from a Star-God into a Sun-God, Sebek combined the two planetary characters of Saturn and Ra in the Solar Dragon. These two being blended in one, there were but five other planets, or *six heads altogether*. A similar reduction of the old Dragon might be traced in the Hindu mythos by means of *Sesha* who is the *Teacher of Astronomy* to Garga. *Sesha* began as the Serpent of Infinity, the Egyptian serpent of the universe and the annual renovation. Next it was the Seven-headed *Nâga* that upheld the Seven Patalas on its heads. Then it became incarnated in Bala-rama who is the essential Soul of Vishnu.[2] Bala represents force considered as the *Sixth* organ of action. Thus the Seven-headed *Sesha* is related to the No. 6, *Vishnu being the Sun-God of the under-world, after the Three Regions and Six directions of space had been founded*. This same continuity of the serpent or Draconian type may be traced in connection with Vishnu with Hea, with Num, and with Sut-Nub or Chnubis. In each instance it becomes the representative of the Solar God in the Sixfold heaven; and in each re-adaptation of the type the Seven-headed serpent or dragon might be described as losing one of its heads and becoming a symbolical figure of Six or S, which when thrice repeated and joined together in accordance with the three regions is SSS or 666, the "Beast" in the final *planetary* phase. We shall trace Sevekh in the Seven-rayed Sun-God of the Gnostic-stones on which the Dragon of the Seven Stars, still identifiable by the seven rays, becomes the Serpent *Chnubis*. Enough at present to point out that on these stones the Solar Dragon with the Seven Rays appears with the sign S S S (triple S's) with a bar for its reverse.[3] The Greek S, like the Coptic, has the numeral value of six. As an ideograph, this is Ses (Eg.), whence the phonetic S retained that value. Thus, three S's may be read 666, the number of the Second Beast in the Book of Revelation. The Beast is doubly identified on the same stone as the Beast of the Seven Stars with the Seven Rays on the one side and the

---

[1] Jamblichus, *De Myst*, sect. v. ch. viii.   [2] *MahaBh.-Santi-p.* 989٢.
[3] King's *Gnostics*, pl. 3.

numerical value of 666 on the other, the *Abrasax* stone being the six-sided cube-figure of the solar foundation. Chnubis the Golden is a continuation of the Egyptian Sut-Nub. We are compelled to employ the type-name of Sut as well as Sevekh for the Son of Typhon! And in Coptic the S is Sut by name. Thus Sut is also identified with the number 6. Again, in Chaldee the name of number 6 is *Shet.* Now it appears from the inscription of Shebaka, who bears the name of the Crocodile God, that one of the most ancient traditions of Egypt alluded to in an obscure legend of the 15th Choiak regarding the once venerated Sut derived him from the south (which still bears his name), and affirmed that his birthplace was in Su-su-su (or S S S).[1] Brugsch Bey also cites other inscriptions in which S S S is mentioned as the birthplace of Sut, and he gives the hieroglyphs as ∏ ∏ ∏ ⊕ (S S S). Here the birthplace of the Beast is named 666. The Birth-place in time would be the beginning of a Cycle, to which the number related. S S S, or Su Su Su, is also the "name of a Man" as a Pharaoh, who is number 43 on the Karnak tablet. Niebuhr tells us how in the year of Rome 666 *the Haruspice announced that the mundane day of the Etruscan nation was drawing to a close.* This points to a form of the Saros under the number of 666, and the name of the Saros in Chaldee has the numeral value of 666. Thus

ש	(S)	300
ע	(A)	70
ר	(R)	200
ו	(O)	6
צ	(S)	90
		666

Various names may be derived from letters which contain the numeral value of 666 or the equivalent of S S S; the Number of the Beast having to be *counted* with understanding. Figures were earlier than Phonetic Letters because they originated as Ideographs. In the Gnosis or Kabalah, the Secret Wisdom was often set forth by means of figures rather than Letters, and the Word had to be transliterated and reckoned up according to numerical values. Hence Irenæus was in a measure right when he gave it as his conclusion that "*Teitan*" was "*by far the most probable name*" (of the Beast) although he was ignorant of the true reason why.[2]

Teitan is the Chaldean form of Sheitan, who is still adored by what are termed the Devil-Worshippers of Kurdistan, Sheitan being our

---

[1] Cols. 15 and 17, Goodwin in Chabas' *Mélanges, &c.*
[2] Irenæus, b. v. ch. xxx.

Satan. The Hebrew Sh is frequently rendered by the Chaldean T. The value of the Coptic Letters is:—

T	.	.	.	.	.	300
E	.	.	.	.	.	5
I	.	.	.	.	.	10
T	.	.	.	.	.	300
A	.	.	.	.	.	1
N	.	.	.	.	.	50
						666

Teitan was the opprobrious name given to the Sons of Heaven in the Greek Legend of the Fall. Hesiod says the Father called the Revolters by an opprobrious name, *Teitans*, when he cursed them and they were cast down into Tartarus, and bound in chains of darkness in the Abyss.[1]

Sut or Sevekh was Saturn under his Planetary Type, and in Chaldee Saturn is Satur, *i.e. Stur*, and the numerical value is:—

S	.	.	.	.	60
T	.	.	.	.	400
U	.	.	.	.	6
R	.	.	.	.	200
					666

The Second Beast whose number was 666 commanded those who dwell on earth that they should make an Image of the Seven-headed Beast that had the stroke of the Sword and yet lived *after it had lost one of its heads*. This therefore would represent the number Six—*Ses*, Egyptian, *Shesh*, Hebrew, *Shash*, Sanskrit.

The Beast that "*had Two Horns like unto a Lamb*" and "*spake as a Dragon*" is the express image of the Crocodile-and-Ram-headed Sebek-Ra; "*and he exerciseth all the authority of the first Beast*," identifies him with Sevekh of the Seven Stars, the Son of the Red Dragon, Typhon, the genitrix of the earliest Gods.

The change from the type of Seven to that of Six is indicated by the loss of one of the heads of the Beast that had Seven heads. "*And I saw one of the heads as it were wounded to death, and his deadly wound was healed.*"[2] This would leave Sevekh of the Seven Stars and Seven heads with only Six when the wound was healed. The change from the Beast that was, and is not, and yet is, explains the change of Sevekh from the stellar to the solar phase as well

---

[1] *Theogony*, i. 207; ii. 717, 729.   [2] Rev. xiii. 3.

as the loss of the horn. The Woman and the Seven Kings are the ancient genitrix and her Seven Children, who were the Gods of Seven Constellations yet to be described. In treating of Sebek as the Gnostic IAO we shall see *how* the Beast that was and was not and yet is took two of the Seven Characters, those of the Sun and Saturn on himself, and so brought the Seven Planetary types under the six heads of the Dragon.

The Third Beast, then, is the same as the Second in a new phase, that of Sevekh the Star-God turned into Sebek the Sun-God, "*with two Horns like a Lamb*," who "*spake as a Dragon*," *i.e.*, a Crocodile. This is the portrait of the Ram-(lamb)headed Crocodile or Dragon in his Solar Character!

The Woman who sat on the Seven Hills, which were also Seven Kings, the Seven Crowned Heads of the Dragon, still sits on the Seven Hills of Rome, where she has never been dethroned.

The old Sut, Sevekh, Satan, or Satur, the Beast of the Number 666 (Stur) came to a curious double ending in the Christian continuations. He was canonized as a saint in the Romish Calendar under the name of St. *Satur;* March the 29th[1] being the Festival of "St. Satur, the Martyr." So that the Divinity of one cult, the Devil of a second, was continued as the Saint of a third.

The *Tan* that rose up in revolt as the natural Darkness, called the Dragon of the Deep, became at last a spiritual terror as the Satan, שׂטן, the rebel against the God of light, the adversary of souls: and thus the Old Serpent or Dragon of physical phenomena has been transformed into a supposed spiritual Being, a *Vice-Dieu* of the dark

---

[1] Chambers's *Book of Days*, vol. i. p. 435.

[2] Elliott[1] has observed that the Kabalists used to ask "*What is the Lily?*" (Shushnah) in the Book of Esther, rendered by Shushan as a proper name in the A. V., "*because both words contained the same numeral value.*" This is given as the No. 661.

שׂ	300	א	1
ו	6	ס	60
שׂ	300	ת	400
נ	50	ר	200
ה	5		
	661		661

But this is to miss the secret meaning. It may be supposed that the Kabalists would use the *He* for "*the* Lily," and also write the name *Hesther* in accordance

---

[1] *Horæ Apocalyptica*, vol. iii. p. 205, note.

who, on the whole, is considered a greater power than the divine;
and who has evoked the more assured belief; for Theology has made
the primal shadow substantial and permanent in the mental sphere;
and from the darkness of the beginning it has abstracted the Devil
in the end.

with that of *Hadasah*. The He adds five, making the number 666. Thus,
H'shushnah for "the Lily" has the numeral value of 666. Hesther is the Hebrew
form of Ishtar or Shetar (Eg.) the Betrothed, and the character of the Betrothed
is performed by Hesther for twelve months.[1] The Kabalistic conceit of "the
Lily," Hesther, and the mystical number is precisely the same as that of the Beast.

The Lotus-Lily was a symbol of the genitrix or Virgin-Mother, who sat upon
the Waters as the Scarlet Lady of mystery and abomination. The Sistrum was
another symbol of the Beast Hes, Isis, or "Seses," a Gnostic name of Isis.
Its name of *Seshsh* contains the three S's, value 666. These were represented by the three wires, that make it a figure or image of the No. 666.

Astarte, also, in a dual or compound character called Isis-Minerva, has
been found under the title of Saosis or 666 when the S's are read according
to the numeral value of the letters. The Beast was of both sexes, according to
the double Constellation of the Seven Stars. M. Renan is of opinion that the
"Man" identified with the Beast is Nero, whose name, when written on the coins
and standards as Νέρων Καῖσαρ, or נרון קסר, which, if each Hebrew letter is given
its proper numerical value, amounts precisely to 666. The present identification,
however, is only concerned with the mythical Beast. The "Beast" is primary;
it belongs to the Astronomical Allegory and the Gnosis in two forms. In one
of these it had the feet of a *Bear*. In the second it becomes six-headed. The
allusion to the man is merely *en passant*. Nothing can be got out of the letters
χξς, as they stand; unless we identified the Beast with *Kakos*, the dragon of
darkness, the Egyptian *Kek*. But there can be no doubt the riddle is numerical.

---

[1] Ch. ii. 12.

SECTION VII.

NATURAL GENESIS AND TYPOLOGY OF THE MYTHICAL MOUNT, TREE, CROSS, AND FOUR CORNERS.

IT has now to be shown, by a world-wide range of illustration, how the Mount and the Tree became two of the chief sacred types and figures of expression for the primitive and pre-historic man. Max Müller has remarked that when the Hindu poets exclaim *"What Wood, what Tree was it of which they* (the gods) *made Heaven and Earth ?"* this means, in the ancient language of religious poetry, *Only of what material were Heaven and Earth formed ?* [1] On the contrary they speak according to the system of Typology which was universal once and interpretable in all lands. It is the same language spoken by Homer when Penelope says to Ulysses : " *Tell me thy lineage, and whence thou art, for thou dost not spring from the ancient Tree nor from the Rock.*" [2] Tree and Rock, the Stock and Stone of all the olden world-wide fetishism.

Hesiod knew that the Tree and the Rock involved great mysteries. In the *Theogony*, the singer being bidden to sing of the race of the ever-living ever-blessed immortals, asks why should he begin by telling tales or blabbing mysteries concerning the Sacred Tree (oak) or the Rock? [3] The " Rock of Israel " was a type of the Progenitor of that people. " *But*," says Max Müller, " *the Hebrews speak in a very different sense from that in which Homer speaks of the Rock from which Man has sprung.*" [4] The answer is that the typology is the same wherever found.

When the son of the chief of the Bushmen who lived in the neighbourhood of the Moravian station at Glenadendal became a Christian, he told the Missionaries that the Bushmen performed a kind of religious worship to Two Rocks, the one representing a male and the other a female. On going out to hunt they implored the aid of these deities to provide them with food. First they went to the male rock and struck it with a stick ; if it sounded they believed the report

---

[1] *Chips*, v. ii. p. 209. [2] *Odyss.* 19, 163. [3] 30—35. [4] *Science of Religion*, p. 42.

was heard in *heaven* and they would have success ; but if they got nothing they repaired to the female rock, which they thought was inhabited by a malicious spirit, and beat it well, upbraiding it, saying ; " *Why do you, by your hidden arms, cause all the game to be shot dead so that we can find none ?* " [1]

The Rock or Mount is also reverenced by the Negroes on the Gold Coast, where it is called *Tabora*, the same type by name as the Mount Tabor, the Egyptian *Tepr* the point of commencement in a circle. The Zulus have the Magical Tree, and the Rock with two holes which opens and shuts at the voice of those who know the secret. [2] The hereditary title of the Chief of Pango-pango, Samoa, is *Maunga*, the Mountain ; as was the Egyptian *Seri* and the Hebrew *Tzer*. " Great Mountain ". is the title of the supreme Divinity of the Santhals. One of the New Zealand chiefs claimed the neighbouring mountain, Tongoriro, for his progenitor. " *This seemingly whim-sical belief,*" says Mr. Spencer, " *becomes intelligible when we observe how easily it may have arisen from a nickname. Do we not ourselves sometimes speak figuratively of a tall fat man as a mountain of flesh ?*" [3] True, but here, again, we have the same system of typology as in Africa, India, and Greece. The Mount and the Tree were primordial types of the genitrix, of Khepsh, of Ri (Ishtar) Hathor Kêd, Parvati, and others. Primally it was the Mount of the North, the birth-place of beginning. Tongoriro denotes the very lofty. In Egyptian Seri is the Mountain (or Rock) and the Chieftain, the Head ; in Hebrew, the God. The Maori Chief claimed descent from the olden Rock or Mountain. The mountain Maunga is named from Mau, fixed, enduring : and the same word signifies a product of Earth. The Chief was descended from the Motherhood in its first form, that of Earth, which was represented by the Mount and the Tree. According to Paul, Hagar the Mother of Ishmael was Mount Sinai, in Arabia. Therefore Ishmael was likewise the Son of the Mount as typical birthplace. It is also certain that Paul knew this symbolical nature of the Mount when he said it answered to Jeru-salem, the " *Mother of us all.*" [4]

The genitrix who was represented by the Mount came to be called the great Harlot and Prostitute, on account of the early status of the Mother. She is still identified by the Rock or Mount as the " Bad Woman " of Hongkong. This is the name of a particular rock on the hill near Wanchai that presides over the illicit intercourse of the sexes. Those who make money by immoral practices still offer her a share of their profits, and burn frankincense at the foot of this Rock, which remains a monument of the Motherhood as it was in the primitive sociology. [5]

[1] *Historical Sketches of the Missions of the United Brethren*, p. 383.
[2] Callaway.   [3] *Fortnightly Review*, 1870, p. 542.
[4] Gal. iv. 25, 26.   [5] Eitel, *Feng Shui*, p. 53.

The mythical heroes of the Parsees were born of the Mount Ushi-Darena, from which they are said to descend with the glory shining on their faces.

The Navajos claim the Mount for their birthplace and attribute their deliverance from the underworld dwelling in the heart of it to the Moth-Worm that mounted and made a way out of the Mountain when he found himself in a world all water.[1] The world all water was the heaven above; the Moth-worm is a symbol of the breathing power. The Indians of Guinea venerate the Tree and Mount under the figure of a great rock that rises sheer up for fifty feet like the trunk of a gigantic stem; this is designated " *Pure-piapa* " or the "headless Tree." [2] In Plato's Timæus the prototypes of our race are spoken of as being inclosed in, and developed from the Great Tree, which is not to be understood except by knowing the history of the Tree as a type of the genitrix. The Lenni Lenape Indians relate that Manitu at the beginning floated on the water and shaped the earth out of a grain. He then made a man and a woman out of a tree. The "Popul Vuh" describes man as being created from a tree named the Tzité. Woman, according to the same authority was formed from the marrow of a reed called Sibac. The Hindus still ascribe genders to the bamboo, reed, or cane; and the female one contains the pith, the male the hard substance. The Sioux Indians have a myth of the primal Man who stood for many ages with his feet made fast in the soil and growing like a tree. Near him grew another tree. A snake gnawed them off at the root, whereupon they walked away as human beings. [3] The Serpent that gnaws at the root of the Tree re-appears as Nidhogg beneath one of the roots of Yggdrasill. But in neither instance can anything be made out of such statements until the typology is interpreted.

The Philippine Islanders narrate how the world at first consisted of Sky and Water, and between these there was nothing but a Glede, which, finding no place of rest, and being weary of flying about set the Water at variance with the Sky; this he did in order to keep it within bounds; and, to prevent its getting uppermost, he loaded the water with a number of islands to settle on and leave the Sky at peace. Then mankind sprang out of a large Cane with two joints that floated about in the water, and was thrown by the waves against the feet of the Glede which stood on the shore and opened the Cane with its bill. A man issued from one joint, a woman from the other.[4] The Tree or Cane with two joints denotes the two sexes that were divided first at Puberty. So Tiri split the Tree into Man and Woman. The one that split the Tree or opened the Cane represents à type of pubescence like the Stone of Pundjel or the Tortoise of

[1] Bancroft, vol. iii. p. 81.   [2] Brett, pp. 314, 375, and 447.
[3] J. G. Müller, p. 109.
[4] Marsden, *History of Sumatra*, p. 303.

Fohi. Here it is the Glede or Hawk, a Kamite symbol of Soul which as the soul of pubescence did divide to distinguish the sexes, or split the double-jointed Cane in two.

As the three sons of Bor were one day walking along the sea-beach they found two stems of wood floating on the waters. Out of these they shaped a Man and a Woman. Odin breathed into them the breath of life; Honir made them to go, and Lodur caused them to speak, hear, and see. The Man they called Ask (or Ash), the Woman Embla. From these two descend the whole human race.[1] A tree was pointed out to the traveller Erman as an important monument of an early epoch in the history of Beresov. When the Ostiak rulers dwelt there in former times this tree was a particular object of adoration. It was a larch about fifty feet high, and its peculiar sacredness was connected with the singularity of its form and growth. For about six feet upward from the earth the trunk had divided into two equal parts and then united above in a single bole.[2] Thus the tree offered an obvious image of the door-way of life. "*Honour your paternal Aunt, the Date-Palm* (says Muhammed), *for she was created in Paradise of the same earth as that from which Adam was formed.*"

The Stake, that is a reduced form of the Tree, still represents the first mother and the later ancestors in the sacrificial feasts of the Damaras; they stick this type of the tree and primal parent into the ground and offer the first portions of the feast to it.

The Veddas who dwell in huts made of bark live in a primitive form of the tree-ark, and their name for the house *Rukula*, means the hollow tree in Singhalese. The Tasmanians returned their dead to the mother's arms under this type, by burying them in a hollow tree.[3] The hollow tree or *Cos* was also a British coffin. The inhabitants of Thebes in the eleventh dynasty, many of whom are negroes, were buried in coffins formed of the hollowed trunk of a peculiar kind of tree, which is no longer met with except in the Soudan.[4] The Tree of the birth-place is yet extant in Germany, north and south, as "*Frau Holda's Tree*;" the common name for old decayed and hollow boles. A hollow tree in or overhanging a pool is still recognised

---

[1] *Prose Edda.*   [2] Erman, *Travels in Siberia*, v. i. p. 464.

[3] The recent fall of an enormous puketea tree near Opotiki, New Zealand, disclosed the fact that the hollow interior from the roots to the first fork, about forty-five feet from the ground, had been filled with human bones. A confused heap of skeletons burst out of the butt of the tree when it fell. A local paper says :—
"A more extraordinary sight than this monarch of the forest lying prone and discharging a perfect hecatomb of human skeletons can scarcely be conceived. Some are nearly perfect while others are mixed up in a chaotic mass of heads, hands, feet, and arms, indiscriminately. All the Maoris here seem to have been quite unaware of this natural charnel-house, and declare that it must have been filled long before their or their fathers' time. Indeed the appearance of the tree fully justifies the supposition that it must have been some hundreds of years since this novel family vault was filled with its ghastly occupants." — *Knowledge*, August 4, 1882.

[4] Mariette, *Monuments of Upper Egypt*, p. 147.

as the habitation of unborn children. A Hessian legend describes the genitrix Frau Holda as a lovely woman in front and behind a hollow tree with a rugged bark.[1] An ancient tree once stood on the Heinzenberg near Zell, which was the shrine of "Our Lady" the genitrix. When the woodman cut it down it was said to utter its moan. At the present time "Our Lady's" chapel stands on the same spot.[2] The chapel superseded the tree, and "Our Lady" who was Holda once, is Mary now. It is the same in Egypt. There the sycamore is sacred to Hathor, the Egyptian Venus, who is styled "Mistress of the Sycamore" at Maturea. In the Ritual the solar god. is said to issue forth from the midst of the copper-coloured sycamore. The tree being employed as a type of the genitrix and birth-place (locality) in one. Maturea is named from Mat an ancient name of An the place of birth, beginning and repetition, where the tree of the Two Truths grew in the pool of Persea, or the tree of life stood in the water of life. To this day the sycamore-fig of Hathor, one of whose characters and names is Meri (and this is likewise a name of her tree as the Meri or mulberry-fig), is pointed to at Maturea as the tree of Mary and her child. In the Arab traditions the divine child Jesus was also said to have been concealed in the trunk of the *Gemaseh* tree, a spider having spun its web over the entrance to hide him from his pursuers. The mother of Confucius is reputed to have been told in a dream by the Black Te that she should bring forth the divine child in a hollow mulberry-tree.[3] The elder tree is an especial type of Holda the old or elder mother, the Danish Uildmoer who, as herein maintained, is one with the Egyptian Urta the bearer, and Irish Arth the Bear. The Earth is of course one type of the bearer under the same name, but the tree would be first recognised as the yielder of fruit. The mother-tree in England is often reduced to the status of a gooseberry-bush, beneath which the babies are found, but it is still a bearer of fruit. The tree as a type of the birth-place will account for the custom of passing diseased infants through a split sapling or the cleft of a stem which, in some cases, may have signified a transference of the disease to a genius of health supposed to reside in the tree.

But primarily the tree typified renewal, and this was a symbolical mode of rebirth from the mother imaged as the tree. Such was the idea in the eschatological phase where the adult was regenerated and born anew in the mysteries, whether · from the tree, the holed-stone, the ark, cow, or any other type of the *rue des femmes*, when the object was a moral or spiritual renewal. The tree was a type of healing when the rags and other tokens of disease were hung upon it by the sufferers praying for assistance. When the Khonds hung up the hands of their slain foemen on the tree it was a type of their deity

---

[1] Mannhardt, pp. 280—3. [2] Grimm, *D. M.* p. 615.
[3] Legge, *Chinese Classics*, v. i. p. 59.

to whom they offered their trophies. In this aspect the tree is equivalent to the "Hill-Altar" of the Jews, upon which they offered their propitiatory sacrifice. "*His own self bare our sins in his own body on the tree*,"[1] is a continuation of the tree itself, which had borne the propitiatory offering on its living altar. But, in all the oldest mythologies the tree is a type of the motherhood, and the child is her branch. The Egyptian Rennut is the nurse, the Rennu is her nursling, and Renpu to renew, be young, is the name of the branch, shoot or plant, as the child of the tree. The genitrix as Hathor is pourtrayed in the tree or by the tree, and as the tree half human in shape. From this she pours out the drink of life and furnishes the food upon which souls are fed.

In one picture the deceased standing with his body on one side of the tree of life, and as a soul on the other exclaims, "*Oh, Sycamore of Nut, give me the water and the breath of life which proceed from thee, that I may have the vigour of the goddess of vigour.*"[2] He receives the water of life as a being of flesh and blood; the breath of life as a spirit, both from the Mother in accordance with the Two Truths, and in their earliest phase. Isis is said to have found the Ark of Osiris exposed on the river Nile, containing the Child, entangled in a thicket of heath or tamarisk, the Aseru, a form of the tree of life,[3] which had entwined about the Ark and Child until both were completely inclosed within its trunk, now grown up into a stately tree. This tree which contained the invisible Chest, or Ark, and Child, was *made into a pillar to support the roof of a royal palace.* Isis being informed of this went herself to Byblus. When she came there, she sat down hard by a well. Here she met with the Ark-tree; "*she begged the post that held up the roof.*" This tree, or pillar, she trimmed of its bushy heath, poured perfumed oil upon it and wrapped the trunk in fine linen, and thenceforth it was laid up in the Temple of Isis.[4]

A similar myth of the tree and child is related of Krishna. One legend describes how he was transformed into the trunk of sandal-wood, or the tchandana tree, and that after being planted in Yamouna, near *Mathurea*, it passed from thence to the holy waters of the Ganges, and these bore it to the shore of Orica.[5]

In the North the ash, which is the tree of life in Egypt, is known as the "Refuge of Thor," because that tree caught and saved him when he was being swept away by the river Vimur, just as the Child Osiris was being swept away, but was saved by the tree, inferentially as the type of a land-mark.

So supreme an emblem of reproduction was the tree in India that the Buddha is fabled to have been incarnated some forty or fifty times under the tree-type, the tree of knowledge, wisdom or enlightenment.

[1] I Peter, ii. 24. [2] *Records*, vol. 12, p. 177. Libation Vase of User-Ur.
[3] *Tamarisk, vide* Book of Enoch, ch. xxxi. [4] Plutarch, *Of Osis and Osiris.*
[5] Creuzer, *Symbolik*, par J. D. Guigniaut, tom. i. pp. 208, 209.

Maurice observes that "*it is a fact, not less remarkable than well-attested, that the Druids in their Groves were accustomed to select the most stately and beautiful tree as an emblem of the deity they adored, and having cut off the side branches, they affixed two of the largest of them to the highest part of the trunk in such a manner that these branches extended on each side like the arms of a man, and together with the body, presented the appearance of a huge cross, and in the bark in several places was inscribed the letter Tau.*"[1] On the central upright stem he says they cut the word "Taramis," on the right hand branch the name of "Hesus," and on the left hand one "Belinus." Taramis represents the Daronwy of the Druids. Taliesin celebrated this tree as the great refuge from the flood. "*What tree is greater than he, Daronwy? I know not for a refuge around the proud circle of Heaven that there is a mystery which is greater.*"[2] Belin, it may be remarked, is an Inner African type-name for the *Young one*, the new thing, the *Rennu* (Eg.).

Belin, is Young, in Kanuri.		*Belin*, is Young, in N'guru.	
Belin ,, ,, Munio.		*Belin* ,, ,, Kanem.	

The Mother of Adonis was said to have been metamorphosed into a tree, and in that shape to have brought forth the divine child.[3] On the coins of ancient Crete the genitrix is pourtrayed, like Hathor or Nupe, in the tree.[4]

In the Phrygian Mysteries, called those of the Mother of the gods a pine-tree was cut down every year, and the image of a youth was bound on the inside. This was on the first day of the feast of Kubele.[5] "*What means that pine,*" asks Arnobius, "*which on certain days you bring into the sanctuary of the Mother of the gods?*" This he identifies with the tree of the genitrix, beneath which the youth Attis laid hands upon himself, and which the Mother consecrated in solace of her own wound.[6]

The "*dark pine*" that grew in Eridu was the seat, shrine, and couch, of the Akkadian genitrix *Zikum*. She who was the tree that bore the child as Tammuz or Duzi. "*In Eridu a dark pine grew. It was planted in a holy place. Its crown was crystal white, which spread towards the deep vault above. The Abyss of Hea was its pasturage in Eridu, a canal full of waters. Its station (seat) was the centre of this earth. Its shrine was the couch of Mother Zikum. The (roof) of its holy house like a forest spread its shade; there (were) none who entered not within it. It was the seat of the mighty Mother.*"[7]

In Egypt the sycamore-fig is the chief type of the tree of life from which the Great Mother, as Hathor, pours out the divine drink.

---

[1] Maurice, *Indian Antiquities*, vol. vi. p. 49. [2] Skene, vol. i. p. 269.
[3] Ovid, *Metam.* lib. x. ver. 500—13. [4] Calmet, pl. 51, figs. 1, 2, 3.
[5] De Sacy. [6] Arnobius, 5. 16.
[7] *Records of the Past*, vol. ix. p. 146.

Hathor was the *Sekhem,* or Shrine of the child, in the shape of the sycamore tree, also this type of the tree, genitrix, womb, shrine, and tomb may be traced back by name to Inner Africa. The typical tree is the—

Dsigma, in Nupe.	*Tsugma,* or *Tsugba,* in Esitako.	*Tagma,* in Ebe.
Tsigmo, in Kupa.	*Tsimo,* in Gugu.	

In this name the *Tes* that is ideographic in the hieroglyphics supplies the T and S which permute in later language. Thus *Sekh* (Eg.), liquid, drink, interchanges with *Tekh,* drink, liquid, wine; to supply with drink; whilst the *Tsigmo* in Kupa becomes *Tugma* in Ebe. In Hebrew the typical tree as the Saqamah (שקמה) is the sycamore-fig-tree. Also we have a species of fig tree called the *sycamine* in English. The fig is an emblem of the womb, the *Sekhem* (Eg.), one of those feminine types like the pomegranate, the Persea fruit, or the lotus which contain their seed within themselves, and it is the fruit of the sycamore-fig-tree. In the African Gura the abode as a hut is the *Saguma.* The Swedish *Skemma* is a store-house for the fruits of the earth. In Egypt the *Sekhem* had become a Sacred Shrine representing the Mother; the abode of Horus in Utero.

The Turks have a tradition that when Mary and the Child were being pursued by the murderers whom Herod sent after them, they came to the tree at Maturea which *having the power of opening and shutting,* opened to receive the parents and saved the child.[1] In this legend the *Sekhem,* or sycamore tree, becomes the Egyptian "*Sekhem,*" which means the *Shut-place,* and Shrine. The typical tree of Inner Africa, the Sekhem of Egypt, Zikum of Akkad, survives in the Koran as Al-*zakkum,* the tree of knowledge; but how different says the text, from the abode of Eden. Here it issues from the bottom of hell, and is planted solely for the torment of the wicked. The fruit of it resembles the heads of devils or serpents (for the word signifies both), so that it is still the tree of the serpent, and the damned are to eat of it and fill their bellies therewith, washing down the fruit with scalding liquor.[2]

The Lord said, "*If ye have faith as a grain of mustard-seed, ye would say unto this sycamine tree, Be thou rooted up, and be thou planted in the sea; and it would have obeyed you.*"[3] This may possibly contain an occult allusion to the tree of the Motherhood which was superseded in the Worship of the Son; the tree of Zikum in Eridu, and of Hathor at Maturea.

The natural genesis of the typical tree is self-evident. Norden describes the sycamore-fig as a very tree of life in Egypt. He says the people almost live off it. This tree is always green and bears its fruit several times a year, without observing any change of season.[4]

[1] Ogilby's *Africa,* p. 73.
[2] *Al-Koran,* Sale, ch. xxxvii. and notes.
[3] Luke xvii. 6.
[4] Norden, *Travels,* vol. i. p. 79.

Ficus sycomorus in Egypt sometimes measures fifty feet in girth. But equatorial Africa is the paradise of the sycamore tree, which grows there to a size befitting the roof-tree of the world.

Captain Cameron describes three vast specimens towering outside the town of Khoko which formed a prominent mark for miles around. One of these afforded ample shelter for 500 people who encamped under its branches.[1] Another type of the food-bestower is the Baobab or Monkey-bread-tree of Central Africa which sometimes attains a girth of thirty yards in the trunk. When it loses its leaves in the dry season, fruit the size of a half-quartern loaf is seen suspended all round it. The wood soon decays and most of the older boles are hollow like those of Frau Holda; these become reservoirs of rain, from which the natives draw water in the dry season, and in the day of need. A magnificent tree of life was the bread-and-water tree for man as for monkey. Its leaves are eaten by the negroes, and the apes are very fond of its fruit which has a slightly acid pulp. Now, one of the old folks' stories told by the Indians of Guiana says the Tree of Life was planted under the rule of *Sigu*, son of Maikonaima, and *in its stem was pent up the whole of the waters that were to be let forth according to measure and reckoning to stock every lake and river with fish.* But, Warika the mischievous monkey forced open the magic cover that kept down the waters and the next minute he was swept away with all living things by the bursting forth of the deluge.[2]

In this account we have the tree typified after the Baobab or monkey-bread-fruit tree of Inner Africa, with its primitive cistern of water and pent-up reservoir of rain, supplying the type of a tree that contained the deluge. The negroes also make artificial cisterns of the large boles of decaying trees. The name of the Norse tree Yggdrasill, is said by Magnusen to signify the producer of rain. Such a meaning has little application in northern regions, but in Inner Africa where the tree collects water and becomes a reservoir of nature or the mother, an Yggdrasill of wet in a burning land, it was indeed divine as the distributor of an element of life which it had caught in a myriad leafy hands held up to the passing clouds for their riches of rain. When we see Nupe or Hathor pourtrayed in and as the Celestial Tree offering the divine food and drink of souls, we have a late picture of the African looking up to the tree of sustenance, of water, and of life itself. So ancient then is this type of the Motherhood that it reaches back to the time when the tree was the cradle and coffin of the race, and the bounteous breast of the mother herself leaning over the human infancy with its nourishment; when man, only a little ahead of the Soko, was born and lived in and on and underneath the tree. The natural type was first. The tree preceded any form of the carven image, however rude; consequently

---

[1] Cameron, *Across Africa*, vol. i. p. 119. [2] Brett.

there are African races with whom the tree has continued from the beginning, and the type has never passed into the domain of representative art.   In Egypt where the type is sometimes found in all its phases, a sycamore tree with two arms is a form of the genitrix who became Hathor in the tree or as the tree personified.   A sycamore with human arms is an illustration of the 19th Chapter of the Ritual ; this image of the two-armed tree being the tree, the cross, and the mother of life all united in one.

A great deal of nonsense has been written concerning the so-called " Tree-Worship," and " Tree-Spirits."   But, the primitive man was not the diseased victim of subjectivity.   The tree that is the African's *Wong* did not become sacred at first because of any inherent " Spirit." Primally the tree produced food and was the support of life, the producer, the mother of life on the physical plane.   It was the mother in the same sense that the mother was the cow, or the earth was the mother, because it was the source of food and drink in the human infancy.

Sahagun says the Mexicans adored certain hills on account of the rain-water which they collected, and the same reason is assigned by the aboriginal tribes of India for their worship of hills.   But here the words worship and adoration are modern, and the sense is modern compared with that of the early men who were glad if the hill or the tree proved to be a cistern of water for their time of need.   Typology shows their mode of representing this hill or tree was as the image of the mother who feeds the child from her breast and still earlier in her womb.   Hence the Mount *Tanga* (in Mose) is the thigh.   The primary motive for looking up to the hill or great tree was want of water and desire for fruit—the early man being frugivorous—the first sense of this source of supply ; the moral and religious came afterwards.   In looking to the hill and tree for sustenance, they had common sense and reason on their side, which is more than can be said for those who have continued the types as fetishes in the religious phase.   The first perception was that of food, drink, and shelter. Hence the tree represented the nursing mother.   The primitive man did not personify the inherent life of the tree as an object of adoration nor adore any abstract spirit of the forest.   He did not conceive of a spirit first and then localise it in the tree.   Animistic ideas belong to a later stage ; to the metaphysics of savages in common with the " fung-shui " of the Chinese, the poetizing of the Greeks, and the modern interpretation of mythology.

Primitive Animism was not spiritual in the current sense. What it was is evident from the genders of American and other early languages in which living things belong to the animate gender, and things dead, motionless or small and mean, belong to the inanimate gender.   The motion of wind or lightning ; the voice of thunder, the renewing life of the tree, these were animistic but not eschatological.   Spirits were not conceived as governing phenomena until the elements had been personified as spirits. The fruit evoked no gratitude to a giver that constituted the intelligence of the tree. Language is able to tell us what the tree was to the earliest human perception. It was the dwelling-place and the producer of food, and sometimes it had food on it; at other times none. This would excite expectation. The Ojibwa name for an object of veneration meaning "*My hope*," would particularly apply to a source of water in a burning land, and still remain an adequate expression when the one conscious cause of phenomena was postulated and worshipped in a later religious phase. The earliest form of gratitude would be a lively sense of future favours. These were bestowed at recurring intervals, and thus evoked or appealed to a sense of periodicity. The tree is one of the ideographs of time, and it bears the name of time itself. Our word *tree* is identical with the Egyptian *Teru* (or Tre), the shoot, branch, or tree of time, carried in the hands of Taht the reckoner of lunar time; and *Teru* (Eg.) is likewise the name of time. This is the chief Inner African type-name for the tree.

Taro, in Legba.	*Atir*, in N'goala.	*Tir*, in Bayon.
Tero, in Kaure.	*Tir*, in Balu.	*Turi*, in Tumbuktu.
Tera, in Mose.	*Atir*, in Bagba.	*Daru*, in Barba.
Tir, and *Atir*, in Papiah.	*Tir*, in Kum.	*Ntera*, in Muntu.
Tir, in Momenya.	*Atir*, in Pati.	

This type is continued in the Egyptian *Teru*, Greek *Doru* or *Drus*, Welsh *Deru*, and English tree. As food-producer the tree became the sign of a season and a teller of time. Therefore the tree that told was adopted as the symbol of a time. On account of its bringing forth fruit periodically, the tree was an Intelligencer to men and a kind of primary Intelligence. The tree that told became the tree that talked and gave forth oracles whether as the sacred palm of Negra in Yemen, or the prophetic oak of Dodona, the Ava-tree of the Polynesians, the tree "Mirrone" of the Congo negroes or countless other sacred trees.

The fact is curiously conveyed in the account of the Antilles Islanders which was given by Friar Pane, who says that certain trees were supposed *to send for the sorcerers and instruct them in the selecting and shaping of their trunks into idols for the temple where they became oracles*,[1] which is tantamount to saying that various trees had certain self-manifesting qualities which were best known to the learned in forest-lore, and these gave them a self-conferred sacred character.

The Siamese follow the "Spirit" of a tree (that which constitutes its essential character) into the boat made from its wood, and continue their offerings to it when it has assumed that shape. This "spirit" we should call "durability" as of oak; or "lightness" as of teak; the quality which constituted its especial character. With us the

[1] Pinkerton, vol. xii. p. 87.

"spirit" of the Cinchona bark is quinine; but the modern medicine was a primitive "spirit." The ancient Tree-spirits are now known as vegetable alkaloids. They have at last revealed their nature. To the early man they only made known certain effects. Still, inasmuch as they did make known they were acknowledged to be tellers, talkers, or intelligencers to men. This habit of self-revelation made the tree oracular to the early mind of man.

The dark side of phenomena being first consciously reflected, dread of an inimical influence would precede a mental recognition of the good. What to avoid would be the first lesson taught by the tree. The tree or plant that produced poison would naturally be considered the abode of a bad character, a power of evil, a tree noted for the malignancy of its in-dwelling inimical element or power. The African Negroes of Senegambia, the Australian aborigines, the Karens of India, and North American Indians, alike seek to propitiate and appease the malicious demon of the tree that sends disease. This was primarily the poisonous tree. But the early man having found it out would simply not eat of it! He did not offer sacrifice to it any more than the dog gives thanks for the grass which he knows to be medicinal; whilst his mind had not yet attained the savage religious phase. The doctrine of early "spirits" is well illustrated by the Bushmen. A caterpillar called *n'gwa* supplies a deadly poison with which they anoint the barbs of their arrows. The poison is fatal even to the lion. They are also said to cure the wound of this poison. They told Livingstone that they administered the *N'gwa* itself *with fat.* "*The N'gwa wants fat,*" they said; having found that fat or oil was an antidote. Now when the Negro in felling the Asorin tree gives it the first cut the spirit of the tree is supposed to issue forth and chase him, whereupon the Negro drops palm-oil on the ground and while the spirit pauses to lick it up the Negro escapes. So the knife that made the cut has to be fed with fat to assist the wound in healing. The doctrine is the same as if the oil were applied to a wound as an antidote to the sting or poison, only the poison is represented as a devourer who has to be appeased by the oil. According to Bosman "*The trees which are the Gods of the second rank of this country* (Hwida) *are only prayed to and presented with offerings in time of sickness, more especially fevers, in order to restore the patients to health.*" [1]

The Tree of Life originated in the tree that furnished food and drink. The Tree of Knowledge was the tree that told. This can be traced into the tree alphabets and other forms of the book. Hence the beech-tree is identifiable by name with the Book-tree; its bark having supplied a kind of papyrus. But here the book and food are inseparable by name. In Egypt the *Buka* is the palm-tree, the branch of which is the Book of Taht. *Buka* is also the Palm-wine.

---

[1] Burton, *Wit and Wisdom from West Africa*, pp. 205, 243. Bosman, *Letters.*

Buk modified into *Buh*, is food, bread. The *Buka*-tree furnished food with its fruit and wine with its liquor. *Pekh* (Eg.) is another form of the word for food, as in the English "*Peck*" for victuals. *Bag* (בג) is food in Hebrew; *Bhag*, in Sanskrit; *Fagus*, in Latin, is the beech-tree; φηγός, in Greek is the oak. Both meet under one name as the bearers of food, *peck*, or *vic*tuals. *Fek* (Eg.) is produce, plenty, and the food-producing tree is of various kinds which may be traced under one name. The food-tree is Buko in Kanyop (Af.); the palm is the Bukeem in Bola; Bukiam in Sarar; Bekiame in Pepel; and Buka in Egyptian. The *fig* is a form of the same name, and in the African Filham, the ground-nut instead of the tree-fruit is the *Fukui*. The corresponding name of the genitrix and giver of food in Egyptian is that of the goddess *Pekh*. To denote ancient descent Hor-Apollo says the Egyptians depict a bundle of papyrus, and by this they intimate the primæval food; for no one can find the beginning of food or generation.[1] This is the papyrus roll or book. The root. of the papyrus was eaten for food and the plant, like the lotus, is a form of the typical tree. It is carried in the hands of the mother-goddesses as the Uat-sceptre of the genitrix who produced the food of the child's life in her own blood (the red food of Source) and nourished it afterwards at her breast. Thus the book and food were both found in the papyrus plant, as they were in the tree. Such an origin as this will explain how "eating the book," as in Revelation,[2] could be spoken of as synonymous with receiving knowledge. Many illustrations of this mode of eating of the Tree of Knowledge might be quoted and traced to the beginning of the Tree as the producer both of food and information. It extends among the Africans and other races to the swallowing of the written letter as white man's medicine or fetish-food. The tree that told communicated the information first of all by means of its fruits and its juices.

Hor Apollo asserts that Education was called *Sbo* (Coptic for learning), *i.e.* Seba, by the Egyptians, which, when interpreted, signifies sufficient food.[3]

The primitive man did not begin by book-making but the later men developed the tree as a type of the Intelligencer which became a book at last, and continued to be known by the same name. Primitive man did not eat of the tree and straightway personify it as the Divine Mother. But the tree gave food and drink as the mother does, therefore, it was the Mother of Life and so survived as a typical mother, exactly in the same way that the milch-cow, or goat, or ass was a mother, only *the tree was first as it did not need to be trained or domesticated*. It is noticeable that the palm-tree of the primæval world was the immediate precursor of man in the garden of earth. It was in the shape of the palm-tree that nature first gave her maternal milk to man, with such a dash of spirit in it as made him wink and

---

[1] B. i. 30.   [2] Ch. x. 9 and 10.   [3] B. i. 38.

wonder, and feel like the farmer whose glass of milk had been slily mixed with whiskey, and who on drinking it off exclaimed lustily, "*Lord! what a Cow.*" The Toddy Palm of equatorial Africa was a cow and a mother indeed! The palm-tree was not only an intelligencer but an inspirer of men; a strange illuminator of their dawning minds.

In Egyptian *Sukh* (or Uskh) is liquid, drink ; *Sukha*, the flood-time. This is our English *Suck ;* the Euskarian *Uisge,* for Water ; Chinese, *Sok* (Suck) ; Latin, *Sugo* ; Sanscrit, *Sić,* for drink, wet, liquid, or liquor. But just as whiskey is a kind of Uisge, the suck of the toddy is a natural sort of whiskey, and the Mother's Milk was found to be *koumess,* ready fermented, when drawn from the tree. In the Zulu Kaffir language the good wife who fills her husband's cup is designated his *Zikisa.* *Zugia* was a title of Juno. Now this root, *Zug, Sukh,* or *Sakh* (cf. English Sack), denotes fermentation and spirit. *Sakhu* (Eg.) is to be fermented. *Sakh* is to inspire, illuminate, mental influence, the illuminator. *Sekht* (a name of Pekh) is a divinity of intoxicating drinks. Thus drink and divinity are found under one name, the first spirit as a mental inspirer being alcoholic. συκος is the Greek name of the fig-tree, from the fruit of which the divine drink was also made. This root, *Sk,* is an Inner African type-name for Divinity ; the deity or demon is

Tshuka, in Ibu.	*Soko,* in Nupe.	*Sogei,* in Kise-Kise.
Dsuku, in Isoama.	*Soko,* in Esitako.	*Sokwo,* in Nufi.
Dsuku, in Mbofia.	*Seakoa,* in Puka.	*Suge,* in Susu.
Soko, in Basa.		

In some African languages there is but one name for God and Devil, as in Marawi, where both are called *Tsoka.* In the country of Kivo the intoxicating Palm-toddy is named *Zogga.* In Dahome the *Soko* is a poison-tree. Both bear the name of the *Spirit,* which is a Divinity in one language and a devil in others. Poison being one of the active principles first recognized because of its effect, that would identify the tree of death ; and in opposition to this the tree that bore the good fruit was the Tree of Life. The typical tree has descended in the Hebrew Genesis as the Tree of Knowledge of Good and Evil, that is, the tree as a natural Intelligencer to men.

The "Tree of Knowledge" in Egyptian is known as the *Kat.* This is also the name of the feminine abode, the womb, and is a title of the genitrix as Kat-Mut. Another name of the feminine interior is identical with that of the fig-tree, which is Kent (Eg.), a type of fertility, abundance, plenty. In several languages the female, or womb, and the sacred-tree have the same name, just as in English the *Pudendum femine* is called a plum-tree. In Spain the plum-tree furnishes an especial wood for images of the Virgin. This arose naturally from the mother being the bearer of the food. She was the Tree of Life.

Kat, the Welsh Gwydd, in the Hebrew form (עץ) Getz, is the typical Tree of Life and of Knowledge planted in the Garden of Eden; and this feminine type will show us how the tree is related to the Fall, because it bears two different kinds of fruit, one of which may be called good and one evil. The typical tree in Hebrew has preserved an Inner African name, Getz (עץ) being identical with

Kedsi, in Nso.	*Odsi*, tree, in Opanda.
Ketsi, in N'ki.	*Odsi* ,, Egbira-hima.
Kodsi, in Kore.	*Etze* ,, Param.
Ekedsi, in Boritsu.	*Itsi* ,, Okam.
Heitsi, tree-like, in Hottentot.	*Keti* ,, Mfut.
Yetse, tree, in Baseke.	*Kat*, tree of knowledge, Egypt.
Odsi ,, Yala.	

In the Ananda Tantram [1] the Aswatha or sacred fig-tree is identified with the Yoni or uterus. In the Yoni-rupam,[2] instructions are given for making the *Bhagam Aswatha patra Vat*, or fig-leaf-shaped vulva as an object of adoration in the Cult of the Yonias, "*Let the cleft in the* MONS VENERIS *be seven fingers wide, bulging out four fingers breadths, and downwards let it be shaped like the Aswattham*" (fig-leaf). The fig-tree, says Magnus, was the first to introduce purity of life among men. Hence the Athenians called the fruit of this tree the *guide* or *guiding-fruit*.[3] This was a mystical Tree of Knowledge, which we shall find connected with the "Fall."

The Aborigines of Victoria have a legend of the tree and the introduction of death into the world. *The first created man and woman were charged not to go near a certain tree in which a Bat* (Bon-nel-ya) *lived. The Bat was not to be disturbed. One day, however, the woman was gathering firewood, and she went near the tree in which the Bat dwelt. It flew away and after that came death. Many among the Aborigines died after that.*[4] It may afford a gloss on this in connection with the Fall to repeat Hor-Apollo's statement that the Egyptians pourtrayed a Bat when they would represent a mother as suckling and *bringing up her children well;* this being the only winged creature that has breasts and teeth.[5] Thus when the Bat which taught how to nurse and bring up the children properly had deserted the Tree of Knowledge or Life, then came death into the world.

In the Polynesian Paradise there grew the "*Tabooed bread-fruit tree*," together with the sacred apple-tree. In old times the Hawaiian priests held that the tabooed fruit was in some way connected with the trouble and death of Kumu-honua and Lalo-honua, the primal pair whose fall is bewailed in ancient chants that describe the eating of the fruit, the breaking of the law and the bringing down of death. The "Tree-eaters" or "Tree-upsetters" were tempted to eat by the Moopela or Ilioha, an artful lying animal and mischief-maker; and

---

[1] C. vi. v. 13, Sellon, p. 70. [2] Ananda Tantram, 7.
[3] Athenæus, iii. c. vi. [4] Smyth, *Aborigines of Victoria*, v. i. p. 428.
[5] B. ii. 53.

they were then driven out of the primal paradise by the "*large white bird of Kane.*" [1]

Those who ate of the forbidden food and fell are mourned over in the native chant, as

"Dead by the feast,
Dead by the oath;
Dead by the law, in
Disobeying the gods."

The genesis of the legend would be in eating of a tree that poisoned or made the eaters of it ill, with later applications of the type.

The Hottentot deity, Heitsi Eibib, tells his son Urisip, the whitish one, not to eat of the raisin-trees of the valley. It is said that when Heitsi Eibib was travelling about with his family they came to a valley in which the raisin-tree was ripe, and he was there attacked by a severe illness. Then his young (second) wife said, "*This brave one is taken ill on account of these raisins; death is here at the place.*" The old man (Heitsi Eibib) told his son Urisip (the whitish one), "*I shall not live, I feel it.*" "*Thou must therefore cover me with soft stones.*" And he spoke further, "*This is the thing which I order you to do: Of the raisin-trees of this valley ye shall not eat, for if ye eat of them I shall infect you, and ye shall surely die in a similar way.*" His young wife said, "*He is taken ill on account of the raisins of this valley, let us bury him quickly and go.*" So he died there and was covered flatly with soft stones, according as he had commanded. When they had moved to another place and were unpacking there, they heard, always from the side whence they had come, a noise of people eating raisins and singing. In this manner the eating and singing ran:

"I, father of Urisip,
Father of this unclean one;
I, who had to eat these raisins and died,
And dying live."

The young wife perceived that the noise came from the side where the old man's grave was, and said, "*Urisip, go and look.*" Then the son went to the old man's grave, where he saw traces which he recognised to be his father's footmarks, and returned home. Then the young wife said:

"It is he alone, therefore act thus:
Do so to the man who ate raisins on the windward side,
Take care of the wind that thou creepest upon him from the leeward,
Then intercept him on his way to the grave,
And when thou hast caught him do not let him go."

He did accordingly, and they came between the grave and Heitsi Eibib who, when he saw this, jumped down from the raisin-trees and ran quickly, but was caught at the grave. Then he said, "*Let me go,*

[1] Fornander, vol. i. p. 80.

for I am a man who has been dead, that I may not infect you." But the young wife said, "*Keep hold of the rogue.*" So they brought him home, and from that day he was fresh and hale.[1]

Dr. Hahn says he has eaten the fruit of this so-called wild raisin-tree, and the result was an attack of dysentery. The natives, having no medicine, often succumb to such attacks. Hence the natural genesis of the type in relation to this particular tree that brought death into the world.[2] Dr. Hahn derives the name of Heitsi from *Heii*, the tree, but admits that he cannot account for the " *ts*." One meaning of it is " to come." This tends to identify Heitsi with the branch, which is his especial symbol. The tree itself is feminine. The child god is everywhere the branch, the coming one. This god, their first man, is continually rising again as the branch from the root; a primitive sense of the resurrection that might suit the modern agnostics. The imagery is also applied to the renewal of the moon, as well as of the human race. In consequence the green branch is still laid on the cairns of the dead, whether considered as the grave of their first man, who is renewed in them, or of their more immediate relatives. Of course, in a later phase, the ancestral tree or root is assigned to the male. Thus the root, and the grandfather become synonymous. When this root is personified it is as *Khū-nomab*, the Mimosa-root, of whom the Lion says, "*Mimosa-root has killed me.*"[3] Now a book of the origines is concealed in this, for the Mimosa is the *Sensitive* plant. One of their typical roots used as charms for protection and images of divine power is the Giraffe-Acacia. The acacia is the Tree of Life in Egypt. The wood is so vital that when dried and planed down in door-sills, it has been known to sprout again. But the *Sensitive* root offers a mental clue to the primitive thought. When they set fire to this root as they lie down for the night and murmur, "*My Grandfather's-root, bring sleep on the eyes of the lion and leopard and hyena: make them blind that they cannot find us: cover their noses that they cannot smell us out ;*"[4] and when they give thanks to their Grandfather's-root next morning on finding themselves in safety, and we remember this is the Mimosa-root, the *Sensitive*-root, we also can lay hold of it as a first link in a chain of that consciousness which culminates in apprehending or divining the mind beyond phenomena, to which the later human appeal is made.

Um *Nga*, in the Kaffir dialect, is the name of the Mimosa-tree, and *Nga* means to *wish*. It is the root of all that implies potentiality and forms the potential mood of the verb. Wishing by the Sensitive-tree, then, is primitive prayer. So the Egyptians wished by the *Ankh*, the life, the living one, when their *Nga* was the king, or the still earlier knot, or the clasped (*Ank*) hands.

[1] *Hottentot Fables*, by Bleek, p. 82.   [2] *Tsuni-Goam*, p. 103.
   Hahn, *Tsuni-Goam*, p. 73.   [4] Hahn, *Tsuni-Goam*, p. 82.

Heitsi Eibib, as divinity or spirit of the tree identifies himself, not only with, but *as* the tree when he says, "*I shall infect you.*" Here we see the spirit of the tree communicating the knowledge of good and evil in the act of warning them against the evil, whereas the subtle Serpent or the sly Moopela tempts them to eat of the tree of death. Thus the spirit of the tree is demonstrably based on the quality of its fruit, and afterwards a motive is assigned to this as an active agent personified.

Alcoholic drinks were taken in the ancient mysteries to induce an abnormal condition and excite the power of prophecy and divination. In the *Rig Veda* the gods are said to get drunk and to obtain immortality by drinking the "Immortal Stimulant"—*amartyam madam*. They all drink copiously the first thing in the morning, are drunk by mid-day, and dead-drunk by night with the third libation. Their followers also drink the Soma-juice to attain the privileges of immortality and to know the gods ; and in their consequent exaltation sing :

> " We've quaffed the Soma bright,
>   And are immortal grown ;
>   We've entered into light ;
>   And all the gods have known." [1]

They felt the " *tulla intoon,*" or supernatural ecstasy of the Finnic Magician, in which he became *the likeness of the spirit in possession of him.*

Even in the Book of Deuteronomy [2] the Jews are commanded to spend their saved-up money in drink as an offering to the deity, which shows that intoxication was a religious rite with them as it was with those who grew immortal by quaffing the juice of the Soma, the Homa, or other types of the Tree of Knowledge. The Tree of Knowledge first supplied the divine drink, which was naturally fermented in the Toddy-Palm. The drink was elsewhere produced artificially from the various *Kavi*-trees and plants, the vine, the Homa, Soma, fig, mistletoe, elder, raisin, and other sacred fruit-trees. The Mexicans made brandy from the pulque-plant, called the Maguey, which is one of the Agaves or Kavis. The Kavi drink was made by the Mangaians from the " Piper Mythisticum," and a root of this intoxicating tree was buried with the dead at Rarotonga to enable the *Spirit*-Traveller to make a fit *Spirit*-offering to Tiki and obtain entrance into his dwelling.[3]

The juice of the Hindu Tree of Life is called the ornaments of the Siddhas. The Siddhas are the perfected ; the spirits of the Eighth Heaven, or the Height, which was first attained by primitive man, who mounted and entered by means of the intoxicating tree. Among the North American Indians we find the notion that immortality consists in

---

[1] Muir, vol. v. p. 90.   [2] Ch. xiv. 26.

[3] Gill, *Myths*, 170.

being eternally drunk, because drink supplied the type of a paradisiacal condition, and the dead-drunk were as spirits among spirits.

The story of the tree in the Hebrew Genesis has been told with this gloss: The Serpent informs the Woman that "*in the day ye eat thereof, then your eyes shall be opened, and ye shall be as Elohim, knowing Good and Evil. And when the Woman saw that the tree was good for food and pleasant to the eyes, and a tree to be desired to make one wise, she took of the tree thereof and did eat*," or partook of it in some way. And "*their eyes were opened.*" The tree was to make them wise. The wise are the Seers. The Persian Magi were the wise men. Seers, Clairvoyantes, fortune-tellers, prophets, are called the wise. The Wizard is the wise man, and the Elohim, as spiritual beings, say, "*Behold the man is become as one of us.*" The tree had taught them the way to enter Spirit-world, and the Elohim were the Elementary spirits or gods of the earliest time and typology.

We are told by Plutarch that previous to the time of Psammeticus, the Egyptian priest-kings were not used to drink wine at all, nor to pour it out in a sacrifice as a thing they thought in any way grateful to the Gods. On the contrary, they shed it as *the blood of those who in ancient times waged war against the Gods* from whose falling down from heaven and mixing with the earth (*cf.* the blood of Belus mixing in the same manner) they conceived vines to have first sprung; which is the reason, they say, that drunkenness renders men beside themselves, and makes them mad; they being, as it were, gorged with the blood of their ancestors. "*These things reported by Eudoxus in his Second Book of Travels, are thus related by the priests.*"[1] There is a cognate tradition extant among the Folk Tales of the Little Russians concerning the origin of tobacco, or "the devil's herb," as it is designated by the Raskolniks. Once on a time there was a witch-woman who is described as a heathen. She led men astray, and a voice from heaven commanded that she should be put to death. This was obeyed, and the enchantress was buried alive. Her husband planted a twig on her grave which grew up into the tobacco plant. The people plucked its leaves and discovered the art of smoking. They smoked and smoked until one day the smoke burst into flame, and they were all consumed.[2] In the Mexican Legends the genitrix Magaguil or Mayaguil is represented as a woman who had 400 breasts (the Dea Multimammæ), and on account of her fruitfulness the creative power changed her into the Maguey Tree that is the vine of the country, from which the natives made their wine. This also identifies the Great Mother with the Tree of Knowledge as a producer of intoxicating drink.[3] The Egyptians described by Plutarch, had passed out of the primitive Typhonian phase in

---

[1] *Of Isis and Osiris.*
[2] The legend is cited by Gubernatis in *La Mythologie des Plantes.*
[3] Kingsborough, *Mexican Ant.*, vol. vi. p. 203.

which inspiration was attained by intoxication.   The giants, the opponent powers, are here identified with the fall from heaven, and wine with the cause of the fall.   We still call wine the blood of the grape.   The first wine in the mystical sense was the blood of the Tree of Life ; and this was actually partaken of in the Eucharist of the mysteries before it was commuted by the blood of the grape, or the fermented juice of other fruits.   The Egyptians were in the position of total abstainers from wine because it was the symbol of the earlier source of uncleanness, lawlessness, and sin against nature; and representative of the dæmons or spirits that were early and elemental, and therefore the "bad" spirits of later thought.   This reaction is especially characteristic of the Hebrew prophets, and is still more plainly set forth in the Parsee Sacred Scriptures.

The priests and prophets of the Devs are called by the name of *Kavi* in the Gathas.   The Kavayas and Kavitayas are the ministers of evil, Stealers of the understanding ; Typhonian in the evil sense. *Kavi* often occurs in the Vedic Hymns.   In Sanskrit the root *Kavi* supplies a name for the *Kāvya*, as those who are possessed of the greatest understanding, endowed with the qualities of the sage, the prophet, the poet, and inspired seer.   But it also denotes a " female fiend."   By drinking the intoxicating Soma-juice the power of *Kavi* may be attained.[1]   In India the Kavis or seers were believed to be divine revealers to men, and were consulted as prophets.   The word *Kavi* is a revelation in itself.   It is the Egyptian Kefi or Kepi which signifies the mystery of fermentation, heat, illumination, and spiritism of the alcoholic kind.   It is applied to fertilization by the inundation ; and *Kap* in the Hok-Keen (Chinese) dialect likewise signifies imbibing to the full, to soak through ; *Keep* being a libation.   *Kep* (Eg.) is Typhon.   The ancient Iranians were worshippers of the genitrix ; as the Devi Drukhs maliciously reminds Zaratusht.   The term *Kavi* was once an honoured name ; a title of the most famous personages of Iranian antiquity, such as Kavi-Husrava (Kai Khusro) Kavi-Kavata (Kai Kabad) Kavi-Vishtaspa (Kai Gushtasp), and in its derived adjectival form Kâyanian was the designation of a whole dynasty of the ancient Bactrian rulers.[2]   They wore the mighty glory which was peculiar to the Kavis, the Iranian heroes before the Zoroastrian times, the glory worn by Yima and Thraetaona, a celestial glory essential for causing the resurrection of the dead at the end of the world ; a light of the life everlasting.[3]   Kavasakha is the name given to those who are influenced by drinking the Kava, and who are the enemies and despisers of the Soma, the later and more sacred drink of India.   Sakha (Eg.) means illumined, influenced, inspired, and the Kava-sakha are the illumined by fermented liquor.   In one passage[4] the Kavasakha is called a Maghava.   Indra is said to turn out the

[1] *Rig. Ved.* 1, 91, 14 ; 1, 164, 6 ; 7, 86, 3 ; 9, 37, 6 ; 72, 6.
[2] Haug, *Essays*, p. 290.   [3] *Zamyad Yasht*, Haug.   [4] *Rig. Ved.* v. 34, 3.

Maghava who follows the Kavayas from his possession. The Maghava and Kavasakha are thus synonymous and in Yasna 51, 15, the Zoroastrians are designated Maghavas.

"*Zarathustra assigned in times of yore as a reward to the Maghavas the Paradise where first of all Mazda himself had gone.*"

"*Kava Vishtaspa obtained through the possession of the spiritual power (maga) and through the verses which the good mind had revealed that knowledge which Ahura Mazda himself, as the cause of truth, has invented.*"[1]

The casting out (or transformation) of the *Kavi* corresponds to the kindred change in Israel. Kep has a variant in Sep (Eg.) for the Spirit of Wine ; and this is the root of the Greek word Sophia, which signifies wisdom and originally meant wine, as the juice of the grape ; the vine being one of the trees of knowledge that were " *to be desired*" to "*make wise ;*" the sap or juice is one by name with *Sapiens.* Also, the Assyrian cuneiform characters which designate the "Vine," or wine are traceable to the compound Ges-tin in Akkadian, which means the Tree of Life.

The connection of the fetish idol with a "spirit" is curiously shown in the religious rite described by Columbus who relates that the West-Indian natives used to place a platter on the head of the divinity. This platter contained the intoxicating *Cohoba* powder which was snuffed up the nostrils by means of a double-branched cane.[2] In this way the Gods inspired them through the powder.

Roman Pane also describes the native priest as coming to the sick man, and then putting himself in communication with "Spirits" by snuffing cohoba powder that "made him drunk," or induced the abnormal condition in which he saw with opened vision, and foresaw and divined, because in this state of trance he was talking with the "Cemis," *i.e.* the dead ; the *Khemu* in Egyptian.[3]

The Spirit was first discovered in the Powder of the fetish herb, hence tobacco became the Holy Herb because it inspired the Seers ; next, the Spirit was discovered, by means of the powder, in the consequent ecstasy, delirium, trance or dream. Then it was believed that a window had been opened into another world, through which the Medium conversed with the dead, who went on living, despite the evidence of the external senses. Primitive Spiritualism was based on the trance-vision now called *Clairvoyance.* As before said, the present writer has had many years' private experience of the Abnormal Condition which could be induced by the look, whether of a serpent or the human eye, a disk, a light, a looking-glass, by anæsthetics, narcotics, or by ecstatic sensation. In this trance the Sensitive believed that she saw and talked with spirits, and observers also considered that other Intelligences than her own could commingle

---

[1] Haug, *Essays*, West, 169.   [2] Pinkerton, vol. xii. ch. lxii.
[3] *Colombo Vita*, Roman Pane, *ib.* ch. 15.

with, and see and talk through her. Whether this be true or false or mixed, we have the means extant in our own day for studying such "mysteries" of the past. The attempt to explain these abnormal phenomena on the theory of imposture is a shallow delusion, even if supported by all the foremost men of science living, and can but tend to their own discredit.

The tree as the Mother of Life, as the teller, and lastly, as the oracle or foreteller, was represented in certain rites by a living woman who was worshipped beneath its branches. Isaiah denounces the "*Sons of the Sorcerers*" who "*inflame themselves with Idols under every green tree.*"[1] Jeremiah says of Israel, "*She is gone up upon every high mountain and under every green tree, and there hath played the Harlot.*"[2] This is termed committing adultery with stocks and stones ; the stock and stone that represented the Tree and the Mount of the genitrix. According to Hosea they sacrificed under the tree "*because the Shadow thereof was good.*"[3] The reader must not suppose that mere congress of the sexes, natural or unnatural, is all that is meant by this harlotry under the tree, whose worshippers were they that "*Sanctified and purified themselves in the Gardens behind one tree in the midst, eating swine's flesh, and the abomination and the mouse,*"[4] and drinking the broth of abominable things, in a kind of Eucharistic rite, incredibly primitive.[5] In the Hindu drawings an altar is pourtrayed beneath the tree ; in one of these the "Medium" is being led to the altar.[6]

This Nautch woman or Temple-Hetæria (Gr. ἑταιρεία) is intoxicated for the purpose of divination. She becomes the Radha Dea to the Sakteyas, and in her state of magnetic sleep, the divinity, in this case, of drink, inspires her to utter revelations.[7] By an effusion of the spirit, a cup of wine, the wine of astonishment, is consecrated for the sacrament, somewhat after the manner of the Cup of Charis in the Eucharist of Marcus.[8] The female was the acknowledged inspirer of the male in the sexual sense, she was his Sakti. This is identical with the Egyptian *Sakh*, to inspire, and *Sekhet*, the double force personified as that of the female. The goddess Sekhet is designated the "*force or energy of the Gods, the astonisher of Mankind.*"[9] Hers was the "*Wine of Astonishment.*" That which was the all-potent charm of the primitive mind, the "Ur-heka," or great magic power in the Hieroglyphics, remained the natural type of pleasure and paradise in the more spiritual phase—if the epithet may be allowed—of the erotic and uterine religion. The *Sakteyas* continued to worship the great magic power of the primitive man. They held that the spirit was of feminine origin.

[1] lvii. 5. [2] Jer. iii. 6. [3] Hos. iv. 13. [4] Is. lxvi. 17.
[5] "I will take his bloods (margin) out of his mouth, and his abominations from between his teeth."—Zech. ix. 7. Cf. the "bloody wafer."
[6] *Tree and Serpent Worship*, pl. 98. [7] Sellon, *Notes*, also the Tantras.
[8] Irenæus, b. i. ch. xiii. 2. [9] Birch, *Gallery*, p. 17.

The Pythoness who spoke with the belly-voice is often assumed to have been a ventriloquist.   But the known facts show that the female professors of spirit-utterance were not supposed to give oracular responses with the vocal organs alone.   Sellon describes the voice of an oracle that certainly could not be ventriloquised.   In various temples the adorers of the Yoni believed that it spoke oracles.   Clement Alexander, Arnobius and Theodoret, amongst others, mention the adoration of the Yoni at Eleusis; and this was considered by some to be the supreme oracle of the goddess Vach.   This voice of the feminine oracle was the original of the Hebrew Bath Kol.

The survival of most primitive customs and superstitions amongst the Jews is proved by the denunciations of their teachers, and the prohibition of their later law-givers.   What the practices really were can only be ascertained by the comparative process.

We shall find that the Tree, the Pillar, and Mount, are interchangeable as types of the motherhood and place of birth.   The Paphian Venus was typified by a conical stone pillar, respecting the significance of which, says Tacitus, we are left in the dark.   It was identical with the pillar or pyramid of Isis-Sothis; a type that is masculo-feminine.

A conical pillar or stone called Lovekaveka was consecrated to a Fijian goddess, Lovekaveka, near Thokova, Na-Viti Levu.   It was a round black milestone with a *Liku*, the female girdle of pubescence tied round the middle.[1] The Natchez of Louisiana likewise worshipped a conical stone.[2]

Kubele was held to lie concealed as "Mother of the Gods" in the Pessinuntian Stone sent by Attalus, King of Phrygia, to the Romans.[3]

The tree, the pillar, and the cross are all three combined in the Assyrian Asherah or Grove; a far more primitive form of which is found in the Hittite or Khetan Hieroglyphics, where it is in the next stage to the *pudendum muliebre* itself.[4]

It has been thought a confusion of metaphor when, in the First Epistle to Timothy, Paul likens the Church *to a house and a pillar*, as basis of the truth.   But, the pillar and House were both symbolically the same.   Pillar, Seat, Mount, Tree, or Abode, was each representative of the Motherhood, whose latest type was the Mother Church.   In a Greek myth described by Pausanias the *tree*, the *mount*, and the *horn* are confounded together.   The Garden of Dionysos contains a kind of Mount Meru which resembles a horn, it is called the Hesperian Horn, and produces the Golden Apples and every delicious fruit of the Tree of Life.   This shows the phase of confusion in which the mythologists appear to be insane to their interpreters, who are innocent of eating from the tree of the Ancient Knowledge.

[1] Lubbock, *Origin of Civilisation*, p. 228, fig. 20.   [2] Lafitau, vol. i. p. 146.
[3] Arnobius, *Adv. Gentes*.   Livy, *Roman History*, xxix. 11.
   Trans. Bib. Arch. vol. vii. pt. ii. pp. 275, 295, 298.

Because of the birth-place the Tree of Life is likewise one with the mount and summit of the world called Paradise. *Pardes*, says Ibn Ezra, is a Garden planted with one kind of tree. We shall see that Paradise and the tree are identical as the type of a world or a first formation consisting of the Mount, the Circle and Cross of the four cardinal points.

So the Iranian "Tree opposed to harm" the White Hom-Tree was planted in the Eden of Aryana-Vaejo, which was one with the Mountain of the World.[1]

The Jambu or rose-apple tree is an equivalent type with the Mount Meru. It stands on an island and the juice of its fruit was fabled to flow in a river of life. The soil of the banks of the river absorbs the jambu-juice, and in being dried by gentle breezes it becomes the Gold termed Jámbunada of which the ornaments of the Siddhas are made.[2] This is the river of Eden that went forth to water the Garden and encompass the whole land of Havilah, the land of the good gold.

The Jambu or Gambu is the Tree of Earth or Jam (Sansk.) and its droppings make the Earth or Soil. This agrees with the Kami tree, a Gum-Acacia in Egypt with which the name of Kami is written as a type of the earth or soil that was actually shed in the Nilotic Valley, as it was fabled to be shed by the jambu tree of the Hindu Allegory.

The Egyptian Tree of Life stands in the Pool of Persea in Annu, the birth-place. This can be followed in the Parsee Bundahish :—

" *On the nature of the tree they call Gôkard it says in revelation that it was the First Day when the tree called Gôkard grew in the deep mud within the abyssal ocean ;*" and it is necessary as a "*producer of the renovation of the universe, for they prepare its immortality therefrom. The evil spirit has formed therein, among those that enter as opponents, a lizard, as an opponent in that deep water, so that it may injure the Hôm. And for keeping away that lizard, Ahura-Mazda has created there ten Kar fish which, at all times, continually circle around the Hom, so that the head of one of those fish is continually towards the lizard, and till the renovation of the universe they remain in contention.*" Again, " *The White Hom, the healing and undefiled, grows at the Source of the Water of Aredvivsur. Every one who eats of it becomes immortal, aud they call it the Gôkard (or Gôkarn) tree, as it is said that Hom is death-expelling. Also in the renovation of the universe they prepare its immortality therefrom. It is the chief of Plants.*"[3] With it they restore the dead.[4]

The tree of the "First Day" and the fabled fount of Immortality are found together, and have one origin and significance. The one is identified with the very beginning of time, the first day. In the Ritual

---

[1] *Bundahish*, ch. xxix. 5.   [2] Wilson, *Vishnu Purana*, 167, 168.
[3] *Bundahish*, ch. xviii. 1—4 ; xxvii. 4.   [4] *Bundahish*, xxiv. 27.

the renewing pool is designated the "*Generator of Years.*" The Tree of Life is pourtrayed in the Monuments of Nineveh with the Two Waters flowing from it in keeping with the Egyptian Persea Tree in the Pool of the Two Truths.

The Myth of the beginning found by the missionary John Williams among the traditions of the islanders of the Southern Seas relates that the heavens were so near the earth at first that men could not walk but were forced to crawl under them. "*This was found to be a very serious evil, but at length an individual conceived the sublime idea of elevating the heavens to a more convenient height. For this purpose he put forth all his energy, and by the first effort raised them to the top of a tender plant called Teve, about four feet high. There he deposited them until he was refreshed, when by a second effort he lifted them to the height of a tree called Kanariki, which is as large as a sycamore. By the third attempt he carried them to the summits of the mountains, and after a long interval of repose, and by a most prodigious effort he elevated them to their present height.*"[1] For this beneficent work he was deified as the "*Elevator of the Heavens.*" The Elevator of the Heavens is also known as Maui in the Hervey Islands, and as Tane in New Zealand. He has been already identified with Ma-Shu, the upholder of the nocturnal heaven. Tane was also represented as a Tree. Here the types of the tree and mount are both applied to the height of heaven. The Egyptian Teve or Tef is the papyrus reed which, like the cane, is a form of the typical Tree of Birth and beginning, especially from the waters of source. The Kaffirs derive their origin from the reed; and so popular is the symbol with the Basutos that they still fasten one over the hut to announce the birth of a child. Casalis tells the story of a prosaic-minded Basuto who acquired the nickname of "*Father Reed*" because he made it his mission to go about denouncing the ridiculous belief that men could be produced from reeds.[2] The reed represents the genitrix and the great-grandfather. So in Egypt Tef, the Reed, bears the name of Tef, the great Mother, and Tef, the divine Father. The reed itself is a hieroglyphic determinative of Sems the Heir as it is with the Kaffirs. The *Teve*, about four feet high, agrees with the Tef or reed as a minor form of the Tree. It was by means of the tree that the vault of heaven was lifted. The tree was the earliest "Strut" or support. By its branching the two halves were stemmed apart and the four quarters founded. By means of the tree space was first penetrated, ramified, divided, and configurated.

This tree of earth, the branches of which were hung with the clustered constellations, is found among the Kasia of Bengal, who affirm that the stars were once human beings but they climbed to the

[1] Williams, *Narrative*, ch. 31.
Casalis, Basutos, p. 241; *Callaway*, Amazulu, pp. 2—58.

top of a great tree whereupon others who were below cut the trunk in two, and they were left aloft in the branches.[1]

The North American Indians preserve the tradition of a tree or vine which carried a whole tribe across the waters of the Mississippi river. They also have an account of their origin through climbing up the roots of a large vine from the interior of Mother Earth![2]

The tree type is employed by the Chinese in two characters, as the tree of earth and of heaven. In the celestial aspect its branches represent the twelve zodiacal signs, like the twelve-branched tree in the book of Revelation. As the tree of Ti-Chi or the Earthly Branches it is the horary of the Chinese twelve hours, equal to twenty-four of our time. This tree is also totemic, as the tree of twelve signs previously explained.

The Lenni Lenape Indians, who have twelve highest Manitus, were accustomed to set up twelve trees or posts in a circle in the middle of their council-house; these trees were then connected together at the top. Into this house of twelve trees twelve hot stones were rolled, sacred to the twelve spirits, four of which were the genii of the four Corners of Heaven.[3]

The inscription of Nabonidus, King of Babylon, was found on four terra-cotta cylinders at the four corners of the Temple of the Moon at Mugheir, the Ur of the Chaldees. This is called the " *Temple of the Great Tree*," which was begun by Urukh, a king who lived long ago. The tree or mount was a figure of the pole and the ancient temples were sometimes built with a planisphere in the roof around the roof-tree.[4]

The starry heavens were taken indoors, and placed upon the astronomical ceilings of the temples of Egypt, Babylonia, and China; and now whilst looking up at the starry dome whether of the building or the heaven of night we for the first time understand what could be meant by *a Mountain which is said to surround the world*, as does the Turkish and Arab Mount called "*Kaf.*" Considered as a mountain this dome surrounded the earth just as did the water of heaven, the first figure of the firmament. This can be proved by the Mythical Alborz (Persian) which is also a Mount that surrounds the world. Of this celestial mount it is said that it has 360 apertures and every day the sun comes in and goes out through one of these.[5] Thus the Celestial Dome, the Mount and Tree, the Pole and Horn-point are identical.

The Apalaches of Florida said the sun had built his own conical mountain of Olaimi, which had a spiral path winding round it, and leading to his cave-temple on the eastern side, in which four solar festivals were celebrated every year.[6] In this instance the natural

---

[1] Latham, *Desc. Eth.* v. i. p. 119.   [2] Schoolcraft, v. i. pp. 14—17.
[3] Loskiel, *Ind. of N. Am.* pt. i. p. 42. J. G. Müller, p. 92.
[4] *Records*, vol. v. p. 145. [5] *Bundahish*, ch. v. 3. [6] Rochefort, *Antilles*, b. ii. ch. viii.

mount occupies the place of the pyramid mound erected elsewhere. In the Ritual the Mount of the Seven Stars and the Four Quarters supplies the type of a house on high, to which the soul of the deceased ascends, and is at rest. This abode is built by Sefekh-abu, whose name of the "Seven-horned" shows that she represents the Seven Stars of the Mount, or the seven constellations called the Seven Hills of Heaven. Here he sits in peace, or changes his quarters according to the direction in which the four winds blow. When the Assyrian gods are discussing their plans of future action after the revolt and fall, it is said of the race, "*In a Circle may they sit*," and "*Let them plant the Vine*" —the new creation consisting of the Circle and the Tree. So the Pippala is planted in Hindu districts as the sacred village tree, the "Chaitya-taru," the tree of the inclosure. It is still a custom with the Khonds, when a new village is founded, to first plant the sacred cotton-tree as a point of commencement, a central mark; and under this is placed the stone of the deity,[2] the image of the mount. The tree, as a lotus-tree, stands in the seventh Muhammedan heaven, at the boundary beyond which no angels can pass, or the creature's knowledge extend.[3] Vast trees used to mark the boundaries of English counties. The great "Shire-oak" stood at the meeting-point of the three counties of York, Nottingham, and Derby, and its branches extended into each like the typical tree of the three regions, in the triple division of the heavens. 230 horsemen could find shelter or shadow under the "Shire-oak." A most ancient Maypole is mentioned in a charter by which the town of West Hatton, Lancashire, was granted to the Abbey of Cockers, and about the time of the reign of King John the Maypole was a landmark that defined boundaries; this, it appears, superseded a cross—the typical Druidic Tree. Thus we find the maypole and cross interchanging as types. The words of the Charter are "*Lostockmepull, ubi crux sita fuit recta linea in austro, usque ad Crucem super-le-Tunge.*"[4] Kemble prints in his *Codex Diplomaticus* a charter of the date of 959, and in this one of the marks or memorials of a boundary line of land is called *Frigedæges-Tréow*, or the Tree of Friday, the Day of Freya, or sacred to Freya, as a Doomsted and Judgment Seat. At Hesket in Cumberland, yearly, on St. Barnabas Day, a court was kept for the whole forest of Englewood under a *thorn-tree* by the highway side, according to the very ancient manner of holding assemblies for judgment in the open air.[5] In front of the ground now occupied by St. Mary-le-Strand there once stood a Cross, at which, according to Stow, "*In the year 1294, and other times the justices itinerant sat without London.*" The Cross is a form of the Tree. The Mount and the Tree were likewise

[1] Smith, *Chaldean Genesis.*   [2] Macpherson, p. 61.
[3] *Al-Korân*, ch. liii.   [4] Dugdale, *Monast. Anglic.* vol. vi. p. 2 ; N. ii. p. 906.
[5] Nicolson and Burn's *History of Westmoreland and Cumberland*, v. ii 344.

interchangeable types of the Judgment-Seat in Britain. The ancient shire-moots and hundred-courts used to be held on the top of the dun, tor, or tut-hill; or under the oak of the shire; or beneath the apple-tree made sacred by the mistletoe—the tree of pure gold, the tree of the lofty summit, as the mistletoe was called. And because this was the tree beneath which covenants were once made and troth was plighted, the white-berried branch is still suspended overhead for the Christmas kiss; the "Tree of the Summit" being a type of the celestial pole. In the Ritual the tree of the "Two Truths" stands in the place of the "Judgment Hall;" and on the tablet of one Tahtmes, a Memphite functionary of the eighteenth dynasty, we find a reference to the Judgment under the tree. The text states that "*on the 30th day of the month Tibi*" (December 16 in the Sacred Year), the "*day of filling the eye in Annu*" (the birthplace), "*the great Inspectors* (or Judges) *come out to the end of the Dais under the trees of Life and Perseas.*" This was the locality of the Judgment, the place of examination. "*Having been questioned thou answerest in Rusta on the 3rd of the month Epiphi,*"[1] or on the 17th of May, in the sixth month afterwards; the two times corresponding to the two halves of the heavens, the hall of the Two Truths, and the Tree of Heaven and Earth, or North and South. The first tree was at the Centre of the Circle, like the Pine in Eridu. An oak-tree standing near Weedon, in Warwickshire, is still pointed out as marking the very centre of all England. Next the type is divided into the Tree of the North and South, to mark two points of reckoning and boundary. The tree was one in the Pool of Persea, in Annu. Then it is spoken of as two trees. "*I draw waters from the Divine Pool under the two Sycamores of heaven and earth,*"[2] says the Osirian in the Ritual. This tree is deposited in the Egyptian planisphere along with the Virgin Mother, and may be seen in the Decans of Virgo, where it shows as the tree of the north.[3]

The Hindus personify a kind of pre-eval supreme being as Skambha, whose name signifies the prop, support, or fulcrum. He formed the first abode, he "*who, with a prop* (Skambha), *held the two worlds apart, like the Unborn.*" He is typified as the tree; and the gods, who are all comprehended in Skambha, are his branches—or, rather, he is the tree-type impersonated in a masculine instead of the feminine form. Skambha is the fulcrum of the whole creation, as the tree, first of two branches and then of four. The two primordial branches are termed those of non-entity and entity, according to the theory that in the first age of the gods the existent sprang out of the non-existent.[4] Here it should be observed that this beginning is theoretical and metaphysical, whereas the actual beginning was in accordance with

---

[1] Sharpe, *Eg. Ins.* pl. 105.
[3] Plate in this volume.
[2] Ch. 97.
[4] *Rig Veda*, x. 72, 2 f. Muir.

observation.   The makers of language and moulders of typology were not metaphysicians.[1]

The Egyptian *Nun*, as phase or condition, place or point of commencement, is negative ; it is identical with Not and None.   But it denotes existence in the negative condition of water, or the firmament considered as water, and *Enti* (Eg.), or entity, which signifies the coming out of, is determined by the flower of blood or bleeding, and the froth and foam of water.   These are the blood and breath (Sen) of the Two Truths of being.   The water, whether below or above, was a first form of phenomenal and elemental existence, and not a theoretical non-existence in the Vedic sense ; and the blood was the mystical water of life.   The natural Genesis of Hindu thought is not to be found in the Hindu writings, but in a far earlier representation, and its myths can only be laid hold of by means of the primordial and physical origines, into which the later speculations have been read.

The Chinese system of "Fung-Shui,"[2] or the "Breath of Nature" said to have commenced with the "*Absolute Nothing*" out of which the "*Great Absolute*" was evolved, begins phenomenally with the "Two Truths" of Water and Breath, corresponding perfectly to the Water and Breath of the Egyptian Mâti, Water, or *Shui*, for Shade and Light.   The female principle became the representative of non-existence, because it transformed into existence as Breath.   The two were essentially one, just as dew is condensed vapour and vapour is rarefied moisture.[2]

So is it with the Hebrew writings.   R. Azariel, in his Commentary on the Ten Sephiroth[3] tells us that he is following the opinions of the Kabalist Theosophists in considering the Deity to be purely negative, by divesting him of all attributes.   The Ayin or En-Soph of the Jewish Kabalah, the Boundless, Endless, or Timeless, is of a negative nature, and in a sense non-existent.   It has the negative nature of the Egyptian Nun, that Negation out of which creation came.   But the Kamitic typology affords us tangible foothold once again in the vast void of metaphysical vagueness.   It shows us the Nun or Abyss as the mother nature who produced the first seven elemental powers and formed, with them, the Ogdoad that was continued by the Jewish Kabalah in which the first of the Ten Sephiroth or Manifestors of the "Ayin-Soph" has seven other names, and the Ogdoad are designated אהיה and חיות, the circle or pleroma of primordial powers.   The Kamite Nun or En, whence Enti existence and Neith the genitrix, was not negative in itself, but only in relation to other things—as the water is negative to breath.   In one form the *Nun* is the New Inundation ; in another it is the Child, called the *Nunu*, English *Ninny*,

---

[1] It is at times as satisfactory to get back to the simplest elements of the beginning as were the signs of the Deaf Mutes to the Chinaman who found himself in a European city where no one spoke Chinese.

[2] *Fung-Shui*, by Ernest F. Eitel.   London : 1873.   [3] 2 a.

Italian *Ninna* and *Nan*, Modern Greek Ninion, which is negative because impubescent. So the *Nun* and the *Nanny* are negative compared with wife and mother. But the Nun (Eg.), Irish *Nion*, as the Heaven or Firmament was actual; so was Nun, as the water or the infant. These were not non-extant. Hence Nun (with its variants *Han* and *An*) signifies to bring. The *Nun* (Eg.), which is the firmamental water in the first vague stage, gives a name to *Nun* or *Nin* the fish in the stellar phase. *Nun* in Chaldee is the Great Fish; *Nuna* in Syriac is the constellation *Ketos*. This shows the passage from the vague phase of water to a definite water-type in a constellation. The *Nun* (Nnu or Nu) was heaven personified as the bringer of the water and the breath of life. And this Mother-Heaven, as bringer, had been the Inner African Mother from the beginning.

Nna, Ina, or Na, is the Mother, in Kabunga.			Nnu, is the Mother in, Yula.		
Nna, Ina, or Na	„	„ Dsalunka.	Nne	„	„ Isoama.
Nna, Ina, or Na	„	„ Kankanka.	Nene	„	„ Isiele.
Nna, Ina, or Na	„	„ Mandenga.	Nne	„	„ Abadsa.
Nina	„	„ Bola.	Nna	„	„ Mbofia.
Nna	„	„ Padsade.	Nna	„	„ Mbofon.
Nne	„	„ Basa.	Ninge	„	„ Landoro.
Ninu	„	„ Kra.	Nina	„	„ Balu.
Nande	„	„ Krebo.	Nen	„	„ Bamon.
None	„	„ Anfue.	Nene	„	„ Pulo.
Nna	„	„ Gurma.	Inna	„	„ Goburu.
Nna	„	„ Koama.	Enna	„	„ Okam.
Nau	„	„ Bagbalan.	Anen	„	„ Kanyop.

Nana, as person, is one with the Mama, and *Kaka*; as name it is from a primordial *Nga-Nga*, the earlier sound of *Na-Na*. The Kaffir *Nina* is either her, his, or their Mother. This was the Mother at the head of the line of descent from whom the Mother-name has been extended to the sense of nationality which is Um-*Nina* or *Nini* in Xosa Kaffir. This type-name is also Vedic, as *Nana*, the mother; *Nana* is the Babylonian genitrix; *Nin*, the Assyrian lady; Nini, the Mother in Malagasy. Mother and Woman are often synonymous, and the Woman in Africa is

Nenu, in Gbese.	*Onya*, in Yala.	*Anye*, in Opanda.
Nyonu, in Hwida.	*Onyui*, in Isiele.	*One*, in Egbira-Hima.
Nyonu, in Dahome.	*Unwai*, in Aro.	*Nô*, in Boko.
Nyon, in Mahi.	*Oniye*, in Igu.	*Ne*, in Bagrmi.

The cow was another form of the bringer of the liquid of life whence the Cow of Heaven; and this bringer in Inner Africa is

Nina, the Cow, in Gbese.			*Ningei*, the Cow, in Kise-kise.			*Una*, the Cow, in Timne.		
Nan	„	„ Koama.	Ningi	„	„ Kono.	Ina	„	„ Mampa.
Nnan	„	„ Bagbalan.	Ningena	„	„ Soso.	Nao	„	„ Legba.
Enan	„	„ Anan.	Nnara	„	„ Biafada.	No	„	„ Kaure.
Nankuye	„	„ Ashanti.	Ana	„	„ Baga.	Nao	„	„ Kiamba.

It was at this stage the No-people and the Nuther-speech were named as forms of the first, which was neuter, because undistinguished by sex. Nene, English, is neither, Egyptian Nunter, or nuter, which is potentially either in a second phase, as is the child, and was not non-existent in the first. On account of this origin *Nin* is the Lord or Lady in Assyrian, and both the Grandfather and Grandmother are the "*Nini*" in Javanese. Metaphysics, Theosophy, and Theology have everywhere perverted the ancient "Wisdom" by introducing their counterfeit coinage in hermeneutical interpretation, but the true types are uneffaced and yet extant as the original coins of primitive human thought, and to these we must trust, as our sole guides in the matter when the natural simplicities have been transmogrified into abstract spiritual or metaphysical profundities. Thus Skambha can be followed to the root by means of the tree-type. The tree was one which bifurcated in the first or solstitial division of the circle above. It became four fold as the tree of the four quarters. Hence the four regions are called the four Arteries of Skambha. The word Skamb in native lists is written *Skanbh*.[1] This recovers the hieroglyphic prop which is the Egyptian *Skhen*. Skhen (Eg.) means to support sustain, and embrace, with the prop upholding the heavens as ideographic determinative. The Prop Skhen Y is a "Strut" with two arms. This, when pourtrayed in the human form, is the god Shu, who upholds the heaven with his two arms, which were also represented by the two stars of the solstices, the two lawgivers North and South, Kepheus and *Cor Leonis*. Further, the Prop, *Skhen*, was personified in the divinity named *Skheni*, who is designated the Two Hands of Ra. In the Solar Litanies the Two Hands of Ra are said to be the god *Skheni*.[2] *Skheni* also denotes the Embracer and Supporter with the arms as well as the Prop and Sustainer; and Skambha or Skanbha is expressly said to embrace all things with his two arms, which represent entity and non-entity.[3] Skambha is identified with all that breathes and possesses soul and *Skhen* (Eg.) signifies to give breath. *Skhen* and *Skhem* are interchangeable as names of the abode of breath and being; and by aid of the form Skhem we recover the feminine type of the shrine, the Mother, who was *Zikum* in Akkad, and whose symbol of the birth-place, the prop and support of being is the tree, the *Sekhem* or Sycamore of Hathor. Skambha then is reclaimed as the tree type which has been divinized according to the later cult in a masculine form, as *Skheni* was personified in Egypt. It is the primordial type that proves the original unity.

The Skambha Prop becomes the Pillar of Stone, *Çkemba* (in the Avesta), otherwise called the Kata, which was erected for the dead.[4]

Skambha and Skheni make the sign of the Cross with their arms extended, and may be figured as the Prop of North and South, or the Cross of the four quarters of the roof-tree of Heaven, which is one with the roof-tree of the house. In English the prop, or roof, is the

---

[1] Monier Williams, *Dicty.* p. 1141. [2] *Litany of Ra*, ch. iv. 8.
[3] Texts quoted by Muir on "Skambha," *Sanskrit Texts*, vol. v. pp. 378—390.
[4] *Vend. Farg.*, v. 36, viii. 26.

Sign-tree, and that is *our Skhen* (or Skan-bha) of the human abode. The Mangaians have the dual tree, but it is applied to the mapping out of east and west. One, they tell us, was planted eastward, facing Mauke; one toward the west, facing Atiu. These were so tall they touched the skies, and their branches put forth and spread and bowed down with their load of fruit within the reach of men. Supernatural beings are said to have dug earth from the hollow of Anaoa and filled baskets, which they hung on the branches of the befriending trees that stooped down to receive them, and then rose up and strewed the soil over all the barren rock until the island was covered with vegetation. One-half of this beneficent work was done by the tree planted eastward, the other by the tree of the west.[1] This is a primitive mode of representing the formation of the Garden of the Beginning, or of making two boundaries in space. Anaoa also agrees with the Valley of Annu in the Egyptian Mythos, and with the Chinese Han-mun. These two trees are considered to be the bifurcation of Tane, the Polynesian and Maori form of Skambha, who is depicted as a tree growing head downwards and propping up the heavens with its roots, because he had to lie on his back and hoist them up with his feet. In Egyptian *Tahn* is to force, to compel, with the determinative prop of the mid-way or divided heaven.

The Great Mother was the one in space who divided into Two Sisters above and below, or north and south, and who was also the Goddess of the four quarters. The water of the firmament was one (the blue heaven), and it was divided into the two waters, north and south, and then into the four rivers of the four quarters. The mount and the tree follow the same law, and are divided to mark the two stations and the four stations. The tree is one and single as a type of the genitrix, the abode of being, the nurse of life. The tree is two-fold, as the type of the being that bifurcates and stems the earth and heaven apart. The tree is four-fold, as the image of the four quarters, the Tat-Tree of Ptah, the tree of four branches shown to Zaratusht.[2] The tree is seven-fold, as a type of the Seven Constellations and the seven regions of a primæval order of things in the earliest time. The tree has twelve branches which bear their fruit monthly, as a type of the twelve signs of the Zodiac. And finally, the Celestial tree of the Kabalists, copied by Kircher, has seventy-two branches, which represent the seventy-two demi-decans of the Zodiac. This is called the Tree of יהוה, and the type affords another proof of the feminine origin of Jehovah-genitrix.

It must be explained that the mythical Mount and Tree fulfil their types in the image of both sexes. The Mount as birthplace was feminine at first, as the Brû, Navel, or Mam, the Mamma-shaped

---

[1] Gill, *Life in the Southern Seas*, p. 171.
[2] *Bahman Yasht.*

hill, but the Pen or Ben is of a masculine nature corresponding to its name. The Ben (Eg.) is pyramidal; and the Pyramid and Obelisk are both male symbols. The Cave in the Mount was feminine; the Monolith erected on the top was masculine, the type being perfected in the blending of the two sexes.

Hence the Triangle is feminine at the base and masculine at the apex. These two were represented in the Great Pyramid with its well of the water-source, the birthplace below, and the " Ben-Ben," or pyramid of fire above. These two are still combined in the feminine nave of the Church and the masculine spire, as they were in the Argha and its mast. By reading backwards we see that the tomb in the earth is feminine in type, and the stone erected above is masculine. This shows the simple nature of the Cairn, consisting of an excavation and an erection; the within and without of the earliest thought; the hole in the earth having the feminine, and the conical pile of stones the masculine, likeness.

The Chinese still select a spot of ground for the burial-place of the dead just where the male and female features are most completely delineated in the natural configuration of hollow and mound which correspond to the uterine excavation and stone-erection of the Cairn; the cave and pen of the mount; the nave and spire of the church. A similar conjunction also constitutes a luck-bringing site for the dwelling-place of the living.[1]

The British " *Combe* " combines this dual nature under a perfect type. It unites both hill and hollow in one formation, hence the name is sometimes identified with the Mount, as in Black Combe, and at others with the hollow.

Liechtenstein, who travelled in Outeniqua-land in 1803, records that the Hottentot grave consisted of a conical pile of stones some twenty or thirty yards in circumference at the base. Sometimes these cairns were called the graves of Heitsi-Eibib, the deity who always *rose again*. He was their Moon-God, and his periodic renewal is obviously related to the lunar phenomena applied to the dead. The phallus was buried in the tombs as a type of re-erection (the Kamite phrase for re-arising), and the monolith, or the conical pile of stones, was erected in the likeness of the male erector and establisher of existence.

The Tree was also feminine at first; the Tree of Life and Knowledge in one; the central tree of all beginning with and derived from the Motherhood. Then it became a dual type, which blended the sexes as twin producers. Finally, the Tree of Life was considered especially masculine, and the Tree of Knowledge was left to the Woman who first ate its fruit. The hollow bole might remain feminine as the Coffin; the root was assigned to masculine cause, and the branch was its product. The Khoi-Khoi still add the fresh

[1] Eitel, *Feng Shui*, p. 50.

green branch when they lay the stone on the cairn, and the branch is held to spring from their Grandfather's Root.

When the Druids shaped the Tree into the Tau-Cross, they were turning it into a masculine Tree of Life ; and in the Cross of the four quarters the Tree had become prominently masculine. Hence it interchanges with the fourfold phallus, and both have one name as the Tat (Eg.) ; and the Cross within the Circle (or in connection with the Ru, the Rosary, or other feminine figure) is the same symbol of the male Tree of Life twinned and blended with the female as the fourfold linga or the four-cornered Swastika in the Tomb, or the Square that is figured with the Circle in the American and British Mounds. Perhaps the most primitively perfect type of this sexual duality is that which is figured in the Long-horned Cairn, the chamber of which has the shape of the uterus within, and the four horns at the corners correspond to the four-footed Cross and the fourfold phallus without.[1] Thus, from first to last, the symbols retain and show the impress of nature's primordial mould.

It was at the top of the tree of heaven—the pole—that the Guaranis were to meet once more with their Adam, Atum, Tum, or *Tamoi*, who was to help them from thence in their ascent to the higher life. Here the Tree of Life becomes a tree of the dead to raise them into Heaven. So in the Algonkin Myth the tree of the dead was a sort of oscillating log for the deceased to cross the river by as a bridge of the abyss, beyond which the Dog—as in the Persian Mythos—stands waiting for the souls of the dead, just as the Dog stands at the Northern Pole of the Egyptian Planisphere,[2] and is depicted in the tree of the Southern Solstice—the tree of the pole which was extended to the four quarters.

Nowhere could the tree type of the four divisions have struck deeper root than in our own land. It was the tree of virile vernal life all in flower as the Maypole, the British Bedwen ; the tree of fruit built up with fruits for the festival of Harvest Home ; the tree of the two equinoxes somewhat belated ; it was the tree of fire at Midsummer, and is still the fire-tree or illuminated tree of light when the Yule-log burned on Christmas Eve is transfigured by fire into the renewed tree of Christmas Day. The fire-tree is solstitial. Thus we have it all round. Moreover, as before said, the tree of these four times interchanges with the pyramid, a form of the Mount of the four corners, and this equivalence of the types affords good evidence of the unity of origin for the total system here called Typology, and shown to be Kamite.

On an ancient gem copied by Maffei the tree is engraved with *four* oscilla suspended from its branches.[3] This is an obvious form of the

---

[1] Mitchell, *Past in the Present*, Fig. 49, " Plan of the Long-horned Cairn at Ormiegill, Caithness."
[2] Plate, vol. ii. *Book of Beginnings*.   [3] Maffei, *Gem. Ant.* vol. iii. 64.

Roman and British Christmas-tree, only the pendants are limited to the *typical four*, according to the Gnosis that has been lost in England, which made it the tree of the four cardinal points. The tree, like the serpent, is a type by which numerous ideas could be expressed. As the serpent was an image of the revolving heavens, or of a polar constellation, so the tree was a fixed figure of station round which the starry serpent twined. This tree of heaven also served for the primitive thought to climb by, to mount, to make the passage from this life into the Paradise first planted on the top, at the centre where they saw the *place of Rest* in the star-lit ocean always moving round. The seven stars of Ursa Major were observed to revolve around the tree or pole, and to make a circuit annually. This was the first circle marked out with the four cardinal points and assigned to her who was called the Mother of the Revolutions, whose name of Teb signifies the first movement in a circle, she who had been the old Typhonian genitrix as the Abyss in Space, and brought forth her brood of seven elementaries in Am-Smen, or Chaos. Four quarters were established by means of this constellation. The Chinese reckoned four seasons by its pointings to the south, east, north, and west in making the annual round. Four types were assigned to the genitrix in her Starry Shape of the Great Bear, which were representative of four elements. These were the Hippopotamus for Water, the Kaf-Ape for Air, the Lion for Fire, and the Crocodile for Earth. The Hippopotamus was given the Ape's Nose and Lion's Feet, and was depicted as a Crocodile in her hinder part. Thus the Great Bear north, the place of the Waters, was the Water-Cow; to the south, the place of fire, she was the Lioness; to the west, the Swallowing Crocodile of Earth; and to the east, the Ape of Breath. In such a four-fold form she was the Goddess of four elements and of the four quarters. These four types of the four quarters and elements once established might be varied, but have never been effaced to this day. Two of them are yet zodiacal, as the signs of the Lion and Waterer. The four-fold Beast of the Great Bear Circle is the original of the beast with four faces, seen in Ezekiel's vision,[1] where the circle is described as a wheel with four faces of the beast which had the likeness of a man, a lion, an ox, and an eagle; also of the four in Revelation[2] where they appear as the lion, calf, man, and bird—the lion, bull, and waterman of the Zodiac. These four characters and four elements were likewise represented by four elementary Spirits, or Genii, who were stationed at the four corners, and who are pourtrayed as *Amset* the human-headed; *Hapi* the ape-headed; *Tuautmutf* the jackal-headed; and *Kablisenuf* the hawk-headed.

In India the typical four may be recognised as the cow, ape, eagle, and serpent which receive the highest honours amongst the totemic or divine types. In this group the cow takes the place of the water-

[1] Ezek. ch. i.   [2] Ch. iv. 7.

cow of the north, as it did in later Egypt; the ape is one with the Kaf-type of breath in the east; the eagle with the solar hawk in the south, and the serpent represents earth in the west. The human was not at first included in the four types of power, force, or faculty. They were four elementaries that represented four elements, as the fish, reptile, animal, and bird; there was no bird even amongst the earliest four in which fire was signified by the lion. The four have variants, but the elements were primordial and permanent. It was the type of Water, the Hippopotamus, or Fish, that was first humanised as the Mother of all, water being the earliest element of life that was recognised, as is shown by the bringer to birth and producer from the waters. Thus Amset, who is the man-image in the later four and who took the place of the genitrix, had an earlier feminine form. This connecting link also serves to prove that the first type of the producer which was humanised was that of the mother, not the male.

The four types that became gods of the four quarters and four elements are pourtrayed in the fragment of an inscription of Psametik I.[1] as the Goddess Uati, Seb (or Sut), Shu, and Ra. Uati represents water; Seb, earth; Shu, air; Ra, fire. In a still later phase the four became four rams or souls of Ra called *Sheft-hat*, the primordial force. This was after the one god (solar) had been compounded from the four spirits or elements to become "*the only God, the original male power of gods and men who reveals himself in the region of light with four heads*" (that represent him as) *the illuminator of heaven and earth by his solar splendour, as the one coming in the Nile stream, as the one granting life to the terrestrial world, and as the air for all men.*"[2] He is still the divinity of the solar *fire*, of *water*, *earth*, and *air !* In like manner Horus is said to be the "*Four superior Gods of the Upper Place.*"[3] The four were first, were elemental, were the types, spirits, genii, or gods of the four quarters, and these were derived visibly from the genitrix of the Great Bear. Water, Fire, Air, and Earth were the four sacred elements of existence; and under the most ancient religion these were kept sacred to all. Under the current Cult they have become the personal property of the few, and the ruling powers no longer guard these natural elements for the whole people, or fitly represent the giver who supplied them freely for the benefit of all.

Proclus, in Timæus, affirms that "in the equinoctial circle the motive power of the universe was especially established."[4] In Yucatan the reckonings were kept by means of a Wheel divided into four quarters; and with the Siamese their dates are arranged on a Cross *i.e.*, the sign of the four quarters. This marking out of the annual Circuit by means of four cardinal points furnished the foundation of the

[1] From *Palermo Trans. Bib. Arch.*
[2] *Great Mendes Stele*, i. 2. *R. P.* vol. viii. p. 95.
[3] Rit. ch. cxxxv. [4] B. i.

Mythos in which the four brothers, genii, spirits, or other figures of the four are stationed at the four different quarters to bear up the heavens no matter in what land or language we may find it. These four are universal. They belong to the first circle that was quartered according to the cardinal points. To quarter is a common term in English. Troops are quartered when they are lodged, and a quarter is a fourth part, whether the quartered get a fourth or not. Our heraldry proclaims the same origin and social stage in the quartering of arms as is found in the four quarterings of the Kamilaroi. It is related by the Iroquois concerning the introduction of their religious mysteries, that the first Mother had four Sons at a birth and died in bringing them forth. These are the four Good Spirits placed at the four quarters to which they point in their ceremonies.[1] Thunder is the voice of these four to whom the Iroquois offer the smoke of *Samau* (Tobacco). With the Algonkins, Creeks, Dacotahs, Natchez, Araucanians, and other Indian tribes, it is an indispensable formula preliminary to any business, to puff tobacco-smoke to the Spirits of the four Corners. The same religious custom has been observed among the Tartars of Siberia.[2]

Brinton has called the Cult of the Red Indians an Adoration of the Cardinal Points, identified with the Spirits of the Four Winds, who were the ancestors of the human race : he points out that the Indian speaks as if he carried the cross inside of him, and expresses himself according to the cardinal points even within his own wigwam. The four "Lineages" of the Tlascalans who occupied the four quarters of the Pueblo of Tlascala; and the Aztecs, who also occupied the Pueblo of Mexico, can in like manner be traced to the same source. The Inca of Peru was "*Lord of the Four Quarters of the Earth.*" According to Prescott the natives had no other epithet by which to designate the large collection of tribes and nations who were assembled under the sway of the Incas than that of the Tavintinsuyu, or Four Quarters of the World.[3] In the Maya, Moscos, and Huasteca languages the names of the four winds or spirits are the same as those of the four quarters. The Dacotah word *Tate-ouye-toba*, for the four cardinal points, literally means whence come four winds.[4] The four gods of the showers also dwelt at the four corners of the earth. Four mighty Manitus were worshipped by the Delaware Indians, and sacrifices were offered to them as gods of the four quarters, the west, south, east, and north. The Algonkins and Dacotahs traced their origin to four ancestral personages, not completely identified either as gods or men, but positively with the four winds and four quarters.[5]

The four brothers in Algonkin were designated Wabun, Kabun,

---

[1] Schoolcraft, vol. i. pp. 317—319.   [2] Nuttall, *Travels*, p. 175.
[3] *Conquest of Peru*, b. i. ch. ii.   [4] Brinton, p. 75.
[5] Schoolcraft, *Algic. Res.* vol. i. p. 139.

Kabibonokha, and Shawno, and these are the names of the four cardinal points as well as the four winds.[1]   Shawno was a Spirit that presided over the south in the Iroquois mythology ; his station being between the Twins and the Crab.   Kabun was the west and Wabun the east.   The Mexicans had four spirits of the wind who carried the dead to heaven, and Brinton refers these to the Cruciform Graves ascribed to the Mexicans.[2]   The Eskimo Abode of the Dead was Sillam Apane, the House of the Winds (or Spirits), and Sillam-Innua was owner of the four winds.   The Mayas of Yucatan looked back to four parents or leaders called the Tutul Xiu.[3]   The Xiu are spirits, chiefs ; and in Egyptian Khi or Khu is a spirit, a Ruler. Moreover, the Khi or Khiu are the four supports of the Heaven at the four corners, who are, therefore, identical with the four Xiu of the Mayas.   But the Khu is an earlier Keb as a lord of the Angle or Corner, and the Four Keb (Kabiri) are the four representative Genii of the four quarters, and of the sarcophagus of the Great Bear, the coffin of Osiris.   These are the Four Assyrian Kubur which were stationed facing the " Four Celestial Regions," as mentioned in the inscription of Khorsabad.[4]

The Yucatees said the sky was supported by four brothers whose family name was Bacab, their individual name being *Kan, Mulac, Ix,* and *Canac.*   These four had been placed at the four corners of the world when it was created, and they escaped when all else was destroyed by the flood.[5]   Amongst the Lunar Mansions the Arabic Al-Hak'ah is in Orion ; the Chinese *Chang* is in Hydra, and the Hindu *Mula* is in the tail of Scorpio.   These names and cardinal positions correspond to *Ix, Kan,* and *Mulac.*   According to the Quiché Myth the four genii were in existence before the creation of the sun ; there being no sun in Tulan-Zuiva, the birth-place called the Seven Caves, where they had lived by star-light.   The Circle of the Seven Stars was thus succeeded by the chart of the four quarters, four gods, or four constellations.   Following this earlier world came the creation of four perfect men, the three Balams and Mahucutan.   A god was assigned to each of the four.   Tohil, the god of fire, Avilix and Hacavitz, together with the fourth deity, given to Iqi-Balam.   It was on Mount Hacavitz, named after the divinity, that the sun was first seen to rise, whereupon the four men were turned into four corner stones.   The transformation and the appointment of the four gods, or men, changed into stones by the sun, for watch and worship, simply denote the making of the four cardinal points of the solstices and equinoxes by means of the four great stars or constellations that first served as indicators in the earliest zodiac of four signs.

[1] Brinton, p. 167.
[3] Ancient MS. discovered by Stephens.
[4] See B. B., vol. ii. p. 469.

[2] *Myths,* 95—98.

[5] Bancroft, vol. iii. p. 122.

There is a Tulan, says an ancient authority, where the sun rises (east), and there is another in the Land of Shades (north), and another where the sun reposes (west), and still another where the sun reposes (south) and there dwells God.[1] These four Tulans are solstitial and equinoctial, they belong to the four quarters, and were established in the Mount of the four corners.

Four of the Brothers Maui, who are a family of Elementary Gods like those of earliest Egypt, are the four supporters of the sky in the Maori Myth. In one version they are described as rending the earth and heaven in twain, and as the four props or supports they stem them asunder when divided and quartered.[2] The four brothers are found in the most ancient Chinese books. In the Canon of Yaou (Shu King), the second chapter of which is entitled the "*Measure of Yaou to secure a correct Calendar in order to promote the work of Agriculture*,"[3] the Yŏ are four persons who are brothers; they are also Four Mountains or astronomical stations. To these four the emperor appeals when the deluge begins to rise, "*Oh chief* (or chiefs) *of the Four Mountains, destructive in their overflow are the Waters of the Inundation. In their vast extent they embrace and overtop the mountains, threatening the heavens with their floods. Is there a capable man to whom I can assign the correction of their calamity?*" The Four Yŏ are the same four brothers previously called Ho, to two of whom is assigned the examining and registering of the times of the spring equinox and summer solstice, and to the two younger members of the house of Ho the autumn equinox and winter solstice. Yaou commanded the Ho brothers, in accordance with their observations of the wide heavens, to calculate and delineate the movements and appearances of the sun, moon, and stars, and to measure the zodiacal spaces. He commanded one brother to reside at Yu-e in the Bright Valley, where he was to respectfully receive as a guest the Rising Sun, and there adjust and arrange the labour of the spring. The day, said he, is of mid-length, and the star is in *Neaou*. You can thus determine mid-spring. *Neaou* is a starry space of the heavens embracing the Seven Constellations or Sieus of the southern quarter in the Lunar Circle. Another brother was ordered to reside at Nan-Keaou and there arrange the *transformation* of the summer and observe the extreme limit of the shadow. The day, said he, is at its longest, and the star is Ho; you may thus exactly determine mid-summer. The Star Ho is identical with the Star Fire, the central star in the Azure Dragon, which embraced the Seven Constellations of the westein quarter (called east by the Chinese) and corresponding to the Heart of Scorpio. A third brother is ordered to dwell in what was termed the Dark Valley and there convoy the setting sun and arrange

---

[1] Brinton, *Myths of New England*, p. 89.
[2] Grey, *Polynesian Myth.* ch. i.
[3] Legge, *Shu-king*, pt. i. ch. iii. ; Chalmers, *Astronomy of the Chinese.*

and adjust the labours of the autumn. The night, he said, is of medium length and the star is Heu. You can thus determine mid-autumn. This was in the natural west of the period, but the culminating star was *Heu* the central one in the Black Warrior, which included the Seven Constellations of the northern quarter, the particular star corresponding to β Aquarii. The fourth brother is to reside in the north, in what is called the Sombre Capital, and there adjust the changes of winter. The day, said he, is at the shortest, and the star is *Maou*. These four stars mark four of the twenty-eight Lunar Mansions or *Sieus*. Kio is the twelfth Sieu, the star *a* Virginis. This corresponds to the star Ho of Nan-Keaou. Uei is μ 2 Scorpionis, in the seventeenth Sieu. Heu exists as Hiu, β Aquarii, in the twenty-second Sieu, and Mao is η Tauri, in the first *Sieu*.[1]

This disposition of the sun and the four points of the year shows the longest day to have coincided with the sun in the sign of Scorpio, and the shortest with the sun in the sign of the Bull. The summer solstice now occurs with the sun in the last degree of the Twins, the winter in the last degree of the Archer. The zodiacal difference is, therefore, that of four full signs, or 8,620 years in time. Hence the necessity for readjustment. The Chinese Tauists have the four spirits of the four quarters named (1) Pek-hé, (2) Cheng-liông, (3) Tsu-chhiok, (4) Hieu-bu, corresponding to the Black Warrior, White Tiger, Red Bird, and Blue Dragon.

Four spirits stand, four powers preside, four winds blow, or four waters flow, at the four cardinal points or the four corners of the Mount in the general myths of the world; this being a primordial type like the Serpent or the Tree. The lotus is also a figure of the Mount Meru in India, and the Kamite original of the lotus as the mount of the four corners may be seen in the Hall of the Two Truths, where Osiris presides as judge of all the world. The earth is here represented by the four spirits, gods, or genii of the four corners, who stand on a lotus before him. This becomes the lotus-tree of Moslem legend. Four immortals are spoken of in the Atharva-Veda as the guardians of the four quarters of the sky.[2] The four spirits appear in the book of Enoch as the four great angels Michael, Raphael, Gabriel, and Phanuel. The four winds or spirits of the four quarters are described by Enoch.[3] The first wind is called the eastern. The second is *" called the south, because the Most High descends there."* The western wind *" has the name of diminution "* because *" it is there that all the luminaries are diminished and descend. The fourth wind which is named the north is divided into three, and the third part contains Paradise ; "* the garden eastward. There is a paraphrase of Genesis ii. 7, in one of the Targums, ascribed to Jonathan ben Uzziel, which relates that when Jehovah-Elohim formed man by two creations, he

---

[1] *Sûrya-Siddhânta*, Burgess, p. 324, for comparative lists.
[2] i. xxxi. 1.   [3] Ch. lxxvi. 1, 2, 3, 4.

collected dust from the habitation of the holy place and from *the four spirits of the world* and mixed from all the waters of the world. Here likewise the four spirits stand for the four corners of the world. In the Book of Revelation[1] the four Angels stand at the four Corners holding the four Winds of the Earth in their hands. According to Milligan the spirits or manes of the dead that returned after death to cause good or evil to befal the living were of *four different kinds*, answering to these spirits of the four corners. In the prose Edda the four spirits are four dwarfs called the east, west, north, and south, who are placed at the corners of the four quarters. In the Scandinavian Mythology the four corners are represented by four horns which support the vault of heaven. The Kabalist throne of the Divine *En-Soph* has four legs and six steps. The four legs stand for the four corners, and the six steps are the four quarters, together with the height and the depth. These form a figure of the Ten Sephiroth. The "four props of Heaven" are identified by a priest of Amen, in the time of Tahtmes III., with the four corners at the "utmost ends of the world." The Assyrian four protecting genii are represented as the human-faced bull, called the Sed, Alap, or Kirub; the lion with a man's head called the Lamas or Nirgal; the Nattig with the head of an eagle, and the Ustur formed in the human likeness. The same four as the symbolical creatures described by Ezekiel.

The Mandans have the tortoises at the four corners of the earth which spout forth the waters.[2] Two tortoises are also found in the sign Libra of an ancient Egyptian zodiac. The stag, phœnix, tortoise and dragon, are a Chinese heraldic form of the typical four. These preside over the Chinese empire; they coincide with the Egyptian phœnix in the south, the tortoise in Libra, west; the dragon north, leaving the stag for the east.

The Aztecs had four chief ideographic signs which were symbols of the four elements. These are Tochtli the rabbit; Calli the house; Tecpatl the flint (or arrow), and Acatl the cane. The rabbit was dedicated to Tevacayohua, god of earth; Calli the house was dedicated to Xiuteucli, god of fire; Tecpatl the flint, to Quetzalcoatl, the god of air; Acatl the cane to Tlaloc, god of water; these correspond to Seb (Tseb) or Sut, for the earth; the hawk (Horus or Kabhsenuf) for fire; Shu (the ape or Hapi) for air, and Amset (or Uati who carries the papyrus sceptre) for water.[3] The Mexican four Great Ages are the age of earth; the age of fire; the age of air and the age of water; and these are based primarily on the circle of the four quarters extended possibly to the Cycle of Precession. The Druids founded

[1] Ch. vii. 4.
[2] Catlin, *Letters and Notes*, vol. i. p. 181.
[3] Boturini, Humboldt, Kingsborough, *Mex. Antiq.* vol. iv.; Gemelli Careri, *Giro de Mondo*, tom. vi. cap. vi. p. 40.

the Quadrangular Caer, on the circle and four corners. They are called by Cynddelw, "*the Druids of the circle, of four dialects, coming from four regions.*"[1] They were also designated "*Bards of the Steep Mount.*" This mount of the circle and four regions was the seat of the throned bards of the Briton's isle; and their seat was the chair of Kêd the genitrix of gods and men; the chair of Cader Idris, as the mount.

When *Tu-wên-hsin* sent his "Panthay" embassy to England, signifying his submission or his desire to become feudatory to the British Crown, his representatives brought four pieces of rock that had been hewn from the four corners of their sacred Tali or mount. They offered all their world in that type of totality. The mind of the oldest races is continually limited to this primitive mould of thought, and their expression and simplicity is not comprehended by the race that now governs them.

Four colours were connected with the four corners. The square at the top of Mount Meru was faced with four different colours; it was white to the east; yellow to the south; black to the west, and red to the north.[2] In the Maya arrangement yellow is said to be assigned to the east; red to the south; black to the west, and white to the north. These four correspond to the ages named after the metals, gold (yellow), silver (white), copper or brass (red), and iron (black); also to the tree of the four quarters shown to Zaratusht by Ahura-Mazda. It is declared in the Studgar Nask that when Zaratusht desired immortality, he beheld the root of a tree on which were four branches, one golden, one of silver, one of steel, and one mixed with iron.[3] An image of the ancient four quarters is described by Daniel as seen in the dream of Belshazzar. It was formed of the four metals, Gold, Silver, Brass, and Iron (the latter being mixed with clay), and is identical with the root of the four-branched tree of Gold, Silver, Steel, and Iron, shown to Zaratusht, which Ahuramazda tells him typifies the four periods that are to come.[4] This figure of the four quarters is to be superseded by a form of the mountain that is to rise up and fill the whole earth; *i.e.*, a mount of the four quarters, as the throne of the one Solar God alone, as it was in the worship of Ra. Another application of the four was made in relation to the square, circle, triangle and crescent; the square being assigned to earth, the circle to water, the triangle to fire (*cf.* the triangle of Horus), and the crescent to air (*cf.* the bow of Shu).[5] The square,

[1] *Cf.* the Assyrian four dominions, each of different language.—*Bull. Ins. of Khorsabad.*

[2] Williams, "*Meru.*"

[3] *Bahman Yasht*, ch. i. 2.

[4] Daniel, ch. ii. *Bahman Yasht*, ch. i. 1, 2, 3. *Studgar Nask.* Haug's *Essays*, p. 126. West.

[5] Remusat, *Notes on the Travels of* Fa Hian *Foe-Koue-Ki*, p. 92; also, see diagram, p. 316 present vol.

the circle, the triangle and crescent were all continued in the Christian iconography as the nimbus, aureole, or glory of the god. "God the father" also wears the *square* disk in the "Disputa" of Raphael. It often appears lozenge-shaped. The Deity wears the *triangle* in a Greek fresco of the seventeenth century. He is seated on the *bow* or *crescent* in other representations, and the *circle* is the common glory.[1]

A type once founded in physical phenomena continues for ever. The four elements yield four spirits of the four elements. The four corner constellations become four spirits. The four winds that blow from the four quarters are four spirits. Four spirits are extracted from the four metals. Four properties of matter are transformed into four spirits. The type was continued by the Kabalists, Theosophists and Mystics.

The whole matter of the Mythos survived with the Gnostics (in a doctrinal phase) who begin with the Great Mother that divided into the two sisters as Sophia below and Sophia above. From the Mother of All Things came the first Tetrad (as it did in the fourfold Apt or Typhon) and from her came the Second Tetrad as a Daughter,[2] a "female from a female." The Gnostic Valentinus derived the primordial Four from a certain duadic being. This tetrad was likewise of a dual nature; it bifurcated and formed the ogdoad of a right and left hand Tetrad, the one being called Light, the other Darkness.[3] These agree with the Quiché four spirits and their four wives. Moreover, according to Irenæus, "The Ogdoad" (composed of the four who were dual) "*is understood as being hidden in the viscera,*"[4] which makes a curious return to the Egyptian spirits of the Four Corners who were also the four Genii of the Sarcophagus, to whose care the viscera of the embalmed mummy were committed to be kept in four different Canopic Vases over which they presided. Now, when we learn from the Berosian account of the Chaldean kings and the Deluge that *four double-shaped personages* came up out of the sea to land in the time of Daos of Pantibiblion, there can be little doubt that these likewise represent the four keepers of the cardinal points who comprised the Ogdoad in their dual nature. Pantibiblion, the City of the Records, was the place of the most ancient Temple of the Sun.

This is how Jacob Böhme applies the four-fold type to the creative nature, "*The four first forms in themselves are the anger and the wrath of God in the eternal nature; and they are in themselves nothing else but such a source or property as standeth in the darkness, and is not material, but an originality of the Spirit, without which there would be nothing. For the four forms are the cause of all things.*"[5]

Irenæus shows us how the four spirits of the four corners were

---

[1] Didron, figs. 4, 21, 22, 38.
[2] Irenæus, b. i. ch. xv. 2.
[3] Irenæus, b. i. ch. xi. 1, 2.
[4] Irenæus, b i. ch. xviii. 1.
[5] *Threefold Life of Man*, chap. ii. par. 44.

continued when he says, "*It is not possible that the Gospels can be either more or fewer than they are. For, since there are four zones of the world in which we live, and four chief winds,* τεσσαρα Καθολιχὰ πνεύματα, *or four Catholic spirits, while the Church is spread throughout the world, and the pillar and ground of the Church is the Gospel and the spirit of life, it is fitting that she should have four pillars. . . It is evident that the Word the Artificer of all* (who in Egypt was Khepr-Ptah), *he that sitteth upon the Cherubim* (which are two beetles in an Egyptian ark), *has given us the Gospel under four aspects, but bound together by one spirit. The Cherubim were four-faced as the Scripture says.*"[1]

A Hindu who was shown the symbolical pictures of Matthew, Mark, Luke and John with their respective man, lion, ox and eagle, explained these in accordance with his own system of divine totemism as the avatars or Vahans of the four evangelists,[2] because they represented the universal types of the four quarters. The four of the Gospels are still appealed to by incantations as the Genii of the four corners of the Children's Bed.

The present writer considers that the "Mount of Transfiguration" in the Gospels according to Matthew and Mark is the Mount of the transformation of the solar god in the Ritual; and that the four in the Mount, the Christ, Peter, John and James are a form of the four Genii, the Hawk-headed Horus (or Kabhsenuf) Hapi (or Kafi) Sut-Anup and Amset. But this thesis has to be developed hereafter.

The "Pantomime" deserves to be preserved a little longer as a witness to the origines of Mythology which were continued in the Mysteries. Nowhere else have the four spirits of the four corners a more perfect survival.

Columbine, the Dove, is the Great Mother, one of whose types was the Dove of Hathor, Menat, Semiramis and Juno. Her quarter is the north, the region of the Great Bear. The clown is a survival of the ape (Hapi or Kafi; *i.e.* Shu) whose quarter is the east, and who appears as the Greek Pan or Orion in an Egyptian planisphere.[3] Pantaloon represents the jackal, the sly, wise counsellor, Sut-Anup, whose quarter is the west. Harlequin is Har the Solar God, who went downward from the south as the sun of the under world, the "Horus (Har) of the Two Horizons" *who transformed and was the cause of the transformation which took place annually in Amenti.* His black mask witnesses to the hidden sun, invisible in the darkness. His magic wand is the sign of the transformation and resurrection. "*I went in as a Hawk; I came out as a Phœnix,*" says the Osirified in the two characters of Horus. This is the Hawk-headed Kabhsenuf. The

[1] Irenæus, condensed from b. iii. ch. xi. 8.
[2] Tylor, *Prim. Culture*, v. ii. p. 217.
[3] Drummond, pl. ii. from Kircher.

Phœnix is a type of the transforming Horus, our Harlequin. It does not matter how or where the pantomime was continued from the miracle play or mystery drama, nor what the explanations hitherto offered may have been; we are solely concerned with the origin and significance of the characters and the persistence of the types. Possibly the pantomime, as we have it now, was re-introduced from Italy, but "Harlequin" is Armoric for the juggler, a reduced shape of the divinity of transformation and wonder-working. Also, in the continuation of the miracle-play still performed in Brittany, the actor who represents the sufferings of Christ in the drama becomes the harlequin in the pantomime that follows, so that he plays the part of the double Horus. Moreover, we can point to the four most ancient British festivals of these four spirits pre-identified with the four quarters of the year, and the four-fold Yule, wheel or circle of the cross. The genitrix presides over the north and the Mother-Night of the year was celebrated by the northern nations, in Britain and Greenland on the night of the winter solstice and the rebirth of the year. The folk-festival following, that of the Fool Plough, establishes the connection with the Great Bear (the Plough); the seven characters in which correspond to the seven spirits; the fool and Bessy to the ape and bear. The Old Fool's Day ("All Fools") belongs to the clown, ape, or fool, whose constellation was probably Orion, the Hebrew Kesil, or the fool. It has been denied that Kesil does mean the fool. But this has to be determined finally by phenomena, and the mythology. The giant Shu was represented by the ape; he is known as the *Keh Keh* an ape, a fool, or a crazy man. In Coptic *Kes-Kes* is the name of Orion, and the Hebrew *Kesil* completes the proof. · The Kehkeh (or Khaku, a variant) becomes our Gec, or Gouk who is the April Fool. The fool, Orion, was superseded as one of the time-keepers in the later mythos, and made a mock of. The ape and fool are identical, and formerly the fool carried an ape on his shoulders as his image. · To "put an ape into your hood" is to make a fool of you. The ape represents the equinox. At Midsummer we have the festival of fire, associated with the name of Baal and Belin. In Egypt Baal is Bar-Typhon, *i.e.* the Sut-Anup of the Four Genii, whose constellation is the dog or jackal. The autumn festival has got belated with the lapse of time; for example, Nutcrack Night at Kingston in Surrey had kept its equinoctial position and was celebrated on the 28th of September, whereas in the north of England it is the vigil of All Souls' Day, celebrated on the 31st of October.[1] "All Souls" is the great autumn festival of the four, and it is now kept five weeks (or 2,600 years) behind the true time. At this equinox the Horus of both horizons or Har-Makhu (our Micha-El) entered the underworld to conduct the

[1] Chambers, *Book of Days*, vol. ii. p. 519; Brayley, *Topographical History of Surrey*, vol. iii. p. 41.

congregated souls and deliver those that were in purgatory. No doubt the nuts were cracked by the living as a ceremony that was symbolical of the deliverance of the dead that were now supposed to be released by the solar god, who descended to do battle with Apollyon the Apophis in the Valley of the Shadow, and lead the waiting multitude of "All Souls" up into the region of eternal light. Another custom, that of diving for apples and catching them with the mouth only, the hands being tied behind, may be interpreted as illustrative of the Horus who saved men in spite of his maimed and fettered condition, as the lessening autumn sun that conquered the adversary and rescued souls under the most adverse conditions which were dramatised and imitated by the actors in the ancient Miracle plays and pastimes. The four Genii or gods of the four quarters, elements, colours, metals, &c., are also deposited in the pack of 52 playing cards. These are based on the four divisions of thirteen to the set, and the four, the ace, king, queen, and knave, preserve their places according to the latest arrangement in which the Sun-God was supreme. Harlequin is the Great One; the ruling power. The Ace takes all the tricks, just as harlequin frustrates all the trickeries. The ace is the Latin *as*, and in Egyptian *as* means the Great One, the Supreme Ruler.

In Central Asia the game of chess which is believed to have *had its origin in the Garden of Eden*, is played by four persons (instead of two as with us) in keeping with the four quarters. The four are likewise known in the British mythology as (1) Cesarea, called the Niece of Noah, and her Three Brothers; (2) as Heremon and three others, termed "four Scots," who first ruled over Ireland. (3) Deirdre and the three sons of Usneach. The Tuatha-dadanan are also said to have built four cities, their Tetrapolis—named Falia, Goria, Finnea, and Mura; that is, they divided the land into four quarters like Nimrod in the plain of Shinar.

In Egypt the four elementals of the four corners were stationed finally as the four souls (or Rams) of Ra in the decans of Aries, the four being compounded into the one God, called Primordial force. The forces were primordial, but the God was final. In the Memnonium at Thebes the four Rams appear as an animal with wings, like those of the Assyrian bulls with the human head; and this, as we have seen, was a type of the later Solar God. A compounding of the one God from the four occurs also in the four-headed Brahma. When this had been effected we hear of the "four Castes" who are "*formed from the body of the Creator*," according to the Hindu doctrine,[1] whereas the body of the Creator had been formed out of four types or characters of the elemental castes. Orpheus sings of

"*One Zeus, one Aïdes, one Helios, one Dionysos.*"—(Fragment 4.)

[1] Muir, *Sansk. Texts*, vol. i. ch. ii. p. 293.

These were identical with the four in Egypt and elsewhere, and may be paralleled with other sets of four in many forms.

Aïdes.	Dionysos.	Helios.	Zeus.	Night.	Morning.	Noon.	Evening.
Uati.	Shu.	Ra.	Seb.	Nor.h.	East.	South.	West.
Chiun.	Lion.	Khem.	Respu.	Winter.	Spring.	Summer.	Autumn.
Miriam.	Moses.	Hur.	Aaron.	Water.	Air.	Fire.	Earth.
Deirdre.	Ainli.	Naisi.	Ardan.	Deluge.	Typhoon.	Conflagration.	Earthquake.
Venus.	Mars.	Sun.	Jupiter.	Fish.	Bird.	Serpent.	Beast.
Amset.	Hapi.	Kabhsenuf.	Anup.	Hippopotamus.	Ape.	Lion.	Crocodile.
Mother.	Child.	Vir.	Old Man.	Mouth.	Nose.	Eye.	Ear.
Columbine.	Clown.	Harlequin.	Pantaloon.	Vegetable.	Spirit.	Mineral.	Animal.
Queen.	Knave.	Ace.	King.	Cane.	Arrow.	House.	Rabbit.
Human.	Lion.	Eagle.	Calf.	Copper.	Silver.	Gold.	Iron.
Ustur.	Lion.	Nattig.	Bull.	Red.	White.	Yellow.	Black.
Human.	Ape.	Bird.	Jackal.	Circle.	Crescent.	Triangle.	Square.
Bear.	Orion.	Phœnix.	Crocodile.	Fomalhaut.	Aldebaran.	Cor Leonis	Antares.

The four-fold compound divinity was also described by the oracle of the God Iao in the Temple of Klaros. This deity being consulted through his oracle as to which of the gods it was that should be adored under the title of *Iao*[1] replied :

> " Know that of gods who exist the highest of all is Iao,
> He is Aïdes in winter, and Zeus at the coming of springtime,
> Helios in summer heat, and in Autumn the graceful Iao."

Here the combination varies ; the god of fire appears twice as Helios and Iao the Autumn Sun (the Child Horus, Elul, Adon, or Tammuz) and Dionysos is omitted. This combination therefore points to the Iao of the three-fold nature already explained who did not include the fatherhood of the Tetramorphic Iao (which has to be elucidated) but it does show the divinity adapted to the four quarters or four seasons of the year.

In Egypt one god of the four quarters was the Tat-Cross of the four cardinal points personified as the four-fold Ptah, and likewise as " Osiris-Tat." In the Inscription of Shabaka[2] the god Ptah is pourtrayed in the four-fold character of " *Ptah-Ur*," " *Ptah-Sen*," " *Ptah-Nunu* " and " *Ptah-hes-urt* " ; he is designated " *Ptah in his four divine forms*." Beneath are four figures in the mummy-shape holding the Tat-Cross. Ptah is a recognised god of fire, the Egyptian Hephaistos. Ptah-*nunu* is god of the water ; Ptah-*Sen*, god of breath ; Ptah-*Ur* is the old first, four-fold (equating with the genitrix Ta-Urt), and Ptah-hes-Urt is the god of the ancient seat. In this way the four-fold god, whether as Ra, Osiris-Tat, or Ptah, superseded the goddess of the first circle of time and the four quarters of the beginning. In the Ritual this god is designated " *Ptah the Great Tat, the Throne of the sun, sole type in the Roofed House*." The type being the Tat-tree of the four quarters.[3]

The " Tat of gold " made out of the body of a sycamore tree and washed with the water of life, was placed at the throat of the

---

[1] Macrobius, *Saturn*, i. 18.
[2] Chabas, *Mélanges Égyptologiques. Troisième-Série.* tom. i. p. 247 ; Goodwin.
[3] Ch. cxli.

dead so that they might pass through the gateways "*turning a deaf ear to the charmer*," the snake Ruhak.[1] This Tree-Tat was symbolically the *back-bone of Osiris*, on which the heavens and the future state of existence were bodily built.

In connection with the compounding of a one god from the four it is noticeable that when the four spirits, gods, or old men passed away, in the Quiché legend, they left in their place a bundle that could never be unfolded as it was without seam. It was called the "*Enveloped Majesty.*"[2] This has been previously compared with the Mummy which in Egypt was represented by and as Ptah, the god of the four-fold Tat-type.

The Mexican god, Napatecutli, appears likewise to be a form of the four-fold deity. His name means the *four times*, or the *four-fold lord ;*[3] the four times answering to the four corners figured by the Tat of Ptah, the four seasons of Iao, Brahma with four faces ; the ram with four faces ; the beast in Ezekiel and Revelation with four faces ; Ptah in four characters, and other forms of the four.

The cross of symbolism has no significance without the circle ; both go together and are indivisible. In the town of Northampton the ceremony of beating the bounds is called "Beating the Cross." The cross or crossing is usually at the centre of the bounds. The week of *going round* to beat the boundaries was also known by the name of "Cross Week."

The Hindu Râsamandala is a circular dance in honour of the young sun-god Krishna. In this the couples of the dancers keep making the sign of the cross with two sticks which they strike together in going round.[4]

The mystic chain of the Masonic and other Mysteries formed by making the circle with the hands of each person crossed derives all its significance from the cross and circle being figured at one and the same time and in one and the same image.

The planets are all crossers of the circle, and each one has the sign of the cross. The symbol of Mercury unites the moon, circle, and cross. Jupiter has a cross underneath a crescent ; Mars an oblique cross on the circle ; Venus a cross below the circle ; Saturn a sickle and cross, and these cross-symbols are all extant as the Planetary Signs of the Crossers.

The great Cross which was discovered a few years since at Callernish (in the Lewis) covered with a bed of peat-moss more than four feet thick that must have taken ages to accumulate, was a chamber sunken near a Circle of Standing Stones ; it was planned according to

---

[1] *Rit* ch. clvi. Birch.
[2] *Book of Beginnings,* vol. ii. p. 100.
[3] Bancroft, vol. iii. p. 54.
[4] Moor's *Hindu Pantheon,* pl. 63.

the four quarters with scientific precision, with the head to the south, foot to the north, and arms extending east and west, 270 feet in length and 27 across.[1]

The circle and four corners are also depicted as a circle and a square. These are two patterns of the mound-builders. They appear both as the *square outside of the circle* and as *a square inclosed within a circle*, in the ancient earth-works of Ohio, America.[2] These squares and circles were also formed with scientific precision. The Chinese have two typical Temples; one of which is consecrated to Heaven; that is *round;* the other to earth, that is *square.*

The circle and square constituted the "Quadrangular Caer" of the Druids, as the circle of the four quarters. And this was a continuation of the Horned Cairns of a prehistoric British race that once extended from Caithness to the Cotswold Hills, and from thence to West Wales. The plan of the Cairn of Ormiegill which is sixty-six feet long, and has nearly the same breadth, shows the *circle within the square*, like the American Mounds, and at the centre of both is the uterine type of the abode, the Egyptian Kha. This cairn comprises the mother's womb, the circle of heaven, and the square (with four corners) of earth.[3]

In the Quiché geography the earth is four-square. It is shaped as a square, divided into four parts, marked with lines, measured with cords, and suspended from the heavens by a cord to each of its four corners and its four sides.[4]

The square was held by the Pythagoreans and Neo-Platonists to be the symbol of earth, and inferior to the circle, the symbol of heaven. The square in the language of heraldry is a diminished or broken circle, the circle being the square perfected. This is imaged by the Swastika cross, the four feet of which show segments of the circle broken and reduced to form the square.

The square is of course an angle of ninety degrees, the fourth part of a circle. Thus the square formed of the four corners is a cross equal to the circle of 360 degrees.

The oldest known form of the Nagari character in use throughout Pegu and Ava is formed of circles and segments of circles combined, whereas the sacred text of the Pali is in a form of the square letter, consisting chiefly of right angles. There is the same contention of circle and square manifested in the Phœnician and Hebrew letters; this is shown by the Ayin, the earliest form of which is round, the later square.

The circle assigned to heaven was the primordial figure, and this was followed by the square of the four corners. Both are

[1] *Notes and Queries,* September 13, 1873, p. 206.
[2] Baldwin, *Ancient America,* figs. 13, 15.
[3] Mitchel, *Past in the Present,* fig. 49, Cairn at Ormiegill.
[4] Ximenes, *Or. de los Indios,* p. 5.

E E 2

combined in the shape of the Mounds, in the Quadrangular Caer (or Ceathar), and both are reflected in the round and square forms of letters.

The square and ring are coupled together in the marriage ceremonies. In Yorkshire it was formerly a custom for the bride-cake to be cut up into small square dice-like pieces, passed over the heads of the bride and bridegroom, and then crossed through the wedding-ring. The pieces of cake were drawn through the ring nine times over.[1] Passing the square through the ring nine times is indicative of the nine solar months of gestation, and shows the relationship of the square to the circle. In a Popish "Hallowing of the Ring" the blessing asked for on the ring is denoted by the sign of the cross, "*Lord, send thy* X (*blessing*) *upon this ring*,"[2] the blessing being one with the cross-sign of multiplying, or the phallus. In this connection of the circle with the cross of the four corners we shall find the origin of the fourth digit being made the especial wearer of the wedding-ring.

In the Hereford, York, and Salisbury Missals instructions are given for the ring to be put *first on the thumb and afterwards on three fingers in succession*, to be left on the *fourth* finger, where it is to remain, the four digits being equal to the four corners. Passing the fourth digit through the circlet is identical symbolically with passing the square of bride-cake through the ring; this is acknowledged, and, as it were, pointed out in putting the ring on the four digits before leaving it at last on the fourth, and going round the four points or corners of the square in the complete espousal with the ring. Many sufficiently prolific mothers who represent the Tree of Life bowed down with its fruitful branches, never take off their wedding-ring from the time it is put on the fourth digit at the altar, little thinking it is the type of fertility, of the Circle fulfilled in the nine months of gestation, and that it signifies progeny in plenty or children for ever. This not being sufficient, the keeper-ring was added to be worn on the same finger, originally as a charm against miscarriage. The cross being a symbol of blessing, this was represented by the ring placed on the fourth digit, and to take it off would be to lose the blessing. Instructions for depicting the "Divine Hand" in the act of *blessing*, according to this typology, are given in a Byzantine manuscript cited by Didron: "*When you desire to represent a hand in the act of blessing you must not join the three fingers together, but let the thumb be crossed on the third finger, so that the first, called the index, may remain open, and the second finger be slightly bent. These two fingers form the name of Christ Jesus, IC. The first finger remaining open signifies an Iota, and the curvature of the second finger forms a Sigma. The thumb is placed across the third finger, and*

---

[1] Brand, *Ring and Bridecake.*
[2] Nicholas Dorcaster, *Doctrine of the Massebcoke*, from Wyttonberge, 1554.

the fourth, or little finger, is slightly bent, thus indicating the word Kristos, X.C. The union of the thumb with the third finger makes a Chi, χ, and the curvature of the little finger forms a sigma, C. And these two letters form the "sigle" or abridgment of Christos." [1] This sign of the cross and circle in one figure is made by the Christ as the Saviour God in the Greek Iconography. It is also made by the Divine Hand reaching out of heaven; [2] which hand is undoubtedly intended for God the Father. Up to the twelfth century, says Didron, the hand represents the Father exclusively. But Didron did not know the relation of the Number 4, or the fourth finger to the Fatherhood. This has to be expounded in the following section. Enough for the present to affirm that the sign of the thumb and fourth finger making the circle does denote the fatherhood, and that this corroborates the reason now assigned for placing the marriage-ring upon the fourth finger.

The fourth digit was considered the healing one, known as the Lech-man, or medical finger. The Greeks and Romans called it the medical finger. It is still used in England for the purpose of rubbing on salve. But the first salve, medicine, or healing signified was that of marriage applied to such ailments as green-sickness. Salveo to save is primarily to be well in health. Hence the Saviour of the world poses as the Lech-man with his thumb touching the fourth digit as a sign of saving and healing, or of blessing. It is the fourth digit on the right hand, the masculine hand which constitutes the healer. This in digital reckoning is number 9, an equivalent to the nine pieces of cake passed through the ring, and the sign of nine months, the period of gestation. The Hindu Buddha is often depicted making the figure of the circle and the cross, both with the hands and the feet, whilst holding a four-petalled Lotus in one or in each hand. The Buddha of Bengal also wears the four-petalled Lotus on his breast, and a hood of *nine* hooded and inflated snakes on his head. [3] These also denote the period of gestation, and, as the present writer considers, show the nine dry months of a year that was first completed by the three months' inundation in Egypt.

The circle and cross are inseparable. The Ankh-loop, the sign of one turn round, consists of a circle and a cross or crossing of the ends. This, however, is not the cross of the later four corners. The Crux Ansata unites the circle and cross of the four corners. From this origin the circle and the cross came to be interchangeable at times. For example, the Chakra, or Disk of Vishnu is a circle. The name denotes the circling, wheeling round, periodicity, the wheel of time. This the god uses as a weapon to hurl at the enemy. In like manner Thor throws his weapon, the Fylfot, a

[1] Gulielmus Durandus, *Rat. Div. Off.* lib. v. cap. ii., J. Beleth. Didron, pp. 407—8, English Tr.
[2] Didron, fig. 52. [3] Moor's *Hindu Pantheon*, pl. 75.

form of the four-footed cross, and a type of the four quarters. Thus
the cross is equivalent to the circle of the year. The wheel emblem
unites the cross and circle in one, as does the hieroglyphic cake and
the Ankh-tie, ⌒.

The *Tat* Cross consists of a pedestal (or stand) with four horizontal
bars or shelves that are *circular*, constituting a kind of altar-cross. It
was used in the temples as the pedestal and fulcrum for supporting
the statues of the gods. The name signifies to establish, and it is the
symbol of stability as the four-fold foundation of a world or an order
of things that was established upon the four quarters. The Tat-altar
(or pedestal) is the equivalent of the mount of the four corners, or the
tree with four branches, or the cross with four arms. The Tat is the
special type of Ptah, the establisher of the four corners in the solar
mythos, but it existed as a lunar emblem for the moon-god. Taht
impersonates the Tat, and says : " *I am Tat, the Son of Tat, conceived
in Tat, and born in Tat.*" [1] As a lunar type it would represent the
four quarters of the moon, for, whether the four corners may be those
of the four stars (or spirits), the four leaves of the lotus, the four
lunar divisions, or the four corners of the solar Zodiac, the cross is
everywhere the sign of the four quarters with the one exception. The
Tat was set up in Tattu, the established or eternal region corresponding finally to the zodiacal sign of the Fishes, the station of the Seven
Great Gods of the Assyrians, the chief of all the four corners because
the solar birthplace.

A most curious form of the cross is given in the *Journal of the Royal
Asiatic Society.*[2] At each of the four corners is placed a quarter arc
of an oviform curve, and when the four are put together they form
an oval ; thus the figure combines the cross with the circle round
it in four parts, corresponding to the four corners of the cross. The four
segments answer to the four feet of the Swastika cross and the Fylfot
of Thor. The four-leaved lotus flower of Buddha is likewise figured at
the centre of this cross, the lotus being an Egyptian and Hindu type
of the four quarters. The four quarter arcs, if joined together,
would form an ellipse, and the ellipse is also figured on each arm of
the cross. This ellipse therefore denotes the path of the earth.
Now the symbol depicted on the Scottish stones and commonly
known as the " spectacles ornament " is, as previously suggested, a
form of the cross of the four quarters ; a symbol of the solstices and
equinoxes. This is also drawn within the ellipse upon the sculptured
stones of Scotland. Sir J. Y. Simpson copied the following specimen,
which is here presented as the cross of the two equinoxes and
the two solstices placed within the figure of the earth's path. The
same ovoid or boat-shaped figure appears at times in the Hindu
drawings with seven steps at each end as a form or a mode of Meru.

The four-armed cross is simply the cross of the four quarters,

[1] *Ritual*, ch. i.   [2] Vol. xviii. p. 393, pl. 4 ; Inman, fig. 38.

but the cross-sign is not always simple. This is a type that was developed from an identifiable beginning which was adapted to the expression of various ideas afterwards. The most sacred cross of Egypt that was carried in the hands of the Gods, the Pharaohs, and the mummied dead is the Ankh ♀, the sign of life, the living, an oath, a covenant, and a pair, or to couple and duplicate. The top of this is the hieroglyphic Ru ⬯, set upright on the Tau-cross. The Ru is the door, gate, mouth, the place of outlet. This denotes the birthplace in the northern quarter of the heavens from which the sun is re-born. Hence the *Ru of the Ankh-sign is the feminine type of the birthplace representing the north.* It was in the northern quarter that the goddess of the Seven Stars, called the "Mother of the Revolutions," gave birth to time in the earliest circle of the year. The first sign of this primordial circle and cycle made in heaven is the earliest shape of the Ankh-cross, ⬭, a mere loop which contains both a circle and the cross in one image. This loop or noose is carried in front of the oldest genitrix, Typhon of the Great Bear, as her *Ark*, the ideograph of a period, an ending, a time, shown to mean one revolution. This, then, represents the circle made in the northern heaven by the Great Bear which constituted the earliest year of time, from which fact we infer that the loop or Ru of the north represents that quarter, the birthplace of time when figured as the Ru of the Ankh symbol. Indeed this can be proved. The noose is an *Ark* or *Rek* type of reckoning. The Ru of the Ankh-cross was continued in the Cypriote R, Ω, and the Coptic Ro, Ρ. The Ro was carried into the Greek cross, ⯒, which is formed of the Ro and Chi, or *R-k*. Thus the Ark (Eg.) sign of the circle and cross survives by name in the *Ro-chi* cross, and the connection of the Ru or Rk with the birthplace can be shown by this name. *Ru* (Eg.) is the outlet, and the feminine *Kha* determines its nature. *Rak* in Akkadian, like the Ru-kha, is the vulva. *Rakha*, in Quichua, is the vagina and the woman. The Rak, or Ark, was the sign of all beginning (*Arche*) on this account, and the Ark-tie is the cross of the north, the hind part of heaven. "*Arka*" in Assyrian is the hinder part, which is represented by the Ru ⬯.

The sign, ♀, occurs as the *reverse* of a Phœnician coin, with a Ram as the obverse. The two represent the front and hinder part, or the familiar Head and Tail. The same sign, sometimes called Venus' Looking-Glass, because it typified reproduction, was employed to mark the hind quarters of valuable brood mares of Corinthian and other beautiful breeds of horses.[1] This was based on the Ru or Ark sign of the crossing in the north. With the Ru sign set on the staff thus ♀, we have the symbol of north and south, or male and female, the south being considered the front, before, masculine. A form of

[1] Raoul Rochette, *De la Croix ansée. Mem. de l'Acad. des Sciences*, pl. 2, Nos 8, 9, also 16, 2, p. 320.

the Ankh Cross found in the fourth pyramid ☥ enables me to prove the origin of this cross as a sign of north and south, because the pillar and base are the Pyramid of Sothis, the dog-star. The Pyramid being both four-square and triangular is a figure of Seven. Hence its name of Hept or Sebt (Sothis) is the name of number 7. Sothis was a masculine or southern type of the Goddess of the Seven Stars, who was thus represented by the Ru of the north and the Pyramid of the south. The top is the *Ru* of the birthplace in the north, and the bottom is the symbol of the south! With the two arms it presents the figure of above (north), and below (south) with the crossing east and west, or right hand and left. *This is the complete Ankh-Cross of Life.*

In symbolism nothing dies. The earliest Ankh-sign is the cross of cord. The Muysca Indians continued this in a very significant form. They used to stretch a great rope-cross consisting of two cords over the surface of a pool or a river, and at the point of intersection they would cast their most precious offerings and tributes into the water. Such was their offertory of the cross; the cross of the genitrix, and of the waters. The cross of rope survived in Britain. Scot in his *Discovery of Witchcraft*,[1] mentions a kind of cross made of a rope's end on Ascension Day, which was looked on as a source of blessings. The Ankh signified life and reproduction, whether made of rope or any other material.

The notion of Payne Knight and Inman, that the cross or Tau is simply a copy of the male organs in a triadic form is radically false. For instance, Khem-Horus is the crosser; he wears the cross on his breast. He exhibits HIS form of the Tat, which is *expressly deprived of two members of the supposed triad of the Tau.* The Tau cross T, our letter T, is connected with the number 9. The Coptic Theta, Tida, or T has the numeral value of 9. In the Greek form the Theta unites the circle and cross *θ*. The T is a numerical three, *a cross of three-quarters instead of four, and so becomes a figure of nine months, or nine divisions of the twelve which were completed by the three water signs,* or the abyss in the north, represented by the 0 of the ♀ cross. But the cross as the Tat and the male emblem have a meeting-point inasmuch as both are types of establishing. De Rossi found a phallus of red coral in a tomb which, as he says, might have been suspected of being Christian did not the presence of this symbol persuade to the contrary.[2] But the emblem was not uncommon in the so-called Christian cemeteries.

There is a cross also composed of a fourfold phallus. This is found on the bosom of the Paphian Aphrodite of Cyprus, likewise on a Greek coin, an Assarion or *farthing* of Chios, which has the female sphinx on one side and the four-fold phallus on the other.[3] The

[1] P. 152 (1665). [2] *Roma Sotterranea*, vol. i. p. 309.
[3] Madden, *Jewish Coinage*, pp. 43—49.

emblem is found on a "Christian" sarcophagus where it occupies the same place as the "Sacred Monogram of Christ" on another marble coffer in the catacombs.[1] Now what is to be made of the

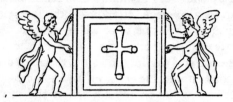

cross of Christ in the form of a four-fold phallus? Yet this occurs amidst the iconography claimed to be Christian. As the cross of Khem or the Khem-Horus only can it be comprehended. The male emblem was from remote times a type of re-arising assigned to Khem, Mentu, Khepr, and Horus, the solar gods who ascended from the underworld. As such it was a symbol of the establisher in Egypt, in the bone caves, in the cemeteries of Rome, on the bell of St. Fillan, or the pier of the old bridge at the Chesters a few miles from Hexham. Indeed, a Buddhist cross in the Asiatic researches is formed of a seven-fold phallic type.[2] The sevenfold linga is an image of the solar power equivalent to the seven spirits of Ra, the seven horses of Sûrya, or the seven tongues of fire; it was a fellow type to the seven Yonis of fire, a numerical figure of masculine force. In the four-fold form it is equivalent to the four-fold Tat of Ptah, the type of stability based on the foundational four corners. Also, as the Tat is a form of the pillar and tree, so is this four-fold sign of the generator treated as the tree of life, with two winged figures supporting it, just as the two cherubs or griffins support the tree in the Assyrian and other representations. This masculine type also appears at Rome under the dignified title of *Soter*.[3] It was as Soter in the phallic sense that Horus the Christ, who, dwelling above, took pity on the great mother Achamoth, whom the Gnostics identified with the woman that had the issue of blood—when she was running all to waste, and her creations were without form, and void; and by extending himself over her cross-wise he imparted to her a figure. As Stauros he was the cross, the Tat, or the four-fold phallus of the Christ in the catacombs.[4]

The Hittite or Khetan cross which is common to Citerior Asia unites the cross of the four corners and the tree. It is pourtrayed with shoots or branches springing from the root and stem, and is therefore a form of the tree of life. The Buddhist cross puts forth leaves and flowers and fruits, and is reverenced as the divine tree, the tree of life and knowledge which produces all that is good and

[1] Maffeus, *Museum Veronense*, p. 484.   [2] *As. Res.* vol. x. p. 124.
[3] Worship of the generative powers. Plate.   [4] Irenæus, b. i. ch. iv. 1.

desirable. It is likewise the tree of the earthly paradise. *Tona-caquahuitl* the "tree of our flesh" is a name of the Mexican cross.

It has been a subject of discussion as to which of the elements was represented by the cross symbol. The truth being that this type of the four quarters also served to indicate the four elements of earth, water, air and fire; earth in the west where the sun descended to the underworld; water in the north, the region of the water-horse; air or breath in the east, and fire in the south, the region of the dog-star. The sun or the soul entered the earth in the west, crossed the waters in the north, breathed new life on the horizon of the east, and soared in the south as the phœnix of fire. The cross of earth is especially represented by the square. The cake sign of land and locality which has the square of earth within the circle, is likewise a cross of earth. This occurs on the British stones and the Gaulish coins. It is also the Chinese sign of Teen, a field, in the ancient characters.[1] This ideograph of land and locality, hence of the town and city, is likewise a symbol of the solar orbit and the equinox; and our cross on the cake or bun of the Easter crossing is identical with the Egyptian cake of the cross, or the cross of earth.

In the baptismal ceremony of the Western Church the making of the sign of the cross was accompanied with breathing three times on the mouth of the child.[2] This was making the sign of the cross of breath, or spirit, at the same time as that of the water-cross, which identifies the dual cross as a type of the two primary Truths.

Another most ancient and illustrative custom is yet extant which appears to preserve the essence of the symbol. It is a mode of covenanting by *crossing with the breath*. It is known in Pennsylvania as a form of oath-taking amongst boys. "*If it is not so I will cross my breath,*" is a saying equivalent to I will stake my life on it. When the crossing is carried out it is done by breathing on the hand and making the sign of the cross over the heart.[3]

Gori tried to get the name of Jesus out of the two Zeds of the Swastika cross of the catacombs by writing Z for J, and Zezus for Jesus. But the fact is that *Seses* is a Gnostic name of Isis, and the SSS Sistrum (the Sshsh) is a symbol of Isis, the sign of the female crossed, the three S's or bars being identical with the *Seses* of the Gnostics. Therefore a six-fold cross may be claimed as a cross of breath. For *Ses* (Eg.) signifies breath and number six with an occult allusiveness. *Ses* also denotes the attaining of land after crossing the waters, as did the annual sun when emerging from the water-sign of the Ram or Pisces. The "Padma-Swastika" is a mystical mark consisting of the lotus-flower; (according to the Scholiast) a four-cornered sort of painting. It is the lotus-cross figured in the palm of Buddha's hand and upon the

[1] Kidd, *China*, p. 94.   [2] Augusti, *Arch.* ii. 441.
[3] *Notes and Queries*, December 23, 1876, p. 505.

soles of his foot, as well as on his breast, the place of breath.[1] The Lotus, the ascender out of the waters, was a symbol of Breath, and the Egyptian Seshnin (lotus) is the opener, uncloser or breather out of the waters.

But breath, spirit, and fire are equivalent types of life. In Egyptian *Ses* is breath ; *Sesit*, flame ; *Sesh* is combustion, also a spirit of wine, *Ziz*, or *Zizit*, was the Rabbinical Bird of Fire or Soul. The Greek " ζησης ! "—*Vivas*—is a form of wishing life and health. *Svas* in Sanskrit also means to breathe and to live. The Svastika, or Swastika Cross, is a sign of life represented by the vivifying fire, and also a lingaic symbol (*Tika* [Eg.] is to cross, join, twist, go together ; and *Tik* in Sanskrit is to go) ; this has the shape of a double Z, and Z Z has the force of *Ziz*, *Ses*, or *Svas*, denoting the life, the breath, the generative fire, of which the Swastika is the Cross.

The Dakotahs have a native name for the cross, which signifies the " *Musquito-Hawk spread out.*"[2] Here the bird is a type of fire. The Hawk in Egypt was representative of the soul and the solar fire. The Creek Indians at their festival of the *Busk* commenced with making the new fire by placing *four logs in the centre of a square*, end to end, so that they formed a cross, the outer ends pointing to the four cardinal points, and in the centre of this cross the new fire was created.[3] This was another mode of making the Swastika or cross of fire. In Egyptian "*Bus*" denotes both fire and protection. This connection of the cross and fire as interchangeable types of protection is likewise manifest in the command for the Hebrews to make a fiery serpent, and elevate it on a stauros or cross pole, which is rendered by the Targum " *Make thee a burning.*" The four-footed Swastika cross has been found on the prehistoric pottery of Cyprus, at Herculaneum, in Egypt, in Ireland, and in England. A leaden figure of the Babylonian goddess Nana discovered by Dr. Schliemann at Troy, has this cross figured on a *triangular* pelvis. The triangle is a type of fire, and the Hindus consider the Swastika cross to be the especial emblem of Agni or fire. Swastika in Sanskrit is the name of various mystical marks and signs, amongst others the cross, and one particular symbol made of ground rice, and shaped *like a triangle* or pyramid, and this triangle or pyramid was a sign in Egypt of the ancient Horus, as the virile one of the triad. The Swastika was also used (in India), for the fumigation of Durga, as a type of the fire that vivifies, after the period of negation or the water. According to De Rossi the Swastika from an early period was a favourite form of the cross employed with an occult signification which shows the secret was not that of the Christian cross. One Swastika cross in the catacombs is the sign of an inscription which reads "ΖΩΤΙΚΩ ΖΟΤΙΚΗ *Vitalis Vitalia*," or life of life. The writer of *Rome in the Nineteenth Century*

---

[1] Moor's *Hindu Pantheon*, plates 70 and 75. [2] Rigg's *Dic. of the Dacotah.*
[3] Brinton, p. 97. [4] Boldetti, also Lundy, fig. 13.

witnesses that Christ was buried before he was dead, according to the Christian reckoning ; "*His body is laid in the sepulchre in all the churches of Rome, where the rite is practised, on Thursday in the forenoon, and it remains there till Saturday at mid-day, when, for some reason best known to themselves, he is supposed to rise from the grave amidst the firing of cannon, and blowing of trumpets, and jingling of bells which have been carefully tied up ever since the dawn of Holy Thursday, lest the devil should get into them.*"[1] On the Friday was *the day of adoring the cross of fire.* A blazing cross was suspended from the dome of St. Peter's, a cross being covered with countless lamps, which had the effect of a perfect figure of fire, shaped cross-wise. "*The whole church,*" says the eye-witness, "*was thronged with a vast multitude of all classes and countries, from royalty to the meanest beggar, all gazing upon this one object. In a few minutes the Pope and all his cardinals descended into St. Peter's, and the aged pontiff prostrated himself in silent adoration before the cross of fire.*"[2] This may explain why the Swastika cross, the fire-cross of India, the cross of the generative fire in Egypt is found in the tombs at Rome. Dante describes the souls in Paradise as kneeling, praying, and respiring inside a cross of fire which forms their world. The cross of fire survives in the hot cross bun, the cake of the vernal equinox, and of the Horus who arose hawk-headed, the hawk being a symbol of the vivifying fire. The hot cross buns eaten on Good Friday are believed to protect the house from fire, which shows the connection with that element. The cross of fire was continued in the "cross candle" of Easter Eve and Pasche, also in the candles that used to be consecrated to "light up in thunder," which was equivalent to making the sign of the cross as the symbol of stability when the powers of darkness, discord and desolation were at work overhead. The cross has now been identified with the three elements of earth, breath, and fire.

The vessel borne in the hands of Chalchiuitlicue the Mexican goddess of water, which vessel is the equivalent of the Egyptian water-bottle Nu, ☋, and the womb-shaped vase of Mena, is *fashioned in the form of a cross.* This we may consider the water-cross, together with the Muysca rope-cross of the water. The Mexican cross is particularly the symbol of rain, the first element of life being liquid. Ankh (Eg.) the name of life and the cross denotes the liquid or oil of life. Martin found the people of the Western Isles in possession of a stone called the "water cross." The traditions said the ancient inhabitants were accustomed to *erect* this kind of cross when they wanted rain, and to lay it flat again when they had more than they wanted.[3] The water cross is likewise made in the baptismal sign of the cross.

The Romish calendar contains several festivals devoted to the glorification of the cross, but the church gives no account of their

[1] Vol. iii. pp. 144, 145.   [2] Vol. iii. pp. 148—9.   [3] Martin, p. 59.

origin, one of these designated the "*Feast of the Invention of the Cross,*" is celebrated on the 3rd of May. Another is the "*Exaltation of the Cross,*" on the 14th of September. This is the same cross which, according to the *Legenda Aurea*[1] was found by Helena.

It is so explained by the Egyptian ascetic Mary (about 400 A.D.) and by Eutychius of Constantinople. It is to Egypt that we must turn for the origin of these festivals of the cross. The Egyptian calendar still preserves some most ancient matter which has been Christianized by the Copts, and brought on without being readjusted according to the Christian dates. For example on the 26th of September, 1878 (30th Ramadan, 1295; 17 Thoth, 1594), is the *Eed-es-Salib*, or Festival of the cross. The equinox is on the 21st of September, and on the 22nd the sun (as reckoned) *enters the sign of Libra*, and Autumn begins. On this day (September 26), the Coptic Christians say, "*We make mention of the glorious cross of our Lord Jesus Christ.*" The festival proper lasts three days, "*beginning with the preaching in the Church of the Resurrection, and ending with the Feast of S. Porphyrius, who is connected with the finding of the holy cross by Helena,*" as it was to his keeping and care that it had been committed.[2] Formerly the Copts assembled on this day at old Cairo, opposite the cross of the so-called Nilometer when the patriarch, after certain formalities, threw into the Nile a silver cross, which expert divers endeavoured to recover. The custom is preserved in some churches by throwing the cross into a basin of water.[3] Salib also signifies "*suspension*" and the water of the inundation is at its full height, and generally stationary for some days about this time, at the end of the three months' flow.

A Coptic local tradition asserts that the suspension of the waters lasts fifteen days whatsoever their height on the *Eed-es-Salib*. This level at the equinox *was the level of the equinox*, which shows how the cross flung into the Nile was a type of the cross founded on the crossing and on the suspension of the waters at the equinox. The inundation is one of the fixed facts of nature, and this suspension of the waters is for ever coincident with the level attained in time at the equinox; and the balance of the stationary waters at the crossing was the real *suspension* on the cross intended by the original ceremonies at the festival of its exaltation. ·

The Nile-cross as a symbol of the new flood of life poured out over the thirsty land, was the cross of a salvation indeed, but what has this festival and sacrifice of the cross at the time of the overflow to do with the cross of the Christian cult? Yet they are both one and the same in Egypt and Rome. For this was the cross that was found by Helena under the guidance of the saint Porphyrius.

· The making mention of the " Cross of Christ," is but the application

---

[1] *De Exaltatione Sancti Crucis.*   [2] *Egyptian Calendar*, pp. 21 and 68.
[3] *Egyptian Calendar*, p. 69.

of a later faith to imagery and customs of immense antiquity. The first rise, the very birth of the inundation, is in the month Mesore (May-June), which is named from the re-birth of the waters and of the child Horus of the waters, who is borne up from them on the lotus. *Mes* (Eg.), means birth and re-birth; it is the root of the Messiah's name, who in Egyptian is known as Mesiata; and Mess-Iah is the re-born Iah. The Horus of the waters was the Messiah, or Mes-Hor, born in the month Mesore, about the time of the summer solstice. He represents the water-source as the Child Horus, and his brother or second self, who is born nine months after-wards at the vernal equinox, represents fire or the sun of the resurrection. If the reader will now turn to the zodiac of Denderah,[1] the child who images the river and the descending sun may be seen seated on the "*Scales*" at the crossing. In the oblong zodiac of Denderah, the Child Horus is enthroned on a mountain with the Balance suspended overhead. In other zodiacs, the sign of the Scales is marked by a measuring rod which shows that the Nilometer was a measure of the inundation. As the Egyptians attained the height of felicity on the summit of the waters at the crossing, it follows that this was the cross exalted and celebrated on the 26th of September.

This was the cross of the waters found at one time of the year, and hidden at another. For the churches of Egypt and Abyssinia also celebrated the festival of the *Hiding of the cross*, the natural corollary to the finding and exaltation; but this feast is unknown to the Roman Church, which considers the others schismatic, in regard to that particular festival. The cross considered to be hidden or lost in later legend was the Nilometer in Egypt; the cross that was found when Nile was in full flood, and lost again when it was at lowest ebb. It was not only the cross that was lost in Egypt, but the Christ also. According to one legend, the Child Horus fell into the waters and was drowned.

At the Autumn equinox the waters begin to fall, the sun to descend, and these were typified by the Child Horus, who suffered and dwindled, was lost or drowned. Isis the Rennu or nurse was pour-trayed as the seeker of her child, whom she found, and reproduced at the time of the resurrection on the Easter horizon. The Rennu (nurse) of Hel (or Har) is probably the *original*, that is mythical Hel-lena. It was the boast of Isis that she gave birth to Hel-ios. In her search she was accompanied by her guide Anubis, one of whose names is *Apheru* the guide (Ap), of Roads (heru). He has the same name as that of the crossing which he kept, and therefore helped Isis to find. He is sometimes called "Aper." His double Holy-House is the *Par*-iu, and Aper-par-iu is the possible original of Porphyrius, the "Saint" who accompanied Helena, and to whose keeping the cross was committed after it was re-found by Helena.

[1] Pl. 1, vol. ii. *Book of Beginnings.*

It is *certain* that the Coptic Christians merely continued the rite of the ancient Egyptians, for with them *the sun still enters the Sign of the Scales on September the 22nd, which is at least 2155 years behind time, or 4000 years if we reckon from the first entrance of the equinox into the Sign; the reckonings not having been adjusted to the change of Signs.* Here then we can identify the cross of the Water.

The author of " Tree and Serpent Worship," [1] speaking of the cross sign on the sculptured stones of Scotland says "*their age is known with tolerable certainty, inasmuch as the greater number of them have the cross itself, or Christian emblems engraved upon them, and these must therefore be subsequent to the age of St. Columbia, who arrived in Scotland apparently in 563, and died in 597.*" And such are our authorities and teachers who have ascribed to Christianity all the symbols that existed before it, and are then compelled to date the oldest monuments after it! There is no greater fraud than that of historic interpretation which begins with things where they are first met with, as we look back on the past. The history thus fabricated from evidence which has been forged for the purpose is at war for ever with all that is prehistoric, and in no other domain of thought could such falsification of facts have been tolerated as in that which is termed " religious."

The Christian Fathers, with the exception perhaps of Clement Alexander, had scarcely enough knowledge of the ancient symbolism to put any perceptible boundary to their ignorance. Augustine [2] recognizes in the sign of the cross the antitype of circumcision, which is the excision of a circle. But in reality the one was the constant complement of the other.

The present writer knew a sailor who had been seized by the natives of one of the isles of the Southern Seas, and tattooed with the cross and circle on the *thigh*. He could not be persuaded that the operators were not avenging his breaches of the seventh Commandment. The inhabitants of the Isle of Anaa tattooed themselves with the cross. The people of Raratonga were in the habit of tattooing themselves with *the cross and square*, side by side; a double figure of the four corners.[3] According to Kahn the Hurons tattoo themselves on the thigh with black figures, sometimes of a serpent, at others of a cross.

Both Protestant and Catholic missionaries who first entered the territory about Hudson's Bay found the adoration of the *tree of the cross* was quite common in those regions of North America as a magic talisman and an emblem of fertility. According to the native Toltec historian Ixtlilxochitl, the deity Quetzalcoatl, who was said to have introduced the cult of the cross, was adored under the sign of the

---

[1] P. 31.   [2] Sermon 160.
[3] Waitz, *Anthrop. der Natur.* p. 32.

cross, which was called the Tree of Sustenance and the Tree of Life.[1] He was also pourtrayed in a robe covered over with crosses. The hair of Toze the great Mother (*cf.* Tes-Neith, Eg.), was carefully arranged on her forehead in curls and crosses; the curls being made to form the crosses.[2] Garcilasco says that a great cross cut out of a single jasper was sacred to the Incas of Peru.

Dobrizhoffer tells us the Abipones were all marked on the forehead with the cross. They likewise wore black crosses in red woollen garments, a custom which was not derived from their knowledge of Christianity.[3] The Cross was discovered in the ruins of Palenque on the tablet of an altar with a bird on the top and a serpent at the foot. It was standing on the serpent's head. The Cross being the type of stability, this would be the Evil Serpent, the representative of disso- lution, the Dragon of Darkness conquered by the cross, or by the bird-headed sun-god at the crossing. The cross was used in Egypt as a protecting talisman and a symbol of saving power. Typhon, or Satan, is actually found chained to and bound by the cross. In the Ritual the Osirian cries " *The Apophis is overthrown, their cords bind the South, North, East, and West, their cords are on him. Har-ru-bah has knotted him.*"[4] These were the Cords of the four quarters, or the cross. Thor is said to smite the head of the serpent with his hammer, or fylfot, a form of the Swastika, or four-footed Cross, and therefore an equivalent to the four-armed cross established on the serpent's head. In the primitive sepulchres of Egypt the model of the Chamber had the form of a Cross. The pagoda of Mathura considered to be the birthplace of Krishna was built in the form of a cross. The type had the same significance when cut in a ground-plan, whether in Egypt, India, or in Britain, as if represented by the Crux Ansata. The cross and Calvary of the Christian Iconography is common on the breasts of Egyptian mummies.

From time immemorial the copper ingots of Central Africa have been smelted in the shape of the Cross. As Livingstone remarks, " *Not as a Christian emblem certainly.*"[5] They were so founded because the Cross was a primal figure of the four-fold foundation. The South Australians dance around the *Palyertalla.* This is a spear upholding a Cross which has bunches of feathers displayed at the ends of two sticks.[6] Humboldt, in his *Travels,* says he met with the Cross symbol and other rude remains of hieroglyphics, similar to those of Egypt, in Kam- katka, the remotest corner of Asia. West Indian negroes employ the cross as a Charm. They carefully cut a bit of paper in the shape of a Cross and stick it on to a child's forehead to take away the hiccough.[7] The sign is identical with the Ankh-Cross, which denotes

---

[1] Terneaux. Squier, *Nicaragua,* p. 493.   [2] Bancroft, vol. iii. p. 352.
[3] Part ii. ch. iv.   [4] *Rit.* ch. 39.
[5] *Last Travels,* ii. 179.   [6] Bonwick, *Tasmanians,* p. 198.
[7] *Contemporary Review,* October, 1875, p. 764.

life, health, sanation. Pliny says that it is sorcery to sit by a parturient woman with the fingers crossed.[1] In both cases the cross signified a stoppage. Making the sign of the cross is as old as clasping the hands to make the sign of Ten, which is the cross. The Maoris practise a mode of divination by means of this form of the cross. Whilst uttering the appropriate *karakia* or *inoi* the hands are clapped and clasped, and if the fingers strike clear of each other it is a good omen, but if they come in contact it denotes a check. This is a mode of making the cross and completing the circle in one.

Captain Warren found the Tau Cross on a Phœnician vase far down below modern Jerusalem. Arnobius (*Adv. Gentes*) recognises with disgust the "handled Cross" made use of in the Bacchus Mysteries. The value of the cross as a Christian symbol is supposed to date from the time when Jesus Christ was crucified. And yet in the "Christian" iconography of the catacombs no figure of a man appears upon the Cross during the first six or seven centuries. There are all forms of the cross except that—the alleged starting-point of the new religion. That was not the initial but the final form of the Crucifix. During some six centuries after the Christian era the foundation of the Christian religion in a crucified Redeemer is entirely absent from Christian art! The earliest known form of the human figure on the cross is the crucifix presented by Pope Gregory the Great to Queen Theodolinde of Lombardy, now in the church of St. John at Monza, whilst no image of the Crucified is found in the catacombs at Rome earlier than that of San Giulio belonging to the seventh or eighth century. So in the earliest representations of the Trinity made by the "Christian" artists, the Father and Holy Ghost (who was feminine as the Dove), are pourtrayed beside the Cross. There is no Christ and no Crucified; the Cross is the Christ even as the Stauros (Cross) was a type and a name of Horus the Gnostic Christ. The Cross, not the Crucified, is the primary symbol of the Christian Church. The Cross, not the Crucified, is the essential object of representation in its art, and of adoration in its religion. The germ of the whole growth and development can be traced to the cross. And that cross is pre-Christian, is pagan and heathen, in half a dozen different shapes. The Cult began with the cross, and Julian was right in saying he waged a "Warfare with the X;" which he obviously considered had been adopted by the A-Gnostics and Mytholators to convey an impossible significance. During centuries the cross stood for the Christ, and was addressed as if it were a living being. It was divinized first and humanized at last.

The Tree of Paradise, that is of the Mount of the four Corners, *was* the Tree of the Cross. According to the legends the genealogy of the tree was traced back to Paradise. Seth obtained a shoot from the Tree of Life and planted it on Adam's grave at Golgotha, where

[1] *Nat. Hist.* lib. xxviii. 17.

it sprang up as the Cross of Christ, and where it was re-buried to be discovered by Helena. So certainly does the Cross of Christ represent the four cardinal points that in the Christian traditions the Cross of Calvary was said to have been made out of four different kinds of wood, the palm, cedar, olive, and cypress, to *signify the four quarters of the world*. Thus does the legendary mould the alleged historical matter! The cross did symbolise the four quarters of the whole circle, and the four different woods are afterwards read into it by the A-Gnostics. The mythological tree of the cross no more consisted of four various kinds of wood than a tree does in nature. The Tree of Life and cross of the beginning is also shown in the colour of the Christian cross. Green was the Egyptian hue of life arising from the underworld as it is in external nature. And after the tree had been planed down into the wood of the crucifix, this was *painted green* as a common representation of the Cross of Christ, which proves the survival of the living tree of the ancient typology. It is yet believed in England, and other northern countries, that the wood of the *true* Cross was elderwood. Some of our peasants still consider this wood sacred, and will carefully look through their faggots to avoid burning it. Not because the tree of the cross was ever made of an elder-stem, but because the elder was one of the trees of life in the north, and a type of the old Mother. The elder is one of the wine trees, a producer of the inspiring juice, and its leaves and flowers are still held to be very healing. Also, there was a sacred festival at which the Romans annually paraded a kind of crucifixion consisting of a dog stretched out alive upon a cross of elderwood. The exhibition was made between the temples of Juventus and Summanus. The Dog was a type of Sut-Anup, the Golden Jackal, who is depicted on the cross, or at the Crossing, as the Gnostic Anubis in what has been termed the "Blasphemous Crucifix," which was discovered on the Palatine wall of Rome.[1] The dog, jackal, and ass are three types of Sut-Anup, who was the Crosser and guide of the Crossing in the pre-solar and pre-Christian mythos. The Elder, one of the hollow trees, identifies the ancient genitrix who was Typhon, the mother of Sut.

The cross that was seen in heaven by Constantine was that of the four quarters. Hence he had himself represented in the solar character as the Slayer of the Dragon. After his victory over Licinus, he was pourtrayed at his palace in Nicomedia with the cross on his head and a transfixed dragon writhing at his feet. This is the same imagery as that of the cross established on the serpent found in the ruins of Palenque. One of the coins of Constantine also shows the Labarum standing upon the conquered serpent. The meaning of this is simply the cycle founded for ever on the four quarters, and the cross is nothing more than a type of duration. So far from the typology showing

[1] King's *Gnostics*, p. 91.

that Constantine was a worshipper of the Christian Christ, it proves that *he himself was the Christ intended*, who was added to the cross and dragon of the pre-Christian imagery. On one of his coins the four-armed Greek cross appears beside a figure of the sun-god (not a pretended portrait of any historical Christ), and on the reverse *Soli invicti comiti*. He was assimilated to the sun-god, whom he represented just as the Pharaohs impersonated Horus or Ra, and in *that character he was the Bishop of the Christian Church*.[1]

Wilkinson [2] remarks upon the (to him) strange and startling fact that the first cross found in Egypt belonging to the Christians is not the cross which was substituted in after times, but the Crux Ansata, the Ankh-*sign* of life. " *The early Christians of Egypt*," he says, "*adopted the Ankh in lieu of the Roman cross, which was afterwards substituted for it, and prefixed it to inscriptions in the same manner as the cross in later times. I can attest that the Ankh holds this position in the sepulchres of the Great Oasis, and that numerous inscriptions headed by the Ankh are preserved to this day on early Christian monuments*." That is, the supposed emblem and proof of a crucified Christ is purely Egyptian, and has no relation either direct or typical to the crucifixion, which has been all along ignorantly assumed to give its significance to the cross. This Ankh-sign proves the Christians to have belonged to the Osirian religion, the Christ of which was Horus, the Christ who was continued by the Gnostics.

When the Christian iconoclasts, in the time of Bishop Theophilus,

---

[1] The *Labarum* was the royal Roman standard, which Lactantius calls "the ensign that was consecrated by the name of Christ;" by which he means the monogram of "*KR*" upon the banner. No doubt this signification was being read into the sign on the standard of Constantine. But there was nothing new in it, whether found in Rome or out of it. The tree and cross are identical ; and as a type the one involves the other. The Labarum was the tree, from *Laba*, Greek, a staff. This is a common type-name for the tree. *Llwyf* is the elm-tree in Welsh ; *Liobhan*, in Irish ; *Laban*, a kind of wood, in Malayan ; *Lipa*, a plane-tree, Polish ; *Luban*, a conifer, Arabic ; *Labanah*, a poplar-tree, Hebrew ; *Labanj*, a plane-tree, Persian, etc. Lep or Rep (Eg.) signifies to grow, bud, branch, and take *leaf*. The vine is a form of the Rep or Arp. The Repa personified was the branch of the ancestral tree, the shoot and offspring of the Pharaoh, called the hereditary highness, the prince, lord, heir-apparent. Now when Constantine is pourtrayed on the Labarum with his child (or children), he is the exact equivalent of the Egyptian Ra with the Repa ; and the coins prove that he was assimilated to the Solar God, after the fashion of the Pharaohs. The doctrine of the Repaship belongs to mythology, in which the Repa was the divine child, the *KR*, *Kar.t*, or *Khart*, who is pourtrayed as Horus on the cross, at the crossing, the representative of the *KR*, a course or circle. Seb-Kronus is called the veritable Repa of the gods ; that is, as the personified course of time,—*KR*, for the course, being a monogram of Kronus. The latest form of the Repa was the lord of the solar course, the Kar whose representative was the *Kart* in Egyptian, the Kurios in Greek, the God *Har-pi-Khart*, *whose image is pourtrayed in the catacombs*, or Har-Ma-Kheru. The cross goes with the tree in the Labarum as elsewhere, because it was the tree of the four corners. The cross is inseparable from the circle, the Kar, or course, and the maker of the course is intended by the monogram of *KR*, whether personified as the *Kart*, *Kronus*, or *Christ*. The typology is so ancient, that the *Repa* is found as *Rupe* in the Maori mythology,—he who was fabled to have fallen from the cross, or at the crossing ; *ripeka* being a name for the cross, the cross-roads, and to crucify.

[2] Vol. v. pp. 283, 284.

about 390 A.D., were engaged in the work of destroying the monuments and effacing the tell-tale past—had they been able to read it
they would have wanted to erase the geological record itself—they
came upon the Ankh-cross, which they were horribly astonished to
find in Egypt, at the end of the fourth century A.D.[1] So ignorant
were they of the age, origin, and significance of the symbol which
they had adopted. The native Christians explained to them that it
was the emblem of life to come, as it was, and had been for thousands
of years. The cross was placed in the hands of the dead, and bound
to their bodies as the sign of life to come. It was figured on the
back of the sacred scarab as the image of life to come. The Ankh
cross signifies life and to duplicate ; and in the Sechuana (African)
language, *Tsela, to cross over*, literally signifies *to live*. The Horus of
the resurrection is pourtrayed with the Cross of life in his hand in
the act of raising the dead body from the Bier.[2]

It may be noticed in passing that the tree and cross of life are
identical, and that the staff or rod is a reduced form of the tree-type.
The rod of Moses was fabled to be a shoot from the tree of life.
But perhaps the most singular form of the rod and staff that was
ever clutched for comfort is that which used to be held in the hands
of a person who was being bled. It was an ancient British custom,
continued until recent times, for the patient at the barber's to sit and
clasp a coloured pole, somewhat shorter than the one outside the
door. The patient was thus holding on to the tree of life whilst parting
with a goodly portion of his own, and supposing that he was saving it
in losing it. This practice, says Brand, may be seen from an
illuminated missal of the time of Edward I., in the possession of
Mr. Wild.[3]

The cross in Egypt was the express emblem of life to come when
the Ankh was a mere noose held in front of the *enceinte* genitrix
as she brooded over the dead in the tomb, the womb, or Meskhen, of
the second birth. This place of re-birth and of life to come was
imaged by Apt, the Hippopotamus Goddess of the Great Bear, who
was represented as the gestator, if not in the crucial pangs of her
travail, in the act of bringing the dead to their immortal birth. It is
this fact which accounts for the masculine symbolry that first accompanies the cross. One of these cruciform figures has a beard, and bears
a fourfold phallus on her breast.[4] In like manner Apt or Ta-Urt, the
old Typhonian genitrix, as well as Mut, has the male member
assigned to her. These are *the symbols of their power as the re-
begetters and re-generators of the dead.* As Apt, she was the crib, the
cradle of new life, the abode of the four corners, or four parts by
name. Therefore she was herself a figure of the Ankh as well as the

[1] Sozom, 7—15 ; Socrates, *H. E.* v. 17; Ruffinus, ii. 26—28.
[2] Denon, *Travels*, plate ; Lundy, fig. 183.
[2] Brand, *Barbers' Signs.*   [4] Di Cesnola.

bearer of the Ankh-symbol. The Ankh was likewise impersonated in the Goddess Ank.

The Great Mother with the Ankh-cross of life to come was continued ·as the Ankh-cross or the genitrix in a cruciform figure. This is a type of the Cyprian Venus. Amongst the images recovered from the ancient tombs of Cyprus by Di Cesnola is one which Dr. Lundy calls the "*Crucifixion of the Great Mother herself.*" It shows a cruciform female figure, and the ligature looks as if the one arm that is now left ·might have been bound to a piece of wood. But the pre-Christian cross does not imply any actual crucifixion. . The Ankh, whether as emblem or goddess, is the cross of life, not of death. So the cross that burgeons into leafy life in the Khetan and Indian symbols, and bursts into blossom in the floriated cross of Rome, is an illustration of the cross of life, the Ankh of Egypt, not the Roman instrument of torture or of death.

Thus, when Krishna is depicted as what is modernly termed "*the Crucified,*" the picture is not a representation of the Saviour made flesh to be nailed on the wood of a tree. The *Stigmata*, the four nail-marks, are visible on his hands and feet, nevertheless he is not nailed upon a tree. On the contrary, *He is the tree*,[1] as Christ is the vine, and the tree is alive, all in leaf, therefore it is a Tree of Life, not of death. It is the tree of transfiguration from one character into another, whether of dying moon or diminishing sun that only waned a while to wax again with redoubled power. This is but the impubescent Child-God who transfigures into the pubescent Bala-rama as virile divinity ; or into the Man of twenty nails, according to the simple typology of digital reckoning. An immeasurable mistake has been made by thinking the nail-mark was necessarily a sign of crucifixion. The earliest *Stigma* ever branded on the human body was a totemic token of puberty, a mark of the male who had duplicated, or crossed the boundary of boyhood ; and who became the completed Man of twenty years of age. This was the origin of the cross that was used as a brand cut in the body, or tattooed upon the thigh, in the rites of *Young-man-making ;* and the natural genesis accounts for the cross being figured as a four-fold Linga or *Tat*, wherever this may be found. Also the original Soter explains why the phallus and the cross should be equivalent signs of power in the practice of *Crucesignation* for the purpose of healing. The pubescent one had crossed and become established in his manhood ; hence he was tattooed with the cross of the four corners, as the sign of foundation. This is the Egyptian *Tat* (a fourfold cross or the Phallus), and *Tattu* is the region of establishing for ever in the eschatological phase, the place where the Tat-Cross was erected when the Child Horus had crossed and been united with his masculine force or virile soul, and the two became one in *Tattu*.[2] The Romans likewise had the figure of a man extended on the cross ; for Minutius

---

[1] Inman, *Ancient Faiths*, Fig. 92.   [2] *Ritual*, ch 17.

Felix (one of the Christian Fathers) in his perplexity at their non-acceptance of the later doctrine of the Crucified, says to them, " *Your victorious trophies not only represent a simple cross, but a cross with a man upon it.*"[1] This figure also was pre-Christian in Rome as well as in India and Africa; whilst the primary form of the man on the cross was that of the young man who was tattooed with the cross.

The Cruciform Witoba has the marks of Nails in the palms of his hands and feet, but there is no crucifix behind him, nor does he represent a person nailed to the cross. Like Horus—as Stauros—he is the cross. Certain figures of the Buddha also show the sign of the nail in the palm of the hand. This is so common that it appears in the little toy-images or fetish figures which are made by the Chinese. No Christian sees this symbol without looking upon it as a sign of the Crucified. If pre-Christian, as in the image of Witoba, it is considered to be a pagan prophecy of the true Christ, or it is denounced as the devil's mode of parodying the divine. Yet the Nail in the palm of the hand never meant the crucified Christ, Buddha, or Witoba, except to the ignorant A-Gnostics. It signifies exactly the same thing as the cross-shaped, four-leaved Lotus displayed by the Buddha in the palm of his hand, or depicted on the soles of his feet.[2] Vishnu, in his Avatar of Vahara, is represented with the nail-mark on the palm of his hand figured within the sign of the square of the four corners in place of the cross.[3]

The Swastika Cross is found as a pattern on the gold-leaf which covers the " bone buttons " disinterred by Dr. Schliemann at Mycenæ. Here the Cross is depicted with *Nails in the four angles.* Bone and Nail are emblems of reproduction, and the gold-leaf corresponds to the gilding on the Nails, teeth, and phallus of the Egyptian mummies. Four Nails equate with the fourfooted Cross of the four corners, and both with the fourfold phallus.

The most mystical signs are the most simple, *i.e.* fundamental; they can only be explained by the natural genesis, and according to gesture-language. The Nail was a sign of No. 20, the *Homme fait;* and it takes the place of the virile member as a token of the pubescent Solar God who had crossed, decussated, or duplicated—for that is the root of the matter—in his second character. Now this second character, being that of puberty, applies equally to both sexes, and so the nail-mark appears in the female as well as the male. In a portrait of Maya (copied into the present volume) the palms of her hands are hidden, but the nail-mark is visible on her feet! Not because she had been crucified, but on account of *her second phase.* She is the pubescent Woman of the Two Truths, the Gestator who in Egypt wore the double serpent for her maternal crown. In the Gnostic sense she has been crossed by Stauros, as is indicated by the scarf-tie and the

[1] *Oct.* c. 29. [2] Moor, *Pantheon*, pls. 69-75.
[3] Moor, pl. 6, figs. 1 and 2.

cruciform nimbus or glory ; the Egyptian "Double Force." The four nails are equivalent to the fourfold phallus worn on the bosom of the Cyprian Venus as the sign of generation or gestation, and this, again, is equivalent to the four-leaved lotus or the cross. Moreover, the Genitrix as Devi, a form of Parvati, is represented with the nail-mark on her foot and a phallus in each hand ; the types being interchangeable.

The Nail, whether as *clavis* or *unguis*,. being a type of virility, its significance becomes apparent wherever the Nail is a symbol. Burton, our modern opener of Central Africa, found that the negroes there would drive a nail into the " *Devil's* Tree " as a charm against disease.[1] The meaning was the same as that of the Nail in the tomb, . the nail in the corners of the Swastika, in the body of Buddha or Krishna ; the nail that figured the masculine potency of the Soter, Saver, Preserver, and Healer, with which the primitive man contended against the Devil, Disease, and Dissolution. It was the weapon of his manhood, whether this might be represented by the nail, the hieroglyphic *nakh*, or *ankh*, pubes, horn, stone, metal, or the member.

Tertullian, in his taunting of the non-Christians with their use of the same symbols as the Christians, asks with regard to the cross " *Doth the Athenian Minerva differ from the body of the cross, and the Keres of Pharos who appeared in the market with a figure made of a rude and shapeless stake ? The origin of your cross is derived from figures mounted on the cross. All those rows of images on your standards are the appendages of crosses. Those hangings on your standards and banners are the robes of crosses.*" As if the cross of Christianity were the original of these ! Whether innocence or impudence, it is imperturbable. Except in a dark void of human ignorance there was no place left in this world for the cross to become the symbol of salvation and the type of immortality by man or god being sacrificed upon it. According to the Septuagint, the cross [2] was the symbol of salvation, just as it had been for ages and in divers forms when buried with the mummies in Egyptian tombs, with no earthly relationship to an historical crucifixion. It was already the image of immortality in Egypt, in Chaldea, Britain, India, America, and the Southern Isles, because it was the cross of life and not a cross of death. And it was the cross of life because it represented the fourfold foundation of the world, the four corners of the human abode ; because it was an emblem of reproduction, an image of duration, a type of the eternal.

There is a belief yet current amongst our peasantry that one can hardly die or pass away in peace beneath the cross-beams called the sign-tree of the house. Many a bedstead has been removed from its usual place under the cross-beams before the departing spirit could get release. Thus, after the cross has been for so many centuries held

[1] Burton, *Central Africa*, vol. ii. p. 352.
[2] Numbers xxi. 8—9 ; and Wisdom xvi. 6.

before the closing human eyes as the sign and token of relief, as the very hand outstretched by an expiring deity to help the dying mortal in the pangs of death, this primitive pre-Christian type of stability, duration, life, and living, remains so potent over minds that are totally unconscious of its origin and significance that they cannot die whilst looking at it or lying under it. The sign-tree, or Skhen-tree (the prop), is the cross-shaped tree of life in Britain, as it was in Egypt, India, or Mexico, and here it also survives as the cross of life in opposition to a cross of death. The cross-type is a continuation of the tree, and it equates with the tree, the mount, and the conical pillar of Aphrodite, all three being primary images of the mother of life and goddess of the four quarters. The mother as the cross was continued in the *Orante*, who was found in an Etruscan tomb standing with extended arms over the laid-out body of the dead.[1]

The same sign is made by the spiritual body just emerging from the dead body in the Egyptian drawings, because it is the symbol of the future life. The Etruscan *Orante* survived in Rome where she forms one of the chief figures in the catacombs. There she is taken to represent the Church and the Bride of Christ. Call it what you may, the cruciform *Orante* in the cemeteries of Rome or the Etruscan Tombs or the tombs of Paphos is identical with the ancient mother of life who holds her cross before her pregnant womb in token of the life to come. She was the virgin mother, too, who produced without the fatherhood, and who reproduces the dead in a later time when the male progenitor or emblem has been added. The identification of this virgin mother with the Church is complete in the words of Clement Alexander, who exclaims: "*O Mystic Wonder! The universal Father is one, and one is the universal Logos or Word; and the Holy Spirit is one and the same everywhere, and one is the Virgin mother. Her I love to call the Church!*"[2] She was the Church as the abode of life continued. She was also the cross as the *Orante*; the cross that bore the Christ of the ancient cult; the tree of which the Messiah son was the branch.

The *Orante* figure is several times found double; one standing on either side of the Good Shepherd, the supposed Christ of the catacombs, like the two divine sisters on each side of Horus; they who call him to come to them, to his abode; with one of them, Nephthys, carrying the house on her head. The latest form of the feminine abode was the *mother Church* who becomes twin because it was so in Egypt.

A figure extended in the shape of the cross, then, whether as a female *Orante*, a Cyprian Venus, or a masculine *Orante*, does not necessarily imply a crucifixion or the crucified. There is a cruciform figure pourtrayed on the Egyptian obelisk of the Lateran Basilica,[3] a male *Orante* standing upon a serpent, which might be interpreted by the Christian A-Gnostic as the antetype and foreshadowing of the

[1] Caylus, *Recueil*, i. pl. 32; Lundy, fig. 188.   [2] *Paed*, i. c. vi.   [3] Lundy, fig. 63.

seed, or Christ overcoming the serpent according to prophecy. But which serpent is intended? The good or the evil one? Here it is *not the Apophis monster but the Serpent of Life.* The two figures are necessary, and the serpent proves that the Orante makes the sign of the Cross of life to come; that is the Ankh.

Another Egyptian cruciform human figure was found in an old Nubian temple at Kalabche, which, like that on the Lateran obelisk, is pre-Christian. It is a man or a divinity with his arms extended crosswise, but without the cross or any other hint of a crucifixion.[1]

Osiris has been found in this attitude. Also Vishnu as Witoba is presented as the crucified in what has been termed the crucifixion in space; the crucifixion without the cross, in which the god himself *is the cross* in a male form, just as the genitrix is the crossed one in a female form, and as Horus was Stauros.[2]

It is true the sun of the western crossing was considered to be the suffering, dying sun. As Atum he was said to set from the land of life. As Horus the elder we see the god on the cross, at the crossing which is represented by the cross-beam of the scales.[3] This is Horus the Child, and Horus " the Lamb," who was described as the divine victim that died to save. But in the Mysteries the matter was rightly explained in accordance with phenomena.

The crossing of the west was on the dark side where Typhon triumphed over the lord of light, and in a sense here was the cross of death, the opposite to the cross of Easter and the resurrection. But whether the mythical Messiah descended into the world of the dead or rose upon the horizon of the east, both the vanquished victim and the overcoming victor were known to be mythical by all except the non-initiated.

The cross of the west is that of the Red Sun of Autumn, who was Atum by name; and this sign of the sinking sun survives in the red cross which Krimhild marks upon the cloak of Siegfried. The solar god in the west, the hinder part, was the vulnerable sun, the sufferer, who was overpowered and overpassed for the time being; and the red cross on the back of Siegfried is intended to point out his one vulnerable and penetrable spot.

Rome had continued and still preserves enough to convict the " primitive Christians " of the profoundest ignorance of the past and of the true nature of that religious symbolism which they had come by they knew not how nor when. As the consciousness of the pre-Christian origines grew, there was an endeavour made to revise and revise; the latest of these attempts being the revision of the New

---

[1] Lundy, fig. 66.

[2] Lundy, figs. 61 and 72. This figure of Witoba has been omitted from Moor's *Pantheon*, edited by the Rev. A. P. Moor, 1859.

[3] Plate, vol. ii. *Book of Beginnings*; also Drummond, pls. 6 and 7.

Testament in the nineteenth century, by the correction of some thirty thousand errors in the "Word of God."

In the fifth century certain believers began objecting to the cross or crucifix being coupled with the Trisagion or threefold form in which the Holy Ghost was invoked. It was urged by them that the heathen would think that God himself had been crucified. The sculptor was accused of *introducing a suffering son* in addition to the Three Persons of the Trisagion. Other Christians are said to have derived from this figure of the cross and trisagion the heterodox opinion that the son, the second person of the Trinity, was divided into two.[1]

This, however, was no late addition. The dual nature of the Osirian son was as old as the myth itself. The two Horuses were the suffering Messiah, the Mother's Child, and Horus the Son of the Father. Their astronomical stations are at the place of the two equinoxes. These two Horuses as the biune one were blended in Hor-Makhu, the deity of both horizons or equinoxes, the symbol of which was the cross because the equinoxes were the crossings.

Proclus says, of the circle and its divisions or its decussation, that "*the one soul and the two souls proceed from it.*" Here the circle is feminine, as it is in the Dove-winged circle of the Persian Triad, or its co-type the winged eye, an emblem of the genitrix. The one soul was primarily feminine; the feminine holy spirit whose symbol is the dove.[2] The two souls are those of the double Horus, of whom it is said the "*one and the other are united. He (the God) is transformed into his soul from his two halves, who are Horus the sustainer of his Father and Horus who dwells in the shrine.*"[3] This blending in one is the reverse to the obverse which is the decussation of the one into the two halves. Horus was the one God of the two horizons, and the cross was the sign of him who "*decussated in the form of the letter X,*" in the two characters of the child and the Virile God; the sun that descended crossed the waters and rose again on the horizon of the resurrection.

Osiris, Isis, and Horus were the Egyptian trisagion. But Horus was biune, he did bifurcate into the suffering Messiah and the risen Saviour, and the emblem of that twinship was the cross, which with the rest of the ancient imagery had been continued by the Christians who knew not what heathens they had been all along; heathen in origin, doctrines, and typology. When they did wake up to the facts one by one they tried to get rid of the proofs, or keep them concealed.

At the end of the seventh century it began to be felt that the supposed actual human history and veritable reality of a personal Christ were in great danger of being submerged and lost amid the mass of symbols and the number of allegorical Christs; and, we are

---

[1] Maitland, *Church of the Catacombs*, p. 164.
[2] *Proclus*, Taylor's translation, p. 114.   [3] *Ritual*, ch. xvii.; Birch.

told, the Church grew uneasy. Wherefore it was decreed by the Council of Trullo, or the *Quinqui Sixtum*, in the reign of Justinian II. that *for the future the figure of the real historic personal Jesus should be pourtrayed upon the crucifix.* It was proclaimed that the Lamb (Egyptian and Persian; also a type of the saviour from the year 2410 B.C.) was to be superseded "in the *images of Christ, our God.*" "*He shall be represented in his human form, instead of the lamb, as in former times.*"[1]

In the eighth century Adrian I., Pontiff of Rome, addressing Barasius, the Patriarch of Constantinople, expressed the opinion that the time had come for the Christ to be no longer pourtrayed as the Lamb—"*Forasmuch as the shadow hath passed away and that Christ is very man, he ought therefore to be represented in the form of a man.*" "*The Lamb of God must not be depicted on the cross as a chief object; but there is no hindrance to the painting of a lamb on the reverse or inferior portion of the cross where Christ hath been duly pourtrayed. as a man.*"[2]

In this particular at least it took seven centuries to transform the typical and mythological cross into the actual and historical, and the sacrificial lamb (or ram) into the human victim; and thus the shadow was at last substantialized by the pre-Christian type being humanized as Christ.

The absence of a human portrait of Jesus is said to prove his divinity. They who adored him as a deity could not or would not pourtray him with mortal lineaments, although they held that he came into this world to be "*made flesh.*" And in the absence of the human likeness he was represented to them by the outcast Pagan gods, by Apollo, by Aristæus, the Good Shepherd; by Orpheus, by Bacchus, Osiris, Horus, and others who are admitted to be *types* in the catacombs, of *the Christ who is not otherwise there.* Rochette shows conclusively that the most ancient images of the Virgin and Christ were of Gnostic fabrication;[3] and the Gnostic Christ was not an historical personage.

In the *Micrologus* of Ivo we find a curious witness to the readaptation of the cross. The "Apostolic Constitutions"[4] expressly prescribe the single cross to be made as the sign of sanctity. The *Micrologus* (about 1100) admits the signs of the single, triple, or fivefold cross in the sacred oblation, whilst the sign of the twofold or the fourfold one was absolutely prohibited.[5]

The origin of the cross as a type of the four quarters was probably dawning on the adaptors. The Syrian liturgy prescribes thirty-six

---

[1] Cited by Didron, *Icon. Chrét.* pp. 338, 339.
[2] G. Durandus, *Rat. Div. Off.* lib. i. cap. iii.; *De Consecratio. Distinct.* iii. cap. vi. Cited by Didron.
[3] *Discours*, pp. 17, 18. Paris, 1834.
[4] Book viii.
[5] *Micrologus de Observat.* Eccl. c. xiv.

crossings, the same as the number of the decans in the zodiac, which were first reckoned by thirty-six crossing-stars. Here then we have the cross of the thirty-six decani (Tekani or Tehani, Eg.), of the early reckonings, continued in a Christian liturgy.

It was prescribed in the *Ordo Romanus* that in consecrating churches the walls were to be signed with the Chrisma in the shape of the cross in *twelve* different places, the number of signs in the zodiac and on the Papal Chair, which, according to Bower, was being cleaned in the year 1662 when the twelve labours of Hercules were found to be pourtrayed upon it.[1]

If there be one thing considered more certain than another, it is that the cross composed of the Chi and Ro, ☧, which reads *Chr*, must be the abbreviated name of Christ; and it is always taken to convey that meaning. Be it so. Yet it is not of Christian origin; and, to go no further back, it appears upon coins of the Ptolemies and on those of Herod the Great, which had been prophetically struck *forty years before the Christian era*.[2]

Who then was the Christ intended? *Chr* answers to and represents the Egyptian *Kher* or *Kheru*, which means the Word, Voice, or the later solar Logos. *Chi* and *Ro* ARE the cross and circle. The Egyptian Khi, ⊂, called the sieve, is a cross; the sieve being made by crossing (Eg. Teka). The Ru, ⊃, is an oval, as on the top of the Ankh, ♀. These are continued in the Greek ☧. The *Kher* then is a dual sign of the cross and circle. The sign ☧ appears upon a coin of the Emperor Decius, with the letter A prefixed. Here the *A, R, K*, are an abbreviated form of ἄρχοντος, which proves that the sign has the value of *RK* when read one way,[3] and therefore *KR* the other. *Kher* and *Rekh* interchange in the hieroglyphics for the "Word." Also *Ker*, for the circuit, course, or turn round, is identical with the *Ark*, a period or cycle of time. The *Kr* and *Ark*, signs of the Cross and circle, or the Crossed circle, likewise correspond; and the Ptolemeian or Greek form of the *Kr* symbol is the later equivalent for the Ark-tie, ∝, which, from the beginning, contained both the circle (ru) and the Cross (Chi). The "Ark" was the sign of the annual circle when it was made by the Great Bear. It denotes a lunar month in the Assyrian *Arkhu*. And the *Rk* or *Kr*, is a circle, or course of time. *KR* denotes a course in Egyptian and various other languages. For this reason the sign appears in Greek inscriptions as an abbreviation for Kronus, the monogram of Time himself.[4] *Kr* is the root of the names Kronus, Course, Circle, Cross, and Christ. Further, *Tek* (Eg.) is a cross, and this explains the sign ☧ found upon the coins of the Armenian King Tigranes, which stands for the first letters (*Tigr*) of his name, or that of his capital, the

[1] Bower, *History of the Popes*, vol. i. p. 7.
[2] King, *Early Christian Numismatics*, pp. 12—13, and others.
[3] Münter, *Sinnbilder der Christen*, i. 33. Stockbauer, 86, 87.   [4] Münter, i. 33.

city of Tigranocerta. In this the cross reads both *Tau* and *Chi* in one, as does the hieroglyphic Tek X, and with the Ro forms the *TKR*, whence Tigr.   Of such pre-Christian signs of the mythical Christ, the author of " *Early Christian Numismatics* " has remarked, " *Although these symbols, as far as regards their material form, were not invented by the Christians, they nevertheless received at this time a new signification,*" [1] which is perfectly true; but the signification read into them by men who were ignorant of their origin, history, and nature is entirely false, and ridiculously delusive. The typology of the catacombs, when interrogated and interpreted by means of the Gnosis, will be found to turn informer and confess that it has been forced to bear false witness in giving its testimony to the truth of historic Christianity.   All such symbols figured their own facts from the first, and did not prefigure others of a totally different order.   The Iconography had survived in Rome from a period remotely pre-Christian.   There was neither forgery nor interpolation of types; nothing but a continuity of imagery with a perversion of its meaning.   The sign A⧈ω is simply composed of a cross bisected with the letter *Iota*. This letter has the numeral value and mystical significance of the Hebrew Jad, which denotes the ineffable name of the *Iao*.   Here it signifies the dual one that decussates in the sign of the X to become twain on the two horizons as did Har-Makhu, the Greek Harmachis, and Khem-Horus, who wears the *decussa* on his breast ages before it appears on the coins of L. Lentulus, and on medals of the kings of the Bosphorus. The *Iota* and *Chi* were read as the initials of Jesus the Christ, which they were, but in no personal sense.   *Iota*, *Alpha*, and *Omega* read *Iao*, even as they did with Hebrews, Phœnicians, and Britons; and they remained just what they had been, the monogram of the biune one, the androgynous deity that *decussated* in crossing the circle; who was also considered Triadic or Tetradic in character, according to the variation of the type in the different aspects yet to be elucidated.

The Christ in the Solar Myth was the Sun-God who, in the form of *Stauros*, the Gnostic Horus, crossed the genitrix Sophia, and gave a figure to her who had been otherwise formless by making the sign of the " *Kr* " or Cross in space.   In the human aspect of the typology there is no male without the female, no Cross without the circle, and the two are finally a form of the natural axis, and copula, the Linga-yoni, which is actually worn as a crown on his head by the Crucified Krishna.[2] The symbolical can only be interpreted by the natural. The AO denotes the being of both sexes with a triadic manifestation. Without the two sexes in conjunction there can be no reproduction.   The Christ who Crossed, whether as Horus the Child, or Ma-Kheru, was the Boy of the Mother who duplicated at puberty, or

---

[1] King, *Early Christian Numismatics*, p. 12.
[2] Inman, *Ancient Faiths*, vol. i. p. 403.

decussated—as it was figured—to become the reproducer in conjunction with the genitrix. Hence the *Chi* combined with the *Ro*, or the Cross within the Circle, has the same significance as the male and female united under other and more evident twin-types of the two sexes. Sophia was crossed and established by Horus the Christ in his sixfold form, which is figured by the letters ⚹, Iota Chi. The *AΩ* beside the sixfold Cross has the same significance as the exclamation of the sixfold Horus, who, when he extended himself crosswise to restrain Sophia, exclaimed "*IAO*," which the Gnostics affirmed to have been the origin of that name.[1]

One special solar-form of the Egyptian Christ was Horus-Ma-*Kheru*, the Horus who was the True Word or Logos. He was the crosser of the circle personified, as the *Word* that made Truth, or as the Word made Truth, because he fulfilled the promise: he crossed. The amulet or charm which Isis hung round her neck when she found herself *enceinte* was called in Greek the True Voice,[2] which, in Egyptian, is Ma-*Kheru*. For one reason, the star-gods and moon-gods were not true timekeepers, and they were superseded in favour of *Har-ma-Kheru*, who was the solar crosser or the Christ, and the *Word* as the *Kheru* or *Chr*, ⚱.

Once, at least, the cross of Christ, together with the Alpha and Omega, is found in the catacombs coupled with the name of *Asaris*. The inscription reads, "*Khr-Ao-Asaris*."[3] *As-ar*, ⬭, is the Egyptian form of the name known as Osiris, and this with the Greek terminal ς is *Asaris*. Osiris is designated "Har-Iu." Har denotes the Lord, the Greek Kurios (Kr having been the earlier form), who is the Lord; and the dual Iu is an exact equivalent for Au (was, is, and to be), the Greek Aω (also the ὁ ὤν, he who is). This "Monogram of the Saviour's name" belongs to Osiris, and to Har-Ma-Kheru in Rome as surely as ever it did in Egypt.

The Latins appear to have continued the Ark or Rek in their Rex which they inscribed on the cross, instead of the ὁ ὤν of the Greek Aureole-cross, with one letter on each of three arms. *Rek* (Eg.) denotes time and rule, whence the ruler or regulus. Rex and Kr are equivalents, and Kher (Eg.) also means the Majesty or Rex applied to Horus the Christ, the *Ma-Kheru*.

As late as the eighteenth century the Christ in a fresco at Salamis is pourtrayed in the act of making the sign of the cross and circle with the first and fourth digit of the right hand. In his left hand he holds the book, the Word (Kheru). He is pourtrayed between the two figures

ⓘⒸ ⓍⒸ

which *contain the Egyptian hieroglyphic for the balance or crossing* (Libra), ⬭ *the Makha,*[4] *still extant as the Greek sign of the scales*

---

[1] Irenæus, b. i. ch. ii. 1.   [2] Plutarch, *Of Isis and Osiris.*
[3] *Lap. Gal.;* see Maitland's *Church in the Catacombs*, pp. 66—76.
[4] See *Zodiacs;* also Didron, fig. 49.

and for a crossing; and Har-Makhu in Egypt was the Christ of the double equinox or horizon denoted by these two signs. Moreover, the student has only to compare the portrait of the Christ treading underfoot the Typhonian types of evil,[1] with Horus standing on the two crocodiles and holding the serpent and scorpion suspended helplessly in his hands, to see that the same type of the Saviour was continued in Italy.

Plato in *Timæus* applies the Egyptian figures in a metaphysical phase. He describes the Creator as making the universe of a spherical form, the most like unto his own shape. When therefore he cogitated over that god who was destined to exist at some certain period of time (which period was annual!) he produced his body according to this same circular pattern, and " The perfect circle of the created god he decussated in the shape of the letter X." That is, he made the sign of the circle and the cross. Proclus explains this decussated circle thus :—" *Two circles will be formed, of which one is interior, but the other exterior, and they will be oblique to each other. One of these is called the circle of the Same, the other the circle of the Different, or the fixed and variable, or rather the equinoctial circle and the zodiac. The circle of the different revolves about the zodiac, but the circle of the same about the equinoctial. Hence, we conceive that the right lines ought not to be applied to each other at right angles, but like the letter X, as Plato says, so as to cause the angles to be equal only at the summit, but those on each side, and the successive angles to be unequal. For the equinoctial circle does not cut the zodiac at right angles. Such therefore in short, is the mathematical discussion of the figure of the soul,*" the Nous or Son of God. Both Proclus and Jamblichus agree that the circle and cross typify the one soul, and the two souls that proceed from it,[2] which primarily signified the year, or the Horus renewed at the crossing where the star or sun emerged from the underworld at the place of the vernal equinox. The two souls are described in the *Ritual:* " *Osiris goes into Tattu, he finds the soul of the sun (the second Horus) there. The one and the other are united.*"

Justin interprets the words of Plato as relating to the crucifixion of Jesus Christ, and says he borrowed his description from Moses.[3] John also asserts that Anthropos was to be lifted up after the fashion of the serpent on the cross. One image of this decussation is the ☧, the Kheru, Kurios, or Koros, the word or logos personified as the son, the boy. *Koros,* says Plato, in *Cratylus,* does not signify a boy, but the pure unmixed nature of the intellect. That is platonizing. The *Koros* or Horus *was* the boy, called the Eternal Boy, the Christ born yearly at the crossing, and the Egyptian *Kheru* was the Greek Koros. The two Horuses were the dying mortal one,

---

[1] Didron, fig. 76.
[2] Taylor's *Proclus,* p. 114.
[3] Justin, *Apol.* i. p. 92.

and the living immortal; the sun in relation to the two equinoxes or crosses of Michaelmas and Easter. These supplied two different types of the crucified to the Greeks and Romans. The Greeks represented the Christ on the cross as dying; the Romans as living, and the two characters of the mythical Christ caused a split between the two Churches. The Greeks reproached the Latins with pourtraying the Lord contrary to all nature, and the Latins accused the Greeks of setting up a figure of the Antichrist.[1] The Egyptians blended both Horuses in one as Har-Makhu, the lord of the double horizon, but they had not to contend with the difficulty of the actual cross and crucifixion.

We learn from Isidorus[2] that it was a custom in the Roman army to mark the names of the living with the sign Τ, or the Tau Cross, but the dead were denoted by a Theta, θ. They had crossed. The Greek Theta, θ, is a kind of Tat by name, which combines the circle and cross. Theta is the Egyptian Teta for the eternal. Tet is the tomb, the eternal abode, the lower heaven. Tet or Tat also means death and the dead. Tet signifies to pass and cross over. Death is spoken of as the passage. " *When my death came*" is literally "when my passage or crossing came."[3] " *Save thou the Osiris from the attack made against him at the crossing.*"[4] " *The Osiris has not been spoken of, seen, perceived, or heard, in the mystical house of Cross-head,*"[5] is said of the deceased. The dead are those who have crossed, and attained the eternal region where the fourfold Tat was set up in Tattu, the place of establishing for ever, which may account for the Theta being the sign of the dead.

It even depended on the cross being three-armed or four-armed as to whether the Christ was crucified with three nails or four. Some sects adored the T-shaped cross and three nails; others the four-armed cross and four nails. Bishop Luke of Tuy (about 1230) maintained that the nails were four in number. This was evident from the existence of *the four genuine nails* which were still preserved, and *which he had seen in four different places*, to wit, Nazareth, Tarsus, Constantinople, and St. Denis. The nails in the hands and feet of Buddha, of Witoba, of Maya, and in the corners of the Swastika Cross, show that the proper number is four, in keeping with the Cross of the four Quarters. The cross on which the Jewish Paschal lamb was *spitted*, was double, and thus corresponded to the two equinoxes or crossings which the Hebrews keep.[6] This cross of the four quarters and two equinoxes constitutes that known as the Cross of Lorraine, which has double arms, and is therefore of a sixfold form. Three French churches are founded on this model. The great English churches of Beverly,

---

[1] Hefele, *Conciliengesch.* iii. 737.   [2] Origen, i. 39.
[3] *Instructions of Amenhat.*   [4] *Rit.* ch. cxxxv.
[5] *Rit.* ch. lxxxiii.   [6] Stanley, *Jewish Church*, vol. i. App.

Rochester, Lincoln, and Worcester, are built on the same plan, as may be seen by engravings in Dugdale's *Monasticon Anglicanum*. These edifices have two transepts instead of one. Didron tries to account for this cross by supposing the upper and shorter arms denote the scroll which was said to have been extended over the head of the crucified.

A Greek cross of the "first ages."[1] has this double figure, and is bifurcated at foot. The double cross is likewise extant in the cross of suffering (the cross of the maimed Messiah Horus), and the cross of the resurrection or the Easter equinox.

The cross follows the tree and the serpent as a numerogram. It is merely twin as the two strokes of the Roman cross and the X. It is three-fold in the T. It is four-fold as the Tat-type of the four Cardinal Points. It becomes six-fold in the form of a circle with the cross and perpendicular Iota. This is a pre-christian monogram found on the medals of the Kings of the Bosphorus and on the coins of L. Lentulus, before the Christian era.[2] The sign consists of six points with the phonetic value of Chi and Iota. These when read backwards—and everything in the Christian symbolism has to be read backwards, from end to beginning,—are *I Chi*, assumed to be the initials of the name Jesus Christ. But the value of the letters has to be interpreted by the figures. This is a figure of six. The numeral value of Chi is 600. This is the sign of the AO reckoned as the one who was of a six-fold nature, like Anu of Babylon, whose figure is the one-Six or six-fold one, because of the natural basis in the four quarters together with the height and the depth. So the Hindu youthful god Kârtikêya is represented with six heads; and the Christ or Horus of the Gnostics has six names, and was of a six-fold nature. The six-armed stauros is identical with the six-fold Horus. *Iota-Chi* denotes the one that decussates in a six-fold form, and is an equivalent for the Hindu Shasha-Linga. This same six-fold sign appears on a lamp figured by Gori and by Lundy, with twelve heads around it, supposed to be the twelve apostles, where this six-fold pre-christian sign is taken by all believers to be the sacred monogram of Jesus Christ. But the absolute solar and Kronian nature of the symbol is proved by the number 52 marked on it in little circles. The spokes image the six-fold division which belongs to space. The fifty-two circles are the weeks of the year, and the "Twelve Apostles" are nothing more than the twelve signs of the zodiac personified as companions of the solar god, just as the original twelve of the round table were the companions of the mythical Arthur in Britain. The lamp undoubtedly indicates the "Light of the World," but as the solar god, not as any historical personage. The lamp has the figure of the female; it is of the same

---

[1] Didron, fig. 96.   [2] King, *Early Christian Numismatics*, p. 13.

shape as the Yoni in the Hindu Naga Linga Nandī,[1] which contains the tetrad in unity, within the type of the female; or, in other instances, the sign of the male power erect within the image of the female, as simply pourtrayed as it is in the gesture sign.

Further, it is well known that a triangle with the apex upward is a masculine emblem, but when reversed, with the apex downwards, it is feminine. The two combined in the double triangle signify both sexes in unity; the six points being another form of the figure of six with the same significance as the six arms, six heads, or six names. The reversed or female triangle is found on a grave-stone in the cemetery of Pricilla, and within this, as within the female figure on the lamp, the cross and Ro (Kr), together with the letters A ω, are depicted and also assumed to represent the personal Christ. The *A O* proves the dual nature of the Christ intended as does the uterine lamp in which the monogram of the Apostolic cross is pourtrayed. The female sign is the Ru ◯, the mouth or uterus of birth. It is the primary circle in heaven and earth, which, as before said, is inseparable from the cross. This is the R of the ☧ sign, and of the monogram "*Kr*"; the circle of the Chi or cross. It is the same female image as the reversed triangle and the uterine lamp, the figure of the celestial birthplace which gave annual rebirth to the solar Christ when he had crossed; he whose symbol in its several forms was the pre-christian cross.

In ecclesiastical heraldic blazonry the single cross is assigned to the bishop, the double cross to cardinals and archbishops, and the triple or six-fold cross to the pope. An utter reversal of the grades if the original had been the supposed Cross of Christ. The types tell the truth, however the written word may lie. The pope represents the six-fold cross that was extant ages before the era called Christian, the cross of the completed solar circle, or, in the feminine character, the triple-cross, the s s s of the *Seshsh* (Sistrum), and a form of the 666, the number of the beast that sat on the seven hills. The pope also wears the mitre shaped like the fish's mouth, the "*os tincæ*" of obstetrists; the *Vesica piscis*, an especial emblem of the mother in Rome. These two are a continuation of the same types as the cross-barred sistrum; the cross within the triangle and the six-fold cross or shasha-linga within the Yoni of the lamp.

The ancient popish ceremony of creeping to the cross *on all fours*, illustrates the cross of the four quarters. This used to be performed on Good Friday. John Bale in his Declaration of Bonner's Articles, 1554, denounces, amongst other customs, that of "Creeping to the Cross on Good Friday featly." Cranmer likewise objected to the custom of creeping on all fours to the cross.[2] The kings of England, also the queens and their ladies, crept to the cross on all fours upon

[1] Lundy, fig. 45; Moor, pl. 83.
[2] Strype's *Memoir*, p. 135.

that day.[1] This figure of the four quarters was accompanied by the egg as a type of the circle—the circle and the cross being everywhere twinned. Eggs were offered to the cross, and the image of the cross was used in collecting eggs on Good Friday.

The Cardinals, as their name denotes, are founded on the cross as the cardinal points of the circle, from *Cardo*, a hinge, a point or nick of time. The double cross of the archbishops is still paralleled in England by the two archbishoprics of the north and south, York and Canterbury. No link is missing in the long chain of evidence that shows the continuity of the mythical cross. It cannot be said that the sun and moon were the parents of an historical Christ, but they were the father and mother of Horus the Christ or Iu-su the Child of Atum, and of Khunsu the Prince of Peace. It is the Mother Moon—the woman arrayed with the sun, and the moon under her feet,—that still brings forth her child at Easter, as she does in the Book of " Revelation," and a bust of the supposed historical Saviour is seen enthroned within a nimbus of the cross between the sun and moon, showing the child of both who was born at Easter. Moreover, *this form of the Father and Mother is pourtrayed on the earliest known crucifix that has the human figure on it.*[2] The solar disk and crescent symbols appear upon the plastic crucifix presented by Gregory the Great to Queen Theodolinde, which is preserved in the church of St. John at Monza. The vernal equinox is the place where the sun and new moon were once more re-united and the Horus or Christ was re-born at Easter; and in the mediæval representations of the Crucifixion the Christ is constantly accompanied by the sun and crescent moon. It is the same luni-solar conjunction that produced the youthful Khunsu in the mythos of Egypt. Our calendar rules for Easter continue the same as in Egypt, and the same full moon which contains Khunsu holding forth the Pig of Easter in the Planisphere of Denderah (*Cf.* the leg of pork especially eaten at that season), still determines the Easter-tide. There has been no break in the bringing on to leave any room for the insertion of an historical cross.

Being pre-Christian, the Cross was not derived from an historical Crucifixion, and can afford no evidence of the fact. The monograms of the Cross *X, KR, Iota Chi,* and others, being also pre-extant could not have been derived from the name of a personal Jesus Christ. The Solar and Kronian Crosses were continued for and as the Christ until there was a personal representation; the Pagan imagery was not even *taken* intelligently, it was only inherited ignorantly.

To recapitulate : the earliest sign of the Cross made with the hands denoted reckoning and repetition; this is extant in the × of multiplication. The first form of the Celestial Cross was described by the earliest maker of a circle, which was a constellation that crossed below the

[1] Brand, *Good Friday.*   [2] Martigny, plates p. 190.

G G 2

horizon. This was made by the Seven Stars in Ursa Major or the genitrix who was personified as the bringer-forth of Time in Heaven and pourtrayed as the *enceinte* Mother, whose Ankh-Cross (the tie or cord) was the figure of life to come (for in *her* was life), and 'of continuity by means of cyclic repetition. The next was the Cross of establishing for ever on the four-fold foundation of the four quarters, with the Tat-pillar as its type, which was first assigned to the lunar god. Lastly, the Sun-God made the circle and the sign of the Cross which might be the Tat of the Equinox and Solstice, or the Swastika with four nails in its four feet; the extended human figure with the sign of four nails in hands and feet; the Cross of the four-fold or the cubical foundation; the four-fold, six-fold, or seven-fold Lingaic cross. The Solar God who crossed was the virile potent one, the victor and conqueror. Hence the Cross became the sign of all that is expressed by the word *KR* (Eg.), which not only means a course of time but Power, Ability, Virile Potency, Support, the Weapon of Power. And in its final phase as the Christian emblem the Cross of death and blood-sacrifice offered to the God of Gore, befittingly fulfils *its* type ; keeps its character, and still gets its drench and drink of human life as the *hilt of the sword* by means of which the dominion of the Cross has been and still continues to be extended *over the globe*.

In the Christian Iconography the cross is connected with the ram and the lamb; in each case the animal wears the cross as a glory, and has another form of the cross for an accompaniment. Again, the name of the fish as IXΘYC is placed at the head of the starry cross.[1]

In the Hermean Zodiac, Pisces is named Ichton, and the fish is the female goddess who brought forth the young Sun-god as her fish,[2] whether called Horus in Egypt or Marduk the Fish of Hea in Assyria; Ichthys, who was the son of the fish-tailed Atergatis at Ascalon,[3] or Ichthys which was also a title of Bacchus.[4] The cross of the ram or lamb, as the symbol of the four quarters is corroborated by the mount of the four quarters which are represented by the four rivers of the "Genesis." In monuments of what is termed by Didron the "Primitive Church," the lamb is frequently seen standing on a mountain out of which the four rivers flow, as a symbol of the four quarters. On a sculptured sarcophagus in the Vatican, "belonging to the earliest ages of Christianity," the lamb is pourtrayed standing on the mount of the four rivers with the monogram A ₽ ω set in a circular nimbus. The same writer also cites a monument of the 11th century in which the four streams are called Gyon, Phishon,

---

[1] Gori, Lacroix, and Didron. Mosaicin S. Appollinario in Classe, Ravenna, 6th century.
[2] Pl. ii. vol. ii. *B. B.*
[3] Vossius, *De Idololatria*, lib. i. cap. xxiii. p. 89.
[4] Hesychius, p. 179.

Tygris and Eufrates, and these are represented by figures of men, nearly naked, who wear the Phrygian bonnet and each carries an urn of one of the four streams. In this, the Mithraic bonnet points unmistakably to the Mithraic lamb, which the Persians adopted instead of the ram, and therefore to the Mithraic Cult. Dupuis shows that the ancient Persians celebrated their feast of the Cross a few days after the entrance of the sun into the sign of Aries, at a time when the Southern Cross was visible by night. If so, that constellation would be the starry type of the newly-found cross of the lamb and the vernal equinox.

This symbolism of the cross and ram and the cross and fish is found on the sculptured stones of Scotland. But wherever found, the sole origin and significance is solar, and the typology belongs to the Cycles of Time.

The ram and the fish were not placed in the Zodiac as anti-types of any personal Christ who was to come in human form, nor did these signs on the ancient monuments catch the light of Christianity by anticipation. The Ram or Lamb that carries or is accompanied by the Cross never did and never could really represent any other fact than that of the Equinoctial Colure in the sign of Aries. The ram has no meaning apart from the cross which accompanies it, as the sign of the crossing and of the four quarters. The cross is borne by the lamb in the form of the Tree of Life. The lamb is standing upon the mount of the four quarters which are represented by the four rivers issuing forth. These are the mount and the tree which have now been traced from their beginning. They are found with the typical lamb, or ram, because that was the sign of the vernal equinox at the time denoted by the typology. The lamb or ram was the Christ of its particular cycle of time which lasted 2,255 years. The Ram-type had been continued in the Indian iconography, as the bearer of Agni ever since the sun entered that sign. During all that time the Hindu God of Fire or Spirit, whose emblem was the cross of fire, had ridden on the young ram as the solar sign of his reproducing power; and the Egyptian divinities Num and Sebek-Ra had been imaged in the sign of the Ram, the head of which they wore. When discovered by Europeans, this figure of Agni on the Ram had to be accounted for as the anti-type of the Christ that was to come. When will the long slumber of common sense come to an end, and all such false deluding dreams be put to flight? During all that time the lamb supposed to take away the sins of the world was offered up by the Jews and others as the victim sacrificed. This was crucified on the cross, and it was continued during some seven centuries of the Christian era as the Christ upon the Cross in the catacombs of Rome. When the equinox passed into the Sign of Pisces the fish became the figure of the Christ on the cross. Hence the fish on the pre-christian cross which is found in Scotland and Ireland and the fish-type which was continued wherever the reckonings were kept. *Pisces* became the sign of the resurrection from the dead for souls, as for the sun, about 255 B.C., and in this sign the genitrix holds up the Dove in her hand. Hence Dove and Fish were continued together along with the Cross and the sign of *KR* in the Typology of the Catacombs. Moreover, the Dove and the Fish are pourtrayed as bearers of the palm-branch which is the hieroglyphic symbol of a time, period, course, or *KR*.[1] Thus the Fish, Dove, Palm-branch, and Monogram, are all grouped together in strict accordance with the *latest* sign of the Resurrection at the Crossing. In the Catacombs the concealed burial-place of the ancient religion visibly becomes the birth-place of the new, and it is there we can see the types in the process of their transformation. The fish became and was continued as the Christ of the new cycle of 2,255 years. Christ with or as the fish appears upon a gem copied by Rochette; His youthful head is resting on a fish, and He is identified by the name of ΧΡΙΣΤΟΥ. Horus in Egypt had been a fish from time immemorial, and when the equinox entered the Sign of Pisces, Horus, who was continued by the Gnostics, is pourtrayed as *Ichthys* with the fish-sign over his head.[2]

This engraving has been called Jesus Christ in the character of Horus, but it is simply the Egypto-Gnostic Horus, the Christ who was first born as the fish of the perfected solar Zodiac in the year (or thereabouts) B.C. 255. The facts are visibly depicted in the celestial imagery;[3] and the type has been continued, for example, in Japan, where the birth of a child is still publicly announced by the villagers under the sign of the fish—a typical paper fish being suspended over the doorway of the house wherein the child has been born.[4] Also

[1] Zodiac in present vol. ; Bosio, *Rom. Sott.* p. 505 ; Lundy, figs. 53 and 55.
[2] No. 231, *Gnostic Seals*, British Museum.
[3] See plate ii. vol. ii. *Book of Beginnings*, also plate in present vol.
[4] *Log of* Lord Colin Campbell.

in modern rites of the Jewish Passover, Leviathan and the Fishes are connected. Leviathan is a form of the Dragon of Darkness which has been vanquished by the Sun in *Pisces* ever since the crossing occurred in that sign, over two thousand years since, when the Fish-type succeeded that of the Lamb. The final facts are that Christ, as the ram, dates from B.C. 2410. Christ as Ichthys, the fish, dates from B.C. 255. Christ, in the human form upon the Cross, dates from the seventh century, A.D.

This is the Gnostic Christ, the Egyptian Horus who for thousands of years had been represented in the act of treading the crocodile under foot, and who is here pourtrayed as the youthful Sun-God representing the Sun of the vernal equinox in the sign of the Fishes.

SECTION VIII.

NATURAL GENESIS AND TYPOLOGY OF THE MYTHICAL GREAT MOTHER, THE TWO SISTERS, THE TWINS, TRIADS, TRINITY AND TETRAD.

WHEN, after many years' research, the present writer discovered that mythology is the mirror in which the pre-historic sociology is reflected, his labour was forthwith doubled, but the fact furnished him with the real foundation for the work he was building. It may be difficult for the modern mind to conceive of the primitive priority (for it is that rather than supremacy in Bachofen's sense) of the Woman; the priority of the sonship to the institution of the fatherhood; of the nephew to the son of the father; and of the types of thought, the laws and ceremonies that were left as the deposit of such primitive customs. Yet these facts, and others equally important, are reflected in the mirror of mythology.

The genitrix as Ta-Urt (Typhon) is designated the "*Mother of the Beginnings*," "*Mother of the Revolutions*" (time-cycles), "*Mother of the Fields of Heaven*," and the "*Mother of Gods and Men*." The priority of the genitrix as typical producer was plainly enough pourtrayed by Tesas-Neith, the Great Mother, at Sais. "*I am all that was, and is, and is to be ; no mortal hath lifted my peplum, and the fruit I bore is Helios.*" [1] The title of the goddess as "Tesas-Neith" signifies the self-existing ; she who came from herself. The genitrix is celebrated as the "*Only One*" in the Ritual. "*Glory to thee! Thou art mightier than the Gods! The forms of the living souls which are in their places give glory to the terrors of thee, their Mother ; thou art their origin.*" [2]

Following this enunciation of the female priority we find that Seb, the *father* of the gods, is also designated the "*Youngest of the gods*." The earlier gods, Sut (or Sevekh), Shu, Taht, and the first Horus, were children of the mother alone. They were created before there was any father in heaven, there being no fatherhood as yet indivi-

---

[1] Clemens, *Strom.*, v. ; Proclus in *Timæus*, i.
[2] Rit., ch. clxv., Sup. Birch.

dualized on earth. Both on earth and in heaven the father was preceded by the Totemic elders and fathers, the mythical Pitris. The Kamite mirror shows us that when the fatherhood had become individualized in the human family it was first reflected by Seb as God the divine Father. Seb, the God of earth and of planetary time, who followed the earlier Star-gods, Moon-deities, and elementaries, was then termed the "*Father of the Gods.*" When the fatherhood became individualized it was applied retrospectively, which often gives a false appearance of beginning with and descent from the father in place of the mother. But mythology begins with and reckons from the female, as in the totemic system of the oldest races.   We can only begin at the beginning ; the god could only be born as the child of the mother. Although the Hottentots have now attained the individualized fatherhood, and have elevated the divine father of the fathers to the supreme place, yet their languages show that the race, clan, or tribe, was always called after the mother, never after the father. Thus the Namas, Amas, Khaxas, and Gaminus have each and all the feminine terminal as their appellation.   They are all children of the mother, and it is the same with the lesser formation in the family, which is likewise named from the mother.[1]

Descent in the female line was universal in the earliest times and most archaic condition of society ; the gens or kin being composed of a female ancestor and her children. The fatherhood is unknown to the primary group, and this status of the human family originated the figure of the Great Mother and her children in the heavens. Also in certain Chinese accounts of the founders of dynasties in the oldest time, long anterior to 2,000 B.C., they were invariably born of no father. One maid, or the Virgin Mother, dreams that she embraced the sun. Another dreams that she suddenly felt a mighty wind in the form of an egg. So the Virgin Mother, typified by the Vulture, Mu (Eg.), is impregnated by the wind alone without the male. Tradition said that the first King of Northern Gaoli had a maid slave who was found to be with child. The King desired the death of the boy who was born, but the mother said that she had conceived him by an influence which came upon her, and which she felt to be like air, as if in the form of an egg. The King, at once afraid to kill, and fearing to keep alive a prodigy, had the child thrown into the *pig-yard*. But it was the rightful heir, who lived to become the monarch.[2]

The sole catholic and universal first producer was feminine. She was the Mother Nature, *La Source*, the Goddess of Beginnings (Taurt), the Begetter of the Universe (Ishtar and Atergatis). The

---

[1] Hahn, p. 145.   The Wyandot mode of stating that descent is in the female line, is, "*The woman carries the Gens.*"

[2] Ross, *Corea, its History, Manners, and Customs*, p 121.

Great Mother, the Grandmother (Inner African), the Godmother, the Old Woman (North American Indian), the Mother Earth (Nin-ki-gal), and Mother Heaven; the mother that opened in the void below or vault above in the uterine likeness of the human parent. This alone is beginning. She is yet extant in the African's and the Hindu's " Mama," and the Papist's " Mary." When a piece of crewel work bearing the motto, " God is my King," was presented to Cetewayo in London, he at first declined to receive it with the remark, " *There is no one over me but the Queen, my Mother !* " [1] He himself was the King, the Bull, as Male; and such was the primitive status.

The lower world, says the Sohar, is created after the pattern of the upper, and everything existing above is to be found, as it were, in a copy on the earth. But this is a reversal of the real process; a result of the later thought which culminated in the Hindu tree with its roots above and its branches below. The lower was first in mythology, as in evolution. The esoteric interpretation was last. The Great Mother, the Virgin Mother, of mythology, represents the human mother, as the first mistress of the home in the pre-paternal phase, and thus mythology helps us to ascertain the natural genesis of such customs as those of the Mother-Right by becoming the mirror to the pre-historic past, which reflects the most Archaic social conditions of the human race. The earliest God known is the Son of the Mother, who becomes her Bull or Male. It was thus with Sut, or Sevekh, so with Taht, Khem, and Khepr; and he who was the consort of his mother was necessarily born or re-born of his wife; and, as according to one Egyptian custom the son took the mother's name, in another the bridegroom takes that of the wife, and both are typical of the primordial derivation from the female with which mythology begins. Non-evolutionists have recently been startled at the rank of the wife and the priority and apparent supremacy of the woman in Egypt as late as the Ptolemian age. A writer in the *Times* has said, " *We shall probably never know how customs so strange and perverse came to be established among a people famed throughout antiquity for their wisdom and learning.*" We never shall, except on the evolutionary theory, and also on the theory propounded in the present work, of Egypt's being the mouth-piece and Inner Africa the birth-place of all such archaic and primitive customs. For example, the same supremacy of the female as mistress of the house, which is shown by the Egyptian marriage documents is extant to-day among the Hottentots. In every house or hut she is the supreme ruler, the *Taras*. Dr. Hahn derives this title from *Ta* to rule, be master; *Ra*, which expresses a custom or intrinsic peculiarity, with S for feminine terminal. *Taras* denotes the Supreme Ruler, the Lady of the house. Out of doors the man is Governor, but the *Taras* dominates within. Her place is on the right side of the house and the right hand of her husband.

[1] *Daily News*, Sept. 2, 1882.

He dare not take a mouthful of sour milk out of a tub without her permission. Should he break the law in such a case his nearest female relations will mulct him in a heavy fine of sheep or cows.[1] When a chief died it has often happened that his wife became the ruleress and queen of the tribe, just as in Egypt. It is also a *Khoi-khoi* custom for the sons to take the name of the mother (the daughters taking that of the father) ; and in Egypt the sons, instead of being called after their fathers were named after their mothers. Neither sons nor daughters could be named after the fathers when these were unknown. When the fatherhood was represented by the solar Râ, then she who had been his mother was called his daughter, and so the great goddesses became daughters of the Râ. This position of the woman is the oldest known in the world, and it is in perfect accordance with natural genesis. The mother was the first parent recognized, as in the mirror of mythology, where *Ta-Ur* (with the Egyptian terminal, Ta-Urt, Greek Thoueris), the old first chief ruleress is the *Taras* of the gods in Egypt.

It was a law of the Basques or Iberians that he who married the heiress should take her name, and have no control over her children. In the event of her death he was not permitted to marry again except by consent of the deceased wife's relations.

The earliest societary conditions and typical modes of expression first established in Inner Africa were continued one way or another by the Egyptians whose laws, literature, and mythology, are a complete Kamite fossil formation deposited by the life of the past. Egypt, as insisted in the previous volumes is the missing link between the Inner African origines and the rest of the world. Remote as the postulate seemed when enunciated by me, every discovery and every day will bring us nearer to *that* truth. Such customs do not commence just where we first meet with them in history ; nor were they established in Egypt in the sense of being imported or adopted by a civilised people. They are simply survivals from the Inner African birth-place.

Neither did such customs arise from a primitive order of chivalry being established for the worship of womankind. Woman was the first known parent, and her priority in mythology and sociology was the natural result. As bringer-forth she was the cow of human kind, and the chivalry was doubtless somewhat akin to that of the bulls, rams, and stags, fighting for the finest females in the herd. Female supremacy was sexual at first but the precedence is afterwards registered in statutory laws. Diodorus had already told us that the Queen of Egypt held a loftier position theoretically if not practically than the Pharaoh himself ; the Ra being a far later institution.[2] The Emperor of China is not yet exempted from performing the *Kotou* in presence of his mother.

[1] Hahn, *Tsuni-Goam*, p. 19.
[2] Vide *Chrestomathie Demotique*, par E. Revillout.

According to the laws of Akkad if a son said to his father, "*Thou art not my father*" and sealed it by making his nail-mark he was fined in a forfeit of money. But if he said to his mother even without confirming it with the nail-mark, "*Thou art not my mother*" he was put into prison and had his hair cut off to humble him.[1] The one was so much more certain a law-breaker than the other. Still more interesting is it to learn that in case of homicide among the Kaffirs the scale of compensation allowed by law was seven head of cattle for the male and ten head for the female.[2]

The reason why the mother was the Ruleress and Tyrant of the House and Home was because she *was the first House or Home* that was recognised. She was the abode of birth, and all early forms of the abode whether of the living or the dead were first named after her. Even the notion that a man is born of his wife abides in the Vedas. But, this did not originate in the fanciful etymology of *Jaya* a wife, from *Jan*, to be born, as explained by the commentators. It must be read by the primitive doctrine. "*A Man's Wife Maghavan is his dwelling; verily she is his place of Birth.*"[3] Simply because the wife was the abode of being like the mother. This may be illustrated in Cornish where *Kuf* is the name both of the womb and the wife. Wife, woman and mother are three personifications of the womb, the earliest house of life. It is also shown by the *Wame*, (Scotch) belly or womb; *Wamo*, (Fin.), woman and wife; *Gwamm* (Breton) wife.

The Cave, Cove, Kof; the Combe, Wem, Uamh, Home and Hamlet, are all forms of the dwelling founded on the female. Also, the chief type-names are Inner African, continued in Egyptian.

Kam, in Yula.	*Kamu* in Munio.	*Ama*, in N'godsin.
Kamu, in Kasm.	*Kamu*, in Kanem.	*Uma*, and *Ma*, in Doai.
Kumu, in Kanuri.	*Gama*, in Bode.	*Koomara*, in Dor.
Kamu, in N'guri.		

This is a general type-name for the womb or belly. The dwelling is

Gomi, house, Kupa.	*Kompe*, house, Gadsaga.
N'gim ,, Munio.	*Kumba*, a pit or cave, Gindo.
N'gim ,, N'guru.	*Gumu*, a village, Dewoi.

We cannot derive the *Gens* (or Kinsfolk), except from the woman as producer; the *Khennu* (Eg). In Ulfila's translation of the Bible (fourth century) the wife is *Gens*, the woman is *Ginio*. And the name is the woman's as that of the uterus, the birth-place of the Gens; the Khentu (Eg.), and Kentu for the woman in Arabic. It has been previously shown how the type-name of the woman ranging

[1] *Tablet of Ancient Akkadian Laws*, 12, 13; Sayce.
[2] Dugmore, p. 61.   [3] *Rig. Veda*, Wilson, v. iii. p. 84.

from *Yoni* and *Gine* to *Queen* was based on the first abode of being. This type-name is Inner African for the belly or womb as

Youno, in Krepee.	*Konyo*, in Toronka.	*Eni*, in Ebe.
N'yoni, in Hwida.	*Kono*, in Dsalunka.	*Ine*, in Opanda.
N'yonu, in Dahome.	*Kono*, in Kankanka.	*Ine*, in Igu.
N'kona, in Saldana Bay.	*Kono*, in Bambara.	*Ine*, in Egbira-hima.
Gine, in Tene.	*Kenu*, in Kasm.	*Hona*, Woman, in Agaumidr.
Ginei, in Kise-Kise.	*Kuna*, in Bode.	*Kento* „ Mimboma.
Kun, in Bulom.	*Kunu*, in N'godsin.	*Kento* „ Musentandu.
Kun, in Mampa.	*Kunu*, in Doai.	*Kento* „ Basunde.
Kono, in Mandenga.	*Gungu*, in Tumbuktu.	*Onda* „ Mbarike.
Kono, in Kabunga.	*Unna*, in Yasgua.	

The Hieroglyphics show the *Khun* is the Abode, the Dwelling, or Inn as it is in the boosing *Ken*. *Khen* signifies *In*, *Within*, the interior, the Hottentot and Bushman *Khoin* for the entrails. The first interior, or inn, was feminine. When we have dug down to a root like this we find it is as simple as one of two, or rather it is one with two aspects; these are the dual of the idea of Within and Without. The female is the inn, or within, and the male is out; Egyptian Uta, a title of Khem, the one who puts forth or jets out; as it is in the Chinese duality of Feng-Shui. This is one of the names under which the typical female can be followed the world round, beginning in Africa as the birthplace for this name of the Birthplace.

Kono, in Maori.	*Kuns*, in Mandan Indian.	*Gean*, in Irish.
Quani, in Tasmanian.	*Ken* or *Cons*. in Cornish.	*Qen*, in Hebrew.
Koona, in Australian.	*Con*, in Old French.	*Quan*, the wife, in Old Norse.
Ch'hen, in Chinese.		

Other forms of the Dwelling continue the name. The village in Vei (African) is the *Ken*, the *Kêne* in Kono. In Egypt the royal court of the palace was the Pa-*Khennu*, and Khennu is also the concubine as well as the organ.

The primitive Man did not know that he came from the "Bright Sky" as his *father*. He who did not know his father on earth could not recognise one in heaven! But he knew that he came from the mother's womb and derived his life there by means of his navel. Hence the naming from the primal dwelling-place. The Goddess who wears the mural crown, or turreted tower on her head, is the abode personified, no matter under what name. Artemis, or Kubelê of Ephesus, is an Asiatic continuation of Urt or Kep. She carries the abode on her head in the shape of the tower or fortress, because, as Ovid says, she first created cities. This tower, therefore, is the type of the later dwelling-place evolved from the simplest beginning, but the earliest habitation was one that could preserve life in the water, hence the Great Mother as the pregnant hippopotamus, which was followed by the fish-type of Hathor in Egypt; Atergatis and Venus out of it. The *enceinte* water-cow was continued as the ark of the Great Bear. The cabin is consequently a type of the genitrix, and gestation is called "*going in the cabin*," the cabin of the boat that was overhung with the *Peplos* of Athena in her procession, and is likewise represented by the Hindu Argha-Yoni.

. The lotus was another type of her who brought forth from the waters into breathing life. The infant Sun-God was pourtrayed as rising up out of the waters on a lotus; not because the Egyptians were in the habit of floating on the Nile in lotuses, but because they had continued that symbol as divine from the time before boats were built. The lotus was the bark of the god and the womb of the genitrix in one; *and when they made their barks of papyrus they were continuing the lotus into the boat* which was lotus-shaped at prow and stern. So was it with the dwelling-place on land. *Baba* is a title of the old genitrix (Typhon); and *Babia* was the Goddess of Karkemish. The *Bab* (or Beb), which modifies into *Bau*, is the opening of the abyss or cavern, void or pit-hole, also called the hole of the tomb and the well; the *Bob*, Arabic, the opening out of which the water wells; *Bebi*, Coptic, to flow and overflow. This Bab became the Bahv בהו or void on which the Hebrew dogma of creation was based. It is also the Babylonian and Byblian Bab called the Gate, but which is more comprehensively the opening, the *outrance*, uterus, or abode of life. So the Irish-Keltic *Brû*, Cornish *Brys*, for the matrix, was the primary form of the Berry, Boro', and Burgh, the earliest habitation.[1]

It is the same with place and *locality* as with house and home. The *lici* or *loca*, Latin, as matrix and womb was the primal place and locality of life, which was externalised by name as the *Lochos*, a lair for lying in wait; the *Llych*, Welsh, a covert and hiding-place; (*Luka*, Hindi, to lie concealed, *Ruka* (Eg.), to hide), and other forms of the lodge or Loggia. With the prefix B we have the covert as the Brû or Brough, and the Brake, a covert for game, whence the Brachen and heath which is *Bruk* in Welsh; *Brag*, Breton; *Brego*, Portuguese; *Bruch*, Grisons. The human covert as the *Brug* (*Bru*, Irish, the womb) became the *Burgh, Burrow, Brix*-ham, *Brix*-ton, *Brigh*-ton, *Breck*-nock, Kaer-*Ebrauc*, and Pem-*broke;* also the *Brigh* (Gaelic), as the tomb. The thought of man began at the starting-point of his

---

[1] THE WESLEY-BOB.
At the time of making his remark on the Wesley-Bob (vol. i. p. 304), the writer did not know that the "Bob" was the sailor's berth on board ship. He argued that the children's "Bob" with the dolls, denoted the birth-place of the genitrix, which is the "Berth" of the unborn child. The "Bob," therefore, is one of the prototypes which survive from the first origin. It is the mother herself in the Australian, Akkadian, and other languages. It is the woman, the female, in various languages. It is the womb or belly in the Kanyop, *Pipas;* Pepel, *Pobob;* Mbe, *Fuburu; Bowo,* or *Bovo,* in Tiribi. In Dutch the *Pop* is the caterpillar's cocoon. The *Beb*, or *Bub*, in Egyptian is the hole, the pit, a primitive type of the berth. In Gaelic the *Beabh*-is the tomb; *Bebo* in Tiwi (African); and *Babisi* in Melon, are hells (in the sky). The *Bab* in Assyrian is the Gate, place of outlet, whence Babylon. But the first Bab is the uterus. Then the hole in the ground or berth on board ship. Hence the Great Mother who personified the abode is named Baba (Eg.); Papa, Mangaian; Babia, Khetan.

own beginning and language consequently bears the impress of its
natural mould.

The cave or Kep (Eg.), a secret dwelling, is the mere lair of earth,
and this bears the name of Kef or Kep, the oldest genitrix; who, in
Cornish and Breton is the *Kuf,* English Wife.   Hathor is the Hat or
Hut of the child.   Hest is the Seat, a Stone-chair being her sign of
the Bearer.   From Hest comes Hesta, Goddess of the hearth and
home.   Nephthys bears the house in outline on her head, and Hemen
(Eg.) IS the seat, the *Home* by name.   Also our word Abode is
identical with the Egyptian *Apt* for an abode, the hold of the vessel,
a cradle and a name of the Great Mother.   In like manner the Welsh
Bedd for the coffin, kist, or tomb, is identical with *Bed* for the uterus,
which was represented by Buto as the genitrix.   In Akkad the
Dammal, or House-Dame, was not simply the House-mother, for, like
Isis, she was the Mother-House, the uterine abode, a household divinity
as representative of the Great Mother.   The monogram of *Uni-Umma,*
the Mother, also means broad, wide, and spreading; what is still
termed a *bowerly* woman; the type of the Mother Great with
Child.

In Adampe the village is the *edume; diambo* in Kisama, *demgal* in
Goburu.   *Itembe* is the Roof in Nyamwezi.   The Irish *diomruck* is a
Cromlech.   The Egyptian *Tem,* like the Scottish Tom, is a fort or
mound; also a village.   The Sanskrit *dama* is a house and home;
Pahlavi, *Demun;* Greek *Domos;* Latin, *Domus;* Slavonic *Domu;*
Bohemian, *Dum;* Polish, *Dym;* English, *Dome*; and Irish *Domh-
nach,* a sacred Shrine or a Church.   The Irish Fir-*Domhnann* and the
Damnonii of Cornwall, are known to tradition as the Men of the
deep pits; they were Troglodites who dwelt in a primitive form of
the *Dum,* a mere hole in the earth.   The *domus* and *Domicile* are
one with the *Dame* and *Dam* in English, and the *Dome,* as Woman,
in Correguage.   Several kinds of Land-Family or House-community
are traceable under the Mother's name.   The Russian *Mir,* the aggre-
gate of the inhabitants of a village, possessing the land in common,
answer to the Akkadian *Mal* and Egyptian *Mer.*   The French
Maorissa of the land-family was a form of the primitive *Mère,* the
Mother, who in Egypt is the Goddess *Mer.*   The Great Mother was
Mistress of the Eight and of the region of the Eight in Smen, as Ta-
Urt or Kefa in the stellar phase, and Hathor in the lunar.   Now
among the Southern Sclaves a form of the House-Community is yet
extant called the Zadruga.   In this primitive institution the House-
Mother and Mistress is the *Redusa,* whose name signifies " *She whose
turn has come,*" *i.e.* to rule the community, which is governed by the
females in rotation, each becoming the Superior or Mother who rules
during a period of Eight days.[1]   She is the social representative

[1] *Laveleye.*

of Ta-Urt in Smen, or Hathor in Sesennu, both of which names denote the number Eight.

The Mythical Abyss was the Womb, the Bab, Kep, Ken, Khem, or Tep of all beginning. Tep (Eg.) means first. With the feminine or dual terminal this is the tepht, the abyss of source, the Hole of the Snake or lair of the Water-Cow. The tepht is synonymous with the English *Depth;* Welsh, *Dyfed;* Shetland, *Toÿt;* Lithuanic, *Dubti;* Hebrew, *Tophet*, in the valley. The Abyss is also represented by the *Tuba* (Xosa Kaffir) or opening; the *Tupe*, Maori, a hole over which incantations are uttered against evil demons whose dwelling is the Abyss of Darkness. The Greek τάφος was a Barrow for the Burial urn, and therefore a form of the Teph as the Abyss from which all birth proceeded in the beginning. The *Tiava*, Butumerah, is the womb or belly; the *Dabu* in Bornu. This name of the primordial place of birth is likewise that of the primal conditions of beginning, becoming, and being, as in the Maori and Mangaian *Tupu*, to open, originate, begin; and the Polynesian *Tafito* for the first and most ancient; *Teva*, Cornish, to grow; *Tyfu*, Welsh, to cause to grow; *Dhov*, to come; *Tubu*, Fiji, origin and growth; *Tapairu*, Maori, the *first-born as a female;* also the Niece and Nephew, the Sister's Children; *Teibe*, Irish, the Mother Nature; *Tyba*, Arabic. In Fijian the *Tubu-na* are the ancestors, but more especially the Godmother. *Davke*, or *Davkina*, is the Babylonian Mother Earth, or the Abyss over which the god Hea presided. The first of the Two Truths being Water accounts for the beginning in and from the Abyss, the Tepht of Source. Tepht (Eg.) is a dual or feminine form equivalent to Teph-Teph, and in Fijian *Dave-Dave* is the name for a Channel from the Source. Mystically the Source is denoted by

Tef (Eg.), to ooze, drip, bedew, menstruate.

Tevah, Hebrew, to menstruate.

Tep, Sanskrit, to distil, ooze, drop.

Dhav, Sanskrit, to flow, to give milk as a cow, to cleanse, purify or, primarily, to menstruate.

Diva, or *defa*, Zulu, first menstruation.

Tabau, Yarra, (Australian), damp.

Davi, Fiji, flow of liquids, expressly from the source.

Tuphan, Arabic, inundation or deluge.

Damu, Assyrian, blood.

Tombo (Xosa Kaffir), fountain, source, spring, shoots, germs, malt.

Tomba, applied to the female at the time of first menstruation.

This root, with its variants, is an Inner African type-name for water and wet,

A Tebi, wet, Limba.	*Dsape*, water, Dsuku.	*Ndsab*, water, Bagba.
Isof ,, Kano.	*Ndsib* ,, Bayon.	*Ndsob* ,, Momenya.
Sabe ,, Toma.	*Ndsab* ,, Kum.	

Teb (Eg.), the Mother of Source, was a personification of the Womb and *Mamma*, and the female breast is named

Debe, in Diwala.	*Debor*, in Konguan.	*Diben*, in Nyombe.
Debe, in Mfut.	*Dibel*, in Kanyika.	*Dibele*, in Songo.
Dibe, in Murundo.		

The procession of the Gods from the Abyss of beginning is not as Taylor the Platonist would phrase it, an ineffable unfolding into light of the one *principle* of all things. Damascius says truly, " *The Babylonians, like the rest of the barbarians, pass over in silence the one principle of the universe, and they constitute Two, Tavthe and Apason.*" [1]

This Beginning is followable. The earliest Myth-makers knew of no *one principle*, or abstract spiritual entity in the Greek or still more modern sense. They observed phenomena and represented objective manifestations. Their beginning was simply the Oneness that opened in giving birth and in bifurcating; hence the type of the female first, the one Great Mother of all. An illustration of the primitive profundity or the beginning with the Abyss of Darkness and the Waters, may be found in the name given to their magicians by the Finns, who call them " *Abysses.*" [2] In like manner the Akkadian Hea, the God of Wisdom and repository of all science, one of whose types was the Fish, another the Serpent, was the representative of the Abyss. The Abyss was in the North; the *Kiba-Kiba*, Fijian, or opening into the under-world. This is *Kheb-Kheb* in Egyptian, a name of lower and northern Egypt. It was also called the Khepsh, or pool of the water-cow, Khep, the Typhonian genitrix who first brought to birth in or from the Abyss. The water-cow (Hippopotamus) Khep, or Keb, has the Inner African name of *Ngabbu* in Fulah. As Khepsh it supplies the Pahlavi *Geush* for the typical Cow which was also the earth; and the Greek *Gaes*. The degrees of development are each preserved. The Earth being considered flat, the Abyss, however sunken and concealed, was still *in* the earth, or in the vast pool (Sh) where the hippopotamus and crocodile had their habitat.

The ancient Mother was pourtrayed as the pregnant water-cow in front and the crocodile behind. Thus she represented the two primal elements of water and breath, or the breathing life which she produced from the water. In a far later, because human type, the Hindu Goddess Mayâ impersonates the Two Truths, the flowing and the fixed, as the un-girt and the up-bound. She hovers over the waters of Source and presses her two breasts with both hands; the feminine fount that streams with liquid life. The face and upper part of her body lighten with the radiance of the fire that vivifies, the spirit of life, the second of the Two Truths. Within the cincture of her scarf she is seen to be the bearing Mother. It is also observable

[1] Cory, *Ancient Fragments*, p. 92; ed. 1876.
[2] Tchihatchef, *Voyage Scientifique dans l'Altai Oriental*, p. 45.

that her figure and aureole of glory form the Cross symbol corresponding to the Ru and three-quarter Cross of the Ankh-sign.
Her scarf also represents the Tie.

In the second phase the genitrix as a personification of space
below and above, of Darkness and Light, of Water and Air, of
Blood and Breath, divides in twain and is then pourtrayed in *two
characters*. A passage in the Avesta, translated by Haug, says, the
"*Wise have manifested this universe as a Duality*." The word
rendered duality is *Dûm*, identified with the Sanskrit Dvam
(dvamdam, a pair), a word that is not found elsewhere in the
Avesta; hence, says Max Müller, it is not likely the uncertainty

GUIGNIAUT, J. D. *Religions de l'Antiquité, Atlas Planche,* 19. No. 103.

attaching to it will be removed.[1] This duality, however, is
shown by the hieroglyphic double heaven the *Tem* or Tem.t,
with the sign of the Twin-total. Also the Chinese *Thima* is
the Goddess of the dual heaven: and *Atem* (Eg.) is the Mother
Goddess of time. The Welsh have their equivalent of *Dvam* in *Dwyf,*
called the self-existent Cause or origin, from which they derive a pair
of divine Ancestors, as Dwyfan the upper, and Dwyfach the lower, or
lesser Cause. These are the dual heaven when referred back to
phenomena. The genitrix of heaven or earth, in her two characters,
was always the producer and bringer-forth in space; and the gods,
whether elementary, stellar, lunar or solar, were produced and brought

[1] *Chips,* v. i. p. 141.

forth by the mother, the sole supreme primordial being in (or as) earth and heaven.

Hor-Apollo points out that the Egyptians thought it absurd to designate Heaven in the masculine, τὸν οὐρανὸν, but represented. it in the feminine, τὴν οὐρανὸν inasmuch as the *generation* of the Sun, Moon, and the rest of the stars is perfected in it, which is the peculiar property of the female.[1] The Heaven, whether Upper or Lower, was the bringer-forth, therefore feminine. Wheresoever the fatherhood is applied to the heaven itself the myth is later. The Two Heavens, or Heaven and Earth, were represented by the Two Divine Sisters as Neith and Seti (or Nephthys), or Isis and Nupe, who were two forms of the first One, the Mother and Sister in the earliest sociology. These Two Sisters were represented not only as Two Goddesses, for in the Cult of Atum at Heliopolis, the Two Sisters Urti, who bore the name of the double-uræi Crown of Maternity, were the Servants of the god. These likewise agree with the Two Women of the Temple that were carrried away from Thebes by certain Phœnicians and became the first who established oracles in Lybia and Greece.[2]

The author of the " Book of God "[3] speaks of a picture of Paradise described in Brahminic theology. At the top of the seven-stepped mount there is a plain and in the midst a *square* table surrounded by *Nine* precious stones, and a silver bell. On the table there is a silver rose called *Tamara Pua*, which is the shrine of Two Women, who are only one in reality, but two in appearance according as they are seen from below or above ; the celestial or terrestrial one. In the first aspect the twin woman is *Briga Sri* the *Lady of the Mouth ;* in the second she is *Tara Sri*, the *lady of the Tongue*. This dual being was depicted in Egypt as Pekht, the Lioness. Pekh means division, and the genitrix divided into the double-mouth. One Pekh (or Peh) is the sign of the hinder part (the back) the North, the mouth of birth ; the fore part (pekh-pekh or pekhti) is the mouth in front and therefore the mouth of the tongue. The double mouth typified the two horizons and the divided lioness was equivalent to the two sisters who represented earth and heaven.

In Chinese poetry the heaven is considered to be both father and mother.[4] But in ancient Egypt, before the time of Seb, the plural parent was female alone ; female above and female below ; female as the emaner of the waters of source (or blood) and female as the mother of breath, the gestator. *Hence Seb also appears as the genitrix.* In Chinese *Tien* is the double heaven or heaven and earth as upper and lower of two. Thus Ti denotes heaven and earth ; and Shang-ti the Supreme One, is of necessity dual, like the Egyptian Penti for the one. The heavens are called Ten or Tien in

[1] B. i. 11. [2] Herod, b. ii. 54.
[3] P. 13. [4] Chalmers, *Origin of the Chinese*, p. 14.

HH 2

Amoy. Tem or Ten (Eg.) signifies the division into two halves, and this is the root meaning of Ten or ten-ten in Amoy, and Tan in Chinese, to cut in two. We have the same duality in *dawn* for morning and *den* for evening.

The Hindu Aditi is the great mother of the Gods who becomes twain. As the mother who yielded milk for them, she is identical with the cow of heaven in Egypt. Aditi was the primæval form of Dyaus, the sky divinity, who appears as such in the Rig-Veda, however rarely. She alternates with Diti as mother of the embryo that was *divided into seven parts*, the Seven who were also called the Seven Adityas.[1] She became Diti in her second character, and is identical in both with the one original genitrix who opens and divides in all the ancient mythologies. The Aryanists who begin with little less than infinitude insist that *Aditi* signifies infinity, or the infinite, as a mental concept. Aditi, says Max Müller, is in reality the earliest name invented to express the infinite! Professor Benfey remarks that the conception of this goddess is still dark. Roth understands Aditi to mean the boundlessness of heaven as opposed to the limitation of earth. Aditi is, of course, the negative of Diti, and it is by aid of the latter that we have to recover foothold in phenomena. Then we shall find that the un-finited is not the infinite ; the unbounded is not the boundless infinitude ; timelessness is not necessarily the eternal. *Diti* in Sanskrit denotes cutting, splitting and dividing. *Thut* also signifies splitting and dividing. *Tithi* is the fifteenth lunar day, the day of dividing. So *Tutua* in Tahitian, signifies splitting in two, and in the Inner African languages we find *Didi* in Timbo; *Didi* Salum ; *Didi*, Goboru ; *Didi*, Kano, as the type name for number two, the divided one. Aditi has a mystical form on certain Hindu talismans under the form of *Athithi*, the un-fixed, the undefined, or un-established; and this was the sole character preceding that of Diti. Aditi was the primordial undivided One, the All, who when divided as the Egyptian goddess of the north, bifurcates in Uati, the dual One ; or as Omoroka and the Cow she is cut in two and becomes Diti the divided. Aditi produced Diti by a sort of self-splitting which may be compared with that of the entozoa, molluscoids and annelids ; she being twy-fold in herself as the representative of the Two Truths.

The passage from a "Mother Heaven" to a "Father Heaven" is easily traced. The upper of the two females represented the breathing force as the inspirer of Soul. This being the superior power of two, it came to be considered masculine, and was then pourtrayed as a male attribute of the motherhood. There is an extract rendered by Bunsen from the "Great Announcement," a work attributed to Simon, the Samaritan, which has a bearing on this change of sex in the heaven. Simon teaches that the root of all things bifurcated in two powers. Of these, the one appears above,

[1] Muir, *Sanskrit Texts*, vol. iv. p. 145 ; vol. v. p. 39 (note), and 147, note.

and is the Great Power, the mind of the universe, *directing all things male;* the other appears below, the great thought, female, producing all things. Hence, being thus ranged one against the other, they form a *syzygia* (a pair, *Copula*), and make manifest the intermediate interval, the incomprehensible Air. In this air is the Father, supporting all things. This is "*him who stands*"—as did Khem-Horus, Mentu or Khepr-Ra—and who was of a dual nature. These Gnostic evolutions, whether Simonian, Valentinian or Marcosian, were but a continuation of the mythical characters in a later phase of thought. The great power was the female inspirer of the male, his Sakti; she who was the primary begetter as communicator of the breath of life; next, begetting was identified as masculine, and the upper was then called the father Heaven.

Our British Druids must have possessed the myths and symbols of Egypt right to the inmost core of the matter. The Great Mother who bifurcates in the two heavens, or the two divine sisters, is represented by Ked in two persons as Keridwen and Ogyrwen. Also her daughter repeats the dual phase. She has two names. As Kreirwy her name denotes the token of the egg (*i.e.* Virginalis) as Llywy she is the emaner of the egg; *i.e.* Matrona. The double daughter represents the two phases of the female nature. Kreirwy is the British Proserpine, she who in the Greek mythos was fated to dwell alternately in the upper and lower heavens, or the underworld. Another form of her name is *Kreirddylad,* the token of the flowing or the mystical period, and this is the original of Cordelia by name. She keeps her character too as the dumb Cordelia of the drama in which our *Sige* of the Druidic Mystery is the Silent one, the Mer-*Seker* (Eg.) type of the flowing (Nile or Nature), as a divinity humanized for ever.

"*Of the Vivific Goddesses,*" says Proclus, "*they call the one older but the other younger.*"[1] These two forms of the Mother appear in the Mangaian mythology as Vari and Papa. Vari is the very beginning in the Abyss, the Polynesian *Sige* who dwells in the Mute land at the bottom of Avaiki, where she is the originator of all things, from the water or mud of source. She is the blood-mother who creates her children from pieces of her own flesh, these therefore are equivalent to the embryos of A-diti. Vari is the first form of the Great Mother and Papa, answering to Diti, is the second. It is Papa who produces the first human being in a perfect human shape, as the Mother of Breath or soul called Foundation.[2] In a dramatic song of creation Vari, the first of the two is celebrated as the source of all, and the singers claim descent from her, the Mother, alone, "*We have no Father whatever; Vari alone made us,*" and "*Vari, the originator of all things, sheltered Papa under her wing.*"

[1] Proclus in *Timæus*, b. iii.
[2] Gill, pp. 1—7.

The mother was the first *papa*, and remains so in some of the oldest languages like the Australian.

Pappy,	mother,	Hamilton, Aust.	*Paapie*,	mother,	Kulkyne, Aust.
Pepie	„	Camperdown, Aust.	*Bab*	„	Akkadian.
Papie	„	Upper Richardson, Aust.	*Babia*,	the Great Mother, Khetan.
Bap	„	Lake Hindmarsh, Aust.	*Vavy*,	female, Malagasy.
Baboo	„	Tyntyndyer, Aust.	*Fafine*	„	Tongan.
Pabook	„	Gunbower, Aust.	*Papa*	„	Egyptian.

True, this is an Inner African type-name for the father, *because the one word first named the producer or duplicator in languages that did not denote sex.*

Mythology keeps the pre-historic record of the past. It shows the mother was the first person distinguished from the herd. Descent from one mother was the first bond of blood. The sister was second. These two are typified as the Two Divine Sisters, Isis and Nephthys, who are at one and the same time the two sisters and wives of Horus in his two characters. The "Two women" appear as the two wives of Jacob "*which two did build the House of Israel*."[1] The King of Burmah has two especial wives, the superior and inferior one. Manaboju, in the North American Indian legends, has two squaws. The Hottentot possesses his elder wife, *Geiris*, the great wife, and *Aris* the younger wife, as did Heitsi-eibib their first ancestor. The Kaffir chief has two typical wives ; one, the great wife ; the other the wife of the right hand ; one being called the Elephantess, whilst his great wife is called the Lioness.[2] And here, although the fatherhood is individualized the mode of distinguishing, dividing, and expanding by means of the two women is still extant. Each of these two wives produces an heir. The first is the principal heir, but a portion of the tribe is allotted to the Benjamin or son of the right hand, with which he constitutes a new clan ;[3] and so they spread abroad, even as men did originally in the first Two Castes. It may be noticed that the Namaqua Khoi-khoi have the two women as their two wives in a curious combination of polygamy and polyandry. With these, two chiefs hold four wives in common between them. This is the twin-wife system doubled, as if they might represent the twin-brothers of Mythology married to the genitrix in her dual character of the two sisters.

The beginning on earth shows why the celestial beginning is with and from the great mother in earth and heaven, whose two characters become the two sisters. And the dual figure of Isis or Neith as the earth or lower hemisphere, and Nupe as the starry heaven represents the two women, the two sisters from whom the Kamilaroi claim their descent. The upper one is a common figure of the Egyptian *Pê* (heaven), and this alone is sufficient to determine a matter previously alluded to, against Brugsch Pasha,[4] who says the Egyptians did not

---

[1] Ruth iv. 11.
[3] Theal, *Kaffir Folk-lore*, p. 6.
[2] Burton, *Dahome*, vol. ii. appendix, 4.
[4] *Book of Beginnings*, vol. i. sect. i.

reckon by the right hand east and left hand west. Their figure of heaven and earth does double duty and *shows* the south as front, the north as hinder part; with the east for the right hand and west for the left. This can only be illustrated by *one figure* in the Egyptian fashion. The attitude of this, the upper figure, *is equal to two figures for south and north as front and back;* and *the position of the face turns the natural left arm into the right, so that we have the face for the south, the hinder-part for the north; the right hand being east, and the left west.* This is supplemented and enforced by the position of the lower figure. When one stands with the face to the north to represent the south, the face and front of heaven, as did Sut (or Sothis), the east is on the right hand, but it then needs another figure to stand for the north as hinder-part, and this would be the other female half. In all typology, the west and north are feminine, the left hand quarter and the hinder half of heaven. In the Isubu language, *Dia da modi*, the female, is the *left*, because inferior hand. Also, when the death of an Australian black occurs after sunset, the nearest of kin, a male and female watch by it all night. Two fires are lighted; one toward the east, the other toward the west, and it is the male who watches eastward, the female westward.[1]

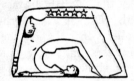

The Goddess of the Great Bear and northern heaven was the bringer-forth in the Abyss of earth in one of two characters, that of the mother earth; in the other she brought forth above as the mother heaven, the feminine Dyaus who was Tep above and Tepht below. The duality of the genitrix which commenced in the division of earth and heaven was finally deposited in the zodiac of twelve signs. First, she was the Abyss of birth represented by the dragon; second, the Goddess of the Great Bear; third, the Wateress with streaming breasts in the Hermean zodiac; and lastly, she was pourtrayed as the virgin mother in the sign of Virgo and the Bringer-forth in the sign of Pisces, where she is half-fish and half-human, and thus combines the two truths of water and breath in one image. Ishtar-Bilit, the genitrix in her dual character of Venus above and Venus below the horizon was worshipped in the temples of Syria, as at Hierapolis, under the form of a statue with a golden dove on her head, one of her names there being Semiramis. Lucian calls Semiramis the daughter of Derketo (Atergatis) whom he saw in Phœnicia as a woman with the tail of a fish, whereas, at Hierapolis she was woman all over. The fish denoted the element of water; the

[1] Smyth, vol. i. 107.

dove signified the soul of breath that was derived from the mother. The breath or spirit of life was first perceived in the motherhood, and the two truths of the water and breath were assigned to the mother. This accounts for the feminine form of the creative spirit in Hebrew. Julius Firmicus observes, "the Assyrians and part of the Africans wish the air to have the supremacy of the elements, for they have consecrated it under the name of Juno."[1] And according to Proclus, "Juno imports the generation of the soul."[2] Dido, who at Carthage was pourtrayed with a beard like the standing image of Aphrodite at Paphos, had a second character in Anna. These two divine sisters, the *bona cœlestis* and *inferna cœlestis* were worshipped, the one, Dido, with dark bloody rites; the other, Anna, the charming one, with cheerful ceremonies. They divided into the good goddess of the upper heaven and the evil one of the lower. Pausanias[3] tells us there was a temple of Aphrodite, and the only such one known to him, which had two storeys, the lower consecrated to the armed goddess; the upper to Aphrodite-Morpho who was sitting veiled with her feet bound. Pausanias thought the fetters showed the attachment of women to their husbands. The tie symbol denotes the gestator, the bearing mother.

One of the legends in the Mahâbhârata, describes Kaçyapas as making two wives fruitful. One is Kadrû, the dark or red one; the other is Vinatâ, the swollen one, that is the gestator, the mother of breath, she who emanes the egg, out of which issued the serpent.[4]

Sufficient has now been shown of the Great Mother in her two phases of the virgin and gestator, also as the two sisters of sociology.

It is the most ancient and most primitive myths that are the most universal; and one of the most universal is that of the Twin-Brothers, born of the genitrix either in her single or her dual character. The Abyss of Darkness, is said, in the Bundahish, to be in the middle of the earth, and to have been formed there when the Evil Spirit pierced and rushed into the earth at the time when "*all the possessions of the world were changing into duality*," and the conflict and contention of high and low began.[5] It is also said in the Bundahish that "*Revelation* is the explanation of both these spirits together"; the two spirits of light and darkness that manifest in space and time.[6] This was in the division or bifurcation of all beginning. The Abyss of Darkness became the hell as antithesis of heaven. The evening and the morning were the twin boundary in the first formation of night and day. And in Hebrew the evening or darkness has the same name as the raven, the blackbird, the *Gareb*, identical with the Latin *Corvus*, old German *Kraben;* old Norse

---

[1] Firmicus, *De Errore*, cap. iv. p. 9.
[2] Proclus, lib. vi. cap. xxii., v. ii. p. 76.
[3] iii. xv. 8.　　[4] *Mahâbh.* iii. xiv. 480.
[5] *Bundahish*, ch. iii. 27.
[6] Ch. i. 3.

Harfn ; Greek *Korōnē ;* Maltese *Hrab ;* Scotch *Corbie,* which modifies into crow. The same word in Egyptian *Khereb* signifies a first formation, the model figure. " *The evening (Gareb) and the morning were the first day,*" and the raven was the type of the dark side. The dove is one form of the Bird of Light. This in Lithuanic is the *Golub ;* the *Golambo* in Polish, and *Columba* in Latin. Both birds were equally types of the first formation and both are named from that origin. The raven and dove are equivalent to the Bird of Darkness and the Bird of Light, which constitute the double-headed type of Sut-Horus and Sut-Nubti in Egypt.

It was argued in the earlier volumes of this work that the legend of Sut-Horus was pre-monumental, and belonged to the time of the Shus-en-Har, to whom an historical period of 13,420 years is assigned. This view has since been corroborated by the inscriptions discovered at Sakkarah. In the later phase the twin-brothers are called the " Sons of Osiris," as was the way after the fatherhood had been established. They are described as having quarrelled and fought for the succession, whereupon Taht intervened, and assigned to each his domain, one having the north, the other the south. Hence, the first division of the heaven, or the land of Egypt, by north and south was the result of the quarrel and division of the twin-born Brothers.[1] These are the Two Brothers of universal mythology, and the myth is now proved to be incalculably ancient in Egypt ; not a later importation from Asia as some had previously thought.

In the Magic Papyrus, the genitrix in two characters which may be identified with Earth and Heaven, or the Two Horizons of the Solar Myth is represented by Anata (Neith), and Astarte, the " *Two Great Goddesses who conceive and do not breed.*" These two are said to be *opened* by Sut, and to be *shut up* or sealed by Horus.[2] The figure of Sut-Horus was at first a dual type of that which is negative and positive in phenomena, whether as the alternate dark and light, or the double lunation, or the twin horizons, represented by the human being, as the impubescent boy, and the virile male ; the one who opened and sealed the genitrix in his two characters. The earliest phenomenal form of the Twins as darkness (Sut) and light (Horus), shows us why Taht, the lunar god, should be chosen as mediator betwixt them and the determinator of their two boundaries, because he came between the darkness of night and the light of day as Lord of the lunar orb.

Sut-Horus then is pourtrayed as the double manifestor of light and darkness on the two horizons, with the heads of two birds, one being the black vulture, the Neh ; the other the gold hawk of the solar-fire. It is a figure of the Two Truths of day and dark, the two elements of water and fire with other applications of the type to phenomena.

---

[1] Pierret, *Panthéon*, p. 49 ; *Ritual*, ch. cxxiii ; Plutarch, *Of Isis and Osiris.*
[2] *Magic Papyrus*, Harris, pp. 3, 9.

Horus was said to duplicate or rise again as the White God. "*Black and crystal are the faces of those attached to him.*"[1] In the Avesta the Good Spirit is white, the Bad Spirit black. *A am ah ve ho*, the white man above, is likewise the Shienne name for god.[2] In the earlier time the White or Light God was the Golden. Another name of this dual divinity is Sut-Nub, the original of Sothis-Canopus in the stellar phase ; and Nub signifies the Golden, Sut is black, like the English *Soot*. The Sut-Horus or Sut-Nub reappears in Australia as War-pil, the male eagle or the hawk eagle who represents the star Sirius (Sothis-Sut), and War who represents the star Canopus. Thus the Egyptian Sut-Har (or Sut-Nub), the dual Har in Egypt is identical with the dual War of the Victorian Blacks ; and the two-faced divinity is represented by the stars Sothis and Canopus. In the northern part of Victoria the natives say the beings who created all things were the eagle and the crow. And the hawk-eagle and crow are one with the bird of light and the black bird which form the dual type of the well-known Sut-Horus, or Sut-Nub in Egypt.

There was continual warfare between the twin-brothers, the crow taking every possible advantage of his nobler foe, the eagle ; but the latter had ample revenge for his insults and injuries. At length the deadly struggle ceased, and peace was established by an agreement that the Murray Blacks *should be divided into two classes, those of the Eagle-hawk, the Mak-quarra, and those of the Kil-parra or Crow* Totem. The same war is described in the Irish myth between the two brothers, Heber and Heremon, and it was perpetuated in Egypt as the war that went on for ever between Sut and Horus, in the escha-talogical phase of the mythos. This identification of Canopus is very remarkable, for, according to Plutarch, Canopus was the helmsman of the Solar God. His wife's name was Menuthis, a form of the old suckler Typhon. In the inscriptions on the tablet of San, Sut-Nub is called the overthrower of the enemies of the Sun in the Boat of Millions of Years. The Golden Sut, the Golden Dog (jackal) was represented by the Golden Star, and a learned priest told Aristides the orator, that Canopus signified the Golden Floor. The Golden Hawk of the Sut-Horus type is one of the golden images of the male Sut.

The Australian Blacks of Victoria account themselves to be very great astronomers. That is, they have preserved some of the primitive types which were first stelled in the heavens. We shall find they have the Great Mother of the Beginnings not only in her earliest phase, as the bringer-forth in Space, but also in Time as the Bear, or Goddess of the Bears and the Waters. The Bushmen also identify the star Sirius as the Great Mother, or the Grandmother of Canopus.[3] Sirius or Sothis was the star of Sut. In its feminine type it

---

[1] *Inscrip. of Darius*, line 42.   [2] Schoolcraft, vol. i. p. 310.
[3] Bleek, p. 18.

represented the Great Mother of Beginnings in the Southern Heaven; and Canopus (Nub) is her starry son, in a pre-solar Mythos. Thus we find the same mythos in Egypt and Victoria, whilst the connecting link supplied by the Bushmen serves as a bridge by which we can cross from Inner Africa to Australia. Although not so obvious in every case, yet the entire system of the most ancient Mythology which Egypt shows to be Kamite, is as surely one and the same in its origin.

The Orientals called the raven the "*Bird of Separation*,"[1] and it is primary, because darkness was reckoned to be first. The Bird of Light issues from it in the double-headed Sut. The rock sculptures of the North American Indians show the contending twins as Gods of the north and south who continue the conflict for ever on behalf of warm and cold weather. The God of the south has two birds, the plover and crow, the equivalent of the hawk and the raven. These are sent out when he wants warm weather, and contests the supremacy of the world with the northern divinity. The crow, however, is the representative of the dark power.[2]

The British Arthur must likewise have been represented by the two birds of light and darkness, for it is an extant Cornish and Welsh superstition that King Arthur did not die but transformed into a *raven*, in the shape of which he is living still. In Jarvis' translation of *Don Quixote*[3] it is said that in the Annals of England Arthur, whom the Spaniards know as King Artus (Art, Irish, is the Great Bear), it is a recorded tradition that Arthur did not die but was changed into a raven by magic art and that he would rise again and reign; "*for which reason it cannot be proved that from that time to this any Englishman has killed a raven.*" The raven is our Phœnix, the Bennu of the resurrection. So the Raven remained a type sacred to Apollo, in Greece, who was the Horus of Egypt.[4]

The earliest form of the motherhood is inseparable from the son who takes a dual shape under various types, as the child and pubescent youth who preceded the fatherhood, or the Child of darkness and the hero of light.

Vari, the Mangaian Great Mother, gives birth to the dual child her Sut-Horus who is half-human and half-fish, the division being like the two halves of a human body. He has two magnificent eyes, rarely visible at the same time. Whilst one shines in the heaven

---

[1] Bochartus, *Hierozoicon*, lib. i. c. iii. t. l. cols. 19, 20.
[2] Schoolcraft, pl. 41, vol. iv.
[3] B. ii. ch. v.
[4] Both birds were united in the Phœnix as they are in our Royston or Dunstable Crow, which is white and black, and is called the *Fineog* in Irish. The phœnix is the Bird of Transformation, and it is an English superstition that the cuckoo transforms into a sparrow-hawk in spring. So in Plutarch's *Life of Aratos*, when the cuckoo asks the other birds why they flee from him, who is not ferocious, they tell him they fear the future sparrow-hawk!

above, the other illumines Savaiki. These are now supposed to be the Sun and Moon, as we find them in an address to Num: "*O thou Lord of Lords, Khnum, whose right eye is the sun's disk, whose left eye is the moon.*" [1]

The first Twins are two Brothers. They consist of a bright being who is held to be divine, and a dark one who comes to be considered devilish, and who began as the devil in physical phenomena. In the beginning the Mother Darkness opened and gave birth to her brood of elementaries as the evil-working powers. This beginning with darkness internal and external, and the starting from the night side of phenomena will account for the dark power, the deity as devil, being the uppermost of two with many of the primitive tribes. It was the dark power born of darkness, whose shadow put out the light, that was first dreaded by the black race; the influence earliest feared and longest believed in, whose type survived in Egypt as the black Sut, the black *Hak* or *Kak*, and the black Osiris. Although the latter were but forms of the nocturnal sun, they continued the type of terror in a psychotheistic phase.

The devil of a God who is recognised by the West Coast Negroes is black, malignant, and mischievous. How should poor Caliban have apprehended otherwise when his chief teachers were wrath and danger; the Blackness spitting fire and growling as if heaven were fuller of wild beasts than the forests of earth; the snap of the crocodile, the sting of the serpent, the stroke of the sun, the whirlwind, flood, and all the torments of incomprehensible disease? If there were a conscious power postulated behind phenomena it must appear of a very bad nature to Caliban.

Burton asked the Negroes of the East Coast about the deity, and they wanted to know where he was to be found, that they might slay him. They said, "*Who but he lays waste our homes, and kills our wives and cattle?*" Such being their very natural interpretation of the intemperate phenomena of nature.

In the Bundahish the Evil demon and Tempter IS the darkness, and he shouts out of the dark his insidious, vile suggestions to the primal human pair, Mashya and Mashyoi. Their turning aside from the right way to worship the dark power is represented as the "Fall." But this form of *Kotou* from fear was primordial, the root of a religious awe, and as such the feeling has been sedulously fostered up to the present time! The Dark Power was primal.

An evil being that is propitiated and flattered or glorified so that it may not work any harm is always found to be related to natural phenomena which are inimical to man. He is connected by the Hottentots with thunder as well as with disease and death. Dr. Hahn shows that the worship of Gaunab, the bad being or inimical power,

---

[1] Inscription of the time of Darius III. Museum at Naples.

who dwells in the Black Sky, was probably of a much older date than that of the good being Tsuni-Goam.

The Gabe Bushmen, the Ai Bushmen, the Nunin, and others, know, fear, and propitiate the evil-doer Gaunab, whereas the good power, Tsuni-Goam, is entirely unknown or unrecognised amongst them.[1] In Mangaia it was the dark god Rongo who was the principal deity of the Twins, and who had to be appeased by human sacrifice. With various other races the dark power is the worshipful, *because* it works harm to man.

Dr. Hahn learned from an old Habobe-Namaqua that Tsuni-Goam was a powerful chief of the *Khoi-Khoi* (Hottentots). In fact he was the first from whom they took their origin. Tsuni-Goam went to war with Gaunab because the latter always killed great numbers of Tsuni-Goam's people. In the continual conflict, however, the good god, though repeatedly overpowered by Gaunab, *grew stronger and stronger with every battle he waged.* At last he grew strong and big enough to give his enemy a fatal blow behind the ear, which put an end to *Gaunab.* But whilst *Gaunab* was expiring he gave *Tsuni-Goam* a stroke on the knee, from which the conqueror received his name of *Tsuni-Goam* or "Wounded-Knee." Henceforth he could never walk properly because of his lameness, but he was victor for the future. He could do wonderful things, and was very wise. He could tell what would happen in years to come. He died several times, and several times he rose again. When he came back there was a great festival of rejoicing. He dwells in a bright and beautiful heaven, and his opponent *Gaunab* dwells in a dark heaven, quite separate from the heaven of Tsuni-Goam.

There are several renderings of Tsuni-Goam's name and story. In Bleek's Hottentot fables we have another version of the Twins. "*At first they were two! One had made a large hole in the ground, and sitting by it told passers-by to throw a stone at his forehead. The stone, however, rebounded, killing the thrower, who fell into the hole. At last Heitsi-Eibip was told that many people died in this way. So he arose, and went to the man, who challenged Heitsi-Eibip to throw a stone at him. The latter declined, being too prudent; but he drew the man's attention to something on one side, and while he turned round to look at it Heitsi-Eibip hit him behind the ear, so that he died, and fell into his own hole. After that there was peace, and people lived happily.*"[2]

Another variant reminds one of the negro chaunt, "*Chase the devil round the stump.*" The two opponents hunt each other round the hole or abyss. We are told that "*All men who came near to that hole were pushed into it by Ga-gorip (the pusher into the hole), as he knew well where it lay. Whilst thus employed there came the Heitsi-Eibip (also*

[1] *Tsuni-Goam*, p. 86.
[2] *Hottentot Fables and Tales*, by W. H. T. Bleek, p. 77.

called Heigeip) and saw how the Ga-gorip treated the people. Then these two began to hunt each other round the hole, saying, 'Push the Heigeip down,' 'Push the Ga-gorip down.' With these words they hunted each other round for some time, but at last the Heigeip was pushed down. Then he said to the hole 'support me a little'; and it did. Being thus supported he came out, and they hunted each other again with the same words. A second time the Heigeip was pushed down, and he spoke the same words, 'support me a little,' and thus got out again. Once more these two hunted after each other, till at last the Ga-gorip was pushed down, and HE *came not up again. Since that day men breathed freely, and had rest from their enemy, because he was vanquished."* [1]

The same conflict of the Twins is celebrated in the legends of the Australian aborigines. The story told by a man of the Wa-woo-rong or Yarra tribe is that "*Pundjel was the first man. He made every thing; the second man (Kar-ween) he made also, as well as two wives for Kar-ween. But Pundjel made no wife for himself, and after a lapse of time he came to want Kar-ween's wives—but he watched them very jealously, and wouldn't let Pundjel get near them. The latter, how-ever, was clever enough to steal both the wives in the night, and take them away. Kar-ween, taking some spears, pursued Pundjel, but he could find neither him nor his wives. In a short time Pundjel came back, bringing with him two women. He asked Kar-ween to fight on the following day, and proposed that the women should fall to whoever conquered. To this Kar-ween agreed, having a different plan in his mind, which was this, to make Ingargiull or corrobboree. Kar-ween spoke to Waugh (the crow) and asked him to make a corrobboree. And many crows came, and they made a great light in the air, and they sang as they danced round. Whilst they were thus singing Pundjel danced. Kar-ween took a spear, and threw it at him, and wounded him a little in the leg, but not in such a manner as to hurt Pundjel much. Pundjel however was very angry, and, seizing a spear, threw it at Kar-ween, and with such good aim that it went through Kar-ween's thigh, who could walk about no more, became sick, lean as a skeleton, whereupon Pundjel made Kar-ween a crane, and that bird was thereafter called Kar-ween. Pundjel was the conqueror, and had the women.*"

In another version we learn that the two beings who created all things had severally the form of the crow and the eagle. The conflict that was waged between the rival powers is thus preserved in song:—

Thinj-arni balkee Mako;	Nato-panda Kambe-ar tona.
Knee strike cow;	Spear father of him.

The meaning of which is "*Strike the cow on the knee, I will spear the father.*"

The war was maintained with vigour for a long time. The crow

---

[1] *Hottentot Fables and Tales,* pp. 78 and 79.

took every possible advantage of his nobler foe the eagle; but the latter generally had ample revenge for injuries and insults. Out of their enmities and final agreement arose the two classes, and thence a law governing marriages amongst the classes.

Mr. Bulmer says:—"*The Blacks of the Murray are divided into two classes of the Mak-quarra or Eagle and the Kil-parra or Crow. If the man be Mak-quarra the woman must be Kil-parra. The children take their caste from the mother, not from the father. The Murray blacks never deviate from this rule. A man would as soon marry his sister as a woman of the caste to which he belongs. He calls a woman of the same class Wurtoa (sister).*" [1]

Here we find the crow and the eagle, the birds of darkness and of light, are the two totemic signs of the people that were first divided into two different castes, just as they are the two symbols of the earliest divisions into light and dark, or the heaven into south and north, which shows what was meant by calling the raven the "*Bird of separation.*" Moreover, we see the beginning with the Dark Power and type, the Black Bird being for a long time the superior one, and the conquest made by the Bird of Light over his brother. This is shown in another way. "Waugh" is one name of the crow and of the "Second Man"—he who was first in time. In the Phœnician legend, according to Sanchoniathon, Hypsuranius and Usous are a form of the two brothers who quarrel and are at enmity with each other. These, the typical dividers, are said to have been begotten when the intercourse between the sexes was so promiscuous that women accompanied with any man they might chance to meet, and men with their own mothers. [2] The Eskimos of Greenland relate that in the beginning there were two brothers, one of whom said, "*There shall be Night and there shall be Day, and men shall die one after another.*" But the second said, "*There shall be no Day but only Night all the time, and men shall live for ever.*" Then they wrestled for the supremacy; the dark one was worsted in the long struggle and the day triumphed at last. [3] The Singhalese have a pair of twins, Gopolu and Menkara, born of a Queen on the Coromandel Coast. The mother died and the twins were suckled by a cow. The brothers quarrelled, and Gopolu being slain was changed into an Evil Demon who sends diseases from his abode in a Banyan tree in Arangodde. Mangara is worshipped as god or demi-god. The Mexican Great Mother who was called the woman with the serpent, and the woman of our flesh, was represented as the mother of the twins. She is depicted on a monument in the act of conversing with the serpent whilst her twin children are standing behind her; they are differently coloured in token of their diverse characters, and one of them is

[1] *Aborigines of Victoria*, by R. Brough Smyth, vol. i, pp. 86, 423, 424.
[2] Cory, *Anct. Fragments*.
[3] Bishop Paul Egede, *Nachrichten von Grönland*, &c. p. 157.

likewise pourtrayed as overcoming or slaying the other. These Twins
were also born of Cihuacohuatl as Two Serpents. Her name is the
Female Serpent, which shows her to be a form of the Dragon Tiamat
and Typhon the genitrix. She gave birth to the Twins of Light and
Darkness as her two serpents. One is, however, considered male, the
other female; and to these the Aztecs referred the origin of mankind.
Hence Twins and Serpents are synonymous as *Cocohua,—Côhua*
being the singular for serpent, *Cocohua* the plural.

The Mangaians relate that the genitrix who took the dual form of
the Two Women, as Vari below and Papa above, bore two children.
Tangaroa, the *fair one*, was the first by right, and ought to have
been the first-born, but was said to have politely given precedence
to his brother Rongo, the *dark one*, just as Jacob gave precedence
to Esau, but recovered the birthright from him afterwards. Rongo
the Dark came up from the *Mute*-land-home of Vari, the first of the
two Mothers who never ascended from the lower world. Soon after
this birth the genitrix, as Papa, the second of the two Mothers,
suffered from a great swelling. She resolved to get rid of it by
pressing it. This she did; the core flew out, and it was Tangaroa.
Another account says that Tangaroa came right up out of Papa's
head, the precise spot being indicated by "*the Crown*," with which
all their descendants have since been born. That is the *double* Crown
which is still considered to be auspicious. Tangaroa instructed his
brother Rongo in the arts of tillage: he was the husbandman of the
Phœnician and Hebrew myths, as Esau is a man of the field. Their
father was desirous of making Tangaroa, the fair one, the sole lord of all
that the parents possessed. So Isaac, the father of the Twins, loved
Esau. But Papa, the Mother, interposes on behalf of Rongo, the dark
one, as Rebekah interposed on behalf of Jacob, to secure the blessing
for him. In each version of the myth the mother had her own way.
Hence, whenever a sacrifice was offered to Rongo, the refuse was
thrown to the mother who dwelt with him in the shades below.
Through the cunning of Papa, the government, feasts, the drum of
peace, all honours and power were secured to Rongo. Nearly
all sorts of food fell to the elder twin-god, with this exception.
Tangaroa was admitted to be lord of *all the red* on earth or in ocean.
This was his lot; the red taro, the red yam, the red chestnut; four
kinds of fish, all scarlet, and all other things that were *red*. This
possession by the fair god of all the red on earth as his share [1] is the
exact parallel of Esau, the red man who is fed with a mess of red.
If Tangaroa is not described as a red man, he has red or sandy hair.
Rongo's hair is raven-black. Here, also, red and black correspond
to the red heaven of Tsuni-Goam and the black heaven of Gaunab
in the Khoi-Khoi myth. It has been previously suggested that Jacob
was a form of the Egyptian god Kak, whose name means darkness

[1] Gill, *Myths and Songs*, p. 12.

or black.   At a feast made by the twin-gods each collected his own kinds of food only, and to this the mother and father were invited. Tangaroa, lord of the red, made a vast pile of all things red, crowned atop with red land-crabs, and all the crimson fish he could find in the sea.   Rongo's pyramid was immensely greater, and the parents said that while Tangaroa's offering carried the palm for beauty Rongo's excelled in abundance.   Tangaroa was so displeased at the preference shown to Rongo that, although he did not kill his brother as Cain did, yet he left the land of Rongo, became the earliest navigator, and went forth to find, or found, a place where he could dwell by himself.   This corresponds to the rival offerings of Cain and Abel.   Abel's were blood-offerings, and Rongo was the god of blood-sacrifice.   In consequence of the preference shown to Abel's sacrifice Cain fell upon him, and then, like Tangaroa, he went forth to build a city in the land of Nod.   According to the true mythos Cain is really the good brother, the light one of the twins, whereas Abel is the dark and disappearing one.   Hence the doctrine of the Gnostic Cainites, who declared that Cain derived his being from the power above, and not from below.[1]   In the Algonkin versions it is the child of light who commits the fratricide.   The sympathies of the Hebrew writers, however, have gone with "righteous" Abel instead of Cain, as they do with Jacob, another type of the Dark deceitful one, instead of Esau.   But how honest nature rises in revolt against the treacheries and sharp practices described in the Hebrew Scriptures!   In a Syrian story relating to the "seven oaks" on a hill in anti-Libanus, told by a native of the village of Zebdani, Cain and Abel, the two sons of Adam, are called Habid and Habil.[2] *The whole world was divided between them ; and this was the cause of their quarrel, Habil moved his boundary stones too far ;* Habid threw them at him ; and Habil fell.   His brother in great grief carried the body on his back for 500 years, not knowing what to do with it.   At last, on the top of a hill, he saw *two birds fighting*, the one killed the other, washed him, and buried him in the ground. Habid did the same for his brother's body and *planted his staff* to mark the spot.   That staff grew up into the Seven Trees.[3]   This shows that Habil was the encroaching dark one, and it restores the true mythos. The two contending birds, and the staff which marks the boundary, appear as in various other versions.

Jacob and Esau are a form of the mythical twins who struggle for supremacy in the mother's womb.   Esau is really the God of Light, the red Tsuni-Goam, or the Red Sun (Atum) of the solar mythos.   Jacob is the demon of darkness, who was Kak (Eg.), the Elemental Darkness continued by name as Kak or Kā (Eg.), the Nocturnal Sun. Jacob appears in both these phases.   Esau the red is the hairy man,

[1] Irenæus, B. I. ch. xxxi. p. 1.   [2] Cr, Kabil and Habil.
[3] Stanley, *Sinai and Palestine*, p. 413.

a type of pubescence. The Jewish traditions, which are worth the *history* in the Pentateuch ten times over, tell us that Esau, when born, had the likeness of a serpent on his heel. This shows two things. He was a personification of the Light-god that bruised the Serpent's head, and Jacob, who laid hold of Esau's heel, was primarily the Serpent or Devil of darkness—hence the wily one, the deceiver, by nature and by name. Esau is said to have sold his birthright for a " mess of *red* " (אדם), and the traditions assert that he was called the *red* because he sucked his mother's blood before his birth.[1] This, likewise, shows him to have been the divinity imaged by the solar hawk, which symbolised blood " *because they say that this Bird does not drink water, but Blood, by which the soul is sustained.*"[2] The Hawk and serpent conjoined are a well-known type of the primordial divinity of a dual nature. In his second struggle Jacob wrestles all night with the opposing Power and becomes a form of the Hottentot " Wounded-knee," who wrestled or fought with Gaunab, the dark and evil being, therefore it may be inferred that Jacob, like Kak, passed out of the elementary into the distinctly solar character of the nocturnal sun, as in other versions of the same mythos.

The hawk and eagle are interchangeable types of the soaring bird of fire or light; the eagle and serpent appear in the following Miztec myth. In this the twin brothers are the two sons of the parents of the gods called the Lion-Snake and the Tiger-Snake. One of these was the Wind of Nine Snakes, the other the Wind of Nine Caves. When the elder desired to amuse himself he *took the form of an eagle*, flying thus far and wide; the younger turned himself into *a small beast of a serpent shape*, having wings which he used with such agility and sleight that he became invisible, and flew through walls and rocks even as through air. The two, therefore, correspond individually to the double Horus who was represented by a Serpent and a Hawk, also to the feathered serpent which was twinned in the Quiché legends as the type of primordial power. These two agreed to make a sacrificial offering to their parents, the gods. Then they took each a censer of clay, and put fire therein, and poured in ground *beleño* for incense; and this offering was the first that had ever been made in the world. Next they created a beautiful garden and left the home of their parents to go and live in it and tend it. They prayed to the gods to shape the firmament, lighten the darkness of the world, and to establish the foundation of the earth, or rather to gather the waters together so that the earth might appear, as they had no place to rest in save only their one little garden.[3] To make their prayers effectual they pierced their ears and tongues with flakes of flint, sprinkling the blood that dropped from their wounds over the trees and plants of the garden with a willow branch.

[1] Eisenmenger, vol. i. p. 646.   [2] *Hor-Apollo*, b. i. 6.
[3] Bancroft, vol. iii. p. 70.

The beginning was with darkness and its division into dark and light, in the elementary stage of the mythos. Eznik, an Armenian author of the fifth century, who wrote a book on Heresies, containing a refutation of the false doctrine of the Persians, says, "*Before anything, heaven or earth, or creature of any kind whatever therein, was existing, Zeruan (Time) existed.*" He offered sacrifices for a thousand years in the hope of obtaining a son, Ormizt by name, who was to create heaven, earth, and everything therein. Whilst he was sacrificing and cogitating Ormizt and Arhmen were conceived in the womb of their mother. Ormizt as the fruit of his sacrifices, Arhmen as that of his doubts. When Zeruan was aware of this event he said, Two sons are in the womb : he who will first come to me is to be made king. Ormizt having perceived his father's thoughts revealed them to Arhmen, saying, Zeruan, our father, intends to make him king who shall be born first. Having heard these words Arhmen perforated the womb and appeared before his father. But Zeruan, when he saw him, did not know who he was, and asked him, "*Who art thou ?*" He told him, "*I am thy son.*" Zeruan answered him, "*My son is well-scented and shining, but thou art dark and ill-smelling.*" While they were thus talking Ormizt, shining and well-scented, appeared before Zeruan who, seeing him, perceived him at once to be his son Ormizt, and handed over to him his rod (the Barsom) and blessed him. Then Arhmen approached him saying, "*Hast thou not vowed to make that one of thy two sons king who should first come to thee?*" Zeruan in order to avoid breaking his vow, replied to Arhmen, "*Oh, thou liar and evil-doer, the empire is to be ceded to thee for nine thousand years ; but I place Ormizt over thee as chief, and after nine thousand years he will reign and do what he likes.*" Then Ormizt and Arhmen began the work of creation ; everything produced by Ormizt was good and right, and everything wrought by Arhmen was bad and perverse.[1] In the Hebrew version of the twins, Jacob and Esau, Isaac the father takes the place of Zeruan. Esau is the first born, but Jacob wins the birthright by deceit: Isaac, like Zeruan, tries to determine which is the true heir by smelling him. When the disguised Jacob came near his father, his father "*smelled the smell of his raiment, and blessed him, and said, See, the smell of my son is as the smell of a field which the Lord hath blessed.*"[2] Jacob is represented as being the "well-scented," like Ormizt in the Persian account.

In some forms of the myth the Two Powers are antiphonal rather than antagonistic; they meet amicably like Satan and the Lord of Light in the Book of Job, or in *Faust*. In an ancient version of the relationship of Sut and Horus the two stand on two opposite eminences in the character, as it were, of two land surveyors, they solemnly agree respecting the natural boundaries of each other's

[1] Haug's *Essays*, pp, 13, 14, West.
[2] Genesis xxvii. 27.

domains and each pronounces the formula, "*The land of An is the boundary of the land.*"[1]

The circle of day and night was also typified by an egg which divided and gave birth to the Twin Brothers. The two Dioscuri are depicted with half of the severed shell on each of their heads as a cap or helmet. The Dioscuri are curiously pourtrayed upon the coins of the Greek city of Istros in Mœsia. The opposition, alternation, conflict or contention of the Twins is ingeniously illustrated. M. Lenormant has pointed out that their two heads seen on the obverse side are there placed side by side but in opposite directions, so that when one of them appears to the spectator in its normal position, the other is reversed, forehead downwards. Chaldaeo-Babylonian art had adopted the same combination to symbolise the opposition of the Twins of the zodiac. Their ordinary representation on the cylinders of hard stone, which were used as seals, consisted of two small figures of men placed one above the other, with their feet in opposite directions.[2]

In referring to the Chaldean form of the Twin Brothers, a fragment of Babylonian legend may be quoted here as a sort of summary of the earliest creations. So ancient is this recovered relic that the entire literature of the Cuneiform Inscriptions, contains nothing with which it has been correlated. It states that in the beginning the great Gods created two kinds of men in the likeness of Birds. "*Warriors with the bodies of Birds of the Desert* (and) *Men whose faces were Ravens. Tiamat gave them suck: their life was created by Bilat-Ili* (the Mistress of the Gods). *In the midst of the earth they grew up and became strong; and . . . . Seven Kings brethren were made to come as begetters.*"[3] The oldest of the Seven Brothers is named *Memangab*, the Thunderbolt. This brief rendering of a broken tablet contains the perfect legend of the Typhonian Creation, with Tiamat, the Deep, in place of the Abyss, Tepht. Tiamat and Bilat represent the two sisters into which the genitrix divided; one gives Suck (Water-source), the other Soul (Breath of life). The two kinds of Bird-men correspond to the dual Sut-Horus, with the two Birds of Light and Darkness for heads; the twins that issue from the egg. Following the twin-birth the total progeny of Typhon and of Tiamat is seven in number, *i.e.* seven altogether. "*The Sons of the Abyss* (there are) *Seven of them.*"[4] These were represented under one figure as the Seven-headed Thunderbolt of Tiamat: "*the Thunderbolt of Seven heads like the huge serpent or dragon of Seven heads.*"[5] Here the first of the Seven is the Thunderbolt by name. This is in agreement

[1] Inscription, *Reign of Shabaka*, col. 16, Goodwin.
[2] Cullimore, *Oriental Cylinders*, Nos. 65, 75, 94. Lajard, *Culte de Mithra*, pl. 26, 1 and 8.
[3] Sayce, *Records of the Past*, vol. ii. p. 109.
[4] Incantation. *Records*, vol. ii. p. 131.
[5] *Records*, vol. iii. p. 128.

with the adze of Anup or thunderstone of Sut. So Thunder was reckoned the primary element by the ancient Chinese; and the Stone from Heaven is the first-born of the Great Mother in certain American Myths.

The ancient Sclavonians had the Twins as the Biel-Bog, a White God, and Czerny-Bog, the Black God. Czerny-Bog was also the dark Deity of the Anglo-Saxons called Zernebok.[1] *Bog* is the common Sclavonic word for God. This is a world-wide root-name for a spirit, found in the *Bwg*, Welsh, ghost, or object of terror; *Bug*, *Puck*, or *Bogey*, English; *Puca*, Irish, goblin; *Puke*, Swedish, devil; *Bogy* and *Boye*, the spirit, ghost, or terror by night, with the blacks of Australia; *Pogooch* (Pine Plain), a spirit; *Buk-ha* (Vayu), distilled spirits; but the Spirit, or God, may be either *light* or *dark*. *Bogi*, in Fijian, is night. *Bogi*, black, in the Inner African languages. The Vedic *Bhaga* is the White One. "*Let us invoke the Victor in the morning* (that is the light which has defeated the darkness of night), *the strong Bhaga, the son of Aditi* (Bhaga was one of the Adityas or Elementaries) *who disposes all things.*"[2] *Bagha* is likewise known as the *Divider*, and the type-name may be traced to the root with that meaning in many languages. *Bagha*, in the Avesta, denotes portion; *Pech*, Breton, a division or piece; *Pagu*, Tamil, to divide; *Phakh*, Vayu, to halve; *Pekh* (Eg.), to divide in two; *Peka*, Maori, the branch, fork, or division in two. So the *Bog* divides into the white and black God, and is identical with the dual Sut-Horus.

The Asvins are a Hindu form of the twin brothers, the twin-born children of Aditi. They date from the earliest phase of the Twin-ship, when the two brothers were simply the representatives of day and dark, or moisture and light, as the dew of evening and the light of dawn. These also were the first who struggled and contended for birth in the womb of the genitrix. Their separate characters have been almost lost in the legends of their twinship, and they have to be divided in order to be distinguished.

The Asvins are born *here* and *there* (*ihehajâte*) on the two horizons of Light and Shade; the one is bright, the other black, like the Sut-Horus. According to the commentator, Yâska, the place of the Asvins is first among the deities of the sky. They are said to "*appear when one black cow sits among the bright cows.*" They "*walk along during the night like two black goats.*"[3] One of them is born in the sky and one in the air. They are associated with two of the elements as moisture and light. So the Twins Shu and Tefnut represent light and moisture. The Asvins are also identified with the Gemini of the zodiac who are Shu and Tefnut in Egypt. Here, how-

---

[1] Sharon Turner, *Anglo-Saxons*, vol. i., p. 217; *Mista, Skogula, and Zernebok, Gods of the Ancient Saxons.*—Scott, *Ivanhoe*, ch. xvi.
[2] *Rig Veda*, vii., 41, 42. Haug's *Essays*, p. 274.
[3] Max Müller, *Science of Language*, vol. ii. p. 490.

ever, two sets of the Twins have been confounded. The Asvins are two males, whereas the Gemini proper are male and female. Heaven and earth are said to be the Asvins who are born here and there, which identifies them with the two divisions in space. It is because they represent the day and dark that their place of meeting and twinning is the twilight, when light and dark are contending in their interfusion. This is called the time of the Asvins, and the nature of the one is to share in the darkness which penetrates into the light ; of the other to share in the light which vanquishes the darkness. Their vagueness has continued from the elementary stage. One form of the twins in Egypt was the double Anubis, a dual figure of the Watch-Dog, in the stellar phase of the mythos. English sailors still keep a watch between four and eight in the evening called the Dog-watch. This is divided at six o'clock (the time of twilight at the equinox !) into two dog-watches of two hours each. From four to six the watch is that of the Dog of the Light, and from six to eight is the watch of the Dog of Darkness. These dog-watches are commonly derived from an idea of a dog sleeping with one eye kept open to watch. But they are really a survival of the double Anubis and the Sut-Horus. These have two different types. In one the heads are two birds ; one light and one black. In the other the heads are those of the dog or jackal. So the dog of Yama is double-headed, one head keeping watch while the other is sleeping ; and this likewise has an alternative type in a double-headed bird. Thus our double-headed dog dividing the twilight watch is a survival of the double Anubis, the black and golden who was Sothis in one character and Mercury in his planetary phase, the watch-dog of twilight both at evening and dawn.

The earliest type of Sirius, the Dog-star, however, was not the dog of Europe, not the jackal of Egypt, not the fox-dog (Fenekh) of Abyssinia, but the giraffe of Inner Africa. This is the *Ser* by name and it was a figure of Sut-Typhon. From Ser we derive the name of Sirius as we do that of Sothis from Sut. The giraffe is an animal that *can see two ways at once without turning its head or its eyes*. This then was the perfect primary type of the fixed and steadfast watcher begotten by that nearness to external nature which belonged to primitive man. The Ser, giraffe, is the proper African type for Sothis. The name is a word of words for measuring, calculating, regulating, arranging, disposing, organizing, renewing, also relating to science and wisdom. The Ser was followed by the fox-dog and the dog. *The giraffe was continued in the gryphon type of Sut-Typhon,*[1] which is often confounded with the Ass. Also the name of the giraffe retains an older or equivalent form of Ser (Eg.) ; and in Khoikhoi the jackal is the *Garib*, and the dog is *Arib*.

In some myths the Twins and their types show that one is the

[1] Pierret, *Panthéon Égyptien*, p. 48, plate.

Keeper of the Fire and the other of the Water. Sut the dark one brings the Inundation and Horus the Solar fire. Both were united in Sut-Canopus. In the Australian myth War, the male crow and brother of War-pil, was the first to bring fire from space (tyrille) and give it to the aborigines, before which they were without it. This can be read by the hawk of fire. Another account of the mode in which the aborigines of Australia first obtained fire is thus given by Mr. J. Browne.[1] A long time ago a little Bandicoot was the sole owner of a firebrand that he cherished with the greatest jealousy, carrying it about with him wherever he went, and never allowing it out of his own care, even refusing to share it with the other animals, his neighbours; so they held a council, when it was decided to get the fire either by force or strategy. The *hawk* and *pigeon* were deputed to carry out this resolution, and after trying to induce the fire-owner to share its blessings, the pigeon, seizing an unguarded moment, as he thought, made a dash at the prize. The bandicoot, seeing affairs had come to a crisis, threw the fire in desperation towards the water, to quench it for ever. But fortunately for the black man, the hawk was hovering near, and seeing the fire falling into the water made a dart towards it, and with a stroke of his wing knocked the brand far over the stream into the long dry grass of the opposite bank, which immediately ignited and the flames spread over the country. The black man then felt the fire and said it was good. Both the hawk and dove are birds of Light or Fire. The Bandicoot is the bird of Darkness, a type of the Water that put out the solar fire.[2]

The first divinity of fire and light was in a sense pre-solar. He began as an elementary or an element, before the sun was a time-keeper and before it was known to be the same sun that set and rose again. For illustration, Ptah is an Egyptian solar-god, and yet not the sun itself, in the later sense. But as a form of the Egyptian Vulcan or Hephaistus he is a god of fire, because the *elemental* was first and the fire or light was primary, whether the fire of the sun, or the lightning-flash, or the conflagration, as one of the elementaries. So was it in India.

Wilford learned from the Hindus that Agni, or Fire, was an Elementary Divinity before the Sun was created, or before the element was concentrated in the solar god,[3] as it was in Egypt, and in Africa beyond,—where *Ogon* is fire simply in Akurakura; *Ikan* or *Agan* in Anan; *Akan* in Bode; and the Yoruban god of blacksmiths is named *Ogun*, with whom we may compare *Ogon*, the Sclavonic god of fire.

It is apparent in the Mangaian and other forms of the mythos that the Sun making the passage out of sight was apprehended as the element of fire in the underworld. The observers saw that in the

---

[1] *Canadian Journal*, vol. i. p. 509.   [2] Smyth, v. i. pp. 460, and 461.
[3] Moor, *Hindu Pantheon*, p. 300.

dark void, the lair of light, between sunset and sunrise, the great fire was rekindled. The god *Maui* descends there to wrest his hidden wisdom from *Mauike*, the god of fire, and there he learns how to reproduce the element at will, *because that was the place where the fire was reproduced*. The god of light and heat was primally the dæmon of lightning and the solar fire. Thus the lame god is the fire god. Hephaistus in Greece, and the crooked-legged antipodal Ptah is a kind of pre-solar sun-god in the elemental aspect; fire or heat having been the first solar type. This fire was almost put out by night when the dark one overcame the bright one. But it was reproduced each day from the fire-place in the nether world by the lame and limping god who warred against the darkness and all its creeping things, as Khepr (Ptah) the transformer and re-creator. *Kep* (Eg.) means to kindle, to heat, to light, to cause a ferment, and this supplied a Kamite root for the name of *Heph*aistus. Thus the god of fire was an early opponent of the darkness and only in this elementary stage do we reach the rootage of the solar Horus. When Sut as Sut-Anubis is said in the later texts to "*swallow his father Osiris*," the sun, there is a reversion to the type derived from the ancient darkness. A perfect identification of the fire with the sun may be found in the Huron myth of the twin-born brothers, the Light and the Dark. Iouskeha, the light one was recognised as the sun who was their benefactor, and but for him they said their kettles would not boil, as it was he who learned from the tortoise the art of creating fire. The tortoise was a type of the ancient Typhon, one of whose names is Kar-tek, the spark-holder, the mother of the elementaries, whose sparks were the starry fires. This beginning with the god of fire or solar heat necessitated such a distinction, for instance, as the later "Sun in his disk," the Aten-Sun of the so-called disk worship and the sun itself as Ra which followed the Har-Sun and representative of fire, in the elementary phase.

In his treatment of the Hottentot myths Dr. Hahn does not distinguish their phenomenal phases. All is sacrificed to the idea of a Supreme Being who is one and the same under various names and types. But this non-evolutionary treatment never can reach the origines. In the Namaqua dialect, for example, Eibi is first. Whence Eibib is he who is the first. And it is said, "*At first there were two* (gods) *Heitsi-eibib and Gama-gorib*."[1] These are the two opposite powers who were elementary. Next Heitsi-eibib can be traced in the lunar phase, and lastly Tsuni-Goam, the Wounded-knee, is the Hero of Light in the solar phase of the mythos, the Nocturnal Sun who brings back the Red Dawn, and is the lord of all things red like Tangaroa.

In the Hottentot, as in the Fijian mythology, the moon is also a type of the Twin Truths. But the moon in its dual lunation had two

[1] *Tsuni-Goam*, p. 56.

different messages for men, just as the natural phenomena are still susceptible of a double interpretation to the theist and the atheist. The moon sent the hare to tell mankind that as the lunar god died and rose again so should they also be renewed and rise again. But the hare played false and perverted the message. She told mankind that like as the moon died and did not rise again, so men should perish and should not rise again. This was the dark aspect of the moon and that was *the true message at the time when it could not be known that the same moon re-arose.* When this fact became known and the moon was recognised as the true prophet of immortality, then the hare was discarded. The moon is now the Khoi-khoi deity who promises men immortality.

In a Caroline-island myth it is said that in the beginning mankind only quitted life on the last day of the dying moon to be revivified when the new moon re-appeared. But there was a dark and evil spirit that inflicted a death from which there was no revival. The dark spirit and the fatal message were first in fact, and the assurance of revival *like* the moon *depended on its being identified as the same moon that rose again.*

Jack and Jill are a lunar form of the twins as we may see in the Norse version of the Younger Edda where they are Hjuki and Bil the twin children of the moon. Hjuki denotes the one who nourishes and cherishes, the increasing new moon corresponding to *Tekh* (Eg.); *Bil* is an interstice, an interval corresponding to the latter half of the lunation; the fall and vanishing of the moon. In the Tuscarora myth, recorded by David Cusick, the Twin Brethren are the Two Children of Aataensic who is identified as the moon and the genitrix of the gods. This was the ancient mother who alighted from heaven on the back of a tortoise and bore her twin sons. The Hurons claimed her as their Grandmother. The names of her twins in the Oneida dialect signify respectively the Light one and the Dark one. According to Cusick they were Enigorio, the Good Mind, and Enigonhahetgea, the Bad Mind, or more accurately the Beautiful spirit and the Ugly one; the god and devil of objective phenomena. The Good Mind wished to create light but the dark one desired the world to remain in its natural darkness. The Bad one made a couple of clay images in the shape of man but whilst he was in the act of creating them they turned into apes. The Good mind formed two images of the dust of the earth, breathed into their nostrils, gave them living souls, and named them *Ea-gwe-howe* or "*Real people.*" This expression alone proves the true myth. The doctrine was not derived from the missionaries, who assuredly knew nothing of the ape being the type of the dark half of the lunar twins, as it became in Egypt.

At length there was a final struggle between the two brothers to determine which should be master once for all. The light one played false, as did Jacob with Esau, and persuaded the dark one to fight him with flags, or, in another version, the fragile wild-rose, as this would be fatal to himself. He then chose a weapon of deer's horn. The dark one was discomfited and went sorely wounded, dropping his blood at every step and wherever the life-drops fell they turned into flint stones. When dying the dark one claimed that he would have equal power over souls in the life hereafter, and on being thrust down into the earth, or abyss, he became the evil spirit, the Satan of later theology.[1]

The two birds of Sut and Horus are the black vulture (Neh) and the gold hawk. The lunar Ibis is black and white and its pied nature typifies the dual lunation. Birds and brothers both appear in the mythos of the Thlinkeet as the twin deities of light and dark. The two brothers are Yethl and Khanukh. The raven is the bird of Yethl, but it is described as a black raven that once was white, the same alternation of black and white as in the Ibis. The white bird is represented as getting black in passing up through the flue of Khanukh's fire-place. This is a form of the Phœnix which transforms from black to white (or into the gold hawk), and from white to black in its passage to and from the underworld, Khanukh's flue.

Another legend tells how Yethl shot the large bird which had a long glittering bill; its name was the "*Crane that can soar to heaven.*" This he skinned, and when he wished to fly he clothed himself in the crane's feathers. The crane is a heron, the hieroglyphic equivalent of the lunar Ibis.

The Ibis-headed Taht was lord of the eighth region, and Yethl was born in the eighth month, and his aunt was watched over by eight red birds called Kun.[2] Yethl supplied light to mankind. In the Thlinkeet tongue Yethl signifies a raven, and Khanukh a wolf. The wolf, or jackal, is a type of darkness. Khanukh is described as raising a magical darkness, in which Yethl, the Light-Bringer, howled helplessly. In a discussion between them as to which is the elder, Khanukh asserts that he has been in the world ever since the time that the "*liver came out from the belly.*"[3] Then said Yethl, "*Thou art older than I.*" Darkness was first, and the blood-source preceded that of the breath. The liver was looked upon as solid blood, and blood as fluid liver, or life; which shows the allusion to the first of the Two Truths in the biological phase. Hence Khanukh is the keeper of the waters, and has to be outwitted by Yethl before he can take possession of them in turn and give new life to the world.[4]

It is possible that the Hindu Krishna and Bala-Rama may be as old as the elemental phase of light and shade. "*Do you not know,*" asks Krishna of Bala-Rama, "*that you and I are alike the origin of the*

---

[1] Schoolcraft, part i. p. 316 ; part vi. p. 166; Brinton, p. 63.
[2] Bancroft, v. iii. pp. 99, 102.
[3] "Seit der Zeit, entgenete Khanukh, als von unten die Leber herauskam." Holmberg, *Ethn. Skiz.* p. 61.
[4] Bancroft, vol. iii. p. 102.

world?"[1]   As the Twins of Creation, in a later phase, Krishna is said to be an incarnation of Vishnu, and Bala-Rama of the Serpent Sesha. But the Twins are earlier than Vishnu, and if not elementary like the Asvins, they were lunar before passing into the solar mythos. One is black, or rather, slate-blue, the other white. Krishna is reputed to have been produced from a black hair of Vishnu, and Bala-Rama from a white hair. The name of Krishna is identical with that of the dark half of the lunar month. from full to new moon. Also Kris (or Krish) signifies to wane, as the moon, to attenuate and become small. Bala means virile seminal force; Rama, the phallic giver of pleasure. Bala-Rama impersonates the pubescent phase, he is the one who waxes in power like the horned moon, whereas Krishna is the one that wanes and becomes the little one, the Child. Yet it is he who conquers the Dragon of Darkness in the underworld, just as the Lunar Child Khunsu is the slayer of the giants in the Kamite mythos. Bala-Rama is named *San-Karshana*, the withdrawing one, or the one who is withdrawn, although the withdrawal was different from that of another Twin with which it has to be compared. In the present instance Bala-Rama gives precedence to the dark one, Krishna, but the double-motherhood of the two heavens is employed, and the two women are both made use of to give birth to the Twins ; Bala-Rama being withdrawn from the womb of Devaki, to be born from that of Rohini.

There is a Babylonian legend of the Twin brothers who are opposed to each other, which was preserved by Ctesias, and Nicolas of Damascus. In this Adar-Parsondas, a solar god, comes every night into the power of his dark rival Shin-Nannaros, who is called his brother. Shin deprives Adar of his virile power. The two succeed each other alternately in their dominion over nature. The elder brother is said to kill the younger, whom he sends to the dwellings of death. Shin, the moon-god, is called the Royal Twin ; Sini (Assyrian), and Shen (Eg.), denoting plural, or twin. The Twins in relation to the moon first personified the double gibbousness, the waxing and waning of the orb. Here, however, the Twins would seem to be luni-solar. Adar is the Babylonian Herakles. But Herakles is also luni-solar in the Egyptian Khunsu, the youthful solar-god who carries the sun and moon on his head, and in whom the Twins were unified. Khunsu is called the son of Amen-Ra and Maut, *i.e.* phenomenally the sun and moon. Both are twinned in him as their child because he typifies the solar light when it was known to be re-born in the moon. The legend thus interpreted supplies a luni-solar link in the chain of continuity, which extends from the elemental to the final solar phase.

The Hindu writers say the black one has never failed to give way to the white one in the eternal conflict of day and dark. But there are two sides to the fact, and in early forms of the myth we see it

[1] *Vishnu Purana*, pp. 519, 571. Wilson.

is the light one who, like Tangaroa and Esau the red, has to give way and go forth on his own account to seek an abiding-place.

This going forth of the parting Twins to found a city or find the second place, is a mode of describing the division of the whole into the two halves, and the two horizons of day and night, light and dark.

According to Bishop Callaway, the Zulus thought the white man made the world.[1] But *their* white man did not originate with the European. It was the light spirit opposed to the dark. In this sense the first world was made, or the world was first made, when the two horizons were distinguished the one from the other as those of light and shade, by the gold hawk and black vulture; the eagle-hawk and crow, or the dove and the raven. In a Tongan form of the myth the elder and younger brothers divide the world between them, each dwelling apart; they were the two progenitors of the black people and light people, or the Noes and Yeas. The founding of a city or building of a temple by a fratricide is one of the common traditions of mankind. Cain kills his brother Abel and then builds the city of Enoch. Romulus slays Remus and the city of Rome is founded in his brother's blood. Olus, or Tolus, was murdered by his brother's slaves and his head was placed beneath the foundations of the Temple of Jupiter Capitolinus. Agamedes, co-builder with Trophonius of the Temple of Apollo at Delphi, is killed by his brother, who carries away his head. The building of a city is of course a late illustration. The establishing of the two solstices and distinguishing the heavens north and south, and marking these by two mountains, trees, stars or constellations would be earlier; these being followed by the signs of the four quarters, and the building of the Tetrapolis above.

Belin and Brennus, the twin brothers of the British legends are, like Heber and Heremon in the Irish, identifiable as a form of the twins of the universal mythos, the light one and the dark one, the prince of peace and the turbulent warrior, combined in the Sut-Horus; and when Belin had conquered Brennus, we are told that he mapped out the island and *made four roads through the length and breadth of the kingdom.*[2] But before cities were built or roads were made a stake was stuck in the ground. We still speak of having a stake in the soil. The stake and tree are equivalents. When the suicide was buried at the *parting of the ways,* or the cross-roads, a stake was thrust through the body as a mode of *fixing;* this being related to the four-fold foundation of the Cross. One of the earliest celestial types is the tree. This becomes twain in the two trees of the north and south; as well as in the rod or staff of Kepheus (Shu-Kafi) whose figure may be found in the Decans of the Waterman.[3] On the Mithraic monu-

[1] Callaway, *Amazulu*, p. 55.   [2] Geoffrey's *British History*, b. iii.
[3] Plate in present vol. See *Œdipus Judaicus*, Drummond, pl. 16, for Kepheus with his staff north and south, a twin-type of the tree which was divided to mark the two solstices.

ments the two trees mark the east and west.[1]   Planting the tree would be a primitive mode of marking the boundary, and in the traditions of Central America there is a story of two brothers, who before starting on a journey to Xibalba, the land of disappearing, plant a cane in the *middle of their grandmother's house*, on purpose for her to know whether they are living or dead, according to the flourishing or withering condition of the cane.   The cane is a sign of one of the four cardinal points in the Mexican symbolism.   Grimm traces this type in the story of the Two Gold Children who leave their father two Golden Lilies, saying: "*from these you will see how we fare.   If they are fresh we are well; if they fade we are ill; if they fall we are dead.*"   The story is wide-spread like the myth of the twins themselves.   Egypt will tell us who were the Two Gold-Children.   They were the twins in a dual stellar phase of the mythos.   Sut-Nubti (or Sothis-Canopus) was the golden Sut of a dual nature, represented double-headed, or as the golden twin ; and the type would be the same if called the double Anubis (the golden-dog, *canis aureus*), or if it were taken for the sun and Sirius, or the sun and Saturn in a later phase.   The reader may see the golden Sut (jackal or dog) in the tree which is planted in the decans of the grand or great mother, Isis, who personates the sign of Virgo.[2]

The "Two Brothers" in Grimm's *Household Stories* are another form of the twins.   First we have them as the rich and poor brothers, the dark one being the rich one, as the dark Rongo is in the Mangaian myth.   With this opening of the tale we may compare an Eastern tradition of the first two brothers of humankind current among the Tshudes, which relates that the elder brother acquired great wealth from his gold mines, but that the younger being envious, drove him away and forced him to take refuge in the East.[3]   The gold mines would be in the West where the light went down.

In the German tale the gold mines are represented by the golden bird which lays the golden egg ; the Roc, or Rekh, *i.e.*, the Phœnix in Egypt.   Then follows the tale of the twins.   These go out into the world, but can find no place where they may dwell together.   So they said to one another: "*It cannot be otherwise, we must separate.*" The huntsman at parting gave them a bare knife, saying : "*If you separate, stick this knife in a tree by the roadside, and then if one returns to the same point, he can tell how his absent brother fares ; for the side upon which there is a mark will rust if he dies, but as long as he lives it will keep bright as ever.*"   The knife is a type of the division.   The younger of the twins becomes the slayer of the dragon which has seven heads, and lies coiled round the top of a mountain.   He cuts off the monster's seven heads and rescues the princess who is waiting ready to be devoured.   Ultimately he marries her and has the usual

---

[1] Drummond, pl. 13.   [2] Plate in present vol.
[3] Schlegel, *Philosophy of History*, p. 95 ; Bohn's ed.

"*half the kingdom besides*"; which dates from the heaven of only two divisions.

The twin brothers are found in the folk-tales of many lands. In the Norse they re-appear as *True* and *Untrue*, where they are still identified with time by means of the year. Once on a time there were two brothers; one was called *True*, and the other *Untrue*. True was upright and good to all, but Untrue was bad, false, and full of lies. Their mother was a widow. They went forth and at evening they quarrelled, when *Untrue*, the dark one, plucked out his brother's eyes. The blind one climbs up a tree for the night and hears the confabulation of the bear, the wolf, the fox, and the hare, who come to keep Midsummer's Eve beneath the tree. From these he learns that he is in the tree of life and healing power, and from its leaves he recovers his sight.

The brother *True*, with his eyes put out by *Untrue*, is one with Horus sitting solitary in his blindness and darkness. In one account Sut wounded Horus in the eye; in another he plucked it out and swallowed it. "*I am Horus*," says the blinded brother; "*I come to search for my eyes*." In the Ritual the eye is restored at the dawn of day.[1] There is also an eye that is the sign of a year. The meeting of the brothers True and Untrue is periodic; the time being at the summer solstice, where the Kamite year began; and Sut, the dark one dominated when the sun began to descend from its highest altitude. The bear, wolf, and fox, together with the hare (which is a North American Indian type) are suggestive of the four quarters. The tree of the solstice is an Egyptian sign, and the ancient genitrix, the mother of the mythical twins who preceded the fatherhood, survives as the widow. *True* of course is finally the victor. Through what he learned from the talking animals he becomes a saviour. He discovers a well of water for the King, and restores his eyesight. He recovers the lost speech and hearing of the young Princess, and gets her for his wife with *half the kingdom* besides. This is a clear and easily-traced continuation of a myth in the reduced form of the folk-tale, but twenty others are just as truly so, even where the likeness is far less apparent. The same types of mythology are minified in the folk- or fairy-tale, and magnified in theology. The Norse *True* is one at root with the Egyptian True Word (Har-Makheru), and with him who was *True* in the Book of Revelation. Dr. Dasent asks how is it that the Wandering Bechuanas have got the story of the "*Two Brothers*," the groundwork of which is the same as the "Machandel-boom" and the "Milk-white Doo," and where the incidents and even the words are almost the same? How is it that in some of its traits the Bechuana story embodies those of that earliest of all popular tales recently published from an Egyptian Papyrus? My reply is,

---

[1] *Book of Beginnings*, vol. ii. p. 291.

because the origin was Inner African and Egypt is the connecting-link with the outside world.[1]

The Twins appear in an American myth, and in a form that *looks comparatively late* in Egyptian mythology. In the Osirian solar phase the child Horus duplicates to become Har-Tema and avenge the death of his father. In the American version the child commands his grandmother to cleave him in twain, in order that he may become the double avenger of his father's death. Thus he is transformed into the duplicated one and is then called by the name of the " *One-Two*." The father of Har-Tema the twin or total Horus, was slain by Typhon, one of whose names is *Stone-head*, another being *Stone-arm*. The father of One-Two is killed by *Stone-Shirt*, and " One-Two " in his duplicated character is the avenger. The shrew-mouse was sacred to Horus in *Skhem*, the place of transformation and annihilation; and in the American Myth *One-Two* transforms into the mouse or mice to make war upon *Stone-Shirt*.[2]

A single type will serve to express different developments and applications of the one primary idea. These vary, according to phenomena, but are determined and limited by the prototypal Two Truths.

At first these Two Truths are simply *day and dark*, or dawn and dusk. Next the twins enter the sphere of time as two stars or constellations on the *two horizons*, or are the two gods of north and south. Then the *double lunation* is personified by the two children of the genitrix, and, lastly, the Twins are the Two Horuses of the solar myth. A glimpse of the mode in which the type was continued with a change of personages may be seen in Indra and Agni, the solar gods who are twinned as the Asvinia; Indra and Agni being the two later divinities of moisture and light, or the solar fire.

The twin brothers are Egyptian in every phase, whether elementary, stellar, lunar, or solar, beginning with the Sut-Horus (elementary), *the twin Lion-Gods of Light and Darkness which the Lunar Genitrix boasts that she bears in her womb; the double Anubis* (stellar), *Sut-Nubti* (stellar or soli-stellar), *Hermanubis or Taht-Aan* (lunar); *and they were continued as the Two Horuses in the Osirian mythos.* Here there is alternation but no contention. The Twins are two representatives of the annual Sun that descends and the Sun that ascends. The first Horus is the child, the impubescent, maimed, or crippled deity, the phantom that fades and disappears or transforms into the virile Horus of the resurrection. Lastly, there is a moral and religious stage in which the Sut and Horus of the beginning typify good and evil, deity and devil, as the final form of the male twins.

The twin brothers in the Avesta can be traced from their natural genesis in physical phenomena as the ever-alternating light and

[1] *Norse Tales*, introduction, p. 54.
[2] J. W. Powell, " Bureau of Ethnology," Washington. *Report*, 1881, pp. 47—51.

dark to their latest phase, as divinity and devil in Ahura-Mazda and Anra-Mainyus. They are called the "Twins" by name in Yasna 30. This description, says Bleeck, agrees with that contained in the Armenian writers, Esnik for example, where they are both the "*Sons of Time*," that is the twins of light and dark, considered not merely as a dual manifestation in space, but also as manifestors of time. We learn that both these heavenly beings, the twins, of themselves manifested the good and the evil, and the wise do rightly distinguish between them ; not so the foolish or imprudent. These two heavenly beings came together in the beginning to that which was the first creation. Whatsoever is living is through the purpose of Ahura-Mazda, who is the life, and whatsoever is lifeless or of death is through the purpose of Anra-Mainyus the destroyer. They are designated the Two Creators, the Two Masters, who are sometimes spoken of as the Two Spirits of Ahura Mazda.[1] And Haug argues that "*in consequence of an entire separation of the two parts of Ahura-Mazda, and the substitution of two independent rulers governing the universe, the unity of the Supreme Being was lost, and monotheism was superseded by dualism.*" He attributes the Persian dualism to a personal Zoroaster, and observes that "*this great thinker of antiquity having arrived at the grand idea of the unity and indivisibility of the Supreme Being, undertook to solve the great problem, how are the various kinds of evil in the world compatible with the goodness, holiness, and justice of God? He solved this difficult question philosophically by the supposition of two primæval causes, which, though different, were united. The one who produced the reality is called the Good Mind ; the other, in whom originated non-reality, bears the name of the Evil Mind. All good, true, and perfect things, which fall under the category of reality are produced by the Good Mind ; whilst all that is delusive and belongs to the domain of non-reality, is traceable to the Evil Mind. These are the two moving causes of the universe, united from the beginning, and therefore called the Twins (Yema ; Sanskrit, Yamau).*"[2] In Manichæism the development of doctrine culminated, and the eternal antagonists were separately enthroned in ceaseless conflict in the domain of what are termed spirit and matter ; the original division of day and night was deepened and darkened into a great gulf riven right through the constitution of all things and the moral nature of man. But the myths do not disclose any deeper meaning by our reading into them the ideas of later times ; we are only imposing on them a sense quite foreign to them in order that they may impose upon us and others in return. Each phase of the mythos out of Egypt can be identified and interpreted by the Kamite Typology from the beginning to the end ; and to the beginnings we must go back to learn.

The mythical twins also became the dual Messiah of theology.

---

[1] *Yasna*, xix. 9, and lvii. 2.   [2] Haug, *Essays*, p. 303. West.

So profoundly ignorant of the doctrinal origines have theologians been that even writers like Gfrörer have maintained the improbability of the Jews being in possession of the dogma of a dual Messiah in pre-Christian times ; and it has actually been contended that after the Christian era the outwitted Jews had to invent a secondary Messiah as the lowly suffering one, the Son of Joseph, who was a failure, because their Messiah, ben-David, had not come in his expected glory.   Whereas, so ancient is the twin-type of the Messiah Son, that the suffering one of the two who was at last represented as the crucified may be found in the New Zealand legend of Rupe, where instead of being crucified he falls off the beam which was laid at the crossing, when he formed the great House of the Sun. This suffering Messiah is as old in Egypt as the name of the month Mesore, in which the *Mesi* (Eg.), or infant Horus was reborn.   He, too, may be seen at the crossing or on the scales of the zodiac, whence Rupe fell, and the sun began to descend.[1]   The double Horus of Egypt survived in the cult of the Gnostics.   Irenæus says of Valentinus : "He also supposed two beings of the name of Horus."[2]   They show, he says, that this Horus of theirs has two faculties—the one, of *supporting*, the other, of *separating*.   Insomuch as he supports and sustains he is Stauros (a cross), while insomuch as he divides he is Horus.   They also "*represent the Saviour as having indicated this two-fold faculty ; first, the sustaining power, when he said, 'Whoever doth not bear his Cross* (Stauros) *and follow after me cannot be my disciple' ; and the separating power when he said, "I came not to send Peace, but a Sword."*[3]   It is a startling discovery for all who ever dip, not to say dive, into the iconography of the catacombs, to find these palpable remains of the dead religion of the pagan past taking life as the divinity of the new.   The twins are there extant, and were often reproduced by the artists of Rome, in whose representations two distinct characters of the Christ are frequently found, and these are generally pourtrayed in juxtaposition. One of the Christs is the Eternal Youth, the "Universal Lad" of the Osirian myth ; the blooming boy Bacchus of the Greek mythos ; the youthful Mithra of the Persians ; the fair Apollo of Greece in his beardless beauty.   The favourite figure, says Didron, is that of a beautiful and adorable youth of about fifteen or eighteen years of age, beardless, with a sweet expression of countenance, and long abundant hair flowing in curls over his shoulders ; his brow is sometimes encircled by a diadem, or *bandeau*, like a young priest of the pagan gods ; a graceful youth, just as Apollo was depicted by the Pagans.[4]   The other Christ is little, old, and ill-favoured, like the bad-smelling one of the Persian Twins.[5]   The two are frequently found together.

[1] Plate, vol. ii. *Book of Beginnings.*   [2] *Irenæus*, b. i. ch. xi. 1.
[3] Irenæus, b. i. ch. iii. 5.   [4] Didron, *Icon. Chrétienne*, pp. 244—256.
[5] Bosio, *Roma Sotteranea*, pp. 49, 65, 35, 91, 253, 363.

Many examples are given by Bosio and others of the twin Jesus; Christ the younger and Christ the elder. The American writer Lundy is pitiably perplexed at what he comes across in the Christology of the Roman tombs. The only possible explanation, he says, of the double Jesus, the young-elder, and the juxtaposition of the youthful Christ and the old one is that this contradiction is intended to depict the two natures in Christ, the divine and the human; the little, old, ugly, hairy man being the human likeness, and the youthful, majestic beardless figure the type of the divine.[1] The treatment is simply that of the Sut-Horus, and of Horus the elder and Horus the younger. The elder Horus, Har-Ur, was the old first one, the mortal, the one who wears the human image, he who was born to descend and suffer and die because he represented the declining sun in the lower signs. Horus the younger was the perennial youth, called the Lord, the Majesty, the God of the Beautiful Face. He was the sun-god, as the Young Immortal, the type of the eternal sonship. It is the same dual type that is traceable all mythology through. So Prajapati was one-half mortal, one-half immortal, and with his mortal half he feared death.

The statues of Dionysos show the same duality as the elder or bearded and the younger or beardless god. The duality is that of Shu, who is expressly designated the "Young-elder" in consequence. It was the duality of Sut-Horus and of the Twins of the Avesta; the primordial type being that of light and darkness; the latest psychotheistic.

The typical twins thus identified as simply a continuation of the type of the Double-Horus, the dual Mithras, the biune Bacchus, the two-faced Janus or Sut and Horus, prove that this twinship could no more pourtray a personal Jesus than the supposed Christ in "Revelation" who is a male figure with female paps, the hermaphrodite divinity of the mythos. These things are unthinkable apart from their origin, and hence they have become the unfathomable mysteries of theology.

Eros and Anteros are a Greek version of the twins. Eros (Cupid) accompanies Venus, the gestator; Anteros represents the negative character; and in some versions he is made the active antagonist of Eros, and shares the character of the Dark Mind in other myths. Plato, in the "symposium," allows us to see that he had not bottomed the Horus or Eros myth. Phædros calls Eros the *oldest*, Agathon the *youngest*, of the gods; and both appeal to ancient versions as their authority.[2] Each was right, for Horus was both. Har-Ur was always the oldest; Har-Ahi for ever the youngest; both were blended in Har-Makheru, the True Word. But he had continued the mythical twin-type, and this he has copied as his portrait of the soul, which he

---

[1] *Monumental Christianity*, p. 237.
[2] *Symp.* 178 c.

calls "double" and says it has *two faces* conformably to its "paradigm," according to the circle of the same and the circle of the different.[1]

Peter, in the *Clementine Homilies*,[2] adverts to the great power, which is also called the Kuria (Mistress), from whom two angels were sent forth, the one to create the world, the other to give the law, "*each of which, on account of his work, proclaimed himself to be the sole Creator*," and thus caused the ancient feud. This is a later form of the twins with the Kuria in the place of the Great Mother. The bird of Light and Shade might likewise be traced all through. Horus, the child, the dark and disappearing one in the solar phase, whose bird-type is the Phœnix of transformation in the lower world, is sometimes depicted with the hawk of his brother flying at the back of his head or skull-cap,[3] the Hawk and Phœnix being the two birds of light and shade in the latest Egyptian form of the myth.

This also survived in the Christian typology as a form of the Dove of the Holy Ghost which blended both birds in one. A Franco-German miniature of the eleventh century shows the Dove with six wings represented *half in light* and *half in shade*, with the fore-part yellow and hinder-part dark. The *Golub* (dove), and *Gareb* (black-bird) are thus blended together, even as the two were twinned in the black and white Ibis of the moon.[4]

The "Two Women" who brought forth the twin brothers were placed in the Zodiac six signs apart. The one, Virgo, was the Virgin Mother of the Child-Horus, the negative one of the twins who is born first, but who, in the solar mythos, has to be re-born, and this time *begotten* by the father, Osiris, or Atum, in the Menti or "re-foundry" of the male generator. This second Horus, the "*only-begotten of the father* (or from a father), *full of grace and truth*"—each phrase may be found applied to Horus, the Redeemer—was re-born of the gestator in the Sign of Pisces; and the dual imagery of the Zodiac, the Two Women and the Two Children who were first born as Sut and Horus, and lastly as Horus the elder and Horus the younger, is perfectly paralleled or preserved in the Gospel according to St. Luke. Elizabeth the *barren*, who is described as *the* barren when she was six months gone with the child John, brings forth six months earlier than Mary.[5] The *barren breeder* can only be understood according to the typology of the mythos.[6] One horizon was the lower, considered to be that of earth, the other that of heaven. The imagery is reproduced by John, who says of himself and Jesus, "*He must increase, but I must decrease.*" "He *that cometh from above is above all; he that is of the earth is of the earth, and of the earth he speaketh.*"[7] The precise characters and relationship of the mythical Twins is

---

[1] Proclus in *Timæus*, b. 3.
[2] xviii. 12.
[3] Birch, *Gallery*.
[4] Didron, fig. 119.
[5] Luke i. 36.
[6] See *Records*, vol. x. p. 142.
[7] John iii. 30, 31.

K K 2

preserved. John represents the element of Water; Jesus the Fire or Spirit. John precedes the Light, as does the dark one in all the true legends, and says, "*He that cometh after me is preferred before me; for he was before me,*" as was Jacob, Ormizt, or Tangaroa, who was first by right of birth, although the latest born.

The description of Mercury in the mysteries given by Apuleius proves how the old Egyptian mythology had found its way to Rome. "*Here, awful to behold, was the messenger of the Gods above, and of those in the realms beneath, standing erect with his face partly black and partly golden, carrying a caduceus in his left hand, and waving in his right a green branch of palm. Close behind him followed a cow in an erect position, seated on the shoulders of one of the devotees of this divinity; this cow being the prolific likeness of the All-parent Goddess.*" Mercury was the Egyptian Sut-Anubis who passed into Taht, or Hermanubis, in the lunar stage. The double visage of black and gold is identical with the black bird and gold hawk of Sut Horus and Sut Nubti.

In the Australian version of the mythos we find the remarkable statement that it *was out of the enmity and final agreement of the Two Brothers that the first two classes originated, and thence a law that governed marriages between those two classes.*[1] Thus the mirror of mythology reflects the primitive sociology and shows us the very bifurcation of the one into duality, as the primary stage of distinguishing from general promiscuity.

Here it will bear repeating that the first of the two original brotherhoods of the Chocta gentes was designated the "*Divided* People," i.e., the people who first divided and became the twin brothers of sociology and legendary lore. This separation of the people into two phratries was followed by the four subdivisions, and eight totems altogether. The Iroquois, the Onondagos, Senecas, and Cayugas likewise began with the dual brotherhood, or twin phratries, the members of which were not permitted to intermarry. The two phratries were divided into eight gentes, answering to the eight classes of the Kamilaroi, which were also founded on the dual brotherhood with the dual motherhood of the Two Sisters at the head of all.[2] Captain Burton found the two divisions and eight totems extant on the Gold Coast. The Twin-Children of the Mother-moon became Totemic with the Arab tribes amongst whom the Banu Badr were named the sons of the Full Moon, and the Banu Hilal the sons of the New Moon. The Greek φρατρία or organisation of the phratry is later. It is founded on the solar triad. Each of the four tribes of the Athenians was organised in three phratries, separately composed of thirty gentes, making a total of twelve phratries and three hundred and sixty gentes. This adjustment corresponds to the four

---

[1] Smyth, vol. i. pp. 423—4.   [2] Morgan, *Ancient Society*, pp. 90 and 99.

quarters, the thirty days to the month and the three hundred and sixty degrees of the ecliptic which corroborates and continues the astronomical beginnings.

The mythical twins are represented by the royal twinship. Royalty in Dahome is invested with this dual character. In one aspect the monarch is king in town, in the other he is king in the bush.[1] In like manner the Egyptian Horus has two titles; one being the "*Youth in Town*," the other the "*Lad in the Country*."[2] So the Pharaohs of Egypt were crowned kings of the double horizon and the Sut Ra continued the dual type of Sut Horus. The Twin-Brothers who divided in the mythos are re-united in the Egyptian Pharaoh. In the "*Foundation of the Temple of the Sun*" at An (Heliopolis) Usertasen I. says the God had exalted him as Lord of both parts of Horus and Sut (Peseshti) whilst he was yet an infant in the womb. The God Amen says to Tahtmes III. that he has "*united the hands of the Pair of Brothers to bless*" the king.[3] Japan until recently had her Tycoon and Mikado, the sacred and secular sovereigns. In ancient Sparta likewise we find the royal twinship or government by twin kings. Also the Samoan chief, whose title is "You Two," preserves the title of twinship founded on the impubescent child and virile male who were united in one at puberty. This is what is meant by mythology being a mirror to the earliest sociology.

The "Two Women" in Egypt are the two sister goddesses, chiefly represented as Isis (Neith) and Nephthys (Neft) who appear on the two sides of Horus, their child and brother, in the act of wooing or worshipping him. The three form that triad which Champollion placed at the head of the Pantheon. These are the dual form of the genitrix that Sut opened and Horus sealed, which equally applies to the later double Horus and the mother on the two horizons. From this origin we derive the two mothers of the child, one of whom may be uterine, and one the milch-mother. The Egyptian Pharaoh had two mothers. It is said in the Inscription of Queen Hatasu, "*Ra consorts with his two mothers, the Uræus Goddesses.*[4] On one side, over one of the doors, at the temple of Dakkeh, it is said of the Æthiopian king, Ergamun, that he was nursed by the goddess Ank, *and born of Seti;* on the other he is "*born of Isis, and nursed by Nephthys.*"[5] Osiris is "*conceived by Isis and engendered by Nephthys.*"[6] Also, the Osirified deceased says, "*I am Horus! I know that I was begotten by Pasht, and brought forth by Neith;*" another form of the Two Goddesses,[7] who are the two sisters of Horus in the drawing on the following page.

To judge from the prevalence of this triadic type, a special litera-

[1] Burton, *Dahome*, v. ii. ch. xvi.   [2] Lepsius, *Todt.* 85, 89.
[3] Tablet at Boulak.   [4] *North Side*, line 5.
[5] Wilkinson, 2nd ser. vol. i. p. 267. Birch, *Gallery*.
[6] *Ritual*, ch. xvii.   [7] Ch. lxvi.

ture must have been devoted to the Two Sisters and their desire for the child, fragments of which have survived. Plato mentions the Hymns of Isis that were 10,000 years old. A Papyrus found in the ruins of Thebes contains what have been termed the "Lamentations," but which are more properly the Invocations or Evocations of Isis and Nephthys. They are the "*beneficial formulæ made by the Two Divine Sisters in the house of Osiris*," and when recited, "*two women, beautiful in their members*," were directed to "*sit on the ground at the principal door of the Great Hall*," holding bread and water in their hands, and having the names of Isis and Nephthys inscribed on their shoulders. These correspond to the two sisters

Urti in the cult of Atum, and Iusâas, whose son, Iu-em-hept, as the Iu-su, was the Jesus of Heliopolis and Pa-Tum. The two sisters invoke the God as the *Babe*.

"Thou who comest to us as a child each month." "Thou comest to us from thy retreat at the time, to spread the water of thy soul, to distribute the bread of thy being." "Come to thine abode." "I am Nephthys thy sister who loveth thee." "Come to Aper; thou wilt see thy mother Neith. Beautiful child, do not stay from her. Come to her nipples; abundance is in them."

Isis cries—

"Come to thine abode, come to thine abode!

God An,[2] come to thine abode!
Look at me; I am thy sister who loveth thee.
Do not stay far from me; oh, beautiful youth;
Come to thine abode with haste, with haste.

I see thee no more,
My heart is full of bitterness on account of thee;
Mine eyes seek thee;
I seek thee to behold thee.
Will it be long ere I see thee?
Will it be long ere I see thee?

---

[1] *Records of the Past*, vol. ii. p. 119.   [2] Osiris reborn of the Moon.

(Oh) excellent sovereign,
Will it be long ere I see thee?
Beholding thee is happiness;
Beholding thee is happiness.
(Oh) God An, beholding thee is happiness.
Come to her who loveth thee.
Come to her who loveth thee,
(Oh) Un-nefer, the Word-made-Truth !

Come to thy sister, come to thy wife ;
Come to thy sister, come to thy wife ;
(Oh) Urt-het, come to thy spouse.
I am thy sister by thy mother ;
Do not separate thyself from me.
Gods and men (turn) their faces towards thee,
Weeping together for thee whenever (they) behold me.
I call thee in (my) lamentations,
(Even) to the heights of heaven,
And thou hearest not my voice.
I am thy sister who loveth thee on earth ;
No one else hath loved thee more than I,
(Thy) sister, (thy) sister." [1]

We find in these fragments the essence of the " Canticles " assigned
to Solomon. It is also evident that some other remains of Egyptian
poetry translated by Goodwin are either spoken in the character of
one of the two divine sisters, or were composed in closest imitation of
the Invocations addressed to the divine lover.

THE BEGINNING OF THE SONG OF JOY AND BEAUTY OF THY SISTER.

" Beloved of my heart, come to the meadows, my brother ; beloved of my heart
(come) after me, thou who art beloved in all thy doings. Thou fair one ! thou who
comest to the garden of one who loves him. The voice of the bird resounds,
occupied with his Uai.[2] Thy love draws me back. I know not how to unloose it
(the bird). Shall I call to my mother that she may come to me ? The bird flies
and perches. Many birds gyrate around ; (thou) art my love alone, my heart is
bound to thy heart ; go not far from me. I go, for I find him whom Amen hath given
to me for ever and ever. Thou fair one ! When thou wast in thy chamber, thy
arm was laid upon my arm ; thou didst survey thy love. I poured forth my heart
to thee in the night. I was as one in my bower ; thou didst strengthen my heart
to seek thee. The voice of the swallow resounds. It saith the earth is enlightened.
How do I wait for thee, thou bird ! I found my brother in his bed-chamber. Go
not far from me. Let thy hand be in my hand, let me be with thee in every
pleasant place." [3]

THE BEGINNING OF THE SONG OF JOYS OF THE FRAGRANT FLOWERS.

" Thou enchantest my heart, thou hast caused me to be as one who seeks, that I
may be in thy bosom. My prayer is to hear the (beat) of his heart ; that I may
behold the brightness of (his) eyes. I fawn upon thee, to behold thy love, O man
of my heart ! Most delightful is my hour of going forth ; an hour of eternity. . . .
I am thy oldest sister. I am unto thee like the garden which I have planted with
flowers and sweet odours. It is watered by thy hand, refreshed by the breezes,
a pleasant place to walk in. Thy hand is in my hand. I remember, and my heart is
joyful at our walking, drinking together ; how I listened to thy voice, it was life to
me to hear it. I bring thy garlands when thou comest drinking." [4]

---

[1] *Records of the Past*, vol. ii. page 120.
[2] *Uaui*, is to discourse, meditate, melt.
[3] A Papyrus in the B. M. rendered by Goodwin, *Trans. Bib. Soc.* v. iii.
pp. 383—5.
[4] From an Egyptian song. Goodwin, *Tr. Bib. Soc.* vol. iii. 387—8.

It is the song of Solomon, matter and music, phrase after phrase, and there is no poetry in literature more full of love-longing. The bosom is also called the "Breast of *Rerem.*" *Rer* was some kind of Egyptian food; the word likewise means a nurse, and to nurse. This, therefore, was the breast for the suckling, the divine child.

The "black but comely" lady of the Canticles says: "*My Beloved feedeth among the lilies,*" "*My Beloved is gone down into his garden, to the beds of spices, to feed in the gardens and to gather lilies.*" Still more occultly, "*I would lead thee and bring thee into my mother's house; I would cause thee to drink of the spiced wine of the juice of my pomegranate.*" This fruit was the emblem of the womb, and was held in the hand of the Syrian Juno; the illustration belongs to the primitive physiology, and relates to nourishing the child before birth in the maternal abode. In the Egyptian song the lady says: "*My sister issues forth angry, uttering all sorts of exclamations at the porter.*" In the Hebrew, "*My mother's children were angry with me; they made me keeper of the vineyards.*" "*I spoke not,*" says the one, "*but my heart remembered.*" The other, "*I sleep, but my heart waketh.*"

In both the feminine triad appear as the mother and the two sisters. Horus is called the brother of the two sisters as Isis and Nephthys and the child of the mother as Neith; the genitrix who becomes twain in the sisterhood. The lady of the Canticles is one of two sisters, and Solomon is their brother. "*We have a little sister, and she hath no breasts.*" But the speaker has breasts that stand erect like towers. This agrees with the two characters one of whom gave the breast to the child, the other being without a breast; hence the female Egyptian figures having only one breast!

The lady in the songs says: "*Thou tookest my breast, thou didst revel in its abundance in the day of* (* * * *)" Nephthys pleads: "*Come to Aper; thou wilt see thy mother Neith. Beautiful child, do not stay far from her. Come to her nipples; abundance is in them.*"

The two sisters and the brother are the children of one mother who represents the abode of being. This abode was figured on the head of Nephthys as the house of breath. Another type of it was the double-turreted tower-crown of Kubele. This is the character of the lady of Solomon's song; she is the wall, the tower, "*her neck is as the tower of David built for an armoury*" like the Kubele crown.[1]

The present reading permits of a sense similar to that claimed by the Christian commentators for their "*Loves of Christ and the Church,*"

[1] The duality personated by the Two Divine Sisters will explain an obscure passage in the Canticles. "What will ye see in the Shulamite?" "As it were the company of two armies." The word Makanaim denotes something double that dances up and down. Fuerst says a "double row of dancing youths and maidens." It is simply the twin-sisters of the double horizon. *Mak* (Eg.) is to dance. *Makha* (Eg.) means the balance, scales, equinox, and the two characters are here combined in the Shulamite, as the mother who divides on the horizon.

only the Christ was the youthful solar god Horus, Iu-su or Khunsu, the "Good Peace" in Egypt; the mythical Solomon, the Hebrew Prince of Peace. The difference between the mythical and the human representation is as great as that betwixt the virgin of Pinturiccio feeding the little one "*among the lilies*" and the fleshly display of one of Sir Peter Lely's painted courtezans.

The child Horus was the Kamite Christ who became the Anointed at puberty. The Great Mother was his Abode and Shrine, or Sekhem. The Abode or House is carried on the head of Nephthys. This type was likewise continued in Rome as the Mother Church, the sanctuary of the divine child.

The primordial genitrix appears as the House of God in the visions of Hermas where she is seen as an old woman because she was the "*first of all creation, and the world was made for her*"; *omnium primus creata est.* She who had been the Abode from the beginning, the abode in life and death, became the Church in the end.[1]

Further, as the Great Mother divided into the two Sisters represented by Isis and Nephthys who stand at the two sides of the child-god, so is it in the imagery of the catacombs, where various examples are found of two female Orante figures which stand on the two sides of the mythical Christ. These two women are believed to symbolize the Church. Being two, however, they are supposed by the religious A-Gnostics to typify the Church under two dispensations of the law and the gospel.[2]

The Christ between them is the good shepherd whose original crook, the Hek, is carried in one hand, by Horus, and his fan (Khu) in the other, as he stands between HIS two *Orantes*, Isis and Nephthys!

Horus is conceived by Isis, the mother of flesh, and generated by Nephthys, the mother of breath.[3] Rhea and Hera were the two mothers of the child Zeus. Bacchus called *Bimater* had two mothers; he was conceived by Semele and brought into the world by Ippa.[4]

The two divine sisters were continued in the Gospels as the two Maries, the Virgin and Mary Cleophas, *both of whom were the mothers* of Jesus. This, that is impossible as history, is perfect according to the mythos—the Christ being bi-mater; and true to the Celestial Allegory, which is illustrated in the Catacombs by the mythical Christ who is pourtrayed in more than half-a-dozen different but identifiable forms.

To recapitulate: first, the Great Mother is personified in space, and as space takes two aspects in the upper and lower hemispheres; she divided and there are two women, the two divine sisters. The great mother bears the twins as male, and these are then assigned to the two sisters. We have now got the characters of the mother, sister, and brother of the earliest sociology. Then follows a pair of twins

---

[1] *The Shepherd of St. Hermas. Vision*, ii.   [2] Lundy, figs. 81 and 149.
[3] *Ritual*, ch. xviii.   [4] Proclus, in *Timæus*, b. ii. sect. 124.

that are male and female, as Shu and Tefnut, the brother and sister who represent the primitive consortship.

The Polynesian twin-brother and sister have their dwelling-place near the great rock which is the foundation of the world.[1] So the brother and sister as Shu and Tefnut the twin lion-gods kept the gates of the north and south on the Tzer Rock, the foundation of the world. The Greeks identified their Castor and Pollux, the Dioscuri, with the Gemini of the zodiac. But the Egyptians distinguished between them. The male twins were represented by the two male lion-gods as Sut-Horus, the Egyptian Dioscuri. Next the twin lions become male and female in Shu and his sister. The first were pre-zodiacal, *or belonged to an earlier inner zodiac*, the two stars being distinguished before the twelve signs were formed, or the brother and sister had been adopted as the Gemini of both sexes. Further, the male and female twins as Shu and Tefnut were also placed in the opposite sign, the Archer, by the Egyptians. On referring to the oblong zodiac of Denderah[2] the reader will see Shu as the Archer twinned with Tefnut as his hinder face. The arrow elsewhere is a well-known symbol of Shu. In this same zodiac Shu appears in the human form, and Tefnut in her type of the lioness. The Archer formed of Shu and his sister exhibits a male-female shape of the Gemini. So that when we find these are the Twins in the sign Gemini, whilst Castor and Pollux denote the twin-brothers, we are able to distinguish between the two different pairs of twins now clustered together in one group.

The Serranos and Acagchemens of California have a myth of the twins who were male and female like Shu and Tefnut in Egypt. They say that before the material world was in existence there lived two beings the nature of whom they are unable to explain. They were brother and sister, and the brother's name signified the heaven above, the sister's the earth below. From the union of these two sprang the first man, *Ouiot*, who was a grand captain. This happened in the north, for they affirmed that men were created in the north, the birthplace in the oldest mythology. In Egyptian *Uat* is a name of the north, and of Lower Egypt, or the Abyss of the Waters, and *Uau* (Eg.) is the name of the captain. In another myth we see the sister following the twin brothers.[3]

The Indians at the heads of the St. Lawrence and Mississippi rivers relate how the first woman descended from heaven and hovered some time in the air seeking where to set her foot on solid ground. The tortoise offered his back, which she accepted as a place of rest and residence. There the spume of the sea gathered about the tortoise and made the earth. The woman found it lonely, and another descent took place. A Spirit came, and finding the woman asleep drew near

[1] Ellis.   [2] Drummond, pl. 6.
[3] Reported by an early Spanish missionary, Father Boscana ; Bancroft, vol. iii. pp. 161, 162.

to her and accompanied with her. The result of this connection was the twin-children of the myth. When she was delivered these two sons came out of her left side; they were jealous of each other, and the one who was an unsuccessful hunter treated the successful one so badly as to compel him to leave the earth and withdraw to heaven. *After his withdrawal the Spirit again descended and returned to the woman, who bore a daughter*, and she became the Great Mother of the North American Indians.[1]

The mother, the two sisters, the child, and the pubescent male, the brother and sister, completed the first group of relations, there being as yet no individualized fatherhood. Following the motherhood simply, a type of the producers was now evolved in the likeness of the male and female twins.

These two different pairs of twins, who were the twin brothers Sut and Horus, and the twin brother and sister Shu and Tefnut in Egypt, enable us to detect and expose another example of the elaborate historicizing of mythic material which was practised by the re-writers of the Hebrew Scriptures; for the story of the twin-brothers is told a third time in the Book of Genesis as the history of Judah and Tamar and of Pharetz and Zarach.[2] In this the red one who ought to have been born first puts forth his hand, which the nurse binds round with a scarlet thread. He then withdraws, and his brother breaks his way into the world. The Nurse, however, identifies Zarach as the one who should have been the first-born, and who is named as the one who appears like the sun, the light, or the red dawn, *i.e.* the one that makes the first *visible* appearance. Pharetz is the dark one, who breaks his way through to be foremost. So Sut was fabled to have broken a way into the world at the wrong time. So, according to Plutarch, Anra-Mainyus, the Dark Mind, broke open the egg-shell to be born first—the egg-shell which images the heaven.[3] The twin-brothers Zarach and Pharetz, the breaker-through, are born of Judah and Tamar, who are represented as relatives and consorts, if not called the brother and sister. Now the male and female twins who consorted as Shu and Tefnut are the twin lion-gods; and Judah was the lion-god in Israel. He is called the lion's whelp, and is represented by the twin lions[4] which were pourtrayed on the standard of Judah and in the planisphere.[5] The lion was the totemic type of Judah because Judah, like Shu, was the lion.

The primitive ideas of the past were expressed, embodied, and stereotyped in images that are still extant. The early men did not begin by conceiving of creative cause and pourtraying it in an Androgynous figure, male in front and female behind. Such a

[1] *Religious Ceremonies of all Nations*, p. 298.
[2] Genesis xxxviii. 27.
[3] *Of Isis and Osiris*.
[4] Genesis xlix. 9.
[5] Drummond, pl. 16.

representation was the *necessary result of beginning with the female, and continuing with the man-ess; the male being added to express progenitorship;* and ending in a type of both sexes which was the male-mother of one cult and the mother-male of another. The mother being first was foundational, the male was additional. The earliest sphinx is the dual female, a figure with a female face and breasts. This is rarely discovered in Egypt. It does appear on the Turin statue with Mut-Snatem, the consort of Horemhebi, and has been found elsewhere. Its rarity, however, is no proof that the feminine sphinx was not Egyptian. It belongs to those types cast out by Egypt which survived in Assyria and other countries among the worshippers of the mother and child. The dual lioness of Pehti and the Ruti, as the two mouths of the horizon, was equivalent to the sphinx that is feminine at either end. But the later and more orthodox Egyptian sphinx was male in front and female in the hinder-part. It was given to the gods in the later religion, not to the goddess-mother. She took her place finally as hinder-part only, the front being assigned to the male-mother as Divinity or royal Pharaoh. The processes of evolution may be traced when we start from a beginning: when we do not, mythology and typology become a maze without a clue.

As before mentioned, in one of the Hottentot songs the lioness identifies herself as the "*Liontail.*" She thus addresses the dying lion, her son: "*Thou yellow child of the* LIONTAIL, *why didst thou not listen to what thy mother told thee?*" Liontail is the lioness; the female is distinguished by and as the hinder-part; the gender by its emblem; the male (*bahu*) being before, or in front. The Liontail in Egypt is Pekh (abraded Peh), the lioness-goddess whose name and sign is that of the rump. In agreement with the lioness as liontail, the mother is the she-bull: "*Thou son of a red she-bull, thou who drankest my milk,*" is the address of a Hottentot mother to her son.[1] So the genitrix under the cow-type in mythology is the she-bull as Astarte, Sothis, and Gayomard.

The name of the sphinx has never been fathomed, but from its dual nature and Egyptian origin, we may infer that the word was based on the Ankh, meaning a pair, to couple and duplicate. *Spu* (Eg.) denotes the creator and preparer. Thus *Sp-ankh* would be the dual creator or biune being, whether considered to be doubly female or epicene.

The personified *Pan* has a prior name as *Phanes*, and still earlier as *Phanax*. He says "the Musians name me *Phanax*.[2] Here again the Ankh as a type of the total is the probable origin of the name. The all in sex was composed of a twin-total, the biune being, and this was imaged by the Ankh, the sphinx and the goat-footed Phanax. Pan is a sphinx, male (human) above, and female (beast) below.

In the mythology of the Vedas there is great confusion of personal

[1] Hahn, *Tsuni-Goam*, p. 73.   [2] Ausonius, Ep. xxx.

characters and relationship. Sometimes the brother is the husband
and the mother is the wife, because of the primitive order and
sequence in the social status. The son became the father; the
brother was the husband and the sister was the wife.

The most primitive human customs were preserved in mythology as
divine. In Egypt the royal brother and sister continued to marry
long after incest was otherwise prohibited, because they typified the
gods like Shu and Tefnut, who were consorts as the sister and brother
of the totemic type, and a form of the mother and her son continued
from the earliest time. The oldest gods are named as the children.
Sut signifies the child. Kebekh is the child of Kep. Hes-Ar is the
child of Hes. The gods are said to recognise him as the "*Eternal
lad himself.*" So Bacchus was called the Eternal Boy. Aten, Adonai,
or Adonis, is the *At* (Eg.) the child, babe, the lad. Ar, Al, or El the
child, supplies the Semitic אל; and the. Ili, Ali, or Elohim are the
companions, primarily the children, the seven elementaries or embryos
of the mother alone.

When Prajapati the lord of creation is said to violate his own
daughter, it is but a result of mythical relationships, which were
based on the primitive sociology. So is it with the biblical stories,
the repulsiveness of which is the result of transforming into human
history that which is only natural in mythology. This apparent
confusion disappears the moment we get the divinities once more
rightly related to phenomena. With the development of doctrine
and the gradual exaltation of the male over the female, the characters
are seen to change positions. For example, the goddess Ishtar is
called "*Eldest of Heaven and Earth*," although in the list of the
twelve great gods she is placed last.

The *fons et origo* was feminine at first, as was acknowledged in the
Roman worship ; Fontus, the father source, was the later object
of adoration. In the first chapter of the Ritual we read, "*I am one
of the gods born of Nu*," the primordial water. Nu, Nun, or Nnu is
the mother of the gods. "*The mother Nu, all birth is received through
her.*"[1] The sun is called the "*eldest born of Nu.*"[2] Sut is the son
of Nu.[3] The serpent is the son of Nu.[4] Nu was the mother-heaven,
the firmament, considered as the celestial water. Yet in chapter xvii.
of the Ritual it is said, "*I am the great God creating himself. It is
water or Nu who is the father of the gods: Petar ref Su.*" The
explanation to be given here, the gloss on the passage, if truly
interpreted, would be, "*The celestial water Nu, Nun, or Nnu and the
firmament were held to be feminine at first, but the later theosophy
made them masculine. It was the mother who came from herself, but
the self-creator had now been made in the male image in the solar
religion.*"

The Greek Ouranos is derived from the Egyptian *Urnas.* Urnas is

---

[1] Ch. lxix.   [2] Ch. lxxvii.   [3] Ch. lxxxvi.   [4] Ch. cviii.

the "*Celestial Water*," that is, the heaven above considered as the water of the firmament. This was feminine, the water of Nupe, the woman-heaven. In the Greek *Ouranos* and the Vedic *Varuna* the sex is changed ; they have become deities who are both male and paternal, in accordance with a far later stage of sociology and mythology. It is the blood of Ouranos which gives birth to Aphrodite and that represents the celestial or biological *Urnas* of Egypt.

The beginning with the two women, as dual heaven, or earth and heaven, still survived after the male progenitorship had been established. Thus it is said of the solar god, "*He comes forth from the bosom of his mother Seb* (the earlier form, Keb, is a name of the genitrix), *born of Nut.*"[1] So when Seb is called the "*Mother of Osiris*," Renouf suspects an error in the text.[2] But the Egyptians constantly think from the phenomenal origin ; and if Seb either as god of earth or morning-star were spoken of as the bringer-forth of the sun—that introduces the idea of parturition, and therefore a feminine phase. It is a matter of typology, and a survival from the beginning. The return to the mother as First Cause is strikingly shown in the "*Praise of Learning*," in which it is said of the scribe that he "*Adores Ra, the father his mother ;*" rightly rendered by Dr. Birch, despite the seeming incongruity. Maspero reads, "*Tuau (or Seb) is his father and mother.*"[3] But that omits the doctrine of derivation from the motherhood. The mother being the primal parent, it was in her image that the fatherhood was founded. The masculine deity Khem, at Denderah, is depicted as the *double-mouth* of emanation, instead of the female. His title of *Ka-Mutf* shows him to be the *Male-Mother*, the second type of the producer or the *Man-ess.* For this reason the male member even is named Mut or Mat (Eg.) after the female Mut, the mother as the emaning mouth of being.

It was the feminine origin which accounts for Num at Philæ being called the "*Mother of mothers ;*"[4] as well as the "Father of fathers." In like manner Jove is designated by Orpheus the "*Mother of the Gods.*" This beginning alone explains that sudden reversion to the mother in the text as the "*father, his mother,*" which according to modern ideas would need to be corrected, like so many more misunderstood expressions. The mother produced the male child who grew up to become her consort and eventually his own father in the character of the generator. At this stage originated the worship of the Virgin Mother and the fatherless child, the *At* (Eg.), which still survives in Rome. But she came to be pourtrayed as a male virgin or male-ess, *to indicate the begetting and creating power, on the way toward the final fatherhood.*

Manu said the male-virgin gave birth to life and light. This male-

---

[1] M. Pierret (p. 55) thinks this is merely "a liberty taken in handling the allegory."   [2] *Hibbert Lectures*, p. 111.
[3] *Records*, vol. viii. p. 156.   [4] Mariette, *Musée Boulak*, p. 113.

virgin, observes Theodoret, was designated *Joel* (Ιωηλ). An Egyptian goddess is denominated the female Horus.[1]

Astarte is called, in a Phœnician inscription, "The King,"[2] whilst Baal is called "Goddess" (ἡ Βάαλ) in the Septuagint,[3] and in the New Testament.[4]

The Chinese Venus, whose immortal peaches ripened every 3,000 years, was called the Western *King-Mother*. In an Akkadian hymn Ishtar the Lady of Heaven, the Queen of Heaven, the opener of the locks of the high heaven, is celebrated as the Begetter. "*Heaven she benefits, earth she enlightens, my Begetter. Queen of Heaven above and below may she be invoked, my Begetter.*"[5] Ishtar has the dual form of the Great Mother who fills the one character above the horizon and the other below.

The Assyrian Zikar or Zikarat signifies the male-female or Man-ess. It is said on the Babylonian tablets : "*Venus is a male at sunrise; Venus is a female at sunset.*"[6] In the Ritual we read of "*Hathor at evening called Isis.*"[7] Also the planet Venus is called Har, the Lord, as Har-Makhu; Har denoting above the horizon. The Peruvians made Venus, the morning star, to be male, and called it Chasca, the youth with the long curling locks.[8]

We have a form of the Zikarat or Male-ess applied to the female in England. This is our "Old *Scratch*," the original of which is the "*Scrat*," the hermaphrodite, the twofold nature exhibited in the mysteries of the Sabbath as the black goat-divinity, afterwards called "Old Scratch" or the devil. "*Scrat*" is also an old woman. Even in the worship of Old Scratch the feminine image dominated, as in Ishtar the Zikarat. The Neeshenams have an Old Scratch, in a ghost named Bohem Culleh, which is of both sexes.[9]

Astarte the supreme goddess, says Philo, placed on her head a bull's horns as the symbol of her lordship. The horns were a masculine type, and these denoted the male-female. The bull-headed goddess is also found on the Egyptian monuments. The ancient Sanskrit literature shows that in early times the bull was eaten as food ; its sacredness was a later investiture. On the other hand, the cow always was and always continued to be too sacred to be eaten. She was the mother of life. The bull's horns added a male character, as did the horns of the female goat. According to Hor-Apollo the Egyptians consecrated a "*two-horned and bull-formed*" beetle to the moon, "*whence the children of the Egyptians said that the bull in the heavens is the exaltation of this goddess.*"[10] In this character the speaker making his transformations in the likeness of natural

[1] Wilkinson, pl. 57.   [2] Schlottman, *Die Inschrift Eschmunazars*, p. 143.
[3] Hos. ii. 8 ; Zeph. i. 4.   [4] Rom. xi. 4.
[5] *Records of the Past*, vol. v. 158.
[6] Sayce, *T. S. B. A.* vol. iii. pt. i. pp. 196—7.
[7] Ch. cviii.   [8] Prescott, *Peru*, p. 40, ed. 1867, Lond.
[9] Bancroft, vol. iii. p. 545.   [10] B. i. 10.

phenomena says, "*I am the bull sharpening the horns—the great illuminator.*"[1] The male character of the feminine moon was derived from its horned phase ; the horn of renewal. The meeting-point is shown by the Kamite *Karn-at*, for a phallus, placed in position as horns. This is identical with the Assyrian *Karnu*, Hebrew *Keren*, Latin *Cornu*, for the horn. Neith and the vulture were both depicted with the male member erect in front of them,[2] whilst Taurt (the Typhonian genitrix) is figured with a phallus for a nose, which makes her masculine in front.[3] These are the equivalents of the bull-headed Astarte, the horned Ashtoreth, the bull-horned beetle, the male-ess, or goddess-lord.

Macrobius observes that some persons corrupt the line in Virgil[4] by reading Dea, goddess, instead of Deo, God, for Venus ; and that Acterianus affirms that in Calvus we should read *Pollentemque Deum Venerem*, Venus that powerful god, *non deam*, not goddess.[5] Servius in his note on this line says, "*There is in Cyprus an image of the bearded Venus with the body and dress of a woman, but with a sceptre and the sex of a man, which they call Aphroditos* (Male), *and to which the men sacrifice in a female dress and the women in a masculine one.*" It was of this cult that a Latin author says, "*There were to be seen in the temples, with a general public moaning, lamentable celebrations, and men manifesting the menstrualia, and exposing with honoured ostentation this blemish of an impure and shameless body.*" Such abnormities (or were they commoner among the earlier races ?) were held to be sacred, like hermaphrodites, on account of their including the signs of both sexes in one, and thus becoming representative of the biune being. Dosiades styles Semiramis the woman with the masculine raiment.[6] Breeches for women were first said to have been invented and worn by her, and men were first emasculated in her worship. She was the divine *male-ess*, the middle type between the motherhood and fatherhood made to partake of both sexes : and men sought to attain the nearest likeness to divinity by becoming intermediates also, called Eunuchs, who unsexed themselves with their own hands, and offered up their virility as a sacrifice. The pseudo-Heraclitus scoffs and mocks at this worship of the virgin-mother at Ephesus, and laughs at her *Megabyzus*, who were compelled to be mutilated because she was too great a prude to be served by a virile male or a man. It was a strange mode of becoming a child of God, or the goddess, and of illustrating the text, "*Except ye become as little children ye cannot enter the kingdom of heaven,*" and yet a literal method of accomplishing it. Attes, the unsexed devotee of Kubele, and Aten, both derive their names from At (Eg.) the child. The child-god was the prepubes

---

[1] *Ritual*, ch. liii.
[2] Champ. *Panthéon*.
[3] Birch, *Gallery*.
[4] *Æn*. ii. 632.
[5] *Saturnal.* lib. iii. vol. ii. p. 24.
[6] *Nimrod*, vol. i. p. 479.

cent, and the worshippers in unsexing themselves were at once conforming to the likeness of the male-mother, called the Virgin, and of her divine infant called the "Eternal Child." This man-ess or male-female divinity was adored as the "*only one,*" since it was of a dual nature unified.

The duality was first of all female : next male-female, and lastly female-male. The male-female and the female-male were divinities or types of two different and opposed religions, according to whichever sex was considered primus. Androgyneity is not a natural but an unnatural fact. Non-sex-denoting language was of necessity androgynous. In typology it is but a symbolic combination like the sphinx adopted to express the two truths of source when these were known to be both male and female. *The first real departure from nature was made visibly manifest when the male organ was typically added to the female as her sign of producing power.* Arnobius derided the "heathen" for praying to deities without knowing of what sex they were, whether gods or goddesses, or the intermediate sex, which is precisely the position of those who have invoked Jehovah ever since the time when the *gnosis* of the incommunicable name was taught.

An Assyrian king calls Merodach, under the name of the goddess Ri, "*the Mother who bore me,*" and he addresses this divinity as both mother and father in one. Merodach is described as a goddess by Jeremiah,[1] "*her* idols are confounded." The idols here are Gillulim, excrementitious divinities. The Seventy sneeringly call her the *delicate* Merodach. Not only is Merodach feminine but excrementitious, that is, menstruating. This is the point of the passage in Isaiah[2] where the parturient deities are mockingly described as being in labour without bringing forth. They bowed the knees and bent the back but were unable to produce, whilst in the act and process of straining, their own life went forth. They merely menstruated. But Jehovah, our Ani-Hva, *he* is the true God whose children are "*borne from the belly, carried from the womb,*" but who says, "*I will bear, I will carry, I will deliver.*" This shows the uterine type continued. Jehovah was the genitrix at first, Jah, or Iao, was a form of the male-female, and when the sun-god became the type of a Supreme Being, the female characteristics also survived. Aten, the Solar Disk, is called "Mistress of Arabia" in the inscription of Queen Hatasu. On a monument of the twelfth dynasty De Rougé found the Sun styled the "*Mother of the Earth.*" In consequence of the beginning with the feminine nature the solar god has to represent both sexes and their operations. M. Deveria points out a curious figure of the Sun having a hawk's head and shedding light in the shape of stars and RED *globules* on a mummied body ; the Sun saying, "*I manifest hidden things, I elucidate the mysteries, I give life to your souls ; your nourishment is in my back ; your souls live there. There*

[1] i. 2.　　　　　　　　　　[2] xlvi. 1, 2.

are waters for you at the station of the abyss; your souls follow my transformations."

The transformations included the male and female phases, hence the Sun or Osiris (or Adonis) was described as menstruating in *Smen*, the original type of the bloody sweat in Gethsemane.[1] As Belus, in the Berosian account, takes the place of Omoroka, and the creation proceeds from his blood instead of hers, so in the Ritual it is said the " *Sun mutilated himself, and from the stream of blood all things existed.*"

This marks the change of sex in the producer, and also shows the perfect identity of the Babylonian and Egyptian typology. Jupiter was formerly the Ju-mater or Jupiter genitrix. Valerius Soranus calls Jupiter the Mother of the Gods. Hesychius identifies Jupiter with Helen. Proclus, in *Timæus*, says all things were contained (ἐν γαστέρι Ζηνός) in the womb of Jupiter. The same writer exclaims, " *Female and father is the mighty God Ericapæus.*"

Brahm begins with the nature of the female. " *The great Brahm is the womb of all those forms which are conceived in every natural womb.*" " *The great Brahm,*" says Krishna, " *is my womb, and in it I place my fœtus, and from it is the procreation of all nature.*"[2] This feminine origin of the imagery alone shows how all beings can be said to have been created from the Mouth of Brahm, Jehovah, and other deities. It is said of Brahm in two characters : " *They who know the divine essence* (Brahma) *in Perusha* (male) *know Parameshthin ; they who know the* HIGHEST *divine Mystery* (Brahmana), *in consequence know Skambha,*" of whom they say " *divine knowledge is the Mouth,*" and who is identified with the dual revealer and the bifurcating one of the Beginning, in whom the two paths of the Sun's two courses meet, and the " *Two young females of diverse aspects, the day and the night, hasten in union*"[3] Here the two females preserve the type of the feminine double-first. Brahm is depicted as the male deity with a pregnant womb, and, as a type of self-emanation, with his foot in his mouth, like the tail of the serpent.[4]

" *The King's uncle found a head of corn with two stalks in two different plots of ground growing up into one ear. Upon this was made the Kwei Ho.*"[5] The god, as figured in mythology was similarly grown from the two stalks of sex, both of which had their single rootage in the motherhood.

The lotus was a twofold type peculiar to the dual motherhood, and the *Nymphæa Nelumbo* has two stalks, one of these being the bearer of the fruit. The fruit, or seed, was the child who grew into the virile male, and thus was constituted a biune being that was twin in

[1] *Vide* vol. ii. p. 37, *Book of Beginnings.*
[2] Moor, *Pantheon* " Krishna," p. 211.
[3] Muir, *Sans. Texts*, v. 381.
[4] Guigniaut, pl. 1.
[5] *Chinese Classics*, vol. iii. pt. i. p. 9 ; Preface to the *Shu King*. Legge.

sex and triadic in manifestation; the mother being the *opening One;* the Child a *duad* in sex, and the virile male a natural figure of *Three.* The deity with four arms is likewise an embodiment of the dual nature. This is not so common in the Egyptian as in the Hindu Pantheon, yet Amen-Ra and Ptah are both pourtrayed with four arms.[1]

One type of the dual divinity is the calf, an image of Ahti, the duplicative abode. The calf, of course, may be of either sex, hence it represents both in one. The calf is the *Au,* and *Au* or *Iu* is a deity with the head of the calf or bullock. *Au* signifies *Was, Is,* and *To-be,* like the A O, or Alpha and Omega. Alpha and Omega are likewise to be seen among the classical curiosities of the British Museum in a terra-cotta imitation of a foot wearing a hobnailed boot on which the nails are arranged in the shape of a pointed A at the toe, and in the form of the Omega at the heel; the beginning and the end is thus figured on one foot. When the present writer was young this same pattern of A and Ω in tips or hobnails was dear to the hearts of our canal boatmen. This epicene nature is pourtrayed by the *A O* of the Mexican drawings, in which the O is entwined about the A, after the fashion of making the capital letter A with the O of a flourish about it thus—

which survives in the symbolism of schoolboys. Out of this biune figure issues the fish or some other type of emanation from the source. The Chinese have the same *A O* or *I A O,* and in Amoy *Iu* signifies first cause, origin, the son and the masculine principle; the three manifestations of the dual One. The Greeks used the letters " *Ie* " " *Ie* " in their religious invocations and evocations. *I E* renders the Egyptian *Iu.* This diphthong of deity attains unity at last in the letter O. " *We worship* O," says Euripides in *Bacchæ;* and with this letter we get back to the beginning where the O or Omega Ω is an emblem worn as the head-dress of Hathor-Isis. It is also the astronomical sign of the Nodes of the lunar orbit, which represents the ascending Node one way, and the descending Node the other. In Egyptian and Welsh *Au* is a plural form, and the calf Au, which might be of either sex, is a dual type. This imaged the A I. of divinity which was of a male-female nature, but to pourtray it as more than human, beyond sex, and as One, it was represented by the castrated male, so that the Eunuch or the Bullock was likewise a final figure of the deity.

The accompanying drawing pourtrays the twins who were Shu and Ma or Shu and Tefnut, the male and female *Gemini* in Egypt; the one being of both sexes. The calf below, with its tongue thrust out, tells the tale in gesture language, as the type of both sexes.

---

[1] Champ. *Panthéon Égyptien*, pl. 5; Pierret, *Le Panthéon Ægyptien*, p. 6.

The beard of the male above denotes the third phase, and thus the figure contains the Trinity in Unity.

Here the beginning in the typology is identical with that of language when it had no sex-denoting words. The child bifurcates into the man and woman at puberty, and the calf into the horned bull and milch cow. The calf represented both sexes in the non-pubescent phase, or the mother and child only in the cult that did not include the fatherhood. Even the bull was made to conform to this type as the ox. According to Varro there was a vulgar Latin name for the ox, viz. Trio. The ox being of a third sex, neither male nor female, return was thus made to the primitive Nuter, or Neuter of the beginning. The Greek τρία is of a neuter gender, in which form the biune one was imaged by the calf, the castrated male, or the ox, *Trio*.

Taken from Guigniaut's *Reliq. de l'Antiq.* plate 13.

The *A Ω* in Revelation denotes the biune being, or hermaphrodite deity, who is described as a man with female paps, and he does not differ in nature from the two-sexed Bacchus, or the Etruscan Priapus, with the male member and feminine breasts. So "*Jesus Christ as Saint Sophia*" is the male-female, identical with Venus-barbatus.[1] Bacchus, the biune being, is called "*Ia*" as one of his titles; that is *IE* in Ionic, the same as *IU* (later IE) in Egyptian, the dual one. Thus Iasus, another form of his title, would be Iesus or Jesus, the *Iu-su* (Eg.), the coming child of a twofold nature. The Gnostic *Iao*, seated on the lotus, is a male-female.[2] Har-Iu is found with female breasts. In the Soane Museum there is a Græco-Egyptian figure of the Child Horus of a female nature, which is only feminine instead of being effeminate or infantile.

The lamb, like the calf, was a type of this biune being, the child of either sex, and representative of both. Horus was the lamb of either sex; Mithras was the lamb of both sexes. The

[1] Didron, fig. 50.　　　[2] King's *Gnostics*, pl. 5, fig. 1.

human child being of either sex, the divine was of both. *This mythical type could only be fulfilled in nature by an hermaphrodite.* The epicene Messiah is described in the "Codex Nazäræus." "*Nebu Messiah shall call the Jews and shall say to them, 'Come ye, behold! I quicken the dead and make them arise again. I pay the price of the ransoming. I am Enos Nazaræus Spiritus, even a Voice being sent that shall give testimony of him in Jerusalem, but he himself will captivate the sons of the men by the allurements of cunning delusions, and will imbrue them with blood and monthly (menstrual) pollution.*'"[1] Such language could not be interpreted without the types on which it is based. It is one mode of describing the biune being of either or both sexes, corresponding to the feminine "paps" of the "Son of Man," the supposed Messiah of "Revelation." In the fragment quoted by the two Clements we are told that "*the Lord, having been asked by Salome when his kingdom was to come, replied, 'When you shall have trampled under foot the garment of shame* (mystically, when the woman shall cease to menstruate), *when two shall be as one, when that which is without shall be like that which is within, and when the male with the female shall be neither male nor female.*'"[2] Which shows an application of the neutral type evolved from the child, calf, colt, or lamb, to the eschatological phase; that which preceded the division of the sexes at puberty is continued as a type beyond sex; the *neuter* image of divinity. Paul identifies the doctrine of this unity in the biune one, the mythical Christ, when he says, "*There is neither Jew nor Greek, there is neither bond nor free, there is neither male nor female, for ye are all one in Christ Jesus,*" who was the biune being, the Alpha and Omega.

When the biune being was finally figured as male in front and female behind, the adorers of the Great Mother are known by the prominence given to the hinder part. Thus when the divinity as Iah showed the hinder part to Moses, that denoted the feminine half of the whole. The Egyptian Peh, or Pekh, is the feminine hinder-part of the lioness, the goddess Pekh; and Pekh and back, as before said, are identical. This cult was continued in the Witches' Sabbath, where all the imagery and actions illustrated the backward way. The witnesses describe how in their circular dances they were placed back to back, and struck each other at intervals. Among the curious figures engraved by Von Hammer there is a naked female form wearing the crown of Kubelê, holding in one hand an image of the sun and moon, both of which have faces turned bottom upwards. This representation was sculptured on a stone coffer found in Burgundy, together with a series

---

[1] "Eisque dicet, vinite videte, mortuos, vivifice et ut resurgant facio, pretium redemptionis solvo, sum Enos Nazaræus Spiritus etiam voce in Jerusalem missâ testimonium de eo dicet ipse autem illecebris præstigiarum filios hominis captivabit et eos sanguine et menstruali pollutione imbuet." Vol. ii. p. 109.
[2] Clement of Alexandria, strom. iii. 12; Clement of Rome, Epistle 2, c. xii.

of scenes indicative of the secret mysteries.[1] The scarabæus was also a
type of the backward way, because it rolled its little globe in an
opposite direction to that of the natural motion of its own body.
Thus it was an image of the moon, that makes its passage from west
to east, the backward way ; and of the sun in its annual motion, which
is the reverse to the order of the signs. This will explain the picture
of the sun and moon turned upside down. In the Witches' Sabbath
the divinity appeared in the image of the biune being, and was male
before and female behind. According to the confessions of the
females He saluted them in front and they saluted Her behind. The
hindward face was the most worshipful, and to this the unclean kiss
in ano, the obscene " Memra" of the Arabians, was given by the
devotees. This was called the goat's face. The goat in French is
Bouc, in Cornish *Bouch ;* and the deity was called the Bouch, the Bug,
Bugan, or Bogy. In this cult the she-goat was a type of the male
(horned) in front, and female behind ; the especial figure of a Hebrew
dual divinity ; a natural sphinx before the male-lioness could have
been compounded as a sphinx. Thus the goat as bouch, the back, as
Pekh (Eg.) rump, and the *back* itself, came to be synonymous. To
back or go back is to buck. To set a back is to buck ; and in the
game of " *Buck, Buck, how many horns do I hold up ?* " we have a portrait of the bouch in the boy who bucks, and at the same time a
glimpse of the mysteries and a survival of a primitive mode of con-
sulting the oracle, which was feminine, and always placed in the
hinder part, whether of the goat, lioness, calf, ass, or sow ; the Adytum
of the Temple, or the Lady Chapel at the end of the Church. The
oracle and behind are synonymous in the Hebrew דבר, or Deborah,
if personified. When the Sabeans made their adorations to the North
it was because that was the feminine hinder-part of heaven.

Typology gives a very different account of the religious origines from
that which has been promulgated by the philologists. According to
M. Renan, for example, the deity as a male Monad was *conceived by
and evolved from the Semitic consciousness.* In his essay on the
" History of the people of Israel," he declares, that whilst all other
races wandered in the wilderness of Polytheism without finding the
one God, the Semite stands first and alone in grasping the idea of
the divine Unity, which all other people have had to adopt from its
example, and on the faith of its declaration. The Semitic race, guided
by its firm and certain sight, instantly unmasked divinity by *a primitive intuition,* and *from its earliest days,* and *without reflection or
reasoning* attained the purest form of religion that humanity has
known. This is that beginning *without nature* commonly called
" revelation !" He further maintains that the *Desert is monotheistic,*
and the one God is the *natural image of its great loneliness !* A sandy

[1] Pl. 38, " Worship of the generative powers."

foundation on which to establish the Eternal! On the other hand, Jeremiah, who knew his contemporaries, affirms that they had a very desert of deities; or, as many gods as cities: "*According to the number of thy cities are thy gods, O Judah!*"[1] Exactly as it was in monumental Egypt.

It has been shown in a previous volume how the gods of Israel had their origin in phenomena like those of Egypt, Phœnicia and Assyria. Hitherto we have been told that the Latin Jupiter is one with the Greek Zeus, and Zeus is the Sanskrit Dyaus, meaning the Father above. But when the Hindus employ the name of Dyaus for the bright heaven, the day, they have adopted one-half of the whole, which in this instance is a circle, that of day and night, as their monad of deity; but the duality of the word *Dyu* is not to be effaced in that way; the twin pattern stamped by the original mould of thought is visibly extant the world over. The bright heaven is one-half of the whole, and the Persians, says Herodotus, call the *whole* celestial circle Jupiter.[2] In Sanskrit *Dvi* is two; *Dva*, two, both; English, *Twy* or *Tvi*; Gothic, *Tvai*; Lithuanic, *Dvi*; Akkadian, *Dub*; Greek, δύο. This in Egyptian is *Ti* (or Tiu), the Irish *Di*. *Tuai* (Eg.), or *Taui* (Tfui) also denotes two halves. The Maori *Tio* for the oyster, the bivalve, shows a perfect type of the two-one under this name. The two halves were the upper and the lower heaven, which were discriminated by various means. There is no Div without duality. Devi has a double nature. Dian is dual because of her double lunation. Deuce is said to have been a Divinity of the Brigantes, who was also described as appearing to women in a male form, and to men as a female; which gives a natural rendering of the duality. The first Dev, as the heaven itself, was dual, as upper and lower, the place of day and dark. Hence the *Div*, in Sanskrit the bright, is the dark one, the devil, in the Avesta; whilst *Dub* (Akkadian) for the white surface of a reed tablet is black in the Irish Duibhe, or Dub. There is no fundamental rootage save in phenomena. The double heaven was solely feminine at first. In Egypt the *Tef*, *Teph* of source, and abyss of beginning, or *Tef* the genitrix, represented by the dragon, the water-horse or cow, was earlier than *Tef*, the divine father; and in India the earliest form of Dyaus was feminine, as the mother heaven; she who was personified as Mahadevi, or the still earlier Aditi. This may explain why Dyaus, the sky, does not occur as a masculine in common Sanskrit, whereas Dyaus does occur in the Veda in a feminine form. *Tep* is the Egyptian name for heaven. In Inner Africa this is

Debo, Heaven, Mfut.   *Doba*, Heaven, Diwala.   *Dioba*, Heaven, Baseke.

In Arabic *Tiba* is Heaven or Paradise. This African and Proto-Aryan root is the Sanskrit *Div* or *Dyu*, whence the names of heaven,

[1] Ch. ii. 28.   [2] L. 131.

day, and divinity; but it did not merely mean to shine, or be bright; that is but the final shimmer of words upon the surface of things, with which the Aryanists begin their interpretation, and beguile themselves. Neither will the primitive myths disclose their fundamental significance to a philology that only penetrates the latest formation of language.

Tep (Eg.) is the Heaven, over; one with our English *Top*. *Tep* (Eg.), means to breathe, sniff, inhale. *Div* in Toda is breath; *Dufe*, Vei, to blow; and the upper was the heaven of breath and light, the lower of the water and darkness. *Diev* in Welsh is day; *Daboi* in Brunka (Costa Rica), is the upper, the heaven of day. *Divi* in Sanskrit is the blue jay (our name for the dove), and *Taubber* is the Bavarian name for the blue or blaeberry; *Div* is the blue heaven. Blue and red, white and black are found under one and the same name as types of the heaven, *because* it was double. For duality, and twofoldness, are inseparable from this universal root.

Dobil, or, *Double*, English.	*Dvi*, No. 2, Sanskrit.
Dub, double, Akkadian.	δυο „ Greek.
Topu, couple, pair, twin, Maori.	*Di* „ Irish.
Dva, two, Avesta.	*Tvai* „ Gothic.
Dube, the zebra, Xosa Kaffir.	*Twi* „ A. S.
Dvi, No. 2. Lithuanic.	*Ti* „ Egyptian.

Where and how then did a male god originate under the name of *Div*, the Father in Heaven, who is found as—

Tef, Divine Father, Egyptian.	*Dio*, God, Zulu.
Dio, the Father-Sky, Sanskrit.	*Dewas* „ Lett.
Dwyf, the Self-existent One, Welsh.	*Deus* „ Latin.
Twisco, the Father, German.	*Duw* „ Keltic.
Tivi, God, Icelandic.	*Dia* „ Old Irish.
Dipti „ Amardian.	*Dhu* „ Arabic.

The evening and morning were the first day, and these were marked on the two horizons by certain stars. In Egyptian the star is the sign of day; it reads both *Seb* and *Tua* (or *Tef*), the *Sebat* or *Tuaut* being the gateway of light that was opened by the star of dawn. *Tuai* (or *Tefi*), is the morning, the morrow-day. Thus *Tuai* is equivalent to Day. The time of opening and closing of day was determined by the morning and evening star, Seb. Again *Seba* and *Tuai* signify adoration, worship, as in the Greek *Seba*, and the time was reckoned by the star of dawn. Now the only planet that can be assigned to the god Seb is Jupiter, the Egyptian *Har-pa-ka*.

Mercury was given to Sut-Anup, Mars to Shu, Saturn to Sevekh, the earlier form of Seb or Kronus. In Seb the fatherhood was first established; he is the youngest of the gods and yet the father of the gods. In him the fatherhood was founded as the god of earth, and *Har-pa-ka*, the Egyptian Jupiter, is the lord of the house of earth, in accordance with the astrological phraseology. There was no father in Egyptian mythology until Seb was crowned with the title of *Tef*.

He is called "*the Lord of the Gods*,"[1] "*the preparer of the Egg*," which was previously produced by the mother alone. Osiris is the eldest of five gods *begotten* of Seb.[3] Seb as the Great Inundator is called the Father of the Gods,[4] the Tef-Nuter; Seb then as Tef the father is identical by name with *Tefi*, modified *Tuai*, the star; the star of day as the planetary morning-star. Now the name of Seb when written with the Tes sign thus ⟶⟧ is Tseb. When written with the Coptic *djandja* ⟨⟩ it is *Djeb*, and with the bifurcation of Tes into T and S (which has been explained), the original word yields both Seb and Tef (or Tûa) as the two names for the star. The form *Tsef* is an Inner African root that has both variants in Tef and Seb, and can be traced thus. *Tseb* is the father, the virile male god, the *elder* or old one. And

Etsafe,	signifies	Old, in Bola.		*Zufa*,	signifies Old, in Kadzina.	
O Tafe	,,	,,	Sarar.	*Zofo*	,,	,, Kano.
Ataf	,,	,,	Kanyop.	*Sobo*	,,	,, Gura.
Defi	,,	,,	Banyun.	*Saib*	,,	,, Wadai.
Ar-safi	,,	,,	Pepal.			

Atef (Eg.) is a variant of Tef, whilst Ar-Shefi (Eg.) is a title of Num as the father-force; the elder or old one. So *Tivisco* who was worshipped as the great Heaven-father is especially called the Father of Mannu, or man. This name of the father is curiously applied in the Accra (African) language where *Tsebi* is the half-brother by the same father, but born of a different mother. In Toda, *Tob* is the father and, in Manatoto, the man as Vir, is *Etobu*. *Sepha* (Sans.) is the emphatic male, the type and token of virility. Both Tef and Seb then are Inner African with an original *Tsafe*, and the *z* is a representative of the Ts, as it is in the Hebrew צ Tzade.

Deo in Gaelic for the life, soul, or divine essence, is pronounced like *Jeo*, which becomes *Jo* in Scotch. This also implies an original *Djeo*. *Jeo* modifies into *Jo*, the equivalent of *Iu* (Eg.), to be dual; and it is identical with the Ju in "Jupiter" or "Juno." Ju, Io, Deo, Jeo, wherever found, meet in a primary *Djf*, *Tsef*, or *Kef*, which is dual in phenomena, in the two halves, two heavens, twin parentage, or two hands, as demonstrated in the "Typology of Numbers."

The Oscan *Djovis*, a form also given to the name of Jove by Varro, continues the Coptic Djandja which deposited the Latin J, and *Djovis* equates with *Tsef*. Tsef or Djef accounts for both Djovis (Djovis-pater, or Jupiter) in Latin, and Tzeus (Zeus) in Greek. All three together with Dev, Dyaus, and Deus are derivable from one original Tsef or Tseb, whence the Tef and Seb as twin names for the divine father in Egyptian. Also, in the Chemmesyan language of North America *Tzib* is the name for man, the father; and this *Tzib* is identical with the African *Tsef;* Egyptian *Tseb;* Armenian *Teiseba* (divine father), Coptic *Djeb* and Oscan *Djovis*. Moreover,

[1] *Ritual*, ch. xxvi.　　[2] *Ibid.*, ch. liv.
[3] *Ibid.*, ch. lxix.　　[4] *Ibid.*, ch. cxxxvi.

in the Central American group of Costa Rica dialects described by Professor Gabb,[1] the Father God is known as *Zibo* in Tiribi; *Zubo* in Terraba; *Sibi* in Bribri; *Sibu*, Cabecar, and *Siboh* in Brunka. Seb then was the first form of the father in heaven founded by the Kamites, and his planetary star was Jupiter, the star of the double horizon, which gave the dual character to it as a star of morn and even, of *Tuai*, or the two halves, reckoned by evening and morning as the day—day as it were on both sides of the dark, the *Twy-light*. The star of the horizon is in keeping with Seb as the god of middle earth, the mundane deity of Hor-Apollo.

Tsef becomes *Tef*, which passes into *Tui* or *Tiu*, whence *Ti* (Eg.) for Two; *Ti*, Chinese, Two, to cut in two, and *Iu* (Eg.) to be dual or duplicative, the equivalent of Ju in Jupiter, the star of the double horizon. The paternal element dominated in Seb or Tef, yet he was of a dual nature, mother as well as father, the Iu-pater or Diu, *i.e.* the dual one.

Jupiter is the lord of the fifth day, and the name of Seb signifies No. 5. As the lord of earth and the fifth region he will be described in the following section. He was a form of Kronus, or Time, in his planetary character. Now time was not founded on any vague bright heaven, but on the revolutions and periodicity of the heavenly bodies. It is here we have need of the distinction between the gods who had their origin in space and those that were born of time. If there be a god Dyaus who was a personification of the sky he cannot be one with Zeus; he would be a divinity of space but not of time. The Greeks knew that their Zeus was Κρονίων, and they called him Κρονίδης, because he *was* a god of time. His brothers, Hades and Poseidon, are not time-gods but gods in space, and neither of these was originally called Κρονίδης.

Pherecydes (B.C. 544) describes Zeus or Kronos as the fundamental cause of all phenomena in nature, distinguished according to the Phœnician tradition, *from* the *Chthonian* or elementary divinities. This makes him a god of time, not of space or sky personified. Moreover, he describes Kronos as the deity dwelling in that part of heaven which is nearest the earth. So the Egyptian Seb is a god of earth and the heaven of day, who declines when Shu uplifts the heaven of night.[2]

Tseb, Djovis, or Zeus, as Jupiter, the planetary, was *Kronian*, because the maker of a twelve years course of time. All the time-keepers are *Kronian* according to their cycles. Sevekh, of the seven stars, was a form of Kronus in the year of the Great Bear, or Dragon. Seb was Kronus in the later planetary time. Dyaus was not Kronian, and therefore cannot be identical with *Zeus*. The sequence shows that Saturn was one with Sevekh, the first form of Kronus, and that Zeus and Jupiter are identical with Seb-Kronus, the first father in

---

[1] *Proceedings of the American Philosophical Society*, 1875, vol. xiv. p. 483.
[2] Pierret, *Panthéon Égyptien*, p. 22, plate.

time or in heaven, who followed Sevekh and superseded the Son of the Mother in the orthodox and anti-Typhonian cult of Egypt.

Not Dyaus, but *Siva*, in a pre-solar character, was the first genuine father in heaven, or heaven-father, represented on the earliest physical plane as the male progenitor and begetter of souls. According to some, Siva was the most ancient and principal god of the aboriginal, non-Aryan tribes of India; he represents the father-god. He is the Mahadeva. Much evidence might be quoted to show that he is the original one of the later solar triad consisting of Siva, Vishnu, and Brahma. One legend relates that the three had a dispute as to which was the supreme being. Brahma, who was seated on the lotus floating visibly alone in creation, seeing nothing but himself on the wide waters, claimed the preeminence. He descended the stem of the lotus to the root, and found Vishnu there asleep. Brahma asked who *he* was. "*I am the first-born*," said Vishnu. This Brahma resented, and he was about to attack him, when Siva threw himself between them, exclaiming, "*It is I who am the first-born. Nevertheless, I will acknowledge him to be my superior who can see the summit of my head or the sole of my foot.*" Vishnu then transformed himself into the boar, pierced through the earth, and penetrated to the infernal regions, where he saw the feet of Siva or Mahadeva. On his return Mahadeva saluted Vishnu as the supreme.[1] Vishnu had then *become* the supreme in the depth as Brahma was in the height; but the god on the horizon, whether stellar or solar, was indeed the first-born.

The masculine soul was, so to speak, discovered in Egypt by Tseb or Tef. Hence Seb is the name of the soul as the seminal essence, "Siva's Quicksilver." This is represented in India by the linga being the especial symbol of Siva, who was the masculine soul and source in person. Siva and Seva are Sanskrit names of the linga, which was likewise the sign of Seb. Siva is identical with Seb by name and nature. He is pourtrayed with the serpent around his neck as the measure of time by years. He wears various other serpents about his person as symbols of the cycles of time. His name—also that of the linga,—is synonymous with the serpent's; Seva in Sanskrit, and Seb or Sep in Egyptian. In the Kamite typology the time-cycles and revolutions are described as *being* the "Serpents of Seb." Ra says to Seb, "*Be the guardian of thy serpents which are in thee.*" Seb-Kronus, or Time, is the great destroyer and renewer.[2] He was fabled to be the devourer of his own progeny whether as Saturn-Kronus or Seb-Kronus. Siva wears the necklace of skulls (together with the serpents of time) which typify the periods of the dead past that have been devoured by him as the destroyer. Kronus, the time-god, was represented in Greece as the swallower of his own children,

[1] Burnouf, *L'Inde Française.*
[2] *Records,* vol. vi. p. 110.

and in an Inner African myth the planet Jupiter is said to swallow his own daughter.

In Egyptian, the wolf also bears the name of the god Seb. At one time the spring equinox was marked by the rising in the evening of the Wolf constellation. This shows the wolf, Seb, to be a type of equinoctial time. The equinox is midmost in time, and was so before the horizon could be midmost in space, as between the upper and lower heaven. Seb, or the wolf, was the god of this mid-region in the stellar stage, before the abyss below and the solar triad were established. The equinox is the station assigned to Seb, and this was represented by a hill. Now Zeus is radically connected with the wolf. The most famous temple dedicated to him was his sanctuary on the Arkadian Mount Lykaios. According to the Arkadians, Zeus was nursed by the nymphs upon the Lykaian Hill. This was fabled to be a sanctuary without a shadow. Pausanias says when the sun was in the sign of the Crab there were no shadows at midday in Syene (the Egyptian Sen or Esné) but that in the temple on the Lykaian Mount there were no shadows cast the whole year round.[2] This hill then represented the Mount of the Equinoxes which the Egyptians placed up in the zenith; the tower in the midst assigned to Jupiter; the mount of the mid-region or earth assigned to Seb. This marks the station of the equinox, the mid-position, where stood the double house of the wolf and Anubis; and when the Arkadians assert that their own Lykosoura, or tail of the wolf, was the first city beheld by Helios, that points to the equinoctial station from which Atum, who was Ra in his first sovereignty, made a new point of departure in the astronomical mythology. Sir G. W. Cox says the same root having furnished a name for wolves, λύκοι, and for brightness or rays, the growth of a myth converting the rays into wolves would thus be inevitable.[3] This, as usual with the school, is an utter reversal of the process. The wolf Seb was equally a type of brightness with the star Seb, and the wolf with all its imagery can be traced in the planisphere, to which our appeal is now made. From the beginning of mythology with the elemental powers, which ruled in chaos before order was established, down to the time when it was finally transformed into the Christian mytholatry, Egypt has preserved the links of the series and sequence.

The fatherhood, first founded by Seb the planetary god, was next represented in the solar mythos.[1] Previously the sun was the Horus, the child of the mother. It was shown in the preceding volume that the change from Abram to Abraham implied the change from the god who was the son of the mother only to the god who was the father.

---

[1] In a previous allusion to the fatherhood, it was said that Atum-Ra was the first father in heaven (*Book of Beginnings*, vol. ii. p. 507). This should have been limited to the solar *régime*. Seb was the first father in the stellar mythos.

[2] Pausanias, viii. 38.   [3] Cox, *Introduction*, p. 106.

Thus, the alteration in Abram's name which followed a change of mythical type is coincident with the appearance of the male triad (Men), the Adonim, who are three in person but one in name. In these the masculine solar triad is visibly introduced. The change first occurred when it was known to be the same sun that went round by night to conquer the powers of darkness and rise again. The completed change from the fear of the dark and angry powers of nature to the worship of a god of light is traceable by means of the sun in the underworld. This was the sun-god out of sight, the *Amen*, who was both the hidden and the coming Ra, since *amenu* (Eg.) signifies to come. The sun in the nether-world is the Regenerator of souls, the Creator of the living, the great Judge of the dead. He is termed "*Master of the hidden spheres; Revealer of the mysterious empyrean;*" he who "*chases away the waters*," as lord of the inundation; he who "*dissipates darkness*," and "*gives eyes to the gods in obscurity*." He is the road-maker of the resur-rection, who "*causes the mummies to come forth*." With this new knowledge a third region of space was comprehended and typified. Previously there were but two regions or horizons, the upper and lower, the earth and heaven of Seb and Nupe, or Isis and Nephthys. Considerable perplexity has been caused by the change from the two regions to the three, and we are sometimes told that the ancients *con-ceived* of the Hades as being within the globe itself. The time was when they had to dig down mentally in that way to get below the surface at all. Before the solar abyss existed the upper and lower were the heaven and earth. In the later, the eschatological, phase of Egyptian or Akkadian mythology, the spirits of the dead, the demons, have their abode in the abyss *beyond* the earth, but in the Finnic mythology this abode was still *on* the earth, however far north; Pohja or Pohjola was a polar region (cf. the Egyptian Pekh for the hinder part, the north) but no Sheol, Hades, or Amenti. It was *not the third region in space*, but the opening of the earliest division.

It has been shown how the third person in the trinity was equivalent to the root of the tree. The Vishnu Purana terms Vishnu the root of the vast universal tree. This figure was also applied to the third division of space, the Abyss or Nadir, which the Akkadians called *Uru* the *root*, for the foundation of the whole which had been divided into three parts with six directions in space. The Pharaohs of Egypt were crowned rulers over the Two Regions, but the three are also mentioned in the *Instructions of King Amenhat*: "*Now thou art a King of earth; now thou rulest over the Three Regions*." In the inscriptions on the sarcophagus of Seti the earth is used as equivalent to Amenti, and opposed to heaven. Also, the sun descending into the underworld is thus addressed, "*Open the Earth! traverse the Hades and Sky! Ra, come to us!*" This we may look on as a survival of the Two Regions in the mythos belonging to the later three. "*Adored be the god Skambha*," says the Hindu poet, "*upon whom the*

City of the Three Worlds rested in the Beginning, as upon its main pillar."[1] Skambha at first sustained the dual division as the prop that stemmed a part and supported the twin-whole. "*These two* (worlds) *the Sky and the Earth, exist, supported by Skambha.*"[2] But, in Vedic Cosmology there are three skies—the upper, the middle, and the lower. The three divisions are elsewhere stated to be the sky, earth, and waters,[3] and these are the same three regions as those of the Egyptian and Chaldean solar mythologies. Vishnu passes through these three regions in three strides; his three footprints being figured in the twenty-third lunar mansion, Sravana.[4] The three footprints equate with the trident symbol; and in some astronomical works, the *Sakalya*, for example, the trident is depicted for Sravana instead of the three footsteps.

Plutarch observes that the trident is the symbol of the third region of the world which the (mystic) sea possesses, situated below the heaven and the air (or earth). The trident is a type of the male triad, and is assigned to the supreme one of the three. This may be Siva in one cult, or Vishnu in another. The god of the third region, the abyss of the waters, was the Af-Ra, in Egypt; Yav or Hea in Assyria; Javeh or Jah in Israel; Vishnu in India. Khnef (or Num) was likewise a form of this solar god; *Nef* being the sailor, the Neptune of the Romans, and the British Nevvy. This was the sun of the waters, the darkness, the abyss; the god who completed the circuit round, the protector by night, the Seer unseen. The Egyptians, says Plutarch, offer incense to the sun three times every day; resin at its rising; myrrh when it is in the mid-heaven, and what they call kyphi about the time of its setting. That was in recognition of the sun of the three regions. In like manner, the gods of Greece were invoked in three forms of gesture-speech. The Olympians on the height were prayed to with upraised hands; the marine gods with hands held horizontally; the gods of Tartarus with hands held down. The sun in the Three Regions is the origin of the masculine triad, the Hindu Trimurti. The Hindus say the sun in the eastern horizon and in the morning is Brahm; from noon to evening he is Siva; at night and in the west he is Vishnu. These three are one.[5] And of these the Indian dramatic poet Kalidasa (who wrote about 50 B.C.) sings—

> "In those three Persons the one God was shown,
> Each first in place, each last, and each alone;
> Of Siva, Vishnu, Brahma, each may be
> First, second, third, among the blessed Three."[6]

According to the Assyrians, the wide heaven is the seat of Anu the King. He is Anu in the height. Bel is lord of the world, countries,

---

[1] *As. Res.* vol. iii. p. 39.
[2] *Atharva-Veda*, x. 8.
[3] Muir, *Sansk. Texts*, iii. x.
[4] Plate in *Asiatic Researches*.
[5] *As. Res.* i. 267; v. 254.
[6] Stone, *Cradle-Land of Arts and Creeds.*

or lands. Hea is the dweller in the deep. These are the heaven, earth, and hell. In the oldest, the Akkadian, cult these three deities are the recognised Zi or spirits of the three divisions.

A papyrus at Turin shows the solar god speaking in his threefold character and as the creator of the "*mysteries of the two-fold horizon*," who says, "*I am Khepera in the morning, Ra at noon and Atum in the evening.*"[1] Speaking generally, it may be said that the Trimurti proper, composed of three male figures, is not Egyptian, although a three-headed and four-armed lion-god found at Meroë is referred to by Rawlinson.[2] There is, however, a solar triad in the *Ritual*, consisting of Atum, Kâ (Kak or Hak) and Hu. In this Atum is the manifestor of the Two Truths, and his two manifestations are personified as Kâ and Hu, who are called his sons. Kâ is the black sun in the abyss. Hu is the white sun in the height. Atum is the red sun on the horizon of the west.

This triad is very ancient and rare. The solar god Hak or Kâ was the child of the mother. According to the present reading, he was a continuation into the solar mythos of Kak, the god of darkness, the crocodile, Khevek (Sevekh), who was the earlier form of Seb, the father-god, and whose name of Khevek would modify into Kek or Kak, whence Kâ, still written with the crocodile's tail. In this way the star-god passed into the solar mythos, and into the triad in which Atum was considered to be the father, and Kâ and Hu are then called his sons.

A doctrinal application of the Tum triad is made in the Tablet of Rameses II. at Kuban.[3] "*Truly thou art the living image of thy father Tum, of An. The god Hu is in thy mouth, the god Ka is in thy heart, the place of thy tongue is the sanctuary of truth, the divinity is seated on thy two lips.*"

The title of Har-Makhu, the Sun of the Double Horizon, distinguishes that God from the Sun of the Third Region, in the Amenti, and preserves a proof of the Har Sun being an earlier solar deity than the Ra of the Three Heavens.

The Chinese male triad appear as Yu, Yih, and Tseih. Yu put a stop to the deluge, when it had broken in, by preparing nine proper channels for the waters. In this work he was helped by Yih, who opened up the forests with fire, and Tseih, who showed the people how to cultivate the ground which had been reclaimed from the waters (Shu-King).

The Chinese symbol of these three regions is made with three horizontal bars, ☰. To denote the supreme ruler of the three spheres the lines are crossed, 王. This forms the figure of the Papal crozier, which is thus shown to be a cross of the threefold heaven, that of the

---

[1] *Trans. Soc. of Bib. Arch.* vol. iv. pt. ii. p. 288.
[2] Herodotus, b. ii. 35.
[3] Birch, *R. P.* viii. 75 ; Brugsch, *Hist. Egypt*, ii. 80 ; Eng. Tr.

hexagram or space in six directions, already identified with the Papal triple crown.

The triad who divide the sovereignty of the universe in the Finnic mythology are Ukko, the old one, the god of heaven above, the supreme one; Ilmarinen, the eternal forger, god of the earth; and Wainamoinen, the friend of the waves. These three were said to have established the celestial vault, fixed the gates of air, and sowed the stars in space.[1]

At one time the Hawaiians had the male triad as a Trimurti named Kane, Ku, and Lono, equal in nature but distinct in attributes. Ku was surnamed Ka-Pao, the Builder or Architect; Lono was Noho-i-ka-wai, the dweller on the water. They formed a triad as "*The one who is established.*" These three were held to have broken up the ancient darkness of Po, the underworld, which shows the dependence of the triad on the sun that passed through the abyss; they created the heavens, *three in number*, as their dwelling-places when they were considered to be distinct from each other. The triadic one is thus addressed: "*Kane-po-lani! O Heavenly Father, with Ku the Builder in the blazing heaven, with great Lono of the flashing eyes, a God, the God of Lightning, the fixed light of heaven, standing on the earth; on the earth of Kane-Kumu-honua, he is God.*"[2]

The New Zealanders also have the masculine triad as the three brothers Maui—the "*elder Maui, the tallest Maui, and the young Maui.*" The younger Maui, as in all the European stories of three brothers, is despised and badly treated by the other two. They leave him at home whilst they go abroad, and do not suffer him to sit at meals with them, but toss him a bone or offal to eat whilst they devour the best of everything. At last he plucks up spirit, and when the elder brothers next go-a-fishing, he takes his place in the boat, and insists on going too. "*Where is your hook?*" ask the two brothers. "*Oh, this will do,*" said little Maui, taking out his own jawbone. This he threw overboard for his fishhook, but on trying to pull it in again found it very heavy. By hauling away at it he at last lifts it, and finds it has brought up the land from the bottom of the deep. This was the first great feat of little Maui, or the sun which made the passage of the underworld. It happened that near the habitation of the three Mauis there lived an old woman called Great Daughter of the Night, a most terrible person. Maui the youngest, however, determined to visit her, and see if he could find anything good. Coming near the spot where "*Hine-nui*" lived, he began to play a tune on his flute. When the old woman heard the sound, she said to her slaves: "*If the man comes down the hill walking upright on his legs, catch him, he's a thief. But if he comes on his hands and feet with his belly and face upwards, be sure not to meddle with him, he is an Atua*" (or God). This little Maui heard, and came upon the old

[1] *Kalwala*, part ii. runa xiv.   [2] Fornander, vol. i. p. 61.

woman as an Atua. He crept into her kumara-store, and ate what he could, besides carrying off a basketful. The other brothers are pleased with the fruit, and the elder thinks he will try his luck, but the young Maui gives him the wrong instructions, and he does not proceed like an Atua, but plays on the flute and goes marching proudly and tall into the old woman's kumara-store, whereupon he is seized and squeezed between the thighs of Hine-nui so hard that he is killed.[1]

The god advancing in a reversed position is the sun in the underworld. The image accords exactly with an Egyptian scene of the sun passing through the hades, where we see the twelve gods of the earth, or the lower domain of night, marching towards a mountain *turned upside down, and two typical personages are also turned upside down.* This is in illustration of the passage of the sun through the underworld. The *reversed* on the same monument are the dead. Thus the Osirified deceased, who has attained the second life, in the *Ritual* says exultingly, " *I do not walk on my head.*" The dead, as the Akhu, are the spirits, and the Atua is a spirit who comes walking upside down.[2]

Little Maui personates the one of the triad who *does* pass through the belly of hades; *does* attain land; the sun that crosses the waters of the deep, the reduced and diminutive winter sun that rises up again and greatens and grows into the glorious conqueror. This is the Jack of our nursery legends, the Scottish Assiepet, Danish Askepot, German Aschenpüttel, who pokes in the ashes and blows up the fire—the solar fire which he has to keep and rekindle. He is the male likeness of Cinderella. Maui is the same as Boots, and Dümmling of the Germans,—the little hero who starts up when the two big brothers have failed and the call comes to him to do the great deed; he climbs up the beanstalk, rides up the hill of glass, asserts the hidden majesty of the ascending sun of morning or spring, and wins the princess and half the kingdom besides. Manifold are the Aryan forms of the male solar triad reduced to the status of a folk-tale, which may be interpreted by the mythos.

The Bull of Hu represented the sun in Britain, and this took a threefold form in the well-known Three Bulls of Hu, which drew out the Avanc monster that caused the deluge; one of these was called the ox that stopped the channel of the waters, as did the Chinese Yu. Nash says : " *They talk of an ox that tolled the bell at Woolwich, and how from an ox he transformed himself into an old man, and from an old man into an infant, and from an infant into a young man.*"[3] This is the triadic transformation of the sun just as it is depicted in the temples of Egypt. The ox was doubtless a survival of the ox of

---

[1] Shortland's *Traditions of the New Zealanders*, pp. 42—45.
[2] *Book of Hades*, Sarcophagus of Seti, Soane Museum; *Records of the Past*, vol. x.
[3] Nash, *Christ's Tears over Jerusalem*, p. 185 (1613).

Hu, the British sun-god. The triad of solar divinities, that passed
into the three brothers of the popular tales on the one hand, survived
on the other in the Christian, Greek, and Roman iconography; not
only in the three identical human persons with three distinct bodies,
but also as the Trimurti with three heads on one body, and even the
one head with three faces.[1]

Sancta Trinitas was one of the names conferred on the triad
composed of three identical persons who were all males. A perfect
example has been copied from a manuscript of the twelfth century.[2]
The three are one, as regards likeness,—the attitudes differ slightly, but
significantly. The right hand one lifts his right hand with upward
pointing fingers, as god in the height. The left hand one makes no
sign, unless with the fingers turned down. The central figure answers
to the god on the horizon.

The Three Kings of Cologne, called the Three Magi, who came
to adore the infant Jesus, are a form of the solar Trimurti. One of
these, Melchior, is black. He represents the sun in the Amenti,
which was pourtrayed as a god, ruler, or king of a black complexion.

The Sun in the Three Regions being the original of the male triad,
the three regions themselves form a feminine triad as their consorts.
On either side there is one who is the source of the hypostasis. This
in the female triad is the Great Mother; she who was the one that
bifurcated into two, when the regions were limited to upper and lower,
now becomes triadic. Sarasvati is said to occupy three abodes. Three
Sarasvatis are also recognised, although details are wanting.[3]

Mahadevi is the great mother who divides herself into three distinct
forms of different colours—black, red, and white—to become Sarasvati,
Sacti of Brahma; Lacksmi, Sacti of Vishnu; Parvati, Sacti of Siva.
When she appeared in presence of the male triad, they asked, " *Who
art thou, lovely` one, and why art thou distinguished by the three
colours?* " In Egypt the Great Mother is called the Mistress of Darkness—that is, the black one; her upper crown is white, the lower red,
which will account for the three colours.

The dual motherhood is expressed by the Gnostic Achamoth, who
is first the mother of material substance or man on the left hand, and
next of spiritual substance or man on the right hand; like the Hermean
genitrix, the Wateress, she divides into the two sisters of the zodiac,
and is then called the " Sophia above " and the " Sophia below." In
a triadic division of the regions, Achamoth is said to dwell in the
intermediate abode, answering to the horizon of the three regions.
" *Her place of habitation is an intermediate one, above the Demiurge
indeed, but below and outside of the Pleroma, even to the end.*"[4] The
" Mother in the Horizon of Heaven " is mentioned in the *Ritual*.[5]

---

[1] Didron, figs. 141, 142.   [2] *Ibid.*, fig. 137.
[3] Muir, *Sans. Texts*, v. 341, 338.   [4] Irenæus, b. i. ch. v. 4.
[5] Ch. clxv. *Supplement*, Birch.

When the three regions were spaced out, the mother *was* the horizon, as place of emanation, the Mut, or Mouth of birth. She is represented in the Vignette as a Deess with *three* heads, one the vulture, one the lioness, and one human; the latter being the wearer of the two crowns in one. The Goddess Hathor, in Egypt, is said to receive the dead in the west as the spotted cow. The British Triads also speak of three cows, one of which typifies the genitrix, Keridwen, the other two being devoted to her service; one was called the spotted cow; the other two were one white and one red, the colours of the two Egyptian crowns of the upper and lower hemispheres. There is a Buddhist emblem called the *Sri Iantra*, in Hindustan, copied from the gates of Somnauth, which will serve to illustrate the three regions—upper, mid, and lower—by south, east, and north, with the corresponding positions assigned to the feminine triad. The diagram is a common one. It is found in the mason's "Royal Arch," and is to be met with in some old English churches. It constitutes the hexagram of the sixfold heaven, or of space in six directions. In the Hindu figure, the three gods and their consorts are arranged with Brahma east, and Laksmi west; Siva north, and Parvati south-west; Vishnu south, and Sarasvati north-east. The order of the Trimurti varies according to the particular cult; all that we are concerned with here is the hexagram.[1]

One name of the most ancient genitrix who divided into the two sisters was *Tef* (Eg.), identical with the Abyss of the beginning. She was continued as Tefn or Tefnut under her lioness-type, and from her name and nature it is now proposed to derive the *Dawn*. The word is common for opening, and to dawn is to open out. In Egyptian *Tebn* means to rise up, spread, illumine, *i.e.* to dawn. But the name of dawn or *Tefn* includes more than the dawn in heaven. The dawn with which primitive mythologists were first concerned was the dawn of womanhood, and the day of procreation. This was a dawn that broke in blood. We speak of the rose of dawn, but they drew their simile from blood; and blood first manifested through a breaking open, as it did in the human dawn. In Egyptian *Tef* means to shed, evacuate, spit, menstruate, drip, and drop, with the flower-sign of bleeding; the bleeding wound, the breaking open in blood, blood itself, are all determined by the flower of blood as the sign of flowing. So in Fijian, *Dave* signifies the flow; *Tevah* and *Daveh* in Hebrew denote the menstrualia. The Assyrian *Dav*-kina (or Dam-kina) is the Blood-Mother. The mother opened in the first of two phases in the red dawn that broke in blood. The first mother divides and assumes the forms of the two sisters, as she did in sociology; one form of this double mother being that of Neith the wearer of the red crown, and Seti of the white crown, whose name is written with the arrow of light, a sunbeam. The three may be described as black night, red dawn, and white day. These reproduced the light, or the solar god,

[1] Inman, *Ancient Faiths*, fig. 34.

M M 2

in three corresponding characters. The dark night represented the hidden sun, whence Mut, the mother darkness, was the consort of the hidden Amen. The red dawn reflected the coming sun and gave it birth.

The verb *Uben* applied to the act is identical with the word *open ;* *uba* (Eg.) is a window as an opening for light, and the Uben of Neith is our opening. Seti, or day, reflected the sun at white heat. Now one image of the reflector was the pupil of the eye; and the two reflectors, as dawn and day or north and south, are also called the two eyes of the sun. The Great Mother, as Mut, Uati, Buto, or Pekht, divides (Pekh, to divide) in the two characters of Tefn and Sekhet, who represent the two elements of wet and heat; the dewy red of dawn, and burning white of day. Hence *Tef* denotes moisture or dew (which is the same word as Tef) ; and also means to drip and drop. *Tef*, moreover, is the pupil of the eye, the mirror in which the sun was re-born of the genitrix at dawn. *Nu* is the heaven or firmament. Thus *Tefnu* (or Tefne) is the reflector of the sun as the opening dawn ; when the dawn reddened it shed blood, and when the dew dropped, the eye wept. Then the mother passed into her second phase as Sekhet whose element is fire, and who is the eye, as reflector of the sun in his fury or double force. These were the two eyes of the sun. The eye of dewy dawn becomes the eye of burning day, or *Tefn* transforms into Sekhet. This is the transformation of Daphne, the dawn, that was poetised by the Greeks. For Daphne does not come from India, and is not derived from any Vedic Ahanâ, which the present writer would explain by Han (Eg.) the young, youth, to go to and fro, the ever-returning; but she is the Egyptian *Tefne*, whose transformation into the goddess of fire or heat was pourtrayed as the metamorphosis of Daphne into the laurel-tree, the wood of fire ; which was only another type of the change from dawn to day, from Neith to Seti, from Tefne to Sekhet, that represented the elemental metamorphosis according to the mythical impersonations. Elaborate explanation may make some of these things look incredibly ingenious, whereas they are only excessively simple. The eye and water were the first natural mirrors, and their application to phenomena is just as natural from the primitive standpoint. The gestator, who in later times carried the artificial mirror, bore an eye on her head in an earlier presentation of the character. Meri is both the eye and the water, as the mirror or reproducer. Also, the two eyes, when used as separate symbols, are painted the one (left) of a red colour ; the other (right) being blue ; answering to the red of dawn and blue of day ; the red of flesh and blood, and the blue of soul. The left eye of the sun is described as shedding blood.[1] The sun is born daily from this eye which is also called the Great Water, the Mirror.

The British Barddas describe Arthur as having three wives, each of

---

[1] *Rit.* ch. xvii.

whom is a character of Gwenhwyvar, the Lady of the summit of the waters,[1] a form of the one that triplicates. The feminine triad is also presented as what are termed the "Three Unchaste Matrons" of Druidical mystery. The first of these three sisters is named *Essyllt*, or Spectacle, surnamed Vyngwen with the white mane, who was the concubine of Trystan. The second is the Lady with the splendid head, Penarwen, wife of Owen, son of Urien. The third is Bûn, the maid, the British Proserpine, wedded to the Flame-Bearer.[2]

The feminine triad, however, was not left to the indefiniteness of space, or of the firmament divided into three and six parts. The Great Mother had other visible types. To say nothing now of the Great Bear, which was a personification of the pre-solar time, there was Venus above and Venus below the horizon fulfilling the characters of the two divine sisters ; and once a year the genitrix was represented by the moon in its annual conjunction with the sun in the place of manifestation, when the child of another year was born. In the cuneiform tablets, the male triad is associated with the moon in three phases. The first fifteen days are assigned to Anu, Hea, and Bel, and the three divisions of five days each in the latter half of the lunation are given to the Great Mother, who triplicates and becomes a triad of consorts, a threefold reproducer.

In the Russian story of the Norka, the fabulous monster is attacked by the two elder brothers in .vain, then by the youngest who vanquishes the beast. The Norka flees to a great white stone, tilts it up, and escapes into *that* world out of this, saying, " You will only overcome me when you enter here." Ivan pursues the beast in the underworld, and there finds a triad of sisters, one of whom dwells in a palace of copper, one in a silver palace, one in a palace of gold. It is the youngest sister who lives in the golden palace. With her the beast is found and slain.[3] In this legend, the triad of the three brothers is conjoined with that of the three sisters, as they are in the hexagram or Sri Iantra.

The triple feminine type is assigned to Bhavani and to Hecate, who is probably a continuation of the Egyptian *Heka.t*, the frog-headed goddess. A Gnostic gem also exhibits a tri-formed female figure. She bears in her hands swords, torches, and serpents. The other side of the gem shows the Cock-headed Abraxas, whom we identify with the Af-ra (Eg.), or sun in the lower world, the sun that triplicated. This feminine triad corresponds to one that accompanies Num (Eg.) who *is* the Af-ra.[4] The Mother of Life, as Ank, wears a crown of hemp-stalks on her head, typical of the weaver of the woof and spinner of the thread of life. She takes two forms, or we may say has two sisters, in Heka.t and Seti, and the three are a feminine triad attached to Num the solar god in the abyss. Again, the genitrix

[1] Davies, p. 187.
[2] *Welsh Arch.* vol. ii. pp. 14—73.
[3] Ralston, *Russian Folk-tales*, p. 73.
[4] King, *Gnostics*, pl. iii. fig. 5.

Neith carries the shuttle or knitter on her head. She too weaves or spins the woof of existence. She also takes two forms, or has (becomes the) two sisters, Isis and Nephthys. These two forms of the feminine triad show us the three spinning sisters of the folk-tales as three Egyptian goddesses, who became the Three Norns Vurdh, Verdhandi and Skuld; the three weird sisters in *Macbeth;* the three Latin Parcæ, and the three Greek Fates, one of whom furnishes the flax, one spins the thread of life, and one cuts it off. According to Plutarch, Atropos was placed in the sun and conferred the principle of generation. Clotho, being lodged in the moon, is she who joins, mingles, and unites; and Lachesis is on the earth, where she adds a helping hand, and with her does fortune very much participate.[1] A German version of the three spinning girls will prove their identity with the feminine solar triad. One of these is quite white, the second is half white and half black, the third is blind. Blindness equates with blackness, and the blind shrew-mouse was sacred to Mut, the Mistress of Darkness. The white sister represents the wearer of the white crown—Seti in Egypt; Sita, the white, in India. The blind one is the goddess in the underworld. The sister who is half white and half black agrees with the spotted cow of Hathor, and the goddess who bears both crowns joined in one. The story of "Little One-eye, little Two-eyes, and little Three-eyes," contains another mode of describing the feminine triad by sight instead of complexion. Three-eyes represents most sight, as the equivalent of most light; the wearer of the white crown. An Arabic expression says, "*al-leyl-a'war,*" "the night is one-eyed," and One-eye personifies the goddess of the lower heaven. Two-eyes, the intermediate, is the goddess of the horizon. In the story, One-eye and Three-eyes are the two imperious sisters, proud of their extraordinary aspect, who both look upon Two-eyes as a most common-place, vulgar mortal, with no possible attraction. "*You are no better than common folk,*" they said to her, "*you do not belong to us;*" they despised her, flouted at her, pushed her about, made her wear the coarsest clothing, and eat offal for food. This is Cinderella.

The story of Cinderella and the Slipper is Egyptian. Strabo tells it of Rhodopis, the rosy-cheeked, who is confused with the builder of the third pyramid of Ghizeh, Neith-Akar, or the perfect Neith. It is said she dwelt at Naucratis, and one day while she was bathing the wicked wind seized her sandal and carried it to the king, who was sitting in the court of justice in the open air, and laid it at his feet. The event was so singular, the sandal so elegant, the king's curiosity so excited that he could not rest until the owner was discovered and he had made her his queen.

The romance was but a later form of the mythos. In the feminine triad, one of three transforms. If we take the moon as the type, then

---

[1] *Of the Face appearing in the Orb of the Moon.*